43

Best Wishes
Georgina
Sammy xxx

GW00468250

EVERY
LIGHT
WAS ON

HARRAH'S CLUBS

RENO

TAHOE

EVERY
LIGHT
WAS ON

BILL HARRAH AND HIS CLUBS REMEMBERED

FROM ORAL HISTORY INTERVIEWS BY DWAYNE KLING

EDITED BY R. T. KING
ASSISTANT EDITORS: MARY LARSON, DWAYNE KLING

UNIVERSITY OF NEVADA
ORAL HISTORY PROGRAM
1999

Copyright 1999
University of Nevada Oral History Program
Reno, Nevada 89557

All rights reserved. Published 1999
Printed in the United States of America

ISBN 1-56475-375-1

Publication Staff:
Production Manager: Kathleen M. Coles
Senior Production Assistant: Linda J. Sommer
Production Assistants: Denise Lane, Beth Opperman,
Marrianne Tipton, and Kathryn Wright-Ross

People used to make fun of the fact that he wanted all the lights to be on, but it was just another part of the whole picture. If one light is out, there's something wrong—it's not perfect.

Holmes Hendricksen

CONTENTS

INTRODUCTION

Casino gambling (or "gaming," as the industry prefers) was made legal in Nevada by an act of the state legislature in 1931. Initially, the majority of Nevada casinos were small establishments containing a few gambling tables, perhaps some slot machines, and a bar. Most operators came from other states, where many had run rigged games in carnivals or had operated illegal gambling joints that were always in danger of being shut down by local law enforcement agencies. Early casinos in Nevada were rough-and-tumble businesses still deeply rooted in the frontier ethos from which gaming had emerged: cheating, profit skimming, and employee theft from the house were rampant. By background and temperament, William Fisk (Bill) Harrah, would seem to have been ill-prepared to succeed in a business operating so far from the center of mainstream American life.

Bill Harrah was born into an educated, upper middle-class family in Pasadena, California, in 1911. When he was still quite young his family moved to the nearby coastal community of Venice, where his father, John Harrah, became a partner in a law firm. John invested extensively (and profitably) in real estate, dabbled in politics, and once served as Venice's mayor. Amanda Fisk Harrah, Bill's mother, was from a long-established Iowa family. Never entirely at ease in the New West of the early twentieth century, she dedicated herself to being a housewife and mother. John and Amanda Harrah had two children; Bill's sister Margaret was four years his senior.

Initially, life in Venice was pleasant for the sociable, prosperous, well-connected Harrahs. Bill's childhood was a comfortable one, largely unremarkable apart from his early interest in automobiles and airplanes—an interest that would become the absorbing passion of his adult life. The Harrahs indulged their youngest child and only son, and Bill's father would buy him practically anything he wanted, including a new Chevrolet roadster for his sixteenth birthday. Bill was an indifferent student in his teens (apparently his parents were unconcerned), but he was always fashionably dressed, had plenty of pocket money, and led an active social life. In other words, Bill Harrah was spoiled.

While Bill was still a teenager, life started becoming more difficult for him and his family when his mother sank into emotional depression. In bad health, unhappy in her marriage, and feeling increasingly out of place in Venice, she first turned to drink and then committed suicide by swallowing poison. Bill was devastated, and his personality seems to have been transformed by the circumstances of his loss. Previously effervescent and outgoing, for the rest of his life he was so taciturn and reserved that many thought him to be antisocial.

Not long after Amanda Harrah's suicide, the crashing stock market of 1929 ushered in the Great Depression of the 1930s. John Harrah's extensive real estate investments were lost. Close to financial ruin and seeking another source of income, he opened a small gambling shop in his sole remaining property on the Venice pier. His only game was the "Circle Game," a quasi-legal variety of bingo. The game would be shut down by the authorities at irregular intervals, but it always reopened, and it returned a steady (if modest) profit to its owner.

Following graduation from high school, Bill completed a year's study at California Christian College to strengthen his weak academic record. Then in 1930 he enrolled at UCLA. He intended to major in mechanical engineering, but in his first term he was caught cheating on a chemistry exam and left the university to work in his father's gambling establishment. The two soon disagreed on how to operate the games, and in 1933 John Harrah sold the place to his son for $500. Bill made it more profitable, but he too had to struggle to keep it going under the scrutiny of law enforcement agencies.

Bill had been driving back and forth to Reno, Nevada, on pleasure trips for several years when, in 1937, he decided to relocate his operation to that little city on the Truckee River where the gambling business was legal. Between 1937 and 1946, in joint ventures with others, he had some success with bingo parlors and a bar on Commercial Row and Center Street, but he was strictly a small-time operator. He was also a heavy drinker who was inattentive to business, and his future did not appear bright. The one thing that set Bill Harrah apart from many of his peers was his insistence on running honest games, but that alone

has never been enough to bring success in the gaming business.

After more than a decade without making any appreciable mark in his chosen profession, Bill Harrah suddenly became more ambitious and started to show some surprisingly bold risk-taking tendencies. In retrospect his actions seem somewhat inconsistent with his pinched personality, but his growing willingness to risk everything on unlikely ventures was to drive the great success that he would enjoy for the next thirty years. Harrah's rise in the world of gaming began in 1946 when he went deeply into debt to become the sole owner and operator of a casino that he named Harrah's Reno Club. (There is evidence that he may initially have had one or more limited partners; if so, that arrangement was short-lived.) It was not long before Harrah's Club was showing a handsome profit and Bill was on his way to becoming the biggest operator in Nevada. First he would make some changes in his personal life.

Shortly after arriving in Reno, Harrah had married Thelma Batchelor, a woman he had known in southern California. The marriage was marked by unhappiness and infidelity, and in 1948 the two finally divorced. After a short courtship, Bill then married one of his dealers, Scherry Teague Fagg. This marriage was to change his personal life in ways that considerably advanced his ability to lead a business. Scherry would not tolerate Bill's constant, heavy drinking, and she badgered him to stop. He eventually got help for his alcoholism, quit drinking (he would not resume until the late 1960s), and began focussing his energy and attention on work. Bill and Scherry were divorced soon after he went on the wagon, but they remarried within a year and were together for a total of over twenty years. (By the time he passed away, Bill Harrah had been married seven times to six different women.)

In 1955 Bill again borrowed a large sum of money to finance a risky proposition. He wanted to create a Harrah's Club at Lake Tahoe by buying some existing properties and rebuilding and expanding on them, and he intended to keep the club open year-round. Harrah's Tahoe Club opened in the summer of 1956. It immediately did great business, but knowledgeable old-timers at the lake predicted that trying to stay open through the winter would be foolish: nothing could induce customers to risk the long trip in hazardous winter driving conditions to do something that was otherwise conveniently available in Reno. The old-timers were wrong. Harrah started a bus program to bring in gamblers from all over northern California. He also began booking nationally-known performers to provide entertainment for his customers when they were not at the tables. In a short time, not only was his Tahoe Club making money throughout the year, it had become more profitable than his Reno club. In later expansions at the lake, Harrah built a four-star hotel and a world-class restaurant that contributed to Harrah's becoming the dominant gaming operation at Lake Tahoe.

Harrah's Club in Reno was also quite profitable through the 1950s and 1960s, but it was overshadowed by the bigger Harolds Club, which advertised nationally. That changed in 1969 when Harrah again took a chance and borrowed a great deal of money, this time to acquire the Golden Hotel and build a hotel-casino on the site. (It was across the street from, and an extension of, Harrah's original casino, and the two properties operated as one.) The greatly-enlarged Reno club offered the same type of high-quality entertainment, food, junkets, and other inducements that were drawing so many customers to the Tahoe operation, and it began to enjoy equal success. Bill Harrah's clubs had become the giants of gaming in northern Nevada. They were to remain so throughout his life.

Much of the success of Harrah's Clubs can be attributed to Bill Harrah's hands-off style of management. He hired people who could get the job done (if they couldn't, they did not last long), and then he let them do it. In truth, he had little interest in the day-to-day opera-

tions of the casinos that were the source of his growing wealth. Automobiles and airplanes were what Bill Harrah really cared about, and he poured rivers of his company's money into acquiring, restoring, and exhibiting them. The world-famous Harrah Automobile Collection (HAC) grew from Bill's 1947 purchase of a 1911 Maxwell. (He thought it was a 1907, but he had been duped.) At the time of his death the collection, housed in a huge complex of buildings including a former icehouse, numbered over 1350 automobiles and about 150 other conveyances such as aircraft and motorcycles. It was conservatively estimated to be worth over $40 million.

During the last twenty years of his life, Bill Harrah spent far more time with his automobiles than he did in his casinos, but his personal imprint on operations remained strong. Harrah had always demanded high quality and attention to detail in all things. His clubs were known for being spotless, tastefully decorated establishments with courteous, well-trained, conservatively dressed staff, and conveniences and comforts that were unavailable in other hotel-casinos. From top to bottom, many employees spoke of being "Harrahized," meaning that they were not only proud to be part of an operation that they believed to be the best of its kind, but that they shared the owner's commitment to keeping it that way down to the last detail.

Most employees went along with the way things were done at Harrah's, but not all were happy. In fact, some felt that their wages were exploitative and that the rigid dress and appearance codes and other forms of employee regimentation were oppressive. However, with the exception of a brief period at the end of the 1940s, discontented workers seem generally to have been in the minority. It appears that for a gaming business, Harrah's really did provide good salaries, benefits, and working conditions. Perhaps this arose from Bill Harrah's fear of unionism.

While Harrah wanted his employees to be happy with their jobs, he was determined not to share power with them or their representatives. This determination translated into a sort of benevolent paternalism that inoculated his clubs against union fever. When the culinary union organized his workers and led them to strike for higher salaries in 1949, Harrah vowed to undo the deed and to set things up so that no union would ever again be able to tell him how to run any part of his business. He initiated salary and benefits packages for workers that were ahead of industry standards, and his employees voted to decertify the union in 1950. Harrah never again had to negotiate with organized labor, but by the 1960s his clubs had fallen behind some others in salaries and wages, and there were more than a few employees who thought that they were being unfairly treated.

Harrah's lavish and extravagant life-style, paid for almost entirely by the company, did not help his image among disgruntled employees. For twenty years he kept a fleet of airplanes at his disposal, including several corporate jets capable of transoceanic flight. He used the planes to transport himself, family, and friends on frequent vacation trips and to gatherings of automobile enthusiasts throughout the United States and around the world. Harrah also maintained a grand personal residence (Rancharrah) on acres of land in the south Truckee Meadows, a waterfront mansion at Lake Tahoe (Villa Harrah), and a vacation resort (the Middle Fork Lodge) in Idaho. He even purchased the town of Stanley, Idaho, to serve his Middle Fork property.

By the 1970s, Bill Harrah was spending so much of his company's money on himself and those close to him that there was little available for planned expansion and improvements. Harrah's was beginning to experience cash-flow problems. Forced to choose between remaining the sole owner and raising additional millions in cash by taking the company public, Bill went for the money with a modest over-the-counter stock issue in 1971. Then in 1973, Harrah's became the first gaming company to have its stock traded on the New York Stock Exchange.

The final years of Bill Harrah's life were good ones both for him and his company. He was immersed in his cars and in a happy marriage, and Harrah's Clubs were being run by a group of highly competent people (most of them promoted from within) who had made the operations so profitable that stockholders were treating them with the adoration usually reserved for movie stars and professional athletes. All was not well, however. Early in 1978, while at the Mayo Clinic for his annual checkup, Bill Harrah learned that an aneurysm was forming on his aorta. It would require surgery, and there was a distinct possibility that the surgery would kill him. He returned to the Mayo Clinic in late June to have the operation, and on June 30 he died when post-surgery bleeding could not be stopped.

Beyond drawing up a will to divide his assets, Bill Harrah had made no plans or provisions for what would happen to the automobile collection, his properties, and his business following his death. Mead Dixon, Harrah's attorney, was named the executor of his estate, which included a majority of the company's stock. Dixon soon became chairman of the board of directors, and he quickly set about trying to sell Harrah's. In 1980 a buyer was found in Holiday Inns, a company with extensive hotel experience but no experience in casino gaming.

Bill Harrah's death marked the end of a colorful era. He was acknowledged to be the top operator in gaming during a period when the largest, most successful casinos were extensions of the personalities of their owners. Following Holiday's acquisition of his company (some old Harrah's hands still insist on calling it a "merger," but it was clearly a sale), things were never again the same at Harrah's Reno and Tahoe Clubs. A company founded and run for forty years by a single man with a strong and idiosyncratic personality—a man obsessed with detail and insistent on the highest quality in everything—had been taken over by a more orthodox corporation, one that was primarily interested in cost-effectiveness, efficiency of operation, and enhanced profitability.

Harrah's two casinos, once flagships of the industry, became interchangeable parts in a corporate empire; but although the clubs lost some of their soul and luster, the bottom line improved, and the Harrah's division of Holiday began a steady expansion that shows no signs of abating. After several corporate reorganizations and changes of name, Harrah's Entertainment Incorporated has emerged as an international gaming juggernaut with assets of over $1.5 billion. None of its money is tied up in an automobile collection.

—◇—

This set of memories of Bill Harrah and his clubs arises from research and interviews done by oral historian Dwayne Kling. Mr. Kling brought forty years of experience in gaming to the project, supported by considerable research into the history of the industry in northern Nevada. He is an adept interviewer and was quite successful in drawing information out of his chroniclers. The interviews address a broad range of topics. Combined, they give a fascinating, insiders' look at the life of Bill Harrah and the operation of his clubs.

Dwayne Kling earned a bachelor's degree in economics and business administration from St. Mary's College. After service in the army during the Korean war he played professional baseball in the New York Yankee organization. A skilled fielder, but unable to hit major league pitching, Kling gave up his baseball aspirations and took a job with Harolds Club in Reno in 1954 as a change person and dice dealer. From this modest beginning, a rewarding career in gaming developed, including a period from 1957 to 1963 when Kling was a dealer, then pit boss, then shift manager, and finally pit manager for Harrah's Tahoe Club. From 1971 to 1981 Kling was co-owner and general manager of the Silver Spur Casino. When that ca-

sino was sold he went on to several other management positions in Reno gaming, retiring from The Virginian Hotel-Casino in 1995 as casino manager.

Following Kling's retirement, Ken Adams, the University of Nevada Oral History Program's (UNOHP) gaming history coordinator, recruited him to work on our Harrah's project. Kling received training in the theory and practice of oral history and joined the UNOHP as an associate oral historian in 1996. In addition to his work for the UNOHP, he is the author of *The Rise of the Biggest Little City: An Encyclopedic History of Reno Gaming, 1931-1981*, to be published by the University of Nevada Press in the fall of 1999.

When the UNOHP began the Harrah's oral history project, it was intended to conclude the work by adding the transcripts of the interviews to our 70,000-page collection of oral histories, where they would be available to students, faculty, researchers, and publishing scholars. However, as transcription neared completion it became clear that the combined memories of our chroniclers told a compelling story that would be of great interest to general readers as well as to experts on gaming history. It was decided to make a book if a subsidy could be found to cover the cost of printing. Several individuals (they wish to remain anonymous) stepped forward with generous gifts, and Harrah's Club in Reno covered the remaining expenses of publication. We are grateful to all who helped.

The book at hand was edited from 2,000 pages of raw transcript. Its oral origins notwithstanding, in general the text reads like that of any other book, but the reader will encounter two unconventional devices that are employed to represent important parts of the dynamic of spoken language: [laughter] appears when a chronicler laughs in amusement or to express irony; and ellipses are used to indicate halting speech . . . or a dramatic pause. As aids to the reader we also provide a glossary of terms and a reference list of

Harrah's employees and others who are frequently mentioned in the text. These can be found at the back of the book.

As with all its oral histories, while the Oral History Program can vouch for the authenticity of *Every Light Was On*, it makes no claim that the recollections upon which the book is based are entirely free of error. This is personal history; this is the remembered past. Copies of the tape recordings of the interviews which are the source of this book are housed in the Oral History Program of the University of Nevada, where they can be heard by appointment.

At every stage of this project we had the enthusiastic and capable assistance of a number of individuals and institutions. In no particular order, we are indebted to the following for their help and their commitment to enriching Nevada's historical record: Phillip Earl of the Nevada Historical Society; Don Dondero; the William F. Harrah Trust; Bob Blesse and his Special Collections staff, UNR's Getchell Library; UNLV Special Collections; Chesa Keane; Rollan Melton; C. J. Hadley; and the UNR Library reference department. We are particularly indebted to those twenty-two former employees of Harrah's Clubs whose stories are recorded here. Their combined memories go far beyond painting a graphic picture of Bill Harrah and his clubs: they provide remarkable insight into fifty years of extraordinary change in Reno, Lake Tahoe, and Nevada's gaming industry.

R. T. King
University of Nevada, Reno

MILOS "SHARKEY" BEGOVICH

*M*ILOS "SHARKEY" BEGOVICH *worked for Harrah's as a dealer and as a shift manager in the 1950s and 1960s. He was born in Plymouth, California, on August 1, 1926, and he has owned his own casino, Sharkey's Nugget in Gardnerville, Nevada, since 1971. His interview was conducted in his casino in May of 1997 and took two sessions to complete. He related freely some of his many experiences in gaming over the last fifty years.*

Begovich worked in and operated illegal casinos in the former mining towns of Plymouth, Jackson, and Sonora, California, in the late 1940s and early 1950s. When those casinos were shut down he went to work in 1956 for Bill Harrah's newly-opened Lake Tahoe casino. He began his career at Harrah's as a dealer, but soon became a box man, pit boss, and eventually a shift manager. His interview is replete with humorous stories of his experiences with headline entertainers and his unique personal dealings with William F. Harrah.

Mr. Begovich is remarkably candid in this oral history. He reveals that he is addicted to gambling and he relates how his gambling problem once caused him to be terminated by Bill Harrah, only to be re-hired a short time later. His tendency to "borrow" Harrah's money to support his gambling habit resulted in his termination once again, and this time Mr. Harrah did not give him another chance.

DWAYNE KLING: Your name is Milos "Sharkey" Begovich. How did you get the name Sharkey?

SHARKEY BEGOVICH: In 1931 Jack Sharkey won the heavyweight championship of the world. His real name was Zukauskas, but when he had first started fighting, the radio announcer had looked up at him and said, "Come on, come on. Give me a name I can handle on the radio." So he thought for a split second. His idol was a great fighter named Tom Sharkey, so he said, "Sharkey, Sharkey, Sharkey." And so that was how he got the name Sharkey.

My real name was Milos Begovich. That was hard to pronounce, and when I was a little boy the boarders at our boardinghouse nicknamed me Sharkey. The name stuck like glue. I mean, from there on out it was so much easier to say "Sharkey" than it was to say "Miloshobelisch Begovich" that the name stuck, and I just kept it and used it in school, on my diplomas, and in my army career. I just made it my middle name, and I've had it for seventy-some years now. So that's how the name Sharkey came about.

When and where were you born, Sharkey?

My mother ran a boardinghouse in Plymouth, California. I was born on the first of August in 1926–born at home in the boardinghouse. My mother didn't go to a hospital; she just had me and that was it.

Did your Dad help run the boardinghouse?

My dad helped. My dad was a monument maker when he came from Yugoslavia. He got here in 1906, and he was in the San Francisco Bay area when the earthquake struck. There was a lot of work for a stonemason or a monument man. He worked there until he made enough money to go to Jackson, California, and then he sent for my mother. When she came over, he went to work at the monument place in Jackson because an old Serbian man owned it, and they had no language problems. He worked there for several years. My parents were going to go back to Europe in 1914, but as they were getting ready to go, trouble started brewing over there, and they were more or less in limbo, waiting to see whether it would be safe to go back over there.

My mother was working in a boardinghouse in Jackson, and the mining company wanted to move them to Plymouth, which is twelve miles away from Jackson. They did move to Plymouth, and then they ran the boardinghouse from there on out. They forgot about going back to Europe. I was the only child out of six–I had two brothers and three sisters–that was born in Plymouth. The rest of them were all born in Jackson. I am the youngest child, and I have one brother, eighty-one years old, and one sister, eighty-four years old, still living in Jackson, California.

I have not been married for thirty-two years. I have one daughter, Mashelle, and a stepson, Butch, who was three years old when I married his mother, and so he's been around

Sharkey (l.), Mashelle, and Butch.

for forty-six years. He's forty-nine now, and Mashelle is thirty-nine.

Do they take a part in the operating of your casino?

Yes, every day of their life, every day of their life. They have been around a casino from the time I opened the Nugget at Lake Tahoe on the first day of July of 1965.

Was that called the South Tahoe Nugget?

Yes, South Tahoe Nugget. Looking for a name for the Nugget, I talked to an old guy from Reno named Lido Costello, and he says, "Call it the Nugget."

I said, "Why the Nugget?"

"Because," he says, "There has never been a Nugget that went broke." [laughter] That's why I called it the Nugget. And it's what they call a free trade name. Anybody can use it. You couldn't stop somebody in Sparks from calling their place the Nugget. I mean, just because Ascuaga has the name doesn't mean that anybody else can't use it. There's a Nugget in Topaz and one in Yerington. There's Nuggets everywhere—Reno, Carson City, anywhere.

To get back to Plymouth, did you grow up in Plymouth?

Right. I went through the eighth grade at Plymouth and then went to Sutter Creek High School on the bus. After graduating from high school, I went straight into the army. I graduated in 1944, and I went into the army in 1944.

I went to Texas for six weeks of training and then went straight overseas, went to the Philippines for a month or so, and from there to Okinawa; was on Okinawa when the war ended and went to Korea and was in the army of occupation for one year. My battalion was one of the first ones that went to Korea to repatriate the Japanese, and we were there to keep peace.

I came back and got discharged at Camp Beale, California, in 1945, right after the war ended. I bought a ranch there in Plymouth in 1945, and in 1945 if you could work on a ranch and make eight dollars a day, you had a good job.

One day a guy by the name of Louie Robbins sold a couple of horses, and he got a hold of me and said, "I'm going to open a dice game up for one night. Come and help me."

I says, "I don't know anything about a dice game."

He says, "You don't have to know anything about it. You just get me what I ask you to get me, and I'll have it in a little box there, and you get it for me." Anyway, the crap game lasted about two hours, and he turned around and handed me seventy-five dollars for helping him for them two hours.

And the next day when I was out working on that ranch in the hot sun, I says, "To hell with this ranch. I want to get me one of them crap games." [laughter] Jackson probably had as many gambling tables, or more, than Reno had in 1945. I went to work there before I was of age. I went to work there probably when I was nineteen years old and started dealing. I've been at it more or less every day of my life since then.

There were probably nine major places in Jackson at that time. It was an unbelievable operation they had there, but they didn't get to run too much longer. From running that crap game I got acquainted with a guy that had a game over in Sonora. So the sheriff came over and asked me if I wanted to come over there and operate a crap game, and I went to Sonora probably right around 1950 and stayed there. It was open and shut, open and shut until 1955.

You say the sheriff invited you to come over?

Yes. That was a common thing, for the sheriff to screen his operators, and evidently the old man told him if they ever opened up the gambling that I would be a good guy for him as far as trouble or anything like that was concerned. I never got in too much trouble–up until I went over there. [laughter]

Was the sheriff taking a cut of your action?

Well, I guess you could call it that. You're talking about figures that are so small that nobody would even want to believe them. But naturally they were interested in keeping it open. I'll tell you how entrenched gambling was: One day I was in a coffee shop in Sonora, and a guy came looking for me. He had all kinds of gold braid on his uniform, and he was the chauffeur for the then governor, Goodwin Knight. Goodwin Knight was there for a campaign speech, and the reason the captain of the highway patrol wanted to talk to me was to make sure that my games stayed open. Goodwin Knight did not want to disrupt anything in that town. Didn't make any difference what it was–he wanted the girls to run; he wanted the gamblers to gamble; he didn't want to disrupt anybody's life. He was just going to be there overnight, and he wanted me to do what I would regularly do. So that was how well it was sanctioned there. It was just accepted, that's all. I mean, it was accepted as a way of life.

Was there more than one casino then, or did you have the only one?

I had the only one in Sonora. It was in a bar called the Mountain Club. I think it's called the Office Bar now.

Were there casinos in Jackson or Plymouth?

No more, no. It got to the point where if you got pinched for gambling, you lost your liquor license. And nobody wanted to jeopardize a liquor license that was probably worth at that time between $40,000 to $50,000. California liquor licenses are a lot harder to come by than they are in Nevada. They didn't have gambling anywhere there was a liquor license involved, because they didn't want to be put out of business.

When you had that joint in Sonora, how many games did you have?

Had three games: roulette wheel, crap table, and a twenty-one table. And they wanted it that way. They didn't want it any bigger. They wanted to keep the big-time operators out of town, and they did keep them out of town.

How many hours a day did you stay open?

I opened at 6:00 p.m. and closed at 2:00 a.m. The primary idea of that was so that nobody would lose their job because they were gambling all night. And I mean, it was as strict as it could be. At a quarter to two they would say the first time a seven shows on the dice, the game is over–they used to say, "When he sevens out." (They had had a couple of awful long hands over there right at two o'clock, and they didn't get closed until 2:30 or so. And they didn't want that, so then they made it the first seven, no matter what it was, that was the end of the game.)

Were you open seven nights a week?

Yes, seven nights a week, and most of our play was local play. None of it ever came from any further away than Stockton, California.

Years ago you told me that you worked with somebody that when you counted the boxes after the game, he would throw all the dollar bills in a closet–he didn't want to bother with them.

Yes. Well, they had an unusual drop box. I've never seen them before or since. They had four paddles on the box. You put the one-dollar bills down with one paddle, five-dollar bills down in another box, the ten-dollar bills in another box, and the twenty-dollar bills in another (there weren't very many hundred-dollar bills around then), and they kept the money separated. So when I was young and would have a date or something, and I didn't want to count the one-dollar bills, I'd just throw them in a safe. I never seen one like it. It had belonged to the Office of Price Administration during the war, and it was about ten foot tall and had fifteen different shelves inside of it. It was a big metal safe, but it had a lot of room to store a lot of things in there. We kept our dice in there and everything. It had more than enough shelves to take care of everything that was used in that operation.

When you had the gambling at Sonora, did you deal, or were you a boss and just walked around?

Dealt every minute. Mainly craps. When anybody wanted to cash out, you kept the bankroll in your pocket, and you just cashed them out with the house bankroll. They'd give you $1,000 at a time, and you would cash out the winners right over the table.

Did you deal with silver dollars then, or was it all chips?

A lot of silver dollars. And the interesting thing about that operation over there was they were shooting a lot of movies in Sonora, one right after the other. And it was not unusual to have Gary Cooper or Forrest Tucker or Ward Bond or Barbara Stanwyck or Burt Lancaster walk in and start playing dice with you. It was the common thing. It was so common it wasn't funny. It was more common to have a movie star at the table than it was not to have one.

What were your table limits?

Dollar minimum to ten dollars maximum. And they made sure that you had signs all over the inside of that room that ten dollars was the limit, in case any investigators came around looking or wanted to photograph the

operation. Everyone immediately knew that it was a small operation. It was like a hometown operation.

Where did you find the dealers to deal the other games?

They would come to town. We had opportunities to get way more of them than we needed. And everybody kept their job. A job was hard to come by, a good job. And on weekends a couple guys from Jackson would come over and work, but it was never a problem getting somebody to deal.

And they were all experienced dealers?

Very, very much so.

But the game was on the up-and-up, wasn't it?

Everything was on the up-and-up— wouldn't have thought of having it any other way. We didn't have to.

What did you pay the dealers?

I think it was twenty to fifty dollars a day, never less than twenty dollars. And if you had a good night, you wouldn't think anything of giving them fifty dollars.

So, what finally stopped the gambling?

The Alcoholic Beverage Control Board was going to pass a law where the Mountain Club would lose their liquor license if they kept the gambling. There had been a bar there for probably a hundred years, and there was no way to keep the game open and maintain a liquor license. It was just impossible.

Did everybody in town know where it was? Was it right downtown?

Oh, it was a landmark, probably ran for thirty years continuously. It ran when Jackson was closed, and it ran through everything. They just seemed to overlook a ten-dollar crap game.

After the gambling closed in 1955, what did you do?

I went up to Lake Tahoe to gamble and to just fool around, and I started talking to a guy that had worked for me named Elwood Orr. He was working in Harrah's. And unbeknownst to me, Harrah's was really short of dealers. Elwood talked to Bill Goupil, and Bill Goupil walked up to me right on the twenty-one table, and he said, "A guy over here tells me you're a pretty good hand around a crap game." He said, "Why don't you come and get on board with us?"

And I said, "I don't think I would like to."

But he was so hard up, he said to me, "Why don't you come up this weekend and give it a try? If you like it, you're welcome to stay here, and if you don't like it, there's no obligation." So I went to work—I think it was in June of 1956—at Harrah's Tahoe.

So you were one of the first employees?

Right, right, one of the first there. I went to work for a guy named Clyde Bittner. He was a shift manager on graveyard. I worked with him for several years before he passed away.

When you started out at Harrah's, was your first job dealing craps?

Right.

How long did you stay dealing craps?

Oh, not very long, a few months. They made me a pit boss that summer. And that was no big deal, because I did have a little bit of knowledge of everything that went on in one of those places. I think in a matter of six months I made shift boss, and that continued on until 1963.

Rome Andreotti dealt with me the first summer. I dealt with him almost daily. He was the shift boss and the overall boss, but he still came down and dealt. That's how Harrah's was just in the beginning. What was happening was unbelievable to everybody. They always thought that tomorrow there wasn't going to be any more action, that there wasn't going to be any play after Labor Day. They were stepping into the unknown, but they were going to keep going.

The reason they kept going and kept it so successful was a bus program that they started that was the most successful thing that ever happened to them before or since. It was just unbelievable. They would bring buses up from Sacramento, mainly, and Stockton and different areas. And there was seldom a vacant seat. They brought in as many people as they could haul. They gave them a free chicken dinner and a free ride and a free bottle of champagne when you went home. Well, it soon got to where the kitchen couldn't handle the free chicken dinners. There was just too many people, so they cut out the dinners, and then they cut out the champagne, and then they cut out giving you the free nickels. And the only way they gave you a break was if you came up late at night when the facility wasn't busy and there was plenty of room for them in the casino.

Bill Harrah always thought that every person he hauled up went over to Harvey's to play. Then Harvey started a bus program, and he always swore that every person he hauled up went over to Harrah's to play. Both clubs started putting different-colored ribbons on the bus customers and stamping their hands, and that was when they first started having counters to go over and see how many people that Harrah hauled up were playing over at Harvey's. And Harvey Gross done the same thing. He sent people over to see how many people he hauled up were playing at Harrah's. [laughter]

It's a joke now, but at the time it was a real serious thing. I remember one night Harvey got upset with something, and he stopped all his buses. The next morning Harrah couldn't believe Harvey had stopped his buses–just couldn't believe it. And I happened to be there, so they sent me over to Harvey's to find out why he stopped the buses. I just happened to bump in to Harvey when I stepped through the door, and I walked up to him and asked him, "Harvey, why have you quit the buses?"

And he says, "Oh, they sent you over here, did they?"

And I says, "Yes."

He says, "Well, go tell him that I fed the cow long enough. I'm going to milk it for a while."

So what could I do but turn around and go back over. I don't think Harrah understood the terminology, but Maurice Sheppard understood it, and he turned around and explained it to him. Well, within a week Harvey started a different bus program that was way bigger than the one that he had previously quit. They all were tied in with different promoters and different guys that were sending these buses up there for x number of dollars.

So the bus program is really what kept them going?

They were the real reason Lake Tahoe got started. Up to that winter of 1956, it was strictly a Labor Day closing for everybody. I mean, they all closed on Labor Day.

Because they knew there wasn't going to be any business in the winter?

Right, right.

Wasn't your brother a state senator at one time?

He was a state senator while I was working at Harrah's. And his area was Amador, Alpine, and El Dorado County. El Dorado County butted right up against the Nevada state line, and let's face it, politics are politics. Harrah's appreciated the fact that if they

wanted the senator's ear about keeping the road open or doing something, it wasn't very hard to arrange for them to talk to the senator. [laughter]

So your brother made an effort to keep the snow off the highways?

In them days they personally had a highway patrolman take them up and down the road after every storm to see if anything had to be done or repaired or anything, and the senator could order it done. The main thing then and the main thing today is Highway 50. With it they survive, without it they die. As was proven again this winter.

Let's talk a little more about Clyde Bittner.

Clyde Bittner was from Montana and came to Reno in the 1930s to open the first keno game in the Palace Club for Warren Nelson. He worked for Warren and was there from the beginning of the keno game. And he knew all about the other games too. He was a Montana gambler before he came to Nevada. He and Warren both went to work for Harrah's after they had the keno game in the Palace Club, and later they both worked at the Cal-Neva. Bittner stayed there until he died. He died a fairly young man. I think he was in his early fifties when he died.

How about Chet Edwards?

Chet Edwards came and went. He may have been working for Harrah's in Reno, and they brought him up to the lake. I bought his house from him when he left Harrah's and went to Vegas.

He was a very, very knowledgeable gambling man. What you called a knowledgeable gambler them days was–if you couldn't detect a deuce dealer or somebody that could switch dice, you weren't a knowledgeable gambler. You weren't smart enough to become a pit boss if you didn't know all the moves a cheater made in order to try and cheat. They tell me now they have seminars where they have these experts come in and show them and teach them as much as is possible to teach them in a couple days about cheating methods. Well, in those days, you more or less had to know a little bit about cheating. Now gaming control has more or less eliminated it, except it will never stop completely. As long as there's two people on the face of the earth, one of them will be trying to cheat the other one. [laughter]

Gambling was more or less nothing but cheating until Harolds[1] Club came along and proved you could be successful without cheating. And, naturally, I feel that way myself. I think gaming does as good a job as can be done. Today, as far as the house is concerned, it's an impossible thing, because you'd be jeopardizing the whole investment. Cheating is a non-existent thing anymore. Casinos would lose their licenses worth millions and millions of dollars. But in the old days there wasn't hardly anybody that ran a club that didn't have somebody that was capable of cheating. Like they say, it takes one to know one.

So a lot of the dealers in the 1940s or 1950s at Harrah's were capable of cheating?

They were very, very knowledgeable. Lots of them had worked where cheating went on. It was more or less an accepted thing. What chance would a truck driver from Santa Barbara have of getting ungodly lucky against the guy that had been working in a gambling place his whole life?

So a lot of the cheating wasn't done on a regular basis—it just happened if somebody got lucky and got a lot of money out?

Yes. Well, they called [these dealers] "stoppers." They would just stop the guy's lucky streak. They tell me that where cheating was really prevalent in this state, they would keep somebody on the payroll on every shift, and a real, real busy night for him would be to make one move or at the most two moves during the whole shift–like I say, to stop the streaks. They didn't stay there and work continuously; they were more or less on call. I could really get into that, but I don't think it's my place to hurt people that are dead and gone. And why even talk about it? You know, during our reign there it was unthinkable. Nobody even gave it a thought. Of course, you had to be on your toes and watching for the outside cheating going on.

Harrah's was always on the up-and-up, from the very beginning. If there ever was cheating going on, it wasn't with the knowledge of the management. It went on between the player and the dealer. And they'll never stop that from happening ever, either.

Just because a dealer was capable of cheating and had cheated in other places . . . when he came to work for Harrah's, he was straight arrow or he would be terminated on the spot, immediately.

Well, I know I took a few people off the table in the middle of a shift, and you probably took several off.

Oh, yes, absolutely! I took several right off the game. You know . . . I mean, hell, when a good deuce dealer looks underneath his top card and sees a six . . . . It ain't no job for him to hold a breaking card back–soon as one comes to the top of the deck, they hold it and go for it when they need it.

If you're cheating for the house, you hold the "right" card, [laughter] and if you're against the house, you hold the "wrong" card; and when you use the key card, it always comes off the top of the deck right under your nose where you can see it. But it may have been held there while ten cards were dealt out from underneath it. When the dealer has sixteen and he comes to a five, he's going to hold it there for himself, and when he needs it—boom! There it is, he knows it's there. There is no guesswork. But it's kind of a waste of time anymore to even talk about it.

Well, it's part of the history of gambling. That's the way it was.

Oh, the way it was, yes. It's not that way anymore, but look at the thousands of Indian places that have opened up where it is as prevalent as it could be. A good friend of mine owned a casino in Laughlin, and he said one of the good things about opening these Indian casinos is all the thieves left Laughlin and went over to where there's nobody looking for them. [laughter] They just work any way they want to work—do whatever they want to do, nobody is going to arrest them. If they caught them, they wouldn't arrest them.

Just the thought of being cheated is enough to keep many players from playing, because everybody wonders when they've lost their money: "I wonder if I got cheated out of my money or whether I lost it." [laughter]

Well I remember you saying that one time at the lake, in probably about 1957 or 1958, when we had been across the street at the Nevada Club.

Oh, yes, the Nevada Club. I often wondered if we got cheated. I later became friends of the manager, Frank Perez, and he was insistent that it never, ever happened. Well, I don't know whether it did or it didn't. No man's going to brand himself a thief, because once you're branded, the brand doesn't come off very easy.

Well, we never won any money in the Nevada Club. We never crossed the street with anything. But there were a lot of places you didn't win any money.

That's right. Harolds Club—the squarest one of them all—was harder to beat than anybody. And they say that Pappy Smith said he didn't want any money that he didn't have

to win at least three different times. Cheating was never thought of at Harrah's Club or Harolds Club. They were the ones that were responsible for taking gaming out of the dark ages.

When Harrah's first started out, they hired experienced dealers, but eventually younger dealers were hired, is that right?

Yes, they started breaking them in, started having dealing schools. The older guys that are working at Harrah's now, that I know, they all started at the bottom ground level and learned to deal there and gained their knowledge while they were working there. Some of them seemed to have it, and some of them didn't. The ones that were really successful, like Dyer and Hendricksen, they started out as a cashier and a bus boy and got to be president and vice-president by nothing but hard work—doing honest, hard work. Wouldn't know the first thing about cheating or anything; never devoted one minute of their time to try and learn anything about it. That wasn't their game, and it wasn't needed. Trying to beat the game on the square is an awful hard thing to do, and it only happens now and then, because people defeat themselves. You don't have to beat them. If they stay long enough, there's no humanly possible way they can win.

So as Harrah's grew, it became a more popular place to work?

Right. They liked to hire a guy like myself with knowledge of the old and the new. There were different things that happened there that nobody will ever know and nobody will believe. And Harrah's, I would say, was lucky that they always had a super sharp guy walking the floor that could detect anything. There are a few men that could be at one end of the casino and have something go wrong at the other end, and they would get a vibration through the air that something is happening that shouldn't be. And I believe that with all my heart. I mean, I know they are few and far between, but they have that one gift of being able to feel something in the air–that something wrong is going on in here. I have been told by a couple different guys that something was going wrong in here, and in a matter of minutes there would be a big brawl break loose in the casino. They could feel it before it happened. They just couldn't put their finger on it.

How big a part do you think the entertainment played in the success of Harrah's?

They use counters so often now. By "counters," I mean people go count the customers in their competition's place, and if the competition has a group in there that had a couple hundred people at the bar, and there was sixty-five in Harrah's, Harrah would like to know who that group is and try to hire them to come across the street and play for them.

In my own mind, entertainment is so successful in bringing people in that it isn't even funny. But a lot of clubs figure that you can make as much money without it as you can with it, so why go through all mountains and mountains of paperwork figuring out whether you made money or whether you didn't make money by having the entertainment there? Some of it is just an exchange of dollars. If your show costs you a couple hundred thousand or $300,000–in today's world that isn't very much for a big-name star to be getting–you have to make $300,000 to get back to square one, to be even. So how many drinks do you have to serve? How much help do you have to hire? How much everything? The show has to bring in a lot of money to pay for the entertainment and still make money.

Harrah's used to change their star entertainers every two weeks, and the stars did two shows every night, and on Saturday night they did three shows. They were glad to do it,

because Harrah's more or less pioneered the star theory. And believe me, they had them all. You didn't see them hiring Pavarotti or Whitney Houston or acts that would cost them so much that they would lose money by having them in their casino, but if they could make money by having them, they'd have them there too.

Yes. Well, by changing the star every two weeks, it gave the people another reason every two weeks to come back to Reno or Tahoe.

Absolutely, absolutely. And they advertised at least six months ahead of time who was going to be there and what time they were going to be there. So if you had a favorite person you wanted to watch, you could plan ahead and come. I remember having an argument with Bill Harrah over Nelson Eddy. Bill said the people that come to see Nelson Eddy don't come to see any other entertainer. He brought a different avenue of money into the place than any other entertainer brought in, because they're Nelson Eddy fans. They want to see him, and they don't want to see Giselle McKenzie or Sammy Davis or Nat "King" Cole. They want to see Nelson Eddy.

So was he sticking up for Nelson Eddy?

No, not really. I had had nothing but problems with Eddy, and I asked Bill why he had him there, and he said because he brings a new source of money into the door.

As you said earlier, you went from dealer to shift manager very rapidly. As shift manager you were in charge basically of the entire casino for eight hours– entertainment, bars, everything. So you must have met a lot of these entertainers when they came to the lake.

Knew them so well it wasn't even funny, because whoever was shift boss, it was part of their job to go ask them if they were having any problems or wanted anything done. And

I think the main reason for that is one night when Louie Armstrong was there, he looked at his watch, and he said, "I'm sorry folks. I have to go pick my Uncle Louie up at the airport." [laughter]

And the next day when Harrah saw where it said the customers were really dissatisfied because he cut his show short, he said, "Well, from now on we'll go ask him if his Uncle Louie is coming." And he said, "If he is, we'll go pick him up and bring him here. Let him do what he is being paid to do, not go off and leave a bunch of unhappy people there." So satisfying the entertainers was more or less a part of the shift boss's job then, and I'm sure it's part of the shift boss's job now.

The main thing the entertainers wanted was cash money, a few hundred dollars to put in their pocket to play around with or to buy a ski jacket or some spending money or to send money home. You would take care of anything. *You* didn't take care of it—you went up and left a message on the back bulletin board, and it got taken care of the first thing in the morning. Or if they wanted money, a cashier came down and brought the money and gave it to them and had them sign a receipt for it, and when they were paid off, naturally, it was deducted out of their pay.

So they took draws on their salary just like regular employees?

Absolutely. Did then and probably still do now. And I would imagine that there's a lot of entertainers' markers still somewhere, sitting up there that never got paid.

Well, a lot of them used that draw or advance money to gamble, right?

Right, and there was a few of them that naturally really abused it. You know, there was nobody that abused it more than Nat King Cole did. It was not unusual for him to have all of his salary drawn in a week and still have another week to go, and then he would get advances on his next engagement. And there were many, many of them that done that—you know, that would have to get a loan to go to the next job. Even if it was only a couple days off, they needed a little bit of money to get them through that time.

In those early days was $50,000 a week the average salary?

Oh, it was not that much money for a long time. I think it was between $11,500 and $17,500. The bigger the room, the more the entertainer wants, which stands to reason. If he can pack 1,100 people into a room every night, he wants more money than he got when you had him in a room that would only hold 110 people in it.

So the entertainers at Tahoe got more money than the entertainers in Reno?

Yes, but in the late fifties, early sixties, the very tops at Tahoe was $17,500. And then it went from there. I don't know what year it was that the lid blew off of it completely.

Speaking of entertainers, could you tell me about Liberace?

He, beyond any question of a doubt, had more heart than any other entertainer. As far as making a sacrifice to help somebody or make somebody happy or do anything that was asked of him, he was the greatest. If you asked him to come and meet somebody or to spend a little time talking to somebody or to take a picture with somebody, he was right there. I never knew him to say no. I've known him to take his clothes off and give them to somebody that wanted them—somebody that thought they were nice. Anything to make anybody happy. He would go to any extreme. He was so thankful and grateful for the way the world had treated him in those days and for the money that he made. And his main gripe was that he didn't have enough time to enjoy life. The demands on him and his time were so great that he didn't have much time for himself or time to do what he wanted to do. I even saw him do shows for different people— maybe a dozen of them couldn't get into his show, so he'd go in and do a song and dance routine and spend more time with them right up close than anybody.

You know, Jimmy Durante was another guy that was always obliging and helpful. A lot of entertainers would look at you like, "What are you asking me to do this for?" It wasn't their style. Their mother didn't raise them the way other people's mother raised them, because they had that "superioristic" attitude. They didn't want to meet anybody, and they didn't want to sign any autographs.

They did their show, and that was it?

That was it. They weren't obliging at all to their fans. And others couldn't do enough for their fans. By the time they got to the big room, they were an established star. From the lounge to the big room was only probably one hundred yards, but it was many, many miles to get from that lounge to get into that big room. Many miles and many years. Louie Prima, in them days, was the hottest lounge act that Harrah ever had. They put him in the big room, and he flopped. He couldn't do it. He wasn't a big room act. But he sure as hell was a great lounge act. He was probably one of the most successful lounge acts that ever played Las Vegas, Reno, or Lake Tahoe.

We mentioned Nat "King" Cole a few minutes ago. He liked to gamble didn't he?

Oh, boy! He'd rather gamble than do anything. He was what you would call an addict. He would play as long as he could get his hands on money. But then again, that's in Nevada. He probably only spent two months a year in Nevada: two weeks at the Sands in Vegas and two weeks at Harrah's twice a year during those years. And the rest of the time he was probably in places where there wasn't any

gambling or the kind of gambling that he liked. I know he was in San Francisco a lot.

Did he gamble more than anyone?

Gambled more than anybody and was virtually an absolute sellout: winter, summer, rain, snow, cold, heat—it made no difference. A lot of entertainers when they didn't fill the room blamed it on everything but themselves. They blamed it on Lent. They blamed it on the weather. But Nat King Cole didn't ever have to worry about selling every seat in the room—didn't matter when, what season, or anything else. And he was good for as long as he played. He was as strong the last night he played as he was the first night he opened.

And ironically, as you said, he lost most of his money gambling.

Lost most of his money, and he was a high living guy that lived every day like it was going to be the last one that he was going to be on this planet. And the way it turned out, he didn't have too many days left.

I remember when he was up there shooting a movie called *Cat Ballou* with Lee Marvin. He would gamble late and stay up a lot later than he had to. Then early in the morning he would go down to the Tahoe airport and get on a jet and jet down to Hollywood and work on the movie and then be back in the showroom that night. And he did that for the couple of weeks that he was there. You know, he punished his body to an unbelievable degree, but he never complained.

One morning I came out of the dressing room with him, and Harrah's had just got their first hot dog machine where you put them giant hot dogs on a grill that rolls around. Well, he spotted that grill, and he went over there and popped his fingers and hollered and danced the jig and just kept staring at them hot dogs. So the very next morning about nine o'clock he calls me, and he says, "Goddamn, Shark, I'm hungry."

And I said, "What would you like to eat, Nat?"

And he says, "I been dreaming about them hot dogs ever since I got home."

So I says, "No problem. How many of them do you want?"

And he says, "Oh, send me over a dozen of them."

So I went down to the snack bar and I says, "Fix a dozen hot dogs to go and have the courtesy bus take them over to the Naify house." I says, "He's staying over there. Take them over there."

So the next morning—very next morning, twenty-four hours almost to the minute later— he called me up on the phone, and he says, "Goddamn, I'm hungry."

And I says, "What do you want? No problem." Which it wasn't. You know how accommodating they wanted you to be—no problem. I happened to have a menu and I read it to him.

He said, "Trout sounds good to me."

I said, "No problem, Nat." I says, "How many? How many of them do you want?"

He says, "Oh send me over a dozen of them."

So I went in the kitchen, said, "Fix a dozen trout to go and take them over to Naify house."

So that evening I'm in the casino, and he had one guy with him that time. His name was John. "Big John," they called him. I'm quite sure his name was John Collins. But anyway, he was a giant of a guy. He shined Nat's shoes and took care of his cleaning and this and that and the other. Anyway, I overheard him say to one of the cashiers, "Who's in charge of sending the King his food?"

As soon as I heard that, I ran around, and I says, "What's the matter, John? Is something wrong with the food?"

He says, "No, not a goddamned thing." He says, "There's eleven hotdogs over there.

There's eleven trout over there on a table." And he says, "They are stinking the hell out of that place." He says, "From now on when he orders a dozen of them, send him one." [laughter]

Did you ever go gambling with Nat "King" Cole?

Well, any time he had any money I did. The main reason I went around with him so much was because he would stake me—he would give me money to gamble with.

One night I went walking through the casino, and he pulled out five hundred-dollar bills, and he put them in front of Sam Dianitto's wife, and she shuffled up and dealt, and she got a blackjack. He reached over and grabbed her two cards and put them in his mouth and snipped them off like a pair of scissors. Cut them clean with his teeth. He wasn't too good a loser. [laughter]

How about Liberace—didn't he play slot machines a lot?

He did gamble at twenty-one when he first started coming there. One day I seen him lose $10,000. He signed a marker for it, and they held it out of his pay. And just kiddingly I asked him a year or so later how come he didn't play. And he whispered to me, "The bookkeepers are still looking for the $10,000 that I lost the last time I played." [laughter]

You know, one time Zsa Zsa Gabor was there. She was only there once, I think. Anyway, she was playing twenty-one, and she wanted a marker. She wanted money, but she didn't want to sign for it. So I says to her, "We probably handle things different here than the way you're used to being handled." I says, "You can have anything you want, but you have to sign for it."

And she said to me, "You know, you're not the kindest person I've come across in my lifetime." [laughter]

I says, "Well, I'm sorry, but that's the way the house policy is here." Well if I remember right, I put the book out in front of her, and she signed it, got $2,500 or something like that. I don't even remember whether she won or lost.

Wasn't Teresa Brewer's husband a heavy gambler?

Yes. His name was Bill Monaghan. When she was appearing, there she was getting $30,000 a week, and I think he drew the whole $30,000 before she did her first show. [laughter] She called me down to the dressing room and asked me what could be done about him not getting any more money. She was crying—crying real, real tears; I couldn't believe how shook up she was.

She did twenty-eight shows, I think, before she was through. The next week he was gone, so he didn't get to draw that. But she was with him for I don't know how long; had five daughters by him. And then they divorced. But I think he spent everything she made during her great years. I heard in Vegas they had a lot of trouble with him, the same thing. He gambled all the time, but she never bet a nickel. She never even played a slot machine. She was a wonderful person. Can you imagine how easy her later years would have been if it weren't for him?

Did Jack Benny and his wife Mary Livingston gamble a lot?

She gambled, and he did too. Whenever he played, he would play five-dollar chips, but he would only play a few hundred dollars worth. When he decided it was time to quit, whatever he had left in front of him in chips, he broke them in two even piles and gave the dealers one pile and took the other pile.

One time when he was there, Harrah's gave them "his" and "her" license plates on two Jaguars that they had parked underneath the big marquee in front of Harrah's. Somebody come and asked me if I would take

him out there and show him his gift. So I got a hold of him and asked him to take a short walk with me, and we no sooner walked out of the door and he spotted those cars then he says, "I really appreciate them giving me a gift, but," he says, "it's going to take two days of sitting down with my bookkeeper to figure how we're going to work this out as far as my taxes are concerned." In other words, "Why did they bother giving me a car?" [laughter] Which was a favorite thing of Bill Harrah's. I remember when he didn't even have one car for them to ride in, and then it wasn't very many years later he thought nothing of giving them a Rolls-Royce. I think he gave Sammy Davis a couple of Rolls. And, oh, Merle Haggard, he gave him two of them—had them delivered. That was when Merle was really big. Bill Harrah asked him one day what his favorite old cars were, and one of them I know was some kind of an old Ford. So Bill Harrah had a couple of them that were completely restored delivered to his house in Bakersfield, and he still has them.

I remember the first day Jack Benny and Mary Livingston came there. Harrah's didn't have a hotel, so they put them up in the motel that Harrah's had right where the parking garage is now. It didn't have a bathtub. It had a shower—big shower—in it, but it didn't have a bathtub. And she couldn't believe it, that there wasn't a bathtub in that room. So they got maintenance to go over there—Austin Raymer and somebody else—and they installed a bathtub right on top of the little sitting room, on top of the floor for her stay there.

Oh, I remember Mary Livingston well. I remember her well. She was very, very demanding: "They do this for me at the Sands, and they do that for me, and how come you don't do it here? How come you don't give me money to play the slot machines? I am a big draw. I attract a big crowd."

I says, "Well they just don't do things that way here." But she would never give anything back.

And Jack Benny never asked for anything?

Nothing, nothing, nothing.

Weren't they usually with George Burns and Gracie Allen?

Yes. I remember when George Burns and Jack Benny "owned" Bobby Darin. They discovered him, and every afternoon they would close the showroom and would go in there, and the two of them, Burns and Benny, would sit in there and offer him advice—he was up on the stage singing—what he should do, giving him a routine. Then later he became a nose-up-in-the-air kid, but he didn't have too long to live anyway. He asked me one day—they had a stage hand there that was crippled—if I could get somebody else to do what the crippled guy was doing, because it bothered him to see somebody crippled around him. He was kind of a funny little guy. But like I say, when they're gone, they're gone.

Were there many other high-limit players?

Oh, there was so many of them there! In them days there was always somebody that was at the top of the hit parade until he lost his money. It was like baseball players and their batting averages. There's a guy on top one day, and next day he's been replaced by somebody else.

Do you remember Harry Belafonte appearing at Harrah's?

Oh yes, I remember him. He was another guy that hated to give an autograph, just hated it. And was a very strange guy, and I'm sure he is yet. He's still appearing. I think he was at Ascuaga's Nugget not too long ago.

Where did the Afro-Americans (or blacks) stay? Was there a housing problem at Tahoe?

Well, I'll tell you an interesting story. The first time Louie Armstrong came to the lake, Harrah's had one door in the back of the kitchen on the little club. And I think Louie had about seventeen people in his entourage, between the band and a sound man and a sound tech and this and that and the other. And he came through the back door several times while he was getting ready to do his show. You know, they always come in and had rehearsals and everything. So I was with Bill Harrah and Malcolm Farnsworth (Red Farnsworth), and I said something about Louie coming through the kitchen. They didn't allow blacks in the clubs then. They used to go up and ask them to leave—I mean just outright. Not very many of them tried to come in, but the ones that did, they asked them to leave. So Red Farnsworth said to me, "Would you go tell Louis that Mr. Harrah would feel honored if he would use the front door?"

What could I do but just go down and find Louis and tell him? I went down and I said, "Louis, Mr. Harrah would really be honored if you would use the front door when you come in and out of the club."

Louis called everybody "Cat." He called me "Cat," too. He says, "Cat, that's awful nice. I really appreciate that, but you tell Mr. Harrah that old Louis is still going to use the back door." And he continued to use it.

Was that in the late fifties or early sixties?

In the late fifties sometime. I think a lounge act called the Treniers kind of broke the barrier a little bit. But security thought nothing of going up and asking somebody colored to please leave. They just weren't allowed in there. And everybody accepted it and left. I don't ever remember an incident.

At that time there were two casinos in Reno on Lake Street. Bill Fong had one, and there was another one. And they didn't have anybody in them but colored people. They catered to them.

You were going to tell me one of the most amazing things that Sammy Davis Jr. ever did.

Well, one night Harry James was in the lounge, and Sammy Davis was in the showroom. Harry James had an old-time jazz singer with him by the name of Jimmy Rushing who sang and whistled, and Harry James would just wilt. He would sit back in a chair and listen to this colored guy sing. So one night Jimmy Rushing said to me–he talked in such a colored talk that it was unbelievable–"Say, Will Mastin, Sammy Davis's dad, he back there?"

And I says, "Yes, he's back there."

He says, "Can you take me to see him? He's an old friend of mine from the Orpheum Theater in New York."

So I take Jimmy Rushing backstage, and here comes Will Mastin, Sammy's father. (Sammy's dad was a little teeny guy.) They hugged, and they kissed, and they hugged, and they hollered, and they danced, and they went through this whole show. Both of them were laughing, and Jimmy Rushing says to Will Mastin, "Is that the little boy you had in the baby buggy back at the Orpheum?"

"Yes, it's him. He's a good one ain't he? He bring home the bacon, don't he?" [laughter] Will Mastin talked just like, "I bring home da bacon." I couldn't believe the conversation between them two old colored guys. Well, Sammy Davis made more money in them days by accident than they made in their whole life. That's enough of that.

–✧–

Gambling was my addiction, and it don't do nothing but hurt you to be known as a player. Who trusts a player? To be a player, you got to be half animal and half man.

I've gambled all my life, but I don't gamble anymore. I've kept myself from it, and the only way you can keep yourself from gambling is don't expose yourself to it. I mean, there's no other way. If you're around a

bunch of guys that gamble, you're going to make a little bet. Who knows what triggers it? Myself, right now in my little world, I don't have to gamble anymore. I can have anything I want; I'm not rich by any means, but there isn't anything I can't buy. I drive an old car, but if I wanted a new one it wouldn't cost me a dime to have one. I mean, it would be a three year write-off, and my bookkeepers can't figure out why I don't. It's just not my style. I just don't like to ride around in a new car. I really don't like to do it.

Well, a true addicted gambler has to be just like a drinker. You can't make one bet and quit. You can't have one drink and quit.

Oh, hell no! There's no such thing as "I've slowed down." What there is, is there's a lot of secret players. They go somewhere, and they're more worried about who's going to see them than they are about whether they win or lose a bet.

But it's crazy to even talk about a guy making a living by playing. That's ridiculous, and on top of that, it's an impossible thing. Sure, you might get lucky. Chet Edwards told me about a guy playing in Reno who won eighty consecutive days–eighty consecutive plays. And by the eighty-fifth day, he was out of money. When the streak left, he went for it all, and that's what happens to a lot of people. If you're satisfied with winning very little money–or even bigger money if you've got it to start with–you might get away with it.

The trouble with the United States of America–I don't care who it is, whether it's some professor or yourself–is greed; G-R-E-E-D. Everybody has got greed. So if things are going right for you, you're going to want more. Greed is what makes gambling casinos. Hitler had Europe. Napoleon had half of the world. They still wanted more. Greed gets everybody. And it will get everybody for the next 2000 years to come or longer, until they set off a chain reaction where they burn every living thing up on the planet. [laughter]

Do you think it's true that if a player wins, he'll win a little bit and quit, but if he loses, he will lose a lot, maybe everything?

That's the problem with every living human. And this idea about limiting yourself to this and that and the other . . . it sounds good, or it reads good on paper, but that isn't the way the human body is put together. Everybody dreams about the big payoff. The best thing that happened in that respect is the big payoff on slot machines, because it could happen to somebody who would never win that amount of money gambling at cards or dice or anything else. If they happen to hit a machine at the right time, they do wind up with enough money to have a good life. Even the way they pay you—over twenty years, which is a joke—it's still not bad for the recipient, for the winner, because he does get something for twenty years anyway. Where if he got it all at once, it would be all gone. Before they instituted that, it happened at the lake. I think a couple of guys won one or two million dollars, and in two years they were not only broke, but it destroyed their whole life.

When did you start gambling?

I started as a teenager around Jackson and in the army. I never outgrew it until I was between fifty and sixty, and I'll carry the curse with me to my grave. I mean it is a curse. Nobody is satisfied with whatever they win.

But you don't play now do you?

No, I haven't for years, not even one bet, because I'm afraid to play. I'm afraid what it would lead to. For example, if you picked up a cold twenty, and a dealer has got a five up

and a five in the hole and then hits a third five and then hits an ace and then catches a fourth five—and you've been watching that game for forty years, and you've never seen that combination come up before—how can that combination come up against me? And so you blow your cool. Whether you show it on the outside or not has got nothing to do with the way you feel on the inside. Invariably, some young kid that's just learning how to deal will pull one of them hands out of the bag to trigger you off.

So, the only way you finally quit was to not expose yourself to gambling?

Right. And I think there's a certain time in your life when you get afraid to play anymore, especially if you're lucky enough to have a few dollars. You know what's going to happen to you if you fool around and gamble.

What was the most money you ever lost in one play?

Oh, way, way more than I ever had a right to lose. I lost a lot of money three different times, probably around a hundred thousand on three plays. I did win a lot of money, too. I made a lot of little scores, but there is no possible way to go against the law of averages and beat the game. You can beat the game any time, but to keep it beat is an impossibility.

Did you play mostly twenty-one?

Well, mainly twenty-one, but what is there to know about twenty-one? I mean, one day you play a certain way, and you win ten bets in a row and lose one and win ten more. Then the next day, you play the same way, and you lose ten bets and win one and lose ten more. There's no way at all to keep the game beat. It's not possible.

There were stories going around years ago that you had a lucky run at Harvey's Wagon Wheel. Is that right?

I did have a big run. The streak lasted five days, and that was basically the only real streak I ever had. I won as much as it was humanly possible to win. Only, in them days the limit was $500: nobody got to bet any more. Look how many years Harrah's went at the lake, and how many years Harvey ran at the lake before they'd let you bet $500.

Yes, and now $10,000 is the common limit in Las Vegas.

A common thing. I don't know how they keep so many people playing for so many years, and they are all a slave to that game. Their families do without the necessities of life. They do without the clothes that they should be wearing and the automobile that they should be driving and the boat that they should be enjoying with their families and everything.

But they've got this so instilled in so many millions of people that I think it will eventually have a great influence on whether our government continues to run the way it runs. The guys that work down in them southern states tell me that for three or four days at the first of the month they're as busy as they can be. And then after those three or four days, they have to wait until the next bunch of welfare and social security checks come through the mail to be able to go again. And you know good and well that a good part of that money should be going for clothing and food, and it doesn't.

So you're saying that gambling is hurting the United States as a whole?

Oh, absolutely! Anybody that thinks otherwise is kidding himself.

Well, on that five-day run at Harvey's Wagon Wheel in 1963, how much money do you think you won?

It was huge. I don't want to say, but I know almost to the dollar. And one thing I did do there that was different: I never waited until I got beat to quit. I just quit when I got scared to play anymore, knowing that I'd blow it all if I got stuck.

But as far as somebody thinking that something big is going to happen to him playing them games–there's no way. There is no way. It doesn't happen. When it happens to one person out of 250,000,000, you read about it in every newspaper in the country. It don't happen very often.

Even after you made that big score at the Wagon Wheel, if you took away the thousands of other times you played where you lost a hundred or you lost a thousand, you'd still be in the hole.

Yes, and anybody else that played for any length of time would be the same way.

Gambling creates a lot of social problems. Look at the respectable women that it's turned into prostitutes, and it's destroyed more marriages than everything else combined. How many households can stay together when the husband isn't bringing home a paycheck? And how many people at Lake Tahoe (when you and I were there) lost a motel gambling? We saw dozens of people come to Tahoe and lose their businesses and leave town. They went back to California or wherever they came from.

Well, then, how do you rationalize running a casino?

If I wasn't running the casino, somebody else would be running it, and it's the only thing I know how to do. But I've constantly observed people, and I just don't understand how they can continually lose, lose, lose; and just can't wait to get the next check so they can lose it, too. [laughter]

I very rarely, if ever, see a story about how many people gambling destroys, because the minute they do they're practically out of business. If they're a newspaper, the club quits advertising with them. And usually the advertising a club does with any local newspaper is the difference between profit and loss. So they're not going to say anything anti-gambling.

When you made that big score at the Wagon Wheel and you kept that money, what did you do?

I never worked another day for another man, and that's from 1963 to today. As soon as I won the money, I went to Korea. I went over there on a gaming venture, and it didn't work out, but I didn't lose any money over there. I went over there with a $10,000 investment and would have been an awful rich man if I would have got to do what I paved the road for somebody else to do.

So there's a lot of gambling in Korea now?

Oh, they have a giant casino now. I imagine it opened about a couple of years after I left. It's called the Walker Hill Casino—highly successful, owned by a bunch of people from the Philippine Islands. They had enough money and everything to carry it through and see it through, and now it's a thriving success. You know, the joint in Korea came about mainly because several thousand soldiers, every week, were going to Japan on leave for a couple of days and spending probably an average of $300 in those two days. The idea was to keep the money in Korea instead of letting it go to Japan.

Was there gambling in Japan?

Well, there isn't a city in the world, whether it's in Israel, whether it's in Bangladesh, whether it's in mainland China—there isn't anywheres that you can't find a place to gamble. They say Castro killed it in Cuba, but there's still places, if you know how to get into them, that are running. There's always going to be that going, because it's a lucrative business.

So your casino in Korea was going to be based on military play?

Strictly military play, but in the far-off future everybody had ideas of chartering people in from anywhere. Today it's the marketing people who make the money. It's unreal, but they're the ones that deliver the customers to the table. And it's getting to be more so that way than ever. Only thing—there aren't enough players that can stay in enough money to keep bringing them over because they get knocked off.

Look at the millions of dollars won or lost in baccarat. When me and you were at Lake Tahoe, they didn't know what baccarat even was. And now it's the big money earner in most of the casinos. Not bigger than slot machines, but as far as table games, they win more money with their baccarat pits than they do with their craps and twenty-one or roulette.

You only lost $10,000 of your money when you went to Korea, so it wasn't a total financial loss for you.

I flew back and forth nine times, and the price of a round trip ticket was $999.

So there's $10,000 right there?

Yes, plus the money I put into it. I took a crew of guys—Hank Decker, Larry Vaughan, Lester Sanborn, and a guy named Toley Sealy—that were going to help run this casino.

They were going to train the help how to deal and so forth, whatever it took. I took an expert from Tahoe in each department with me over there. All my people were very knowledgeable. They weren't like a great deal of casino owners.

A good part of the owners didn't even know how to gamble. The ones I knew intimately and knew well, naturally, some of them did; but Bill Harrah or Harvey Gross, they never understood the basics of a craps game. They didn't know what the odds were, double odds or anything. I remember different owners of casinos would come to the lake when we were there, and they didn't know the basic "elementrics" of playing. But they hired the people that really did know what they were doing to work for them.

Yes. Well, especially Bill Harrah. One of his main things was delegation of authority.

Delegation. And he done a great job of it. And as far as Rome Andreotti was concerned, that's where he came in. He did understand gambling. They did put him in charge, and he delivered the bottom line that they liked to look at. So they weren't going to change him. They'd have been crazy if they did.

Yes. I feel he was a great contributor to the success of Harrah's Club pit department.

Absolutely, absolutely. He kept the thievery at a minimum. He kept everybody in line. He didn't let any department lose any money. If they did, his theory was get rid of them and get somebody in there that did know how to run it where it won't lose any money. And no matter what business you run into, if more money goes out the door than comes in the door, it isn't going to be there very long.

You left Harrah's Club in 1963, right?

Right. But before that, I don't even remember what year it was, I went and took money that didn't belong to me out of the safe and went to the Wagon Wheel and lost it. In the morning I told Bill Harrah what I had done. He loaned me the money to put back in the vault, and he let me continue to work there. After I had paid the money back (which was a substantial amount of money), I went to Reno one day, and I wrote a bunch of bum checks, like $15,000 worth, and I got that credit on the strength of the job that I had at Harrah's. So I went to him again the following morning and told him what I had done. And he loaned me the money so I could put it back.

For the second time?

Second time. Well, wait a minute—I'm not through yet. I paid that back, and not long after that I went to Reno, and all I could get was $5,000 in three or four places. Well, I got that and lost that. The next morning, I met him at 6:00 a.m. in the hall. And nobody was more disgusted with themselves than I was with myself.

I said to him, "I've done it again."

And he said, "I'm not going to even ask you how much. I'll try and help you, but me and you are drawing the line today. It is all over." He says, "It makes no difference whether I'm in London, England, or whether I'm in the Fiji Islands." He says, "Every three minutes the thought crosses my mind: I wonder what he's doing today." [laughter] "Well," he says, "my money is one thing. My mind is another. And you're damn sure not going to get them both."

So I says, "Good enough."

He never said "You're fired." It was just over. That was all.

I went to work at the Mapes hotel in Reno. A couple of nights before Christmas, I'm crossing the street between the Mapes and the big bank building there, and I heard a voice from behind me say, "How's it going?" I recognized his voice and I turned around. He didn't even look down at me. I'd already stepped off the curb.

I says, "Going all right." I says, "They treat me good. They pay me well. What more could I ask for than that?"

And he said—looking straight ahead— "You don't belong there. You belong back with me."

The light changed, and I went to work. He went wherever he went, and I was at work maybe a half hour, forty-five minutes, when Murray Jacobs come walking in there and walked over to me and said, "They want to see you down at Harrah's Club."

And I said, "I can't go down there right now. I'm working."

I sure as hell didn't want to lose that job, so on my lunch break I walked down to Harrah's. Bob Ring was there more or less waiting for me, and he looked up at me when I walked into his office and says, "When do you want to come back to work?"

And I says, "Well, they surely haven't mistreated me down there. I want to give them whatever time they want or until they get somebody to replace me." I worked there a couple of weeks longer and went back to work for Harrah's—in Reno, not Lake Tahoe. Later I got transferred back up to the lake. It's a long story.

So you took money from the safe and lost it gambling?

Yes. But see, I'd be not telling you the truth if I didn't tell you that I took money many times before that and wiggled off the hook and won enough money to put it back. Naturally, came the day when I didn't win it back. The first time I started out real small, only took four or five hundred. And then I got to where I was taking thousands out of there, and I pulled that out several times.

Well, I doubt if anybody's ever done that as many times as you have.

Oh, I don't think so. I don't know how many times I wiggled off the hook. The bad thing about it is time-you only have eight hours before the shift is going to change. It worked many times, but it finally caught up with me.

Well, you worked twelve to eight. You were graveyard shift manager from twelve to eight, so you had to get it back by eight o'clock in the morning.

Oh, hell, I knew the timing better than they did. I mean, I knew the time and knew how to stall the guys from counting out. A couple of times I'd get there, and I'd stall them around until I could get the money back in there where it belonged.

One thing Harrah did ask me was, "I want you to answer one question for me."

And I says, "What's that?"

He says, "Did anybody know you were taking this money?"

And I says, "Absolutely not."

Had I have said yes, which a couple of guys did have a good idea what was going on, they would have been terminated immediately. He would have probably kept me and fired them for not telling.

Well, somebody had to kind of cover for you while you were gone or knew where you were and knew how to get a hold of you.

Oh, I had a knack. It was so easy to do that part of it. I can't mention names. Even if they're dead now, I can't mention their names. Those guys sweated more than I did when I went over there. They knew where I was at and what I was doing and had seen me go back and forth maybe two, three times into the vault room and right back across the street to the Wagon Wheel.

To go back to the first time I got caught.... When I went up to Bill Harrah and told him, he never said a word. He sat there and stared at me. I told him what a hopeless disease I had and said that whatever had to be done, I would accept it, and no matter what happened, he would get his money back. I did have a ranch at that time that was worth a lot more money than what I owed him.

He sat and just stared right at me for several minutes. It seemed like several hours to me. Then he picked up the phone, and he called a guy named Andy Iratcabal to please come into his office. Andy Iratcabal came in with a big yellow pad of paper, and Bill said to Andy Iratcabal, "Sharkey has really got himself a bad problem." He says, "He took some money out of the safe, went across the street and blew it. I want to replace the money; and in turn, Sharkey will pay me back."

So, I'm just sitting there. Andy Iratcabal said in a real sarcastic tone of voice–like I was a rattlesnake sitting there–"And just how do you intend to pay this money back?"

Bill Harrah spoke up in a voice that I never heard him use before. He said, "Andy . . . Andy . . . Andy! I didn't tell you to ask questions. I told you to do what I wanted you to do." He says, "He doesn't know what his name is. He doesn't know where he is. He doesn't know what he's done." He said, "Give him four or five days to come down to earth, and then talk to him and work that out. Now is not the time to work that out." So, in four, five days, I sat down with Maurice Sheppard and Andy, and we worked out a payback schedule. Naturally, I never told a soul about any of these things because nobody wanted the word to get out.

Did Bill Harrah take a mortgage on your ranch?

Absolutely. They drew up some papers and took a mortgage out on it. And like I say, I paid it back, way ahead of time.

You probably made a score and paid it back?

That's the only way I paid it back. But I didn't pay it all back in one lump. I had to get lucky three days in a row and win $3,000 or so and apply it to what I owed.

Eddie Crume was the boss in Reno. Usually when I paid the money back, to keep everybody from wondering what was happening, I would go down to the Reno club and pay it back. Sheppard was familiar with what happened, and he would take care of it. He kept it quiet because it might have started an epidemic if they would have found out what I had been doing.

A few years later, when I finally got lucky and beat the Wagon Wheel, you would've thought I was the biggest crook in the whole world. They were acting like I was cheating them and everything else. You know, as long as they can beat you, they'll beat you forever. But if you beat them three times in a row, they're liable to come over and tell you they don't want your action. "Take it somewhere else." It's still that way.

They changed the dealers and changed the decks, but when you get really lucky, it doesn't make any difference what they do.

Just like when you were running the pit– the dice would be hot, you'd go in and get some new dice from a new company and new edge work and everything, and they still run hot. That didn't stop the dice from running crazy, right?

That's right.

If you could do it that way, there would be nothing to being a pit boss–just go get some new dice and put them in.

Yes. So actually, when you borrowed the money and then paid it back, you continued to work at Harrah's until 1963?

Yes. For some reason or another, they didn't fire me.

Well, that says a lot about you, and it says a lot about Bill Harrah, too.

Oh yes. That's what I always say. I could never say a bad word about him. He could've sent me to the penitentiary.

You know, all these books people write, like the book written by Mead Dixon . . . they all write about how important they were to the success of Harrah's Club. That's all bullshit. Harrah had more dedicated mules working for him than anybody I knew. He had guys that took great pride in being a janitor. They came to work a little early, and they stayed a little late. They didn't get paid for it. But he had janitors; he had men in stores; he had men in every department that were proud to be a part of Harrah's. You don't see that anymore.

I went up there with a guy here a year or so ago, and they had an ice-cream cart selling ice cream. There was a little ice cream being dropped on the floor, and this guy with me, Stew Carnall, said to the girl selling the ice cream, "I don't think Bill would have approved of this had he been here."

And she said, "Bill who?"

He said, "Bill, the man that put the roof over your head and the floor under your feet, and the guy that's responsible for getting you your paycheck every two weeks."

Well, she still thought, "Who are these two guys talking about?"

Well, that seems to be one of the secrets of Bill Harrah. He got so much out of so many people.

He had so many dedicated, loyal people working for him. He commanded that respect. I don't know how. And I think it was a primary reason behind his success at the beginning. After you get so big, it doesn't make any difference, but in a small operation,

if the bartender doesn't show up, it's a crisis. You have to find another bartender or tend bar yourself. Or a food waitress. At Harrah's, if ten bartenders don't show up or ten food waitresses don't show up, it's no problem. They either let the bus girl become a waitress or bar boy be a bartender or they have a few extra on every shift just figuring on knowing there's going to be a couple of them that aren't going to show up.

I remember a few of the porters that he had there. One of the guy's names was Ray Olsen, and he took such great pride in his job. He was a supervisor over half a dozen other porters, and he took great pride in seeing that everything was as clean as humanly possible. He had people in every department that way. He had stage hands that were so meticulous that every light, every wire, everything was working and doing what it was supposed to do.

That seems to be the undefinable quality of Bill Harrah, how and why he got so much loyalty and devotion from so many people.

He commanded it from me, and I have good reason to feel that way because, like I say, he could have put me in jail. Instead of that, he helped me. I mean, he really did. How many men do you meet like that? If that don't command something out of you, why, what does? They should have drowned you when you were born in a sack like a cat and got rid of you if that don't command respect from you.

The secret of the success of the whole Harrah's organization was the unbelievable people that he picked to work for him. Naturally, there was some bad ones, very few. And he always had somebody running the bottom line operation, the gaming operation. There might have been two hundred employees down there, and he always had one person that was smart enough to detect anything wrong. Nobody got the best of the club for long. He was very lucky in being able to get the quality of help and the loyalty of help that he had working for him at the beginning. His success was so much greater than he expected it to be. When he first went to Tahoe, he only intended to be there for the summer, and look what it is now in the winter!

I wonder sometimes if people thought of Bill Harrah as a father image. Perhaps he was like a father that they were trying to please?

Well, if you were lucky enough to be close to him, which I was, and to be able to get his ear, he was one of the finest, kindest men I ever knew. I mean, my case is a shining example. He should've just discarded me the first go around. Instead of that, when he did let me go, he took me right back. If he'd help somebody like me, who wouldn't he help?

He found out that there's not enough time in the day to listen to people that come to him, so he made himself inaccessible to all the five-and-dimers, you might say. If he hadn't have, there wouldn't have been time enough to take care of anything else. He was a shining example. He paved the way. He was the Napoleon Bonaparte of the gambling industry, the Ty Cobb of the gamblers, and I learned a lot from him. I learned to give everybody at least a second chance—maybe more.

Notes

1. Harolds Club, named for Harold Smith Sr., is properly spelled without an apostrophe, based on a decision made by club management in the 1940s.

2

JAMES CASELLI

*J*AMES CASELLI *was born in Ely, Nevada, on December 28, 1936. He worked at Harrah's for twenty-eight years, starting out as a part-time change person in 1958. He eventually worked himself up to the position of slot department manager, and twelve years later he was promoted to shift manager at Harrah's Club in Reno. Caselli was the first slot manager in northern Nevada to be licensed by the state's gaming commission.*

Jim Caselli was a knowledgeable chronicler and was happy to participate in this project. His interview was conducted at his home in September of 1998 and was completed in two sessions. In it he tells of being hired by Harrah's in 1958, and he describes the chain of command in the slot department and how he rose up through that chain to become department manager. Caselli explains that at Harrah's the slot department was actually two departments. One part consisted of the slot machine repair people, and the other consisted of slot department personnel who worked on the floor selling change, paying jackpots, and seeing to the customer's needs.

Of interest in this interview are Mr. Caselli's recollections of some of the innovations in slot machines that were developed at Harrah's, such as change lights, meters, and preventive maintenance. He also tells us why Harrah's used Pace machines for so many years and where they purchased those machines. There were no slot machine distributing companies such as Bally's and IGT in those days,

and Mr. Caselli tells how Harrah's coped with that problem. He reveals that at one time Harrah's tried to develop its own slot machine manufacturing company, but that the project never came to fruition. He also describes the premium point program, a giveaway promotion developed by Harrah's which played a large role in increasing the volume of slot play.

Caselli asserts that Rome Andreotti played a pivotal role in the rise of Harrah's, and he develops this idea in some depth. Andreotti may have been an effective executive, but no single person (with the possible exception of Bill Harrah) can be credited for the success of the company's operations. Harrah's Clubs were industry leaders in personnel training. Caselli shares memories of training sessions (not all of which were greeted with enthusiasm by every employee), and he candidly discusses Harrah's racially-biased hiring practices—practices which were common to the gaming industry well into the 1960s.

JAMES CASELLI: I was born in Ely, Nevada, on December 28, 1936. My dad was an engineer for the Nevada Department of Transportation—it was called the State Highway Department in those days. I grew up in Ely and went to high school there. In high school I met Kayleen, my future wife. Kayleen went on to business college in Salt Lake City and then went to work in Reno. We were married in 1958, and we have four children. Three live in Reno and one in San Francisco.

After high school, I went to the University of Utah for a while; then I came to Reno in 1956. I got a part-time job and then started going to the University of Nevada.

DWAYNE KLING: How did you happen to go to work at Harrah's, and when did you go to work there?

I was looking for a job. I had just turned twenty-one, and they were hiring change people for part-time summer jobs. That was in July of 1958.

And when school started, did you go back to school?

Yes. I was working full-time and going to the university.

How long did you continue at the university?

For about another year, year-and-a-half.

What changed your mind? Why did you decide to go into gaming instead of finishing college?

Well, I liked the gaming business, and I wasn't that good a student, to tell you the truth. [laughter]

What did you like about gaming? You started as a change person, right?

I liked the interaction with people. I was only on change maybe six, seven months at the most. I started working there in July, and

then in November of that year I joined the army reserves and went to Fort Ord for six months for basic training. When I came back, I think maybe I was only there two months on change before I was promoted to a key man. That was the next level in the structure of the slot department. George Johnson was the department manager.

Was there a shift supervisor?

Well, in those days they had what they called a key man. And then they had a new position that they put in when it got a little busier called junior floorman. [laughter] You were kind of a key man but without an apron, and you ran one section of the club. (In those days we only had one club, and that was the Virginia Street club.) That entailed getting fills for the cashiers, putting cashiers' money up, OK'ing jackpots of certain amounts, verifying jackpots of certain amounts, making sure that the break schedules were run properly.

Did they also have a jackpot payoff person?

That came later in the system. When I first started there, the payoff was signaled with one, two, or three fingers. You would go to a machine, and if it was a single jackpot, a $7.50 nickel jackpot, it would be a one-finger payoff; a $15 dime jackpot would be a one-finger payoff; a $32.50 quarter jackpot would be a one-finger signal. What they called the "lowest jackpot amount" would be what we called the "signal."

The cashiers in those days were required to know all the slot machines in their section. They had a form, and when you would hold up your finger, they would write down the machine number and put your initial after it. Then when you paid so many, you'd go back to the booth, and she would look up how many fingers she had seen and the amount and then pay you that amount to build your bankroll back up. And I believe our bankroll was only $150. You were reimbursed in cash for the number of jackpots you had paid and reimbursed the premium points that you had given out. You used to keep track of the jackpots that you paid and the type of jackpots you paid by counting your premium points. In those days you got fifty premium points for a single nickel jackpot, a hundred for a dime, and two hundred and fifty for a quarter. They were in different colors—red, green, and blue.

So when you said "one," that was a single jackpot, a $7.50 jackpot on a nickel machine; and a "two" would be a $15 nickel jackpot?

Right. A $15 nickel and a hundred premium points or two red premium tickets.

So the $15 nickel jackpot was a bonus type of jackpot?

Right. And it took the key man to pay it. The change person saw it and verified it with you, but it took a key man to pay it. A single jackpot, anybody could pay.

So the shift supervisor was in charge of that?

Right. And he had to OK jackpots above seventy-five dollars, up to five hundred. More than that, it took the shift manager on duty to OK it. At that time, in 1958, Harrah's in Reno had somewhere around 354 slot machines.

That makes you realize it wasn't very big in 1958.

No, it wasn't, because in 1958 they hadn't moved across the street to the old Grand Cafe area yet.

So you basically only had the one club?

Yes. The bingo parlor was over in the Grand Cafe area, and it maybe had only two or three slot machines. The only casino was on Virginia Street.

Well, it sounds like Harrah's had the procedure down pretty much in slots just like they did everywhere else.

Harrah's always had some sort of procedure for doing anything. It was in place when I started there and continued on, and they were very, very strong on procedure.

You mentioned George Johnson and said he was the slot manager when you came to work there. What happened to George Johnson? Did he stay with Harrah's?

George Johnson got demoted and became a keno writer. He must have been slot manager for five, six years. He'd been there for quite a while.

So they just weren't happy with his work, and they moved him?

Well, George had some personal problems.

Who replaced George Johnson?

I'm trying to think. I'm thinking it was Max Lewis for a while.

Max Lewis did work in Reno for a while before he came to Tahoe. Did Ed Posey ever work in slots in Reno?

No, Ed never worked in Reno, but he was the slot supervisor at Lake Tahoe then, and he was later the slot manager there. Ed Posey and I were slot managers for a while at the same time. He was slot manager at Tahoe, and I was slot manager in Reno.

Where was Bob Contois when you went to work at Harrah's?

Bob was working at the lake, and he came down to Reno later. I can't remember exactly what year. It was somewhere between 1962 and 1966. He was slot manager for four or five years or better.

You became slot manager in what year?

In 1966 I replaced Bob Contois as slot manager.

To get back to your promotion or your advancement in the organization: you started out as a change person, then you went to a key person, and then the next step was junior floorman. And the next step was what?

Shift supervisor.

So a shift supervisor was the highest you could go prior to becoming a slot manager or assistant slot manager?

Yes.

Was there a separation between the slot department, the actual people on the floor selling change, and the slot repair shop?

Yes, there was. The slot repair shop reported to Bud Garaventa. Bud was in Reno then. The floor people reported directly to the assistant general manager or to the general manager of the club.

Do you recall who was slot repair shop manager?

Joe Dubois.

So the slot department was very separate from the slot repair people?

Yes, they were. And even Bud didn't have any direct control over the floor operation. We worked as a team, but we didn't all necessarily report to the same people. Although the shop manager would report to the general manager, we on the floor reported directly to the assistant general manager of operations.

So you really weren't that involved with Bud Garaventa in your department?

Not on a day-to-day basis, no.

I know a lot of people started in Harrah's and in other clubs as change people and other entry-level positions and went into the pit or the keno or other departments. Did you ever have any desire to work in the pit or any other department at Harrah's?

No, I really didn't. I tried keno because Gene Diullo was an old friend from Ely, but I just couldn't get the hang of the pen. In those days Gene had his own method of writing a keno ticket, and you better write it right–the oriental method is really what it was. And Gene was a stickler on marking spots. He was a tough taskmaster. You would have to spend, if you went to keno school, hours standing there practicing learning how to make spots and to write ticket prices.

It was very important in those days that every stroke was identifiable.

Yes, it was. Keno writers took great pride in how well they wrote a ticket and how clear they could condition the ticket. You know, write four out of eight and the price and all of that. It was like artwork more than it was like writing keno.

So you didn't have any desire to continue that at all?

No, I didn't. At that time I was moving up fairly rapidly in the slot department, and I just didn't have any interest in it.

I had been around gaming all my life in Ely. My stepgrandfather and my great-uncle both owned establishments in Ely, so I had been around cards, and it wasn't a novelty. Dealing wasn't a novelty to me.

Did you ever feel that the slot department was kind of looked down on or not given the recognition that it should be given compared to the pit or keno?

No, I didn't really think that I felt the department was slighted. It was a matter of personalities in the pit. And this is from a slot perspective–we always knew that we were as good as the pit and that we made as much money. It was the dealers and the floormen that wandered around saying, "*I am a dealer. You are just a slot person, or you're just a slot supervisor.*"

It seemed like the pit had always had this great aura about them in the early years. In the early years the pit did out-drop the slot department; and they had this great ego about them, and they were not too shy to let you know. [laughter] But they never bothered me too much because I knew what my position was and where it fit in with the company. If they wanted to run around like they were gods, that was all right. We always said that when they promoted somebody to a floorman, they gave him a suit that blew up and blew his ego up and everything else. Didn't give him any more smarts; it just gave him more ego. [laughter]

Let's get back to your route of advancement in the slot department.

Well, I went to a junior floorman, then to a floorman, and then in 1962 I was promoted to slot shift supervisor. During this time, the slot department was developing new procedures–Bud and the slot shop had come up with meters on the slot machines. We had the first metered slot machines in the state. I will be glad to tell you that. And when you paid a jackpot, you had a jackpot slip, and you put down the meter number on that slip. Then you would turn your jackpot slips in to the cashier, and she reimbursed you for it.

Please, go into detail on how those meters worked. Explain the different types of meters, and explain what they tracked.

Well, we had started out with no meters, and it was that old one finger, two finger system. The number of fingers you held up signaled the amount of the jackpot. That method had a lot of problems. If you were a key man and didn't get up to [the cashier quickly to] get your jackpots, when you got up there chances were you may not get them. There was [sometimes] a little collusion going on. You could end up being short for that night because somebody else [another key man] had already claimed your jackpot, or the cashier had put the wrong initial down for the jackpot.

So somebody else would get your money. Is that what you are saying?

Yes. So when checking out, particularly if you were a key man and you didn't get right up to the booth to collect your money, you might end up a little short.

Did they penalize you for being short?

No. You never had to make it up, but it would go against your record. This was recognized as a flaw in the system, so Bud and the shop–and I think Rome [Andreotti] was involved with it–came up with meters on the slot machines. They had a meter for every jackpot amount–a single jackpot, a double jackpot, or a special jackpot.

So the meter had three rows?

Could have up to four. They had a meter for every type of jackpot on that particular machine. And that meter in the old days, on the Pace machines, operated on what they called the "pay finger." In the old days the reels would stop, and the machines had a finger that would drop in and find a hole, go through it; and then on the top of it, it had a switch. The finger would break the switch, which would make the meter turn. Then in the morning they would come in and they would take what they called "beginning meter readings." Then twenty-four hours later they would read them again. That would give them the number of the different types of jackpots that were supposed to have been paid in that twenty-four hour period. Then accounting would go through *all* these jackpot tickets and make sure that they all matched up.

And they read the meters every day?

Yes, they read them every day. And the meter should have gone up a number equal to the number of jackpot tickets you had for that machine for that particular type of jackpot.

So then someone matched the meter readings against the paperwork that was turned in?

Right.

That was quite a lengthy process, wasn't it?

Yes, it was, and it was time-consuming for slot audit. (That's when they first came up with the idea of a slot audit.) But by doing that, they had a control on the jackpot ticket and the premium points. They would know exactly how many premium points were supposed to have gone out on that shift.

Had there been a lot of hanky-panky with the premium points, also?

There was a lot of hanky-panky with everything.

What year was this happening?

This is probably in the 1960s. Yes, it was in the sixties when Harrah's came up with the meters.

Who read the meters every morning?

The coin crew. When we dropped the slot machines, there was a drop crew and a meter-reading crew, and the meter readers would stay ahead of the drop crew. The day started after the first meter was read; the graveyard started the day.

So they dropped all the slots every day?

Every day. Yes. As long as I was there they dropped every day.

Would you explain a little bit more of the function of the drop crew?

The drop crew is the employees that pull the money from the machines. They drop the buckets. They pull the buckets out from underneath the machines and empty them.

What did you use for drop buckets?

In the beginning they were like big money sacks, canvas money sacks, that were held on hooks underneath the machines so any overflow of the slot machine went into the sacks. When the payoff tubes were full, then the money went into those drop bags. There weren't any hoppers on the old machines. They just had payoff tubes. I think a nickel tube held seven dollars; and a dime, ten; and a quarter, fifteen. There wasn't very much coin in a tube, and when that tube filled up, then the coins would spill over and go into the drop bag.

The payoff tube was a long tube in the front of the machine, and it had the circumference of the coin of that particular machine. It sat on top of what they called payoff slides. You had six payoff slides. Basically you started off with a two-pay slide. The two-pay slide would just hold two coins.

And the two-pay slide was a cherry?

That was a cherry. Then if you moved up in payoff, it would open that slide plus the next one up, which was three; the next one was five. It was a five-coin payoff, which meant you opened up the bottom one, which was a two-pay, and the next one was three, so now you had a five-coin payoff. Then you had a ten-coin payoff. Oranges were ten, so then you had another five. Then you got the plums, which were fourteen, so you had another four-pay slide. Then you had bells, which were eighteen. So you had another four-pay slide, and then you had two left for the jackpot, because the machine always dropped twenty coins when a player hit a jackpot regardless of the denomination.

It's so simple when you look back on it. In those days the slot machines were so simple. They didn't have all these things like bonuses and progressives.

Yes. All the payoffs listed on the front of the machine were controlled by the reel strips and the number of holes you could punch in a disk and the number of slides you could get in the machine. [laughter] It was a rather simple mechanical device, and basically every machine, every denomination, *was* the same. The only difference would be the denomination of the coin. The basic machine was the same. You could take the clock mechanism, the reels, almost the entire machine, and you could change it from a nickel to a dollar just like that! All you had to change was the head, the escalator, your drop tube, your payoff tube, and the slides to the denomination you wanted to change it to. So it was really very simple.

In those days the reels actually controlled the payoffs. Each wheel had what was called a star wheel, which looked like a gear. Each star wheel had the same number of teeth as the reel had symbols, and as the reels were spun, the clock would unwind. As the clock unwound, it would move a bar (the timing bar). Resting on the timing bar were levers called stops. The timing bar moved from under the stops. This allowed the stops to drop into the teeth on the star wheels stopping the reels. Then you had your pay fingers that would be released by the timing bar. The pay fingers would hit the disk, and you had a disk with holes punched in it corresponding to the

payoff for each reel. When they found a hole, they'd just go through it. That would release another set of fingers behind the slides and allow the drop slide to move forward and drop the appropriate amount of coins.

Explain the clock a little bit more.

A clock is a timing device that would wind up when the handle was pulled. It was geared so it would allow the reels to spin for a certain length of time. The randomness was the length of time the reels were spun. The length of time was controlled by how fast the clock was unwinding. As the clock unwound, it would move the timing bar, releasing the reel stop for each reel. This controlled the number of revolutions each reel would spin. This timing was set so that each reel would spin a revolution and a fraction of a revolution. For example, number one reel would spin one and one-quarter to one and one-half revolutions; number two would spin two and one-quarter to two and one-half; number three would spin three and one-quarter to three and one-half revolutions. The actual timing, because it was a mechanical device, wasn't all that accurate. But anyway, as these reels were spinning, the randomness was generated, because as it spun you didn't know exactly where each reel was going to stop.

At this time (the late 1950s and the 1960s) all of Harrah's slot machines were Pace machines. Is that right?

Yes, they were. And they were all single coin machines, except we had what were called piggybacks. They were one machine above another machine, and you could play one coin in each machine and pull one handle.

Did you have to put a coin in both machines?

Yes, you did. You couldn't play it singly.

So that was a primitive multi-coin machine?

Yes, it was, because the way the handle was set up, there was no way you could play one machine without playing the other. If you tried to do one, the other one would lock up.

Also, at the time I started we had about ten left-handed machines. The handle was on the left-hand side.

How about the customer next to him?

Well, all the left-handed machines stayed in one row, and we had, I think it was, ten left-handed nickel machines. They were all in one row because you couldn't mix them up.

Well, that's unique. I've never heard of that before.

It didn't work. They just didn't get enough play.

We were talking about some of the innovations that Harrah's started. Was the jackpot meter the first meter that was put in?

Yes.

Then later on they installed more meters, is that correct?

Well, when the meters were started, they were started on everything. Harrah's was not one to take and try it here and there. It either worked, or it didn't work.

They put them on every machine?

Yes, they were put on every machine. We went along like that until about 1964, somewhere in there, and then we went to what we called the Mark Sense jackpot system. This was the first use of a computer to keep track of jackpots. We used the old computer cards, the kind you used to mark with a special graphite pencil. The jackpot ticket was one of those big long IBM cards, and it had all the payouts on

it. You had to write the machine number, and then you could Mark Sense the meter number and everything else into it. Those you turned in to the slot booth. Then they went to the computer room, and they were read by the computer, which gave you what the hand accountants had been doing: the number of jackpots, the sequence, and the amount of money.

Why did Harrah's stop using Mark Sense?

Well, it had its problems. The business kept growing, and because of the Mark Sense system we ended up having to use wireless microphones (which were small radio transmitters), because you had to call in to the booth the machine number and the meter number. The cashier would put them down on her paperwork so she could balance her jackpots against what she paid out.

Right around 1968 we hired a man by the name of Bill Archer as our new director of computer services. He and I got to talking about the system we had, and so we sat down and designed a true computer system. We started off using an old IBM analog machine. It was designed to open doors, close valves, and do all those kinds of things. [laughter] Well, Bill was very knowledgeable in the computer industry, so he went out and looked at this, and we started working with it to make it so we could actually keep a running total of the meters. It would tell you whether it was a good meter or a bad meter. It would automatically total each person's number of jackpots. In other words, it was a semi-automated system.

So we worked on that and went to Rome and talked to Rome. Rome said, "Fine, I like the idea. Start on it." Rome was very patient with us. We had a lot of fits and starts. The system was called System Seven, and I think that, actually, the name of the IBM computer was the System Seven computer. Well, Bill developed a method of converting the analog computer into a digital computer so that we could use numbers. He wrote a program to do that. When we first started out doing the Mark Sense system, the only method that we had of communicating between the computer and the booth was the old nixie tube display.

What is a nixie tube?

I don't know the exact engineering term for what we called nixie tubes, but they looked like these weather signs you have now, with little light bulbs, and they would give us the numbers.

So "nixie" was just a nickname?

Right. I can't remember the company that made them. So we started off with that. There were no input pads. So with the help of a gentleman named Johnny Ward, who was in our electronics department, we took an old decimal pad, an entry pad like a telephone pad, and converted it to binary code. Not a decimal system, but the computer language. And we worked, and we worked, but we couldn't get the signal right. But back east, Cincinnati Bell took the System Seven and used it for directory assistance. And in doing that, they spent four or five million dollars in getting a small communication device that would talk to it. It had a TV screen on it and an entry pad, and it was set up to talk to this System Seven. So we worked on that, and Rome was very patient with us. Finally we got it working and demonstrated it. It did work, and we went to that on all the machines.

What year do you think it was that you got all the bugs out of the system?

It was right about 1972. I think we worked on it almost two years. Rome would ask us for progress reports, but he was very patient, and I think we brought the whole system in for $70,000.

To get back to the meters again, did the machines have a coin-in and coin-out meter?

No, they did not. It was not a requirement of the state. In fact, there were very few requirements then by the state. You didn't have to have your reel strips registered, and you didn't have to have the information on hand that you have to have now for every machine that shows exactly what the payoffs are and what the percentages are. In those days, they felt that the industry would police itself, because anybody who was taking advantage of the customer wouldn't get the business because the next guy over would have it.

You can't do it now, but Lincoln Fitzgerald and the Nevada Club for *years* had what they called, I guess, "loss-leader machines" for lack of a better word. They would have real hot nickel, dime, and quarter machines that would just pay off fantastically, and they'd move them around the place every day. They'd just change out the mechanism. So today you'd have a nickel machine, number 1, and somebody would come in and play it, and they would just win all kinds of money. Well, at midnight that machine mechanism would move over into nickel machine number 101. And they would do the same thing with quarters. You can't do that today. Today the machine number and the case number always have to match. They used to move machines around all the time as kind of a bait for the customer.

So the meters were developed, and then System Seven came along, and we just used the existing meter system and wrote the procedures for it. Harrah's ran System Seven clear up into almost the 1980s on the mechanical machines.

So it was well worth it?

Yes, it was. The slot percentages went up two or three points. Every time we changed the method of accounting for jackpots, it seemed like the percentage would go up two or three points. [laughter]

Was there that much internal leakage?

That much internal leaking, yes. Then as systems went along, people developed methods of getting around it, and you would see a drop in the win. But when we first went to the meters, we lost five old-time cashiers that had been there for years.

Did they voluntarily retire, or they were asked to leave?

Basically, they were asked to leave; they were asked to retire.

Well, as you were saying, every time you're working to figure out some way to stop cheating, there's somebody else working to cheat the new system that you put in.

Yes. And the old-timers in the gaming industry used to say, "If you keep the inside clean, you don't have to worry about the outside."

◇

Harrah's was the first casino to put *timers* on the change lights. They had a timer originally that if you didn't answer the change light within twenty or thirty seconds, the change light would start flashing. They had decided that they didn't want anybody to wait any longer than twenty seconds for change to play a slot machine.

It is amazing what Harrah's did, isn't it, when you think about things like that?

Yes. We were talking about jackpot payoff people. They came into existence when we went to the meters. From that time on, change people didn't pay jackpots. We had special jackpot payoff people.

Yes, they called them "JPOs," didn't they?
Yes. That's all they did, just paid jackpots.

Could you tell us about what they called "candles" at Harrah's?

They were a series of lights that were located on top of the slot machine, and they were broken up into layers. The top light was for your single jackpot, and then the second light was for the double jackpot, and then whatever special type of jackpot you may have was the bottom light. They were narrow and gave the appearance of a tall candle.

So the light had a different color for different jackpots?

Yes, and the candles were different colors. On nickel machines the top light was red, all dime machines were green, all quarter machines were yellow, all half-dollar machines were brown, and all dollar machines were blue.

So a customer could also tell by looking at the top color on the candle the denomination of the machine?

Yes, they could. *Plus* the old metal cases were painted the same color, so you could walk in, and if you wanted to find the quarter section, you just looked for the yellow-topped candles or the yellow-colored case. And we kept all the denominations together. They weren't mixed.

You said the top part of the machine was painted?

The case that the mechanism sat in was painted the color of the denomination.

I thought the cases were all silver.

The front of the case was silver, but the back of the case was the color of the denomination.

I think that was a good idea. Nowadays all the machines look alike.

Well, I have a comment on that. Casinos have lost their uniqueness. They're starting to get it back now, but when they first went mechanical, they lost any individuality because all slots in every casino looked alike. A Bally was a Bally was a Bally was a Bally. And Bally was the first one to bring in the electrics. Your glass on them wasn't unique. You didn't know whether you were in one store (one gaming establishment) or another one, because all the machines looked alike, and Bally wanted a tremendous amount of money to give you custom glass.

To a certain extent that's true today with these modern-day slot machines. If you walk into a lot of these places, you can't tell–if you were just looking at a slot machine–which establishment you're in. In the old days the machine case, the design, the colors, the reel strips were all different. Everybody had their own distinctive reel strip so that you knew exactly where you were just by looking at the machine. Harolds Club had the covered wagon; Harrah's had the sultans; the Nevada Club had Mr. Nevada. Everybody had their own *distinctive* looking slot machine with unique reel symbols.

Right. I think that was a big selling point.

We always thought it was, because then they knew exactly what they were playing and where they were playing. When they came in with tons of new equipment and new manufacturers, they lost that. They went from the club promoting themselves on their slot machine to depending upon the customer wanting to play a specific type of machine, a Bally or an IGT or a Universal or whatever. The clubs were hoping that the customer would like playing IGT machines more than playing Bally machines.

The companies got into a rivalry on their own machines, and for a while there the gaming establishment let them get away with it. It wasn't like, "I want to play at Harrah's because I know that the payoff is better." It was, "I want to play where there's an IGT machine." Does that make sense to you? It wasn't establishment oriented; it was product oriented.

Yes, and you could find the same slot machine in Raley's or Scolari's.

Right. Now there are some clubs that demand their own custom glass and their own custom card backs. You've seen them on IGT, where the card back on a poker machine will be the special card back of a particular casino. They've gotten back into specialization more, but when they first came out with the electronic machines, it was almost like you could walk anyplace in the world, and you didn't know which club you were in. Under Bud Garaventa we resisted Bally for years.

Do you think Rome kept Ballys out, or do you think it was Bud and Bill Harrah?

Bud, Bill Harrah, and Rome–all of them.

Why was that? It wasn't just Bally though; they kept IGT, Sircoma, everyone out, didn't they?

For a while, yes. They wanted to be distinct to themselves. The problem was that we couldn't manufacture our own machines fast enough to meet the demand, and the customers demanded . . . all these customers now were going somewhere else and playing those machines, and they were coming back to Harrah's and saying, "Well, do you have such and such machine?"

And you have to say, "No, we don't." Harrah's kept mechanicals probably (along with Harolds Club) longer than anybody else.

The Nevada Club did too for quite a while.

And the Nevada Club, yes–the three of them. And the Cal-Neva, to tell you the truth. It wasn't until the new ones like MGM came in that you saw the big influx of different manufacturers.

Well, when Mr. Harrah or Bud Garaventa or Rome were keeping these other companies out of Harrah's, were both the lake club and the Reno club full of Pace slot machines only?

That's right. Then they did go out and bought machines from an Australian company called Aristocrat. What the Aristocrat did was take the old Pace patent and update it. The old Pace, you took and adjusted everything with a pry bar. Basically all the adjustments were mainly prying something to fit. What Aristocrat did was to take all the points that you would have to adjust and made them adjustable with screws or nuts and bolts. They used to say in the old days that in the Pace slot machine you only needed three pry bars: large, larger, and a goddamn big one. Of course, you also needed a hammer. [laughter]

During that time Bud and the people in the slot shop had developed one of the first multi-coin nickel machines. It was a mechanical machine. In the head where the coin dropped through, they put a mechanical switch that acted like a counter, and you could play one to five coins in it. Because the counter was mechanical and because the machine was mechanical, it was a nightmare to keep adjusted. But it was an early attempt to create a multi-coin machine.

Then they developed one that was an automatic machine. Well, it had a problem because they had an electric motor in it, and it was geared so low that if a coin stuck, you could almost watch the mechanism eat itself up. This motor with all this heavy gearing would just take and crunch the ratchets, and you could almost *watch* the head disappear down inside the case when a coin got stuck. [laughter]

Why did Harrah's want Pace machines only?

At the time, and this is before the electricals and the electromechanicals, they felt the Pace was the most dependable machine made.

Did Harolds still have Pace then?

Harolds still had Pace.

I've heard that that's one reason Harrah's went with Pace, because Harolds had them.

Could have been. Also, I believe that there were a lot of Paces in Montana, Wyoming, and other states that had gaming and outlawed it. They would go up and buy warehouses of Pace machines that they got out of Montana, Idaho, and Wyoming.

So they bought hundreds, possibly thousands?

Right. Then Pace went out of business. They weren't manufacturing machines, but Harrah's bought up all these old cases and mechanisms. And then during the later years Harrah's would go out and buy them up in carload lots. Harrah's had warehouses full of them.

I didn't realize they had that many.

Oh, yes. Whenever we opened up a new club or had an expansion, they would renovate them and fix them. In fact, they were practically completely rebuilt. There was a company here in Reno called Nevada Air

Products that used to make the slides and the disks and the clocks and everything that you couldn't get from the factory.

Oh. So there was a part source?

Yes. Nevada Air Products did it for years. It was a lucrative business for them because there was so many people who were still using the Pace machines.

You know, another thing about that individuality. Didn't Fitzgerald have all of one kind of machine?

Yes. Fitz had all Jennings, and Harrah's and Harolds had all Pace machines. Now, Bud never liked the Jennings because they had what they called a chain escalator. It came across the machine, and so the coin was carried across the top of the machine on the chain. The Mills slot machine was the same way. You could see those coins going across the machine, whereas the Pace had what was known as the circular escalator. The coin would drop down, and the circle would go around and you could see the coins going around until they dropped into the pay tube. Bud didn't like the chain because the chain was too hard to adjust and too susceptible to breakage. It was a *long* circular chain; it must have been a good ten inches long. There was a space on that chain to hold the coin, and it would move across and then drop a coin when another coin was put in. The escalator was only about three inches in diameter, and half-dollar and dollar machines had a straight escalator that only held one coin. So when a coin was put in, the previous coin dropped right down into the payoff tube.

We were talking earlier about buying slot machines out of Montana and Idaho.

Yes. Montana was a *big* supplier. Right around the 1950s, Harrah's had gone out and purchased whole warehouses full of Pace machines that had come out of Montana. You

would get them into the slot shop to recondition them, and a good percentage of them would be rigged so they couldn't pay jackpots because of what were called "percentage stops." They had plugged the holes so you couldn't get a jackpot. There was no way the machine could stop on a jackpot. It would take an axe to win a jackpot! [laughter]

And these were machines that had been in operation in other states?

Yes. They had been in operation in other states as well as in Montana.

So you knew no one had ever hit a jackpot on that machine?

Yes. It was impossible.

So that was the way operators in other states operated?

It was illegal gaming and basically just overlooked, so why worry about jackpots? [laughter] They kept about everything they got in.

So Harrah's just stashed away those slot machines they bought, and then as they expanded at the lake or in Reno, they would put them on the floor. Of course, they went over them with a fine-tooth comb.

Yes, they were completely rebuilt. Basically, they used just the frames and the cases. The actual guts—the clock, the slides, the disks, and the reels and all that—would be remanufactured if they weren't in good shape.

Do you think they bought thousands of machines from these other states?

I have no idea, but they had a considerable number.

When you were slot manager, who did you report to?

I reported originally to the general manager, who was Al Fontana, and Mert Smith, I believe, was the assistant when I became slot manager.

So you reported to the general manager, not the assistant general manager?

Well, I reported to Mert. But you'd have to say that you reported to Al. [laughter] Every day a manager was required to walk into Al's office and see him and report to him. He didn't care what time it was, but once a day you would report to Al, and he would go over the day's activity with you and the daily reports that were written by your shift supervisors. At Harrah's, every shift supervisor had to write a daily report of what had transpired on his shift. Al would go over that, and he would have the numbers of what had happened: your wage hours, the amount of drop, the jackpots, everything pertaining business-wise to the operation of that day, and you would have to go in and discuss it with Al. And you learned real quick that before you went and saw Al, if you were smart, you'd first go to the business office. You would get all the day's figures, you would review them, you would review all the daily reports from all the shift supervisors, so that when Al started asking questions, you could answer them.

Because he had all those figures already?

Yes. He had all of those. And what you learned real quick with Al Fontana was that you never tried to b.s. him on the numbers. If you didn't know what he asked, you would say, "I don't know, but I'll get back to you. I'll look it up, Al. I don't know the answer to that." But if you tried to sit there with Al and come up with what he considered a roundabout answer, and you really didn't know what you were talking about, then you were in deep trouble. And he was a yeller, and he was a screamer.

It seems like he was pretty efficient, too.

Yes, he was. You just had to understand Al. I mean, he had one of these personalities that if he wasn't yelling, he wasn't talking. Italian! [laughter]

I went into him one day, and he jumped on me about something. Well, I knew what it was, and I just looked at him, and I said, "Al, do you want to sit here and yell and scream about it, because I can do that, or should both of us sit down and discuss it like gentlemen?"

And he looked at me and said, "Well, all right, Jim." He liked people, basically, that would kind of stand up to him. If you let him yell at you, he'd just keep going. If you said, "Hey, whoa, let's sit down and discuss it," then Al would be all right. He liked needling people. He had people that he just loved because they wouldn't say anything to him. They just let him keep going on and on, and he just loved it. He loved to push that needle in. He was a great one. But he knew the business.

He'd been with Harrah's a long time, hadn't he?

Oh, yes, he had; Al had been with them a long time.

I think he was there when Harrah's opened in 1946.

He was. He came out of Colbrandt's, I think, as a dealer.

Yes, and he came out of Lovelock originally.

Yes, out of Lovelock and then Reno. No, I liked Al. I know there's a lot of different opinions about Al, but I always got along just fine with him.

Was he was replaced by Mert Smith?

By Mert Smith, yes.

Did he leave the organization after that?

Yes, he did. And then for a while, Al was running companies that were in bankruptcy.

So you reported to Al when you started. Who reported to you?

The three shift supervisors, and then I got an assistant slot manager so we could cover the twenty-four hours. That was one of those things—one year I'd have one, and the next year I wouldn't. We'd have those reorganizations of management, and they'd say, "Well, they're not needed," and we'd go along. And then somebody else would say, "Yes, they are needed," and we'd put them back. [laughter] Organizational structure had a tendency to change.

It possibly had something to do with the revenues that were coming in?

Oh, yes. Yes, in the old days you knew that when you turned your budget in, it would get approved. Then come November you would be asked to cut your entire staffing by 10 percent. Even though your budget had been approved, it was mandatory to cut your staffing by 10 percent. [laughter] So if you were smart, you tried to go in with the budget at 110 percent for those months, knowing that you'd be required to take off 10 percent. But if you were trying to be really honest about it, and they told you to cut your winter staffing down to nothing, you could not argue, "I do not have a surplus. *I am where I should be.*" That argument didn't fly. Cut it 10 percent. That was Rome. Rome was a great one for reverting the numbers.

Did you have much contact with Rome?

Oh, I had quite a bit a contact with Rome, yes.

Even though you were going through the manager or the assistant general manager, you still saw Rome?

Right, I still had quite a bit of contact with Rome. I had the opportunity to work with Rome in 1964. I worked with Rome as what they called a "scheduling analyst" for four months. During that four months I went with Rome to every budget meeting for every department in Reno, and then he and I'd sit and talk about it, so I got a real good understanding of Rome and how he did things. His philosophy was to go down through a budget or a monthly review and your comparison of this year to last year, and if you missed one, he was always going to get you on another one, because you answered two questions: where the department was with the budget and where the department was month-to-date or year-to-date compared to last year's actual. Once a month you'd have to sit in a meeting with Rome.

Then during the budget process you'd do the same thing. But Rome would take a budget, for example, that had been turned in for a department (in those days it was a computer printout—we had gotten sophisticated with a computer printout), and he would go down and pick some line item very insignificant in the whole total picture, and he would ask a question. "Why is your miscellaneous pencils or miscellaneous . . . ?" or whatever it was—it would be a small line item—"Why has it gone up from last year by one percent?"

"Ah, uh, ah." And then the guy would start b.s.ing him, because who's going to worry about a budget item that's one percent of the gross, right? But Rome would ask that question, and if the department managers started trying to snow him, and Rome knew he was getting snowed, he'd just turn around, and then he would start at the top. And then the man would answer line item by line item by line item by line item.

Did he do this with every department manager?

Every department manager. And what I found out was that if you paid enough attention to all your numbers, and you had an answer–"Well, Rome, due to this fact, we changed this product which created the increase. You can check with the business office."–Rome then would feel, "Well, if you're not going to b.s. me on this little one, you're probably pretty good up here." He would use that just to test the department manager to see if he really knew what was in his numbers.

So you were lucky enough to sit in with him when he was going over everybody's budget?

Yes. He'd go over your budget once a year when you prepared the budget. Then when the budget was prepared, every department, Reno and Lake Tahoe, would have a monthly review, and Rome would sit in on every monthly review. And here again, the best answer you could give him if he asked a question and it was something that slipped you, you just looked him right in the eye and said, "Rome, I can't answer that, but I'll have the answer by this afternoon or tomorrow morning." He'd be satisfied with that. But if you tried to take and b.s. him–and he had a knack of knowing whether you knew what you were talking about or whether you didn't–then you'd be answering questions for two hours. Because then you'd have to explain in more detail than you normally would, and he'd be relentless.

Well, you sound like you enjoyed working with Rome.

I did. Maybe I'm only one of two, but I enjoyed working around Rome. Rome used to spend quite a bit of time on the floor in Reno because his office was there. I got to know Rome early when I was key man, and he was always a friendly, tough man. There was

the right way, the wrong way, and Rome's way, and as long as you knew that and you knew what he required, he wasn't hard to work for.

He was tough in what way?

Attention to detail, procedure . . . and the procedures were the way *he* wanted the procedures to be.

He had to OK them all?

He had to OK them all. He was to the point; and basically, I think at times he scared people.

Intimidated them?

Intimidated them. Right. *I* never found him intimidating; maybe I'm one of the few. Chuck Yeager used to say the same thing. We never seemed to have any problem with it, but we'd started out early as supervisors going to meetings with him and kind of getting a feel for him.

You grew up with him?

Kind of grew up with him. Well, I was twenty-one and had been around, so it was kind of like we had grown up with him. Now, not that he couldn't be unreasonable and not that he couldn't scare people, but he wasn't, from where I sat, as bad as everybody made him out to be. A lot of times Rome was used as the axe. Whatever a bad job needed to be done, Rome did it. [laughter] He was the one that carried out the tough decisions. I don't know if that makes sense to you.

Yes, it makes perfect sense.

Bob Ring would never make a tough decision in his life. Bob Ring was the nice old gentleman or the nice gentleman. He was friendly and all of this, but he wouldn't make those decisions. Bill didn't want to do them. That wasn't his job. So that left Rome to be the policeman and the bad guy or the German shepherd on a chain. That's what they used Rome for.

And so, basically, if you're the axe and you're using the axe, you get the reputation of being an axe man.

It sounds like he did what Bill Harrah wanted him to do. It wasn't like he was doing it for himself.

Rome did what he was told to do. No, he was not out on a flight of fancy by no means. And they used him like a dog at times. [laughter] He'd work twenty-four hours a day if you'd put it to him.

I was a slot shift supervisor the first big meeting I ever attended with Rome—I'd been in smaller ones with him—and they had instituted a program called junior management. This was one of the first attempts by Harrah's management to improve the quality of their supervisors. An assistant pit manager by the name of Jim Keller, from Lake Tahoe, and I had to do a report on starting an employee drink ticket. This was before they had employee drink tickets, so Jim and I worked up a report on cost and how to go about giving an employee a drink ticket on a paycheck. We made the report to Rome and then to all the senior executives. The only one that was missing was Bill Harrah. Because we were in operations, Jim was sitting on one side of Rome, and I was sitting on the other.

After we had given our report, Rome said, "Stay boys. I want you to sit here with me." So we sat there, and they brought out samples of shoes that they were considering for a company-approved, cocktail waitress shoe. They must have had a dozen different styles of shoes, and they're passing all these shoes around the table, and they all keep looking down at Rome to see what Rome likes. Rome kind of leans back, and he looks at me and says, "I want you to watch this." And they bring out this one, and it looks worse than a

work shoe. I mean, it's the ugliest shoe you ever saw in your life. Rome takes it out, and he says, "You know, I kind of like this shoe."

He hands it down, and all the way around that room, "Oh, this is the shoe, this is the shoe, this is the shoe." And they start to talk about how they're going to buy this shoe, right?

Rome's sitting there, and he says, "Well, wait a minute. One of you hand me that shoe again." Rome looks at me and says, "Naw," he says, "I really don't like this shoe."

It goes around the room, "No, this isn't the shoe, this isn't the shoe." Well, finally they pick a shoe.

We get out of the meeting, and Rome says, "Let's go have a cup of coffee." So we went down to the employees' lounge. Rome is sitting there, and he says, "You see that?"

I says, "Yes."

He says, "You know Jim and Jim, there are times when I wish somebody would tell me no." He says, "It gets rather boring sitting in meetings and listening to that." He says, "All they would have had to do was say, 'Geez, Rome, that's an ugly shoe.'" [laughter] He says, "Now, did I teach you anything?" And from that time on with my dealings with Rome I always tried to be honest with him and straightforward.

People wouldn't argue with him. He'd say something in a meeting, they'd flat clam up. It wasn't wise to argue with him, but you could always bring up, "Rome, have you considered the other side of this coin, or have you considered these as consequences?" and then sit and talk to him. You *knew* when Rome finally said, "I don't care," or gave the indication that the discussion was done, it was going to be done his way, but he never minded anybody who approached him *indirectly* with an idea. You never said, "I think this is nuts," or, "You're wrong, Rome." You approached it from the other side: there's another point of view, or have we considered this? And you could discuss it with him. One thing you never wanted to do was say, "I don't think it's right," because that would put him right on the spot.

Yes. That's true of anybody. You have to give them a way out.

I think Rome probably kept the gaming not under control, but in a direction. Rome had the ability, and it was because of his strong personality that he directed gaming so that everybody knew what gaming was supposed to be and where it was supposed to go, which to me was a strength in Harrah's.

Well, the only thing that I see is that he stayed with Pace slot machines too long, if that was his decision.

It might have been. Well, both him and Bud, but at the time—we're going back into 1978, then the 1980s—at the time there wasn't a real good product to buy. Bally mechanical was a piece of crap. You'd bang it on the side, and if you hit in the right spot and hard enough, it'd start paying off. It had *all* kinds of mechanical problems. That's the one that they had in Vegas, and somebody found out that they had mechanical switches in them. They were just reed switches, just electrical contacts made with reed switches. They found out in Las Vegas that if you took agent 409, which is an electrostatic fluid, and sprayed it down the head, it would close the contacts, and the hoppers would just start pouring out. I mean, they were really a piece of junk, and that's what Bud and Rome didn't want.

Hadn't IGT come into existence yet?

No, IGT hadn't come into existence. So the time frame we're talking about, the Pace machine was probably the best piece of equipment on the market. They hadn't gone to all the electronics. We bought some of the first electronic machines, and those were

kenos. The electronic keno machines and then the electronic twenty-one machines.

Please explain an electromechanical machine.

Well, it's a mechanical machine, except it used electricity to run the hopper and determined pays by timing it, rather than using a mechanical slide. They were the first ones with hoppers.

So slot machines went from mechanical to electromechanical to fully electronic?

Right.

Were there electronic machines before the computers came in? Could that be another type of machine, a computer machine?

No. It's almost like learning how to walk. In the electromechanicals you were still using a mechanical device, a switch, to read things, as opposed to reading a spot on a disk with using an LED or some electronic device. So it was the hybrid between the mechanical and the computer machine.

It was just another step up and more sophisticated?

It was another step up, right. The first ones that came out were, I believe, the electronic keno machines and the twenty-one game. I believe the twenty-one game came out before the keno game. And then the company that developed the twenty-one game got in real trouble because they took cards out of the deck, so they lost their license.

Did they put in a computerized deck that had only forty-eight cards or less?

Well, yes. They would take out the high cards in order to control the percentages. So you may have only had three queens in a deck. [laughter]

So the Gaming Control Board finally found out?

They finally caught up with them. When they first came out, Gaming Control wasn't sophisticated enough to really review the entire program and make sure that all the cards were in there. The company's theory was, "Well, why do we need fifty-two cards? We're only controlling the percentages."

Gaming Control came back and said, "No, you're not. This game is not a slot machine. It is a twenty-one game. It is controlled by having fifty-two cards in the deck; that's what controls the odds on it, and you control the percentage of the game by how much you pay off on various combinations. Or you take all pushes and those kinds of things. You can't do it like a slot machine and say, 'OK, I only want one jackpot symbol on each reel.' If it's a fifty-two card deck, you *have* to have all fifty-two cards in it."

So those kinds of things came out as an evolvement. Then IGT and then Bally got more sophisticated. And then too, the computer industry kept getting better and better with smaller, more intelligent chips and smaller packages.

Let's go back to when you were slot manager. Were you responsible for the scheduling of each shift?

As slot department manager I was responsible for the numbers, but the shift supervisors were responsible for scheduling their own shifts.

And how about hiring?

I did the hiring. In those days, most of the time the department managers personally interviewed every person. Now, if I was really busy and we were doing a lot of hiring, I might send the assistant or one of the better shift supervisors over. But everybody that was hired was personally interviewed by somebody in the department.

And you had less turnover in those days?

Yes. But then you got to understand that in those days we weren't worried about offending anybody either. [laughter] You didn't have to hire any minorities or someone who was aged. And if somebody wasn't pretty enough or too heavy, you didn't have to hire them. I'm not saying whether it was right or whether it was wrong, but that's just the way it was. Harrah's had a certain appearance code, and you *must* fit it. If some guy came in with tattoos all over his arms where you could see them or had bad acne, he wouldn't be hired.

The slot department, because it was an entry department, was always given the responsibility to hire with the idea that these people were going to go to the pit or to keno or become cocktail waitresses. In the old days all the dealers, and basically most of the cocktail waitresses and keno writers, came out of the slot department. They didn't go out and hire cocktail waitresses or dealers or anything else.

So you naturally wanted to have good personnel in your department for a couple of reasons?

Right. Also, in the winter when the pit was cutting back, they would get ahold of the slot department and say, "I've got ten dealers that I'm cutting off the schedule because we don't need them, that are just first-time dealers. Jim, can you find a place? Take them back in the slot department through this winter, and then we'll put them back in the pit in the spring."

So going into the slow time, the slot department would always try not to replace people and wait for the pit to cut down and then hold them for the next year. And the old pit managers always used to say they may have been somewhat of a problem the first year–they weren't the best people–but the second year they made sure that they didn't get put back in the slot department. [laughter] It was just something we all worked together with.

One thing we haven't touched on is wage ratios.

Wage ratios were the total wages for the department during the day divided by the total drop of the day. And you lived and died by that particular number as a department manager.

What was an acceptable wage ratio in the slot department at that time?

I think at that time it was probably about 2.1 percent. [laughter] Somewhere in there–1.9 to 2.1.

And you were given that figure daily, is that right?

Yes. We were given the wage ratio daily, and we had to answer on a daily basis. You also had to answer daily on why you had overtime.

So if your wage ratio was, say, 2.4, you would explain it to the general manager or the assistant general manager?

Originally, it was to Al Fontana, the general manager. Al didn't trust those kinds of things to his assistant, but later it was to the assistant general manager. They would question us as to why we ran such a high wage ratio, and we would say it just happened to snow that day, or we had bad weather and we couldn't react fast enough to send people home. You had better have gotten down to the club and double-checked everything and made sure that it was an anomaly that caused

it, not that you were just trying to run more help.

Were those figures kept on a daily basis?

Daily, weekly, monthly.

Per shift also?

No. In the slot departments you couldn't get a per shift drop and hold because you only dropped once during the twenty-four hours. In the pit you could get it by shift because you dropped every eight hours.

Was it tough to keep it in line?

Well, it meant that you paid a lot of attention to what was going on on the floor. Even as a department manager in the old days, you were expected to be in at least once or twice a week on every shift, but they didn't really give a damn whether you worked two hours, four hours, six hours, or twenty-four as long as you knew what was happening in your department.

Now, if something went wrong, bring your sleeping bag and you better spend some time there. [laughter] They were real good about requirements. You weren't required to work twelve hours straight–you could come in and work two hours during day shift, if that's what it was, and then two hours on swing. They expected you to be informed of what was going on, personally, on each shift.

If you were an eight-to-four department manager, you didn't last long, because the shift managers on each shift wanted to see the department manager at least once a week and have coffee with them. And on graveyard they did not want to see you come in at four o'clock, five o'clock in the morning or seven o'clock in the morning; they wanted you in there like from midnight to two when there was business. Just coming in early in the morning did not qualify . . . nooo. But they didn't require you to be in at eight o'clock in the morning. If you went in and worked swing shift, you weren't expected to be in at eight o'clock in the morning. You'd come at ten or one or two o'clock in the afternoon. They were real good about that. *But* in the long-run you ended up putting in lots of hours.

And six days was automatic, right?

No, five. But by the time you came back and did reports, they got their forty hours. [laughter] The worst thing you could do is come in at eight o'clock in the morning and leave at four.

You wouldn't be around very long if you did that?

No, not in the old days. Which, to me, made sense, and I grew up with it. It was a twenty-four hour operation; you had a twenty-four hour responsibility. During the later years when Holiday Inn came in, everybody was an eight-to-four employee. I think there were department managers that didn't even know they had a swing shift or a graveyard. You'd never see them. They just sat up there and ran things. When you worked for guys like Mert Smith and Bob Contois and Al Fontana, you *better* be around all twenty-four at least once or twice a week. Contois used to come back every Friday night himself; he'd make the tour of the town, and then he'd come back to the club. And every department manager better be there about eleven o'clock, because then he would hold his little coffee session with all the department managers. [laughter] Mert would come back at night; so would Al. They might come wandering through at any time.

When you were department manager, were you responsible for the slot mix or the slot floor layout, and could you explain those terms?

The slot mix is the percentage of nickels to dimes to quarters to halves to dollars. It's your mixture of the various denominations. The floor layout is how you've got your aisles set up and which machines you've got next to each other, and just generally how the floor would look and what machines it would contain.

Were you responsible for that at all?

No. That came from Bud in the slot shop. They would get our input. Bud controlled the percentages, the types of machines, and the slot shop would do the layouts with our help, but it wasn't the slot department's responsibility to sit down and actually do the floor layout or the mix of machines or the percentages.

As slot department manager at Harrah's (and sometimes I've regretted it) you were responsible only for maintaining the customer end of the business. The machines themselves, you didn't have any responsibility for it. Now, you were responsible for low hold. If the numbers weren't good, you were responsible for it, but you weren't responsible for the mix or the percentages or the types of machines.

Was Rome involved in that, too?

Rome was very deeply involved in that. Rome and then later Mando Rueda.

In the 1950s, 1960s, and 1970s was there any method of keeping track of your good slot players? Was there such a thing as tracking a player?

Not formally. Not like they do now. But we were all expected to take and keep the names of good customers and know all the good players, because they were still inviting players to golf tournaments and the New Year's party. We always had a big New Year's party, so you had to know who your good dollar-players were. It just wasn't as formal as it is now. And some of it was that in the old days, comps were left up to the shift manager or the supervisor. He had to recognize and know a good player, and it was his discretion how much he wanted to give him.

It's not like they do now, where they've got a special formula that you have to play X-amount of dollars for X-amount of hours, and that will earn you a hot dog. [laughter] I was working there when they first put that system in, and, to me, that system–although it's valuable–can lose a lot of good players. You could walk in and make one bet of five grand, lose it, and they would qualify you for only a hot dog because you didn't play long enough.

Well, a lot of places still use it.

Yes, because when the bean counters come in–excuse me for using that term–they're uncomfortable with letting an individual make a decision that's good for business, because it's subjective; it's not objective. So we've got to have this objective method of grading a player: "Voilà! Here's what we do. We'll come up with this complicated formula–the average bet times the length of play times the mythical number, the factor. That will tell us how much money we made off of him on an average." Therefore, the decision becomes objective, not subjective. But it's still a subjective decision no matter what you do, because you better hope the guys keeping track of them are doing it right or putting the right numbers down.

Now, when you get a comp report, you have this nice neat report that gives you all of this against what the guy got, so accountants are very satisfied. They can match the numbers, and now they got their numbers they can play with. Voilà!

Yes. And no one is endangering their job or risking their job by giving someone a steak dinner when he can't prove that he was worthy of it.

Right. Or comped a room or put him in a show.

So in your days, when you were on the floor as a slot manager, you'd just carry a book in your pocket to write good players' names down?

Yes, we always had a little Paulson Dice daily planner. Couldn't live without the Paulson Dice daily planner. That was in the pocket from the time I was a shift supervisor. You kept track of the good players in there, and their names would appear in daily reports, much like the pit players. You had to put down so-and-so or anybody winning or losing X-amount of dollars, and that went on for years.

You mentioned the golf tournaments and the New Year's Eve parties. Were there any special marketing or advertising programs directed toward slot players only?

No. The period that we're talking about there wasn't any really direct marketing like there is now with the slot clubs. There was no direct marketing even for pit customers, to tell you the truth. We would go through the reports at the end of the year plus all the records that we had, and if you're a good enough player, you get invited to this, this, and this–whatever happened to be deemed appropriate for your level of play. There wasn't a great scientific formula for doing that. In the big golf tournaments, that was mostly pit players. Very few slot players qualified for that, but that was all right too, because most of the people that played slots weren't golfers anyway. The golf tournaments eventually got a lot of deadbeats.

Actually, I think that's what killed the golf tournament. Eventually there was just too much dead wood.

Not only that, they got so expensive that they couldn't justify the cost of the tournament. They got to the point where they were spending way more than they could possibly take in on any one night, and their philosophy was always, "Well, look at these people. They spend a lot the rest of the year." Well, that may have been true. And knowing Harrah's, you still could have had them, but the two annual ones they used to have every year got to the point where you were giving away $500 a person in tee prizes. I mean, Countess Mara *sweaters* and Le Baron slacks, and this was a *tee* prize. [laughter] The cost just got out of line. It kept growing, and nobody would pull the costs back and say, "OK, you know, this is neat, but can we afford it?" The daily prizes were fantastic, then the big prize at the end and the hole-in-one prizes. It got carried away, and it finally ended up killing itself.

Now, where you got the new, modern, corporate management, every damn thing you do has got to be proven by fact or figure. So you start analyzing, and depending on how you want to do the cost analysis, you end up not having any promotions because you can't prove their value to an accountant's satisfaction. *But* neither can marketing prove some of their great big programs that they come up with. They don't seem to understand this marketing contest is going to cost you dollars. Does it seem funny to you?

Yes.

"We'll spend millions on marketing, but if one golf tournament costs us $100,000, you ought to be able to prove it's worth $100,000. This million-dollar promotion may just keep us even; but we understand that, so that's a whole different ball game." I never could understand that concept. Maybe that's because, I came out of gaming.

The premium point program at Harrah's—do you know when it started?

The exact date? No, I don't. Somewhere in the early 1950s they came up with it. It was

an extra bonus that Harrah's gave away that nobody else did. It was a hard program to duplicate, because Harrah's had been doing it so long they had gotten it down to a fine art, but it was expensive.

How did it work?

You had to hit a jackpot. For example, if you hit a nickel jackpot, you got twenty-five premium points. It was a red ticket–twenty-five points.

So when they paid you the jackpot, they gave you this ticket?

Yes. Then if it was a double nickel jackpot, you got two tickets, and so on and so on and so on.

So different jackpots paid different amounts of premium points?

Yes. Different amounts of money and different amounts of premium points, and that was on all denominations. Premium points in the old days could be redeemed at the premium point booth for merchandise, and they had all kinds of merchandise: irons, radios, jewelry, anything you wanted. You could write orders to stores on them. You could use Harrah's premium points almost the same as cash. You could buy liquor and cigarettes. You could buy anything in the world. You could pay your power bill.

How did you pay your power bill?

You would go to the premium booth, and they would write you a cash voucher for X-amount of dollars.

In later years, when they were screaming about getting rid of premium points (that they cost too much), what nobody really realized is that the premium point cost was built into the reel strips. It was already built in. So if your nickel machines were holding, let's say, 15 percent, you might have 14 percent with the machine, and the other 1 percent was the premium point cost. So it wasn't like somebody had come up and said, "Oh, let's give this actual bonus." When it originally was conceived, the costs were figured into the reel strips.

So the philosophy was, "I'm giving you something for nothing. But really I'm not giving you something for nothing, because I'm shorting your payouts on the machine."

Yes. "I could let you hit a few more cherries, but I'm not going to. I'm going to give you premium points instead."

Wasn't it a great program?

Oh, people loved it! People loved it!

And it lasted for how many years?

Oh, criminy, clear into the 1980s.

So it lasted for at least thirty years. Did it go out after Holiday Inns took over?

Yes. If you got to looking at the numbers and what the cost was, it was astronomical. I can't remember the exact figure, but it was a lot. They got to looking at that and thought, "Do we really need it?" And you couldn't convince them that it was built into the machine. They didn't understand that. What they understood was, "Yes, it may be built into it, but if we eliminate it, look how much more money we will make."

Premium points must have been a good incentive for people to come back into the club.

Yes. People that collected premium points would *faithfully* come in to play Harrah's slot machines because of premium points. Nobody else in the world offered premium

points. The wife is playing slot machines, and she goes to the premium booth, and they got a lamp in there. It's two thousand premium points. Well, she's only got 1,575 premium points, right? So she says, "I got to go back up and play because I want that lamp." The chances are she'll make it, but maybe she won't. She could just end up with her 1,575 premium points, and we'll take whatever money she had. [laughter] So there is some real good psychology to it.

Harolds Club and a few of them tried to do it with their payoff plus system, where they did it automatically. It was like a player club—you put your card in, and you got so many points. Every time you hit a jackpot you would get so many points, which you could go and redeem. It was an electronic type thing. What killed them was that when they went in and did the program, nobody considered the reel strips against the number of points they were giving away.

So they really were giving something away.

Oh, yes. It ended up being way more than what it should be. Plus, you got it not for just hitting the jackpot; you got it for the amount of coin you put in, which was like it was front-loaded. You didn't make them win anything. Just sticking your card in there and playing it and getting so many payouts would amass points for you. With the premium points system, you had to hit a jackpot, so you put up a hurdle right there to keep the cost down. It wasn't just a simple matter of putting the coin in.

At Harolds Club (where I worked from 1988 to 1989), because I was involved in it and I had already been doing it, I was looking at these numbers. I said, "Did you change the reel strips? Are we changing the reel strip?"

"Oh, no! No, no. We don't have to." [laughter]

I mean, "You're giving all these points away, and that's going to affect the gross profit."

"Well, it doesn't have to come off the slot department. This is a marketing project."

You know, I'm one of these kinds of guys: It doesn't make any difference what you want to call it, you're still going to be expending all these dollars.

Didn't some clubs try S & H Green Stamps for a while?

Yes.

And that didn't work for some reason.

What defeated most clubs and defeated most of those programs was the control. You have to have a method of controlling those tickets at the booth—how they get to the booth and how they get paid off. You have to have very good methods of controls, because they're just like money.

When I was a slot department manager, we had a floorman who was making premium point fills. He would get them in big thousand-point rolls, but they weren't getting to the booth. Now, I was slot department manager, and I had assumed (my fault) that the business office every day reconciled fills to the booth against usage through the number of jackpots, and that ought to be fairly close to the number of fills. They weren't doing that; they left that end open.

Even though we were putting the starting and ending numbers of the premium points on the cashier's checkout sheet and putting in the number of fills that they got and giving them their total, they never tied the cashier fills back to the booth. In other words, the floorman would go over to the cashier's office and say, "I need a roll of five-hundred point coupons." Then he'd just keep them. No one ever went back and tied the number of fills from the cashier's office to the slot booths. He figured it out: "All I have to do is just go over here and ask for a roll; they give it to me." He was right . . . until we caught him.

That was a very good program. I know it was a big part of Harrah's for a long time.

It was, and the premiums were all top-dollar merchandise, too.

Harrah's once tried to build their own slot machines.

I was out of the slot department when they got into that; but yes, they were going to build their own electronic slots, and they got Summit Engineering involved. In my opinion, that was Rome's decision. Rome had envisioned this slot machine that would keep track of everything in the world: door openings, number of times the reel spun, this, that, and everything. You would get this computer printout, and it would tell you the world.

They first started out trying to do this with a regular mechanical machine, which you can't do because it's not accurate. There's no place you can get an accurate reading out of it. They worked and they worked and they worked on this, but Rome would never concede. I talked to him once, and I said, "Rome, why don't you just pick what you think the most important points are that you need and get those working? Narrow it down. Narrow the focus down. You don't need to know whether reel number one spun one-and-a-half times this one span. Your scope is too broad."

So then they ended up doing that, and they hired experts to come in and do all this, but they didn't have the wherewithal. They hired an engineering company and all this, but they just didn't have enough wherewithal to compete with IGT and the rest of them. It was kind of foolish, I think.

Did they plan to build them just for their own casinos, or were they going to sell them to other casinos?

It was going to be for Harrah's only–Harrah's priority machine. Bud was more involved in it than I was. I was a shift manager by then.

It just kept stumbling. They had one engineer that came up with a random program–well, he had it programmed so that if you hit a cherry, it was impossible for it to ever come back again. You couldn't repeat the cherry on the machine, and he built that into the program. [laughter] When the state picked it up, they said, "Why . . . ?"

Bud and Rome got on him about it and said, "Why did you do that?"

"Well," he says, "I didn't think you'd want to take two hits in a row." [laughter]

Jim, tell us about the training programs and seminars that Harrah's had.

They were under the direction of Bob Brigham, who I believe was corporate vice-president, human resources. He started a series of management training programs that were designed to teach new supervisors how to supervise and to aid older supervisors in becoming better supervisors. We had one or two almost every year for several years.

How long did they last?

They were one hour, sometimes two hours, sometimes a half day. It all depended upon what type of program we were putting on.

Did Bob Brigham conduct the meetings, or did he bring in outside groups?

No. What he did was use available supervisors. Ed Wessel was involved in it, and I was involved in it, too. We got some of the material from Bob and then turned around and made our class agenda. The class agenda would be more tailored to Harrah's than it

would be to a college student. If you were conducting a management training session, you had the option of taking and changing the basics to where it fit Harrah's more than it did just general businesses. It worked quite well because it wasn't so much academic as it was real life in certain cases. But there was some academic teaching in there, too, you know–the principles of management, the hierarchy of needs, and all that. [laughter] When we did those kinds of things, we tried to make them as interesting to a group of gaming supervisors as possible so you didn't lose their attention.

When they first started out, Brig was conducting them with the whole group. There was Maggie McGuire, Bobbie Hall, Andy Marcinko, Bull DeMarco–a whole bunch of the *old*-time gaming pit people in this class. They just didn't cotton to Brig and his academic approach to supervision. [laughter] One time . . . . I can't remember what the class subject was, but Maggie spoke up, and he says, "Bob, I may not know the distance from one end of the string to the middle, but I *know craps.*" [laughter] And he had to put up with comments like that.

Brig would say that you have to give quality to a man's work; that if he just offered a guy a hundred dollars a day to polish his shoes, there was no job enrichment and fulfillment in that. You wouldn't find very many takers. I can't remember which one of the old pit bosses spoke up and said, "You want to pay me a hundred dollars to polish your shoes, Brig? I'll do it any day of the week for that. You won't embarrass me." [laughter]

When we first got it started, they started with the old-timers, and they were rebelling against it. In those days, I was the slot shift supervisor and not too long out of college, so it was kind of fun for me and the younger ones to match wits with Brig. But the old-timers . . . it was like you were trying to get a mule to start. I wish I could remember all the comments. Every day there would be a snip and a snipe and a snipe and a snip. [laughter] Later on then, when we got really into the training for new supervisors and then for other supervisors, we ran into less and less resistance. And then some of the older pit bosses were phased out one way or the other. A lot of them by that time were gone. Maggie McGuire left and Bull DeMarco was gone, and Bobbie Hall. There was a whole group of pit people when I started there in 1958 that by 1963, 1964 were all gone. They couldn't adjust to the change.

It was sad in a way. Some of those guys had worked for Harrah's for ten, fifteen years, and some had been there since Harrah's had opened.

Yes. Some of them had come up with him from Venice.

Actually, it was their own fault for not adjusting. You have to adjust in life. You have to make changes.

They were just not going to adjust.

Anyway, we put on these training seminars, and we did it for a year. Ed Wessel was involved in it, a young man by the name of Chuck Yeager, Bob Ring Jr., and myself. We were all either shift supervisors, assistant department managers, or department managers. Brig picked the ones that he wanted to train, and then we gave the classes.

Did he sit and observe?

After they got going he would come in, but he left you pretty much to your own devices.

We went into *all* kinds of trainings. In some years it was whatever the latest vogue was in management training, and I can't remember how many of them there were. We would take and modify them. And then, over the course of the years, we finally ended up

with a fairly good, constant program, and we were using pretty much the same material. I was quite involved in it.

Were they held in Harrah's?

Yes, in the conference rooms. I acted as management training coordinator for the program. I was the slot department manager, and I kind of reported to Brig and Joe Specht (the personnel manager) on the training. I reported to them, and I also developed a lot of training classes for Harrah's and conducted quite a few classes for a number of years.

So actually, every supervisor got quite a bit of training?

Yes, they did. That was one of the things that kind of bothered some of us when Holiday Inns came in with all their training programs. They treated us like we didn't know anything and we were hicks from the bush and had never conducted any training programs. We'd been doing it for . . . oh, by the time they got in there in 1980, we'd been doing it since 1966.

A bunch of us were very, very involved in it. In fact, some of the floor supervisors like Eddie Wessel and myself and Chuck Yeager and Bob Ring Jr. were probably more involved in the training than Personnel and Human Resources were because they were developed within the gaming departments. The supervisors' class just wasn't for the pit; it was for all supervisors. But every year we'd have training classes of a different kind, and it kept going. So when Holiday Inns came in with all their fancy educated university professor-type programs, and they brought in guest speakers and all that, they kind of treated Harrah's like, "You guys don't know anything, never did know anything, and you ain't going to learn anything either."

We'd been doing it for years in small groups of ten or fifteen or twenty. We'd even go down into some lower levels like key men and box men, so that with this training program we were trying to give them some ideas of what it takes to make a good supervisor.

Well, Harrah's did have (and still does have) a tremendous reputation as far as a proving ground or training ground for all kinds of gaming employees. And part of it must be attributed to the training that you guys did in the 1960s and 1970s.

I was the training coordinator, but I got a lot of input from Ed Wessel, Chuck Yeager, and Bob Ring Jr. We all developed these ideas, and then we'd run the classes by each other to see whether they made sense. We even had our own textbooks typed up. We took it right out of management training books and then altered it to suit our needs. I know Wes [Ed Wessel] came up with some real good things, and he typed it up for the pit when he was the pit manager. Then I took it, and I used it. So like I said before, in the old days we all kind of worked together. I guess there was competition, but it was like everybody was on a team. That was my perception of it.

Competition without contention?

Right. That's a very good way of putting it. And I think some of it was because there were no job interviews like for shift manager. You were anointed . . . if that makes sense. [laughter] But because of that, it made it feel like you weren't competing for the job. Do the best job you can do with the department you got, look good at what you do, and perhaps you'll be recognized and moved up. You don't get it by making the pit manager look like an idiot or picking on him in a meeting and calling him names. [laughter] It was like, if

we all work together, whoever gets it, gets it because that's the one they wanted, not because you weren't prepared.

Did they also have get-togethers at Villa Harrah at Lake Tahoe?

Yes. Both the Reno and the Lake Tahoe supervisors would get together once a year for a dinner with Bill Harrah—dinner and a cocktail party.

Was that for their spouses, also?

No, it was just the gaming management from both places.

Were they all male at that time?

Yes, except they did have one gal that was in charge of wardrobe, Maggie Beaumont.

It was to get the Reno and Lake Tahoe management and everybody together once a year to strengthen ties. Because, if you remember, there was a strong rivalry between the two properties. They were fun times. I enjoyed those parties.

Would Bill Harrah get up and say a few words?

Oh, yes, he would say *very* few. He was not a talkative individual. I remember I was up there one year when he had just built the "Jerrari," which was a wrecked Ferrari mated to a Jeep Wagoneer. It was the ugliest car you ever saw in your life. It was painted that Harrah's green, and it just stood out. [laughter] Harrah's green and salmon pink, those were the colors. I was standing there talking to him, and I asked him, "Bill, why did you build the Jerrari?"

And he very quietly said, "Jim, I wanted to buy an Aston-Martin." (Aston-Martin had come up with an all-wheel drive car that particular year.) "I went to England to buy it, but they don't make it in left-hand drive. So I decided to make my own." That was the end of the conversation.

Tell us how the Jerrari came about.

Well, Bill had had a safety engineer—and I can't recall his name—who was bringing back a brand-new Ferrari from San Francisco. And as you come into Reno, the bridge coming into Verdi has a curve in it; he was doing 150 miles an hour and missed it. He lost it and slammed that Ferrari sideways into the first bridge abutment and then rolled it clear across the bridge; but he didn't get killed. The seat belts were racing types—he had a full racing harness on, and they were hooked directly into the frame. The only place in that car you could have sat and survived was the driver's seat. The abutment had come through the passenger side all the way to the transmission.

The Ferrari was buckled in half plus rolled, so they didn't know what to do with it. The engine was fine, and the transmission was fine. It was in fairly good shape. It didn't hurt the front end—the passenger side and the top got most of the damage. They cut the front end off and mated it to that old square-box style Jeep Wagoneer; put the Ferrari engine in it and mated it to the Jeep transmission, which made it a four-wheel drive. They had to do a ton of machine work just to get it together.

So now he could drive a Ferrari with four-wheel drive?

Yes, a four-wheel drive Ferrari. [laughter] But it was this ugly thing that went down the road, and it had this box on the back and then that real steep, sloping Ferrari front.

Did he drive it for a long time?

No. I think it was more a "let's see if we can do it" kind of thing. It wasn't driven all that much. It would overheat—the radiator wouldn't get enough air in it, and it would overheat.

But, to get back to the training, that went on for quite a while.

Oh, I think that's an important part of Harrah's. At that time it was probably the only casino that had any kind of a management training program. Now many of them do. Of course, there's a lot of things Harrah's started that a lot of clubs do now.

Yes. One year a bunch of us went eight weeks to the University of Nevada business college for a course in principles of management. That was real interesting. Then some years we went to Middle Fork Lodge for a week and had seminars there. Brig would go along, and it would be a combined Reno-Lake Tahoe training session.

Did you have a certain degree of recreation there as well?

Oh yes, very definitely.

What made Harrah's such a successful organization?

I think it was a shared goal. You knew what was expected from you from the top to the bottom; everybody had a niche. Everybody had something to contribute, and everybody was expected to contribute. There weren't too many secret agendas. What was known was known. Bill Harrah's basic principle of gaming was customer, customer, customer—take care of the customer, take care of the customer. And we would do lots of customer service training: how to take care of customers, and what was expected out of the employee. They were consistent in how all the rules were applied, both to employees and to customers. You had a procedure, darn near, for going to the bathroom.

That was the bible. That's what the benchmark was for everybody–how well you followed the procedures. They didn't change; they stayed the same. And when they were training dealers . . . and I know a lot of it was Rome–he wanted people that did the same thing, because they were easier to watch, particularly in the pit: If you have somebody in the lookout, and you're teaching the dealer how to bury his hole card, Rome wanted him to bury it by *his* particular method, because then the man in the lookout could see if there was a deviation. So you were trained by Harrah's to do everything a certain way. If you were working the crap game, you'd take and pay. There was a sequence of doing that that was by procedure; there was no totaling of payoffs unless you were really on an excellent crew on a real high-limit game. You would have to take and pay, take and pay. Twenty-one games the same way.

Slot department–the key man had procedures of what you could do and what you could not do in the slot machine. Booth cashiers had procedures on how their money was to be set up, how the paperwork was to be handled. Everything was done so that you could take a new hire in the pit or anyplace else, and it wouldn't take you forever to teach him the job if he was of normal intelligence. [laughter]

And they did it the same whether they were in Reno or Tahoe?

Or no matter where you were in Harrah's. And because of that, I think people could come in and know what to expect. Twenty-one players would know the Harrah's dealers dealt a certain way. The crap dealers or change people handled people in the same way. There were procedures on who could pay jackpots and who couldn't. Generally, everything was mapped out. And with a *very* strong emphasis on customers and customer

service. I used to say that the only difference between Harrah's and any other gaming establishment in the world was the people we employed and how they treated the customer. Everybody has table games; everybody has slot machines; everybody's got keno. The defining difference was how well the customer was treated, and that's what made Harrah's.

I think some of it, too, was Bill's uniqueness in wanting to have, in the beginning, real leather on bar stools and in coffee lounges; trucks running around with white sidewall tires. [laughter] It was just an overall persona of *the best*. It percolated down through to everybody, clear down to the bottom. Oh, we were a proud group those years! We worked for Harrah's. "I'm a *Harrah's* employee." Whether it was good or whether it was bad, it made people feel like they were brought into things.

I know for a fact that in some cases, like when we were developing new procedures, employees were involved. We would maybe bring in a shift supervisor or somebody else to write up the procedure, and then we would always get together a group of employees who had to use it. We'd give it to them and say, "OK, go through these procedures and make sure they work. We want to know–do they make sense to you? Can you follow? Is there anything that you think we should change to make your job easier? This is what we want, but maybe you have a better way of getting there. So make whatever changes you want to make before we finalize this procedure." (We were a little more liberal than the pit department because we were writing different types of procedures on how to use the new payoff system or something like that.)

And as part of the training, too, wasn't someone always being prepared for the next step up?

Oh, yes. You always had an understudy. Yes, there was quite a bit of that kind of training.

So if you left, someone had been trained to take your place. Very seldom, if ever, did they have to go outside the club.

Very, very seldom. Harrah's was almost straight in-line promotion. In-line everything. Harrah's hired *very*, very few outside dealers. Once in a while they would; if somebody knew a real good dealer, they could get him hired. But 99 percent of all the dealers in those days were trained at Harrah's. Everybody bought into the program, and *normally* when somebody was promoted, everybody had worked with him and had an idea of how he worked. It wasn't like bringing a stranger in and you would have to find out what kind of a guy he was. You wouldn't have to have that honeymoon period where you were trying to learn about him—you knew if this guy was demanding, he was going to be demanding when he got promoted; if he wasn't, it was something else. If he was a jerk, he was going to be a jerk there, but you knew how to handle him as a jerk. Does that makes sense? [laughter]

Yes. And he also had to follow Harrah's procedure.

Definitely.

And if he was a jerk or a good guy or a hard-driving person, he still had those procedures to follow.

Yes. I guess it was toward the late 1960s or early 1970s, when people were starting to rebel against society, that we started to get dozens of complaints from employees about the procedures. You know—"Why can't we do it our own way?" I always tried to explain to people that the procedures were there as much as a protection to the employee, if not more so, as anything else. All they're asking you is to do it a certain way. If you do it that way, even a poor supervisor or a department manager or a club manager can't do anything to you. Just show up for work on time, follow the procedure, and you got a job for life; and you don't even have to be all that good.

As long as you dealt, sold change, or did a cashier job according to the procedure, they were there to fight for you. Because remember, we had the Board of Review in those days. If you terminated an employee, and they went to the Board of Review, you would *have* to prove which procedure was violated, when it was violated, and how many warnings had been given. Now, if you couldn't come up with that, you may have the employee back again. So the procedures were there to protect people's jobs. I used to give this example: You go to work for, let's say, the Horseshoe. (I don't mean this is bad; I'm just picking up the name.) A pit floorman comes in some night and looks you in the eye and says, "You're gone."

"Well, why?"

"I don't need a reason."

Well, at Harrah's he would have to have a reason based on attendance or shortages or procedure violation. There always had to be a reason, and it was always based on procedure.

Let's talk about some of the individuals that you think were most influential in making Harrah's successful.

Oh, without a doubt, Bill himself.

How did he command respect?

It was in a very quiet manner. The man wasn't that impressive when you first met him and talked to him, but he had good people working for him. He had people who worked with him who had his respect, and he respected them, and he let them do the majority of the work. Now, Bill, as far as I know, would never give a direct order. Most of the time it was in the way of a suggestion. That's what I've heard. And I've been around him. It was, "Don't you think we should do this?" And that was like saying, "Get it done."

And he had people like Rome, Bob Ring Sr., Shep, Lloyd Dyer . . . oh, I could go through a number of people that he had working for him.

And his search for excellence, his attention to details. The fact is that you went around and you made sure that in a slot booth the match holders were full. There were no posted, handwritten notes in the cashier's office or anyplace where the customer would see them—not even in private offices could you have a posted, handwritten note. Everything had to be typed. Nothing Scotch-taped to the walls—any sign that was going to be in the casino had to be made out of plastic or had to be a first-class sign. I remember walking through the casino and checking all the ceiling lights to make sure that every ceiling light was on. The philosophy was that if you don't pick up on the little things, you won't notice the big things. Attention to detail, attention to detail.

Restrooms—you walked into a men's restroom; it was dirty. You might clean it yourself or get somebody in there, because it had to be absolutely, spotlessly clean at all times. There was no excuse for it not being clean. The whole area—the rug on the casino floor. Wrappers . . . the minute a coin wrapper hit the floor, either a change person picked it up and disposed of it, or a porter would come along and dispose of it. But it all went with this personification that Bill Harrah built up of Harrah's being excellent. It was just his persona that came through—the large semi-trucks with white-sidewall tires that had to be specially made; real leather seats on the bar stools. Coffee shops had real leather in the booths!

Little things, like he would only serve the best whiskey. Old Crow, Smirnoff, Cutty-Sark—those were the bar pours. Now, nobody in the world at that time was pouring Old Crow, Cutty-Sark, Smirnoff vodka, and Gilbey's gin as a bar pour. [laughter] These weren't premium drinks; these were the bar pour! So all of this together adds up to give the customers the feeling that they were walking into *the* best; they were going to be treated to the best, and the accommodations were the best. It just built up, and it also built up with the employees.

And he selected the right people to follow through with all those ideas.

Yes, he did. He had good people who understood him and what he wanted.

Did he and Bob Ring work off each other to a degree?

Yes, they did. Bob was a phenomenal man when it came to memory. If he met you once, shook your hand and learned your name, he would never forget it. And he was kind of like the father figure. He was the quiet one that worked very quietly like Bill, and Rome was the watchdog. But their personalities worked together—what was one's weakness was another one's strength. They built up the team for the most part. They complemented one another in their skills.

Another example might be Mr. Sheppard and Lloyd Dyer. Shep was very quiet, and Lloyd was outgoing, more of a people person.

Right. The chemistry worked. And I think that it worked very well in the most part because, up until Bill died, this team had been built up to a certain extent by promoting from within. Whether the person came from the lake to take a job or whether the person was from Reno, it didn't make any difference. It was a promotion from within, so that the common goal had been instilled in them from the time they started at an entry-level job until they got to where they were today. That common goal was there.

To a certain extent, hiring within limits your resources and your ideas. One of the big complaints I always heard is that you got too inbred with your ideas. No new ideas came in.

But on the other hand, you had a team that knew how to work together and knew what the common goal was, and you didn't have to redo it again.

There were a few failures along the way, but there would have been just as many failures if you had hired from outside.

Very definitely. I don't think the failures were due to hiring from within as much as to a bad choice; or there was something about the individual that didn't come out until . . . . What's that old principle?

The "Peter principle."

The "Peter principle." They got promoted beyond their capabilities. It's all human nature. I don't know that you will always make the correct choice of who you promote, no matter how much testing or how much everything else you've got, until a man sits in the chair.

That's right. Well, let's get back to the slot machine business for a while. In this day and age there's so many more dollar players than there were before. Do you think that's mainly because of inflation? The nickel doesn't have buying power?

Basically, there's a strong correlation to economics. [laughter] Nickels now are pennies. When you go to the store now, you use more nickels. Everything is priced to the nickel, where it wasn't then, and a dollar had more value; a dollar could buy more. And I strongly believe that economics has a part in it.

Then you have to remember that in the beginning, years ago, slot machines were recreations for old ladies and old men, and that's the way they were perceived. They weren't perceived as a high-roller-type game. They were just a grind game. The gals or women that came in played slot machines while the husbands played craps or twenty-

one, and that's what the industry had grown up believing. Then as we got further into it, people came in that had money that liked to play slot machines. And from that, it just kept growing and growing–growing until right now slot revenues gross in some places more than the pit.

So it's gone from this little stepchild down here–"We got to have you to take care of the old ladies"–to now, "We want you because we're losing pit players." Now the slots are the drivers. So the pendulum has kind of reversed, and I'm not so sure it's right or wrong. I think you need both of them. They're of equal importance. You just have to manage them a little bit different for resources.

In the early days, the 1950s and the 1960s, didn't you know most of your dollar players?

Not *most* of them; *all* of them. You could call them by name. I think in Reno our dollar section had twenty dollar machines. The dollar section was two rows in front of the dollar booth, and that was plenty of machines. We also had some half-dollar machines in there. That was in 1958, and that lasted probably until 1970. There just weren't that many people that played dollars. Nickels were the big game; dimes were a big game.

Now you seldom see dimes, and you seldom see halves.

Halves weren't a bad denomination, but now I don't think you can buy a dime machine. You'd have to have a special order, and there's a reason for that. Dimes are a real hard coin to handle, because they're so small and so thin they jam up. They used to jam the slides–they'd jam up in the head of the escalator where the coin went through. When you'd go to get a pay, you'd get a dime. They'd stick together. Hoppers were the same thing. They have a read-out unit. Some of them were switches, and some of them were lights–there were various methods. A dime is awful small, and down in the hopper where your hopper plate pulls the coin out, you'd have dimes stuck between it and the bowl. They're an ill-conceived coin as far as the game is concerned.

What impact do you think the multi-coin machines have made?

With a multi-coin machine, what you've done is turned a nickel machine into a quarter, or a quarter into a dollar machine. You've just upgraded the player without him knowing it. It's just an upgrade. We tried multi-coin machines on the mechanical slots using a mechanical switch that would keep track of the coins played, but with primitive electronics it didn't work. When the computer would allow you to do this, there was no reason not to. I mean, it just opened up a whole new market. And *because* of this new market, the slot departments are dropping, in most casinos, as much, if not more, than the pit games. So the multi-coin has enabled the casino to have, theoretically, the same amount of players "headcount-wise" and get a lot more slot drop.

What are your feelings on things such as Megabucks and Quartermania, these huge progressives that are tied in throughout the state?

They are what the customer wants.

The customer does want it?

They *must*, if you look at the amount of money that is being played. You know, the old theory in gaming is you may not like the idea, but you better give the customer a chance to make the decision, because in the final analysis, he's the one that's going to make the decision whether any game is viable or makes money. What casinos are doing more and more is putting in innovations and new types of games in the slot department. You've got a tremendous amount of different

types. They're all the same principle, but they *look* different to the customer. They're all based on the number of symbols on the reel, you know. [laughter] But they can change the look of the symbols. They can do a lot of things to where it looks like a new game to the customer.

And they have some slots with many different games on just one machine.

Yes. I'd have to sit down and think about all the different names, but they all have the capability of playing four or five different slot games. You can play keno (you can play four or five different keno games); you can have craps; you can have roulette, red dog. I mean, you can have as many games as your electronics will allow you to have.

Another big change is the bill acceptors.

Yes, bill acceptors speed up the entire process. You don't have to handle coin anymore–makes the count a lot easier. Technology has allowed the gaming industry to make greater strides in the area of slots than in other departments. Now, I guess you can't call them slots; they're probably "coin-operated gaming devices." Whereas the pit, to a certain extent, is still stuck with its original rules. Twenty-one is still played, other than some variations, the way it started out when the game was invented. Craps, the same way. Keno to a certain extent. So those games were limited just by their rules, whereas a gaming device can come in all shapes, sizes, and looks. Keno has become inhibited because the slot department started getting the bigger payoffs. Keno is no longer the queen of payoffs.

Keno is almost a dying game, don't you believe?

It is as a station-operated game; it isn't as a gaming device. On the new machines now you can play "way" tickets, top and bottom.

Where before we used to just have to play a straight ticket, now you can play not "true-way" tickets but many different kinds of tickets. Plus, keno is a very labor-intensive game. For the amount of money that you can make off of keno, it's very, very labor-intensive. Now, with the new electronic keno, you might as well play a keno machine, because you just go up to some guy, give him your money, and he puts it in a card reader. All you do is you see the balls come up; and you can see *that* on a coin-operated device. It's a game that takes up a lot of floor space, but traditionally large casinos have had to have a keno game.

You have very few brush games anymore. I think maybe the Cal-Neva is the only one that's got a brush game. That's probably because of Warren.

They'll probably have a brush game as long as Warren Nelson is alive.

It was like you had a bingo parlor at Harrah's as long as Bill Harrah was alive. They didn't get rid of bingo until after Bill was dead, because he felt that to be a casino you had to be a full-service casino and make bingo available to the public.

He might have had sentimental attachment to it also.

Well, I think that was part of it, too. But that was the way things were done.

What year were you promoted from slot department manager to shift manager?

1976.

What did a shift manager at Harrah's do at that time?

A shift manager was the one individual on property capable of solving any problem at that particular time. That's kind of a broad thing, but the philosophy of having a shift manager started, I understand, with Bill Harrah. He wanted somebody on property who could make a decision which would affect a customer then and now, so that the customer did not have to wait until the next day to get his problem resolved. Plus, he felt that there should be somebody on property who was a quasi-general manager. That is what you were.

You were in charge for eight hours?

You were in charge, and you were "he," "she," and "it" on that property in charge of everything. If there was a problem, they only had to call one person. If there was a problem, you knew what the problem was and what the solution was.

If there was, let's say, a dispute between the kitchen and maintenance, which there always was . . . . [laughter] "They're not fixing my oven; they're breaking it." Well, when it came to a head, it was the shift manager's responsibility to get the two together and get it solved.

Customer disputes. If there was a customer dispute over a payoff, pit, or any of the gaming departments, it was up to the shift manager to make the decision. It could go either way, either the customer or the company. But a decision would be made at that particular time at that instant, and nobody would have to wait until the next day. That was the philosophy behind it. It was a hard job to explain. You didn't do any budgets, you worked eight hours, and all you did was sit there and answer questions and solve problems and grant credit.

So every shift was different?

Oh, yes! Every shift was different. Every day was different. You had different problems on day shift than you had on swing shift than you had on graveyard. It was one of those jobs where it's kind of hard to explain what you did to earn what you did, but you were there in case there was a problem.

And some days you had very little to do?

Some days you may just sit in the employee lounge drinking coffee with supervisors and with employees. Another day you may be running your tail off. You couldn't even get lunch. I mean, it was kind of volatile. It was a fun job because it was so varied in its application. You were the one who granted credit: after people got to their credit limit, it was up to the shift manager to make the decision of whether they got any more or not. Shift managers controlled the hotel-room line–how many rooms you would keep for comps.

Shift managers controlled the seating in the Headliner Room and at Tahoe. It was up to them to see how many seats they wanted to keep for good customers and how many they were going to let go to sell to the public. That was their realm of responsibility, which gets you in real bad trouble, because Bill Harrah had a philosophy that there would never be a show without at least a hundred people in it. You would have to fill the room. In Reno in the wintertime we got some shows that . . . *oh,* they were bad. We would have to pull people out of the casino and *chase* them in there so that the entertainer wouldn't be playing to himself. [laughter] Oh, and not only did you do that, but one of the big things was you never overbooked the room. Whoa! If you overbooked the room (and it was your responsibility to control that, especially when you were on swing shift), you got in trouble. Rome would say, "How many people did you send away? We do not do that. We do not overbook the room." So they kind of had you on a two-edged sword when it came to the room. [laughter]

When the shows were slow like that, and you took people out of the casino or out of the bar to put them in there, did you comp the show for them?

Of *course.* [laughter] It was an expensive proposition as far as the company was concerned; but I always felt, "If that's the way he wants it done, that's the way it's going to be done."

At the end of your shift, what would you do?

You wrote up a daily report of what happened.

Where did you get all the facts for that daily report?

You'd get the facts from the pit, the slots, whatever, and it wasn't a *big* daily report. It was just pertinent information of what happened: big winners, big losers, basically any problems that arose–customer disputes or anything–so that people would know what was going on on that shift. And it was important that you got it to your general manager or that he got it in the morning the first thing so *he* could read it and be prepared to answer any questions that he was going to be asked by Bill or Rome or Bob Ring or anybody above him. In Reno, I can remember if you worked graveyard, if anything went down–I would imagine it was the same with the lake–you would call the general manager in the morning about six, six-thirty depending upon who you were working for, and fill him in on any major happening in the morning, so when he hit the door, he already had the information before the reports came down.

So you oftentimes made phone calls in the middle of the night?

Oh, yes. You were supposed to call in any keno winner over twenty-five thousand dollars, any big pit win. And I can remember when I was first a shift manager, we had a twenty-five-thousand-dollar keno ticket hit about three o'clock in the morning, and I called up Mert Smith. He wakes up, and I can tell he's about three-quarters asleep, and his question to me was, "Why are we paying it?" [laughter]

Now I'm thinking, "Uh ... because, Mert, he got an eight out of eight on a dollar and ten-cent ticket. I have gone down. I have checked all the draws and the microfilm. Everything is fine. It's there."

And he goes, "Oh, oh, oh, oh. All right."

So I'm sitting there thinking, "OK, I know what the procedure is." I said, "Mert, how about I don't wake you up in the middle of the night? Tell me what time you get up in the morning, and I'll be damned sure to call you then."

And Mert says, "You know, that sounds like a good idea, and just be sure to do it." [laughter]

Did you work mostly graveyard?

I worked all three shifts, but I worked quite a bit of graveyard. I was shift manager, I think, ten years–1976 to 1986. I was a special casino program manager for a year.

What did that entail?

Junkets. I was the junket rep in Reno. It was a special program where you had representatives in cities that would get groups together, and they would bring them into Reno.

Was that the same job that Dan Orlich had?

Dan Orlich was over it to a certain extent, but we still reported to club management. The lake's program was much better than the one that Reno had. They had *much* more to offer at the lake than we had at Reno. It was a good program, but I'll be perfectly honest with you–I didn't particularly care for the job. You have to be on the road talking to the junket reps, and it was a salesman job to me more than it was an administrative job.

So you traveled to a lot of the cities where the junket reps were, or to foreign countries?

No, I never left the continental United States, but I just didn't like to be on the road that much. When we started a Chinese program (and I was quite involved with the development of that), that only involved going to San Francisco, which wasn't bad. The program took somebody, and I'm trying to think of some names of people–I can't right now–who really liked to be on the road and were the salesmen type. I was always more of an administrator than I was the salesman. I liked doing the budgets and writing the procedures and doing the programs and coming up with different new programs. I didn't like the salesman part of the job. I was only there for a year.

In any of the jobs that you had over the years, did you ever have much personal contact with Bill Harrah?

No, I did *not* have any personal contact with him other than when he would come through the club; but to work directly with him or to report directly to him, no I didn't. He never forgot my name. For all the years he walked through he would give me, "Hi, Jim," and this low wave. It was a wave just about hip high with his hand as he walked. He did that to everybody.

So he waved kind of sideways?

Kind of sideways with his hand. It'd be, "Hello," whichever your name, and this little wave, and look straight ahead and keep on going. It was like this ghost kind of sauntered through and anointed you with that little wave. [laughter]

Yes, and everybody said, "Oh, there goes Bill Harrah."

Yes. "Make sure that the carpet's clean. Which way is he headed? Send the troops out ahead of him." [laughter] He would come down to the Headliner Room, because at that time we didn't have a portico or the big entrance like there was at the lake. It was right out on the streets. Well, we would have to know the exact time that he was coming so we could get pylons out there and almost a red carpet, so that when he pulled up he did not have to wait in front of the hotel to come through and go to the Headliner Room. And then you made sure that the back stairwell going down to the entertainers' dressing room—which was carpeted—was clean and that that area was spotlessly clean. We knew what his route was (he never deviated from it too much), so you made sure that everything along that route was "A-number one."

So he kind of presented a challenge, if that's the right word?

Yes. Well, *all* of them did. One of the things about working in Reno on day shift that nobody liked—I didn't really mind it—was that you had all the executives coming to lunch every day. Every day they would come down through the casino, and in about an hour or a half-hour, when they got upstairs, you would get a ton of advice on what to check. They would call the general manager. The general manager would call the shift manager, and then you would have to go check the particular area. So you got so if you were smart, about 11:30 you started your tour. And you knew they generally didn't deviate too much from the route, so you went down there and made sure there was enough change help or not too much change help. You made sure that the pit limits were right and the pit staffing looked all right . . . all the lights were on. Because sooner or later you would get a telephone call concerning that. I've often wondered how did swing and graveyard manage without all this other help. But it kind of got to be a challenge to see if you could stay ahead of them.

You were at Harrah's, Jim, for several years. Could you tell us some of the changes that occurred in hiring practices during those years?

The slot department in Reno was the first department in Harrah's to hire a black American. Bob Brigham hired—and I can't remember his name—an athlete at the University of Nevada. He worked for about one week. And it wasn't his fault, but I think he had been given to believe that all he had to do, because he was an athlete at the University of Nevada, was show up for work.

What year was that?

I think about 1966. And he didn't work out. So then they sent us another one. And I'm trying to think . . . I know his first name was Napoleon. "Nap" is what we called him. *Excellent*, excellent employee. And because he was, I think it made a big impact on hiring any more in the future. It was the slot department's responsibility to take care of him and not show any fears or prejudice . . . which, if you had been there in the late 1950s and the early 1960s, you would know was very prevalent, because they weren't even allowed to come in the club.

Right. Was he hired specifically for any special reason?

He was hired to meet a quota and to have an African-American working at Harrah's. Fortunately, he turned out to be *very* good, and he ended up in the pit. He worked for me as a floor supervisor. He was an *excellent* employee.

Did you say earlier that African-American people weren't even allowed in the club?

Oh, no. They were met at the door and told that Bill Fong's New China Club is where they wanted to go play. It catered to them.

Do you recall ever having any incidents over that?

No. It was almost like it was an accepted fact until what . . . 1963, 1964, when the black movement started. Then is when (and I was a shift supervisor then) everyone *allowed* them to come in. Then you had to put in your daily report how many "collegiates" were in the club on your shift playing in your department. The term "collegiate" was the code name for an African-American.

It is amazing that there never were any problems. I never heard of any problems. I told several of them, and I'm sure you've told them or had security tell them, that they weren't allowed in the club.

Yes, it was required of you. It was your job. I don't think there was any racial prejudice. I would like not to think so, but you either did it or you didn't eat.

I always remember a shift manager who was *real* biased. I was a shift supervisor when an African-American and a white lady came in and sat at the bar. Now, this particular shift manager . . . you could just see the *steam* rising in his head. And he walks over to the bar, and he looks at this couple, and he says, "You, *out now.*"

And the black man or the African-American . . . he says, "You can't kick me out."

He says, "I'm not kicking you out. I'm kicking this piece of white trash that you're with out."

And I'm standing there, and I say, "You can't do that."

He says, "Yes, I can. I didn't kick him out. I kicked her out."

They both left. Well, you always knew that Nevada was considered the Mississippi of the West. It just happened. And then it changed, slowly changed.

How about the black entertainers?

Black entertainers never stayed in the hotel. No. They were fine with that.

And so naturally they didn't come into the casino or gaming area either?

No. It was just a period of change. I can remember we had a series of meetings on when we were going to do it and how to do it and when to do it, and there were a lot of problems with the older supervisors. The older supervisors had a considerable amount of bias, but it worked out.

Did you notice any problem with other customers when the black people started coming in?

No. All the dread that everybody had feared that this was going to turn into . . . what was going to happen never happened. You found out that most people that came in the casino—regardless of the color of their skin—if they're well-behaved, they're well-behaved; if they're not, they're not. There isn't any one particular group of people about whom you can say, "These are troublemakers."

Harrah's was upscale enough so that we didn't get what you consider trash of any kind. They didn't come into Harrah's, mainly because they knew that . . . I don't care whether you're white, black, pink, green—you didn't get away with the stuff that you could get away with over in Bill Fong's. What type of place you run has a definite influence on what kind of customer you draw. So it didn't make any difference. We didn't draw lower-economic blacks, just like we didn't ever draw real low-economic whites or orientals or anything else. This was just the way the place was, so you didn't have that problem. I never perceived any problem.

I'll tell you a story: Nap had been working there for maybe a year, and he had been promoted. (Napoleon Jones, I believe, was his name.) We had promoted him, and he was doing a real good job. Then I get this call from the personnel manager: "Get over to my office immediately."

So I walk over there, and I said, "What's wrong?"

He says, "You got to fire Napoleon Jones." I said, "What?!"

"Well, you have to fire him."

I said, "Before I fire the man, you better give me a reason." [laughter]

"Well, he insulted a white change girl. He made a run on her at the bar and insulted her. You got to get rid of him."

I said, "No, I don't. I'm not going to. I'm going to go back and sit down and talk to everybody before I make the decision to just up and fire him. Whether it is Nap or anybody else, you people aren't going to tell me who I'm going to hire and who I'm going to fire." I used to war with them all the time, and I said, "Let me talk to Nap."

"Well, all right, but you're going to have to fire him, because we got this complaint from this white gal that he very crudely put the moves on and insulted her."

I said, "Well, that don't sound like Napoleon to me, but I'll go back." So I called Nap in and asked him about it.

He said, "*Jim,* you mean that girl complained about me?"

I said, "Yes, Nap."

He said, "I'll tell you what happened." He says, "I'm there with . . . ," and he named off a bunch of key men and somebody else. "We're at the bar . . . ," which everybody used to do in those days, "drinking." [laughter] "She was sitting there. She made a run on me. I didn't want to have anything to do with her. I tried to ignore her, and she just kept coming on and on and on, and I finally told her, 'Please leave me alone. I'm not interested. I don't want to have any part of you. *Get* lost.'" He says, "I may have been in the final moments a little bit adamant and maybe even a little bit crude on how I told her to leave, but I did not start it. I didn't do

anything." And he said, "You go talk to so-and-so and so-and-so and so-and-so."

So I got all the key men, everybody involved, and they all told the same story. Nap did not start it, and whatever she got from him (which they said wasn't as bad as she made it out to be), he just told her he didn't want anything to do with her and basically didn't like sluts. [laughter]

So I went back to personnel, and I said, "Now, you guys are the ones that for about a year or the last six months have been promoting all this damn racial . . . ," and I was pissed. I even went to the club manager. I said, "I don't understand this. You're in here promoting all this great race relations and how we're supposed to handle these people and how we can't be biased, and the first incident that comes up, I have personnel and all those people yelling at me to fire a good employee." I said, "We can't have it both ways, guys, and I'm pissed."

We could have lost a damn fine employee over it. Al Fontana said, "Well, that's not right, Jim."

I said, "I know it's not. What really ticks me off is we've been going to meetings, we've been told how bad we are and how we have got to alter our ways, and here's one of our teachers demanding that we fire one based on a rumor." I said, "It doesn't make any sense. So we are either going to have it one way or another." It was a transitional phase. If you want an honest opinion, though, I am not so sure that in some cases that that prejudice didn't continue for a long, long time.

Were you a shift manager when Harrah's was sold to Holiday Inns?

Yes, I was.

Did that affect your job in any way?

Not in the beginning. Not as long as Rome was alive. [laughter]

So when Rome left is when things really changed?

When Rome died. Rome was the buffer between Holiday Inns management and the gaming. While Rome was there, for some reason, they didn't want to make any great decisions. When Rome died, things changed, because now they didn't have to go through Rome. So a lot of jobs, a lot of procedures, a lot of things that we did that they didn't understand or didn't want to understand–and maybe they were right or wrong–immediately started changing.

So they had tremendous respect for Rome?

Yes! Yes, they did. And then about that time Dick Goeglein left, and Dick had gotten to be a fairly good supporter of gaming.

Who replaced Dick Goeglein?

Phil Satre, one of Mead Dixon's cohorts.

So your job wasn't affected until Rome died in 1984?

1984, right. After 1984 it started changing.

Did you notice any difference in the quality of the cleanliness of the club or the quality of the service that was given?

No. Up until 1986, when I left, that was still paramount. It was more how the internal organization worked and what was expected and what wasn't expected, and it was a change. It was a very definite change. The shift manager job became suspect because the Holiday Inn people could *not* understand this job. They didn't want to understand it. They *couldn't* understand it because they couldn't define it on paper. You couldn't just sit down and write this, this, this, and this; so therefore, it became a job of, "We don't know why we have it, so as soon as we can get rid of it, we will get rid of it."

At that time they were going through this big phase that authority and responsibility should be bucked to the lowest level. "And so we don't need this guy [the shift manager] in here. The shift supervisor in the slots can handle *all* the slot problems, and the shift supervisor in the pit can handle the pit problems and maintenance." Well, I never agreed with that. I guess they can, but what happens if you get them warring together? You need somebody right then and there to solve the problem or a customer complaint.

It was just a difference in philosophy. They could not understand–and we were very well paid at the time–how you can pay a man this much. He didn't do any appraisals, he didn't do any budgets; he didn't do any of these things. All he did was just walk around the floor all night long doing nothing.

They would not ever really come down and get involved with it. Joe Francis was in a meeting one time in Greentree, Mississippi. They were going through some training classes with a whole bunch of Holiday Inns people–I think it was their Search for Excellence program that they were putting on. He was in with these guys, and they were all doing this role-playing, and Joe got up. He says, "You know, guys," he says, "I've got five or six shift managers that make more decisions in one night than you people do in a whole *year* of working." [laughter]

He must have gone over good.

Oh, yes, he did. [laughter] I liked Joe. He was one of the good guys. But you couldn't explain the job to the Holiday Inns people.

Basically, the one rule is common sense and good judgment.

That's all. And make a decision. The worst thing you could do if you were a shift manager was not make a decision. If you made a wrong one, you might hear about it, but you wouldn't get chastised. At least you made a decision.

When I worked in Reno the thing was, "Well, now that you've thought about it, would you do the same thing again?"

If you said, "No," they would say, "Why did you make it?"

You'd say, "Well, I made it for this reason."

"Well, that's fine. But perhaps in the future if you have this, maybe you would consider something else."

The worst thing you could do is not make a decision and buck it up to somebody in the morning, because that got you in trouble as a shift manager, and you didn't get raises. They may not get rid of you, but you became rather suspect of being a good shift manager.

They wanted people who were fairly strong-willed, weren't afraid to make a decision no matter who it affected, and then could answer the next morning in a fair and consistent way. He [the shift manager] had the mantle at the time, which kind of ticked some department managers off. During the later years they'd be in there complaining, "Shift managers made this decision, and it doesn't apply."

The problem was we had a pretty strong core group, and we had some young department managers. What they didn't know is we probably knew almost as much about their department as they knew. In fact, we knew more, because we were there during the shift when it was happening. Towards the end, you didn't see a department manager past five o'clock at night. They had gotten into this eight-to-five routine, and you just didn't see them. But they would complain if you mishandled something. In the old days we didn't complain about the shift manager; we went back and tried to talk to him and find out why he did it and what he wanted done.

What year did you retire from Harrah's?

Retire? They eliminated the position of the shift manager! [laughter]

Oh, you were terminated?

Yes. Well, they didn't call it that, and I think they were ridiculous. In July they eliminated the shift manager position. They called a big meeting and said, "Geez, gentlemen, we're going to tell you something. We have eliminated the position of shift manager. However, we have these other jobs that you can re-apply and interview for," which is like telling you you are history.

Who were the seven shift managers? Do you remember?

Myself, Jack Julius, Steve Shaw, and four others. I'd have to stop and think about it; the names just don't come.

So they all left Harrah's organization?

All except one, and he was one of the newest ones. And I can't remember his name. He had come out of the pit. He went back as a pit shift supervisor.

There were seven of us. I was working day shift, and the bunch of them that worked the other shifts came in because they had gotten a call that there would be a meeting with all the shift managers at 9:00 a.m. They had been called. This wasn't pre-set; they had been called. So they walked into the shift manager's office: "What's this about?"

And I looked at them, and I says, "I'll lay you odds. You guys want to make a bet? Today's our last day."

"Oh, no. No, no."

If you'd been there long enough, you knew people, and you knew. So I said, "No, I think they're going to fire us."

And they said, "Oh, no. Oh, no, they wouldn't do that. We're going to get a *raise*."

"No, no. Tell you what, guys. Each one of you lay a hundred-dollar bill on the table. I'll cover it." [laughter] Well, they wouldn't take the bet. We walked in, and that's what they did–they fired us. It was just shortly after

Wayne Jeffries had taken over as the general manager. He was the vice-president of hotel operations for California and Hawaii, and they moved him in here.

Did you work in any other gambling after that?

I went to work for Harolds Club for nine months. The last dying gasp of Summa [Corporation]. That was a real trip. Then I went to work as general manager of Hobey's Casino-Restaurant in Sun Valley, and I worked there for eight years.

Were there table games there?

No, it was all slots. The area just wouldn't support table games. Very nice little operation.

❖

In the old days the slot machines were quite vulnerable. You could do things like ratchet the machine. Ratcheting relates to the method in which you pulled the handle. If there were parts worn, you could "walk" the reels, which means you could rotate the reels around to bring up the symbols you wanted.

Another cheating operation you had to be aware of was double coining. If a machine was not adjusted properly, you could jam two coins in the escalator. This would allow you to play without putting a coin in the machine, which was known as "free-playing" the machine. They could play it forever, so you had to watch for that.

Then in the old days you had what were called rhythm players. A rhythm player could influence the clock by how slow or how fast he played the machine. What he would do is he would get the clock spinning so it would come up with a certain revolution. If he pulled the handle right—and it took a *lot* of skill to do it— he could influence it so that the number one reel would only make one complete turn, and he would get exactly the same symbol on the next play. Some of them would go in there and do it just for cherries. If they were trying to

get a bar, they'd want to hold the bar on the last reel. That *really* changes things. If you can keep the bar on the last reel, that really affects the percentage.

For a person to be a good rhythm player and affect that clock, did there have to be a defective part in the machine?

No. It just depended upon the clock or if the machine had what they called anti-rhythm devices. One was a rod that stopped the clock every time the machine was played. Another was an elliptical base on the timing bar for each reel stop, so when you had that elliptical base changing, you had the length of the reel spin changing also. You tried doing it with different types of gearing in the clock so that the clock itself had a variation in how fast it spun. The art of rhythm playing kind of died out, because it took a lot of practice to be a good rhythm player. You had to have a lot of patience, and you had to really know how to do it.

Then we had a rash of people coming in one time that were breaking ratchet dogs. They'd slam the handle down and then come *right* back up on it real quick. And if you were real quick and fast, you could snap that dog off, and then you could ratchet the machine. I had to go to court over that, and I had to put on a demonstration.

On how it could be done?

Yes. And I did it the first whack. [laughter]

But there was all that and the rhythm playing and double coining. Then when the first battery-powered electric drills came in . . . oh, the slot cheats loved them, because they could hide the drill in their pocket, then come around to your case front and drill little holes in your case front so they could insert wires and manipulate the reels. When you checked any large jackpot, you had to make sure that there wasn't any holes in the front of the case. Then what they started doing was after they drilled the hole, they'd take a regular silver Crayola and dub it over.

How about stringing a machine?

Stringing came in with the electro-mechanicals. Stringing was when you put a fine string on a coin, normally a quarter, then dropped it down the head. They would feel the switch click, then they'd just pull it up and drop it again, pull it up and drop it again, pull it up and drop it again. So they're using the same quarter over and over. Then the clubs came up with string cutters, which sometimes worked and sometimes didn't. In those days the coin acceptor was an all-mechanical device. Nowadays LEDs read the coin as it's falling, and if it doesn't see it in the right sequence, it stops. There's a lot of electronic methods of prevention now, but in the old days there were just mechanical coin acceptors. The coin went in the acceptor and closed a switch. You could put a coin on a string, hit that one switch, and then pull it back up.

Slot cheating used to be a misdemeanor, not a felony. In fact, card cheating wasn't a felony. It was also a misdemeanor in the 1950s and the early 1960s, which meant if you got caught, it wasn't a serious offense. That's why some clubs were a little rough when they caught cheaters. There were some places that if you got caught cheating, you'd be lucky after they got done with your hands if you'd be able to hold a broom. Especially card cheats. They would break the fingers of card cheaters.

Gaming has come a long ways.

Oh, yes. But they felt that that was their protection against whatever it was, because to arrest them didn't do any good. So some places around the state would get rough reputations. "Don't be caught cheating in that place." Harolds Club was one.

They banged people around?

Yes. They had some tough security guards there. They had that one Indian–he would handcuff them and throw them over the coat rail in the security room and then put them out the door head first without opening the door. Harrah's had a couple of them that were that way, too, but all that has changed now.

3

DOLORES CODEGA

*D*OLORES CODEGA *was born in Chattanooga, Tennessee, on January 14, 1924. She became the first female pit supervisor ever to be employed by Harrah's in its Lake Tahoe casino.*

This interview of Dolores Codega was conducted in the home of Dwayne Kling, the interviewer, in June of 1997. Mrs. Codega was at first hesitant to become involved in the project, but later seemed to enjoy participating. The interview was completed in one session of two hours.

In this oral history, Mrs. Codega relates how she came to Reno during World War II and describes her first job in Lincoln Fitzgerald's Nevada Club. She started in the Nevada Club as a change person, but Mr. Fitzgerald seemed to take a personal interest in her and taught her how to deal craps, roulette, and twenty-one. Of note is her account of dealing to LaVere Redfield, who is acknowledged to have been Reno's premier roulette player in the 1950s. Mrs. Codega was a dealer in the Nevada Club from 1945 to 1958 before leaving Reno with her husband, Leonard, to work at Harrah's casino at Lake Tahoe.

Mrs. Codega recalls her early days of dealing at Lake Tahoe and her experiences conducting a school for dealers. Later she became one of the instructors in a school that taught customers how to play the pit games. When she was offered the position of pit supervisor, she was enthused at first, but after thinking it over she changed her mind and tried to

turn down the promotion. However, Harrah's management wouldn't let her, and she became a pit supervisor in 1962. Because she was a woman she encountered prejudice and animosity from some employees when she became a supervisor, and she had encounters with management regarding equitable pay. However, she never had any problems with Harrah's customers. In 1999 it has been only a few years since female pit supervisors were a rarity. Dolores Codega was truly a pioneer.

DOLORES CODEGA: I was born on January 14, 1924, in Chattanooga, Tennessee. My mother died when I was born, and my father, I never remembered him. He was gone when I was about two. I was raised in Louisiana by my grandmother. I had one brother, and he was killed in World War II.

DWAYNE KLING: How did you happen to come to Reno?

During World War II I came out here, and for a while I couldn't get a job. I lived on my savings until I finally got a job at the Nevada Club owned by Mr. [Lincoln] Fitzgerald. That was my first casino job.

Were you hired as a dealer, or did you start out in another job?

Mr. Fitzgerald let me carry change while he taught me to deal, and so it worked out real nice that way. In those days, if they wanted you to learn to deal, they grabbed you and said, "Here we go," and they taught you how to deal. [laughter] I would carry change for eight hours, and then when I got off from that, I would practice dealing. I learned all three games—roulette, craps, and twenty-one—at the same time, so when I started dealing, I could deal all of the games.

Mr. Fitzgerald took a personal interest in me, and he stood there and showed me how to deal. I learned roulette first; he thought that was the hardest, but for me that was the easiest. Craps was the hardest for me, because, like I told him once, he thought I was smarter than I was, and he just put me behind the table and said, "Go to it." [laughter] But roulette was my main game, and I loved it. When I started dealing, top pay was fifteen dollars a shift, and it took me seven months to get to top pay.

That sounds like you moved along pretty fast.

Yes, I did. But like I said, I had him teaching me, and he not only taught me the games, but he taught me lots of other things–how to watch a game, how to protect the game and to see if somebody was "doing something" to you. He'd come right out there and do it. As soon as you turned your head, you better believe he was going to walk in there and do something to you. That was his method of teaching you to be alert. So you really learned to watch your game! I'd look at him and say, "I don't like to play with you. You cheat." [laughter]

But he wasn't really playing with his own money, right?

Oh, no. He was just teaching you how to deal.

Did the dealers make any tips (or tokes) in those days?

Very few; nothing like they make today. And the way Fitz worked it was, he took all the tokes from all the games into the office, and then he divided them up between all the dealers on a twenty-four hour basis. You never made much–you were lucky if you got two dollars! [laughter]

Two dollars was an average day in tips?

Right.

I have heard stories that he used to keep some of the tips himself. Do you believe that story?

No, I don't. I know better than that. Mr. Fitzgerald was a nice man. If he liked you, there was nothing he wouldn't do for you. If he didn't like you, though–I mean, if you were just somebody that came to work, went home–then he had very little to do with you. He liked someone that put forth an extra effort or tried to do something extra.

You started working for Fitzgerald in the Nevada Club in the war years, around 1944. How long did you stay with him?

I left to go to work at Harrah's Lake Tahoe when they opened the Stateline Club in 1958. I was married then to Len Codega. Len had been working at Harrah's Reno, so he transferred to Lake Tahoe, and I came from the Nevada Club.

Had you ever met Bill Harrah or seen him before you went to work for him?

Oh, yes. I had spoken to him. Everybody ate at a little restaurant around the corner, the Grand Cafe, owned by John Petrinovich. Bill Harrah was friends with all the dealers, and he would come over there, and he always spoke to me. And when I went to work at the lake he walked down the hall one day, and he says, "Well, it's good to see you're with us!" [laughter]

When you first went to Harrah's at Lake Tahoe, did you start as a dealer?

Yes.

There weren't too many women/girl crap dealers at that time, were there?

No, there weren't. I am not really sure of this, Dwayne, but I think Fitzgerald was the one who started women dealing craps. And women were good at it. I remember one night Len and I were both dealing at Harrah's, and we came in to work at midnight, and it was busy. Somebody put us on the same crap game, and I backed off. I said, "No, they won't let us do this."

The pit boss said, "You're going to do it tonight. We want you and Len to deal here for an hour."

"OK!" [laughter] So Len and I looked at each other, grinned real big, and said [whispers], "Quiet." We had the quietest game you ever heard in your life. There were silver dollars all over, but you didn't hear any noise when we were dealing. We found out later that there were quite a few people up on the catwalk watching us.

Did they schedule you like that on purpose?

Yes, they did it. Somebody decided they wanted to see us deal together, and it thrilled us both because we knew we dealt a good game. We were real pleased.

I should comment that dealing a quiet game is a compliment.

Yes, because usually you hear the clang, clang, clang of silver.

Do you remember when and by whom you were approached to become a pit supervisor at Harrah's Club?

Actually, I was approached by Rome Andreotti in 1962. I had known Rome for a long time, and I was not afraid of Rome like everybody seemed to be. I remembered when Rome Andreotti was dealing the wheel at Harrah's, and I was still at the Nevada Club.

So you used to go over and watch Rome deal roulette and visit with him?

Oh, yes. He was a great dealer; he just fascinated me.

So you learned by watching. He wasn't teaching you; you were just observing him dealing?

Yes. That's something that dealers used to do in the early days. They would find somebody that was a good dealer and watch them deal. That's the way I learned twenty-one. So when he approached me about being a supervisor, I said yes. And then about a week later he came up, and I said, "I've changed my mind." [laughter]

So you initially thought it was a good idea?

Yes, but I knew the hardship I was in for, too.

Was your husband, Len, already on the floor?

Oh, yes. Len was on the floor, my daughter was dealing up there, and one of my sons was a radio announcer on radio station KOWL at Lake Tahoe. He was a disk jockey there, and my youngest son was carrying change, so my whole family was there.

As I recall, you and another lady by the name of Dorothy Blevins went on the floor at the same time.

Yes, on the same day. The only thing is, I went to work on the day shift, and she went on that night on swing shift.

So you were the first female/lady pit supervisors at Harrah's Lake Tahoe?

Yes, but there was a lady in Reno, and I don't know when she went on the floor, but it's my understanding that she went on before us. Her name was Bessie Peterson.

So you think Bessie Peterson went on the floor before you?

Yes, I do, that's what I heard.

But your niche in history is guaranteed because you were the first female supervisor or lady pit boss at Harrah's Lake Tahoe.

Yes. Well, I went on eight or ten hours before Dorothy did.

You went on at eight in the morning, and she probably went on at six in the evening.

Yes. They couldn't have us working together. That always burned me, because men worked together; why couldn't we?

Well, times have changed, it just takes awhile. Now you walk in some pits, and all you see is ladies.

Yes. And at that time we couldn't work the same pit or the same hours, because it was only she and I, you know.

Did it remain that way for quite a while, that just the two of you were bosses?

Oh, a long time; I dare say four years at least.

Well, you said when Rome first offered it to you, you thought, "Gee, that's a good idea;" and then when you thought about it a little bit, you told him no. What changed your mind?

The main reason was because I knew there would be a lot of talk. I knew that we were in for a bad time—the men weren't going to let it rest. And I thought, "I don't need that." When I told Rome I had changed my mind, he says, "No, you haven't." [laughter] He says, "You'll make it."

Do you think that there was ever anybody else approached at Lake Tahoe besides you and Dorothy?

No, I don't. I think at that time Dorothy and I were just about the only ones that knew three games and really knew what we were doing, because you'll have to admit that most of the men did not know three games.

Right. Even today there are very few men capable of dealing three games.

That's something I never could understand: if they were going to put them on the floor to watch the games, why did they have to come to me and ask me about a payoff on a wheel?

When you went on the floor, were you required to wear special uniforms or special outfits?

Yes! Suits! I still have a number of knit suits hanging in my closet. [laughter]

Did Harrah's buy them for you?

Oh, no! I bought them. Then they came and told us we could wear pantsuits. I had three or four pantsuits that I wore at home, so the next day I merrily put on my pantsuit and said, "Thank you, Lord!" because I knew it was going to be more comfortable. And, too, I could wear low heels. Up to that point I had been wearing spikes, because I'm short, and to see over a dealer I needed those heels. So anyway, I got told off the next morning.

Somebody didn't like your pantsuit?

The manager of the club–I can't remember who it was–came down, and he told me to go home and change. And so then I explained to him that the lady that was taking care of uniforms said it was OK to wear a pantsuit.

The club manager had told you to go home, and you said that the clothing lady said it was OK to wear pantsuits. So who won the argument?

I did. [laughter] I told him, "Call her and ask her and see that I'm not going against the rules." So then we got to wear pants, and we wore just a nice business suit to work.

Do you have any recollection of what you were paid starting out as a pit supervisor?

Dwayne, I believe it was thirty-five dollars a day.

That was about average pay for a floor person at that time?

Yes, at that time.

Do you think you got less than the starting men?

No. I checked into that. [laughter] But the only thing is that I had a harder time getting a raise. It was *very* difficult, very difficult.

So there was a little bit of prejudice raising its head because you were evaluated by a male?

Yes, right. There was a *lot* of trouble getting raises. And then they would come to you and say, "Well, you're making thirty-six dollars now."

"Is that right? You're sure you can spare it?"

"Well, we wish it could be more." But a man, he got a two-dollar raise, and he didn't know three games. It made me mad.

And if you got in any trouble, you got a pay cut. Poor Dorothy Blevins was always having hers cut! [laughter] Dorothy would get in trouble, and they'd cut her pay. I never had mine cut, because I think I would have raised holy hell if I would have. I just couldn't get a raise.

Did you notice any animosity from the dealers when you first became supervisor?

Yes, from some of the females, but I was ready for that. But I can't remember having any trouble with the male dealers, because a lot of those guys I taught how to deal.

Did the male pit bosses help you as far as explaining policy or procedure or help you read the table?

No, most of them didn't know themselves. And that's the truth. I'm not being nasty or anything, it's just like I told you–I can't even begin to pick out the ones that knew three games. Many female dealers used to be resentful, because they were dealing a game, and a male pit boss is telling them what to do, and he couldn't deal it himself.

I recall in that time frame at Harrah's that few of the men knew how to deal twenty-one or roulette.

Right.

So you'd have a man that had been dealing craps for a year or two supervising lady twenty-one dealers that had been dealing twenty-one for many years?

Yes, right.

How about the customers? Was there any problem with the customers?

I never had any trouble with customers. I could sweet-talk them and buy them a drink or cup of coffee or send them to dinner and take the time to explain why something had happened, and it usually worked out beautifully.

If a man would go up to an irate man customer, the customer would maybe flare up, but in most cases it'd be pretty hard to flare up at a lady supervisor. So that worked to my advantage.

So an enjoyable part of your job was the customer relations and the friends that you made?

Yes.

Were there a lot of good memories like that of customers and people that you worked with?

Yes, there still is. We go someplace to eat, and somebody'll say, "Hi, Mrs. Codega!" or "Hi, Dolores!" And I turn around, and I can't remember who they are. But I just assume that they're former customers, and I start talking to them, and even today it makes you feel good.

Harrah's Tahoe experienced phenomenal growth during the fifties, sixties, and seventies. What, in your opinion, were the reasons for that growth?

I think the people working there helped Harrah's make it grow. I really do–the average employee, the dealer, and the pit boss that made the customer happy.

Did you see Bill Harrah very much in those days?

I saw him in the Reno club a lot. I didn't see him as often in the Tahoe club, but his father was there a lot, along with his wife, Florence.

And they observed things and watched things?

Yes. Especially old Mr. Harrah. He was Johnny-on-the-spot, and if you did something wrong, he saw it, and you heard about it, too! [laughter]

In the late fifties or early sixties Harrah's started a school for customers. Could you give me some recollections on that?

Well, Harrah's would choose so many dealers and set up tables with old roulette chips, where they wouldn't get mixed in with the real chips on the tables. Each customer would get so many chips, and we would teach them where to bet, what to bet, and what they were betting on.

So you were basically teaching them how to play the games and how to spend their money?

Right. It was a lot of fun, and the customers enjoyed it. Almost all those customers would play later with their own money. I always liked to tease people, and I got called down about that a couple of times, because I teased too much. Harrah's didn't like me to tease them. I'd say, "Come on now and bet. That's our money, not yours." And they'd laugh like hell and put out more money on . . . you know. To me this was good relationships with the customers, because they'd laugh then and just have a good old time, and that's what you wanted.

Did they have a certain time of day that they had the school?

Yes. If I remember correctly, it was eleven o'clock in the morning and around three or four in the afternoon, and each session lasted about a half hour. We furnished them with the basics of the games. A lot of people didn't know how to bet on the big six and eight; or they didn't know about come bets, so we would explain it to them and take their money and put it on there and then tell them that's the odds they could take, et cetera. That way they weren't intimidated by the game, and they wouldn't come over and put one little dollar on the line and stand there for hours!

Was there a charge for these schools?

Oh, no.

Do you feel that frequently the customer did come back and play with real money?

Yes, I do. Not much at first, because people are that way, but then they'd come back with a couple of bucks or so and put it on the line. Then they thought, oh, they knew what come bets were, so they put one out there, and pretty soon you had a customer. Then they'd say, "Oh, hi, Dolores. Did you tell me to do this?"

It was probably a great motivator to get people to play, and it was probably a real money-maker for Harrah's.

That's right, it really was, because I think they continued it for many years.

Was there anything that set the average Harrah's employee above or apart from other casino workers?

I would say no. In Reno, when I first was there, we were all good friends. Wherever you worked, if you had on a white blouse and a black skirt, you didn't walk down the street without waving to some of them. As you well know, the doors were not shut except in the wintertime, and you would see those people,

and you'd wave to them and become almost friends with them.

Well, you, of course, taught the customer school, but I also know that you taught dealer schools for quite a while. Would you give us a few of your memories of those schools?

Yes, I will, because that was some of my fun times. I really enjoyed that. I taught roulette, I taught twenty-one, and I helped two of the boys teach craps. That was the one time I had the authority over all of them! I mean I was the big man on the totem pole. [laughter]

You were the head instructor?

Yes, I was the head instructor and that was really great. Sometimes I had as high as fifty in a class. But it was easy for me.

And that class included all the games?

No, fifty just in the twenty-one class. I've had as many as twenty-five in the roulette class, and it's difficult to have that many, because you have to teach them not only to use their brains but also to use their hands. Craps school is not really that bad. In craps school you start out with one thing–like, first you start with the line and the proposition bets. After you teach those, then you move to another two–maybe the come bets, the big six and eight, and things like this. It's easy to teach this way, but I never could make any of the men see this. They wanted to teach everything all at once and have bets all over the place. I think you just confuse the issue when you do that. I know my brain wouldn't accept it.

How did those employees get selected to go to dealers' school?

They applied for it, and then the pit manager's office made the final selection.

Didn't you do that when you were pit manager, Dwayne?

Yes, and we based it on their work record as far as not missing any shifts and getting to work on time and customer complaints or customer compliments.

One of the big problems at the lake was the difference between summer and winter business. All of a sudden you needed as many as 100, 150 dealers, and I have often wondered exactly how much money Harrah's lost by using all those student dealers who really didn't know how to deal. They didn't have the experience, and the pit bosses didn't know what they were doing either.

After your student dealers went on the floor and were actually dealing live games, did you have to watch your students?

Yes. I would go up in the catwalk and watch them from there, because I felt that I was making them too nervous when I was standing next to them.

Were there many people that didn't pass?

There were a few I flunked out, but not many.

Did you give extra time to people that were slow learners?

Yes, I did. I gave them extra time, but some of them just didn't work out. Some of them just were not cut out to be dealers. They either didn't have it in their heart or in their head. Some of them I don't think ever went to public school, because of their arithmetic. Some of them you could ask, "What's two and two?" and they couldn't answer you.

Roulette's one of the hardest games to learn, because you have to know so many payoffs. I tried to teach in a way that was very simple, so if you knew your multiplication tables, you could deal the wheel.

Did a lot of the dealers memorize the payoffs?

Yes, they memorized the payoffs, but when you get up above that memory work, you have to be able to multiply it out. I tried to teach them the easy way, but a lot of the older dealers wouldn't listen to me.

Even then the wheel wasn't as popular as twenty-one, was it?

No, but if you had a good game on the wheel, you had a lot of money at stake.

Did Harrah's have some high-limit roulette players?

Yes. They had some *very* big players. Jack Androvich used to come up at least every two weeks. He would *really* put it to you! And I'll tell you another thing—he knew the payoffs. You make a mistake on a little bet, and he was *right on* your shoulder. [laughter]

Androvich was such a good player, they used to let him spin the ball.

Yes, yes. I didn't like that.

They would let him spread hundreds of dollars out on the layout, and then let him go behind the table and spin the ball. I never knew of anyone ever doing that.

Fitzgerald did it once or twice, and that was when we had LaVere Redfield, the millionaire, playing on the game.

So Fitzgerald let Redfield spin the ball once in a while?

Yes. Redfield really didn't like to do it, though. He didn't know how to do it right, but he'd do it once in a while. One time he wanted to do it when I beat him out of seventeen thousand dollars on one spin. I only had two numbers I could spin him out on, completely out, and I got one of those numbers. [laughter] Then he didn't ever want me to spin the ball again! Redfield loved roulette–he bet the outside and the inside; he bet everything. That's the reason that I only had two numbers that I could roll him out of everything. The numbers were three and ten, and I rolled ten. Then I had to count the money as I brought it in, because Fitzgerald let him play on credit most of the time, and you had to keep up with every bit of money that he put on that table.

So he would just spread the chips around, and you had to add up at the end of the roll how much he had bet?

Right. Fitzgerald would lift the limit on everything, and it was hard to keep up with what he was going to lift the limit on. Fitzgerald had been shot,[1] and he had to sit most of the time. He usually sat by a window in the rear of the building, and the wheel that Redfield played on could be seen from that window. Fitz would hold up his fingers, and that would tell me how much Redfield could bet. If he was losing real big he would want to raise his limits, and that's the way it was done. Fitzgerald had made a little system with me, and if I wasn't dealing the wheel, I was watching it. If he wanted to raise Redfield's limit, he would just give me a hand signal. So I knew all the time what was going on.

Do you think Redfield was the biggest roulette player that ever played in Reno?

He was the biggest that I've ever known. Nobody could keep up with him. Every club in Reno wanted to get Redfield away from Fitzgerald, so they would offer the moon, but they couldn't produce. [laughter]

To get back to Harrah's Club, how many years did you teach the dealer school?

For several years. I can't remember exactly how long.

Did the dealers you taught stay at Harrah's for a long time?

Yes. Some of them, as far as I know, are still there. I haven't been back to Harrah's since I left in the middle or the late seventies.

Did you go to work at another casino after you left Harrah's?

No. I had a ceramic shop, and I started working there and teaching art and ceramics up until about five or six years ago, and then I had to give that up because of my health.

So you worked in the gaming industry from the middle or early forties until the late seventies, well over thirty years?

Yes.

Were most of the years pretty enjoyable?

Yes, they were. I love people. The people were all very interesting to me, and I'm just sorry I can't do it now! [laughter] There comes a time when you get too old to really do things like that.

If you had the chance, would you do it all over again?

Yes, I think I would. Some of it wasn't so happy, but others was really great.

Note

1. Lincoln Fitzgerald was a co-owner of the Nevada Club when he was shot by an unknown assailant on November 18, 1949, shortly before midnight, as he was leaving his home to go to work at the club. The shotgun blast caused damage to his spinal cord and other internal injury, requiring surgery and several months of hospitalization. After he was shot, Fitzgerald was rarely again seen

in public. He lived in a guarded apartment in the Nevada Club, and people who saw him were carefully screened. The cause of the shooting was never learned, and no arrests were ever made. There was suspicion that Fitzgerald possibly was shot by former members of Detroit's "Purple Gang"—that Michigan's two most-wanted fugitives may have sought money from Fitzgerald, who had been a prominent Detroit gambler before coming to Nevada.

4

MARK CURTIS

*T*HIS ORAL HISTORY *interview was conducted in the home of Mark Curtis in March of 1997. Two sessions were needed to complete the interview. Mr. Curtis initially declined to be interviewed, but eventually he accepted and was cooperative and enlightening.*

Mr. Curtis was born in Oklahoma City, Oklahoma, on September 19, 1921. He came to Reno after World War II and enrolled in the University of Nevada, from which he graduated with a degree in journalism in 1951.

Curtis was hired by Harrah's in 1956 and was soon put in charge of publicity and advertising. In this oral history he tells of the early days of Harrah's Lake Tahoe casino, the bus program, the opening of the South Shore Room, the preparations preliminary to the Winter Olympics of 1960 held at Squaw Valley, and the immense worldwide publicity that the Olympics generated for California, Reno, Lake Tahoe, and, in particular, Harrah's.

Curtis describes the problems of advertising casino gambling when such advertising was tightly controlled by federal regulations. He was the originator of a well-known advertising campaign that used the phrase, "I hit the jackpot at Harrah's." This allowed the name of Harrah's to be prominently displayed on billboards and all types of advertising without using the word "gambling."

Curtis eventually became vice-president of public relations for Harrah's, and he relates many of his personal experiences with Bill Harrah. He also discusses in depth the management team of Harrah's, which included Bob Ring, Lloyd Dyer, Maurice Sheppard, Rome Andreotti, Holmes

Hendricksen, Joe Fanelli, and George Drews. Of special interest are recollections of the public relation effort put forth by Harrah's when Bill Harrah was attempting to win the favor of the financial and banking centers that would be needed to make Harrah's a public company.

Additional topics of interest include the World Classic Car Festival held in Japan in 1971 and the worldwide advertising campaign that was initiated to promote the back-to-back appearances of Frank Sinatra and John Denver at Harrah's Lake Tahoe.

This oral history provides an inside look at the advertising and publicity that helped make Harrah's the "Cadillac of the gaming industry." Mark Curtis passed away on June 24, 1998. He was seventy-six.

MARK CURTIS: I was born in Oklahoma City, September 19, 1921. My father was a private oil man who drilled his own wells, which accounted for the area we were living in—Texas and Oklahoma. He was an oil man all his life. As a younger child, I moved around in Oklahoma and Texas. Then, during the Depression, my mother and I came to Phoenix, Arizona, to be with the rest of her family because of difficult times, perhaps. I had no brothers or sisters, so it was just my mom and I.

When I graduated from Phoenix Union High School in Phoenix, Arizona, I went to junior college in Phoenix for a year. Then there was a threat of war, and they were drafting, but a friend of mine and myself figured there wouldn't be a war, so we decided we would get in the aircraft industry. We went to Long Beach, California, and on Sunday, December 7, 1941, Japan attacked Pearl Harbor. I went to work for Douglas Aircraft the next day. I worked there for a couple of months before I was drafted into the air force. I was discharged from the air force in 1945 in Washington, D.C.

When I came back from the service, my fiancée was working for the congressman from Nevada, Berkeley Bunker. We decided to live in Washington since she had a good job there, and I would look for work. But we got married here in Reno. We then went back to Washington, and I worked for Eastern Airlines, one of the first GIs that Captain Eddie Rickenbacker hired. I worked at the National Airport, or whatever it was called in those days, taking reservations and so forth.

When my first wife became pregnant, we moved to Phoenix, and I worked in radio. After we'd had our first child, Mark, I decided I wanted to go back to school. I'd heard a lot about the University of Nevada journalism school when I was in Washington, so I decided I'd come out here and go to journalism school. I started at the University of Nevada in 1949, and I graduated in 1951.

DWAYNE KLING: When you got out of the University of Nevada, was your first job at Harrah's Club?

No. At that time I didn't have any interest in or know anything about Harrah's. I was working in a travel bureau at the Mapes on weekends, and I was working for United Airlines at the airport. United and Eastern were very close, business-wise. I sort of segued from those jobs during school, and then I started a little so-called advertising agency with another guy named Ray Ward. Later, I started doing radio—a radio show on KOLO and KWRN, two different stations. I did that quite a while and stayed pretty much in advertising.

Then 1956 I wrote a letter to Bill Harrah and said, "With all the things that are going on at the time,"—he had just bought the place next door, the Frontier Club—"and the way you're expanding here and at the lake, you're going to need some good advertising and PR." Very audacious letter. [laughter] And I never heard a word. A few weeks later a couple of guys walked into my office and pretended to be representing some eastern outfit. They asked me a lot of questions, and a couple of days later I got a call from Harrah's to come over for a visit.

The people that came in, were they an outside efficiency group he hired?

Well, Bill Harrah had started hiring these consulting groups, Stanford Research and a couple of others. He and Bob Ring had stopped drinking, and so they were suddenly getting down to business. As I recall, they had me come over to see a guy named Joe Harbaugh. I'm really not quite sure, but I think they hired me in the publicity department.

Did they hire you as an individual or did they hire your firm?

They hired me. I learned pretty much what they were doing in a few months, and then Joe Harbaugh quit, so they gave me his job. Later, he returned and wanted his job back, but they didn't give it to him. They handed me the advertising department, also. That's when we first started engaging an advertising agency. We hired Walter States. He had a local agency. Then Harrah's went so-called "big-time" and hired an outfit called the Richard Meltzer Agency from San Francisco. Later I hired Tom Wilson and then went to Hofer, Dietrich, and Brown in San Francisco. I was trying to work up the advertising, trying to improve it.

When you worked with agencies like that, were you a middle man between Harrah's Club and the agencies?

Yes. I had a small department that did a lot of the work, but the agencies produced all the print and all the radio, and we just worked together.

What year did you start that program?

1957.

So the lake club had opened in 1955, Harrah's had bought the Frontier Club in 1956, and now they were getting ready to expand across the street at Lake Tahoe, is that right?

Yes. That's when I went to work for Harrah's. I was in their employment when they opened up Sahati's Country Club at Lake Tahoe.

The bus program is undoubtedly the major reason for Harrah's success at the lake in the late fifties. Was the bus program in effect when you went to work for them?

It was not in effect. And I know the big question is how the bus program came about. I think it was Bill's idea. I don't know how it came about, but it was one of those things that he would likely come up with–"Oh, why don't we try this, or why don't we try that?"– just out of the clear blue. And then we brought the agency from San Francisco, Meltzer, into it. They're the ones that got it on the road.

The real beginning of Harrah's success was the start of the buses from Sacramento and other northern California cities. I can remember we'd be at Lake Tahoe having a meeting in the Quonset hut on Friday night, and somebody would yell, "The buses are here!" We'd all run down and see how many people were on the buses! [laughter]

I often wonder if Harrah's would have made it if they hadn't had that bus program.

Well, everybody thought it was crazy to go up there in the first place. Nothing happened after Labor Day, so what are you going to do in the winter? You must know what they're thinking: "Well, let's try buses and make it easy for people to get here." And it worked from the very beginning. Just an amazing idea. Of course, the whole industry, in later years, took it up one way or the other. How many thousands of buses come to Reno every week even now? We were at one time the biggest user of Greyhound buses, second only to the U.S. Army.

When you were given Joe Harbaugh's job, were you in charge of advertising, publicity, and public relations?

Yes.

Were you overseeing all the advertising in both clubs, or were there advertising departments at the lake and Reno?

No, we were all together, as I thought we always should be. After I retired, maybe shortly before, Holiday separated them, and I thought that was a bad idea. I always thought it was more powerful to be able to say "Reno and Lake Tahoe." Harrah's was the only one that could ever say "Reno and Lake Tahoe," and I thought that was a very strong statement.

In the early days, the forties, fifties, and sixties, there were many federal restrictions as far as advertising casinos—what could be mentioned and what couldn't be mentioned. Could you tell us a little bit about that, Mark?

Well, there still are restrictions, and I think they're ridiculous. I was just noting the other day that any other business can use gambling as a metaphor. What I saw was TWA had a roulette wheel in its ad, and that's ridiculous. Gambling can't advertise its main

business, yet other businesses can use gaming equipment in their ads.

Due to those restrictions, we talked about jackpots on our billboards: "I hit the jackpot at Harrah's"–that advertising theme went on for many years. And postcards–"I hit the jackpot at Harrah's." And entertainment was a big deal. That was the number one way we kept our names out there.

Were those restrictions federal regulations or state regulations?

Federal regulations. You couldn't mention gambling at all. You couldn't mention roulette, slots or any gaming devices. You just had to keep your name out there. If it was

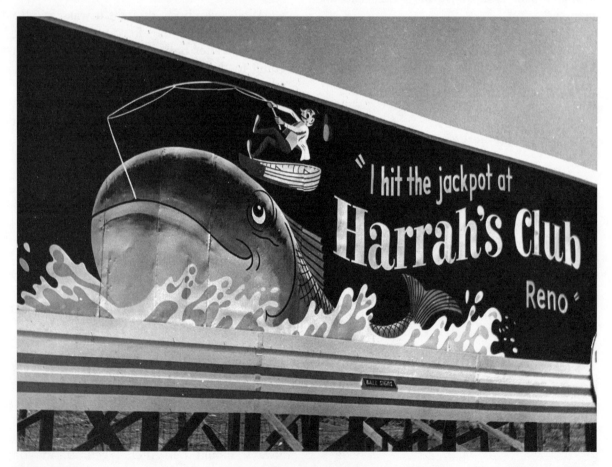

"Due to those [advertising] restrictions, we talked about jackpots on our billboards: 'I hit the jackpot at Harrah's.'"

outdoors, pertaining to entertainment, you made comments like "Nevada fun" or "Nevada excitement." There was no doubt in anybody's mind what you were talking about, but they didn't want you to say it.

Entertainment, of course, played a big role in Harrah's success. Was part of the reason for entertainment so that Harrah's could advertise their clubs more?

I'd say there were three reasons: The first one was to have a real draw—I mean to have an attraction that would bring people into the club. The second was to keep your name out there. The third was to be able to take care of good customers, to be able to comp them in the shows, and even in those days, to comp public officials, which was another way of taking care of them, which was illegal, of course. But it was very beneficial to be able to invite senators and so forth to your dinner shows and lounge shows.

Was there a separate advertising budget for entertainment?

There was just one advertising budget. We did segregate it, but it was just the general advertising budget that we worked with.

There was nothing that said, "Well, 80 percent's going to go to entertainment," or anything like that?

Oh, no.

So lots of work was done by these advertising agencies throughout the history of Harrah's Club?

Yes. Agencies were always very important.

To get back to entertainment: In December of 1959, Harrah's opened the South Shore Room at Lake Tahoe. Were you involved with that opening?

Yes. That was great. It was pretty well timed with the opening of the Olympics. The showroom opened December of 1959, and then the Winter Olympics opened in February of 1960 at Squaw Valley.

The opening of Harrah's South Shore Room on December 19, 1959, was a big occasion. The room was filled with all the top people in the area, politicians and so forth; and of course, the governor, Grant Sawyer, was there. The funny thing was that the entertainment director, Candy Hall, introducing at the stage, forgot the governor's name.

Each guest was given a silver cigarette box inscribed with the date of the opening and the name of the headliner, Red Skelton. Just prior to the opening, while the room was still torn up and nobody could quite believe it would ever be prepared in time, we were all taken in the room to have a test on which beef we thought was best, eastern or western. We were each served—there were ten of us—two pieces of beef, one marked with a blue cow and the other with a pink cow. And then we voted, and it was a tie. I forget which one we finally ended up with.

We considered the 1960 Winter Olympics a great opportunity to get Lake Tahoe's name out to the world and to get Harrah's name out at the same time. We lined up all those great stars, international stars like Dietrich, Skelton, Borge, to be there during the Olympics. The place was full every night. It was pretty much comped, because all those people in the Olympics were worn out and too tired to go to the show, but if it was comped they would find the energy to attend.

The South Shore Room served its purpose in getting the word out, but as far as being tied in during the Olympics, it didn't work very well. We had been working for a year before that to tie it in. We even brought in top sports writers from all over the country exactly one year in advance for a preview of the Olympic site. And we did a motion picture of the Olympic site that syndicated on television.

Mark Curtis and his wife, Ruth, at Squaw Valley, California. *"The Winter Olympics opened in February of 1960 at Squaw Valley . . . . We considered the Olympics a great opportunity to get Lake Tahoe's name out to the world and to get Harrah's name out at the same time."*

We did everything we could think of to tie in Harrah's and Lake Tahoe.

Ticketing was done by lottery, because that little valley couldn't handle everybody that wanted to get in there, so, a year or so in advance, people started writing in for tickets, and the ticket winners were chosen by lottery. We had every employee write in for tickets, and by the luck of the draw, we got four hundred tickets. We put those tickets in a customer's hand—four hundred tickets a day, every day of the Olympics. Some might have tickets for three or four days, and it was a logistics nightmare to make sure that customers got one of those tickets every day

and were transported to the games and could hang out in the hospitality house and see what the venues were. It was incredible!

How long did it take to get from Harrah's to Squaw Valley?

I'd say forty-five minutes to an hour.

Did Harrah's go out and rent a bunch of vans or buses to transport the customers to the Olympics?

Buses, cars, and some customers were able to take care of their own transportation. But we tied ourselves close to that. It was like we were running the games–we had an office there at Squaw Valley.

Did Harrah's furnish rooms? Did you have to assign motel rooms for all your better customers?

Oh, yes. We had to do all that.

Also, at that time there were no hotels on the south shore of Lake Tahoe, and all the motels were on the California side of the state line.

Yes, they were. And we depended on California motels until Harrah's Tahoe Hotel was built in 1972 or 1973.

Earlier you were saying it didn't really work out that well during the time of the Olympics, but did it benefit Harrah's in the future?

It did the job. It established Harrah's; it established Tahoe. Everybody knew where it was, and from then on business was great. In other words, it was just like this whole new vacation land had opened up, and suddenly everybody knew about it. It was a real turning point, not only for Harrah's, but possibly also for Lake Tahoe.

During the years we're talking about, Mark, the words "public relations and advertising" were used so much, and now you hear the word "marketing." All you hear is "marketing." To people that aren't familiar with the word "marketing," what's the difference, if any, between marketing and advertising and public relations?

Well, I'd say marketing is a lot more scientific. It's directed to specific groups. It takes into account publicity, public relations, advertising–but I'd say mostly advertising. And, of course, it includes the property itself, the way it handles the property, the facilities, the games, the slots. It's all tied together. But it's very bottom-line oriented, as opposed to just making it look great and getting the name out. I think it's good in some ways; in others, I

don't know. But there is a real difference. For example: Advertising would be just throwing it out in the wind, putting up a billboard here and a billboard there.

We just went for numbers and people and keeping the name in the public eye. Now they're much more, as I said, scientific and direction oriented and measured. They measure the results of everything. We weren't doing anything different; we just didn't know what we were doing. [laughter]

Were casino hosts used much in the early days?

Yes, they were.

Do you recall any specific hosts that were with Harrah's for a long time?

I recall Bill Jones, because he was identified in our big *Wall Street Journal* story about the company. They talked about Bill Jones taking care of a problem with one of Bill Harrah's dogs out at his estate.

Do you remember Frank Perez at Lake Tahoe?

Yes, and Russ McLennan and, of course, Curly Musso. He was general manager at Lake Tahoe for a long time, and when he retired and stepped down, he worked as a host. A prerequisite of a host is knowing a lot of good customers, and those men were very qualified. A good host also has to develop new customers and take care of good customer's needs such as meals, shows, rooms, et cetera.

When you were doing advertising work and working with ad agencies, were you responsible for newspapers, radio, TV, the entire ball of wax? Who did you report to then?

Yes, I was responsible for all media advertising, and the first person I reported to, of course, was Joe Harbaugh.

Did you ever report directly to Bob Ring or Bill Harrah?

Yes, I did. I reported to Bob Ring. He was vice-president then. I forget the sequence when he became president. He had picked up all of Bill's Virgo qualities ten times over. He became so detail oriented, it drove me crazy. He was such a stickler for every little thing.

Today you might say he became a clone of Bill Harrah?

Oh, he took it much farther. I think he originated the pointing out of the dust on the light bulbs and fingerprints on the glass. Everybody was like that, but I think Bob was the guy that started that trend. Anything on the floor, he had to pick up. I think he overdid it. It didn't hurt, but it drove me crazy. [laughter]

I remarked once to Bill Harrah, "He knows *everybody's* name."

And Bill said, "That's his job!" [laughter] "I can't remember *anybody's* name." Bob Ring knew everybody–employees and customers both–which is a great talent. He was number one in that area.

Was he involved with public relations?

In a personal way, in a different manner. He had a great personality, and everybody liked him. So he was good for Bill in that way, because Bill was . . . I don't know how to say it, whether he was shy or withdrawn, but it took him a number of years before he could really be comfortable in his role.

Did Bob Ring have good access to Bill Harrah? Could he get his ear?

Oh, yes. Everybody could have, *but* too many were intimidated. I found that people did not take advantage of Bill's accessibility, especially in my second go-around at Harrah's. They didn't approach him enough.

He was quite open, available, but I think just his presence and his aloofness intimidated people. I never had a problem with it. I did not mind calling him up and asking to go to lunch with him in his private dining room. I went with him on a number of trips alone, which others did not look forward to.

I wasn't that much of an outgoing, back-slapping guy. I was actually just the opposite. I was very quiet, and I didn't have the feeling that it was my job to make a *friend* of everybody. I did not mind sitting quietly with Bill on the plane for hours at a time. That did not bother me. Other people felt that something had to be going on, but that never concerned me.

So most people would be intimidated by Bill Harrah?

Well, perhaps intimidation is not the word. It was that quietness of his and trying to keep a conversation going. I don't think intimidation is the word; awkward might be better. He was just a quiet guy, but once you got him going, he was very talkative, very effusive. I can recall many private occasions with him when we'd travel abroad and be in a restaurant and just talk.

When you traveled with him, did he have his wife with him, and did you have your wife with you?

Sometimes. Once we went to Europe, to Nice and Monte Carlo. We took one of the boys, John, over there and put him in a Swiss school. There was just Bill and I and his son, John, and the steward of the plane, Karl Thoeni, who would cook and take care of things on the plane. He was great. It was always very pleasant for me, but I think it would be trying on other people who were used to things going on. There's no doubt that Bill's presence kept a lid on things.

I have heard some people say Mr. Harrah was almost god-like.

Exactly. At annual meetings, after the meetings, walking around, you would see him head and shoulders above everybody. Everybody started going to him for autographs, and he was always very gracious. People were looking at him like there was some kind of a presence there.

Yes. [laughter] Well, he really was to someone that didn't know him.

Exactly. I think while he was still alive he became a legend. He was gone, of course, before we went into Atlantic City, but it always amazed me to see how his legend grew. His picture turned up in everybody's office, and they had no idea who he was. I think his presence is still felt. I think his name probably comes up every day somewhere, somehow, some way. I think they're still talking about him in Memphis or Reno or wherever. In less than forty years, he went from the owner of a small bingo parlor to the owner of the largest gaming casino in the world.

Were you responsible for arranging and orchestrating media conferences and press conferences?

Yes. And there's another thing where he had control. He believed quite strongly that too much was not a good thing.

Too much publicity?

Yes, too much publicity. He always reminded me to make sure we were not overdoing it. He gradually loosened up on that to where interviews would be arranged. But he was not a Donald Trump. He knew intuitively the extent to which he should go. And he also knew the power of his persona just being there. He was certainly not dumb about what his power was.

He had this great reputation for being on time. And "on time" does not mean five minutes early. "On time" means on time—in

the door at ten o'clock. We'd be sitting there, and the second hand would be going to ten o'clock, and then the door opens. He worked on that. I mean, I know he was working on that. I've said it would not surprise me if he was standing outside the door for thirty seconds waiting for the second hand, because he *knew* that had an impact. [laughter]

And what would his reaction be if the meeting were at 10:00, and he was there, and you or someone came in at two minutes after 10:00?

The meeting started at 10:00 regardless of who was not there. And you would pretty well be ignored until you worked yourself into it! [laughter]

He wouldn't exactly give you a dirty look; he just ignored you?

Right. And he would wear his watch on the bottom of his wrist so he could just glance at it casually instead of staring at it. Especially when he had an appointment, and it was in fifteen minutes, and somebody was going over their time limit. [laughter]

Was he hesitant when you'd say, "We're meeting the press today"?

Bill was very careful to arrange those meetings well in advance, because he had a calendar that was unbelievable. I mean every minute was accounted for. He's got it down there, and it's eight weeks in advance, and he knows where he's going to be, and he knows what he has to do, and he's already picked out his clothes. So he's well prepared. He knows what's got to be done. But you had to give him some time. You didn't do it the next day.

When we went public, he knew and demanded media conferences, and he insisted on appearing. I remember one of our first financial meetings in New York. As usual, he was standing there alone in the room, taller than anybody, and somebody came up to me and said, "Are you Bill Harrah?"

And I said, "No."

Standing alone made people even more hesitant to go up to him. He was six feet-two, and that gave him an even more dominating presence.

Do you think he was really shy and an introvert, or was he just happier being by himself?

I don't think he was introverted, and I don't think he was shy. I just think he was a quiet guy that would not initiate anything. He would wait to be approached, but that was the problem–people were afraid to approach him. He was very accommodating and polite once approached. I did many private things with him; with writers he was very good. He was just a quiet guy. If you were around him enough, you knew how to deal with him, but somebody who had never met him before, to draw him out was a little difficult.

You were employed twice by Harrah's Club?

Yes. I got fired in 1962 and came back in 1970.

You say you were fired. How did it happen?

Bob Ring just got mad at me. I don't really know why. I never really knew what triggered it. I was in San Francisco, and he called me up and said, "I want to see you at my office, eight o'clock tomorrow morning." Didn't sound good. When I showed up he told me, "You're fired; you're through." And the only explanation I got was something like, "You're an empire builder." He felt that I was too big for my britches.

Were you trying to take too much of a leadership role?

Probably. I think I had become pretty cocky, and it probably was beginning to wear on some people, especially Bob. I didn't give up easily on ideas, and I was probably running a bit too much, just going after stuff without clearing it with Bob Ring. Some things just seemed so insignificant that I just did them.

The funny thing about the firing is that in 1959 when Ruth and I got married, Bob Ring was my best man. [laughter] But I never felt any animosity toward Harrah's. I knew there had to be a logical reason for my firing. I never had anything bad to say about Harrah's. I still thought they were the best. And I still remained friends with most of them. Even with Bob. I can remember, in the interim, setting up things for other clients that had something to do with Harrah's, and even being in Bob's office taking pictures, and he was always very cordial.

Do you think Bob Ring ran your termination by Bill Harrah?

I don't think so. I heard later Bill was a little surprised. And I'll tell you a funny story: After I came back to work, we had a dinner honoring people who had been there twenty or twenty-five years. It was a pretty big dinner, and there were a number of speakers. I was asked to say some things about Bob Ring, and I talked about what a nice thing it had been when he had been my best man, and how we had been in this little room in that lodge next to the club at the lake where a few people had gathered. I talked about the low lights and how nice it was. And then I said, "And two years later in an equally quiet, serene atmosphere with low lights, he canned my ass!" [laughter] Canned it!

He said later, "I didn't do that, Mark."

I said, "Bob, I'd never forget you canned me!"

Yes, you never forget who fires you. [laughter] You might forget who hired you but never who fires you.

Yes, right. But even then there was never any hard feelings. I think he got over it pretty quick.

When Harrah's opened the Golden Hotel in 1966, were you working for Harrah's?

No.

And that's the same year that what is now known as Sammy's Showroom and was earlier called the Headliner Room and prior to that was known as Harrah's Theater Restaurant was opened. Is that right?

Yes. I missed out on the opening of that room, and the opening of the hotel.

Talking about openings, tell us a little bit about a gentleman by the name of Lou LaBonte.

Lou LaBonte had this restaurant in Auburn, California, and there was a relationship there between Lou LaBonte, Bob Ring, and Bill Harrah. He was a good customer, and he'd bring people up, and he arranged some bus trips and that sort of thing. Everybody from Harrah's usually stopped at Lou's restaurant on their way to or from the Bay Area, and it was a close relationship. I think they tried out a lot promotions on him like giving away ash trays, matches, et cetera.

Wasn't there a tradition established where he was always the first one invited to an opening?

Exactly.

So if Harrah's opened a hotel or a restaurant or anything, Lou was always there. Was he always the first one to register?

I don't know that he always was, but he was always among the guests.

Let me ask you about Clifford Irving and his biography of Howard Hughes. Could you tell me a little about that, Mark?

Well, first of all, Leon Mandel, in his book, exaggerated my role. The way it worked was that this book was coming out, and Frank McCullough, who was an editor of *Life*–I forget whether he was in Asia, or whether he was editor of *Life* in the western United States–and Howard Hughes had established a great relationship, and Hughes trusted him.

Trusted Frank McCullough?

Yes. And *Life* announced that it was coming out with the real story on Clifford Irving, and Bill says, "Well, see what you can find out about this before it comes out."

He had an interest in Howard Hughes or in Clifford Irving?

In Clifford Irving. He wanted to know if this was going to be the true story. I had to start making calls, and I can't believe how this happened. I called *Life*, and I said, "I want to talk to somebody about this Clifford Irving story coming out next week. I understand he's going to be revealed or exposed."

I was told: "You should be talking to so-and-so." In other words they practically admitted it was true. *I* never got to anybody else, *but* I told Warren Lerude, who was editor of the paper here at the time.

I said, "Listen to this story. They practically told me that they're going to reveal this guy next week and how they are going to do it."

Lerude followed up on it, and he got to somebody, and the local paper ran the story about what was happening to expose Irving. Of course, the way that Mandel wrote it is that it was my inquiry that had prompted *Life* to explore the story, which was altogether baloney. Bill on many occasions sought information on things before the fact. He just wanted to be the first to know.

Do you suppose that maybe Irving had contacted Mr. Harrah about the Howard Hughes will?

No.

He just happened to take an interest?

Yes. He was a voracious reader. He read everything; he took every magazine in the world–newspapers, three or four television sets. He kept up on what was going on in the world, and if something hit him once in a while, he just wanted to know more.

Did Bill Harrah have a particular interest in Howard Hughes?

Oh, sure. Has anyone told you the story about Hughes trying to buy the place?

No.

Well, Hughes wanted to buy Harrah's at the lake. Robert Maheu contacted Bill, and they had these late-night telephone calls, which really intrigued Bill. He loved that. That's all he did. And Maheu said, "Would you sell the place?"
Bill said, "Everything's for sale." Bill really didn't want to sell it; he just put an enormous price on it.
And Hughes came back and said, "That's just a parking lot with a roof on it." [laughter]
I also recall some lined tablet paper with Hughes's writing on it that said "when you ask him this, and he says *this*, you say this. But if he says this . . . ." I mean, it was a script, and Howard Hughes had written it. I don't know where I saw that or how I saw it, but it did exist. Anyway, I think Bill was intrigued with the late-night meetings.

So he probably didn't ever meet with Howard Hughes.

No.

It was always with Robert Maheu?

I don't even think he met Maheu. I think they just talked on the telephone.

How about the Harrah's Automobile Collection and the Horseless Carriage Club? Were you involved in that?

To a degree. Bill made sure that all of us were involved in those big meetings that he'd have at the lake. At the big club meetings, everybody had a duster and was in a car. Ruth and I went on a number of them. I can remember one in Virginia City and many at Lake Tahoe. He loved those meetings. I don't how many others of us loved them. I think Bob Ring was into it, and there were a couple of others here at the time that were very much into it. But many others were just going because they were expected to be there. They were quite well attended, of course, because he did such a nice job with them.

Did he do that to publicize Harrah's Club in any way?

No. It was just his personal love, but he understood enough to know that it helped the club to have all those people there. But his first priority was with the cars, and whatever fell off of that was great.

Would you expand on the Horseless Carriage Club?

Collectors of antique and classic cars from all over the country, and even abroad, belonged to this club. Bill became quite prominent in it as he became more interested in old cars and added to his collection, which, of course, became the world's largest. His reputation grew quite quickly, because he did such marvelous jobs of restoration, and he had all these restoration people and facilities available to him.

He became almost a god in the automobile collection world.

Yes, he did. Here is a story I've heard many times: One of the first cars he bought, he had restored, and he was so proud of it. He was showing it off to somebody, when somebody else pointed out to him that one of the parts of the car was incorrect, and that it really belonged to another car. He said, "That'll never happen again!" [laughter]

After that he would have manuals made up far in advance of the start of restoration. *Every detail* that had to be done, where you got them, and getting all the pieces together before the job even started. Incredible!

So he wanted perfection in his automobile collection as he did in everything else?

Absolutely! Were you ever out there when he was in his heyday of restoring?

No.

It was marvelous! The offices and the libraries and the restoration area, people in white coats . . . . It was just incredible!

I've heard that he would come in the downtown club, check in, read the daily report, and then he'd go out to the collection.

Yes. He had a routine. He went out there every day. I'm not sure how early he went out, but he was there every day in his office checking things. He had a big staff, and it was a big drain on the club.

Oh, do you mean money-wise?

Yes. He knew that, and I think that Mead Dixon points that out in his book. I think that Bill said, "I can sell everything and just keep the collection." And Mead said that he didn't have any idea what it cost to keep that thing going, that the casino was paying for the collection, and it wouldn't have lasted very long without the casino's revenue.

So, you feel he loved the collection more than the casino operation?

I think he loved the casino business, but as far as where he'd rather be any day, I'm sure it was with the cars. He did have a definite passion for Harrah's itself and what he'd done with it and the things it allowed him to do. It allowed him so much, so many different ways to express his perfection. His imprint was everywhere. However, I do think he also loved the casino gaming business; it was his business.

Harrah's Automobile Collection was a great statement about the kind of company Harrah's was. I can't think of any other company that had something of that value to give back to the public. In other words, to make something really worthwhile out of gaming proceeds that the world could enjoy.

Because the collection spoke so highly of the company, we used it quite often in publicity and PR, and just the fact that it had the Harrah's name and belonged to that company meant a great deal. It brought great people to the area—well-known people, car builders, Ferrari and the like, who then learned about the company overall.

I always felt that the automobile collection was a very important and unique opportunity for a gaming company, although that was never why it was planned or collected. It was put together strictly because it was a passion of Bill's, and it was something he thought could contribute to history.

The collection was located in Sparks, on East Second Street. The building is still there. It was previously a big icehouse, then Harrah's completely gutted it. Part of it was the workshop and the library and a small museum of other items that he had bought perhaps in the late fifties. The museum was formerly known as Parker Lyon's americana museum out of Los Angeles. It was located in the lobby. After you entered the building, you went through the workshops and saw them working on the cars. Then you went out into a warehouse or a big building that had been built specifically to display the cars–rows upon rows of cars.

How did the customers get there? Did they go directly to the collection, or did they go to Harrah's and take shuttle buses?

They did both. They had a system where customers could win tickets to the automobile collection, but you could also buy tickets there. Most people went directly there. And, of course, there were many enthusiasts during this time that came from all over to see the place, and as its reputation grew, it became larger. It just had its own particular attraction. They'd go out sometimes in buses that came up from other areas–I mean busloads of people, and the parking lot was also usually pretty full.

Do you recall what year it opened?

Yes, on February 24 of 1962, that's the first time the cars were on display. He'd been collecting for some time before he opened, and I had taken people through the collection before it was open to the public. In fact, I took Clark Gable through there.

Was that when he was here for the filming of Misfits*?*

Yes. And I can compare times because *The Misfits* was shot in 1960. It was also interesting because Gable recognized a Duesenberg that he had once owned.

Mark, you mentioned that the collection was quite popular with customers. Do you have any idea how long it took them to reach their millionth customer?

Well, I'd say it took some time. As an attraction, it became known mainly as people

passed through town, but as its national reputation grew, the numbers grew. I think it is said that we reached a million customers by 1970. But after that I recall that we were averaging about three hundred thousand a year, as the collection grew and as our promotion grew. He charged a nominal fee to get in, just a very slight fee. I don't recall what it was, but at the time it seemed almost nothing.

How many cars were in the collection?

Well, I think we had on display one time perhaps twelve hundred. Some of them were not fully restored, but they were in good enough shape to be exhibited. Then there were five hundred more cars waiting in line to be restored, so I'd say in his total he had at least seventeen hundred cars.

Mr. Harrah did not require that we come to him with all the advertising of the club, but he was very interested in what we were going to do with the automobile collection, not only in publicity stories but also in advertising. I made the mistake once of putting up a billboard with a car that had a monocle windshield–a Stutz-Bearcat–and the headline was, "Varoom into the past at Harrah's Automobile Collection."

Bill called me, and he said, "That car doesn't varoom. An Indianapolis race car varooms."

And I said, "Well, can it zoom?"

And he said, "OK, it can zoom." [laughter] He was very sensitive as to how the cars were presented.

It's been asked, "Did Bill Harrah like to delegate authority?" Yes, he did. He felt that they spent enough time finding the right people, so they should know what they were doing. He didn't want any surprises. He wanted to know what was going on, but you did not to have to ask him what to do. You just kept him informed. I did go beyond my authority in that billboard. I shouldn't have done that, because if he'd have known in advance, he would have caught that.

As I think we mentioned before, he spent a lot of time out at the collection.

Yes. As I recall, he usually had a time he was out there—certainly by after lunch. And he spent a lot of time there looking at the progress of various cars. He knew more about them, I think it's been said, than anybody, even all the car experts. He had this phenomenal grasp of every car and its detail.

Bill also seemed to love entertainment and entertainers.

Oh, yes. When we got entertainment, he really began to enjoy the entertainers. He got to know every one of them, and that's when he started coming out of his shell. He would spend time with them, have them to dinner, and he got to know every one of them personally. And, of course, his reputation for taking care of them, their rooms and their dressing rooms and gifts (he gave great gifts) and cars . . . limousines, a driver, whatever they wanted—Rolls-Royces or Ferraris—while they were there, and sometimes *giving* the cars to them. Nobody could match that. The word got out quite quickly, and that's why so many stars just had to be asked once. [laughter] Frank Sinatra even asked his people to approach Harrah's, because he wanted to appear there.

Did you get involved with the entertainers much in the advertising of themselves, or did you work with their agents?

I worked mostly with Holmes Hendricksen. I got to know a few of them, but Holmes was the guy—he and Doug Bushousen. They knew them all, and they had great reputations in the industry as far as how they dealt with the entertainers. I worked mostly with Holmes on the advertising. Holmes was

very into it and kept a hard eye on it, because he wanted to represent them well, and he wanted to make sure that they were all being advertised at their proper strength. So I'd say mostly working with Holmes was the way we handled advertising.

Well, Holmes told me recently that the advertising campaign for the John Denver-Frank Sinatra back-to-back appearances at Harrah's Club in the seventies was the greatest bit of entertainment advertising he'd ever seen or ever been involved with. Would you, as creator and the architect of that campaign, give us an in-depth look at all the things that were done for that show?

Well, he seems a little lavish in his praise there, but Holmes put that deal together. I think he worked with Jerry Weintraub, who had John Denver, and the attorney for Sinatra, Mickey Rudin. I really don't know who came up with the idea, but you can say that Holmes immediately saw the great value of it. He had this huge, established, all-time star, Sinatra, and he had this young guy coming up who was as big as he was going to get—two different generations. We had a couple of months to work on this, maybe more. It was so big that I was really intimidated with what in the world you could do with this, because we knew it was more than filling the room. I mean if there ever was an opportunity to say what this place, Harrah's, was, this was it.

I really worked with a lot of people to establish what we could do. I worked with a guy in San Francisco that used to be here in Reno, but has since died, Harry Murphy. I needed a line; I just needed something that really said it. And I think it came out in San Francisco, this back-to-back idea. The picture, which I'm sure you're familiar with, has them standing back-to-back. It was shot in Connecticut and San Francisco. Denver was in Connecticut and Sinatra was in San Francisco, and there's no way they're ever going to get them together. So this guy

Murphy just started to set up these diagrams and points and the height of stools and backgrounds for both locations. So both of those guys, all they had to do was walk on. The light intensity and everything was all set; they simply had to walk on, sit on the stool, fold their arms and take a picture. They came out absolutely perfect. We put the two pictures together, and that was how that picture came to be.

As to the next part of it: Holmes and I were discussing how could we really make a big deal out of this, and that's when we started talking about putting these billboards up in all these incredible locations. We had signs in London, Tokyo, New York, San Francisco, L.A., all over the world. The billboards simply had those two guys there sitting on a stool back-to-back, and the wording was, "Back-to-back at Harrah's Tahoe," and the date.

Harrah's began accepting reservations thirty days in advance of the show, and on that day there were six hundred thousand attempted phone calls in a matter of twelve hours that backed up the circuits to Bakersfield, California, and absolutely disrupted the service. Pacific Telephone and Nevada Bell said, "Don't *ever* do that again!" [laughter] In other words, attempted calls may mean one person is trying ten times, but the point is that all that happened in a twelve-hour period. It was just an avalanche of calls.

It's an astounding number. Did the phone calls continue for the next several days?

Yes, but not at quite that volume, because everybody knew by the second day the reservations would all be gone. I forget how many people could actually see the show, but I think it was about fourteen thousand. We had two shows a night for two weeks.

What you also have to remember is that Holmes had such a reputation in the industry that these kinds of things were brought to him so he could put them together. I don't know that anything like that would ever have been possible anywhere else. It was just that the people like Rudin and Weintraub and the principals themselves knew that it would be well done.

Holmes was able to get many stars like Sinatra and Denver and things like that going simply because of his reputation in the business. His integrity and honesty helped Harrah's build a great reputation with entertainers—not just because of how they were kept and taken care of, but how Holmes dealt with them personally. I don't think that kind of management or reputation is out there anymore.

He also had this great *respect* for advertising and promotion. He knew instantly what you could do with something and what it would be worth beyond filling a room. He didn't miss a thing. He didn't miss a detail. If a sign or a poster was going up six minutes late, he knew about it.

So was he following through on Bill Harrah's perfection?

Well, yes, but I also think this was Holmes himself. He took a great interest in everything that we did, and he really drove the quality of the advertising.

As you said earlier, there was no problem to fill the room. You wouldn't have had to do anything to fill the room, except let people know that Sinatra and Denver were appearing there.

Yes, and it's hard for some people to understand that. What advertising is for, or what entertainment is for, is to let the people know who you are and where you are. And that was one of the great advantages Harrah's had, and Holmes knew that.

Yes. I imagine some entertainment directors would object to that, or they would be advertising their entertainment as opposed to the entire property.

Yes, there's an attitude like that now, even locally, that after you have taken care of the attendance and it's full, just don't do anything. But that isn't the way it should be. It should sound exciting all the time. Now they have shows for weekends only that they advertise way out in front. In other words, they'll take advantage of the name, even though it won't be here for a month, which is fine. They're still establishing the quality of the entertainment of the property, even though they are talking about something that is a month away, and it works. Ascuaga's Nugget does that a lot; Caesar's Tahoe does that a lot.

It's just a whole different perspective. Entertainment costs so much. I remember when we had the chorus girls and all that other incredible stuff–the chorus line, the house orchestra, the entourage that comes with the entertainer. There were a lot of residual expenses then.

Now there's very little entertainment in Reno on a daily basis. There are a few big names that come in on weekends, and that is about all.

Well, big names can't afford to do this anymore. They don't get enough out of a showroom. It has to be a concert. You might get a big name at Vegas in some of those big rooms, like you had Streisand. She got a million or five million or whatever. I can't think of anybody else who does that anymore. You have these built-in shows–Siegfried and Roy and those follies–but there aren't any names that lend themselves to that venue that can afford to do it today.

Getting off the subject of entertainment, were you with Harrah's when Mr. Harrah was involved in hydroplane races? Didn't he have a hydroplane called the Tahoe Miss?

Yes, he did. I was involved in the beginning of the hydroplane era. Guy Lombardo had a boat, also, but I lost out on most of that. I think that might have been in the early sixties.

I was curious why it died out. Charles Mapes had a hydroplane, also, didn't he? And they used to race at Pyramid Lake, and they used to race at Tahoe a lot. I thought maybe you were involved at that time because that's about when you were with Harrah's.

No, I wasn't. The guy that was involved with that was Gene Evans.

To return to your career, Mark, when you were first fired, you said you were trying to be too creative and doing too many things of your own volition. Did that change when you came back?

Well, I like to explain it by saying that I was very far out, and they were very conservative when I got fired. I was probably really too cocky. When I came back, Bill was dressing very mod, had had a couple wives in between, including Bobbie Gentry, and I had calmed down. [laughter] We just sort of grew back together. The guy that really got me back was Wally Warren. He and Shep were pretty good friends.

Who was Wally Warren?

Wally Warren was the dean of public relations in Nevada. He *invented* public relations. And he was a lobbyist (a wonderful guy), and he was my mentor. He had great companies he represented–Harrah's being one–and a great mind. And he was my advisor. Constantly he would throw me business. He and Shep started talking and decided that I should come back, or maybe Wally talked him into it–I don't know. But they approached me, and that's how we got back together.

So Shep is the guy that actually brought you back to Harrah's?

Yes, it was Shep . . . definitely Shep that got me back, but he and Wally worked together on it. Shep was very helpful. I don't know if he had to do any spade work before I came back or not. But I was greeted very warmly by everybody, including Bob Ring, and I started out again as a publicist, which became public relations. Then they came to me one day and said would I also take advertising. Then I became director of advertising and public relations. Then in 1976 they made me a vice-president.

Earlier we were talking about whether you were encouraged to be creative. Were you more creative when you came back, and were you allowed more freedom when you came back the second time?

Yes, Harrah's was very open. The thing I appreciated most was that everybody had a great interest. They gave a lot of attention to advertising, and I was able to present my stuff to the advertising committee. It was composed of Bill and Bob and Shep and Holmes. I'd run things by Holmes first, but we always took them to the full group. We didn't always make it, but I'd say generally they always supported whatever we wanted to do.

So you worked closely with Holmes, because so much of the advertising was about entertainment.

Exactly. And that's how I think Harrah's established its great reputation and aware-ness, because, as I say, we're the only ones that could ever say Reno *and* Tahoe in advertisements. We had these billboards everywhere advertising who was appearing in Reno and Lake Tahoe. That sent *a big message*–when you had two big stars on one board.

Yes, and most of the entertainers would appear at both properties eventually.

Yes, that was part of the deal. If you had a big star at Tahoe, somewhere along the way they had to come to Reno. [laughter]

When you came back in 1970, did you go to Bill Harrah with an idea, or did you go through Holmes?

Well, first of all it was a guy named Chuck Munson, who I reported to. On entertain-ment I went to Holmes, but on the general stuff I went through Chuck, and then, of course, to the management committee.

Chuck Munson was the first of my supervisors, and then Holmes Hendricksen and later Jim Rogers, who is now vice-president/general manager of Harrah's Reno. He came to us with an M.B.A. from the University of California. A bright young man.

As to another supervisor, Maurice Sheppard: Was he really shy, as much introverted as sometimes pictured? Yes, I think so, especially when he was troubled by something, and he worried about everything. It must not be forgotten how important he was to the business of the company. He was the main reason it became so proficient in conducting business and actually where it got its reputation as a highly business-oriented organization. Harrah's got a lot of its respect because of Shep. I don't know whether to call him introverted, but he was within himself because he did worry a lot about the company. He fought for those things that he thought were important, and he was very valuable to the company over the years in setting it up as a business-like organization. I also think he was responsible for hiring all those consulting firms, like Stanford Research and those people.

He was also the guy that developed the daily report. The report gave you a profit and loss statement every morning, for everybody, from every part of the casino—the restaurants, the slot area, whatever it was, it was all right there in front of you. Unheard of at the time, and, of course, there were no computers at that time.

When the stars and entertainers were at Lake Tahoe or Reno, did they have their own agents and their own publicity people with them?

No. I'd say that we handled that completely, and that was one of the things entertainers liked about Harrah's—the way we promoted them. We took the entire responsibility of promoting the entertainer, of course, with their approval, and we had a regular routine. They were on our billboards, and then there was an opening ad that went in the California papers and on radio. However, the promotion of the shows was entirely up to us. It was again part of Harrah's reputation—because of Holmes—that we would take care of their publicity as soon as we booked them. I mean we started promoting them immediately.

Even weeks and months ahead of time?

Oh, yes, of course. We'd use the columnists for that—people like Earl Wilson in New York—to let people know that big things were coming up.

Was it hard to get the names of the entertainers planted in Earl Wilson's column?

Well, no. But you always had to come up with a good angle. I think Harrah's was probably the first one to really use all those columnists to our advantage, because we found that a line in Earl Wilson was every bit as important as a full story in the *Chicago Sun Times*. It got that much readership. Just a mention, because of his great syndication, was invaluable, and we had many columnists that we worked with in that respect.

How about Herb Caen in the San Francisco Chronicle*?*

Herb Caen was very good. I don't think Herb was a real fan of Nevada, but he was always nice. And if we had something important, like Sinatra or something like that, and had an angle on it, he would be happy to use it.

Did that come under your department?

Yes.

So you contacted the columnists?

Yes. Well, of course, I didn't do all that. I was head of the department, but we had other people, like a man up at the lake or several people up there. Candice Pearce, whose title was manager of public relations, had good contact and good relationships with many of those people. We all had some kind of distinct relationship with certain people which we would foster.

Is that the same Candice Pearce who is the city councilwoman now?

Yes, it is.

Did Walter Winchell have a column then?

Yes, he did. And he used things about us. We had a guy that I hired in New York named Jackie Cannon. He was the brother of Jimmy Cannon, the great sports writer. Jackie was probably one of the last of the old-time column planters. He had clients whom he tried to get mentioned in all his columns. I was introduced to him by Joey Adams, a great comic. Joey's wife, Cindy, also had a syndicated column and she also used some of our things.

Jackie Cannon became an invaluable asset to our publicity, especially dealing with columnists in New York, which was very important.

Did he get paid on a salary basis?

Yes. Holmes also gave him the job of taking care of our requirements when we came to New York–getting us in shows, in certain restaurants, and taking care of details like that. He was a great guy, I mean a typical New Yorker. And his brother, Jimmy, of course, was a very great sports columnist. I can remember being in Sardi's one night, and Jackie introducing me to Lauren Bacall.

The first World Classic Car Festival was held in Japan in 1971. What role did Bill Harrah and Harrah's Automobile Collection play in that event?

Well, first of all, the name was just for that event. I don't think there ever was another one. This promoter in Japan came to us, and he wanted thirty cars. He wanted to, of course, pay for the shipping of the cars to Japan.

So the promoter borrowed the cars from Bill Harrah?

Actually, he leased them at a very good price. But, nevertheless, the big concern was how they would be transported and protected. Even with all the preparation, there was still lots of work to be done on them after they arrived in Japan, because of the salt air and exposure. The cars were a big hit, and their presentation was a very big deal. Even some of the royalty of Japan came.

The cars were displayed in Tokyo, Osaka, and Kyoto–big crowds. And the event was even noted in our congressional records as a gesture of friendship from this nation to Japan.

Did Bill Harrah attend?

Oh, Bill Harrah was very prominent. People were constantly crowding around him. There was a lot of Japanese attention, press conferences, et cetera. And because of his height and his somewhat aloofness, he was an immediate attraction. Bill himself was as much of an attraction as the cars.

Did you go to Japan with Mr. Harrah?

Yes, I did. I was there for the entire presentation, and we felt that it was a very worthwhile thing to do. It did bring a lot of attention to Harrah's. And as we know, the Japanese people are great visitors to the United States, so it had an impact for the company as well.

The festival lasted about two weeks, and the promoter spent lots of money. They could not do enough for you. Japanese have this thing about gifting their visitors. They made our stay very comfortable and constantly had us visiting or touring something, and we stayed in great hotels. They would give you great gifts on arrival and great gifts on departure. We thought the thing that the promoter appreciated most was when we gave him the hood ornament of a Bugatti Royale on a pedestal. We silver-plated it, and he was overwhelmed, but he was not to be outdone. The things that showed up after that were incredible. You couldn't do him one better!

Did many people go with you and Mr. Harrah?

Well, of course, all the technicians, the people responsible for the cars–there was quite a crew. They wouldn't let anybody touch those cars except Harrah's people. I can't recall how many technicians there were, but there had to be at least ten who took very sensitive care of the cars as they were being shipped around.

Possibly one of Bill Harrah's proudest moments–he must have had many–was when Harrah's became a publicly traded company in 1971 and then later when Harrah's was listed on the New York Stock Exchange in 1973. Could you tell us your part in publicizing those events?

Well, that was a very unusual period, because here we were, a gaming company, an entertainment company, and we were suddenly dealing in the financial world. I didn't know what I was doing, and I don't think anybody else really did either. We *knew* that we shouldn't be publicizing the listing of Harrah's on the New York Stock Exchange, but because it was the first truly gaming company to be listed on the big board, it did get a lot of attention. When we went there to be on the floor for the first day of trading, when that HRR, the symbol, went across the screen for the first time, it was very much of a thrill. Bill was very proud of that moment, and there's no getting around the fact that one of the reasons we did it was because his lifestyle had changed, and he needed some cash. The stock issue was an immediate success. It started trading at sixteen, and the rest is history.

Harrah's was listed on the New York Stock Exchange 1973 and first went public in 1971 as an over the counter stock. Was it more difficult to become a publicly traded stock or more difficult to get listed on the New York Stock Exchange?

I think the most difficult part was for gaming to finally be accepted as a business. George Drews was largely responsible for dealing with the financial community and establishing our integrity.

George was the vice-president of finance or perhaps senior vice-president of finance. He personally went to New York and dealt with many of these financial firms. He convinced them what a solid company Harrah's was, and he was responsible for the high bond rating we received. I don't recall right now, but it may have been as high as triple-A.

He was extremely instrumental in establishing Harrah's financial reputation and instrumental in getting Harrah's listed on the New York Exchange, which of course, was a great coup. It was difficult to get there, and it was only by the proof of those couple years–with our reports and so forth–that the New York Exchange finally accepted us; and as I

said, we were the first *pure* gaming company to be listed.

Did your department or you personally try to create an image for Harrah's?

We've always "sold" a very business-like company, and I think that contributed to Harrah's success in becoming a publicly traded company. It was difficult to maintain some kind of a balance between what we really were–a big entertainment company with a lot of flash–and then this responsible business. It was dealing in altogether two different areas. It was like night and day. At the same time we managed to make this entertainment business, this glamorous business, become accepted as a legitimate business. We didn't back down at all from what we were. We did not try to soften the image of a gaming company. We presented it exactly as it was, and I think that probably had as much to do as anything with getting on the exchange. I think after we got on the New York Exchange, we finally got a front-page *Wall Street Journal* story that told all about us, which was absolutely the greatest thing that ever happened.

Gradually, business writers of business publications took a great interest in us, because we were one of a kind, the first. They came to us. We were the experts in gaming; any questions they had about the industry, they came to us first. So that also helped to establish Harrah's as a very professional, stable, business-like company.

Did magazines like Forbes *and* Newsweek *come to you?*

Yes. All those publications. We had it all to ourselves for quite a while. They came directly to Reno, so I had a lot of contact with them, and I still do. A guy that I corresponded with recently, Frank Lalli, is now senior editor of *Money* magazine. He was representing *Forbes* at the time he did a story on us, and those are contacts that grew over a period of time. I forget who the guy was who did the *Wall Street Journal* article, but we must have spent a week with him, showing him around the company, et cetera.

To put it in the proper time frame, it was long before gaming opened in Atlantic City, so gaming was really foreign to the East Coast.

Oh, yes. That had its advantages and disadvantages. There was some argument that we should present ourselves in a more low-key and austere manner, but Bill at the beginning said, "This is what we are; this is how we should be perceived; and we won't downplay anything–the games or anything. This is the business."

When Harrah's first went public in 1971, it was the same time construction began at the Lake Tahoe hotel. Is there any connection between going public and the construction?

Well, of course. But equally as important as raising money for the hotel was Bill's personal needs. He simply had no cash, and he was living a whole new lifestyle. He owned a lot of things and was worth a lot of money, but he had no cash. So he had more than one reason for going public. He had to borrow money for the hotel and to support his personal spending.

The hotel construction at Lake Tahoe began in 1971, and the hotel was completed in November of 1973. Do you recall some of your activities and duties then as far as publicizing the opening of the hotel?

Naturally it was a big event, primarily because of the quality of the place. It was so immaculate and so beautiful in its construction and the magnificence of the rooms. The rooms cost $100,000, which was unheard of at that time. The furnishings and the televisions in the bathrooms and all the amenities that

were in the rooms made them expensive. It was immediately–although it didn't receive it–perceived as a five-star hotel. The opening festivities, of course, were the usual big names, not only in entertainment but also in state government. The Summit restaurant was one of the key places that we used to help promote the property–that and the big shows.

Did Bill Harrah have a lot to do with the planning of the hotel?

Certainly. They had a mock-up built in the Reno hotel, in one of the construction areas, of exactly what each room was going to be like–its exact square footage, its exact furnishings, the almost bay windows that jutted out from each room so you could get more of a view of the lake. They played with that for I don't know how long to get it exactly right, and he was there every minute. He picked up all these ideas in his travels from all over the world, and he made notes *forever*. He hadn't missed a thing.

Do you think the hotel opening in 1973 was as big or bigger than the South Shore Room opening in 1959?

I've never thought of that. But I think probably the South Shore Room. First of all we probably had eight hundred guests in the South Shore Room, and there was big-name entertainment, like Marlene Dietrich and Red Skelton and Victor Borge. I think that that probably caused more of a splash. However, I do think the hotel itself was also a very big event.

By 1973, when the hotel opened, people were probably used to Harrah's doing great things?

Yes, but I think the hotel opening was still a big thing. It was an altogether different thing, but it certainly fit with the quality of the South Shore Room, so those two things together became a big attraction. The first tower was only 250 rooms, and it was just like this little square thing going up in the air. Not until they added the second tower and they continued the building did it really have the outside appearance of a major hotel.

Did it eventually get a Mobil five-star rating?

Oh, yes, and they had it for quite some time. It also received the AAA five-diamond rating. It was one of only seven hotels in the United States at that time that had both a five-star and a five-diamond rating.

We talked earlier about Frank Sinatra appearing at Harrah's Club at Lake Tahoe and what a draw he was. Do you have any anecdotes or remarks about Mr. Sinatra that you would care to mention?

Rome Andreotti (l.) and Mark Curtis. *"Rome Andreotti . . . became the expert of experts in gaming and in how to furnish a casino and how to display the games."*

Well, to me, getting Sinatra to appear at Harrah's was the greatest thing in the world. And I recall this vividly–Holmes Hendricksen doesn't think it happened this way, but Sinatra's people actually contacted Holmes about his coming to Harrah's. I remember very vividly being in the Plaza Hotel in New York City, in Bill Harrah's suite, and Holmes came in and said, "Guess who wants to play for Harrah's?" And he said, "Sinatra," and both of us just absolutely dropped our mouth open. That was a big thing.

The other thing was, in his first appearance there and his first night on stage, he said, "I play some great places in the world; I play Caesar's in Las Vegas–a wonderful company, a great showroom, and a great hotel. But," he said, "Caesar's compared to Harrah's Tahoe is a toilet."

That's pretty strong! The crowd must have really responded to that.

They certainly did.

People like Sinatra were one of reasons that Harrah's was the unqualified leader in entertainment and in the gaming industry for so many years. Were there any specific individuals that helped make Harrah's so successful?

There were several key people who were just perfect for the positions they held. Holmes was certainly absolutely perfect in his handling of entertainment and had the great respect of the business because of his integrity. Also Lloyd Dyer brought so much to the business. Especially his concern about the retirement plans and bonuses and that sort of thing for the employees and management. I think but for him, a number of us would not be quite as well off as we are today. And then Shep, of course, who was so important; Rome Andreotti, who became the expert of experts in gaming and in how to furnish a casino and how to display the games; and George Drews, because of his financial acumen. George was one of those who was recruited from outside the company. Harrah's had a very strong lineup of managers and officers that ran the company.

You mentioned most of them came from within the club, except for Mr. Drews. Is that right?

Yes, but I should have also mentioned the arrival of Joe Fanelli in 1971 from the Mayo Clinic, who became the vice-president of food and beverage.

That's the Mayo Clinic in Rochester, Minnesota?

Yes. The Kahler Corporation owned the hotel, the clinic, and so forth. Joe made Harrah's an institution by the food that was presented in the various restaurants. He was absolutely the top of the line.

However, most of management grew up with the company. Bob Ring came up here with Bill Harrah from Venice, California. Bob Ring, I should say, was also extremely important. He was actually the personality of the club, because he knew everybody, and he knew how to treat them. His golf tournaments were legendary, and he was extremely important to the beginning of the company and where it went. I can't think of any others—of course, there are many others—but I could go on forever. I do think the ones I mentioned were the key people who made the company what it was.

So three of the factors that made Harrah's a success were entertainment, food, and great relations with the customers?

Yes, and the treatment of people. The development of high-rollers was important to any casino—being able to accommodate them when they wanted to come; sometimes picking them up in an airplane. We had great casino hosts who were mainly under the supervision of Dan Orlich, Bob Ring, and Rome.

I've heard it said that Bill Harrah was quoted as saying: "Try to treat everyone like you would like to be treated yourself."

Well, that's exactly true, but that's not exactly an original thought. That's almost a mandate of God. He just made so much out of it that it became his philosophy. He really meant what he said, and he made sure that everybody thought that way. I don't think he invented the concept, but he certainly carried through with it.

Do you feel that Bill Harrah was a visionary who had long-range plans for his casino, or was he an opportunist that happened to be at the right place at the right time?

He was a visionary. He was the leader of the industry. The industry looked up to him. Everybody knew how important he was and what kind of a reputation he was setting for the industry. I've often said that when Harrah's went public, he was carrying on his back the reputation of Las Vegas, which was not easy. He gave the entire industry a good reputation. He was definitely a visionary. He created opportunities.

Going to the lake was entirely visionary. Nobody in their right mind would go up there for three months in a Quonset hut, but he made it a year-round success. Nobody else thought of how to get customers up there in the winter. So many details that came from his thinking—the fresh rose in every room every day, no dust on light bulbs, no fingerprints on the mirrors—were carried out by everybody. Everybody had that mind-set.

Did Bill Harrah have many friends, associates, or acquaintances that spent time with him?

I think in Bill Harrah's definition of friends, he had lots of friends. He had friends in the antique classic car area, he had entertainer friends, and he had other friends. But by his definition, friend did not mean close relationships. He didn't play golf. He didn't bowl or do any of those things. Some people who defined themselves as a close friend might have overstepped a little bit.

When he traveled, he would take his wife, or perhaps somebody in management. But when you traveled with him, you were not sitting there chatting with him, although he did spend time with you. And, of course, having entertainers to dinner was a programmed thing; but he wanted to do that. I think he would consider Sammy Davis Jr. a friend; I think he would consider Sinatra a friend–even though he'd only spend perhaps one evening with them during their appearance.

He had a list of birthdays, and one of my jobs was to compose a congratulatory telegram to each of those people on their birthday. Once he missed one, he got the wrong date, and the guy said, "Thanks very much, but it's not my birthday!"

I think Bill thought he had friends. But in the sense of most people, where you're close and spend time together on the golf links or doing other things–no, he didn't have that.

Someone has said that Frank Sinatra and Bill Harrah were quite similar as far as their demand for punctuality and getting things done in a proper way. Did you ever notice that?

Yes, I would say the same. Their perfectionist attitude about what they did and how they did it were quite similar.

Did you ever know of anyone who was actually privy to Bill Harrah's private thoughts or feelings?

Not his intimate thoughts and feelings, but he did confide sometimes to various people. When I traveled with him, something would come up once in a while, but I don't think that was because we were friends. I remember when he got a million dollars when we became a public company, and he said, "You

know what I'd like to do is put this in my pocket and walk around the block."

Also when the divorce from Bobbie Gentry was final, he made a couple of comments, but they were not terribly revealing. It was just interesting that he would talk about it, and the comments were mostly jokes on himself. He did not mind a joke on himself, and he was able to withstand what might be embarrassment to other people by just walking around like nothing ever happened.

Another time Bill told me about the vice-president of entertainment before Holmes. This guy would come to his office, and Bill would talk to him, and it drove Bill crazy that he never had a pencil. Never had a piece of paper. Bill would say, "How do you know what I want, and how do you know what to remember?" It drove him out of his mind.

One day he told me that he had the plane set to go someplace at seven in the morning, and he woke up late. He ran around getting everything ready and packing his bag and getting dressed and jumping in the car and speeding off. Then he suddenly realizes it's his plane. He can get there when he wants to. So he just slowed down. That was an intimate thing that he revealed, and he was laughing at himself.

Then there was another case where he said he went to get fitted for some ski boots up in Idaho. He was sitting in this room, and they poured this plaster around his feet to get his size, and he said, "It actually flashed through my mind that somebody would come in here and gun me down!" [laughter]

Mark, do you recall where you were and what you were doing when you heard of Mr. Harrah's death? Did you have any inkling that he was in bad physical shape?

I think that Lloyd told us that it was serious. I think you know the story about how he went back to Mayo because when he was in Hershey, Pennsylvania, he had dropped by to see how he was doing, and they told him that he had an aneurism and said that he should come back right away. I think Lloyd was pretty concerned, but I really didn't grasp it. As you know, it hit him on the last day of the fiscal year, June 30, 1978. I think the news came out in the afternoon, and we just started dealing with it. I was aware that it absolutely knocked the business out of the opening of the Sahara Reno. It threw a damper over everything else that opened that night–the Circus Circus and the new Money Tree.

His death had quite an impact on the community and on Lloyd, of course, and on most of the employees. Getting through that funeral was tough. A lot of people turned out. Bobbie Gentry was there, which surprised me. I think his other wives were there too. John Denver was there, and he sang during the services. He was buried in Idaho.

Did you go to Idaho for the funeral?

No, I don't remember the funeral in Idaho. I just remember that he was buried there. I have visited the grave in Sun Valley, Idaho.

Did you have a feeling, or did anyone sense, that when he died that was really going to be the end of Harrah's Club as you knew it then?

I don't think so. I had no idea. I think we knew it would still be Harrah's. How it survived, of course, had a lot to do with Mead Dixon putting that deal together. He put that deal together with Holiday Inns, which everybody despised, and so we became acquired–another fateful day–on February 28, 1980.

I remember a story somebody told me about Bill. They thought that he probably knew he was going to die in the Mayo Clinic. He's standing out in front of his big, white house, with his poodles, looking off into the horizon, like he's contemplating. I don't know who observed that, or who said that, but I think it's been indicated to me that he had a good idea it was a pretty dangerous operation. However, I don't think *I* knew how serious it was. I knew it was serious, but I did not realize how serious.

Well, he was actually a young man when he died. He was only sixty-seven years old, and that's quite young.

Sure is. Let's see, today he would be–he's ten years older than I–so he would be eighty-five.

I remember once at a meeting, when John Kennedy was elected president, Bill said, "You know, this is the first time in my life when the president's younger than I am."

[laughter] Well, we mentioned briefly that Harrah's was sold to the Holiday Inns February 28, 1980. What effect did the sale have on you personally or on your job?

It was a very unhappy time. Luckily I had a guy from Holiday Inns that was a pretty good guy to work with, but people were dropping like flies. I had to deal with a couple of probably the worst–and I use this cautiously–assholes from Holiday Inns, and I have no idea how they ever wound up working for a company like Holiday Inns. A marketing guy and a PR guy–both absolute bullshit con artists who were out to show everyone how it was done. I think my biggest question was, "How in the world did they ever get a job with that company?" Talking like they did and doing what they did! They were womanizers; the only reason they'd ever come out here was to get laid. It was just disgusting, and I had to deal with that. Later, Darrell Luery came in and was able to get in between me and them. But it was sad to see things change, especially the attitude toward advertising and PR and quality–as much as they denied things would not change, they, of course, did change.

There was a time there when Goeglein, the president, called me in and said, "I want you to leave." He simply said, "We just don't need you anymore."

I went to Rome, and I said, "What the hell's going on here? Why would they do away with this position?"

Rome stepped forward and spoke up for my job. Also, there was a consultant in New York named Joe Snider, who worked for Holiday Inns. And by natural attrition he came to work for Harrah's. He was an advisor, and he came out here and sat in various meetings and so forth. He was very well thought of by Mike Rose and many other people with Holiday. He was a typical New Yorker; always wore a fedora. He sat in on a couple of my meetings, and he took me to breakfast one morning and asked me about being fired. We talked about it, and the result was he went to Goeglein and said, "You're making a big mistake." And Goeglein *canceled*! [laughter] I mean I was back! I don't know who this guy was, but he sure had power.

I became quite close to him and became friends with him. I never knew what his contribution was or how good he was, but Holiday Inns thought highly of him. He used to always carry three-by-five cards in his pocket, and he would always write notes and give them to people. The notes expressed his thoughts, which were always well taken. For some reason this guy took a liking to me, and he saved my job. I have no idea how he did it, but Goeglein backed right down! [laughter] He had that much power.

I have no idea why they thought so highly of him. Maybe he was just better at whatever it was he did! He had a way of saying things philosophically. I had a guy there once that I wanted to put in a job at Atlantic City, and I had to take him to see Joe Snider. We had breakfast in the Plaza Hotel in that corner restaurant at the corner table, his favorite table, and he was asking the guy, "What's the Boy Scout oath? What's this, what's that?" It

was just a blizzard of those kind of questions. Then we shook hands out in front of the hotel, and Joe left. This guy looked at me, and I looked at him. [laughter] But the guy had to get Joe's approval or OK, and I guess he didn't get it. The guy didn't go to work for us because of that!

When did you retire from Harrah's, Mark?

I retired in 1986. I stayed as a consultant for two years until *they* could find somebody I could spend a little time with, and then I left. I like to be ahead of the curve. I was sixty-five in September of 1986 and I retired that same year.

Did Holmes Hendricksen stay longer?

Yes, he was there until two years ago, and he was very highly thought of by Phil Satre. He still had an office there, but his role was becoming less important, and they listened to him less. All the new guys who were running the place had their own marketing ideas, and they just went right by him.

What are you doing now to keep busy? Are you completely retired, or are you with an advertising firm?

No, I am completely retired except for writing a little bit, but I keep pretty occupied.

5

LEE DeLAUER

*L*EE DeLAUER, who worked in several key positions while employed at Harrah's, was a willing and enthusiastic chronicler while being interviewed in his home in Reno, Nevada. Two sessions were needed to complete the interview, which was held in May of 1997.

Mr. DeLauer was born in Oakland, California, in 1925. He entered the United States Marine Corps after graduating from Oakland High School. Following service in the marines, he enrolled in the University of Nevada in 1946. While in college he played semi-professional baseball and ran a boarding table for the university's football team.

After receiving a bachelor of science degree in business administration, DeLauer served Harrah's as an independent auditor before being hired as the office manager of the newly-opened Harrah's Lake Tahoe casino. In this oral history he goes into detail about the bus program at Lake Tahoe and about some Harrah's executives, such as Bob Ring, Red Farnsworth, and Maurice Sheppard. DeLauer eventually transferred to the public relations department. From that perspective he discusses the Winter Olympics of 1960, held at Squaw Valley,

the opening of the South Shore Room at Lake Tahoe, the golf tournaments put on by Harrah's, and details of Harrah's management meetings.

LEE DELAUER: From about the time my father was eight years old to when he was fifteen years old, he was in a reformatory in Ohio. His brother and a bunch of friends, who were kind of street people, were sneaking into a circus when a cop got murdered, and they were all put in prison. When they got out of prison, authorities put my father and his brother on a freight car heading west, and they ended up in Oakland, California. He spent about thirty years with Scripps-Howard. He had a self-taught, great, mathematical memory. He also traveled to Australia, New Zealand, the Philippines, and Hawaii as a professional boxer and made a little money that way.

My mother was from Oakland. Her father was the first Presbyterian minister in Oakland. They still have a church cornerstone with my grandfather's name on it, John Giambruno. My father was French-Italian from northern Italy. My mother was full Italian—a little bit of Siciliano and a little bit of Roman in her.

I was born in Oakland in 1925. I had two older brothers. I went to school in Oakland, and I spent all my time on the playground. Because I was slow and little, I couldn't play basketball, but I was a tough little guy, and I played baseball and football at Oakland High. I played with some great athletes. One of them was the great Jackie Jensen, and there was another fellow, a year older than Jensen, named Boyd Anderson that was even better-looking than Jackie. (Boyd went in the marine corps with me.) I played on a championship baseball team in Oakland, I was the smallest man on the football team, and I was also the captain of the East team in the all-star football game between East and West Oakland.

In 1943, when I was seventeen, I joined the marine corps. I am proud to say that I was a combat marine. I was a gunner in an amphibious tank, and I made two first-wave landings. I got blown up on Guam, and I still have fusions in my spine. I was on the first wave in Okinawa—I have some shrapnel from being in northern Okinawa for awhile. Right after Okinawa, I turned myself in, flew home, and got operated on at the Mare Island Hospital.

I was an outpatient, and I started going up to Lake Tahoe and the Feather River area. An old coach of mine got me a job (while I was still in the marine corps wearing a brace) as an athletic director of a boys' camp. On the brochure they had Jim Aiken[1] listed as the athletic director, but I did all his work. I left that boys' camp and worked a month at the Cal-Neva Lodge at Lake Tahoe. At the Cal-Neva I met Bill Beko (who was later my roommate), Jack Hailey, and Aiken, and they helped me get into the University of Nevada. So, that's how I came to Reno.

I started school in September of 1946. I pledged Sigma Nu fraternity, and I was very active in the fraternity. During those years, I was involved with food, and I fed the football team for a couple of years. From that, I got the idea to open a boarding table for veterans that didn't go into fraternities. My boarding table was located in the Blue and Silver, which was next to the Wolf Den on Ninth Street. I operated it for an entire year. I was serving all those veterans when the Korean war started in 1950. All the late veterans that didn't see combat in World War II got re-called. The marines wanted me to re-enlist and run a tank company. Luckily, I turned it down. In December of 1950, they got the shit knocked out of them in making a beachhead in one of MacArthur's great blunders in Korea. So, it was one of my better decisions. It probably saved my life.

When I lost all those veterans, I started a boarding table for the football team and made the mistake of giving them a lot of credit, and I lost a lot of money. But the one thing I didn't do was, I didn't sue anybody. And everybody loved me. I made all my friends in Reno because of that move. And maybe it was a good investment. I don't know.

DWAYNE KLING: Between the school sessions, during the summer months, did you go back to Oakland, or did you stay in Reno?

Well, I went back one year, and luckily I did, because while I was down there, my dad passed away with a heart seizure while fishing with me off the Golden Gate. Because of that I decided to stay in Nevada permanently. The next summer, I think it was 1948, Buddy Garfinkle and I were the only University of Nevada kids that played for the Harrah's Club baseball team. Also on the team was Wes Barkley, whose sister was Harvey Gross's[2] wife, Tommy Hill, and Andy Marcinko. And of course three guys from St. Mary's—you [Dwayne Kling], Stan Dembecki, and Carroll Canfield.

Tell us a little bit about why the casinos sponsored the teams in those years.

Well, in those years, you know, Reno was a great sports town. Semi-pro baseball was very popular. And in the San Joaquin Valley of California, softball was awfully popular. Harolds Club had a championship softball team. I played softball for an outfit called Du Pratt's, but on our fraternity team, we had Thornton Audrain, Al Barbieri, and a fellow named Frank Tachino, who were probably the best pitchers in Nevada softball. Again, I made a lot of friends. I didn't know anybody when I got here. Athletics was a big thing in those days.

When we played for Harrah's, nobody could spell the name because everybody thought it was Harolds Club. Every place you went in the west—Utah, Idaho, Nevada, California—you'd see "Harolds Club or Bust"; it was a big thing. When our team was traveling we used to go in John Harrah's car. He had a big Packard convertible.

So, baseball was a way of getting the name out into the public?

Yes. We went to Susanville. We went all over. The year that we had this good team, we played Harolds Club for $10,000. Now it doesn't sound like much, but then it was a lot. The game was played at Moana Stadium. In those days Bill Harrah and Bob Ring were big drinkers. Harrah wasn't a big gambler at the time, but Harold Smith was, and there really wasn't a hell of a lot of love between the two organizations that I can remember.

Bob Ring and a guy named Al Lansdon were the contacts for Bill Harrah. Harold Smith went on the pitching mound before the game and declared the bet as $10,000. I didn't start the game, but in the middle of the game I was sent up to pinch hit. Two or three people were on base, and I happened to connect with one, and I hit it to right field and hit the fence; and I laughed so hard, I fell over second base and only made a triple. I should have made a home run. Then, you and Dembecki got some hits and we beat them real bad.

Bill Harrah and Bob Ring won $10,000 on the game, and we were big heroes. Everybody loved us for a couple of days.

Where did you meet your wife?

Well, she was a popular southern Nevada girl. She was from a famous ranch family in Lincoln County called the Conaways. Her name was Geneve Conaway. She was really an exceptional horse woman, and she had been in the Helldorado in Vegas a few times. She liked baseball and went to the games with Scherry Harrah. They became good friends when Geneve was in college, and that friendship lasted for a long, long time.

So, you met your wife at the University of Nevada?

Yes. We were married twenty-five years with three children. She was quite a gal and an asset to my success in life.

Shortly after I got out of school my father-in-law died, and there were estate problems. There was a big cash flow problem, so we went down to Caliente. We lived down there about three years. We had our second child down there. We liked Caliente. I liked the people, and I had a wonderful mother-in-law.

My brother-in-law ran the ranch, but he didn't like animals. He was a great farmer and very astute with the BLM policies. We had a range fifty by sixty miles, and he was quite busy with that. I spent maybe the last nine months down there just riding and branding cows. We branded about 900 of them one year. We culled the herd down from about 3,000 cows to about 1,000 cows, and the ranch started making money, but I decided I wasn't a rancher. I didn't want to be a rancher, and my wife actually missed Reno (she liked northern Nevada) so we decided to go back to Reno.

Pat France was working at Harrah's Club. He was the head cashier. I knew Pat from the University of Nevada. He and I were house managers together. He was the house manager of Sigma Epsilon house, and I was at Sigma Nu. Pat offered me a job in the cashier's cage, and the same day I was offered a job at Semenza & Kottinger, an accounting firm. Gambling wasn't that acceptable then, and my wife was always guided by the respectability of her mother, so she asked me to go to work for the accounting firm–which I wanted to do anyway.

There were a lot of accountants that worked for Semenza & Kottinger, and if you wanted to be a CPA in Nevada, you had to work for S & K. We worked long hours, and we didn't get very much pay, but they were good to us. We had some super clients, and we learned a lot, but I never became a CPA. I wanted to start making some money, and CPA's in those days didn't make any money. I had two children and had just got through paying off all my debts, and I didn't owe a dime. I bought a Meyers house, and I was respectable. Across the street was Ed Reed who ended up being a federal judge and was my friend in college.

I stayed with S & K for three years, and because of my ranch background, I became real close to Joe McMullen, who was from Star Valley. Joe was the accountant for lots of ranches in Alturas, and he took me along to carry the briefcase. I was always a good cost accountant; I wasn't a real good accountant, but I could cost. My mind went into units and so on. So, during tax season, we did all the ranches. And during the summer, they would assign you to do a gambling joint. (In those days we called them all gambling joints.) One summer I spent a month at the Riverside learning the cashier's cage. (The Riverside was a premium hotel in those days.)

Did you also do audit work at Harrah's?

What happened was that Joe McMullen was a junior partner at S & K, and he was doing Harrah's Club; and then, all of sudden, Harrah gets involved at Lake Tahoe. Joe spent a little time up there, and he knew my background of ranching and the boarding table I had ran in college. He also knew I had written a study that I called "Portion Control." So he knew I understood food. Because of that Joe assigned me to Harrah's Club. They segregated the Lake Tahoe bills (Tahoe wasn't open yet), and I ended up auditing the Lake Tahoe function.

Harrah's had hired John Hastings as the manager of their food operation. No one in Harrah's knew anything about food. The summer before, I had been the resident auditor at the Cal-Neva, and (I'm using names because I hate thieves) Del Monte Meat had a kickback going with the chefs at the Cal-Neva. I caught them, and I made a big deal out of it with my lovely Italian voice. That's why I'm so obnoxious. I'll never forget them. I can even identify them now. There were three cooks, and I remember waving the invoices, and everybody denying they signed them. [laughter]

Anyhow, the first time I go to Lake Tahoe, Shep drove me up in his own station wagon.

We found out we were both Sigma Nu's. We found out that we both knew a lot of people in Reno, and that I was not a newcomer. We were both enlisted men in the service. He was a sergeant, and I was a corporal, and for some reason, we just became friends. We hit it off right away.

This is a true story: I went down into the kitchen the second day to meet John Hastings, and one cook looked at me, and I looked at him. I said, "Geez, I know you." The guy took his apron off and took his knives, wrapped them up, and walked right out and quit. He walked right out the back door. Hastings looked at me, and I said, "You guys don't want those kind of cooks at Harrah's." Hastings pretty near wet his pants. Two days later, he quit.

I didn't ever say a word to him, but I went upstairs, and I said to Shep, "The one thing I learned years ago when I had my own restaurant is that you don't leave the back door open, Shep." He went right out and hired twenty-four hour security. I then went down to Reno, with his permission, and ordered a big food scale. And we did two things: We watched the back door, and we weighed the meat. [laughter] And we taught the security guy how to count the cases that came in. Everybody thought I was the greatest food man in the world.

Did you go to work at Harrah's after that?

No. I stayed there for the summer. I had been moonlighting, and I had three jobs. I was the Little League baseball commissioner, I did the books for the meat company, I did the payroll for a milk company, and I had my job, and I lived like a king. But I was having trouble because, when I'd go home Saturday afternoons from Lake Tahoe, I'd spend the next twenty hours doing the work I was doing for those other two companies plus the baseball program. At the end of the summer Shep had just been promoted to controller, and he asked me if I wanted to come to work

for Harrah's Club. I think the only reason my wife approved was the fact that she never saw me, and she figured she'd see me a little more. So, I moved to Lake Tahoe and went to work for Harrah's in 1955. They opened in June of 1955, and I went up there three weeks after it opened. But I wasn't an employee. I worked for S & K until I went to work, officially, for Harrah's Club on November 1, 1955.

What was your first job?

Well, I was hired as office manager. My problem was that I liked to work, and I knew a little about everything. I knew about purchasing, so we developed a purchasing department. I knew all the thieves in the food business, and we reorganized who we bought from. We were the first ones to start buying in Reno. Lake Tahoe had never bought in Reno before. They were always using Sacramento or Stockton. Reno didn't have that many big food places at that time. We changed to a Gardnerville milk company; I forget the name in Gardnerville. It sounds funny, but I did a little bit of everything.

The cashiers were so busy, and Pat France was so busy. The cashier's cage was a constant problem, because they went from a little place in Reno to a place where there was really some action. We had tons of action. The old saying during the winter was that you could either shoot a cannon through the casino or you were packed. It was a high-low deal, very valley-peaked then, which was hard to schedule. We had no personnel office, so in my office, if you want to call it that, we did the interviewing. We didn't do the hiring. Harrah's always let department heads hire, but we screened them. We just did everything.

So, Pat France was the credit manager?

Yes. Harrah's had never had big credit like they did at the lake. In Reno a twenty-five dollar check was a big thing. Up there there were bigger checks because a guy would come up less, and they'd spend a little more money. And credit took a little more work. Pat did a super job on credit. That's why Rome Andreotti liked Pat. Rome was the swing shift manager, and he would never OK a check in his life. Yet he had the busiest shift up there. Pat had to work the whole shift with Rome, and I used to kid Pat that I had to do his work because he was doing Rome's.

Rome Andreotti was not one of my favorite people. I thought he was overrated. There were so many good people that worked for Harrah's Club. In this period we're talking about, about two years after this period, Holmes Hendricksen and Lloyd Dyer came to work there. And they were super, especially Homer [Holmes' nickname]. On first impression, Lloyd probably had a better personality, but as you got to know Holmes, he had the better personality. But, work-wise, Holmes was astute, besides being a good golfer. [laughter] They were two good guys. They were high caliber people.

There were very few college graduates that went to work in the gaming industry then. I happened to be one of the first. A lot of guys had gone to college for a year, but they never finished, and nobody had even heard of "personnel" at the time. Personnel, in the early days, was a secretary.

Red Farnsworth was a guy that was important in Harrah's. He eventually became a vice-president of Harrah's Club. He was very underrated. Nobody ever knew even who Red Farnsworth was. All he did was watch Bill Harrah's cash, and that was pretty important, because Bill Harrah had valleys and peaks with cash—one day he'd have cash, and the next day the cashier's cage was down to zip; had chips in it, but no cash. Red was great at converting coin into currency and so on, and as far as I know (and I checked everybody out), he had fingers that wouldn't take a penny.

Red was an old circus and carnival man—he had apprenticed handling cash for the circus. Lots of gaming people came from carnies. Old "Pappy" Smith from Harolds Club was a carny guy, John Harrah was. Harrah was an attorney, and he was mayor of Venice, but he was also a carny guy with bingo. He and Bob Ring used to sit there and figure out the angles of how to pop a balloon, and they were really great, which eventually led on to their keno thinking. All these things magnified in the northern Nevada gaming industry. And I don't mean it facetiously, but there was nothing in Vegas.

One thing about Harrah's, they paid good. They didn't pay as good as Vegas, but they would give you a lot of fringes. I never made any real big money at Harrah's Club, but I had a company car and a full expense account, and I could take my wife and family to dinner once in awhile. It just gave you a whole different way of life. And I always said Bill Harrah never wanted you to become real wealthy, because you wouldn't work for him any longer. And I always said he wanted you to spend about $1,000 more than you made in a year so that you'd be in debt. [laughter]

⋅⟡⋅

In 1955 Bob Ring and Mr. Harrah went down to California to meet a fellow named Ackerman. Ackerman was the biggest person in the country in transportation. He controlled a company called California Parlor Cars. It was a spinoff from Greyhound. Ackerman was the president of all the Greyhounds before they split into Greyhound West, Greyhound South, and Greyhound whatever. So Harrah and Ackerman made a deal, and then Bob Ring followed through. They hired a fellow named Jim Woods from Reno that was famous in transportation.

When I first started full time for Harrah's Club, I put a cost system in for buses the first day I was there. The bus program was run by a PR guy from Reno, a guy named Joe Harbaugh. He didn't know as much about buses or accounting as that wall over there, but he was a good guy. And somewhere along the line–how it happened I can't tell you–I ended up running the bus program.

In those days, we ran four or six buses a day out of Sacramento. (We just had Sacramento.) They were Greyhound buses, and the problem was when they made the deal, they gave Greyhound a guarantee. I think they were thirty-seven seat passenger buses in those days. Say they gave them a guarantee of thirty a bus–well, if they only had twenty customers, Harrah's still owed them for ten empty seats. But if they had thirty-seven customers on the bus, and there was guarantee of thirty, they didn't get credit for the other seven. You could see it after about two invoices, and it wound up being a debit-credit account.

We had a phony deal, because on weekends, even in the winter if the road was clear, we were running quite a number of buses out of Sacramento. (During the time we're talking about, the bus program was the biggest expenditure Harrah's had. It was five million bucks, and it really got big. We expanded into San Francisco and Oakland for awhile. We tested San Jose and Tracy, but it didn't work.)

One of the next problems was that we didn't know who got on the bus. Bill Goupil and I were having lunch one day with Bill Harrah, and Bill Goupil said, "Lee and I were talking, and we figured out a guy could save three dollars a day by traveling the Harrah's Club bus." (Bill Harrah has his eyes wide open.) Goupil says, "He buys a ticket in Sacramento and gets a refund from the casino when he gets to Lake Tahoe. So now he's got the cash. He had to invest in the first ticket, but now we give him a split of champagne and a meal. The guy's got drunk. He had a meal. He had a nice trip through the pines of Lake Tahoe, and he still has his three dollars." [laughter]

We then put a security guard and a representative at the bus depot in Sacramento. At first, we had a Greyhound guy we paid overtime to, but then we hired a guy to screen the passengers.

You would just look at them to see what they looked like?

Yes. We just looked at them and their appearance and so on. Anyway, we would screen the customers.

You couldn't screen them for the amount of money that they had on them?

No, but how they looked and their appearance. We really watched who got on the bus.

As far as their nationality?

Yes, and a few other things.

One day I got a call from my bus representative in Sacramento, and I said, "What's going on?"

I can't quote him exactly, but there was either one or two–actually they didn't use those terms in those days–civil rights workers, or, in those days, it was the NAACP, and he said, "They want to get on our bus."

And I said, "What did you do?"

He said, "I don't know what to do."

I said, "Tell them the bus doesn't work. Cancel it." And I said, "Tell them you had to cancel the whole thirty-nine people." So we canceled that bus. Then they went over to Stockton the next day, and I canceled that bus. [laughter] Then I phoned Bob Ring (he always wanted to know what was going on), and I also entered it in the Harrah daybook system.

About a week later, we start getting letters from the NAACP, and everything was referred to me. Harrah was a great straight-liner, so everything came right down to me because I had made the decision. I said, "Hey, that bus didn't work." We stayed with that decision, and we did it for a few more times, but we finally changed our policy.

But this was not just Harrah's in those days. Actually, most casinos did not cater to the black people, did they?

Only a few casinos did. We never eighty-sixed a black person, but nobody catered to them. They'd come to cash a check, and nobody would cash the check. You'd say, "Geez, we need your driver's license." We didn't encourage them to come in any part of the building.

◇

Joe McMullen gave me an old car to drive to work. He was getting rid of it, and he gave it to me. It was an old Plymouth, probably a 1937 or 1938–they all looked alike in those days. So I had this old Plymouth. Johnny Desmond[3] was appearing at Harrah's, and he wanted to go to the west side of the lake or something. I say, "Hey, John, take my car." So I gave him the car.

Later that night Bill Harrah came by my office, and while he's there Johnny Desmond puts the key back on my desk. He thanked me, and then they talked for two or three minutes (that's a long time with Harrah), and then they left.

The next Sunday, Bill started talking to me about the problems with entertainers, and I said housing was a big problem, and the other big problem was they were bored and they had no transportation. Boy, the next day, we had a company car up there. I mean that's how he reacted. [snaps fingers]

So then we went into housing. Somewhere along the line, I met Rose Naify. Her family owned the Naify theatre chain, and they were quite wealthy. She came up to me one day and says, "We have this big home right on the state line off of Park Avenue, right down by the dock, and I'd like to rent it to Harrah's Club." So I brought it up to Bill, and the next day we leased that place. It became the first entertainers' home. I used to say, "The one thing about going to work at Harrah's Club as an entertainer is we entertain the

entertainers." It became a slogan, and I take credit for that one.

Was there an entertainment director at that time?

Yes. Lee Frankovich bought the entertainment for awhile; then Candy Hall for two or three years. Candy Hall was good. Entertainment was a dirty business. Everybody accused everybody of kickbacks. Bob Ring would get mad at you if you drank, and Candy would have a drink once in awhile, but Ring would forget that these guys are working till three and four in the morning. Sammy Davis would always get mad if I didn't have a drink with him. But I've always said, "When a guy gets off in the daytime at five o'clock or six o'clock, and he drinks till seven or eight, nobody gets mad at him. But if a guy gets off on graveyard at ten o'clock and drinks to twelve, he's a drunk."

Now, an entertainment director comes in about eleven o'clock in the morning. He answers all these phone calls and meets with people, then he goes home and naps for two hours, and he has to be there for the first show. Well, he could run out of gas, and if he does and then has a belt or two, then he is a drunk.

If the entertainers want you to have a drink, and you don't have one, you're rude. Eldon Campbell ended up being fired because Ring thought he was a drunk. And poor old Eldon was just working late hours. Of course, Bob worked all the time, anyway. Bob didn't need to drink: he was an AA. He'd had his share earlier in life, but he was an asset to the company.

Harrah's was run really good, and the guy that really followed Bill's thinking was Bob Ring. Ring was a great company guy. He knew how Bill thought. He wasn't a yes man, but he never would argue with Bill in front of anybody. Bob was a good guy to work for. Just being around him taught me an awful lot. It was like getting a master's degree.

When they needed a PR guy at Lake Tahoe, they offered me the job, and it was such a big increase in salary I just had to take it. I liked working for Shep because he was always honest with me and he gave me a lot of freedom, but I didn't make any money. By this time I've got three kids, and I am devoted 100 percent to Harrah's Club. So I took the job, got a raise and a company car, which is a big thing.

Were you PR for just Lake Tahoe or for Reno too?

Just for Lake Tahoe. About that time Mark Curtis came to work for us as a PR director. And it was kind of funny, because, although my title was public relations, I was really doing the buses, the entertainment stuff, the public relations, and I was just doing everything. I was on the management team for Lake Tahoe, except for industrial relations. They would start the management meeting, and they'd have entertainment first, then public relations. Then they'd have the industrial relations parts, which was company policy, then everybody'd leave. The big part was entertainment and public relations and advertising.

Who was the advertising person?

Dick Meltzer. He had an ad agency. He was the guy that did the big thing for Harrah's. He was really good, but when he got some big national accounts, Bill Harrah didn't think he was devoting all his time to Harrah's Club, and when you work for Harrah's, you work for Harrah's.

He also had the same dumb tendency I had. He would . . . the word *argue* is a bad word; *disagree* is a bad word too. But if you tried to explain your side to Bill, he'd turn you off, and once he turned you off, Ring could feel it. Now you keep going, you keep talking, not knowing, and now Ring starts getting in the conversation. Pretty soon, Harrah . . . he just didn't want to talk about it. Then Ring would carry on the pro and cons of it. And you'd end up with kind of a half-way little

argument. Harrah wouldn't do the argument, but Ring could tell. It was really a game they played.

The management meetings were held at Lake Tahoe on Thursdays and Reno on Wednesday. I'd go to the Reno ones about once every month. They weren't too bad. But I'll tell you, those ones at Lake Tahoe–I used to call them the "blood bath." I'd go over to Harvey's and get half gassed after the meeting. You'd go in there, and you'd be grilled for an hour or two. And I'm telling you, you had to have every answer!

Who was asking most of the questions?

Bill would go over some of them. Bill would start, and then Ring would step in. Later on, Rome tried to get into the act, and he had about as much ability as that light shade. In about one sentence I could cut him in half, because he was just being a "yes" man. All he was was a "yes" man. And you know, you could sit there and keep your job for a hundred years just by not saying anything . . . . And that's why I never had a job over the years. [laughter]

In the early days, we were very active in community service organizations. What we were trying to do at Lake Tahoe was to show them that Harrah's was reputable, that we were part of the community. I remember I was appointed to the clinic board for Harrah's Club, and that's where I met Bill Ledbetter.[4] He and I became big buddies, which eventually led to the creation of the Barton Hospital. In the early days we didn't have a doctor or a hospital at Lake Tahoe. The Barton and the Lampson families started the drive to build the Barton Memorial Hospital, and the entire community got behind it. Harrah's helped a lot with various fund raisers being held at their facilities.

When you were in public relations, was this prior to the Squaw Valley Winter Olympics?

Yes, this was before that. Mark Curtis was the guy that handled most of the Olympic coverage. Mark had a great rapport with Harrah. I've known Mark for a long time, and I like Mark, but I never could communicate real good with Mark. He and Bill had the same kind of personality, and they communicated great. Well, of course, this made a lot people, especially in Reno, a little jealous of Mark. Mark and Harrah visualized, they realized what was going to happen in Squaw Valley. Nobody knew where Lake Tahoe was in these days. In New York, they didn't even know about Yosemite. They knew Reno, the divorce capital, but nobody knew anything about Lake Tahoe. So anytime you got it mentioned, it was great. For years it was "Squaw Valley, Lake Tahoe," which was a big thing for us. That started it.

Alex Cushing had done a great job to get the Olympics there. You've got to give him a lot credit. Also, you have to give Wayne Poulson a lot of credit. Wayne was the guy that had the vision of Squaw Valley, not Cushing. But Cushing got the Olympics there, not Wayne. But anyway, those two guys saw the potential.

Mark and Bill went up to Squaw Valley, and Mark got the idea of having a hospitality house, mainly to entertain the press. Harrah's leased Cushing's house, and we did big PR there.

One thing about Harrah was that he had enough vision to see that we had to start promoting customers. We've got this big showroom, and, although they had good customers in Reno, the big customer list started building from Lake Tahoe. At the time I was doing PR work, and I made a deal with *Queen For A Day*.[5] I did a lot of *Queen For A Day* giveaways in Hollywood with Jack Bailey. Mark had a good rapport with Army Archer[6] from L.A., so we started opening up the L.A. market about that time.

Harrah's also had about a hundred seats to the hockey games, every game. The only thing my wife ever asked me for in twenty years at Harrah's Club was to go to the hockey games. She fell in love with hockey, and I had to take her. I had to get permission to use one of those seats so she never missed a hockey match. She just loved it. It was really funny. Here's a ranch girl from Caliente, Nevada, that loved hockey, so we were there a lot.

Just prior to the Olympics Bill Harrah opened up the South Shore Room. Do you have any memories of the opening show with Red Skelton?

I remember when Red Skelton walked out on the stage and said, "Just think what God could have done if he had Bill Harrah's money." It was a beautiful room, and Red Skelton was quite a guy. I became a real good friend of he and his wife. He was asthmatic and had trouble breathing. The problem we had with a lot of entertainers at the lake was that they'd go up there, and during rehearsals their voices would crack because of the altitude. So most of them got wise. They'd have their directors do the rehearsing. But if some of them hadn't worked for a week or two, they weren't any good. I remember Teresa Brewer was one of them, and another was Gogi Grant. Even some of the men singers, like Harry Belafonte, had trouble when he went up there. It was just the high altitude and the dry air. Dry humidity. So you'd have to warn them.

Do you have anything you could tell us about the Harrah's golf tournaments and how they got started?

We decided at a management committee meeting to have a golf tournament. The key to a golf tournament was to have a lot of volunteer help, but Harrah's wasn't a volunteer organization. They paid for everything, and they used their own employees. So when we were talking, I brought up the fact that Jackie Jensen[7] had held some golf tournaments in the Bay area. Jensen held a tournament every year that helped promote his Bow and Bell restaurant in Oakland, but it was for charity, which was super. He had used a fellow named Alex Stewart to run his tournaments, and so we hired him to run the golf program and be the golf coordinator. Stewart stayed with Harrah's the entire time as the golf coordinator. The first year we gave him $5,000, and you would have thought it was a million dollars. He believed in details (everything had to be perfect), and he was one of the reasons why the Harrah golf tournaments were so successful.

What was the purpose of the golf tournaments? Was there more than one purpose?

No, there was really only one purpose. The golf tournament was a customer promotion. By that time, the South Shore Room was in operation, we owned the Stateline Club, and we had that lodge right next to the Stateline Club.

So it was used to promote the Harrah's name and also to bring in big customers, so good golfers weren't necessarily invited?

You had to be both. You had to be a good golfer and a good customer. At first we didn't have too many celebrities, but we found out that good customers like playing with entertainers. When a good customer came up when I was playing golf with Jack Benny, I might ask him if he would like to play with Benny. They all liked that. They liked being around the celebrities.

The good gamblers liked being around the action, and the entertainers liked being around the action. So the entertainers had fun playing with a guy that could lose $50,000, and vice versa. Everything Harrah's did was a pyramid action–in other words, more than one purpose for doing something.

We charged some of them. We comped very few when we started, but we gave them more than that back. We took over the Tahoe

Inn, and we made sure they all had good rooms. We picked up the tab there. It wasn't a free golf tournament. Even the good customers at the first stages paid. I remember Alex Spanos wasn't a good customer at the time–he talked like he was, but he wasn't. He was probably worth $500 million or more, but he only got invited because he was a friend of Art Berberian, and Art was, at the time, probably Harrah's number-one customer.

Let's go back to the early days of Harrah's Club around the 1950s when Bill Harrah and Bob Ring were still drinking. Who was really running the club then, or who was keeping an eye on the club?

They kept an eye on it from the bar. [laughter] I first got involved with Harrah's Club when I went over there as an auditor in 1954, and I went to the lake in 1955. Then in 1956 they bought the Frontier Club. By that time, the May Company had set them up, I think, in 1952.

How do you mean, "set them up?"

They gave them an organization chart, number one. Then Bill was made the president of a private corporation that had been created. I forget what John Harrah did– John Harrah was always active, but I don't know if he had a title. I'm not sure. Bob Ring was the number two guy. Pat Mooney was the number three guy, but he and Ring didn't get along. Mooney was in accounting. Mooney was very progressive for an accountant in those days. Red Farnsworth was involved because he handled all the money. Those were the four main guys.

Was Maurice Sheppard involved in anything?

Well, he was the office manager until Mooney left. Shep was a real good detail guy, but he was real quiet. He wasn't an outward guy, but he was a loyal hard worker. But then Mooney left. I'm sure Mooney left because

Bill made the decision. It either had to be Ring or Mooney, because you could see an internal clash.

For a long time Ring was leery of Shep. In the first place, Shep never was on the floor. In those days, if you weren't on the floor, you weren't anything. Shep had been an accountant since graduating from the University of Nevada, but he didn't become controller until after I joined the organization.

Do you think Bill Harrah made the decision to go with the May Company?

It had to be Bill Harrah. I wasn't there then, but it had to be Bill Harrah. It had to have been in 1952 or 1953. That's when, I think, he quit drinking, and that's when he settled down. I think they realized that they weren't going to make it otherwise. (In this period there was some talk . . . I can't verify it, but there was a fellow named Fred Vogel whose mother was a friend of John Harrah and Bill Harrah. Fred Vogel wasn't as old as Bill, but he was a little older than me, and the talk was that his mother loaned Bill some dough when he needed some cash.)

One thing that came from the May Company study was the creation of a public relations department. Joe Harbaugh became the first public relations guy. They bought him a red station wagon, and his job was to go up and down Highway 40, which is now I-80. His job was to go to motels and restaurants and leave ashtrays and matches with Harrah's logo on them. Well, everybody thought it was something stupid, but people that owned these places couldn't afford ashtrays.

In the history of Harrah's Club, whether it was a customer or an operation or a sign location, they would screen it to make sure it was good. They wouldn't say, "OK, we're going to put up ten signs . . . ," or, "OK, we're going to service ten motels." They had to be ten *good* motels. They had to be ten *good* restaurants. Harbaugh did a great job. I'm going to give Joe a lot of credit. He didn't stay

long for a lot of reasons, but he was there long enough.

About that time I went into public relations, and I took John Gianotti into our department. He ran the motel program full time. He went into motels up and down Highway 395 and Highway 50. The motel program was real big in those days. And the reason motel owners liked Harrah's Club, where they might not like the Mapes or the Riverside or any hotel in Reno, was we didn't have any rooms. We were not competition. We'd say, "Hey, we're not going to steal your bed from you." All they had to sell was a bed. All we had to sell was pit, slots, entertainment, and food, so it was a great marriage.

You'd go into a good motel and give the guy a case of matches and a case of ashtrays. That was how Harrah's developed the market. It was by little things and by being consistent. You wouldn't ship a guy some ashtrays and then forget him for ten years. You'd go back, maybe every six weeks, and ask him, "Did your customers like Harrah's Club?"

"No, my customers said that a Harrah's Club dealer was rude." Well, then the detail again. Our motel rep would write a little note. I'd see it, and I'd get it in the daybook, which was the big thing, as you know, at Harrah's Club. And somebody would follow through. Usually, when I'd see it, I'd follow through. But it depended on what department you were in. And boy, we might not know the dealer's name, but we'd have a meeting back in the club and narrow it down to the shift.

That was typical Harrah's Club. There were a lot of reasons for its success, but they started from scratch and became successful. And I'm not knocking Harolds Club–Pappy did that, and he was the first guy, but the family didn't continue doing it, and he never had the real good executives. You've got to have good executives; you just can't have a couple of bosses making all the dough. If you want good department heads, if you want good shift managers, you've got to pay them.

But one thing about Bill Harrah–after he paid you, he worked you.

Well, the motels were a big thing at that time. On the five miles between the state line and the junction there had to be dozens of motels.

Right. I remember when I had customer relations, I had fifty-six people working for me. Harvey Gross had just built his hotel. He had two hundred rooms, and it looked just like the Holiday–they were built by the same architect . . . piece of shit. So what we did was double our motel program, and we kept saying, "Hey, that dirty Harvey's, they've got your customers."

Then we did another thing–we put an Oriental bus program into Reno. Al Fontana [Harrah's Reno general manager] wanted to do his share of the bus program, so we put in a special one, but we only ran two buses twice a day. This was just for Reno, and it was just for Orientals. But boy, we treated them good! We had a super location on Stockton Street in San Francisco, and we had *all* the Orientals. Our bus rep was an Oriental, and we had three of them that could speak all the dialects. (We found out, with Orientals, that half of them couldn't understand the other half.)

Next we started a screening process. If a guy trying to board the bus was dirty or something, we'd say, "Well, you can't go to Reno." We'd say, "Go down to Jeanette's." (She had the bus program to the Horseshoe.) So pretty soon, now we have only the elite. We have two thirty-seven passenger buses in the morning and two more in the afternoon.

We'd give them hot chicken soup while they were waiting for their bus. That got us compliments. Then we'd give them a box lunch, because we didn't make any stops. We made sure they had bathrooms on the buses–Greyhound had to give us bathrooms. And that bus program, for about three years, was the best program we ever saw.

We worked hard on that program, and we used to do daily costs. Bill knew every day what all the bus programs cost; the box lunches cost about $2.65. Now, I felt these bus customers to Reno were worth about forty, fifty bucks a person. One day there was a meeting in Reno, and they knocked out the box lunches. I was out of town and missed the meeting. Well, that program fell in half and never did recover. You just don't take away things from people, and that was one of my *big* arguments with Rome Andreotti.

Could you tell us about your work with the community affairs department at Harrah's?

What happened was I got passed over for being a vice-president. And, consequently, I wasn't on the management committee anymore, but I got a better job. I was named director of community affairs, and I worked for Shep and Bill Harrah personally. But I got bored. I'm a great company guy if I can give you my input, but if I can't give you input, I don't want to work for you because it's stupid. And after about a year, I got bored, but during that year I went to many meetings for Harrah's Club, and I did many different things that were good for the community.

I was one of the founders of and first president of Barton Hospital. I was the chairman of the airport commission at Tahoe, and I got the airport expanded. You know, Harrah did a great thing for the airport. He bought the land around the airport because when it first opened, the first landing strip, about 6,500 feet, was a quarter of a degree off, so the whole alignment of the land was out of kilter. When the strip was expanded to 10,000 feet, the alignment problem was solved. I was responsible for putting the control tower up there, with the help of Senator Cannon. He did it. We borrowed the land from–with a county guarantee–Placerville, which was in Eldorado County. And it was owned by the Barton and Ledbetter family. We bought it, and then we held it in trust. And every year the county would buy certain parts of it back and get reimbursed by the federal government. So in five years, Harrah had his money back. But if it weren't for Harrah, they wouldn't have had a good airport at Lake Tahoe. Nobody ever knew about that.

It was like the reservations: We would make probably 5,000 room reservations a week–free–for all the motel owners at Tahoe. We'd have their availability through our San Francisco office, and we'd just automatically do it and then teletype it to them the next day. Nobody even knew about it. It was just good customer relations.

The Ledbetters from Harvey's Wagon Wheel started running little courtesy buses from the motels to their club. So, typical Harrah's Club, we didn't want to do little buses. Through Jim Woods–actually, Jim Woods fronted it, but we financed it–we got the Yellow Cab franchise. And Bill Harrah wouldn't have a bad cab. He went back east personally to check on the construction of the cab frames and bodies. Bill's remark was, "I don't want people hitting their head when they're getting in the back seat." So we would have made reservations for a customer in San Francisco; the customer would come to that motel; and when he was ready to come to Harrah's, he would call the dispatcher, and the customer relations department would then send the Yellow Cab to his room. Then all the customer had to do was sign his name. He didn't have to pay the Yellow Cab. We had great drivers–they were clean; they weren't winos. This is just another kind of thing that Harrah's did.

There was some big money play at the lake. My famous story . . . I wasn't there, but it's a true story: When they opened Harrah's Club at Lake Tahoe, they decided to take the drop boxes off only once every twenty-four hours. Bob Ring, the shift manager, Bill Goupil, and Bill Harrah went in to count the money. They couldn't leave once they started, and Harrah got so tired of counting money that day–I don't how long he was in there– that he never went back in the count room,

ever! And they started counting every shift after that.

I can't remember what the other casinos were doing, but there was just a lot of money at different times, and, of course, a lot of times there wasn't. But I always said we sent more money down than Reno sent us up. [laughter] And we never had an armored car. Farnsworth would put it in the trunk of his car. Later on, we did have armored car delivery.

—❖—

In 1963 I resigned from Harrah's. Sewage was always a big problem at Lake Tahoe, and a friend of mine and I formed a private utility company. After about two months, the California South Tahoe Public Utility District wouldn't let us use their right-of-way, and the whole thing fell apart. So then I became a consultant. I helped J. K. Bourne put in his Round Hill sewer plant. I was responsible for that, and I did a lot of consulting work for the Bourne family after that. So I helped export the effluent out of Lake Tahoe, and I was the driving force behind the construction of Barton Hospital. I always felt those two things should get me into heaven. [laughter]

Next, I became the chairman of the Douglas County Planning Commission. I was the first appointee on the original agency–the others were elected officials. But then I was getting bored again, and since I loved the casino business, I got back in it. Hughes Porter owned the Riverside Hotel, and he had leased it to these guys from Stockton who quickly lost two million bucks. (They put about a million bucks into refurbishing the Riverside, and then they lost a million bucks operating it.) When they were a little late with a payment to Porter, Porter arranged a deal that enabled me to become a partner in the Riverside and be its general manager for a little over a year.[8]

Late in 1964 we sold the Riverside to a group led by Bernie Einstoss. I had moved my family down to Reno, but now I wanted to go back to the lake. The Tahoe Sahara was opening, and I thought about going to work for them, and then I saw Bill Ledbetter, my old pal from Harvey's. He offered me a job at Harvey's setting up a customer relations program. It was probably the easier job of the two, so I went to work for the Wagon Wheel in June of 1965.

I really learned the food business at the Wagon Wheel. Also, I put together a customer relations program that turned out to be real successful. Harvey Gross knew a fellow named Joey Yip who controlled the Oriental gambling in Stockton, Lodi, and Sacramento, and was well known in San Francisco. He had been put out of business by the Kefauver committee. They called him Uncle Joe, and I'm going to tell you, if he knew one Oriental, he knew two billion of them. And he was great. He didn't know anything about credit, but he knew a lot of people, and everybody he knew could spend five hundred or a thousand dollars. Well, it doesn't sound like much, but when you know a lot of them, they add up. Joe would never OK a check. Old time gamblers, they were all cash guys. I call them "Del Monte gamblers," you know, where they put all their money in tin cans and they smell like tomatoes. That's my old joke. Anyway, with Joey Yip's effort and a little bit of my encouragement, we really competed with Harrah's.

I didn't make an awful lot of money at Harvey's, but I did good, and I had fun. I really enjoyed learning the food business from their chef, Mr. Wallers, and the hotel operation from Dick Schofield. He was great—probably as good a guy as I've ever been around.

About how long did you stay at Harvey's Wagon Wheel?

Five years. And then I had a chance to run the Holiday. A corporation in Arizona had hired me. I went to Reno and reorganized the Holiday, but they couldn't get licensed. When they couldn't license, I went to the Gaming Control Board. They put me with Nate Jacobsen, who owned the King's Castle

Hotel-Casino at Incline Village. I liked Nate Jacobson, but I couldn't work for those guys from Vegas—they were different kinds of guys—and I wanted to move back to Reno so my kids could go to high school there.

My son had gone through a little drug problem at the lake, and I had put him in a prep school in Arizona. I knew I couldn't afford to put all my kids in prep schools, so I went down to Reno and saw Shep, and he talked to Bill Harrah, and I became the only executive they ever hired back at Harrah's Club. I must have done a good job the first time, or they felt sorry for me. [laughter]

I went back to Harrah's in October of 1969. In fact, the day I went back was the day the hotel opened up. Actually, I'm sure the reason they hired me was that I explained what I had done for Harvey's and how I had worked the front desk into the pit. I had learned this from Bernie Einstoss and the old gamblers—you know, the front desk is very important to the pit. There was a little pit, about eight games, by the front desk at Harrah's. I wanted to be able to raise the minimum bet there from one dollar to three dollars and then go right up. Rome and Mert Smith wanted to go from one dollar to five dollars, and I said, "No, there's certain times you should go from one to three."

So Rome and Mert said, "Well, we have to have a unit bet." It took six weeks to get the three-dollar chips. We used them one day, and they were a bust. We took them out and started using tokens on those six or eight games. In one day we made $18,000 more. It was a great location, by the front desk. Guys waiting to get into the hotel would make a bet, and it was great.

You could move the minimums from one to three to five to ten. Women would play a three-dollar game; why have a one-dollar game, you know? To me, a one-dollar game, even in those days, didn't pay the dealer wages, didn't pay the heat bill or the wear and tear on the carpet. They found that out in the slot machines: a nickel won't do you any good, but five of them make a quarter. It's the same unit deal. Anyway, we made a lot of money at Harrah's Club, and I feel very responsible. Another thing I did at Harrah's Club was improve room service. They didn't know anything about room service. Anyway, we wound up teaching them how to run a hotel, and we made the Steak House the best restaurant in town, although I didn't work in it.

See, the one thing I had going for me was the fact that I could always see Shep (which I very seldom did), so I had a line to go see Bill if I wanted to. Now, a few times I did go see Bill, but I never went to Bill about any individuals, not even about Rome. When everybody stalemated me on baccarat, I remember going right to Bill with Shep and telling him what baccarat was doing in Vegas. And when they put it in at the lake, and they wouldn't put it in Reno, I went to Bill again. Then they put it in, but they never ran it right. I found out that they had two different sets of rules–Rome again. Liberal rules at Lake Tahoe and stringent rules in Reno. And we blew some good customers. I mean, you have to be consistent.

Reno is not a baccarat town; but I had some customers at the time that really wanted to play baccarat, so I'd end up putting them in the limousine, and we'd go to the lake. I'd go with them, so I'm up there with no authority except to OK money, of course. And it was getting to be a bore. I got tired of bringing customers up there, so I'd teach them how to play craps. Then Shep got sick, and that kind of broke my heart. He was my friend.

My years with Harrah's Club at the end weren't happy. I had to fight Rome on everything I did. I had to do everything the hard way because Rome was my boss. Rome was probably a nice guy, but we clashed. He and I had had a personal problem at the lake, and he brought it back. He kept it with him. He brought the personal problem into the business, and that was wrong.

After I was back five or six years, Rome finally found an excuse to get rid of me. I didn't mind him firing me, because they did make a big payment to me, but he clouded my name for a long time, and he shouldn't have, because I didn't do anything. Everything that I did, I had to fight him, but I won all the time.

You worked at Harrah's, the second time, from 1970 to about 1976?

Yes, 1976, something like that. When I tried–with some customers–to buy the Horseshoe, and Harrah found out about it, he fired me without any notice. But the funny part about it was, just before we made the deal at the Horseshoe, I was going to be their first key employee to ever be licensed. So when they fired me, they couldn't have fired me for the job I'd done. They wouldn't have had me be a key employee. And what they did was–it was typical Harrah's–they paid me for a year, but they paid me through an attorney, Clark Guild. It was kind of severance pay deal.

Did you go to work anywhere that year?

Well, I was all lined up to go to work at the MGM. They had just opened up, and they phoned Rome to see what kind of a guy I was; and Rome said it would serve no purpose having me work there, because I was always trying to buy a casino, which was wasn't quite true. I had told Harrah's when I went back that I would never, and I never did, take any Harvey's customers back into Harrah's Club. It was not my style. But Harrah's said, "Well, you're going to take our customers to the MGM," and I said, "No, I won't. I just want to go to work for a big outfit." We'd failed to buy the Horseshoe, and there weren't that many other good places around to buy. I just wanted to go to work, but Rome shadowed me for years.

By shadowing, you mean that whenever you'd go to get a job, he would say something?

Yes. I'd have to use Harrah's as reference, and by that time, Shep's sick as heck. And Lloyd Dyer didn't know anything about operations, so they'd always pointed to Rome, and Rome just put the kiss of death on me.

Do you have any last story or recollection of Bill Harrah you'd like to mention?

The last one is a sad one, because I wasn't at Harrah's when Bill died. Most of the time I worked nights in Reno, and when Bill didn't have anybody else to have dinner with, he'd have it with me. We got along good, because he liked some of the stories I'd tell him. And then he'd tell me a couple. But before he went back to Mayo for his heart deal the first time, he was kind of nervous about it. In fact, he didn't really eat a heck of a lot of dinner. By then he was having a glass of wine or a drink or two. (After he divorced Scherry, I think he had a few belts.) He knew I liked wine, so we did have some wine. He explained what they were going to do at the Mayo Clinic, what he thought they were going to do, and what his problem was.

When he came back, I don't remember whether I went to see him in his office or if we had dinner again, but I said, "Geez, aren't you glad you weren't nervous about any of it? It didn't matter how bad you felt, you turned out good."

And he said, "Yes." Because Bill didn't show you his feelings, but he was very happy, and I'm sure he was happy with his new marriage.

I'd see him a little bit after I left Harrah's Club, but not much because of my conflict with Rome. Soon after that, he died. When he went back for his second operation nobody expected him to die. It was a sad way to go. Bill was a private guy, so he died privately, and that's the way it was. It was a sad thing, because he did a lot for a lot of people.

People have different opinions of Bill, but the one thing I felt he did for the industry was he brought respectability to the gaming industry. Good people liked going to work for him, because you weren't working for a bunch of hidden interests. He was careful who he surrounded himself with, and when you worked for him, you had to be pretty careful. Bill was good. He brought dignity to the industry, and people forget that. Plus, he raised the salaries, and he was the first guy that made women pit bosses and women executives. Bill wasn't a pioneer when it came to minorities or blacks or pinks; but when it came to women, he always treated them with respect, and for a casino, they made pretty good money. You've got to give him a lot of credit there.

Bill Harrah was the best in the industry, along with Pappy and maybe a couple in Vegas. But as far as Benny Binion and those other guys . . . you know, they couldn't carry his socks, as far as the real way to run a casino. That's all I have to say.

Notes

1. Jim Aiken was the University of Nevada football coach at the time.
2. Harvey Gross was owner of Harvey's Wagon Wheel, now known as Harvey's.
3. John Desmond was a very popular singer in the 1940s and 1950s who appeared at Harrah's in the 1950s and 1960s.
4. Bill Ledbetter was a top executive at Harvey's Wagon Wheel for many years. He was also owner Harvey Gross's son-in-law.
5. *Queen For A Day* was a long-running radio and TV show that selected a contestant and gave her her wish for one day. Jack Bailey was the master of ceremonies.
6. Army Archer was a noted Hollywood columnist.
7. Jackie Jensen was an All-American football player at the University of California and a major league baseball player for many years.
8. In February 1963, Hughes Porter purchased the Riverside Hotel with a $3.5 million loan from the Southwest-Southeast Pension Fund of the Teamsters' Union. In July 1963, the following

individuals, doing business as the Chapter S Corporation, leased the Riverside gaming operation from Hughes Porter: Calvin (Red) Swift, Jack Streeter, Leonard Wykoff, Don Hall, Cliff (John) Sanford, John Sommers, Ferdie Sievers, Richard Fraser, James Ensign, and Neil Johnson.

In June 1964, Hughes Porter facilitated an arrangement under which Lee DeLauer purchased 25 percent of the stock in the Riverside's gaming operations, the Chapter S Corporation controlled 25 percent, and the remaining 50 percent was left in treasury (unused/unpurchased) stock. Having 50 percent of the *owned* stock, DeLauer had operational control and was made general manager of the Riverside Hotel. The gaming operations began bringing in money, and the fortunes of the Riverside were looking better, so in October 1964, following a meeting in Chicago with teamster leader Jimmy Hoffa, DeLauer and the Chapter S Corporation joined together and took over Porter's loan from the pension fund, thus purchasing the Riverside. Within a month, the hotel and casino operations were bought by Bernie Einstoss, John Richards, and Andrew Desimone. DeLauer remained with the Riverside for a few months to complete various business transactions.–ed.

6

EUGENE DIULLO

*E*UGENE DIULLO *was Harrah's first keno manager. Diullo was born in San Pietro, Italy, on March 14, 1913. He came to Ely, Nevada, in 1921, and moved to Reno in the 1930s.*

Diullo was interviewed in his home in Reno in May of 1997. He was an extremely friendly and cooperative chronicler, and the interview took two sessions to complete.

Diullo grew up in Ely, played on the Ely High School state championship basketball team, and worked in casinos in Ely in the 1930s. He tells of coming to the Reno-Lake Tahoe area in the late 1930s, working at the south shore of Lake Tahoe in the summers and at the Palace Club in Reno during the winters. He had learned about keno in Ely, but his first casino job was that of a bartender. He eventually went to work in the keno department of the Palace Club.

Mr. Diullo was hired by Warren Nelson to work the graveyard shift at Harrah's on the day that Bill Harrah opened his first casino, June 20, 1946. He later became a shift supervisor and still later became Harrah's first keno manager.

This oral history describes many things about keno that have never been openly discussed before.

Most of the early-day keno writers were from Montana, and Diullo recalls some of them from the Palace Club. He discusses how early keno writers cheated and stole money from the house and how various measures were put in place to prevent this. In addition he goes into some detail about the art of keno writing, explaining how writers held their brushes and how a keno writer's stroke was as individualistic as his signature.

EUGENE DIULLO: I was born in Italy in a town called San Pietro on March 14, 1913. My parents were both born in Italy, and my father came to the United States when he was eighteen years old and worked in the coal mines in Pennsylvania. He evidently had met my mother before he came to the United States, and he went back to Italy and married her. Then he came back to the United States to work so that he could have enough money to send for us. I was conceived in Italy, and I didn't see my father until I was seven years old.

When my mother and I came to the United States we came directly to Ely, Nevada. My father had moved from Pennsylvania to Ely because there were a lot of countrymen of his working in Ely, and they had sent for him, because they had a job for him. They stuck together as countrymen.

DWAYNE KLING: Do you have any brothers and sisters?

I have one brother and one sister. They are both younger than I am and they were both born in Ely.

I have been married to Lena Digino for fifty-seven years, and we have three sons. Our oldest son, Gene, is a therapist, and lives in Springfield, Missouri. Our second son, Robert, is in Las Vegas working as a shift manager in the Monte Carlo, and our third son, Dennis, lives at Incline Village and is a property manager there.

I came to Ely when I was seven and grew up there. I went to White Pine High School and graduated from there in 1931. In high school I was involved in football, basketball, and track. We won the state championship in basketball in 1930, and we were invited to the national tournament in Chicago. At the national tournament, we won our first game. We defeated Cambridge, Maryland. We were defeated in the second game by a team from New Jersey. That was one of the biggest thrills of my life, to play in the national tournament.

After I completed high school, I went to work in McGill for Kennecott Copper Company. I worked in construction for a few years, and then I became a bartender at the Miner's Club in Ely. I also learned how to write keno at the Miner's Club.

My first job in the Reno/Lake Tahoe area was at the Stateline Country Club on the south shore of Lake Tahoe. I worked there the summers of 1940 and 1941. It was owned by Nick Abelman, Steve Pavlovich, and Burt Riddick. I had worked for Burt in Ely, and he asked me to go to work at Stateline.

At that time the only other clubs there were the Main Entrance and the Nevada Club. Where Harvey's is now, there was a Baptist church. (The church utilized the property as a summer camp for their members.)

The clubs were only open about three months a year, at the lake from Memorial Day to Labor Day. Most of the people who worked at the Stateline Club in the summer went to Reno and worked at the Riverside Hotel when the season ended, because the same three people owned both places.

What did you do in the winter? Did you go back to Ely, or did you go to Reno?

I went back to Ely in 1940. Then in 1941 I moved to Reno. Lena and I were married in 1940.

What did you do that winter in Reno, after you came back from Lake Tahoe?

I went to the Palace Club as a bartender. I worked as a bartender for only a short time before they needed keno writers, and I was transferred to the keno department at the Palace.

In December of 1941 the war started. What did you do then?

I moved to Oakland and worked in the shipyards down there. I stayed at the shipyards until after the war was over. I came back to Reno in 1945 and went to work at the Carlton for a short time. When Bill Harrah opened up his casino on Virginia Street, Warren Nelson[1] asked me if I would like to come over there as a keno writer. He opened in June of 1946, and I worked the first graveyard shift.

Who were some of the shift supervisors? Did they have a keno manager then?

Well, my understanding was that Warren Nelson was to be the keno manager. He purchased the keno equipment, the blower, and he set up the counter. But he never did become the keno manager. Instead he went into the pit.

Did each keno shift have a shift supervisor?

Whoever picked up the bankroll was considered the shift supervisor. At that time Jim Brady ran the swing shift, Dick Trinastich had the graveyard, and Pete Savage had the day shift.

Why did you happen to take up keno? Why didn't you go into the pit and be a dealer? Did you ever think of that?

Yes, I did think of it, and while I was working at Harrah's, a lot of the keno writers would practice dealing on their lunch break. I tried to break in on twenty-one and the wheel on my breaks, but the shift manager on graveyard didn't encourage me to learn the games. So I stayed in keno.

You said earlier you learned keno in Ely. Is that right?

Yes. I learned how to write tickets in Ely, but my first keno job was at the Palace. I just wrote in Ely on my own; I didn't get paid.

When I first went to work at the Palace, the pay was seventeen dollars a shift, and that was in 1941.

The pit always paid more than keno; in the early days of gambling, keno was always second to the pit. They pushed us around. Whenever they wanted room for slot machines, they would move a keno counter. They moved the keno counter several times while I was employed there. The pit got all the glory. And, of course, the bigger wages. Pit people always made more money than we did.

There were several pit people that started in keno and went into the pit department—people such as Warren Nelson, Clyde Bittner, Ken Watkins, and others. Was that the main reason they left keno, to make more money?

Yes, it was strictly a monetary decision. They made more money in the pit than they did in keno. Also, there was more chance for advancement in the pit. There were very few general managers that ever came out of keno. Mostly, they were pit people. The only one that I can recall was George Gilgert, who was club manager at Harrah's Tahoe.

George was working at the lake in the keno department when I was sent up there in the summer of 1963. They had problems in the keno department, and I went up there to straighten them out. We ended up firing the keno manager, the assistant keno manager, and several other people that were in the keno department. It was up to me to appoint someone to take over the keno manager job, and I chose George Gilgert, because he was the one that helped me the most up there. He never shirked on assignments, and he always had his work in on time.

He did a great job as a keno manager, and he eventually became assistant club manager, and then club manager. He was the only person that went from keno to being a club manager. He died at a very young age. I'd say he was probably like fifty-five or so when he died.

At the time that I went to work at the Palace, there was a *lot* of cheating and stealing. Keno was an easy game to cheat. They didn't have an audit, and people used to steal the management blind. One of the big changes during my career was in the microfilming of the games and the security of the games. Bill Harrah was really a stickler on security. He didn't want to lose a penny to anybody unless it was won honestly.

Keno was really a loose game that everybody could get to. A lot of inside help weren't loyal to the management at all. They thought of different ways that they could cheat the game, and there were a lot of them. I went through a lot of people, and every time that I saw how they could cheat it, I tried to find a way to stop it. I evidently did all right, because I stayed there as a keno manager for years, and there were a lot of people trying to get my job, which I found out about in a roundabout way. But they never got rid of me. Evidently, I did a good job.

Well, honesty is a very big thing.

That's true. I didn't believe in stealing. I thought if I had to steal, I'd go find a job someplace else.

When you started in keno, of course, it was called "racehorse" keno. It was called that for two reasons: first of all, to distinguish it from the Chinese lottery, which was illegal; and secondly, to distinguish it from a bingo game. Would you explain why they called it racehorse keno?

Currently, keno tickets just have numbers on them, but in racehorse keno they had racehorses' names on the bottom of each number. When you called a keno game, you called the number and the racehorse. "Number one on Nanny D, number two on Sunk . . . ." The numbers represented the jockeys.

So, you did call the number and the name?

Yes. You would call, "Number one, Nanny D; number two, Sunk; number eighty, Bright Lady."

I'm now looking at keno tickets from Harrah's Club in 1950, and some more of the horses' names are number fifty-one, Tut-Tut; number fifty-two, Casey; number fifty-four, Minty; and number seventy, Black Tom. Did every club in town have the same horses' names on the keno ticket?

No. Not all the clubs used the same names, but I think Harrah's copied the horses from the Palace. It probably was because Warren Nelson came from the Palace to Harrah's. He probably used some of the same horses' names. And, actually, nothing was copyrighted, and it didn't really make any difference.

When was the word "racehorse" dropped?

It died out around 1955. Keno was exciting in those days when the callers called out the horse's name. Customers visualized a race track and imagined they were betting on the ponies. Some customers selected the numbers because of the horses' names.

Well, did different callers add more excitement to the game?

Yes. Some callers were more colorful than others. John Morris was one of the best. He would sound just like a race track announcer. He would begin by saying, "They are off and running," and as the last two balls were going to be called he would say, "They're in the stretch, and here comes jockey number eighty on Bright Lady, and the last winning horse is number one on Nanny D." Customers loved it when he called a race. It was almost like being at the race track.

Another thing you mentioned to me earlier was the individuality of a keno writer's stroke of his brush. Could you explain that?

You could tell what writer wrote a certain ticket by the characteristics of his spots. Some writers would drag the brush and roll their wrists as they lifted the brush from the ticket and leave a little tail at the end of the spot. Others would drag their brushes without rolling their wrists, and their spots would look like a smudge. Each individual had his own method, and his stroke was as personal as his own hand writing.

The keno brushes were imported from China and were made of pig or camel hair. A good brush, properly broken in, would last about a week. Some of the better writers would solder their brushes a quarter of an inch below the handles. This helped retain resiliency in a brush. Those writers carried their brushes with them all the time. We frowned on that, because when they went on a break, sometimes there wasn't a workable brush left at the station. The relief writer would then have to get a new brush. It took time to soak a new brush, and so our productivity went down, and by making the customer wait, we hurt our customer relations.

Why did they like to keep their own individual brush with them?

Well, they broke in a brush, and they were comfortable with the resiliency of the brush. They took a lot of pride in their work. Some of the writers were like artists. The spots, conditioning, and price stood out like a picture. Curtis Harwood, who worked for the Nevada Club, wrote the most outstanding tickets in town. Some customers kept his keno tickets for souvenirs.

There was an art to writing a keno ticket, and the key was how you held the brush. Writers that came from Montana held the brush like the Chinese writers did. Jim Brady,

who came from Montana and was an excellent writer and a good instructor, taught many dealers how the brush should be held. The brush should be positioned between the thumb and the index finger, and the middle finger held the brush. The handle of the brush rested between the middle finger and the third finger. That positioned the brush handle, and your thumb was vertical to the ticket.

The wrist was cocked so that the heel of your hand rested on the keno counter. The brush never changed position while spotting, pricing, or conditioning the ticket. When spotting, you rolled your wrist, and when pricing and conditioning, the entire arm was used. When copying a customer's ticket, you spotted from right to left and from top to bottom.

Your first keno job was in the Palace Club. How did you happen to get hired at the Palace?

I was working there as a bartender, and they needed keno writers. I knew Jack Mullen,[2] and he introduced me to Warren Nelson, and I was hired in the keno department.

Was it more money to write keno than tend bar?

Yes, it was. Bartending was not a lucrative job. The customers didn't tip at all, and if they were drunk they often became belligerent, and you would get into a lot of arguments when they didn't want to pay for their drinks. A bartending job was not very desirable.

So keno was an easier way for you to go. When you first went to work for Harrah's in June of 1946, who were some of the other people working in Harrah's keno game?

Well, there was Jack Seymour, Jim McDonald, Jake Sigwart, John Howells, Noel Pryor, Pete Savage, Jim Brady, Walt

Connelly, Bill McGarry, Milo Smith, John Larsen, Jack Furman, and many others.

What year did you become keno manager at Harrah's?

In 1957. Prior to that there was no keno manager. The three shift supervisors, Pete Savage, Tommy Cavanaugh, and myself, ran the keno game.

You were called a "working" keno manager. What was that?

As a working keno manager I would run a shift. I checked tickets, ran the games at a steady pace, and handled customer questions or complaints. Customer relations was a top priority. I worked all three shifts: two swing shifts, two day shifts, and prior to my promotion I was working the graveyard shift.

When you were keno manager, who did you report to? Did you report to Rome Andreotti?

I knew Rome from when he started dealing roulette wheel–his wheel was right in front of the keno. I knew Rome real well, and I considered him a friend, but he was stubborn. Sometimes he had ideas that he thought were the only way to go, and I used to argue with him. One time he got real mad at me, and he says, "I'll let you have your way, but if you screw up, it's going to be your head." That's the way he put it. Rome had a lot to say about all departments, but I reported to the club manager, who at that time was Al Fontana.

Was Harrah's considered a desirable place to work?

Yes. The main reason people wanted to work at Harrah's was the benefits they offered, including holiday pay, which meant that anyone who had been employed four months was eligible to be paid for eight holidays a year. Also, anyone who had been

employed for one year was eligible for one week paid vacation, and after two years you were eligible for two weeks paid vacation, and after five years you got three weeks, and after fifteen years it was four weeks, and after twenty years you got five weeks paid vacation.

Harrah's also had a board of review, and that was a place where you could contest your termination and get a hearing from your equals. Along with that they had a merit program where you could get a pay raise based strictly on merit. Another real popular benefit was the employee's party. Once a year you and a guest would be invited to go to a cocktail party and a dinner show at either the South Shore Room at Lake Tahoe or the Headliner Room in Reno.

Were you given a lot of freedom, as far as who you could hire or how many you could schedule on a shift?

Yes, but club management kept a check on the wage ratio. Department managers were trained to schedule according to the volume of business. If your wage ratio was too high, you immediately heard about it. Your wage ratio was a figure derived by dividing the amount of keno write by the cost of wages.

An important part of keno is to get a certain amount of games out per hour. Did Harrah's have any procedure regarding the amount of games per hour?

We tried to run the games as soon as we got the tickets in, and the more games you got out, the more revenue you'd take in. We tried to set a pace, but there were times that you had a lot of volume, and it took longer to get the tickets processed. You couldn't always run a game when you wanted to. At our lake club sometimes the lines were so long that you had to cut off a game. You'd just say, "No more tickets," and run the game. But that created a lot of disgruntled customers. You'd have to tell a customer, "You'll be first in the next game. Just stay where you are."

The shift supervisors would write a report describing the type of action on the shift, how many games they ran, any customer complaints, and of course, any big winners. We tried for a game every five minutes—twelve an hour. But there were times when the volume was heavy and it was impossible to call a game every five minutes. One shift supervisor, in his report, said, "We ran seventy games. The action was light." Well, what else could it be, but light? [laughter]

Did Harrah's break in many keno writers?

Yes, especially during the summertime. Management recruited college students from out of state, and we would enroll them in keno school, and in about ten days they were ready to write keno.

Do you recall when women first started in keno?

I don't recall the exact year we started using women in keno. It was probably about the time they started using women twenty-one dealers, so it was in the late 1940s or early 1950s.

Harrah's was the first to employ keno runners, and it was because of a lady that was playing twenty-one. She had to leave the twenty-one game to go to the keno counter, and she said to the dealer, "Why don't you have someone collect these tickets for me so I don't have to leave the game?" Well, Harrah's had a suggestion box, and the twenty-one dealer put the suggestion in the suggestion box, and we started using keno runners. That happened around 1952 or 1953. Harrah's was the first casino to use keno runners, but it wasn't long until they were all using them.

Are there many ways to cheat a keno game?

Yes, there are lots of ways. I can't think of them all, but I know quite a few. Before we went to surveillance cameras and microfilm, keno was a pretty easy game to "get next to" if you were a dishonest employee. If a keno writer had an outside agent, it was pretty easy to run in an illegal ticket, because there was no cameras on the game.

The keno game was audited daily, and if a shortage showed up we would check it out. If the shortages occurred on days that a certain writer was working, and there were no shortages on his day off, we would sit in the catwalk over that writer and watch his movements. Most of the time we caught the guilty person. (On one occasion we observed a female keno writer giving a customer change for a fifty-dollar bill when he had only given her a one-dollar bill.)

When I first started writing keno at the Palace Club, the keno balls were in a wire cage. The cage was between two stainless steel posts. The base that the posts were mounted to was made of wood, and it was bolted to the keno counter. The cage swiveled around the posts so that the keno balls would get a good mix before the draw. The cage had a round top that screwed on the top of the cage. On the bottom was what they called a gooseneck. The gooseneck had a trap with a spring that was manipulated with your hand to release the keno balls, one at a time, from the cage, and they were placed in a ball rack so everyone could see the winning balls displayed.

Anytime keno balls were handled, there was a chance of changing the balls or holding out balls. A caller could, when placing the keno balls back in the cage, swivel the cage so the balls that had been in the rack (the previous game's winners) would go to the bottom of the gooseneck and be drawn out again as repeaters. Manipulating the balls was one of the most prevalent ways of cheating in the early days.

There was a writer who wore black cuffs up to his elbow. He would place his left arm in the money drawer, and with his right hand he would stuff currency in the cuff. He always left the counter before quitting time and then would empty the currency out of his cuffs into his pockets. He got away with it because it took place at the Palace Club, and they never audited their keno game. To me, the poorest way to run a keno game is without an audit. Anybody can put a twenty-dollar bill in their pocket, and it can't be accounted for, because if you don't audit, you are just counting money–not money against tickets.

Once several years ago in Harrah's, a new guy was promoted to assistant shift manager, and the first thing he did was to terminate the keno audit. He stated that it was not needed. (To this day I don't think that Bill Harrah was aware of it. Bill was very strict about security. He would spend hundreds to save five.) I reported to the club manager that the audit had been terminated, and he just shrugged his shoulders. The keno audit was not resumed until the assistant manager was transferred.

In those days no one wanted to get involved in turning in employees who took money. If most people saw anything, they would just turn their head. In those days a snitch was frowned on. One of our keno bosses saw something shady in the pit one day, and he reported it to management. He was interrogated as if he was involved in the scam. He said that he would never get involved again. If anyone ever got caught it was usually by one of the owners. When I worked at the Palace in 1942 the owner was John Petricciani.

A friend of mine knew a former keno manager at the Nevada Club who had been fired for stealing. This character used to hold keno cheating schools two or three nights a week. In the school they would rehearse the technique that they were going to use to cheat the club. The caller would set up the procedure. The club used an automatic punch; and when the ball was drawn, the number of the ball had to be placed in a designated hole, and then the punch automatically punched out the number.

The caller would intentionally punch the wrong hole so that there would be a mis-punched book (the paper, sometimes called a "screen," that was used to check the winning keno numbers). This would cause a commotion and a frenzy, as now a new book– with the proper numbers, the proper game numbers, and the date–would have to be made. While all this was going on, an illegal ticket would be put in on the game. The collaborators would give someone $100 to collect the ticket and then split the winnings.

This guy that taught the cheating schools and set up those illegal tickets once set up an illegal $25,000 ticket at Harolds Club. The way he did it was to mark a ten-dollar one-spot that was turned into a ten-dollar eight-spot by his confederate after the winning numbers were called. Management suspected it was an illegal ticket, but they paid it off rather than cause customer resentment. He was finally caught and wound up spending two years in jail. When I told you there was a lot of cheating in keno, I wasn't kidding.

Originally the balls were in a wire cage. After the wire cage, then what was the next step? Where were the balls kept then?

After the wire cage they had what they called a squirrel cage. It was a large bowl, kind of like a fishbowl, and they kept the balls in it. When a game started the caller would turn on a switch, and that would turn on a blower and create air pressure in the bowl, and the balls would be pushed up to the neck of the bowl. At the top of the neck there was a little gadget that was held down by springs, and you could spring that so one ball at a time would come up in your hand. After you got twenty balls, you turned off the blower and the remaining balls would settle to the bottom of the bowl.

The problem with that setup was that the keno caller was still handling the balls, and he could drop a ball or palm a ball and hold them out for the next game. You didn't have to hold out too many balls to affect a game. If somebody was playing a three-spot pretty heavily, why, it was pretty easy to hold out two or three balls.

The piece of equipment that was put in to replace the fishbowl was called "rabbit ears." The rabbit ears prevented anyone from handling the balls. I don't want to brag, but I was the one that came up with the idea of rabbit ears. I submitted the idea to Bob Ring; and soon after that, one was built in our experimental shop.

The rabbit ears was an attachment to the bowl, and it was shaped like a "Y," hence the name rabbit ears. The air pressure would propel the balls upwards and into the rabbit ears–first ten balls in one "ear," and then the next ten in the other "ear." Then the game was over and the blower was shut off.

These rabbit ears cut the cheating down considerably, because nobody touched the balls. The only way you could cheat would be if the caller called the wrong numbered ball. And that was done too! They would call the number nine whether it was in the ears or not, and the other person, who was in on it, would light up number nine. They did this especially on graveyard when there weren't many people around.

I never got any credit for the rabbit ears and never got any money for it, but they knew I had come up with the idea. They were manufactured in our experimental shop by Lee Jellison, but there were only two made there–one for the Reno club and one for the Lake Tahoe club. They proved to be highly successful, and it wasn't long until all the clubs were using them, and most of them still do.

Could you tell us what a "pit ticket" was?

On September 19, 1955, the keno limit was raised to $25,000, and Bill Harrah was concerned about the security of the game. He was concerned that someone would try to do something illegal in order to get that $25,000, so before we booked that limit we went into what we called "pit tickets."

What we did was put two spindles on the keno desk. Every ticket that could hit the limit was placed on one spindle, and the other spindle was used for the ordinary tickets. Then, before we called the game, we made duplicates of all the limit tickets, stapled them, and sent them to the pit. The pit supervisor would initial them, put a time on them, and put them in a locked box. If a large winner hit we would go to the pit and have someone unlock the box, retrieve the ticket, and check to see if we had an inside ticket on the keno desk that matched it. If we did, we of course paid the ticket.

About the same time we started the pit tickets we heard that in Las Vegas, at the Stardust, they were filming every ticket that was written. So Rome Andreotti, who was in charge of gaming at that time, and I went to Las Vegas to look at their operation. When we got back Rome said, "Well, you better look into purchasing a microfilm camera for Reno and Lake Tahoe." They were very expensive, but we bought two of them. They were Remington Rands, and they were huge. They had to be hand fed, and we filmed every ticket we wrote, and we did away with the pit tickets.

Then we found out that there was a way to get around the camera. If there was a thief working, he would hold out a group of tickets and then mark a winning ticket after the game was called and then film it. Because of this we came up with the idea of putting a spacer on the film. When you turned on the blower to mix the balls up, it automatically activated the camera and put a small space on the film. If any ticket was filmed after that space, you knew it was illegal.

Harrah's pioneered the spacer in the microfilm camera, and pretty soon every casino copied it. But we weren't fully satisfied with just the spacing in the film. We had a camera installed in the catwalk that automatically started when they started drawing the balls. The camera was set up so that it would take a picture of the empty rabbit ears; then it filmed the balls going up each side, and it showed the rabbit ears full of the twenty winning balls, and it filmed the game number. We had a processor downstairs where we developed the film, and we saw that the winning tickets were in order before we paid the ticket. It was a great security factor. Nobody could hold out any balls, and it did a lot to eliminate cheating.

Later on, instead of having one big camera that the keno supervisor fed all the tickets into, we had individual portable cameras where the writer, after he wrote the ticket, would feed it through the camera. It made it a lot faster, because the supervisor didn't have to feed all the tickets through the camera himself.

How many years did you work for Harrah's Club?

I worked for thirty-two years, from 1946 to 1978. During that time there was a lot of growth and a lot of expansion. When I retired we were running four different keno games and had two out-stations.

You probably knew a lot of the executives pretty well; for example, Bob Ring. Did you ever associate much with Bob Ring?

Yes. Bob was very friendly to everyone. He knew everyone by name. I considered myself a real good friend of Bob.

Did you ever visit with Bill Harrah?

The only time I was one-to-one with Bill was when the limit was raised to $25,000. He had me come up to his office, and he said, "Gene, I will not book that ticket unless you come up with a sure way that they're not going to screw me out of my money." And that's when we started the pit ticket.

In 1946, when the club first opened, Bill spent a lot of time there, and he spent most of the time at the bar. I worked graveyard, and when I'd get off shift, he'd be at the bar. When I came back the next day, he was still at the bar. [laughter] They said that he would go home, shower and shave and get an hour or so of sleep, and come back. Bob Ring was with

him most of the time. Bill's father, John, would also be there a lot. In fact, he had a room above the club that he lived in.

In the early days at the club, things were very lax. There were things that were going on there that somebody should have caught. That's why Bill went through two or three bankrolls. It was just too lax, and it was in all departments. There were a lot of people taking advantage of the fact that Bill Harrah and Bob Ring were drinking so much. Nobody was watching the store, and the shift managers just turned their head.

What do you think turned Bill Harrah around? Was it his doctor or his car wreck or his wife Scherry or something else?

I think that all those factors combined caused him to straighten up. And also he got the May Company in there as advisors. May Company wouldn't let him operate the way he had been operating. That helped pull him off drinking. And when he married Scherry, I think she was a big factor in his quitting drinking and getting down to business. Bob Ring, his right-hand man, also quit drinking when Bill did. Then they were both more alert to what was going on in the club.

Harrah's was famous for their celebrity golf tournaments and their high roller golf tournaments. Were any keno players every invited to those tournaments?

Yes. We had to submit a list of keno high rollers. They wanted people that really spent a lot of money playing keno. There weren't as many keno players that were considered high roller as in the pit, but we had a few that were invited. In the pit, it's pretty easy to lose five or ten thousand very quickly. In keno, it's a little harder to lose that much in a short time, but there were keno players that sat there and played a whole shift, and they would play a handful of tickets. It amounted to a lot of money at the end of the shift.

How much money would a keno player have to play to be considered a high roller? How many tickets and what price of ticket would he have to play?

Well, some of those high rollers would bet $100 a game, and we wrote at least five games an hour. So, they could be spending as much as $500 an hour.

When you started working in keno, what was the limit payoff for the game?

The limit was five thousand dollars when I started, and then it jumped from five to ten, and then, from ten to twenty-five. And after I got out of keno, they went up to fifty thousand dollars.

Do you recall what year the keno limit went from five to ten thousand dollars?

Yes, in 1953. The first operator to go to ten thousand dollars was Pick Hobson at the Frontier Club.

When did the limit go to twenty-five thousand dollars?

In 1955. It started in Las Vegas, but I don't recall in what club. And it went up to fifty thousand in 1979.

Bob Ring (l.) with Gene and Lena Diullo at Gene's retirement party in 1978.

When you started out in the 1930s and 1940s, how long did it take you to become a supervisor? Did you have to learn all the payoffs and check all the payouts?

You had to be able to check tickets and know all the way tickets and know what was legal and what was illegal, as far as tickets. And you had to be able to figure out the payoffs. Usually, they had a checker that was more knowledgeable than the writers, and when the writer called in the serial number on a winning ticket, the supervisor would figure out the payoff. In other words, the writer would turn around to the supervisor on the desk and say, "Ticket number 0863," and the supervisor would holler back "$17.80." And then the writer would pay the ticket.

When our keno game got so large that we had four keno games in the club, we put a room in downstairs that was used only for checking tickets. All the tickets were sent down to the checking room, and we had one, or sometimes more, checkers working there. We had intercoms so that we could call back and forth from the check room to the counters and tell the writers what to pay. And, of course, we had pneumatic tubes to send the tickets down to the check room.

So this replaced what you were just talking about, where the writers and the checkers would call back and forth?

Yes, this replaced that system, and we didn't have to use checkers on the counters. Now they have computers, and I'm told that a person doesn't have to know anything about keno. The computer does everything. After the game is called, all the winners are printed out, and the supervisors or the writers don't even have to check a ticket. So now you can become a keno writer almost overnight and a keno supervisor in a very short time.

Was there was a limit on how much the keno writer could pay?

They only had so much money in the drawer. Usually, an amount like $100 or $200 was paid by the game supervisor, who would come down with money from the bankroll and pay the ticket.

Gene, you retired from Harrah's Club in 1978. Do you ever go downtown and check out the keno games?

No. Very seldom. Oh, occasionally when we go out for dinner, I might look at the keno operation, but I never mark a ticket.

Did you used to mark a ticket once in a while, when you were working?

Oh, yes. I used to like to play keno. In fact, I won $1,700 on a ticket at the King's Castle or one of those clubs at Incline Village. That was my biggest winning ticket.

Do you have any regrets that you stayed in keno for so long? Did you ever say, "Gee I wish I had gone into the pit"?

Well, I had a chance to become a shift manager. They were breaking me in, but when the opportunity came I turned it down. Rome Andreotti said, "Well, at least you know what you want."

Notes

1. Warren Nelson later became co-owner and general manager of the Club Cal-Neva at the corner of Second and Virginia Streets.
2. Jack Mullen was one of the original keno supervisors in the Palace Club keno game.

7

GEORGE DREWS

G *EORGE DREWS was born in Wilmington, Delaware, on February 22, 1930. He was the executive vice-president of finance and administration for Harrah's when the company was sold to Holiday Inns, Inc. This oral history interview was conducted in two sessions at his home in April of 1997. He was a willing and candid chronicler.*

Mr. Drews's early years were spent on Long Island, New York, and he was graduated from the United States Coast Guard Academy in New London, Connecticut, in 1952. After three years of active duty in the coast guard he returned to school and was graduated from the Harvard Graduate School of Business in 1957.

Drews was one of the first high-level Harrah's executives to be hired from outside the organization. He began working for Harrah's as a controller in 1971, was eventually promoted to the top financial position in the organization, and served in that capacity until 1980.

In this oral history Drews gives the reader an inside look at finances and accounting at Harrah's, including details about the daily report that was designed and first put into use by Maurice Sheppard. Mr. Drews also remembers William F. Harrah and discusses the management team of Harrah's (especially Rome Andreotti) and his many trips to Atlantic City to research the area for Harrah's expansion there. He also offers an interesting

appraisal of Mead Dixon, who became chairman of the board of Harrah's upon Bill Harrah's death.

Perhaps most important, Mr. Drews discusses the many problems Harrah's had when it attempted to go public. He relates how the New York money people looked with disdain upon a gambling casino and how the management team of Harrah's convinced them that Harrah's was a legitimate company and was not owned and operated by gangsters and hoodlums. The pioneering work that was done by Harrah's to make gambling acceptable to New York financial people opened doors for others in the gaming industry to go public.

GEORGE DREWS: I was born in Wilmington, Delaware, February 22, 1930. My mother and father both came over from northern Germany in about 1928. My mother was a housewife, and my father was a marine engineer, a naval architect. He worked with one of the largest naval architectural firms in the country–it's called Gibbs and Cox. He helped design most of the destroyers in World War II and also the ship which was the fastest ship in the world at the time, the *United States.*

I grew up in Staten Island and lived there from the age of four through eighteen. I went to Curtis High School. After I got out of high school, I went to and graduated from the U.S. Coast Guard Academy in New London, Connecticut, with a B.S. degree in engineering. After graduation I went to sea for three years as an officer in the coast guard. I had various positions, such as navigator, chief engineer, gunnery officer, et cetera. Our duties were mainly patrolling in the north Atlantic off the coast of Greenland. This was during the Korean War, from 1952 to 1955. I stayed in the reserve quite a few years after that and eventually became the commanding officer of a reserve unit.

In 1955, I went to the Harvard Graduate School of Business. During one of the summers when I was going to Harvard I worked at the Electric Boat Company in Groton, Connecticut, on nuclear submarines in the planning part of the business–planning and costing. I received my M.B.A. degree in 1957, and I was in the top fifth of my class.

DWAYNE KLING: When you received your M.B.A., did you stay in that area?

I was employed by Curtiss-Wright in Fair Lawn, New Jersey, and worked in the financial side of the company. They were building reciprocating engines–which were being phased out–and just getting into jet engines, the ram jet. So it was a big engine manufacturer.

How did you happen to come to Reno, and when did you come to Reno?

Well, there's a few moves in between. I was with Curtiss-Wright for about a year or a year-and-a-half. Then I went to Raytheon in Massachusetts and worked on missile systems. I was business manager of some of the engineering departments there. I wasn't in the technical end, but I was in the business end of high-tech.

I was with Raytheon for about nine years, and then I was hired by a recruiting firm to go to work for Varian Associates in Palo Alto, California. I had a number of interesting jobs there. I started with the radiation division, which made linear accelerators. They were huge machines that shot atoms half a mile. Some of them had to be put underground. We also did a lot of R & D projects, and one of the first things I found out was that we were losing a large amount of money. These were fixed price R & D contracts, sometimes for three million dollars apiece. The contracts defied the laws of physics. So one of the first things I did was get us out of that R & D business, which was really high risk and created huge losses. Instead I took what we already had and made commercial products out of them. For instance, two of the products we had were called the Clinac 35 and the Clinac 4, and these were basically radiation devices for curing cancer. We commercialized them, particularly the Clinac 4, and it is used in probably most of the hospitals in the United States now; in fact, I think Washoe Med has one.

From that I went on to be the international controller for Varian, and I was controller of twenty-four companies overseas, mostly in Europe, but one in Australia and one in Japan. My headquarters then were in Zurich, Switzerland. I commuted there; I didn't live there. Later, I was named group controller, which was the highest finance position at Varian. Then I was given a second position at the same time, which was group controller of the instrument group. The instrument group had about eight divisions, so I was controller of a lot of entities in the company.

How did you get to Harrah's?

I was teaching evenings–and this was a volunteer thing–financial management for non-financial executives, and I was teaching that to the engineering people in Varian. All of the top people are invariably scientists with Ph.D.'s. You almost need to have a Ph.D. to be at the top of any of those divisions, because they are all really into very advanced technology. They are all aided by business managers or controllers, who are always their number-two men. Typically, the scientists would have very little business knowledge, so I volunteered to teach this course on finances.

American Management Association somehow got wind of what I was doing, and they gave me their course. I looked at it, and they said, "Well, what do you think of it?"

I said, "It's awful." [laughter] I thought I'd really hurt their feelings, but I hadn't. They said, "Well, why?" And I told them point by point by point by point what was wrong with it, and told them what I was teaching was much better. Apparently they were really impressed, because they had an assignment from Harrah's–probably from Lloyd Dyer or Bob Brigham–to hire somebody, and they called me. I was really amazed, because I thought I had insulted them. But they called me to see if I wanted the position of controller at Harrah's. I didn't know the difference between Harrah's or Harvey's or Harolds, and I said, "Well, hardly."

Then they said, "Well come out and see us," and they just kept calling and calling and calling. I went out to Reno probably six times. That would have been 1971.

When they called you, was it the personnel office calling you or Bob Brigham?

I think it was Bob Brigham. He was a Harrah's VP then–the VP of personnel. We didn't have "human resources" then.

I did come out quite a few times, and I'd go to shows (I saw Bobbie Gentry), and I just became more and more fascinated with the company. The company was private at that time, and nobody had ever seen the books of the company–absolutely no outsider, except maybe the financial people and the executives of Harrah's itself. But they showed me the books, showed me absolutely everything. I was really impressed, and I did a lot of research. I didn't want to get into gambling; I mean, I was a high-tech person, and I thought, "maybe they're crooked." I did a lot of research with the Justice Department, the FBI, and the University of Nevada. I did a lot of checking. It took me a long time– probably six months–to make up my mind. I think Lloyd got frustrated. He was at the bottom of the Grand Canyon at the time, and he placed a telephone call, probably to Brig, and Lloyd says, "He's either got to get off the pot or nothing's going to happen." So I made up my mind and said yes. I was really impressed with the company, but I was very, very wary.

So you came to work there in 1971?

Yes. I knew it was a good opportunity, and it's one of the best moves I've ever made. You always move to something higher, and the job was good. It was an exciting life, and, boy, those days were just wonderful. I mean, what a company that was!

Were you married then?

Yes. I was married and had three sons.

So it was a big move for you?

Yes, but we'd moved across country from Boston to the Bay Area. So this was a little less of a move.

So when you moved to Reno, the glamour and the excitement were part of it?

Yes, but mainly it was because Harrah's was an incredibly good company and the people were fantastic.

Who was president then?

Shep [Maurice Sheppard] was president and Lloyd Dyer was executive VP of finance and administration. I started out as controller. As I remember it, every two years I had a promotion. After controller I was made treasurer, and I appointed Dave Thompson controller. Then I became VP of finance, and later I became executive VP of finance and administration.

Were you over both casinos? At that time they only had two places, right?

Yes. The whole thing was actually run from Reno. We had management at Tahoe and Reno, but the corporate structure was all in Reno. We traveled to Tahoe all the time.

How often did you have a meeting on a regular basis?

Well, we had all different kinds of committees. We had wage and salary; we had a finance committee; we had board meetings—things of that sort, so I'd say that probably every other week we were at Tahoe for our meetings.

Were you on the entertainment committee?

No, that's about the only committee I wasn't on. They wouldn't let me on that one, I think, because they wanted to spend so much money! [laughter]

And they were afraid you'd shoot them down.

Yes, that's right!

Previously you were saying that when you were vice-president of finance, there was a controller at each property.

They weren't controllers. They were called business managers, and what they did is they kept the raw books which were the drop and hold and the various expenses of the property. But they weren't even accountants. They were really bookkeepers, but they reported to finance. Finance had the accountants that put everything together. We had, for instance, a daily report where we had a profit-and-loss statement of the casino every day.

I've been led to believe that Maurice Sheppard started the daily report. Is that right?

Yes, and it has continued on ever since, or at least through 1980. [Holiday Inns, Inc. acquired Harrah's in 1980.] It would show the actual drop and hold for the previous day. It had wins and losses by sections of the casino, and it had them by kind of game. It summed everything up, so that there was an actual final number. Things like salaries, wages, and expenses were based on previous experience. The daily numbers were incredibly close to the actual report at the end of the month; there was very little variance.

Was food and beverage also on the report?

Yes. We never had profit in food, by design, but we knew what the margins were in food, and those were actuals. And we knew what the estimated labor was, so we knew what the profit-and-loss was of food and beverage, as well as the casino, plus every subsection of it. We could also watch hold percentages and we were alert to any changes, especially if percentages went down.

How many people had access to the complete, total daily report?

Well, I would say . . . and I'm guessing a little bit, but at the corporate level it was probably all of the VPs, and at the property level, people like Reno club manager Mert Smith and the Tahoe club manager Curly Musso.

So you and, of course, other people would analyze that report–Lloyd Dyer, Sheppard, Bill Harrah. Everyone would analyze that report, and then if there were problems you would go to the particular department?

Yes, but usually we could research it pretty much with the numbers. The daily report was something that was handwritten. What we did, also, and I started this, was we published what we called a White Book. It was titled "Harrah's Financial Statements," and it came out once a month and went to all of top management: Rome Andreotti, Lloyd Dyer, Joe Fanelli, Holmes [Hendricksen], and the business managers at Reno and Tahoe. I think I started that in early 1972. It was published every month and got more and more elaborate. It had a financial review at the beginning, which summarized earnings, revenues, gaming, hotel, food and beverage, expenses, payroll, and so on. And then we had sections on variances, looking at hold and gross profit, administrative expenses and so on. And then it went into a lot more detail. We compared, for instance, eight years worth of data on hold and gross profit, pre-tax profits, things of that sort.

Did the White Book go to all the stockholders?

Oh, no, it was distributed only in house. There was a lot of detail, and I was told by the top banker at the Chase-Manhattan that we had better controls at Harrah's than they had at Chase-Manhattan Bank. He was sincere about it.

So the White Book evolved from the daily report?

Yes. Except it had a lot more information in it, and it was once a month as opposed to daily.

When the company went public, you only had to turn out quarterly statements. Is that correct?

Yes, that's correct.

So this was an in-house report that helped management in several different areas?

Yes, and it covered all levels of management, right down to the individual department. We had quite a few departments at both properties, so it really covered everybody, and we always had a comparison of this year's period with the previous year's period and with the variance. We looked at variances pretty closely.

Harrah's had always had their only financial relationship with FNB [First National Bank of Nevada], with Art Smith. [Arthur M. Smith Jr., president of FNB, 1967-1984.] We had a terrible bank loan of twenty-two million dollars at a high interest rate, and there was no competition with any other bank whatsoever. We dealt with only one bank, FNB. That was it, and it was really inbred. I thought that it was very bad for the company.

Does that association with FNB go back to loyalties between Bill Harrah and Mr. Questa [Edward J. Questa, president of FNB, 1952-1962] from years past?

Could be. I don't know. Art Smith was real close to Shep and vice-versa, and the company never wanted to go out and look for loans from other banks. I thought it was bad not to have competition, because you don't get good rates that way. First National Bank had all of our assets pledged, which really locked us up, because if we wanted more money, we had to go to them, and they could tell us what they were going to charge us. So I said, "What we need is a money-center bank.

As a public company we can't be held up like that." I said, "I'm going to New York, and I'm going to talk to every major bank." I talked to Chemical Bank; I talked to Manufacturers Hanover, Chase-Manhattan, to every major money-center bank in New York. And everybody laughed at me, and they said, "You're going to come back with nothing."

All the Harrah's people laughed at you?

Yes, and they told me it was a total waste of time, but I kept at it. I met a lot of people, and most of them were very wary of us. Finally I found a fellow by the name of Harry Abplanalp. He was one of the top bankers at Chase, and I got him out to the company many times. I went back there many times; I talked to all of their people, and finally we got a loan from them, which was a major event. Bill Harrah said one of his dreams was to do business with Chase-Manhattan. I mean, he was thrilled! We went to Chase-Manhattan, and when he saw David Rockefeller's office, it was like we were kings. It was an amazing thing. And FNB was so mad, so jealous you can't believe it.

That was the start of a lot of things. Later, in 1976, when we needed money we went down for mortgage bonds. In order to get a good rate on bonds you have to have a bond rating. That was very difficult, because nobody in the gaming industry had ever had a bond rating before. Everybody was so suspicious; everybody thought we were Mafia. I did an incredible amount of work back east with Standard & Poor's, Moody's, and Fitch's. It was really hard to get them to give us a good rating, and you really need a good rating to get a bond at all; and especially to get a good rate of interest.

I just went back and back, and then I had them out here, and we met socially. One time I called Phil Hannifin, who was head of the Gaming Control Board. The financial people didn't know for sure that we weren't crooks, and they wanted to know more about how we

were regulated and so on. They basically believed in the financial structure of the company—that it was an incredibly good profit maker—but I needed help on the regulation part of it. I called Phil, and I said, "Phil, can you come to New York with me?" This is probably on a Sunday, and I said, "Tomorrow." And goddamn it, he did go. He was wonderful; I tell you, he was incredible! He just reeked of being aboveboard, and he really handled it well. I think he really helped convince them—he was the thing that turned it over.

We finally got an "A" rating, which was *incredibly* good. Hilton didn't have an "A" rating; Warner Brothers didn't have an "A" rating. Hilton's John Giovenco, head of all of the Hilton Nevada hotels at the time, called me and said, "How the hell did you get an 'A' rating?" He couldn't believe it—I think they had a double-"B" or a triple-"B" or something like that at the time.

That was a real coup. As a result of that, we were able to do twenty million dollars of convertible debentures in 1976 at a rate of only 7.5 percent. Later we did fifty million dollars of mortgage bonds through Paine Webber; actually, we did both transactions through Paine Webber. After that I got Merrill Lynch to be our underwriter, and I did a lot of work with Merrill Lynch towards the end. So we went from really nothing, to a regional investment banker that took us public, to Paine Webber, to Merrill Lynch. I found out later that Bill Harrah really was tickled that we were able to do all those things.

How much relationship did you have with Bill Harrah on a one-on-one basis? Did he give you ideas, or did they just hand you the ball and you ran with it?

I would say I had almost no personal relationship with Bill Harrah. Shep and Lloyd were always the interface. He would hear me all the time, though, because I was in every single finance committee meeting and I always made all of the presentations. I was in every single board meeting for almost ten years.

However, as I said, I had almost no personal contact one-on-one with Bill. Bill listened and I talked–that is the way it worked. The reason I talked, of course, was because at finance committee meetings I made the presentation, or I asked the questions and so on. Bill really just listened; he almost never said anything. I wasn't on the board, but I was the chief financial officer almost that entire time. Bill knew what I was doing; he knew what all the financial matters of the company were and so on. But I would

say that in ten years I never heard him make a comment. He listened.

At the annual meetings it's fair to say that I probably answered 90 percent of the questions. Bill Harrah would get up and open the meeting and welcome everybody with about a three to four-sentence speech. Then Shep or Lloyd, whoever was president, would make a general kind of speech, and then I would go through all the financials of the company. We would get hundreds of questions, literally, from the floor. Typically, every year we had eleven hundred shareholders show up.

Where were the meetings held?

George Drews addresses a shareholders' meeting. In background, l. to r.: Charles Franklin, Maurice Sheppard, and Bill Harrah. *"At the annual meetings it's fair to say that I probably answered 90 percent of the questions . . . . We would get hundreds of questions, literally, from the floor. Typically, every year we had eleven hundred shareholders show up."*

They were held–alternating between Reno and Tahoe–in the convention centers. It was a *huge* room when we'd open it up. Hilton at the time had thirty-eight people at an annual stockholders meeting; we had eleven hundred, *even* in a snowstorm. And a *tremendous* loyalty. People would ask us for our autographs and take our pictures and things of that sort. It was just like you were stars. [laughter] It was amazing. Of course, we always did so well and everybody was making so much money–the stockholders, I'm talking about–that they were just fans of the company. Plus it was an excuse to go to Harrah's.

Most of our stockholders were customers, so it was an excuse to come to Reno or Tahoe and go to the meeting and then play twenty-one or craps or engage in some type of gambling. The more they played, the more money the company made, the more they made, and so on and so on.

How did Bill Harrah handle that exposure to the public?

He'd sit and wouldn't talk much.

Did they ask him for autographs?

Yes, and people became real fans. I mean they came year after year after year. You'd see the same people, and we got to really know them and be good friends with them.

Well, I'd heard before that Bill Harrah delegated much of his authority, and you're certainly verifying that.

The only time, and this is kind of humorous, when we really had an interaction with him was when he wanted to do something that we didn't want to do. Then we fought it.

When you say "we," are you saying you specifically, or "we" meaning the management team?

Well, myself and Lloyd and Shep . . . the management team. If we thought something was just a pet project, like wanting to build a big auto collection [museum] on I-80–which absolutely wouldn't work, and we were convinced of it–we would fight it. We stalled it and did things of that sort. We knew it wasn't in the best interest of the company, and we were able to delay the I-80 construction. It would have lost a lot of money, because cars do not draw gaming customers. We couldn't make thirty slot machines or forty slot machines at Harrah's Auto Collection [in Sparks] pay off. We had slots out there, and we lost money on them.

So there was no actual face-to-face confrontation. If he wanted to do something, you would stall and try to make it go away?

Yes. I probably shouldn't say what I just said, [laughter] but we were open about it. We never hid anything from him; we just told him it wasn't a good idea. We wouldn't give him any money, even though he owned virtually the whole company. And if he wanted to do it, he'd say, "We're going to do it," and we'd have to do it.

Bill Harrah is famous for his attention to details and punctuality, and most accountants, comptrollers, and financial people are pretty much detail lovers, also. Did you get along good with Bill Harrah in those areas?

I don't know if Bill really knew the numbers at all. I think what was probably important to him was that somebody was taking care of the details. I don't know if he understood the numbers or even cared. I think in the total sense, he cared. He'd certainly be concerned about the hold percentage or somebody stealing or something like that. The story you've heard a million times is he was always looking for light bulbs out, so all the top management spent half their time looking at light bulbs. And again I'm kind of kidding, but we were certainly alert to every detail. We were always supposed to go to the shows, and I'd go to one show in Reno one week and the show in Tahoe every other week. If we had a chip in a glass or the slightest thing wrong with anything, we reported it. We had to report it. In our daily report every customer complaint was written down, and where it came from. Was it food and beverage? Which restaurant? And so on. Every complaint. And we responded to everything. We had to. We also had to observe ourselves, and, as I said, if there was a tiny chip in a glass, that was written down. Things of that sort, that kind of detail. Courtesy and friendliness were really the key words in the company.

It sounds as if he felt that if you took care of the little things, a lot of the big things would take care of themselves.

Yes. But he never got into things like talking about staffing or the size of a department or cutting costs—never a word. That was management, and I'd say that one of the most influential people in management was Rome Andreotti. He was criticized a lot for nitpicking and being tough and so on, but in my opinion he was the heart of the company, because he had most of the operations under him.

Well, he was quite loyal to Bill Harrah, and, of course, so many of you people who were with Harrah's a long time were loyal, too.

Oh, absolutely, totally loyal. Not because we had to be; it's just that we were.

Well, do you think part of it was the thing that he did—give you so much power of decision that you really felt like you were the boss in a way?

Well, I think it was because it was such a great company that we were so proud to be there. We always wanted to make it better and

better. I think he created that atmosphere. We were so enthusiastic about the company that we didn't need any kind of prodding at all. Never. Absolutely never. We were always just absolutely doing our best.

The other thing is if somebody didn't do their job and wasn't superb, they were gone quickly. However, there was never a fear for the people that were good employees. There was *never* a fear of getting fired; but if you *weren't* a good employee, you were gone. No ifs, ands, or buts about it. He wouldn't tolerate any inadequate person, and management wouldn't. I mean, it's not that Bill did it personally, but management would not tolerate somebody that wasn't really a good worker.

Yes. There had to be people a couple of tiers down that were in management that Bill Harrah didn't really come in contact that much with, but, say, Lloyd Dyer or Shep would come in contact with them, and they would eliminate them before they caused a problem.

Yes, and Rome [Andreotti] would be on Mert [Smith] and Joe Francis or George Gilgert and Doyle Mathia or whoever was involved. He'd be on them every day, and, boy, he was tough on them! But he was the most insecure person I've ever seen in my life.

Rome and I were good friends, and he would for some reason confide in me. You'd think he would be anti-finance, because controllers and finance people are always on operations people's backs. However, he was very close with me, and he would tell me all of his thoughts, his insecurities. He'd say, "Well, what does Lloyd think about me?" and this and that and the other thing. "What does Bill think?" And I'd always have to bolster his ego. But he would never show that to anybody else, I don't think.

He was incredibly competent, probably not well educated, but he really knew the numbers; he knew gaming; he knew food and beverage. He was tough on the guys like Joe

Fanelli. They'd all complain about him at times, but they also thought the world of him. But underneath all that, he was really insecure. I thought the world of him.

Were there any other people that were dominant, or did it revolve around Bill Harrah?

Well, if we first talk about the people directly under Rome ... for instance, the general managers at Reno and Tahoe and the auto collection ran their organizations in detail, but they were almost extensions of Rome. I mean, he was so close to them all the time that they were really subservient to him. Rome almost ran the entire organization, including food and beverage, in detail.

Bill Harrah–although I never saw him being involved in management at all–did travel the world, stayed at the finest hotels, and brought back ideas to improve the hotels and service and anything that had to do with the auto collection. He was very, very close to that. He was kind of the spirit of the company–I don't want to say a ghost, but if he was *not* there (for instance, let's say he left the company or died), it would be a totally different company; it wouldn't be the same thing at all, because he had certain principles and standards that had to be met, and we were devoted to that concept. Sometimes we criticized it if we thought it was way too expensive. For instance, we were initially appalled at the two bathrooms in a hotel room and TVs in the bathroom, things of that sort. But years later that proved to be an incredibly good concept. It was the talk of the world. Bill Harrah was more of a spirit, and I can't tell you how it worked or why it worked, but it did. It probably would never work in any other organization.

It's been said that Bill Harrah wasn't too concerned with the return on the investment. He just wanted to furnish good facilities for the customer.

Right. Yes. I don't think he really cared that much about financial success as long as we had enough money to do what he wanted to do. I think he was proud of what we did, but he never demanded it of us. We were proud to increase at a certain percent a year and make more and more money. We did really well during those years, during that ten years until Holiday took over. But we didn't do it because we were driven to do it. We just wanted to do it.

Harrah's had already started to go public when you came to work there. Did you finish the project?

Yes. We had a lot of meetings on getting organized to go public. To go public you need to have your financial statements in order, and they have to be recast into a public format. We had a strictly internal format at the time, so there was a lot of financial work to be done.

Bill never really wanted to go public. He didn't want to–I don't think–give up control, but everybody thought that he should be able to have liquidity in his estate. Everybody's going to die someday, and he had everything in the company and no way of paying taxes. If he had to pay an estate tax, there was no cash to pay it. I mean, it was a huge amount that would be due, and going public provided the liquidity to pay the taxes. We did a very, very small offering. If I remember correctly, it was only three and a half million dollars. I'd have to research that to be sure I'm right.

I remember one of the early meetings we had with the underwriter. You have to have a "use of proceeds." In other words, you have to answer the question, "Why do you want the money?" And we didn't need any money. We absolutely didn't need any money. We did, however, have to come up with a "use of proceeds," and we couldn't figure out any reason to say, "This is why we're going public, because we need this money for this and this project." Finally we came up with the notion that we were going to put a second floor on the

Headliner Room, so that was our use of proceeds. We didn't really need money for that, and I don't think we were going to do it anyway, and the bottom line is we never did it.

The reason a "use of proceeds" is important is so the public thinks that the money we're putting into the company is going to improve the profits of the company and that it's going to enable them to do a certain project which is going to make a lot of money, and therefore the profits are going to be bigger, and so on. Anyway, we went public with a dumb reason for going public, and were still very, very successful. We went public, I think, at sixteen dollars a share, and it just kept skyrocketing after that—split two for one, and so on. But we never did the project.

You never built the second floor?

Never did, never will. [laughter]

You said Bill Harrah didn't really want to go public. Did someone have to convince him?

Yes, the underwriters and the lawyers. Mead Dixon, and I think Lloyd Dyer and Shep were behind it. I think Bill didn't want to show anybody the figures. It had always been a closed-book company. No one, no outsider *ever* knew anything about our volume or profit. I'd say secrecy was one thing, and then having the public tell you what to do was another. You've got to meet certain requirements all the time, and you can't do the things you necessarily want to do—you can't buy maybe a hundred automobiles; you can only buy thirty. [laughter]

After Harrah's did go public in the fall of 1971, did you take more of an active role in the company? Did going public have anything to do with you progressing through the company?

It made the job a lot more difficult, of course, because we had to publish quarterly reports. They were a new format. Once we

overcame that, it wasn't that bad anymore. But I think my role became more important because of the need for outside financing, having money-center banks in New York as opposed to just FNB, having access to mortgage bonds and to convertible debentures. It wasn't only bank loans. We had long-term financing—you know, like a thirty-year loan and things of that sort, and a permanent loan. Also, we got away from having to pledge all our assets just for a single twenty-two million dollar loan from FNB.

Financially we became much freer. We had access to cash and we could grow more rapidly. We could build the tower at Tahoe; we could build a second tower at Tahoe; we could build a tower in Reno—things of that sort which we couldn't've done before with just the twenty-two-million-dollar bank loan.

So going public made it easier for you, as far as having access to finances?

Yes. It was even more than making it easier—it made it possible. It wouldn't have been possible with just FNB.

Yes. Harrah's possibly would never have built the hotel at Lake Tahoe?

I would say no.

Plus possibly many other expansions. So your job was easier as far as having more access to money, but it was more difficult or a larger job due to all the other details?

Yes. Then we had annual meetings, of course, and we had to answer to shareholders—why this and why that, and so on. But they were never negative meetings. I tell you, it was just like a fan club; it was unbelievable. Unbelievable. [laughter]

You originally went public as an over-the-counter stock, then went on the American Exchange, and then the New York Stock Exchange. As you progressed to larger exchanges, did the process become easier?

We pretty much had to start over the counter. Unless you're a giant company, you don't go on the New York Exchange. You have to have a certain distribution of stock—so much stock in so many states, things of that sort. But it was a real coup to be listed on the New York Exchange, in terms of prestige, credibility of the company, things of that sort. It added a lot of credibility to the company.

As I recall, it was the first solely gaming organization to go on the New York Board.

I believe that's true, and certainly the first one to have access to capital at money-center banks and to receive the kind of rating that we had.

It appears as if you were the major contributor as far as getting the company public.

No, not actually going public; but once we were public, of establishing relationships with the financial community. That meant Paine Webber, Merrill Lynch, the banks in New York, and the rating agencies, Fitch and Standard & Poor's. We really needed the money from going public to do the Tahoe hotel, and we needed things like the mortgage bonds and the convertible debentures to do Towers One and Two.

Do you remember the cost of the hotel at Tahoe?

Boy, I'm probably wrong . . . it might have been only twenty-eight million or something, but I'd have to really look back. Maybe Lloyd remembers better than I do. I'd rather not say. It was incredibly expensive per room. It was double, triple, or quadruple any other room ever built, which we all yelled about, but later on it paid off.

One time we looked into diversifying out of Reno and Tahoe into recreation-oriented

businesses. However, Bill was against going into Las Vegas, so even though that was a great opportunity, we absolutely were not allowed to even talk about that. I think the main reason was the unionism in Las Vegas. That was probably his big reason for not wanting to go there—it wasn't for a lack of opportunity. We did look, for instance, at buying Sun Valley, and we made a trip there. We looked at buying Hollywood Park, related kinds of things, but none of them ever really worked out to be a good fit. Gambling was such a lucrative business that it was almost impossible to beat what we were already doing. The opportunities we had at the time, since there weren't other legalized states, were really limited to Atlantic City and to Las Vegas.

I heard a story that during the extreme gas shortage in the United States in the early seventies, Bill Harrah thought about buying an oil company. Were you aware of that?

Yes. I was kind of involved in it, and the gas shortage was a very serious threat to Harrah's. As you probably remember, there were long lines of people trying to buy gas in San Francisco, even in Reno. It was very hard to get gas, and we went into major advertising programs that said we were "only a tank away," which probably helped a little bit. Most of our market was northern California and to some extent the northwestern states, and most of our customers drove to Reno, so the gas shortage really had the potential of killing us. We did various things, such as put in gas stations for our customers so that they were assured of gas when they got here.

It became so bad that you couldn't even be assured of getting gas anyplace. You hated to drive all the way to Reno and then not have the gas to go back. So we did do gas stations, and we did look into buying at least one oil company. I remember we went to Texas and looked at a company there, and Lloyd, Charles Franklin, and myself explored buying that company. We never did go through with it, but it was a thought. That way we could have tied up a certain amount of gas to guarantee us fuel, but it wasn't too long after that that the whole situation cleared up, so we were OK.

When you say gas stations in Reno, did Harrah's actually lease gas station properties?

Yes. As I remember, at Tahoe the gas station was actually within the facility. I think it might have been either in the parking garage or just outside it. We also had something in Reno that was right next to the facility.

When your customers came here, your good customers, you saw to it that they could go to this gas station and get gas?

Yes.

Did you give them the gas?

Oh, no. We just made it available.

What were your thoughts when you heard that Mr. Harrah had died? Did you have any inkling that he wasn't feeling well?

No. In fact, he walked by my office when he was on the way to surgery. He had already scheduled a river trip for six weeks after the surgery, and he just waved at me and said, "Bye, George." He looked like he was in perfect health. Nobody expected him to die. But it was a real tragedy, because then Mead Dixon took over.

Mead Dixon didn't play much of a role in the business prior to Bill Harrah's death, did he?

No. No. He didn't know anything about the business, but the day Bill died, he knew everything. [laughter]

When Bill Harrah died, did you have any idea that it was going to be necessary to sell the company?

No. I found out later. I became the chief guy in valuing the company. There were a lot of conflicts of interest with the various parties. We had representatives of the estate–I think we had Dean Witter representing the estate to sell the company. We had Merrill Lynch valuing it for the company, and then we had somebody else valuing it for something else. We had three different sets of underwriters. My job was to price the company, to do a five-year forecast and come up with a value of the company. I did the forecasts, and they were pretty high. They were growing very rapidly over five years, and people tried to cut me down so that the company would be worth less and it would be easier to sell. But I was still working for Bill Harrah, even though he was dead, and all I cared about was getting the most money for the owners of the company, which was the public and Bill Harrah's estate. We had underwriters for the buyer, which was Holiday; we had the estate; and we had the company. So we had three different sets of underwriters. I was constantly being prodded by Mead and by Holiday to lower the estimates, which would make the price lower.

At the time I believe the value I came up with was three hundred million dollars. Mead and Holiday wanted two hundred million dollars or something like that. Here I am, working for a dead man and defying the people that are going to be my future bosses, which is Holiday and Mead. But I'm working for the stockholders and I'm working for the estate, and I stuck by my guns. It was a dumb thing to do if you wanted to have longevity, but it was the right thing to do in my opinion, and I would never do it any different. I wasn't, as a result, popular with future management. I don't mean Lloyd and Shep when I say that. I mean Mead and Holiday, because they had to pay probably a hundred million dollars more for the company. I think I did the right thing, and I'm proud of it.

Do you think Bill Harrah knew the workings of his will as it related to Mead Dixon being completely in control of the company?

Probably not. He may have known it technically, but maybe not how it would really work.

Most other things he had, he had boards or management committees where there was input from three to six or eight people, is that correct?

Yes.

And the way his will was written up, Mead Dixon had complete control, right?

Yes. He [controlled] all the shares. He said, "I'm going to make myself chairman."

Somebody said to him once–I'm not going to say who–"Well, you can't be chairman."

And Mead says, "Why?"

The other person says, "Nobody likes you." [laughter]

But Mead made himself chairman, anyway. Mead was a very, very smart guy. Very smart.

Who made the decision that Harrah's had to be sold? Was it because of taxes?

I think it was Mead, and partly for taxes, maybe; although maybe we could have raised it. I think we could have raised the money ourself with a public offering. But Mead stood to make a lot of money; his law firm stood to make a lot of money.

On the sale?

Yes, yes, yes. I was violently against selling the company, which again was not a popular position with the future management.

But actually, the only person that could make the decision to sell was Mead Dixon. Is that right?

Yes. I really don't know where Lloyd stood. I just plain don't know, but I think he kind of had to go along with it.

George, I know you were very active in Harrah's Club checking out the Atlantic City area before they opened there. Could you tell us how it came about, how you happened to go back there, and how Harrah's got involved?

The only growth opportunities for Harrah's were in Las Vegas or what was to become the Atlantic City gaming market. When we heard about legislation in New Jersey to legalize gaming in Atlantic City, I became very interested, and with Lloyd's blessing went out there numerous times in the last half of 1977 and early 1978. The gaming was actually legalized in June of 1977, and Resorts International opened on the Memorial Day weekend, May 28 of 1978. That was a very exciting time because the business for Resorts was so phenomenal.

I was there the night of the opening and the morning after. In fact, I was there early in the morning, and Steve Norton was still doing the count at four in the morning. Steve was head of finance at the time, and Jack Davis was the president of Resorts International. We were to find out later that in the first nine months of operation, Resorts had earned enough to completely pay for their property. To give you an example of the casino win, in talking with Steve Norton, who was vice-president and general manager of Resorts, they were doing approximately $450,000 per day in win.

I asked Steve to compare his expected profits with our Tahoe operation, and he felt that they could do one and a half times that of *all* of Harrah's, Reno and Lake Tahoe both, and they were in a facility half our size. When I was there, the volume of play, even at 1:30 in the morning, was incredible. People were waiting out on the street, on the boardwalk, to get in. They had crowd control; they had a lot of security; they had high-stakes people. It was just a phenomenal business. There were actually people paying people to get ahead of them in line, to get up ahead so that they could get in sooner.

Some of what I'm reciting now is from a memo that was written to Lloyd Dyer on a trip that we made June 26, 27, 28 of 1978. In a letter to Lloyd, with a copy to Shep, I pointed out that Shep and I were extremely impressed with the potential of Atlantic City and repeated a statistic that approximately fifty-five million people, or 25 percent of the population of the United States, is within a one-day's drive of Atlantic City. I also mentioned that the city had good highway access and we probably wouldn't even need a hotel except in the winter.

Well, the dates there are interesting. Bill Harrah died June 30, 1978, and you were back there just a few days prior to Bill Harrah's death. So if you were investigating then, it would indicate Bill Harrah had expressed an interest, or Lloyd Dyer as president had sent you back to Atlantic City to check it out.

Yes. I'm not sure exactly what Bill's position was on that, but certainly Lloyd was for it, and I believe Shep was, too, because Shep was on this trip. We were both very favorably impressed.

Had any other executives gone back there prior to that time and expressed a like or dislike for Atlantic City?

I think around that time Lloyd may have been there. We were there constantly through December of 1978. I mean, I must have made a dozen or more trips during that time. I know Mark Curtis went at one point, and Lloyd and Mark and I took a helicopter trip to survey the property from the air. I had already researched virtually every property on the boardwalk. Most of the boardwalk at that time was dilapidated hotels and empty land. The hotels were doing essentially no business, and,

therefore, we could acquire the properties very quickly.

I looked at probably twelve to fifteen properties; met the owners and in some cases negotiated prices. We were ready to option the properties. Some of the properties were the Sheraton and the Ambassador Hotels, which were owned by Marvin Ashner, and we actually had a letter of intent out to him at one time. Other properties we looked at included the Holiday Inn that Steve Wynn eventually bought and the property that became Caesar's, which I believe was the Howard Johnson at the time.

I met the governor of the state, the senator, Steve Persky, and his legislative counsel. We met virtually every key person in Atlantic City, and I think we had a really good relationship. I would say that after Resorts, we were the first people really sincerely interested, and Steve Wynn was there at the time, too. We talked about splitting properties with him, and we talked about partnerships with some other people.

I have a press clipping dated January 25, 1978. This was in the Atlantic City newspaper, and it's titled "Harrah's Exec Tours A.C." Lloyd and I and Mark Curtis were there, and the opening sentence is, "It's going to be a gold mine." That was my quote. I also said, "The only danger is that it will be too successful," explaining that if the resort is too successful, other people will legalize gaming in other states. In any event, it's quite a nice article. We talked about our enthusiasm for the city, and this was January of 1978, which was six months before Resorts even opened and five to six months before Bill Harrah died.

We pursued what we thought was the best property even to the point of getting an option. Mead Dixon came to Atlantic City with Lloyd and myself at one point, and later we had a number of other people, including Mert Smith, Holmes, and Bob Martin come to the area. We did a lot of things, including pricing out construction costs and actually preparing an organization chart–doing everything that you need to do to get an operation opened quickly. The key, of course, is tying up the land.

On one of the trips (and this would have been later in 1978), Mead was with us. Mead walked around the city and the boardwalk and said to me–he almost shouted at me– "This is the stupidest thing I've ever seen! I mean, this is crazy to go into Atlantic City, absolutely stupid." So we were shot down cold and couldn't do anything about it. I think this was at the time that he was already chairman, so it must have been not too long after Bill Harrah died and Mead took over and exerted his opinion.

It was several years before Harrah's actually got into operation at Atlantic City. I remember writing a memo at one point that said, "If we delay even six months, we lose forty million dollars and maybe a lot more than that." Harrah's eventually optioned or leased the land next to Resorts International, which was a parking lot, and never did anything with it. Finally, in November of 1980, Harrah's opened the Marina property.

Harrah's lost a good two years there. It's a shame that Mead delayed the opening, because we could have made a lot more money, *a lot more money*. And as I said, in those early years, when it was really hot and you had almost a monopoly, we could have made more money than Reno and Tahoe combined on one site.

There was much less competition in those early years.

Yes. We would have been the second casino there, and it's interesting to read in Mead's book[1] that he takes credit for pioneering Atlantic City.

It appears as if he actually was the person who put the damper on Harrah's New Jersey expansion.

Yes. He also said that management was so stupid and didn't know anything about Atlantic City at all; and of course we were very knowledgeable about the area.

By the time that Harrah's did move to Atlantic City, Holiday Inns had taken over Harrah's, and you, along with Lloyd Dyer and a few other executives, had left the company. So you didn't get to participate in the opening of gaming in Atlantic City, is that right?

Not for Harrah's, no.

George, you worked in several top-level organizations throughout the country, and you've been associated with and exposed to several top management people. How do feel about the management team at Harrah's Club, compared to management in other companies you worked for?

I'll start with some of the companies I've been with. They include Electric Boat, Curtiss-Wright, Raytheon's missile systems division, and Varian Associates–all superb companies. And I would say that of all of them, Harrah's was the finest by far. I've never seen such an outstanding management team, people that were so devoted to the company and had such tremendous spirit. I mean, it was really a great team. The guys were smart, and they were good managers and good people. They were also talented people as far as getting along with other people, a necessity in the gaming industry.

We had incredibly good spirit, and we really wanted the company to be the best. Also, there's clear evidence that we *were* the best. Everything we had was dominant– everybody knew that Harrah's was the finest company, the finest hotel-casino, without question. The bond rating we had was the highest bond rating, not only in the casino industry, but in all of entertainment, even Warner Brothers. Financially, we were structured, we were very profitable, we had a very rapid growth, and I don't know how you can do that with mediocre management.

Most of the top management team came up through the ranks of the organization. They started out at Harrah's in various capacities and worked up into their top jobs. However, I believe you were one of the first people that came from the outside that was hired directly into top management at Harrah's.

Yes, I think that's true. Joe Fanelli and I were hired about the same time and at basically the same levels. Joe was head of food and beverage for the combined operations, Tahoe and Reno, and I started as controller. I believe that we were both hired at the director level and then later promoted to vice-president, and then I later became executive vice-president.

Also, I was probably the first outsider that was ever shown the books of the company before I was hired, which really amazed me, because there was an incredible amount of secrecy in the company in terms of anything to do with the financial results.

You mentioned that everyone worked hard because they wanted to work hard. Did part of that possibly came from the fact that Bill Harrah demanded that in a subtle way?

Yes. I think without him ever saying it, he demanded absolute excellence. If a manager wasn't excellent, he was reprimanded; he was told what was wrong. We had appraisals; we were constantly informed about anything that we did wrong and occasionally right. But we were not motivated by fear, not at all. I still don't understand it. I don't understand how he did it. There was a mystique and an aura about the company, of course, that changed dramatically after Holiday bought the company.

So most of it came from Bill Harrah himself in one way or another.

I think his presence in some way did that, yes.

Did anyone look at him like a father figure—like, "I'm trying to impress my dad," or "I want to impress this person"?

I don't think we tried to impress him at all. I don't think we ever tried to impress him, but that's just my personal feeling.

Did you have much association with Bob Ring?

I only knew Bob socially. I don't think in the seventies that Bob really had a function in the company. He was vice-chairman and had an office, and I think he was kind of a spiritual father, if I could say that, to all of us. But he didn't really have a direct management role. Bill may have confided in him and talked to him—I have no idea. I know he knew virtually every employee by name. A tremendous person, had a tremendous memory, a tremendous knowledge, and he knew a lot of customers. He was a *very* social person, a really fine person to be with, and everybody liked him.

Was Harrah's Club still having golf tournaments when you went to work there?

Yes. I remember at least one tournament I played in, which was at Incline, and we would give a Rolls-Royce if somebody made a hole-in-one on a certain hole—that type of thing. The tournaments were very popular.

Did the golf tournaments end when Harrah's was sold to Holiday?

Probably. I'm not sure, but I think almost everything that was good went away.

What did you do after you left Harrah's, and what are you doing now, George?

For a while I was doing some consulting with firms such as Harvey's and a little bit with the Mapes. Six Flags Over Texas–there were some bright people running that company, and they wanted to get into gambling at that time, and they contacted me. I even did a little bit of consulting for Bob Guccione, who invited me out to lunch in his brownstone, which Judy Garland used to own. We had lunch together with he and Kathy Keaton. As you know, he later built the Penthouse Casino.

Then I joined a company called Sircoma in June of 1980. I quickly renamed the company International Game Technology. I was the president and director and later became CEO. I was with IGT from 1980 to 1986. I helped organize the company. Si Redd[2] had fired every key person, including the head of the computer operation, the only computer operator, the executive VP and so on, and he had something like three hundred people reporting directly to him. We needed management, and I brought that in–consolidated the Reno and Las Vegas facilities, which had competitive duplicate products, and in 1981 took the company public. As you know, it's been extremely successful. I was the person that conceived of Megabucks and developed it, and I started us in video lottery and started the S-Slots. We didn't have spinning reel machines when I came. We just had video, so I got us in the regular slot machine business, as well as into the lottery in Nebraska and things of that sort.

I retired in 1986 at the age of fifty-six. I've been doing some occasional consulting since then, but I am basically retired. Four years ago, I became associated with Bally Gaming, which is the spinoff from what was Bally Manufacturing. Bally Gaming is a separate company that builds video and reel machines, and since I had done this for IGT in Australia, Bally asked me if I would get them started in Australia. I became president and chairman of the board of the Australian company. I started the company from scratch, hired some key people, hired software people, engineers, and so on. We're now licensed in virtually every state in Australia, have a good presence, have a full software staff for designing games for the Australian market, and we've received our first major order–putting machines into the hugely successful Crown Casino in Melbourne.

So Bally is there manufacturing machines. They don't have any gaming casinos themselves?

No. We've basically been importing the cabinets and the boards and things of that sort from the U.S. We're importing the whole machine, but all of the games are original Australian design because it's a totally different market.

Those games are so successful that the United States people asked us to put the games and machines here. We're actually bringing the games that we developed there back to the states, where they're much more successful than the local games. But at the moment we're strictly an engineering and management and sales operation. As soon as we hit a certain level of orders, we'll actually assemble machines there. The Australian and New Zealand market is currently the second most important gaming market in the world. It's incredible.

Notes

1.   *Playing the Cards That Are Dealt: Mead Dixon, the Law, and Casino Gaming.* Reno: University of Nevada Oral History Program, 1992.
2.   William S. "Si" Redd was president and principal shareholder of Bally Distributing, a subsidiary of Bally Manufacturing. Redd started International Game Technology (IGT) in 1978 to produce video gambling machines. He is considered the father of the video slot revolution.

8

JOAN DYER

THIS ORAL HISTORY interview of Joan Dyer (wife of longtime Harrah's president Lloyd Dyer) was conducted in May of 1997 at her home. She was cooperative and eager to participate in the project, and the interview was completed in one afternoon.

Joan Dyer's story is unique. She was there at the beginning of Harrah's at Lake Tahoe as an entry-level employee, and she was there as the wife of the president of Harrah's when the gaming giant was sold to Holiday Inns in 1980. Mrs. Dyer, who was born in Alameda, California, on February 8, 1938, first came to Lake Tahoe in the spring of 1958. She was attending the University of California at Berkeley at the time, and, looking for a seasonal job to help defray her college expenses, she hired on as a payroll clerk at Harrah's. In this oral history she remembers some of the problems she encountered in her first years at Lake Tahoe, such as getting out the payroll under primitive conditions and coping with living in the as-yet undeveloped Lake Tahoe area. The extreme ups and downs of business affected not only the club, but also the financial lives of Harrah's employees.

Mrs. Dyer also discusses Harrah's strict personal dress codes in the late 1950s and some of

the problems that the company encountered when it first put all its employees in uniforms. Other memories include trips to Europe with husband Lloyd and Mr. and Mrs. Harrah, experiences with other executives' wives, and memories of William F. Harrah's funeral and her part in its planning.

JOAN DYER: I was born in Alameda, California, on February 8, 1938. One of my grandfathers came to San Francisco in the 1800s to participate in the gold rush but ended up in the food industry. When the 1906 earthquake hit, he moved his family across the bay to the island of Alameda, and the family is still there. Basically, I'm the only one that ever left. They're all still there.

In 1852 my father's family came across the country in a covered wagon, also to participate in the gold rush, but ended up in Loyalton, California. Because it was such a green valley and they were ranchers, they stayed there forever and ever. My grandmother was raised there, and she rode a donkey to school in Chilcoot. She had a great time growing up, but when the Western Pacific railroad came through Loyalton there was a way to get out of the valley, and so ultimately that branch of my family also moved to Alameda, California.

Both my parents went to Alameda High School. They met shortly thereafter and they were married in 1937. I was born in 1938, and I also went to Alameda High School. So it just went on and on. After I graduated from high school I went to the University of California, Berkeley for two years. I was one of those oddball February graduates, so I started at U.C. Berkeley the Monday after I graduated from high school. All I had was two days off. It was very strange. I was there for exactly two years, and then I took a break and I went to Lake Tahoe in the spring of 1958.

I had worked for the *Oakland Tribune* part-time through two years of high school and two years of college in the advertising department. So when I arrived at Lake Tahoe, I went to the *Tahoe Tribune* to work in the advertising department. I quickly learned that you needed knee-high boots to march through the snow during a very heavy winter and to go door-to-door to businesses to sell advertising. I also quickly realized I wasn't going to eat if that was the only money I was going to make. [laughter]

Lucky for me, Harrah's was hiring. I was only twenty years old, so I knew I couldn't work on the floor, and I really didn't want to—I was intimidated by that anyway. So I went to apply for a job, and the fact that I had been a math and science major at Berkeley—which had no validity to the business world—they thought I might be really great with numbers, so they put me in the payroll department, which consisted of two people in the roof-top of the Quonset hut that was Harrah's at that time. And that's how I started—it started out as "just a summer job."

We only had two desks in the business office; so accounts payable and receivable worked the day shift, and then we switched and the same two desks became the payroll office at night. The office was at the top of the Quonset hut, and if you were over five foot eight inches you couldn't work there. You'd hit your head. The first day I met Bill Harrah, he was coming in off the stairwell from the roof, and the first stair down was a drop of about three feet. He just sort of fell in, and with his hands he grabbed the side of the wall. That was my first sighting of him.

He was very tall, so he had to sort of crouch to get down in there. He looked at me and he said, "You're not twenty-one are you?"

I said, "No, sir." And that was the end of it—he just kept walking. [laughter] I guess I looked pretty young. Anyway, that was my introduction to Bill Harrah.

I met Lloyd Dyer that late spring. I made his paycheck and Holmes Hendricksen's paycheck so they could go on vacation to a golf tournament in Las Vegas. Harrah's had a voucher system whereby you could get your pay three days early so that you could leave on a trip on Friday instead of waiting until Monday. They had to come up to the office personally to get that check, and that's how I met them.

In those days the way Harrah's and all the casinos operated was that from Memorial Day to Labor Day, gentlemen did not get a day off. They worked a seven-day week, and women worked a six-day week. So our romance was over cups of coffee on breaks. It wasn't a lot, but we did see each other on the beach, and I always say Lloyd fell in love with my mother's salad dressing. I worked the swing shift, so I worked from 4:30 until midnight, and I'd have an early dinner. Lloyd would come to the house on his break and have dinner with us, and he just loved that salad dressing. So he had to hang on to me. [laughter] In September, when I was going to go back to school, Lloyd asked me to marry him. I was smitten. Of course I married him, and the rest was history.

Part of the joy of the early years at Harrah's was the people—so many fun characters that I will always remember. It was such a melting pot. We had all come from somewhere else; we all had a story as to what brought us there. We shared those stories in

Lloyd and Joan Dyer ca. 1958. *"In September, when I was going to go back to school, Lloyd asked me to marry him. I was smitten. Of course I married him, and the rest was history."*

full, because we were living for today and we were so busy and worked such long hours. Everybody had a good time, and I never felt there was an attitude problem. You were so busy, you didn't have time to worry about it.

There was also a seasonality to the whole thing. You knew there was an end in sight. Summer was wild, but boy, the day after Labor Day you could roll a bowling ball down the middle of Highway 50, because the traffic stopped! [laughter] Then we could relax and get to know each other; and then, as you got further into the wintertime, the working schedules began to shrink. Employees were hoping for all the hours they could get. I was lucky in the payroll office, because I was pretty much a full-time person at that point and I didn't get my hours cut; but certainly people in the pit and in the slots did for the obvious reason: there were no customers.

My hours were about the same year around, but the crunch of the volume varied. The payroll system at that time—long before computers, of course—consisted of little pink-and-green pieces of paper that employees signed in on every day. At the end of the week we counted all these little pieces of paper. We had two huge NCR check printing machines—they were about four feet wide—and we typed in and calculated by adding up on a crank adding machine (not even an electric one) the totals per week and then printed the checks out. A few years later we got a little more sophisticated, and a better printer was purchased at Harrah's Reno. Then we literally drove the payroll down off the hill to the Reno store, it was printed, and then we drove it back the next day.

One snowy night there was a terrible accident at the Mt. Rose intersection at Highway 395. Tony Ortez, who was the supervisor of the payroll at that time, was in the accident. He was not injured, but the car was, and Harrah's Tahoe payroll was scattered all over the Mt. Rose highway. [laughter] Somehow we did get it put together. I don't remember the particulars, but I remember the panic. That alerted everybody to the fact that there had to be a better way. I think we went back to doing it at each club. Then, of course, computers and other things came along and life changed. [laughter] But that was long after I was gone.

In August of 1960 there was a huge fire on Donner Summit that lasted for about four days. Three of those days, the greater Lake Tahoe area had no electricity, but payroll had to go out during that time. Although by then we had several electric adding machines, we still had a couple that were hand operated. So we elected to do the payroll by candlelight and with hand-cranked adding machines. We hand-wrote every check, and we did get the payroll out on time. I lived in a little rental house at that time that had a gas hot-water heater. The other two women in the office lived where there were electric hot-water heaters, so everyone in the office came to my house and showered and did their laundry so that we could indeed get to work and do what we had to do. It gave everybody a wonderful pioneering spirit that we were able to get through that period with no problems, and everyone was very happy to get their paychecks on time.

DWAYNE KLING: Was there a strict dress code in the business office?

Yes, there was a dress code. For the most part we maintained the same dress code as the workers in the pit. After a few years we were allowed to wear business attire. Women always wore black or gray skirts—no trousers were allowed unless it was heavy winter, and then we could wear ski pants and the Harrah's white shirt with the red embroidered Harrah's logo on the back. Earrings were encouraged so that you looked put together, but they could only be the size of a quarter, and they could not have anything on them that dangled. Really, the dress code was fairly simple, and getting dressed every day was fairly simple.

All the gentlemen sent their clothes to the cleaners and their shirts to the laundry, and when you would go into Bobby Page's Cleaners you would see dozens of Harrah's Club white shirts lined up on hangers. The girls always did their laundry at home, and I can remember having white starched shirts hanging around waiting to be ironed. You had to be dressed perfectly—in the pit or in any department—and your shirts had to be pressed, starched, and look appropriate.

Harrah's concern about appearance ultimately led to the creation of a wardrobe department. Pauline Trigeré, the famous clothes designer, was hired as a consultant to design our first uniforms. I remember going to the fashion show she put on to show us what we would be wearing, and I remember a lot of murmuring in the audience like, "Oh my gosh! I'm not going to look like that model when *I* have that uniform on."

The biggest controversy was over the cocktail waitress uniforms. When I started in 1958, they wore the same white shirts that we did, but they wore soft pistachio green skirts. Now, Pauline Trigeré put them in scanty little uniforms. They were tastefully done and they weren't nearly as scant as they are today, but there were some senior cocktail waitresses that were pretty unhappy with them. They truly felt that it was discriminatory (although we didn't throw that word around in those days), because there were two of them that were probably fifty years old, and obviously they couldn't wear those costumes. So they were placed in cocktail waitress positions in the restaurant, where they were dressed like everybody else. They were not allowed to work in the bars or the entertainment areas where the tips would have been much greater. Naturally, there was some disgruntlement there.

What year did Harrah's start their uniform program?

Late in 1959 is when the program started.

Didn't they go through several different styles and colors of uniforms?

Oh, yes. One was a turquoise blue, sort of silk chiffon with huge sleeves that hostesses wore. And the sleeves got into everything and tangled around everything, and then the skirt swooped. And if you had too much hips . . . oh my goodness, you looked like a Sherman tank with a drape around it! So there were a lot of modifications that became more practical.

I always thought the pit people looked the best. They looked very starched and put together. There was also a time when there were vests that went over the shirts. Later they experimented with the color of the ties from black to red–I don't remember the sequence of that, but the dealers always looked very put together and professional. Of course there were rules about cuffs for gaming security reasons. Men couldn't have French cuffs and women couldn't have ruffly cuffs. They had to be plain and only single button, because the dealers might tuck a chip through their cuff and up their sleeve.

Were the uniforms being worn at both Tahoe and Reno?

Yes, and there were different uniforms for every department. Each department had their own identifying color and style.

Did Harrah's ever furnish any kind of housing for their employees at Lake Tahoe?

Not in the very early days, but they did experiment with it in the mid-1960s. However, it was quickly determined that the cleanliness standards of Harrah's were not being lived up to by the employees that lived there as tenants. And it became a question of whether or not Harrah's had the right to dictate policy to employees in their off hours. It opened a huge can of worms, and Harrah's quickly got out of the housing business. I don't know that it lasted more than one year.

After you were married, did you keep on working?

Yes, I kept working. I had a child in 1959, and in those days the policy in so much of industry in general was you could work when you were pregnant as long as no one could tell by looking at you. [laughter] As soon as that began to occur you were usually "out of there." I did get special dispensation because I came in the back door and went to the office, and nobody really saw me anyway; plus, they kind of needed me. At that point, as things were growing, they didn't want to have to break in anybody new. So I worked probably into my seventh month of pregnancy, and that got us into the summer.

I remember the opening of the South Shore Room in December of 1959 with Red Skelton as the star. At that time Lloyd was the scheduling supervisor. He attended every show for two weeks just to see how many employees were needed to operate the room efficiently. He would keep tabs on how many bus boys, how many waitresses, et cetera, were working. Mr. Harrah left nothing to chance. Lloyd had to work a split triple shift, the two night shows plus a four-hour period during the day. A very unusual but a very terrific assignment that he will never forget. [laughter]

Were you still working in payroll?

I was still in payroll, right. Payroll was the only place I ever worked. I had my child in June, and Louie Tyler, who was the head of security, had a delightful pair of daughters that he volunteered to babysit for me if I needed to go in for a few hours to work on the payroll. I worked on a hit-and-miss basis, and it worked out fine for everybody.

So, I worked very sporadically through that first year of my child's infancy, but the following year–this would have been 1960–Harrah's had a little slump in the spring, and things weren't so good. Everybody's hours got cut back a bit. Lloyd's hours were cut back, too, and he really considered moving on to another occupation.

We had been offered a position in California, and we went and looked at it, but Lloyd wasn't really thrilled with the offer. He decided we would stick it out at the lake. I went back to work full time, and that helped us out a little bit. We worked different shifts so we could take care of the child and not have to hire a babysitter. I worked nights and he worked days. Then he was made assistant slot manager, and suddenly he had a full-time job and an increase in pay. That sort of set our track. We were committed. We were there forever. We both loved Lake Tahoe and we loved the people. There was never another thought of, "Well what else are we going to do when we grow up?" [laughter]

It was a fun job, and a lot of our really best friends came out of those years. I worked full time for the rest of our time at Tahoe. Then in February 1962 Lloyd was named assistant chairman of community affairs, and we were transferred to Reno. That changed our life forever.

Did you go to work in Reno?

No. I became pregnant with my second child, so I officially retired in February of 1962, and I never went back to work. Of course, I always stayed affiliated with Harrah's, because our friends were Harrah's people and our life was very involved with Harrah's. Lloyd worked a six-day week as everybody did then, but we were just John Q. Citizens in the neighborhood.

I enjoyed living in Reno. We were in a really nice neighborhood with green grass, sidewalks, and neighbors who weren't all in gaming. I felt it was a good environment in which to raise a family. However, that only lasted two years, and then Lloyd got another promotion. He became director of community affairs, and that necessitated a move back to Lake Tahoe. I remember the weekend of President John Fitzgerald Kennedy's funeral

we had to go and look for a place to rent at Lake Tahoe, and it was cold and dismal and snowing. Nobody wanted to do this, but we had to do it because we had to be there by December 1, 1963. Fortunately, we were able to rent a house on Kingsbury Grade so we could make the move by the scheduled date.

We first rented a house and then decided that we would build a house in the Skyland subdivision on the Nevada side, near the lake. We were able to move in by June 1, 1964. I enjoyed the neighborhood, although it was a scary neighborhood if you had little children, because they could hide behind huge boulders and you wouldn't know where they were. More than once I had a two-year old missing for a few hours and I was panicking that he was either on the highway or in the lake. But we got so that we all watched out for each other's kids. One great couple, who were our next-door neighbors, Nancy and Joseph Ciatti, became dear friends, and they kind of oversaw us. She was like my surrogate mother, which was very nice.

In the fifties and sixties Lake Tahoe was just pine trees everywhere–no landscaping. The lake itself was beautiful, but I can remember on gray days when the lake reflected that gray sky it could be so depressing. And frankly, I was going through culture shock–having been at U.C. Berkeley and in a very enriched environment and suddenly coming to Lake Tahoe, that had nothing in the way of culture. Fortunately you could get in the car and drive to somewhere that had a little culture if you weren't snowed in, or if you weren't too busy to get off the hill. In the winter, when things slacked off a little bit, we could go to San Francisco, and that was really a treat.

How long did you stay in Skyland?

We were there just over a year when we got word that Lloyd was becoming a vice-president of the corporation and we would have to move back to Reno. He needed to be on the job right after Labor Day of 1965, so we started looking for houses in Reno. We wanted to be settled by the start of school, as our oldest boy was ready for kindergarten. We had a hard time finding a place; it was just one of those years when there wasn't much available in Reno. Of course, we finally did find a house, and we're still in it thirty-one years later.

It wasn't the house we really wanted. It had a whole lot of things wrong with it, but the location, location, location was perfect. I checked the school districts out. That was very important to me. Also, Lloyd didn't want to be out very far. We never wanted to be commuters, so "close in" was the byword, and it also was an area with trees. All the properties behind us were twenty or thirty years old already, and they had big trees that I could enjoy. Since then that's recycled; now I have big trees and almost more than them. I have this jungle syndrome. I over-plant because I was always afraid I'd never live in the house long enough to see it mature. But we've been here thirty-one years, and we've remodeled this a lot, and we've loved living in Reno.

After you came back to Reno for the second time and Lloyd stepped up in the organization, was he then considered to be in middle management or top management?

It was upper management. At that time I believe there were only three vice-presidents in the organization, and he was one of them.

By being in upper management, were you and Lloyd, as a couple, expected to entertain?

No. In fact it was discouraged. The theory was that if business people came to Reno they would much rather have dinner at Harrah's and see a show than come to my house. However, we did do a lot of escorting of people. If Lloyd had a gentleman in a meeting, then it was my job to entertain the

wife. I made a lot of drives up to and from and around Lake Tahoe, Virginia City, Truckee– I made the circuit. I remember a lady from New York City who wanted to go antique hunting, and I hadn't done too much of that. So I received quite an education, because there weren't too many places in Reno at that time that had antiques. But it was a fun assignment, and we met a lot of very interesting people.

In the late 1960s and early 1970s Lloyd was vice-president of finance, dealing mainly with people from New York City. He was looking for money to finance the expansion of the casinos and the building of the two hotels. That was his prime focus. When the decision was made to take the company public and make a stock offering, he worked two or three years on getting that to happen.

We met a lot of very interesting people who were fascinated by the gaming industry and thought that we must be a different breed of cat than the John Q. Citizen that worked for an insurance company or a bank. I can remember going to meetings where they almost hoped you would be wearing a pin-striped suit and a yellow shirt, but the Harrah's people came in looking like FBI agents. They were dressed in conservative suits, and many of the men wore the crew cuts. Bill didn't like long hair and absolutely outlawed mustaches. He wanted you to look like "Joe Clean," and certainly anything but a gambler, so we perpetuated that image.

When you looked around our pit, many of the dealers were college students who had come to Harrah's from all over the United States to work summer jobs and stayed to make it their career. They were the polished young kids of America. They were good people and they had integrity. The last thing in the world we would think of was somebody being dishonest. So Harrah's was really a paradox of what the public thought gaming was. And most of that was due to Bill Harrah himself. His standards were continued when the entertainment world became a part of

Harrah's. Entertainers were astounded at how well they were treated, and actually pampered. Harrah's employed special people that knew what the entertainers liked to eat, or if they wanted starch in their pillow cases. And the level of class in everything Harrah's did was always there, whether it was the soap in the hotels and the quality of the towels or the joy of working with Henry Conversano, the decorator who did Harrah's Tahoe. There wasn't anything red, and there wasn't a piece of fringe to be found. There was subtlety and elegance, and that's what Bill liked.

Also, he was fortunate enough to surround himself with people who followed through with his ideas–people such as Lloyd Dyer, Holmes Hendricksen, and people of that calibre. Without realizing it, he demanded absolute respect. He didn't seek it; it just came, mostly because he was comfortable to work with. He'd certainly have his moments, and he could be temperamental and he could be silent. (Silence was always the killer.) But he had high standards, and he always kept a little notepad in his shirt pocket and he made notes about everything. In management meetings those notes were acted upon. I remember one thing that came out of a visit to Monte Carlo: that was white gloves on some of the janitors. It was a short-lived experiment that was really a pain in the neck, but at least they tried it. And I think some of those kinds of things that were somewhat pretentious and beyond the limits of class were a laugh, but they were tried.

In many businesses people's promotions are oftentimes based to a degree on their wives or their wives' behavior. Did you ever notice anything like that in Harrah's?

I did. There was a time when there were a few wives that Bill didn't care for. The biggest infraction was being too "chatty." He didn't like chit-chat. He hated cocktail parties where you had to have a chit-chatty conversation. He'd just turn around and walk away from

you. And, of course, good manners trained all of us that you do make social conversation. So it was hard to know where to cut that off. He didn't want to come to our house particularly. He did that very little, occasionally a barbecue. But he wasn't really comfortable. We'd go to his house. He was more comfortable with that arrangement.

Through the years, with his different wives, Lloyd and I did get involved in two things that were extracurricular with Bill. One was the car collection and the Horseless Carriage parade group. Lloyd was even driving cars in parades every now and again, which was kind of fun, and I got dressed in the period costumes every once in a while and would ride in the Horseless Carriage parades.

We were not active in the golf tournaments, because Lloyd was not a golfer at that time. However, I went to the ladies' events and was a "worker bee" along with all the other executive wives, and we would stage a luau or conduct a fashion show.

The other thing that Lloyd and Holmes Hendricksen got involved with was the Phi Delta Theta fraternity. When Mr. Harrah found out that both Lloyd and Holmes were Phi Delta at the University of Utah, he had lunch with them one day and said, "I think it would be a good idea if we did something for that fraternity on the Reno campus. Why don't you guys get that going?" We also found out that John Ascuaga was a Phi Delta at the University of Idaho. So suddenly we had some power packs to work with on this, and I became the grunt-work secretary for this effort. We put in a call to the University of Miami at Oxford, Ohio, where Phi Delta Theta had been founded and where their archives were, and we got a huge list of names from greater northern California, Nevada, and Utah. We tracked down a lot of Phi Deltas in the area, and it was amazing how many there were.

The first event we put on, we had sixty people. Bill Harrah and Scherry came, as did John and Rose Ascuaga. After that we'd have

One of the Horseless Carriage Club parades stopped outside of the old Harrah's Bingo parlor, ca. 1960. *"Lloyd was even driving cars in parades every now and again, which was kind of fun, and I got dressed in the period costumes every once in a while and would ride in the Horseless Carriage parades."*

two events a year that one or the other of them would host. Pretty soon we had all the executives from Miami, Ohio, coming out, and it got to be a "big do." We were either at the Villa Harrah or in the South Shore Room, and we had great parties.

The ultimate thing was to establish a chapter on the University of Nevada campus, which we did. Lloyd and Holmes were very involved. I think Lloyd was the secretary-treasurer of the alumni association for fourteen years. [laughter] We kind of were in it forever. It now has a life of its own, and Lloyd has stepped back from it, as has Holmes. But it was a great time, and Bill was just thrilled that this happened. He was very grateful to the Phi Deltas at UCLA, because he was so shy at that time and they helped bring him out of that a little bit. He just felt a real kinship to those people.

Did you ever know of any people that were turned down for a promotion or demoted because of their spouses' behavior?

I don't know of any that were ever demoted, but there may have been a couple that were "skirted around" for promotion because of their spouses' behavior.

I only know of a couple of cases where Bill preferred if certain wives weren't always included in all the activities. For the most part he just tolerated it and kind of ignored it, but usually the biggest offense was if you were a little too chatty. He didn't like that. He seemed to like me—we had a comfortable, but obviously distant, relationship.

Lloyd and I were always invited to the big parties with the Lawrence Welk group, as were other executives, and we always made an effort to go when he wanted us there. However, there were a lot of others that didn't go, and I don't know if they were asked and preferred not to go, or what the story was, but we were always there. And then, of course, in the very late years we were thrilled to make a trip to Australia with him and later to spend a month in Europe with Bill and Verna. It was the trip of a lifetime. I had to pinch myself.

I was always one to remember that no matter what or who you are, remember where you came from—you always go home and wash the socks and clean the toilets. Don't get on your throne. Don't think you are a big deal. I remember after Lloyd became president of the company, I was in a grocery store, and I met a lady who said, "I can't believe you're doing your own shopping." I just looked at her like, "Are you kidding?" And then I thought, "Is that what people think?"

There was a brief time when we considered getting a bigger home, mainly as a status symbol to say that we were what we were. Then we began to think: "But that isn't who we are. We still are who we are, and we may live in different circles and certainly are high flying, with all the entertainers and all of that . . . ," but it was OK to be who we were, and Bill didn't press us to get a different home. All he ever cared was that you lived in southwest Reno. He didn't like you to live in any of the other three quadrants. As long as you were in the southwest, it was fine.

The Sheppards and us were the two that didn't really get into the big prestige houses. We did build a swimming pool in 1972, and the main reason for that was in those days we did not take a summer vacation. In gaming, even though we were in the end of it that was pretty much year round, you didn't take a summer vacation. We could have taken off in the summer, but we didn't want to show other employees that we could be off when they had to work.

For example, even during the five years Lloyd was president of the company, he always went to work on Christmas Eve and Christmas Day. He always walked through the pit to make everybody else feel like, "Hey, you know we're *all* working here." We wanted people to realize that we weren't way up here

and they weren't way down there. I know in the later years of the company—after our time—that faded away a bit. People just didn't make that effort.

We came up through the ranks and we were always one of them. It wasn't us versus them. We were always very gracious to all employees in all the departments for that reason. We were never the "Ugly American" or the demanding executive. If Lloyd felt something was wrong, he didn't deal with it face to face; he wasn't a real demonstrative person. In the board room he could scream and yell if it was necessary to get things corrected, but we always tried to be very sensitive to people and their feelings.

I think the key thing you touched on was that you came up through the ranks. You both began at entry-level positions. Currently, most CEOs have never been at that level.

That's right. They come laterally from some other industry. I remember two very special people in our lives early on were Hal and Beulah White. Hal was a shift manager at Harrah's Tahoe. He had come out of Elko as a musician and then got into the gaming business. He had been in World War II, fought in the Battle of the Bulge, and had seen some pretty heavy action. At Lake Tahoe he used to grumble, as we went to the time clock, "If they just would quit trying to run this like General Motors and run it like a gambling joint, everything would be fine." [laughter] And we'd all just laugh.

Beulah was a hostess in the restaurant and a pretty tough cookie as a waitress, very efficient, full of laughs and just gave us another dimension to our lives. She was another surrogate mother of mine. The day my first child was born, Lloyd was a scheduling supervisor and was splitting his time between Reno and Tahoe in that position. One day when Lloyd was in Reno I was with Beulah, and I didn't even know I was in labor when she said, "I think we need to go to Carson to the hospital." Because, of course, there was no hospital at South Lake Tahoe. We called Lloyd in Reno and said, "We'll meet you there." [laughter] So she took me, which was very gracious of her. That's an example of executives' thoughtfulness in the early years.

Earlier you mentioned you spent a month in Europe with Bill and Verna Harrah. Was that a business trip or a pleasure trip?

It was a combination of business and pleasure. A whole lot of fun and some business. There were really three main reasons for the trip. The first reason was that in October of every year Bill went to Italy to select his wardrobe from the Brioni tailors. He would go there for fittings, then do something else, and then come back and pick up the clothes.

The second reason was to go to Stuttgart, Germany, to visit the Mercedes works, because at that time Bill was the Mercedes and Ferrari dealer for Reno. The third reason we went was to participate in the London-to-Brighton Run. This is an event of antique cars aged 1904 or older. We were to ride in a Panhard-Levassor that had been shipped from Harrah's Automobile Collection to England. Harrah's chief mechanic, Clyde Wade, and another mechanic went with it. The London-to-Brighton Run had been an annual event for seventy-five years. It was more of a parade and an excursion than a race, and Bill just relished it.

The day of the run was a cold and blustery day, but there were huge throngs of people in Westminster Park. Well, we went about a mile and a half, and the car broke down. Then I realized why Bill brought the mechanics. We also had a lorry—a truck—and a Daimler-Benz limousine with a driver along with us. I thought, "We aren't even out of the park, and we have to have mechanical repair." We had gone over Westminster Bridge, but we weren't fully out of the park. So they fixed the car, and we started off again. Then it started to rain! Now, all these cars, this vintage of 1904 or older, have no tops, so we knew we were going to get wet. We were all pretty-well bundled up and dressed appropriately, but when we started to get wet Bill just stopped the car and said, "OK, you and Verna get in the Daimler-Benz." They went a little bit further, and pretty soon he and Lloyd were getting wet, so then Lloyd got in the Daimler-Benz and we're following along. Bill decided to stick it out, but the rain got heavier and heavier, and then the car broke down again. They couldn't get the car started, so they loaded it on the lorry, and then as a little parade, we three continued on to Brighton.

It was amazing—these very stalwart gentlemen from all over the world soaked to the skin, making it to the end of the run. There was one gentleman from Oklahoma who brought over his own white Rolls-Royce to follow his antique car, and his wife rode in the Rolls-Royce. [laughter] It was a very different group of people. When we got to Brighton we stayed in a lovely small hotel. That night we went to a black-tie, gowned event, and everybody was recoiffed and dried out, and we had a very gala evening—fun memories in that regard.

Some other fun memories include flying over the Swiss Alps on a clear October day and having lunch as we viewed the beautiful Alps. We were in Bill's private plane, a GII, and he took along Karl Thoeni, a waiter from the South Shore Room, as the food steward, plus *three* pilots in case of emergencies. One day we landed in Helsinki, Finland, in a huge snow storm—I remember coming down, down, down through the storm, and then all of a sudden we saw the tops of the fir trees, and bingo! We were on the ground. Jim Barnett was one of the pilots, and I remember he turned around to me and said, "Today we earned our salary." [laughter]

I thought, "Oh, my god! I'm glad we're on the ground." [laughter]

They were great pilots. That was one of the joys we had all the years we were at Harrah's–great airplanes and the fantastic caliber of the pilots that we had on those airplanes.

The day that Harrah's bought the GII, Bill and Verna and Lloyd and I got in it, and we flew to Boise and back, just for fun. He just wanted to see what it felt like. Bill was pretty silent through the whole trip, and after we came back and got off he says, "Guess that's what $4,000,000 will buy." [laughter] It was great.

We had a company car for a lot of years, as many executives did, and as you moved up the ladder your car got better and better. When Lloyd was executive vice-president he had a twelve-cylinder Jaguar. Although we loved it, it needed work a lot. It was pretty temperamental. So, soon after Lloyd was made president he went in to see Bill, and they were laughing about something, and Lloyd says, "You know, I'd love to have a different company car."

And Bill said, "What would you like?"

And Lloyd said, "I want a Ferrari."

Bill was so thrilled that anybody even wanted to drive one of his Ferraris that they left that moment for the dealership. There was a used one–he didn't have to have a new one–one-year old. And Bill said, "Let's go try it." Lloyd liked it, and so he took possession of this bronze-colored Ferrari.

At that time our children were all teenagers, so they were pretty thrilled to have a Ferrari in our garage. But we had our own rules, as did Harrah's. We had no family members drive the Ferrari except Lloyd, and of course it only sat two. So as a family of five, we never went anywhere in it. [laughter] But it looked smashing in the driveway.

One time it died on us on the top of Spooner Summit as we were rushing to a dinner show at Harrah's Tahoe. Fortunately, one of Harrah's limousines was going the opposite way, and they spotted us and pulled over. The limo driver said, "I'll call on my car phone and get help here. I'll turn around the limo and take you where you're going." So we just jumped in the limo and left the Ferrari sitting there.

But it was a fun, fun car that Lloyd drove for three years. Then for practical reasons we changed to a 6.9 Mercedes. Bill Harrah got the first 6.9–there were very few of them allowed into the United States, and he got a brown one. One day he was receiving an award in Gardnerville from the Western Peace Officers Association, and we drove there with him in his brand new 6.9 Mercedes. There was no speed limit then, so we zipped right through Washoe Valley, and he was so thrilled with it he said to Lloyd, "You really ought to try one of these." So that was our next car.

The whole automobile "thing" was fun, and it was a joy to watch Bill around his cars. He was a Teddy Bear with them. He purred like a kitten. I enjoyed being a host to some people on a few occasions when he took us through the car collection and talked to people about why he had each car. One was Henry Kissinger, and Mr. Kissinger was very grateful for the tour and was fascinated with the cars. Bill took such great pride in knowing all about them, and, of course, the car collection building was pristine. You could eat on the floors. Every car was perfect, and all the mechanics that worked there thought they had died and gone to heaven. What greater place could there be?

Did you meet any of the executives or their wives when they came into the organization?

Yes. Actually, prior to the sale of Harrah's to Holiday Inns they had a three-day gathering of a great many people at Lake Tahoe. We had two events. One was at the Villa [Villa Harrah], where we hosted a big luncheon. The other was a dinner in Harrah's proper in the convention room, with a question-and-answer phase with facilitators. One of the lasting memories of that dinner is everyone having to stand up and identify who they were and how long they'd been with the organization. It stunned the Holiday Inn people, the longevity that Harrah's people had. For instance, at that point top management of Harrah's had all been with the company at least twenty years. Five or six of us stood up and said that. Then the top five people from Holiday Inns stood up and said two years, eighteen months, three years, and so forth. It was a complete contradiction. Very different.

The founding gentleman of Holiday Inns, Kemmons Wilson, was out of it for the most part at that point. I believe he was deceased soon thereafter, but it was so very obvious that theirs was a different philosophy. It quickly reminded us of the stick-to-it-ness and loyalty that everyone cultivated unknowingly to Harrah's and to Bill Harrah. The reason we were where we were was because we liked what we did; we liked who we did it with; and there was a great sense of pride in the end product.

Those are some of the main reasons for Harrah's success—those things you just expressed?

Right. Bill Harrah was able to cause things to happen because of the type of people that he had working with him . . . with him more than for him. I can only remember one or two occasions when people that he brought in from the outside to do specific tasks at mid- to upper-level management didn't fit in and were let go or moved on. For the most part everybody rose to their inner selves' best expectations. I think there were people that succeeded at Harrah's that didn't know they had it in them, but they rose to the occasion because the task was set forth.

Bill hired people for the expertise that they had, but he was often surprised at some of the expertise they carried in their hip pocket. He found out who knew how to do what. Some people were strictly gaming oriented, and that's where they stayed; but for

that reason, they did that well. They weren't ever considered for upper management and they weren't given the opportunity to come through the ranks, because they didn't bring another area of expertise with them.

What a lot of people don't realize is that it takes more than just gaming knowledge to operate a gaming casino.

Absolutely! First of all, it's a business, and that's the strata it had to be brought to. I think in the beginning that didn't exist. All of a sudden you had to manage that money; you had to be accountable for that money. Taxes were involved. Credibility. Paperwork. And suddenly you were a business. This happened in the early 1940s, when things began to grow, and particularly after World War II. That's when Maurice Sheppard became involved, and he was an accountant. He was a number pusher and a good one. He was often at loggerheads with Bill Harrah over his spending, because Bill didn't really care what some things cost. It was Shep's burden to pay the bills and to try and tell Bill Harrah "no" once in a while.

I think all of the top management, from time to time, had to tell Bill Harrah "no." His acceptance varied according to the mood of the moment, and often in the later years the mood of the moment was set by his personal marriage situation. If his marriage was on the rocks and things were bad, I think it was very difficult in the board room. Lloyd was very quiet about it. He didn't bring a lot of that home, but I could sense the mood. There were times when it was very tough, particularly in the tenure of Maurice Sheppard as president of the company, there were a lot of tense years, and it was difficult.

When Lloyd was president, was Bill married to Verna most of the time?

The majority of the time, right. And Verna made Bill happy—they were like "two bees in a buzzer," they got along so good. They both loved to read; they both took an afternoon nap. They just fit together, and she was really good to him. She was a nice person and still is.

So it was possibly Bill's happiest time in life?

I think so. It was certainly one of them. His little boys were growing up. They were still pretty young, and Scherry had custody of the two boys; but he would visit them a lot, and they weren't causing him any difficulties or any problems. They were little, naughty, spoiled brats once in a while, as good kids can be, but, basically, that part of his life was OK.

I think Scherry and he obviously had had their ups and downs. They had had a lot of good times, but they were more contemporaries, so I don't think she kowtowed to his wishes quite as much as Verna did. Also, [Scherry] was way more bogged down in the Horseless Carriage thing. She took on the great responsibility of trying to keep a lot of those things going that later wives really weren't burdened with. By then it had phased out. The automobile collection had a life of its own, and Bill's wives didn't have to get involved in that.

Bill had his moments. There was a real transition when he went from short haircuts and grey flannel suits for everybody to when he was having his own mid-life crisis, and suddenly he was mod with sideburns, bell-bottoms, and neckerchiefs. But simultaneously with the fashion and the personal statement, he was having emotional difficulties with wives. And so it splashed over to the business. I never saw him angry at a wife at a function, but I saw silence at times, which was his mode when he wasn't happy. But he was really a homebody. He loved his home. He had pets, and he loved being at home. He didn't really seek an outside world. His outside world was the automobile collection, which was his Saturday routine. He was out there on Saturdays, and he loved it.

After Bill divorced Scherry he had a little routine he went through. The first thing he would do when he dated a new person would be to send her to the Mayo Clinic, because he was a great believer in that. (It was where we all did go, by the way.) If she was in good health, that was great. If she needed a little help, that was taken care of too.

Did he send them to Mayo before or after they were married?

Before they were married, but while they were dating. He just believed that everybody should have a good physical and should go to the best place. After Mayo, they usually got a very nice mink coat and then a Ferrari, and if they were really lucky they got a big diamond ring. [laughter] So that was kind of the sequence of things. Yes. Lloyd went through all of those romances.

Then upon Bill's death, it fell on us, before they even got back with the remains, to start putting together the funeral. It was like having a huge family that you didn't really know that well. We had all the ex-wives at the funeral. We strategically placed them so that none of them sat next to each other, but they were all there. Every ex-wife was there, including Thelma, his first wife. I remember going to the church—St. John's Presbyterian Church—and the minister, Mr. Barrett, was wonderful. I knew his wife because she was a counselor at Reno High, and they were willing to let us come in and put in sound equipment and wire it so the services were audible to everybody. Lloyd helped work with Verna on the list of who would be the pallbearers, and we got John Denver to come and sing.

It was quite a spectacular event. Of course, there wasn't a spare seat in the church, and there also wasn't a dry eye in the audience. I hadn't really been through anybody's death that was close to me family-wise, and it was very emotional for me.

Did a feeling of gloom and depression permeate the club after Mr. Harrah's death?

Yes. It was brief, and it was especially tough on management. All of us had to rise to the occasion and be strong for everybody else, but I think right at the top it was, "Hey, this is too big. This will go on. Nothing will happen. We're going to keep this the way it was." And of course the burden then immediately came upon the executors to try to deal with that, and hence a whole lot of problems were unveiled. The reading of the will, I don't think was a real surprise to anybody, but dealing with the financial picture was a difficult few years for the executor. But that's another story.

Lloyd resigned as president of Harrah's when it was taken over or purchased by Holiday Inns, Incorporated, in 1980. Is that right?

Yes, that is correct.

You've been involved in many community and civic affairs over the years, haven't you, Joan?

Yes. Like every other parent I started doing things with my kids, such as PTA and scouting. Then I got more involved in volunteerism. I became a member of the Junior League of Reno in its fledgling days, in early 1972. By 1974 I was president of that organization, which was a great growing time for me, and I met a lot of great people who were very no-nonsense and very time accountable. One thing that came through to Lloyd and I with twenty-five years at Harrah's was being time accountable and punctual.

In 1976 I was asked to join the board of directors of the Sierra Arts Foundation and to spearhead an effort to get arts in the schools. And in September of 1977 we started the Arts in Education Program, for which I still work. I had to raise money for it, so I had my first experience in being what I call a "professional beggar"–writing grants and going to the school district for money–and learned about

matching dollars. And that, "Yes, we'll give you $10,000 or $20,000, but you better go match it somewhere else." Through Sierra Arts and their wonderful staff and development people, we have been doing that ever since.

I probably over-stayed my welcome in the money-raising a little bit. In fact, a very diplomatic gentleman who did work on a consultant basis for Harrah's, and was a lobbyist forever and ever in the legislature, named Wally Warren, took me to lunch one day. And he said, "You know what? You need to back off this asking business, because what's happening is everybody you go to asking for money for your thing thinks they can then go to Harrah's–because you're married to the president–and ask for money." I was so naive that it had never even crossed my mind that people would do that. So I did back off asking for money. I kept doing and working with the program, but I wasn't involved in raising the money.

Getting back to the arts, weren't you recently given an award a few days ago?

Yes. I was very honored. The governor gave me the Distinguished Service to the Arts Award for the State of Nevada, which was great.

That's quite an accomplishment.

Well, I believe in a lot of things, and if I believe in it, I work for it. I'm on the University of Nevada Foundation Board; I raise money for the University of Nevada ski team; I'm on the board of public TV; and I just finished a six-year term on the board of directors and the executive committee of the United Way of Northern Nevada and the Sierras. But I'm starting to back away from the board positions. I think it's time for some young blood, like my children's age group.

My son Greg is thirty-seven, and he's very active in his community of Sacramento,

California. Jonathan, who is thirty-four, lives in Reno, and he's been on a project with the Nevada Museum of Art to raise some money. My daughter, Robin, is thirty-three, and she lives in Sun Valley, Idaho. She's just a "hard worker bee." She's very involved in the community, and she enjoys it. Yes, we all try to give something back.

And everything in your life "goes back" to Harrah's?

You bet. And really I have to take—for my personal side—one step beyond that to Lake Tahoe. That's what brought me to Nevada—Lake Tahoe. When I was a teenager and in high school a lot of us would come to the lake, and I fell in love with the mountains and Lake Tahoe. And actually Lake Tahoe brought Lloyd to Nevada. Lloyd, being a New Yorker, fell in love with the West and the blue skies, and he came west to go to school and then he fell in love with Lake Tahoe. And here we have stayed for those many wonderful years.

9

LLOYD DYER

*T*HIS ORAL HISTORY interview with Lloyd Dyer, husband of Joan Dyer and president of Harrah's from 1975 to 1980, was conducted in the office of the William F. Harrah Trust in Reno, Nevada, in March of 1997. Two sessions were required to complete it. Mr. Dyer was cooperative and helpful with his time and information.

Mr. Dyer was born in Pittsford, New York, on July 15, 1927. He first took a job with Harrah's at Lake Tahoe in the summer of 1957 in order to earn enough money to complete his education, and he never left the company.

In this oral history Dyer modestly remembers his rapid rise in the Harrah's organization and describes the various positions that he held. His expertise was in finance, and he recounts the many real estate transactions that he was involved in while he was vice-president and later president of the organization. Those transactions included the purchases of the Golden Hotel, the Overland Hotel, and the Palace Club. Additional topics of interest include Dyer's personal recollections of Bill Harrah, with whom he spent a great deal of time. Dyer's many anecdotes about Harrah are not only revealing but humorous. Mr. Dyer's account of Bill Harrah's marriage to Verna Harrah and the last years of his

life gives us a fresh perspective on the gaming giant's character and personality.

LLOYD DYER: I was born in a small town–Pittsford, New York, a suburb of Rochester, New York–on July 15, 1927. My father was from Maine, and my mother was from Boston. When they got married my dad was offered a job–I don't recall what it was at the time–and they moved to Rochester and then subsequently moved to the small town of Pittsford, which had a population of about 4,000 people. They lived in that town and other neighboring towns until my father passed away in 1970, and then my mother moved west to Los Angeles to live near my sister, who was teaching school in the L.A. area.

DWAYNE KLING: Do you have any other sisters and brothers?

There were six of us. My second oldest brother passed away about five years ago, and so I have three brothers and a sister left. I have one brother who is a retired school principal, and he lives in Vermont. I have another brother that's retired from Eastman Kodak that lives in Arizona, near Phoenix. And I have another brother who's a retired FBI agent that lives in Tacoma, Washington. My sister, who's a retired school teacher, lives in Arcadia, California.

Did you grow up around Pittsford?

I went through the Pittsford school system and graduated in 1945, and then subsequently went in the army. After I was discharged, I worked there for a couple of years. Then I went west and started college in Utah.

How did you happen to go to college in Utah?

When I was in the military in Fort Dix, New Jersey, I met this gentleman from Provo, Utah, and we became friends. So when I was discharged at Camp Stoneman, I took a train from Oakland to Ogden and from Ogden to Provo and spent two weeks with him. I was

just absolutely fascinated with the mountains and the country, and I made up my mind I would come back some day.

I went home and worked on a golf course for about six months and then went to work for Eastman Kodak in a production job. I managed to put away a little money and then talked my older brother into going to college. We applied and were accepted at Brigham Young University in Provo, Utah. I knew nothing of the University of Utah at that time.

In the fall of 1948 we started at BYU. At that time they had something like 3,500 students, and today I understand they have about 40,000. Out of the 3,500 students there were probably a hundred non-Mormons, and I spent more time going off campus having a cigarette [laughter] than I spent on campus. [laughter] I lasted four quarters and left for home.

Next I went to Denver University and enrolled in a hotel management school. I went there for the winter quarter of 1950, and I decided that if my father didn't own a hotel, I was going to be a cook the rest of my life; so I got out of that program and went back home again. I took a part-time job at Kodak for a while. Then I enrolled at the University of Utah, and I graduated from there in 1953.

When I graduated from college, what I wanted to do was go to law school, but I didn't have any money. So I worked as a brakeman for the Southern Pacific and was employed out of Ogden, Utah, but was sent to Carlin, Nevada, and worked from Carlin to Imlay, Nevada. Eventually I worked out of the Sparks yards and worked on the "extra" board–worked all over this division and stayed there for two years to earn enough money to go to law school. I went to law school for a year at Utah, and now I'm out of money again. So I went back to the railroad for a while, and later I worked for a finance company in Salt Lake City.

Holmes Hendricksen worked for Harrah's in 1956. (The reason Holmes went to work there is that there was a shift manager by the name of Hal White, who had a son, Wayne, who also went to Utah. The three of us–Holmes, Wayne, and myself–all belonged to the Phi Delta Theta fraternity.) The following year, April of 1957, Holmes went back to Harrah's to earn enough money to return to school and finish his master's degree. Then I went to Harrah's, and Holmes got me a job through Pat France. (His real name was Pat Francellini.) Pat was cashier manager, and Holmes talked Pat into hiring me. I soon discovered that I could work twelve hours a day, seven days a week. I thought, "Hell, I could work for a year and earn enough money to go back and finish law school."

I remember the first day I met Pat. He had an old Studebaker, and the only bank at Tahoe was the Bank of America down at the Y,[1] which is about five miles away. Pat says, "Come on. I'll interview you in the car." Well, he had the car trunk full of coin. He had all the coin from the slot drop in the trunk of his car. Halfway to the bank he ran out of gas, and I had to push this goddamned car filled with coin into the gas station to get gas. Maybe that's why he gave me a job–he probably felt sorry for me! [laughter]

Holmes was the swing-shift supervisor, and I was just a cashier. I worked eight hours a day in the cashier's office and took an hour break and then went back and worked upstairs making coin banks for the change people for another four hours. So I worked twelve hours a day, and I did that until January of 1958. I worked seven days a week. Never took a day off. Holmes did the same thing, except he only worked eight hours a day. Then we took three or four days off in 1958 and went to Las Vegas to watch the Tournament of Champions, a golf tournament.

At about that time I met my future wife, Joan. She was working in the business office at Harrah's. She was a junior at the University of California and had come to Harrah's for a summer job. After we met she decided to stay

over, and we were married that following September.

In the meantime I'd had a couple of promotions. Harrah's created a job called "employee counselor": If an employee had a personal problem or a job-related problem, they could come and talk to me confidentially about their problem; then I would try and work it out with the club manager, the assistant club manager, or the department managers. I worked on that both in Reno and Tahoe. Later that job was eliminated because management felt that the supervisors should be doing what I was doing. If a supervisor is doing a good job, you don't need an employee counselor.

My next job was a scheduling supervisor. I was in charge of scheduling and involved in the scheduling of most of the departments in Reno and Tahoe. I would go into a department, look at their schedules, watch them operate, see how the shifts worked, and make suggestions. Maybe they needed a person here and a person there. The idea was to tighten labor in each department so that we didn't have any unnecessary employees in the various departments. The first job I had was scheduling the South Shore Room when it opened in December of 1959. Red Skelton opened the room. He was there for two shows a night for three weeks. I would go in during the dinner show and watch the bus boys, the waiters, and the captains work, and then I'd go to the cocktail show and do the same thing. I did it for three weeks, and then I wrote a report on my observations.

Who did you report to?

I reported to Rome Andreotti. Rome was the assistant club manager at the lake at that time; Eldon Campbell was general manager.

While you were observing the South Shore Room, did you evaluate any other departments?

Yes. I'd go through the slot operations (I didn't get involved in the pit; the pit kind of took care of itself) the cashier's department, and just about every other non-gaming area. The job soon kind of went away. It was felt that we'd done as much as we could and that the department managers should be doing their own scheduling and doing it right. So I went back to the cashier's for a short period of time, and then I wound up being the slot department's assistant manager. I worked for a fellow by the name of Max Lewis. I worked for Max quite a while. Then Mr. Sheppard, who was vice-president of community affairs at the time, had an opening for an assistant. I was recommended to him, and he interviewed me, and I got the job. Getting the job necessitated a move to Reno. That happened in January of 1962.

Shep had an office at Tahoe and Reno, but his main office was in Reno. All of management had an office at the lake. Even though they lived in Reno and operated out of Reno, they would come to Lake Tahoe for a day or two almost every week to attend management meetings and to meet with the employees who reported to them.

When I moved to Reno I was involved in the leasing and the acquisition of real estate. That more or less became my field of expertise, real estate, but I also worked in community affairs with Shep. Community affairs meant lobbying for city council members, county commissioners, state legislators, and working with Shep in the state legislature as a lobbyist. I also worked with and lobbied with the supervisors in El Dorado County in California and the county commissioners from Douglas County, Nevada.

To go back a few years—there was a fellow by the name of Lee DeLauer that came to work at Harrah's in 1956 from the Kottinger & Semenza accounting firm, and he worked in the business office with Shep. Shep hired him in the early 1960s to be Harrah's lobbyist in El Dorado County and Douglas County. When Lee left Harrah's in 1963, Shep sent me back to the lake to take Lee's job in the lobbying and public relations area. I also continued to work with Shep in the real estate and in leasing warehouses for antique cars.

When I first went to work for Shep, I think Bill Harrah had about six cars and a garage on Lake Street. And then slowly, as we were accumulating cars, we needed warehouses for them. I don't remember what year it was, but Harrah's rented the old PFE [Pacific Fruit Express] icehouse in Sparks and the adjoining property. That's where the auto collection was located. But there were also a variety of warehouses around town that housed newly-purchased cars. When they were restored they were brought back to the old icehouse that we had rented from John Dermody.

To get back to Lake Tahoe in the 1950s and the early 1960s when you worked there: were there any special employees at Harrah's Club that were unique as far as being interesting characters or people that had worked in gaming in California or elsewhere before coming to Tahoe?

The one guy in particular that I remember was Phillip "Curly" Musso, who was a shift manager when I first started at Harrah's and who eventually became club manager. Curly came out of Vallejo and was in a horse book operation there prior to World War II. When he was discharged from the service he came to Lake Tahoe, and he and a fellow by the name of George Cannon actually started Heavenly Valley. He and George Cannon also owned George's Gateway Club that Bill Harrah first leased and then purchased from them. That became the original Harrah's Club at Lake Tahoe.

Did you ever work with Frank Perez?

Yes. I knew Frank Perez well. When Harrah's bought the Nevada Club, which was adjacent to the Stateline Club on the south side of Highway 50, Frank was running it for the owners, Clyde and Bud Beecher. Clyde was the father and Bud was the son. Frank had also been involved in running gaming operations on ships off the coast of southern California and gambling clubs in Palm Springs.

Frank was a real character and a very neat guy. He was a crippled man–he had one leg shorter than the other and wore an elevated shoe. Frank was really what you would call today a casino host. He knew the high rollers, and when they would come in he would put them in the showroom, would grant them credit and do whatever was necessary to make them comfortable in the club. He was the first casino host that we had.

Were the employees' work ethics different in those days?

Yes, probably they were. I think what Harrah's did, and a lot of casinos did, was to have a core of employees that worked year 'round. Most of them were of little education, and, at the most, maybe high school graduates. Very few were college people. Then in the summer times when the business was really busy, they hired college kids, and that's how Holmes Hendricksen and I went to work at Harrah's.

The reason I didn't go back to law school is that I had these promotions, I got married, I enjoyed what I was doing, I really loved the gaming business, and I just stayed. I remember telling Holmes and also my wife, "With a college education, if a guy keeps his nose clean and works hard, God knows where he can go in this company, because there aren't many people here that have an education, including top management." Even Bill Harrah didn't finish college. I think he was a junior when he quit.

As I said, I'd had two or three promotions within a year, and when I went to work for Shep, I thought, "My gosh, the way things are going, my next step could be to a vice-president." I felt that there were real opportunities for me at Harrah's.

So did you set a goal of being vice-president or possibly even president of the company someday?

Yes, I did. I think at that time my job was director, which is different than a director on a board. It was a title that we had in mid-management. There was a director of services or director of public relations, and I was director of community affairs.

Did the directors report to the vice-presidents?

Yes, they did. I don't even think we had senior vice-presidents then. Bill was the president, and Bob Ring was general manager.

In 1965, when we were looking to borrow money to build a hotel at Lake Tahoe, Shep told me that two names were brought up at a management meeting as candidates to fill the newly created position called vice-president of finance, whose job would be to go out and raise money to build a hotel at Tahoe. Bob Martin and I were the two names that were brought up to management, and I got the job. So, in September of 1965 I was transferred to Reno, and I've been here ever since. Our offices were upstairs in the bank building on the northeast corner of Second and Virginia Streets, where Planet Hollywood is now. I still continued to handle the real estate, but was not involved in community affairs. John Gianotti took over my job at Lake Tahoe. I still reported to Shep, and my job was to find the finances needed to build the hotel at Tahoe.

At that time we used to borrow money from First Interstate Bank–known then as the First National Bank of Nevada. We would borrow money from First National Bank of Nevada to the tune of about three million dollars every winter, and we would pay our vendors and pay our bills. Then in the summertime we would earn enough to pay the bank back. But we were always behind the eight ball. We never got even. I remember talking to Shep and/or Bill about it, and I said, "This is kind of dumb, because we are paying a high interest rate and we are slow in paying our vendors back, creating a real PR problem in town. What we really should do is get a long-term note of some kind, get even, and then take our time paying it off." They agreed, and I remember going over to talk to Joe Sbragia, who was in charge of lending at First National of Nevada. We borrowed five million dollars and paid everybody off, and from that point on we didn't owe anybody.

Then it was my job to try and raise the money to build a hotel at Tahoe. We had a great rapport with the Greyhound Company because of the contracts we had with them— Greyhound special buses (not scheduled buses, but special buses) would bring players up from Sacramento, Stockton, Modesto, San Francisco, and Oakland. We were getting buses probably five or six times a day. Most people would stay for two or three hours; play, eat, drink, get on the bus, and go home.

They weren't special junket people? They were regular customers?

Yes, they were regular customers, but they would get a refund when they got there. When the buses first started, I think the refund was about $2.00 per customer. Because of our volume of business we had a great rapport with Greyhound. More on that later.

Also, Mead Dixon knew a banker in New York, so Mead and I went back to New York to talk to him at the Bank of New York. They told us that they didn't feel there were any conventional banks that would lend us money. The only way we could get any money would be through some venture capital people or through insurance companies or maybe some corporation that would lend money to us.

They introduced us to a gentleman by the name of Sam Silverman, a very brilliant man who had graduated from Columbia Law School. He really was a "money man" in the old sense of the word, a very refined gentleman. He told us that he was so busy doing other things that he didn't feel he could help us, but he would introduce us to a gentleman by the name of David Shuldiner, who was a protégé of Sam's. Later when I met David Shuldiner, I negotiated a deal with him where he would get half a percent of any money that he found. When I called Shep and told Shep that I had met David, he said, "Bill Harrah wants to know what kind of a man he is." I said, "He's a 110-pound Jew with a 100-pound brain." [laughter] Bill thought that was so funny. David is still alive today and still a dear friend, and when I go to New York occasionally, which is once or twice a year, we still get together and have either lunch or dinner.

Did he find you five million?

David first tried through insurance companies. I remember one was Connecticut General (I can't remember the others), but to no avail. He had a connection with the Greyhound people, and we met with the president and chief executive officer of Greyhound, Fred Ackerman. They agreed to loan us ten million dollars at 10 percent interest. The prime rate was about 5 percent, so it was really costly money. We were just about ready to make the deal when Ackerman kicked it up to 12 percent. I went to Bill and I said, "This is ridiculous. We might not even be able to pay this back. This is dumb. We shouldn't do this."

About this time Bill was getting divorced from Scherry, and it forced him to go public, which he didn't really want to do, but it was the only way that he could get money to pay Scherry and at the same time raise money to build a hotel. So we did go public. Bill was so against going public that he asked me to hire a consultant. He said, "I want you to hire a consultant to tell me why I shouldn't go public." And I did. I hired a man out of Portland, Oregon, and he wrote a ten- or twelve-page report on why we shouldn't go public–but we still had to go public. Bill needed the money, and the only way we could expand was with public financing.

We were the first pure gaming company that ever went public. We went over the counter first; then we went on the American Stock Exchange; and finally we went on the New York Stock Exchange. I remember going back to New York with Bill and Shep and others, and we met before the American Stock Exchange board of directors. I remember looking at the board, and you would think you were at a funeral. They were the coldest looking men you ever saw, and in my mind I thought, "I bet they all think we have a gun under our armpit." [laughter]

There was nothing cordial about it at all, but they did let us go on the exchange. We were already an over-the-counter stock. The company that took us public was Mitchum, Jones & Templeton. They later became Paine Webber.

When Harrah's went public in 1971, had they already purchased the Golden Hotel?

Yes. I had negotiated the acquisition of the Golden Hotel from the Tomerlin brothers in 1966. It had burned down in 1963, and the Tomerlins re-built the first floor, the showroom, and re-opened the gaming. Then they put up three stories of exposed steel– that's as far as they got, and they ran out of money. So, in 1966 we stepped in and acquired it. We remodeled it and reopened

l. to r.: George Drews, Charles Franklin, Lloyd Dyer, unidentified, William Harrah, Ralph Phillips, and Mark Curtis. *"We were the first pure gaming company that ever went public. We went over the counter first; then we went on the American Stock Exchange; and finally we went on the New York Stock Exchange."*

the property in June of 1966. I don't remember what we paid for it, but I negotiated with the Tomerlin brothers, and they thought we were Santa Claus! They weren't making any money over there, and they were just delighted that we came along. They had a union, and we did not have or want a union. So our labor lawyer, Nate Burke, said in order to keep the union out, we would have to shut the operation down and terminate everybody. Then if they wanted a job, they would have to go to Harrah's and go through the personnel office. So we shut down for a few months, and we opened without the union.

Harrah's first hotel was actually the Golden Hotel?

That's right.

Did you have a showroom there?

Yes. they had a theatre-restaurant there when we bought it, and we re-named it the Headliner Room. I don't recall what the Tomerlins called it. Then the name was changed to Sammy's Showroom in the 1980s.

So your main job was acquiring real estate and trying to find financing?

Right. That's right.

Where did you come up with the financing to buy the Golden Hotel?

There was a consortium of banks that put that deal together for us through First National Bank of Nevada.

Was there a master plan for this expansion to Center Street?

No, not really. Because of our poor financial position, we couldn't afford to buy. What we did do, however, was to lease and get an option to buy the property, and we set the purchase price at the time that we leased.

When we exercised the option to buy, we got credit for the lease money against the purchase price. So, even though we weren't in great financial condition, by leasing properties with a five or a ten-year option to buy, by the time we exercised our option to buy the property, it was worth five, six, or seven times more than what it was when we set the option price. Bill was very smart and had the vision to see that.

At Lake Tahoe we leased twelve acres from the Park Cattle Company, and as I recall, we leased twelve acres for ten years with an option to buy. We set the purchase price at the time the option was made. I was only slightly involved in it, but I remember Bill said, "Let's offer Brooks Park . . . what shall we offer him? We are going to lease it, but we have to have an option to buy. We can't build a building on it and then ten years from now lose it. We have to have an option to buy."

And so somebody said: "Well, $50,000 an acre." Somebody else said, "$100,000 an acre." Bill said, "$350,000 an acre."

Shep and a guy by the name of Andy Iratcabal, who was our treasurer and controller at that time, couldn't believe what Bill said. Andy said, "You can't offer him $350,000 an acre. That's way, way more than what it's worth."

Bill says, "Offer it." And it was so much over what the value of the property was at that time that Brooks Park accepted it. But I think Brooks is sorry today. It is the only piece of property at Lake Tahoe that he ever sold, except for the First National Bank Building; and at the time we exercised our option, that acreage probably would have sold for a million dollars an acre.

Bill Harrah had great vision, and I think he pictured that the value was going to be so much more in the future that if he could set the price today–knowing in his own mind what it would be worth in the future–he could make a hell of a deal, which he did.

Harrah's Reno and Tahoe properties kept expanding, and some people looked at it as if it just happened that way. But a lot of vision and planning was involved in those transactions.

Yes, and when opportunities came along to buy, or the necessity to expand came up, it made sense for us to make a deal. We bought the Overland from Pick Hobson in 1978. I negotiated that acquisition. The Greyhound bus depot was right across from where the Center Street Harrah's property is today. Greyhound wouldn't sell, but they would consider an exchange, so we actually built the new Greyhound bus depot where it is today. I acquired that property; then we gave them the money to build that facility.

You gave it to them?

No, but with the money we gave them for the land that they owned, and the old bus depot, they had enough to build a new bus depot. Then we expanded to the south, and we bought all the way to the corner, which is where the Hampton Inn is now.

That transaction was a result of the Overland acquisition. We bought the Overland, and I don't remember what the price was then. At today's terms it probably would be rather modest. Half a million dollars would have been a lot of money. Harrah's was doing extremely well, and Harolds Club was doing well, but the Overland wasn't really doing that well. With the money that we paid Pick, he bought the Riverside.

Wasn't that part of a three-way deal to get Jessie Beck out of the Riverside?

No. We weren't involved in that at all. We didn't buy the Riverside and make an exchange. We bought the Overland from Pick, and he took the money and bought Jessie Beck out of the Riverside.[2]

Bill Harrah has been quoted as saying that he believed in the delegation of authority, yet it's also been said that he made most of the decisions. Could you give us your thoughts on whether or not you, as president of the company, had the freedom to make a lot of command decisions?

I think Bill didn't really want to run the company. Bill didn't really want to make decisions. He wanted his management to make decisions, and he wanted me to make decisions but to tell him what the decisions were.

I often thought: "Boy, this is one I'd better talk to Bill about before I make the decision." But Bill didn't want you to go in there and say, "Well, what do you want me to do, Bill?" He wanted you to make a recommendation. Then he'd say, "Well, that's fine," or "Maybe we ought to do it this way. Have you thought of this?"

Bill was extremely cordial and polite to work with. I can only remember once that I heard him say, "Well, that's the dumbest thing I ever heard in my life." It was a recommendation that I had made to Shep, that we ought to sell the Lake Club to Harvey's, because here we are operating across the street and we're competing with ourselves. We were drawing people from the Stateline Club across the street, and they were either going in Harrah's door or they were going in Harvey's door. I said, "We ought to sell the Lake Club to Harvey and put the money in the Stateline operation."

It was such an obvious move that I think Bill was mad at himself because he didn't think of it, so he said, "That's the dumbest idea I ever saw." But within thirty days we were negotiating with Bill Ledbetter[3] to sell the Lake Club. We had originally leased the Lake Club from Phillip "Curly" Musso and George Cannon. They owned the facility, but Senator Ken Johnson owned the land. We had to buy the land from him, and we lease-optioned the building from Curly and George. We sold the operation to Harvey's in 1967 for $3.5

million, which was a lot of money then. The entire property was only about two or two-and-a-half acres.

But Bill definitely delegated. By the time I became president, I think the company was running very well. Shep had it in good shape. Bill was very happily married to Verna; and Bill had a summer place up in Stanley, Idaho—the estate still owns it—and he was more interested in spending time in Stanley and being involved in the automobile collection than he was in the day-to-day operation. He would go to work around 9:00 and then go to the auto collection. He would stay there until 11:30, come downtown, have lunch; and by 1:00 or 2:00 go out to the auto collection again, and then home. In the 1970s Bill didn't really want to run Harrah's on a daily basis.

Did he run Harrah's in the 1950s and 1960s?

Harrah's ran by committees at that time. There was a management committee, and there would be an agenda. Bill ran the meeting. He would bring up topics, and we would discuss them and a decision would be made. When I was president we still had a management committee meeting. (We called it the executive committee meeting when we were publicly owned.) We would really only meet once a month, and it was more of a board meeting than anything else. I would see Bill when he was in town probably at least every other day, sometimes every day. Things would happen or decisions were made, and I would keep my notes on a legal pad and discuss them with Bill.

I knew when Bill came to work—he had to go by my office—and I'd wait until he was settled. Then I'd call his secretary and tell Bill I'd like to see him, and he'd call and say, "I'm free now." So I'd go down and talk to him. Once in a while he'd come down and sit in my office and go over things; and Bill was all business. I might have ten items, and we would cover them all in fifteen minutes and he would be gone. We would make decisions

right now, or he would approve or disapprove of what I did and it was all over.

I never had a bad moment with Bill Harrah. I think I heard Bill say "Jesus!" once or maybe "Christ!" once. He rarely swore. He was an extremely polite man. He never raised his voice. He wasn't a man of temper. I think I saw him pound the table once, and that was when he was trying to be emphatic about something. He was an easy person to deal with, but he was a perfectionist. He just wanted everything to be right. If you had a meeting at 2:00, you could almost watch the second hand. At 2:00 he would walk in that door, and he expected everybody else to be prompt.

Shep started a program when he became president that was extremely valuable. He had all of the directors—and there were probably ten or twelve of them who reported to vice-presidents, and there were six or seven of them—write a status report. The status report had to be in Shep's office on Friday. It told Shep what everybody had done during the week and what that person was going to do the next week.

Monday mornings we had coffee in the conference room on the fourth floor of the building where Planet Hollywood is today, and all the VPs would meet there. (Bill wasn't there. Bill never met with us then.) We met at 8:30 or 9:00, and each vice-president had copies of all of the status reports. Shep would conduct an informal meeting. There might only be five or six things that he wanted to ask about or comment about or make notes on. Then he would meet with Bill—next time he saw Bill—and say, "Do you have any comments on the status reports?" Or Bill would send them back and say, "Tell Lloyd to see me," or "Have Holmes see me."

We talked earlier about the decision to go public. Didn't Bill Harrah have to make the final decision on that?

Yes, he did. He owned all the stock and didn't really want to go public. He liked being private, and he understood some of the reasons why you don't want to be public. When you're public, you're exposed. You have to be thinking of other shareholders—it's their money and not yours. If you spent your money flying an airplane that the company owned, and it was your company, it's no big deal. But if some other shareholders own it, then you have to be careful about that sort of thing. They can, and do, question you on what you do and what you don't do. So, even though he didn't want to go public, he did; and yes, it was his final decision.

One philosophy of management is to find out what the boss wants and try to give it to him. Do you feel that this philosophy was carried out within Harrah's management team?

I think it was in the earlier years. And I think Bill was making most of the decisions up until when Shep became president in 1969. Bill didn't want a "yes man," and he told me that, and I think he probably had told others.

And he always wanted to go outside to get a consultant to make a study and tell us what we were doing that was right or wrong. One such study was titled "Perpetuation of Excellence." The consulting firm was amazed at how well organized we were and how we ran the company like General Motors.

The day that I became president Bill and I had lunch together, and he said, "I want you to understand this—the bottom line to most corporations is the most important thing." He said, "I still own 70 percent of the company, and the bottom line isn't that important to me. I do want shareholders to appreciate and join in our profits, but the three things I want done are: I want the customer treated properly; I want the employees treated properly—if we do that we won't have to worry about unions; and I want the place maintained and clean at all times. If we make money after that, fine." He said, "That's my philosophy." And really,

what he's saying is that if you do all these things you will make money.

Lloyd, Bob Ring was considered by some to be Bill Harrah's most trusted employee for many years. Do you feel that way? Do you feel that Bill Harrah delegated very much authority to Bob Ring?

In the late 1950s, early 1960s, my knowledge of the management structure was that Bill was making the decisions and would tell Bob what he thought we should do. We did have a management committee, and they did meet and talk about things. Bob would then carry it on down to the club managers and/or the shift managers, and any communication that had to go up to Bill went through Bob. Bob would bring it to Bill.

Bob was insecure, in the respect that he wasn't the type of person to make decisions on his own. He always brought the subject up to Bill Harrah, and the question to Bill was, "What do you want to do? How do you want to do it?" And then Bill would make the decision.

I would say that Bob was a very trusted employee of Bill. But I think all of management were trusted employees of Bill. [laughter] It was an extreme camaraderie. There was extreme loyalty to Harrah's, which means loyalty to Bill.

I asked Bill Harrah one day why didn't he give contracts to his management. And his response was, "I don't believe in them." And he said, "And besides that, I don't see anybody leaving here, so they must be happy. I don't have to give contracts."

Did Bill Harrah have any friends in the early days? Were people like Virgil Smith his friend?

I think Virgil Smith[4] was in the early days before I knew Virgil or even knew Bill Harrah. And these stories came primarily from Virgil Smith. I was on a trip with him for a week back in 1980. I asked Virgil about their relationship, because I knew that Virgil had been in gaming for years and years. Virgil thought the world of Bill. Once Bill asked Virgil to be his partner in his Virginia Street casino, and Virgil said, "No, Bill. I'll bankroll you, but I don't want to be in partnerships with you." Which I thought was a little bit strange, because in later years Bill didn't really want to be partners with anybody and was even reluctant to go public; he didn't even want to be partners with the public.

To get back to Bob Ring, I would say that if Bob was a friend of Bill's, it was more in Horseless Carriage affairs that they had in Reno, Tahoe, and other areas. Bob had his own antique car, and so he participated with Bill in those things, but as far as hanging out together, they never did. I don't ever recall Bob even having dinner in Bill's home. I was president of Harrah's for five years, and my wife and I had dinner with Bill only twice during that period of time, at his home. We had dinner with him in the showrooms, from time to time; and in fact, the week before Bill

passed away, he and Verna had Kenny Rogers, Steve Martin, and their wives, along with Joanie and I, to dinner at the Villa Harrah at Lake Tahoe. It was kind of strange, because Steve didn't say a word for probably an hour and a half, but Kenny Rogers was very charming and open and down-to-earth.

I was glad he was there to carry the conversation, because Martin just sat there and ate and didn't say a damn thing. That was the last dinner that Bill had with any entertainers. He went back east a week later and went to an antique automobile museum in Cleveland. From there, he went to the Mayo Clinic, had his examination, had his operation, and passed away at the Mayo Clinic on June 30, 1978. I've often thought that Bill was such a methodical person, such a precise person, and such a perfectionist, that he [intentionally] died on the last day of Harrah's fiscal year. Perfect planning! [laughter]

Bill Harrah often entertained visiting performers at the Villa Harrah, his guesthouse at Lake Tahoe. *"[Bill] and Verna had Kenny Rogers, Steve Martin, and their wives, along with Joanie and I, to dinner at the Villa Harrah . . . ."*

But I really don't know of anybody that was a close friend of Bill's. Of course, I would usually see Bill every day, but sometimes I would not see him for a week because he'd be out of town. I'm sure that was probably true when Shep and Bob Ring were presidents. Socially, Bill didn't have any friends, and I think by his own choosing. If Bill had a friend, it would be his wife, because he spent all of his time, when he wasn't working, with his wife and his family.

When I say no personal friends, I'm saying Joe McMullen, who was Harrah's accountant, was not his friend; neither was Mead Dixon, who was Harrah's attorney. Bill had a tremendous amount of respect for Mead as an attorney, but they were not close friends.

I know from talking to other people that Bob Ring was Bill Harrah's best man at some of his weddings, but that would, evidently, not necessarily mean he was Bill's best friend.

That's right. I remember one wedding . . . and I'm not sure which one it was–if it was Bobbie Gentry or which gal it was–that Bill Cosby was the best man at Bill's wedding.

Who were some of the other people that were around Bill?

The person that worked with Bill more than anybody was Shep. I remember in 1963 Shep told Bill Harrah that the club should be doing better than it was, should be making more money, and that other than Bill there wasn't any leadership. And Bill asked Shep at that time, "Do you want to be the president?"

And Shep said, "No. I think you should give Bob Ring the opportunity to be president. He's been with you ever since you came from Venice, and he has been the general manager. You should make him the president." So Bill did.

Then in 1969 Shep went back to Bill and said, "It's not working." [laughter] "We should

be making more money, and we're not running this thing as a proper business."

Bill said, "Then I think you should be president." And that's when Shep became president. He was the president from 1969 until I became president in 1975. Over those years there were probably differences in opinion and of styles of management between Shep and Bill, and I think that's why Shep stepped down and I became the president.

Could it have been because they were both of the same personality? They were both very quiet and very retiring.

It could have been. Shep was an accountant by profession, so he was more conservative. There were times that Bill was a spendthrift. And Bill, sometimes, wanted to do something, but the club couldn't afford it. He would become upset because they couldn't, and Shep would say, "Bill you can't do it. We don't have the money, don't have the money, don't have the money." [laughter] Bill got tired of hearing that after a while.

I had a different philosophy than Shep did when I became the president. The day that Bill made me president, I told him that I knew that he was the major shareholder of this company, and there were going to be times when I was going to disagree with him on management decisions. I said, "I'm always going to tell you how I feel and what my opinion is, and you may say, 'Well that's all well and good, but I want to do this anyway.' I'm going to do it your way. But I'm always going to let you know I'm not going to be a 'yes' man. I'm always going to let you know if I think it's the right thing for Harrah's; if it's the wrong thing for Harrah's, I'm going to tell you that too." So we had that understanding from the very beginning, and we had a good rapport because of it.

It sounds like you had a good relationship.

Yes, we really did. I wasn't a "yes" man, and sometimes I did play little mental games with him. I remember once he called me in and said, "You know, Tahoe gets cold in the winter, and people walk out and they don't know how cold it is, and they don't know whether they should wear a coat or not." And he said, "I think we should have an outside thermometer in every room at the hotel."

And I thought to myself, "My God, what the hell is that going to cost?" So I sat on it for a while, got to thinking about it. And I was up at the lake one night and stayed over and turned the TV on in the morning, and there's the weather report for Lake Tahoe with the temperature on it, and I said, "Thank God it was on television." The next time I saw Bill I said, "Bill, we won't have to spend the money for the thermometers. All they have to do is turn the TV on."

He said, "That's fine." [laughter]

Well you are more of a "people person" than Shep or, of course, Bill Harrah. They probably were very comfortable with you around to do most of the talking.

That could be right. I think everybody that worked for Bill Harrah respected him and had a tremendous loyalty to him, including myself. But a lot of people, because Bill was such a quiet person and such a recluse, had a fear of him. They were scared of him when they were around him. Maybe I was too dumb to do that, but I have always had a sense of humor, and Bill really did have a sense of humor. You could play with his mind a little bit, too, and he would laugh about it. One-on-one, Bill was just like you and I talking, but if somebody else came in the room, then he'd clam up. I remember going with Bill to Europe–Joanie and I went over there with Bill and Verna in 1976; it was when Carter was elected president. I thought, "My gosh, I'm going to be with Bill for a month." I'm wondering, "Is it really going to work? How is everybody going to get along?" And it worked

out fine. I mean, if Bill wanted to talk to you, he'd talk to you. Or if I had something really important to talk to him about, I could, whether we were on the plane or having dinner or having a cocktail. There was never a problem.

Did you keep in contact with the club while you were in Europe?

We had daily reports that each member of management had on their desk by 11:00 in the morning. We had a daily P & L[5] from both Reno and Lake Tahoe. We had a count in the showrooms. We had a count in the hotel rooms–how many hotel rooms did we rent the night before. There were very short summaries in each department: the pit, the food, the bar . . . the parking lot even . . . entertainment, everything. We called it the "day book," and the day book probably was three pages long.

The thing that Bill was really interested in when we were overseas, and generally what came to his mind first, was what was the count in the South Shore Room or what was the count in the Headliner Room, which was our showroom in Reno at that time. Also, he would be in touch with his secretary every day. He'd call her on the telephone, and she would tell him what the P & L was for the day and what the count was in the showroom. And if something unusual happened, she would tell him. When I'd see Bill for lunch, he'd tell me what was going on or if something had come up.

I don't know if I told you this story or not: When I became president, Rome Andreotti was executive vice-president. Rome said to me, "This goes back a long time, but whenever we've had a big winner or a loser, we have always called the boss, whether it was Bob Ring or Shep, regardless of the time." He said, "Do you want me to wake you up in the middle of the night and tell you when we are losing?"

I said, "No, because it doesn't do me any good to find out. If we lost a lot of money, I'm going to feel bad about it. If we made a lot of money, I can smile about it the next day. If the place burns down, please call me, but other than that don't call me about something I have no control over." [laughter] I think Bill felt the same way. Bill really wanted his management team–and I think it was a slow process over the years–he wanted the management team to run the company.

His last year of life, he told me he was very happily married and he said, "I'm going to spend the summers in Sun Valley, Idaho." He also had a place in Stanley, Idaho, which is about seventy miles north of Sun Valley. He said, "I'm going to stay there." He said, "I'm going to come back once in awhile to see a show. You can call me and be in touch. If something unusual happens, give me a call. Otherwise, I don't want to hear from anybody. I just want to spend my time with Verna and have fun." And that's what he did. So a lot of times it was management by exception. If something exceptional came up, I would tell Bill about it. Otherwise, I didn't bother him with it.

Do you think his attitude changed because he knew was close to dying?

No. I don't think he knew he was close to dying at that time–Bill knew he had an aneurism of his aorta. He had had an operation on his aorta at the Mayo Clinic in 1972, and at that time they told Bill that he'd probably have to have another operation on his aorta in six years. Whether he had a pre-exam here and found out that the aneurism was growing or progressing, I don't know, but he went back to Mayo knowing he would have the operation.

The day before Bill left he changed his will, and he changed some of the trustees of his estate. I saw him and talked to him for about half an hour before he left that day. I said, "I've always heard you don't tell a gambler 'good luck,' but I've got to say good luck to you anyway."

And he said, "I'm a gambler." Then he said, "The operation is 90 percent in my favor and only 10 percent that it's not going to work." Later I found out that the night before he went in for the operation, he told Verna that he had not been telling the truth, because he didn't want to alarm anybody, but he really only had about a 10 percent chance in the operation. It was 90 percent against him, and of course he didn't come out of the operation. He knew then, and he may have had some thoughts before . . . I don't know.

Bill was interested in the automobile collection and spending time with his wife, going to the shows, but he really didn't get involved in management in the last year very much. He was very happily married at that time. I remember Bill telling me that the happiest four years of his life were when he was married to Verna.

Was your trip to Europe in 1976 a business trip? Or were you just relaxing?

Bill had an appointment in Stuttgart, where the Mercedes manufacturing plant was located, and I went over to take a look at a gaming operation in Monte Carlo that the Loew's people owned. There was a possibility that we might be able to do something there. It was also a pleasure trip. We went to the Scandinavian countries, and I spent some time with Joan in France when Bill was on business in Stuttgart. Later we went to Italy. Bill went there every year and bought clothes from a particular tailor there in Rome. We were also in London and spent a couple of days there. We were gone just about thirty days.

⟡

In 1977, Joanie, my wife, and Bill and Verna plus Mark Curtis and Mead Dixon flew over to Australia in Harrah's GII. We were interested in starting a gaming operation there and were laying the groundwork with the political people there to see if we could get licensed. It was a long, drawn-out thing, and we didn't get a license.

Had you been to Australia before?

I had made about four or five trips there doing the groundwork on this project, and Mead Dixon was with me on most of those trips. We had met the premier of New South Wales and also the people in Melbourne and Canberra, which is the capital. We were doing a PR thing–getting acquainted and letting them get acquainted with us. At that time there was a labor government, and it was very difficult getting approval for any gaming in Australia.

At that time Harrah's had a big oriental market. Did you go to any of the oriental areas?

Mead Dixon and I went to Hong Kong and met with one of the Chinese gentlemen that was bringing customers to Harrah's. I can't think of the name of the gentleman, but he brought Chinese high rollers twice a month into primarily Lake Tahoe, but also to Reno.

So he was a junket representative there, and you just touched bases with him?

Yes. He invited us to come knowing we were in Australia. He told somebody in Reno, "Why don't they come by Hong Kong and have dinner with us?" And we went in and had a thirteen-course dinner with him and some of his friends.

There were several management people that stayed with Harrah's a long time. You mentioned Shep, who was there for almost thirty-five years. You were there a long time. Holmes was there a long time. How about Joe Fanelli, the food and beverage director?

Joe came from the Kahler Corporation, which owned hotels in Rochester, Minnesota. We got acquainted with Joe because most of top management went to the Mayo Clinic for annual physicals, and Joe was running the food department there. Rome Andreotti hired him when we had an opening, and Joe became the vice-president of food and beverage for Harrah's in 1971.

Rome Andreotti was also with Harrah's a long time, wasn't he?

Rome was with Harrah's from 1946 until he passed away in 1984. Rome had the general managers and all the vice-presidents, except the vice-president of finance, report to him. The financial people reported directly to me. Rome had a long career in the management of Harrah's. He started out in 1946 as a wheel dealer, and he was a shift manager at Lake Tahoe when I started working as a cashier there in 1957.

Rome was a different sort of a person, an extremely loyal, hard-working guy. He was unforgiving of people that made errors. I think if Rome had a fault, it was that if a guy made a mistake, he wouldn't give him a second chance. I think it's probably normal that if a person makes the same mistake twice, then he's got a real problem. But I think if a person makes a mistake, and if you have a lot of money invested in him, in training and years with the company, that you should try to salvage him; but Rome didn't feel that way.

Rome understood gaming very well. I remember once I told Bill Harrah that I wanted to take out some slot machines in Lake Tahoe and put in an oyster bar, and I also wanted to take out a bunch of slot machines in Reno north of the premium booth on the Center Street side and put a lounge there–a place where people could sit and have a drink. Bill said, "I think that's just absolutely wonderful." He says, "You know, if we left it up to Rome, he'd put slot machines in the men's room." [laughter]

Did you win that battle?

Oh, yes, I won that battle. Rome might give you his opinion and he might not. [laughter] Rome was a little bit like Bob Ring. He would go the way he thought you were going to go.

Rome was very loyal to Bill, but he was not a good delegator. He'd rather work sixteen hours himself than delegate, and he didn't let other people make decisions. They would have to come to him and ask for a decision, which was a little bit unfortunate, because I think a good manager is one who hires good people and then gives them the rein and lets them run their own show. I believe you should always be informed by your managers of what they're doing, but you should let them make decisions. That's the only way they can grow.

Isn't that what Bill Harrah did?

Yes. Whether he planned it that way or not, he'd give his managers pretty much free rein. If a person made a mistake and said to Bill, "This is kind of a dumb thing. We really shouldn't have done it." Bill would say, "Well, let's go on with life. Let's turn it around–do it the right way." He wouldn't be that upset with the person if they told the truth and didn't hide anything.

Harrah's had unparalleled growth from the 1950s through the 1970s and was praised in magazine articles as the General Motors of the gaming industry. But it's also been said by some parties that there was no management development program in Harrah's and no career planning program. Do you agree with that statement?

No. Not at all. We were highly structured, and, long before any other casino, we had a written job description for every position. The people knew exactly what their responsibility was and they knew what their authority was. If you were a dealer, for example, you were in

the training mode to become a pit boss. And if you were a pit boss, you were in the training mode to become a shift manager. Maybe some of the training wasn't highly structured, but it certainly was there. Anybody who was an assistant was training to become the boss in that department. I think we had excellent in-house training programs, and we also sent people to seminars to help them in their training.

Another good example of our managers' abilities was that whenever a new operation opened . . . . For example, I remember when the Sahara opened at Lake Tahoe, half of their staff came from Harrah's. [laughter] The Sahara management was delighted to steal them because they knew they were well trained. That was also true with MGM when they opened in Reno. We lost help because our people were so well trained.

Actually, most of Harrah's top management came up through the ranks, including Rome, Shep, myself, Holmes, and many others. The only "outside" people in top management were Joe Fanelli and George Drews, vice-president of finance. We did have some people in the personnel department that we hired from the outside that didn't work out, but there were others like Joe Specht, who started out as an employee counselor and eventually became vice-president of personnel.

There was a gentleman named Red Farnsworth who was with the organization for a long time. Do you have any memories of Red that you could share with us?

Yes. Red was a great man. He was a man with little education, a self-made man. When I met Red, he probably was fifty-five, maybe even sixty, and he had worked in carnivals all his life. I don't know what he did in the carnivals, but he had worked in them all his life. He must have met Bill in Venice, and when Bill started out in Reno, Red was head of the cashier department. Then Red got into personnel and actually started what is now called the human resources department. He also started the employee counselors program that worked with employees if they had problems.

Harrah's was the first casino to have a board of review and employee evaluations. Was Red Farnsworth instrumental in those programs?

I think he probably was. I'm not positive who put them into effect, but they were certainly very valuable tools for Harrah's. If an employee was terminated, they had the right to go before a board of review. There were three representatives on the board. There would be the representative from the personnel department, a representative from that employee's department, and a representative from another department. Whatever decision they made, it was final. Sometimes they put the employee back to work and sometimes they didn't.

We were a non-union company. We weren't anti-union; we were a non-union company. We knew, and Bill Harrah knew, that the only way you could keep the unions out—and we felt we didn't need unions to tell us how to operate our business—was to treat our employees right. We knew we had to have good supervisors that knew how to treat the employees right.

There are often times when a union will get into a department or into a business not because of a wage dispute—they may get in because there is no security within that department or because they have a supervisor that's not treating them right or they are unhappy with their work. The employee counselors that we had were kind of an ear to the ground of what was going on. If we had a supervisor in a department, and he was always having a problem with his employees, something was wrong with that supervisor and we would make a change.

We were lucky in keeping the unions out of Harrah's. When we bought the Grand

Cafe, we had to accept the culinary union. What was remarkable about that was within a year we called for a vote, and the employees voted the union out. So that speaks pretty well for Harrah's management.

What were some of the other factors that helped Harrah's become such a great organization and helped to keep it a non-union company?

Well, there were many things. I'll start with the way Bill Harrah felt, and I think I told you this before. When I became president, Bill told me that there were three things that were really important to him. The first one was that the customer was treated properly. The second one was that the employees were treated properly so that we could operate without unions interfering with our business. And the third one was to keep the facilities physically in top shape. (We probably had more janitors per square foot than anybody else.)

Bill Harrah felt that if you take care of the little things, the big things are going to get done, which is a little bit opposite of the way many other people feel. For example, I remember years ago the shift manager would walk outside the casino and make sure there weren't any lights out in the billboards or over the sidewalks. It was a big deal if a light bulb was out; you had to change it. Scotch tape was forbidden in public areas at Harrah's—no memos, licenses, or notes could be taped to cash registers or on the wall or the door or anywhere. It was a bugaboo of Bill Harrah's that paintings on the wall oftentimes are crooked, but if you put two hooks there and you level them and then hang the picture, it's always going to be straight. So anything that went on the wall—and I'm sure this came from Bill—anything that went on the wall had to have two hooks; not one, but two hooks.

The physical atmosphere of Harrah's was different than other casinos. Early casinos were dark, not well lit. You would go in and it would take ten minutes for your eyes to adjust to what was going on in there. I don't know if it was Bill who did this or not, but we always had windows in our casinos, and you could see in or see out. It was always well lit in our casinos, and it was a cheerful atmosphere. We hired good people–good consultants–to match paints with wallpaper and carpeting. Of course, all of it had to be approved.

Everybody was very pleased, in particular, with the Harrah's Tahoe facility. A designer by the name of Henry Conversano designed the interior of that facility: the carpets and the colors, the wall, the wood, the lighting–everything, including the hotel rooms.

When we were planning the hotel at Tahoe, Bill Harrah said, "I want to have two bathrooms."

And everybody thought, "There isn't a hotel in the world that has two bathrooms. Why would you want to have two bathrooms?"

Bill says, "I want to have two bathrooms so that when a gentleman and his wife are in the room, he can use one bathroom and get ready for dinner, and she can use her bathroom."

Those rooms at that time cost $125,000 a room. That was the cost of the hotel–$125,000 per room. And that's the figure that you would use when you figured out what hotels cost– just by the room–whether you had public area or not. At that time any other hotel probably was $60,000 or $70,000 a room. Today, I would guess the Mirage in Las Vegas is probably $300,000 a room. I mean, the prices have just gone crazy. But it was quality.

I wasn't involved in that decision, but I remember at the time that management thought Bill was crazy. Why would you want to have two bathrooms in every room? (We also had a TV in each of the bathrooms.) But when the hotel opened, everyone talked about our hotel and they talked about it for years after: "I'm going to stay at Tahoe. Can you believe it? They got two bathrooms. My wife likes it. I like it. It's great. It's great. It's the

only hotel in the world that has two bathrooms and a television in every bathroom." (As a matter of fact, when we had the GII, we had two bathrooms in it, one for the crew and one for the passengers. But that was Bill Harrah.)

There is no doubt that Bill wanted to make money, and he did make money, but if we did the three things that he wanted to do and we made five million dollars after taxes at the end of the year, that was fine. Even if he knew that if we hadn't have done those things, we would have made ten million dollars, he didn't want to make the ten million. The five million was OK with him.

When Bill Harrah passed away, we had the funeral here in Reno, and after the funeral we invited people to the Villa Harrah. I met Steve Wynn there–Henry Conversano, who was Harrah's hotel designer and interior decorator, introduced me to him. Mr. Wynn said to me, "I never met Bill Harrah, but I admire everything that Bill Harrah has done, and I'm going to copy him. I'm going to be the next Bill Harrah of Nevada and of gaming."

I looked at him and I thought, "Boy, you got to go a long ways to do that." But I think the man has really done it. In *Fortune Magazine* two weeks ago they gave the ten best-managed public corporations in the United States. Number one was General Electric. Number two was the Golden Nugget's operation–Steve Wynn's. Steve has a reputation for taking care of his employees; he has great entertainment; his facilities are spotless; and he takes care of his customer, just like Bill did. He set his goals and he accomplished them.

There is one fellow we haven't talked about at all that was very important in Harrah's Club for many years, and that's Holmes Hendricksen.

Yes. Holmes was a very important part of Harrah's. I'm prejudiced because Holmes and I are best of friends, and we were fraternity brothers at the University of Utah. He first came to work for Harrah's in April of

1956. He went back to school, then returned to Harrah's in April of 1957, and I started in May of 1957. We roomed together until I got married, and Holmes was the best man at my wedding. Holmes worked his way up from a cashier to head of the cashiers department. Then Holmes was shift manager, assistant club manager, and eventually club manager.

Around that time Bill Harrah and Shep decided to make a change on Pat France. Pat France had been vice-president of entertainment, but they put him back on the floor as a casino host. And I remember Shep coming down–I was executive vice-president at the time–and he said, "We're rearranging the entertainment department and we've got to have someone to take over. Do you recommend anybody?"

I says, "Yes, I recommend Holmes Hendricksen."

He said, "Why?"

I said, "He's single. [laughter] He likes music and he can stay up all night and drink with those entertainers. And he's loyal, and he'll just do a hell of a job for you." (Holmes was the general manager of Harrah's Tahoe at the time.) So Shep went down and told Bill what my recommendation was, and Bill says, "Perfect. He's the guy."

Holmes always *blamed* Shep for that promotion, because Holmes really liked the gaming. He liked to be the general manager. He didn't want to be vice-president of entertainment. He liked to be around the players, and he liked Tahoe because he was away from Reno management. [laughter]

Holmes did an excellent job. Bill Harrah was very fond of Holmes. Holmes developed loyalties with many of the entertainers, and I can't think of anybody else that ever did. Holmes became especially close to Frank Sinatra, and Holmes is still a very close friend of Bill Cosby. All the entertainers liked Holmes. Holmes used to go to the shows and have dinner with those people, and he would go down and see them after the show, and if they wanted to have a drink after their second

show, he'd be there. If they needed him, he was there, and he just did an excellent job. He just recently retired from Harrah's.

It sounds like he was involved twenty-four hours a day.

He was. Holmes got married about seventeen years ago, and he has a son who he is very fond of. He loves to play golf, and he is enjoying his life now and he deserves it. Even as a married person he handled that job very well, and he was probably on the road 60 percent of the time. He'd be auditioning shows in Las Vegas, in Los Angeles, in New York, wherever they were. I think we were the first club that Willie Nelson worked for as a nightclub entertainer.

Well, I'm sure that other people were on the entertainment committee, but Holmes must have carried more weight when it came to the final decision on who did or didn't appear at Harrah's.

Yes, he did. We ruled by committees, and we had several committees. Some were meaningful and some were not. I think the most meaningless to Bill was the management committee, but he went to their meetings. [laughter] The two committees–and I'm exaggerating a little bit–that Bill was really extremely interested in were the entertainment committee and the advertising committee, believe it or not. He wanted to see what those billboards were going to look like, and he wanted to see what the ads in the newspaper were going to look like. Mark Curtis was vice-president in charge of advertising, and, to me, he was the advertising guru of gaming and is still a dear friend of mine today. He just really did a great job.

When I was president I sat on the entertainment committee, the advertising committee, and the management committee. Holmes would audition a new act, or maybe we would see a new act on "The Ed Sullivan Show," and he would talk to Bill and talk to the club managers about the act. The club managers always sat in on the committee, because we didn't want them to think that we were putting in *their* showroom only acts that we liked. We wanted to make sure that they also liked it. Some of the general managers were also involved in auditioning some of the entertainers. Sometimes we'd book two to three years in advance because *they* were booking that far in advance.

The entertainers had a great love affair with Harrah's and a great loyalty to Harrah's. We paid Sinatra less than he was paid in Las Vegas, and we paid Bill Cosby less than he was paid in Las Vegas or other places because we treated them right. We had a big boat on the lake that they could use. We had a villa, a huge mansion up there where they could bring their families and stay. We brought all the help in, we cooked for their families. They could either drive a Cadillac or Rolls-Royce, or if they wanted to be chauffeured around in the limousine, that would be arranged. It was almost a working vacation for them.

Another thing that was really important to Harrah's were the golf tournaments. I only started to play golf nine years ago, and I'm sorry I didn't learn years ago because those tournaments were fantastic. I'd go to the stag parties that they had and things, but I didn't play. I remember one year a person hit a hole-in-one and won a Rolls-Royce. Now, a hole-in-one in a lot of tournaments, you might get a new bag of golf clubs. But we gave a Rolls-Royce. One year there were two hole-in-ones! And it was settled by a roll of the dice, which was unique. [laughter]

The golf tournaments were held the second week of June. What was amazing was, invariably there was a snow storm one of those days. [laughter] The guys couldn't play golf because of the snow, so they would all go to the casino, and we made big money off of them. Years later, everybody had to have a golf tournament. The Nugget had it. The Mapes had it. They had them all over Las Vegas, and after a while we had to do away

with them because they were breaking all of the players. And so the golf tournaments were no longer scheduled.

When you held those tournaments, were you looking for golf shooters or crap shooters?

We were looking for gamblers. We invited personalities too, but a lot of the gamblers that were invited to the golf tournament were horrible golfers. They came because they liked the festivities, and they had great parties, great dinners, and a lot of fun; plus, we gave away great prizes to everybody. They all got something when they signed up, and it didn't cost them anything. Today, for that kind of a tournament, it would probably cost an individual $3,000 or $4,000 to enter it.

Do you feel that Mr. Harrah's second divorce from Scherry Harrah had any great impact on his management of the company or on the operation of the company?

No, I don't think so at all. Bill's wives did not get involved in management. What he talked to them about at home or over dinner, I have no idea, but they weren't involved in management.

Bill was a marrying kind of a person and he didn't want to live alone. After he divorced Scherry, he married about five ladies within the next six or seven years at the most. Every woman he married, he took them to Mayo and they got a physical. [laughter] Then he took them to Europe, and they stayed in the same hotels and they went up to Stanley, Idaho, and they stayed in the same place there too. But his wives were *not* involved in the business.

As times changed, styles changed, Bill changed. If it was a hairstyle, he'd get the latest hairstyle. If it was loud sport clothes, he'd get loud sport clothes. He was very immaculately dressed. He had a tailor in Los Angeles and he had a tailor in Europe. I remember when we went to Rome with him, we were there for three days. He was measured. Then they brought the cloth out for him. Then they put him in it and just pinned everything on him, and then they sewed them all up and they went on the airplane with us when we went home.

If he found a pair of gym shoes he liked or sneakers or casual shoes, he'd buy one pair for his place at the lake, the Villa Harrah; he'd buy one for his home in Reno, one for the place in Sun Valley, and one for the place in Stanley–buy four sets; four of everything.

In Reno he had a walk-in closet that was probably ten by twenty feet, pretty good size. And everything in it was numbered. There would be a number *one* on a sport coat, and there would be a number *one* on the shirt that went with that sport coat and a number *one* on the tie and a number *one* on the shoes and a number *one* on the socks. I mean, the guy was a perfectionist. When he grabbed that sport coat, there would be the tie, the shirt, and the whole works. He'd just jump right in them.

How were the numbers attached–not with scotch tape? [laughter]

No, no. No, they weren't attached with scotch tape; they were on hangers like the kind you get when you check your coat in a restaurant.

That plan was a great time saver, too.

Oh, yes. Time was extremely important to Bill. I'm glad you brought that up. To successful people like Bill, time is very important. One day Bill called me from the airport after he had got off the Falcon, and he said, "You know, these guys land that plane and they do well. Then they run that plane all the way to the end of the runway. Then they turn and they come back. Why don't they stop at the first turn?" He said, "Look at all the time they're wasting."

I said, "Well, I'll find out." So I got ahold of the guy who was in charge of the aviation department and I asked him.

He said, "If we stop at the first turn, we're going to be burning brakes, we're going to be changing brakes more often."

And I told Bill. He says, "I don't care if you got to change them every day, let's stop at the first turn." [laughter]

He wanted to get a helicopter to fly from Reno to Tahoe when he would go to the shows there. I thought, "Well, here's another expenditure of two or three million dollars." So I went out to the hangar and talked to the pilot, and I says, "You know, at five o'clock in the afternoon or six when Bill goes to the dinner show up there, the turbulence could be so horrible as to throw the helicopter over."

The pilot said, "No, helicopters have flexible blades. They just go with the turbulence–it doesn't bother them a bit." [laughter]

So then I had to figure out something else, so I told Bill, "By the time you leave your office or you leave your home and you drive out to the airport and you get in the helicopter and you get cleared for takeoff and you fly up there and you land down at the airport and then you have to take a limo back and forth, it's probably going to be about an hour and a half. You can *drive* there in an hour, and you *like* to drive."

So he says, "You know, you're right." He said, "Forget the helicopter, I'll drive." [laughter]

He went overseas once and he noticed that the janitor in some hotel wore white gloves, so we tried that for awhile. Every janitor had to wear white gloves. Do you remember that?

Yes, I remember that. [laughter]

That's where that came from. Bill was an idea man, and he was not afraid of using other people's ideas. He told me once, "I'm lucky my name is Harrah–it sounds like Harold, and that is why we called our club Harrah's Club. People were confused–they really thought they were going to Harolds Club, because it was much better known than we were, but they actually came into Harrah's Club. Then when we got more widely known than Harolds Club, we changed it to Harrah's and cut the Club off." [laughter] But he said he didn't ever mind using other people's ideas.

When I became president, I asked Joe Fanelli, the vice-president of food and beverage, "What does Harvey's and the Sparks Nugget have a reputation for?"

Joe said, "I don't know. What?"

I said, "Food. They have a super reputation for food." Harvey's Sage Room had a great reputation. John Ascuaga had a great reputation for food. He had an oyster bar. I said, "I want you to go over there and go through all those restaurants at John Ascuaga's and see if you get some ideas to use.

Bill told me, "You know, that's really great." He said, "You know, we don't always do everything right. Other people do things better than we do. And if they do, let's find out what they're doing and let's copy it." He wasn't afraid of change.

I remember once Bill told me, "I want to have a casino on every road into Nevada [where it enters the state]. I want a chain of them." We even looked at the possibility of buying some land near Boomtown. I went down to Laughlin when the only thing at Laughlin was a gas station and a very, very small casino with no rooms and one restaurant.

Bill and I and (I'm not sure if it was Verna or Scherry) went up to Twin Falls, rented a car and drove to Jackpot and looked that operation over. George Cannon owned a place there, and we took a look at that. We knew that we could buy that. But we were doing other things at the time, and we were always stretched for cash. One thing I mentioned to Bill was unless it's really a great operation and unless we really can afford it, we got to be careful doing this, because we're

going to spread management. And how much money are we going to make? I mean, we make five million here. We're going to make fifty thousand there and we're going to spend half our time looking at that joint and watching it and spreading management out. If we can't really have a big operation, we shouldn't do it. And we never did do it.

When I asked Bill the reason he didn't go to Las Vegas over the years, he said, "They're all unionized down there, and I don't want the unions. If I have a joint down there, they're going to make me have a union up here."

I said, "I don't really believe that. You know, we're miles apart. Hell, we could be in Canada as far as the distance between ourselves and Las Vegas. If we were in Boulder City, that's different, or Mesquite, but we're too far away."

I convinced Bill that we could go to Las Vegas, and we may even have to accept a union, but at least that union wouldn't have to be transferred up here to the Reno-Tahoe area. So, prior to Bill's death, Mead Dixon and I went down and took a look at the Aladdin. Then I took Bill down and we looked at the Aladdin. We also looked at the Dunes as a possible purchase. The Aladdin was a bad operation because the entertainment showroom was a separate complex– people could go to that and never go into the casino. So we said no on that. The Dunes was a possibility, but that was in the spring of 1978, just prior to Bill's death, and we never got into it.

What about this area west of town, Harrah's World? What were his plans for that?

What Bill wanted to do was move the auto collection. It was in a warehouse area in Sparks. It was really in an old Pacific Fruit Express icehouse, and it certainly wasn't displayed properly. Bill wanted to have a perfect museum to show his cars. We owned thirteen hundred automobiles at that time, but probably only about four hundred had been restored.

He sent my wife and I to Europe with the fellow who was the head of the automobile collection at that time, Doyle Mathia. We did Europe in one week. We were in Italy, Germany, Switzerland, France, Holland, and London; and we looked at lots of automobile museums over there and got some ideas. When we came back, we acquired over three hundred acres, which would be the southwest and the southeast corner of McCarran and I-80, and we hired an architectural firm out of San Francisco to design a museum for us. We had some great ideas on how to display the cars in different angles and different lightings, and some where the wheels would be turning and lots of different things. We were also going to put an old steam train out there and some old airplanes.

We had 360 acres there, and Bill wanted to build a museum right now! Maybe he was thinking that he didn't have a lot of years left. Bill was sixty-seven when he died, so he still wasn't an old man. I told him we couldn't put the museum out there by itself, and he said, "Why not?" I said, "We could not afford to run that museum. We can't afford to build it and run that museum. We have to have gaming. We have to build a hotel with gaming. We get that up, then we can put the museum next to it." And he agreed to do that. But subsequently he passed away and it never got developed. After Holiday bought it, they sold all the property.

So you actually did purchase the property?

Oh, we had it all purchased, yes. I was involved in most of those acquisitions. Shep was involved in a couple. At that time Shep had a different job–he was senior vice-president of community affairs, but he was also involved in real estate. He did the leg work, and I was making the decisions on the real estate. We had to put together five different parcels to make that deal, and we

actually built the bridge that is still there. We paid $600,000 for the bridge that joins both properties across McCarran.

In Bill's last years, was it difficult for you to get access to him?

No, not at all. In fact, we had a lodge on the middle fork of the Salmon River which I had acquired for Harrah's back in about 1967. It was a very nice retreat and a nice hunting and fishing lodge. (Bill didn't hunt, but he did like to fish.) He was either there, or he was at his place in Stanley or his place in Sun Valley. We could always talk by phone, and a couple of times I flew up there and sat down and discussed things with him. So, access to Bill was no problem, and he made that very plain: "If you ever need me, I'm there. I'm available. If you got to fly up to see me, fine. I may not fly down to see you, but you can fly to see me."

So you went ahead with your management meetings once a week?

Yes. We used to meet every Monday morning with management and review the status reports that Shep had started, which were extremely valuable tools. Bill got those in the mail; everything we got, he got in the mail. And he might mark them up and send them back to me with: "Why, why, why?" So, access was no problem.

He made some changes in his will. Would you expand on that?

[Shortly before Bill's death] he made some changes in his will and also the trustees. The trustees of Bill's estate wound up being Bruce Thompson, Mead Dixon, and myself. However, Bruce declined because he wanted to stay on as a federal judge. And Mead and I– which is what the will said–we had to pick a replacement, and we picked Joe McMullen. And then, when Mead Dixon died, Joe McMullen and I picked John Sande.

We are the trustees of the Harrah's trusts.[6] One trust is for Bill's widow, Verna. She gets the income off of her trust for life, and when she passes away, her children will get the principal. The two boys, Bill's two children, were both adopted children. One is John Adam, the other one is Tony Lee. They each have a trust. John is thirty-two and Tony is thirty this year, and those trusts will go away when they're forty years old. By "going away," I mean they'll receive all of the principal from those trusts when they are forty years old.

Were they blood brothers?

No, they are no relation. Bill and Scherry adopted them through the Mayo Clinic. They went back there for years having physicals and told the powers-that-be there that they would like to adopt children. They couldn't have any. So somehow these two children were recommended to Bill and Scherry for adoption, and they adopted them in the middle 1960s.

Did you have any role in the decision to sell Harrah's to Holiday Inns?

Not really. Mead was the executor of Bill's estate, and he was like Bill Harrah. He could do anything he wanted. He voted the stock, and he voted to sell to Holiday. I wasn't involved in the decision, but I was involved in the negotiations. I met with the Holiday people in Memphis and also in Las Vegas, but Mead made that decision. Perhaps it wasn't the best decision for Harrah's, for Reno, for Tahoe as far as the continuation of the way Harrah's operated things, but it was the best decision for the estate, because at that time the Holiday stock was around $36 a share, and ultimately it was around $75 a share. So the estate became very valuable by selling to Holiday.

After Mead Dixon made the decision to sell, did he then look for a purchaser?

Actually, I think Holiday came to Harrah's. They knew that Bill had passed away, and they wanted to know if Harrah's could be acquired. Mead then immediately started to negotiate with them. He controlled all the shares, so naturally, he had the power to do so.

Holiday made a smart move when they bought Harrah's. The book value of the Harrah's auto collection at that time was $12 million, and Holiday sold virtually the guts of the collection–they left only 100 vehicles here. They sold the best ones, and with the amount of money they made from the various auctions they held, they made enough money to pay for the acquisition of Harrah's–over $100 million.

When Holiday Inns purchased Harrah's in late February of 1980, I was notified by the powers-that-be in Holiday that they wanted to make a change with me. They wanted to put their own people in management–people that they had worked with over the years. That's when Dick Goeglein came in as president of Harrah's and Mead Dixon stayed on as the chairman of the company. Holiday gave me a substantial compensation with a three-year contract not to compete or not to go in the gaming business. I had to stay out of the gaming business for three years. I was happy with that, because I would not have been happy running Harrah's for Holiday. I was happy running Harrah's with Bill Harrah, but the new company–the Holiday Inn–was not exciting to me at all. I'd been there long enough. I had a good retirement, and I was pleased to get out.

What positions have you held and what boards have you served on since leaving Harrah's?

I was on the board of directors of Security Bank. I am on the board of Southwest Gas, which is a utility out of Las Vegas, and when they acquired Nevada Savings some years ago I went on that board also. At that time I got off the Security Bank board, because you can't be on two bank boards at the same time. Last year we sold Primerit Bank, which was the forerunner of Nevada Savings and Loan. Those are the only public boards that I've been on. I was on Harvey's board for a few years, but the chemistry wasn't there for me with the family. It was more of a family corporation—it wasn't a public company at that time—so I resigned for that reason.

So you're managing three trusts now: one for Verna, and one for each of the boys.

Yes, and they have a total market value of about $300 million.

I've been out of Harrah's since 1980 and I don't miss it at all. I don't have any regrets. Joan will tell you that I'm *actively* retired. We spend a lot of time with our children and our grandchildren, and I play golf and hunt and do some fishing with friends and my family, so I'm very pleased with my life. Joan and I still go to events and we still go to dinner at Harrah's and other facilities, but neither one of us really likes to be downtown with all the crowds anymore. We had enough of that in our life. We lead a pretty private life now. I only know about three people that are still employed at Harrah's that were there when I was there. It's been a lot of years, so there's been a lot of changes.

In closing, Lloyd, do you have any interesting stories or any more remembrances of Bill Harrah that you'd like to pass on before we close down?

Well, there are probably several. Bill was a private person with private thoughts (he didn't volunteer anything), but I've always been a very curious person, and I don't mind asking. Many times I asked Bill about this or that, and one day I said, "How did you ever come to Reno? What got you here?" And this is the story he told me: His father ran a bingo

operation in Venice, California, and he employed about thirty people. So it was a big operation, but it was on again, off again, depending on who was the chief of police. I don't know how much he had to pay them to keep it open, but Bill's father got tired of being shut down all the time, so he said, "I'm going to sell it."

And Bill says, "Why don't you let me run it?"

So John, his dad, said, "Fine." And so Bill did run it until he got tired of it too.

One day in 1937 Bill got in his car and headed north to Las Vegas—Bill is telling me this story. And he said Las Vegas probably had 15,000 people in town if they had that many at that time. And Bill said, "I was in the worst sandstorm I ever saw in my life that day in Las Vegas. And I said to myself, 'This place will never amount to anything.' And I went north and that's how I got to Reno." [laughter]

[I think this story also reveals something about Bill Harrah:] When Joanie and I went to Europe with Bill and Verna, I think they had thirteen pieces of luggage and we had four. [laughter] When we arrived in Rome, one cab hauled all the luggage and the other cab packed Joanie and myself and Bill and Verna to the hotel. Before Bill had left on the trip, his secretary had given him an envelope full of the native money of each country we were going into. So when we went into France, England, Italy, Denmark, Norway, Finland, and Germany, Bill had an envelope of francs or lira or whatever. When we were loading up the cab in Rome he said, "By the way, I do all the tipping." [laughter]

I had brought 100 one-dollar bills that I figured I would tip with, plus I had other cash. When Bill said, "I take care of all the tipping," I thought, "Well, that's pretty easy." All the concierges knew him, and all the managers in the hotel knew him, because he went to Europe with every wife, and he made a lot of those trips. [laughter] As soon as he walked in the door, they knew who he was, and he wanted to keep that relationship, because he

Lloyd Dyer (l.) and Bill Harrah on the *Thunderbird*. *"It had two Italian diesel engines in it, and it was all mahogany and teak with a stainless steel top—it was a gorgeous thing."*

always got great service from them. So that made it easy for us. We didn't have to tip. [laughter]

Another thing that was interesting happened probably about 1963. Emerson Wilson, an attorney in town, a very neat guy and maybe the sharpest real estate attorney in Reno at that time, called me one day and said, "A friend of mine is an attorney in San Francisco, and his client is George Whittell. You know who George Whittell is?"

And I said, "I've heard of him, but I don't really know him."

He said, "Well, he has the Thunderbird Estate at Lake Tahoe, just a little bit south of Sand Harbor. He's got a boat called the *Thunderbird*, that he had built in Detroit in

1938. They put the boat—and the boat is fifty-eight feet long—on a railroad car and hauled it to Truckee (at that time there was a railroad from Truckee to Tahoe), and that's how they launched the boat. Anyway, he is getting up in years and he doesn't know Bill Harrah, but he knows of his reputation and that whatever he does, he does first class. He wants the boat to be taken care of properly, and he knows that Bill Harrah will do that and he may be the only person who could do it, so he wants to sell the boat to Harrah's."

I said, "Well, how much does he want for the boat?"

He says, "$50,000."

It had two Italian diesel engines in it, and it was all mahogany and teak with a stainless steel top–it was a gorgeous thing. Subsequently we did buy the boat, and Bill Harrah put two Allison airplane engines in it. (Harrah's had a guy by the name of Harry Volpi, who was an expert on boats and airplanes. Harry got the boat out of there and got it going, and we took it to the auto collection, cleaned it all up, put a new finish on it, and changed the engines.) Allison airplane engines are what were in the P-51 Mustangs, and when you started that thing up, you could hear it from here to Placerville. [laughter]

[When Bill bought the boat,] my job was to take a check for $50,000 and deliver it to somebody at the Whittell Castle at Lake Tahoe. As I drove down there, there were police dogs all over the place barking at the car. When I got to the castle a lady came out, and I said, "I have a check for Mr. Whittell."

And she said, "He wants to see you."

I said, "Oh, really?"

She said, "Yes."

I said, "Well, what about the dogs?"

She said, "I'll call the dogs off." She did.

So I go in, and he's sitting in a wheelchair in a terry cloth bathrobe. His nurse's name– the lady that met me–was Ruth Casey. I got to know her and Mr. Whittell quite well over the next five or six years, and the only thing I ever saw him in was in a wheelchair in a terry cloth bathrobe.

Mr. Whittell was an eccentric person. He had a ten-acre estate at Woodside, California. On his estate he had wild animals like lions, elephants, and tigers. When he was eighty-two he was wrestling with one of his tigers or lions one day and broke his hip. It never healed, so he was in a wheelchair until he died at the age of eighty-seven.

Bill was very interested in buying property around Zephyr Cove, and Mr. Whittell owned all the land from Zephyr Cove to Skyland. At one time he owned 20,000 acres of land on the east shore of Lake Tahoe that went from the lake all the way up to the ridge. That included Sand Harbor, and

it included all of what Incline Village is today. He bought it in 1932 for $300,000–all of that property. Today a single residential lot, 100 by 180 feet, at Lake Tahoe on the water would be a minimum of $650,000.

Did Mr. Whittell ever meet Bill Harrah?

Yes. In fact, it was really funny. I took Bill up to the lake with Scherry and introduced them to George Whittell. It was a brief meeting, and then Bill went down and saw the boat. (He hadn't seen the boat before he bought it.)

Bill really liked meeting George Whittell. So I told Bill, "Well, if we want to keep this relationship going, maybe what we should do is try to see him every few months. I'll go one quarter, you go one quarter, and we'll take turns."

Bill said, "No, we'll go together." He says, "I don't want to go alone–we'll go together."

I said, "OK."

About that time Mr. Whittell had moved to Woodside, and he never came back to the lake. So I'd call Ruth Casey, and we'd set a date to see Mr. Whittell. We always saw him at two o'clock in the afternoon. We'd fly down in Harrah's plane, land at the San Jose airport and rent a car. Bill and I would drive up to within three blocks of his estate and get there at 1:30. (We'd leave enough time to make sure we were there on time.) At three minutes to two we'd start the car up and drive in. We always arrived promptly at two, and Mr. Whittell never got over it. "How could you leave from Reno and arrive promptly at two o'clock?" [laughter] He didn't know we were sitting outside the gate for half an hour.

We did that, and we gave him a gift every Christmas, and then he was concerned about the maintenance of his place at Thunderbird Castle, which had 360 acres. So we took care of the maintenance for about three or four years. It probably cost us about $25,000 a year to take care of it. We're the only people that never asked him for anything. We were always doing things for him and being nice to him, and he liked us because of that.

When we'd meet him in his office at Woodside, he must have had the furnace up to 100 degrees. It was so hot in there, Bill and I could hardly keep awake. We would walk around stretching and trying to stay awake. We would talk probably for an hour, sometimes two hours; he was really an interesting guy.

Before he died in 1967, he sold us two Duesenbergs. We bought one for $4,500 and the other one for $5,500. Either one of those cars today would be worth $700,000 or $800,000. We really got a hell of a buy on those cars. I think Holiday has since sold both of them.

After Mr. Whittell died, I took a gentleman by the name of Jack Dreyfus, of the Dreyfus mutual fund company, on a tour of Lake Tahoe. He was interested in buying Whittell's Tahoe land holdings from Whittell's estate. He negotiated a deal to buy all of the property that was left, and there was still probably around ten or twelve thousand acres. He paid $13 million for it. Subsequently he sold everything to the Forest Service except the 360-acre Whittell Thunderbird Castle and estate, all of the Zephyr Cove property, and the valuable lake-front property at Skyland. He kept that for himself. Part of that property recently sold for $30 million. Where the castle is now is up for sale for $60 million. So Mr. Dreyfus made a good deal.

Whittell High School at South Lake Tahoe is named after George Whittell. Also, I should mention that Mr. Whittell inherited his money from his father, who had checkerboarded most of the primary real estate lots in San Francisco. That's where Whittell got his money. He was known as Captain Whittell because he was a captain in the Italian navy in World War I. (I don't know how he got involved there.) He also was a friend of Frank Buck and did a lot of hunting in Africa way back when. But, later on in life, he became a conservationist and didn't like people that were hunters.

George Whittell left the bulk of his estate to the Humane Society, but there isn't one Humane Society—there's a Humane Society in Reno; there's a Humane Society in San Francisco, et cetera. So any or all of the Humane Societies that applied for it have part of his estate, and that's why the Humane Society has such a nice facility here in Reno on McCarran.

And that's my story.

Well, it was a good one. Thanks, Lloyd.

Notes

1. The intersection of U.S. 50 and S.R. 89, west of South Lake Tahoe.
2. Other sources have different versions of this three-way transaction.
3. Bill Ledbetter was the CEO of Harvey Gross's Wagon Wheel Casino.
4. Virgil Smith was a longtime Reno gambler who owned and operated several casinos in Reno from the 1930s through the 1970s. He was a partner of Bill Harrah in John's Bar in 1943 and loaned Harrah money in 1946 to open his first casino.
5. P & L is the abbreviation for a profit and loss report.
6. In 1997, when Joe McMullen died, Holmes Hendricksen was named a trustee.

10

GENE EVANS

*G*ENE EVANS *was born in Baltimore, Maryland, on October 12, 1920. He grew up in Annapolis, Maryland, and came to Reno after World War II.*

Following graduation from the University of Nevada with a degree in journalism, Evans moved to Elko to work for the Elko Daily Free Press. *He was elected to the state assembly and served in the legislature for three sessions. In 1959 he returned to Reno to take a job as a publicity and public relations man for Harrah's, staying with the firm for eleven years.*

Gene Evans was a candid and frank chronicler who wasn't hesitant about relating his memories. The interview was conducted in his home in July of 1997 in two sittings. In this chapter, which is excerpted from a lengthier, broad-ranging oral history, Evans tells of his involvement with the promotion of the 1960 Winter Olympics at Squaw Valley, the work that he did with the Harrah's celebrity golf tournaments, and his role in covering the kidnapping of Frank Sinatra Jr.

Several other important subjects, not directly related to the history of Harrah's Clubs, are addressed in Mr. Evans's complete oral history, which is in the research collection of the UNOHP. They include a revealing account of how, as the co-author of AB144, Evans helped push that bill

through the assembly and the senate to the desk of Governor Grant Sawyer, who signed it, creating the gaming commission and making the procedure of getting a gaming license in Nevada a privilege, not a right.

GENE EVANS: I was born October 12, 1920, in Baltimore, Maryland. Shortly after I was born, my father, Clarence, who was a streetcar conductor or a brakeman, deserted my mother and ran off with a younger woman. I guess in those days you could do this without benefit of divorce. If you didn't like your spouse–you had an argument or something–you just left. That's what he did. He left, and my mother and I were from then on just mother and son; no father. I had one brother, but he died shortly after I was born. That might have been one of the reasons why there was a breakup. I never talked to my mother about it, and she's never really told me too much about it, and that's been fine.

I lived in Baltimore until I was about ten or twelve. My mother never remarried. However, she met a gentleman from Annapolis who was an official with the athletic department at the naval academy. She became enamored with him, and we subsequently moved to Annapolis where I enrolled in the school system. She never married the fellow, but they were very, very good friends. He was an awfully fine man. As a matter of fact, at one point along the line after I grew up there, he was going to get me an appointment to the academy. I could have gotten it very easily too, except I took a physical and was turned down: When I was seven years old, I was afflicted with infantile paralysis. Today they call it polio myelitis, but then it was just plain old infantile paralysis. It paralyzed the left side of my face, and I had no movement. As a matter of fact, I was rather a disreputable looking kid, I guess, from what I heard and the fights I had to get into because people called me "crooked mouth." Anyhow, I was unacceptable for the academy, but I spent most of my early childhood in Annapolis. I went to the grammar school and high school there, and after I graduated from high school, I came west.

My mother had a sister living in Los Angeles who was married. I didn't know about it until I met him, but my uncle was heavily involved in a rubber factory in Los Angeles. After we moved out west, I went to work for him at the Kirkhill Rubber Company and worked there for two years. I saved whatever money I could because I wanted to go to college; I saved enough for at least one year to go to Washington State in Pullman, Washington.

I had never played football in high school; we didn't have a high school football team in Annapolis. We had soccer, and soccer, of course, is very big today, but very few colleges even had soccer teams then. When I went to Washington State as a freshman, I learned that they didn't have soccer, so I turned out for the freshman football team and was what we'd consider a walk-on today. Well, I made the team and was also starting quarterback. Get a load of that: quarterback in a single wing, which was a powerful formation then! From that I got the equivalent of a scholarship or what was called a grant-in-aid to play for the varsity.

[After serving in the army in World War II, I enrolled in the University of Nevada to play football on an athletic scholarship. When a knee injury ended my playing career, I continued my education on the GI Bill.] I graduated with a journalism degree in 1948. A regent at the university by the name of Chris Sheerin owned a newspaper in Elko, Nevada, called the *Elko Daily Free Press.* He offered me a position when I graduated. I took the job as city editor of the *Elko Daily Free Press.*

DWAYNE KLING: How many years did you stay in Elko?

I was in Elko eleven years. [In 1957 I was elected to my first term in the assembly. While in the assembly, the most important thing I did was co-author (along with Howard McKissick) AB144, the act establishing the Nevada Gaming Control Board. In my third term Bill Harrah offered me a position with Harrah's,] so in 1959 I got out of the newspaper business and went to work in the publicity and public relations area for Bill Harrah. Mark Curtis was already covering public relations, advertising, and marketing and was the overall department head. Bill wanted to know where I wanted to fit in, and I said, "Well, I don't know anything about advertising, particularly. It's not my field; public relations is." So he offered me the position as public relations director, and I worked in conjunction with Mark at that time. Actually, I worked for Mark for only a minute, and then Mark left Harrah's for a while.

When Mark left, did you take over his position?

Bill offered me the whole deal, but I told him that there were some areas I didn't feel qualified to handle. For instance, the advertising department: I had experience in advertising, but I was not what I would consider an expert in it. I suggested that I could handle the publicity and public relations end of it and some promotion, because I had been involved in promotion heavily in other areas, but as far as the advertising was concerned, no. I didn't want the responsibility. So we split it up into segments—public relations and advertising. We formed an advertising arm, and I just took over the public relations portion. Later, Mark came back and took over the whole thing again because he had good background in all that.

I was at Harrah's for eleven years, and then I went out on my own. During the time I was at Harrah's, I became involved with Bill in a lot of different ways. Bill was very big in classic antique automobiles, and as a consequence, he started his own collection. But he soon found out he had a problem with that. And he did have a problem! He was trying to write it off as a promotion investment. I talked to him early on about how he was handling it, and I said, "Well, we should play this up as it being a part of the total Harrah's operation, as an attraction." So when I handled the publicity for the club,

every time I wrote something about the automobile collection, I'd always use it–in print–as an adjunct to the Harrah's operation.

Sure enough, in the course of time Harrah's was audited, and the feds were going to really nail him on all the money that he had declared as an investment and as a write-off as a promotion for the club. I have to tell you, he was really concerned. I'll never forget the auditor. The internal revenue person who arrived on the scene was really going to come down on Harrah's–Bill particularly, as the sole owner of the club. When this fellow was in Bill's office, Bill called me and says, "Can you come over, Gene? I've got an internal revenue person here. Can you come over and talk to him?"

"You bet," I said, "I'll be right over."

Early on we had installed a system of keeping news clips. Every ad or every story that we ever wrote, or that Harrah's was in, we'd clip. And I had a secretary that would make a monthly and yearly scrapbook of all the publicity that Harrah's had received. So I got a couple of guys in the office, and we took over these big books and set them down. The internal revenue guy looked at them and said, "What are these?"

And I said, "This is your answer here."

Then he says, "What do you mean, my answer? Why are you here?"

I said, "Well, this is all the publicity that this automobile collection has been involved in as far as a promotion of the club."

He started looking at them and went through about three books at random looking for stories about the collection. And every time that we wrote about the automobile collection, it was always as a promotional part of the operation of Harrah's Reno-Lake Tahoe. Finally he says, "Hey, it's good enough for me," walked away, and case was closed. [laughter] Bill always thought that that was the smartest thing we had ever done in that area. We became good friends.

[As a youth] I had had polio, and my face had been paralyzed. Well, Bill was a very dedicated advocate of Mayo Clinic, and he would send all of his top executives back there. Even though I was not in his top management, he sent me to Mayo too, because he just thought I should go, and I thought that was great. One day I got a call from him. He said, "I've got someone here that I want you to talk to." I went over to his office, and there's the head of the plastic surgery section of Mayo. He had come to Reno, and he wanted to look at me. He wanted to see if they could do something for my face. So Bill Harrah actually saw to it that I got cosmetic surgery, which straightened my face out and closed up one eye a little and made me look a little better than I had looked. Bill Harrah paid for it, and I always was extremely grateful to him for that. He didn't have to do that. As a matter of fact, he didn't have to hire me to begin with, because the navy, marine corps, air corps wouldn't take me, but Harrah did. So I always was a Bill Harrah fan and still am to this day.

That had to cost thousands of dollars, even in those days.

It cost quite a little money, and I was extremely grateful for it. I became an extreme advocate or proponent of Bill Harrah and his operation. He, in my opinion, epitomized [the principles of] the Gaming Control Act, and it was from some of the things that I had discussed with him that it had all come about.

So he was kind of the man behind the Gaming Control Act?

Yes, unknowingly. One of several, because we were going to come up with *something*. I took this bill that we've been talking about (AB144), not only to Bill Harrah, but to Harolds Club, to Las Vegas, and even to Newt Crumley. He had some problems with it for a while, but he came around.

Was Mr. Crumley in the Holiday [in Reno] at that time?

Yes, he was in the Holiday. I never went to Elko [to see him] because I didn't need to.

To return to your career at Harrah's, did you ever get involved in community affairs?

It's interesting that you should ask that, Dwayne, because originally a gambler wanted to keep away from that. He didn't want any exposure—most gamblers didn't want the spotlight on them at all. But over the years after I had polio and I was out in Elko, I became very, very interested in the March of Dimes and things of that nature. For some reason my persona has been that I want to help somebody where I can, if I possibly can. Well, when I went to work for Bill, we were involved in very little community activity in Reno. Bill kind of stayed out of it. But I finally got him talked into being more exposed in community affairs. "You got guys here like Bob Ring," I told him, and I said, "Hell, Bob and some of your other executives are naturals to be involved in all these things." As a consequence, Harrah's slowly became involved and became a force in the community. I felt then and still do that if you're going to be a part of the community and you want acceptance, you have to participate.

I was sort of the company's public relations, press relation, community service advocate. I served on lots of committees while I was at Harrah's. Other people at Harrah's sort of steered away from too much involvement. I leaned strongly the other way. I felt that we should have key people to represent Harrah's in areas of influence. I always said this to Bill Harrah, and he agreed with it. I said, "Bill, they passed a law legalizing gambling." I said, "It went through the legislature, and one of these days somebody can get up and say, 'I want to put in a bill that's going to outlaw gambling,' and when they do, then it's going to take votes right here in Carson City. If you got people involved, and they believe in what you're doing . . . ." In other words, if you're an honest gambler supporting your community and state, you're "coppering your bet," is what it amounts to. And he agreed. That's when Harrah became more involved in community activity than he had been before. I don't take full credit for that, but I believe I had a strong influence in having that come about.

When you worked in community affairs, did that involve any lobbying in Carson City during any legislative sessions?

On some occasions I'd go over to discuss something, but I was not an official lobbyist. Harrah's lobbyist was Maurice Sheppard. That was his big job there. That was almost his entire job when the legislature was in session, but on more than one occasion I would help Sheppard in areas where he needed some information or needed some advice.

And you probably still knew a lot of people in the legislature?

Oh, yes. Grant Sawyer said to me one day when he was governor, "I can't understand why Bill doesn't use you as his personal representative, because you're the only one in that whole organization, and even in gambling, that has the ear of the governor."

To go back to AB144, let's talk about that a little bit more, Gene.

There was one thing in AB144 that was extremely controversial, and you may have run into this. It was called the "dealer's registration." If you remember, every dealer who went to work in the casino gaming industry not only had to register, but had to go on record and be finger-printed. The dealer's fingerprints were kept with the Gaming Control Board for future reference.

A lot of people who were working in Las Vegas had worked in Reno and went to Vegas (or vice versa), and when they went to work for a casino, they were asked the question, "Where did you work?"

"Oh, I worked at Harrah's in Reno."

"Why did you quit?"

"Oh, I just couldn't stand the climate. I wanted to come down here." That wasn't necessarily the real reason. The dealer could have been involved in something–maybe dealing seconds, or maybe in some fashion doing something that wasn't in the best interest of gambling and the casino. So the state kept a record. If you were registered, the dealer now would have a record that would follow him wherever he went. Many of the dealers were very upset about this, because they figured that what they did, whatever it was, maybe they could change–maybe they got a bum rap, things of that nature.

Dealer registration was one of the real controversial issues . . . but not so much from the owner's standpoint. If you were a dealer, your record followed you wherever you went. That was a security thing, a safeguard for the industry. Because there are a lot of guys out there–and you may have run across some; I knew of some–who were very much in it. You probably will remember (and I know from when we were discussing this in the legislature) the big thing about cheating in a casino was not so much the house cheating the gambler or the client or the customer, but more the dealer working with a confederate coming in and doing what they call "dumping," or collusion, between dealers and customers. That's where the big bucks were being lost by casinos. Anytime a guy got nailed on that, if he's going to work somewhere else, that establishment should be aware of the dealer's past record. That's what this was all about. Well, we finally got that settled, and it did pass. The dealer registration became an integral part of the Gaming Control Act.

The gaming commission then required the thing called the "eye in the sky." Harrah was an innovator in that–the first "eye in the sky" went in at Lake Tahoe when he built the casino up there. The gaming commission was so turned on by it that it became a requirement for all casinos. That came about for two reasons: one, it really put the dealers on their good behavior; it brought to a screeching halt the shenanigans going on with the dealer working with someone else. But also, more importantly, it protected the customer. The idea was to catch a dealer who was dealing seconds, or dealing from the bottom of the deck, or whatever the little sleight-of-hand tricks were. And that was the whole reason, or the basic reason, for the "eye in the sky."

It also protected the dealer, because a pit boss or casino official that didn't like a dealer just couldn't go around and say, "Oh, Gene's dumping off the table."

Yes. It was a two-way street. I thought it was a very important part of the whole package–part of the continuing effort to keep gaming honest. Surveillance has been improved tremendously over the years and is now a big factor in keeping gaming honest on both sides of the table. That's what we were planning and thinking about when we were drafting the Gaming Control Act.

A thing that I always liked about Bill Harrah–Bill Harrah wanted to have as clean a game in his casinos as he could put forward within the constraints of the law. I remember when we were talking about passing the legislation, before it became law, that giving the customer a fair shake was a high priority for Bill. In other words, if you came in the casino and you put a dollar down on a twenty-one game, you wanted to know that the card that came up was the card that you were rightly going to get. If you were playing craps, you wanted to know that when you threw those dice, they were going to come up

according to lot; that they were going to come up however they stopped. You trusted the dice weren't going to be shaved, crooked, or loaded. You wanted to know they were "clean" dice.

There was all kinds of hanky-panky in those early days. Well, "the eye in the sky" was very, very instrumental in bringing about not a complete halt to it, because everybody out there is still trying to figure out a way to beat you, but a lot more honesty to the games–again, from *both* sides of the table.

Many people that I have talked to that worked at Harrah's say that Bill Harrah wanted the customer to be number one, and that included all things, not just food and beverage and hotel rooms. But as you just mentioned, he also wanted the customer to be number one when it came to getting a good shake on all the tables.

Exactly right. And that was one of the key things that we ran into in discussing this bill at the very beginning–how we were going to upgrade the image of gambling. That was my number-one concern, to improve the image of gambling.

Continuing on the subject of images, wasn't Bill Harrah extremely concerned with employees' appearances and the appearance of the casino?

Oh, absolutely. In my dealings with Bill and talking about it, I got the feeling it was a fetish. He was a nut for cleanliness. You couldn't have an ashtray on the table for ten minutes or five minutes before somebody came by, emptied, washed it, and put it back for you. You couldn't have cigarette butts or stuff like that on the floor for four or five minutes before some maintenance guy came around and swept them up. The keno girls and all the girls that wore the short skirts, they better have their seams straight on their stockings or they were in trouble. [laughter] It got to be funny in some instances, but that was Bill Harrah, and that was his mode of operation. He was a cleanliness nut. But it worked. That was the thing that Harrah's was known for. When you went to work, you had black slacks and you wore a white shirt and a tie, and your pants had to be pressed. You walked on the floor, you better be in good shape or you weren't going to be on the floor for very long. You were going to be sent home.

That was the thing that impressed me with Bill Harrah. I made a comment to Wallace Turner that Bill Harrah is the only person in the gambling industry that I would work for, and that was because of all of these things that I had run into in my first meeting with him. I had a good interview time with him and saw him on several occasions afterwards, and I really was impressed with the man and his attitude. That's why Harrah's became the number one house in the state.

There was an incident that attracted national attention when you were at Harrah's: the kidnapping of Frank Sinatra Jr.

As I recall it, he was a singer with the Tommy Dorsey band. It wasn't the original band, but it was one that had been made up of a couple of Dorseys and a couple of people that played with him when they had another group. They were playing at Harrah's in the lounge, and Sinatra Jr. was singing with them.

We used to put headline entertainers in the north and south lodges, and because he was Frank Sinatra's son, he was in one of the lodges rather than staying with the band, which we put in a nearby motel. Junior was staying in the north lodge when I got this phone call to get right to the lake, there was something happening that I had to handle. And I said, "Well, what's the problem?"

"Well, get up here now. We got a problem," I was told. "I can't tell you what it is. All I know is we got a lot of FBI people up here. It has to do with Sinatra's boy." The caller was the shift manager at Harrah's Tahoe, and I couldn't get any more out of

him. So I got in my car and went up to the lake. When I got up there, I found out that Sinatra Jr. had, in fact, been kidnapped, and there was great confusion. The FBI and the police had taken over, and they were cordoning off different places and, in general, throwing their weight around. I was told, "You can't talk to anybody."

And I said, "Whoa, whoa."

And they were saying, "Well this is an investigation, and . . . ."

I interrupted and said, "Look, you're in Harrah's. Mr. Harrah owns this place. Whatever is happening here, he's as much or more concerned about it than you are. This is his operation. I'm the public relations person here, and I want to see that we're treated properly, pure and simple, Mac."

When the head of the FBI in Reno came up, he took charge of the investigation. He knew me, and he says, "Hey, this kid's OK. He's all right. You're talking to Mr. Harrah now when you're talking to him."

I hadn't called Bill at all; Bill wasn't aware of it, but he would be as soon as we worked it out and we knew what the score was with Sinatra Jr. There was a question of whether he had just taken off on his own. All kinds of things were happening. There had been a phone call, as I recall, which kind of alerted us to the fact that there was something a little unusual about all this. Finally it was determined that he, in fact, had been kidnapped when a ransom note appeared demanding $70,000 or some amount of money. I don't remember all of that exactly. At that time the FBI didn't want anything out on it yet, and I can understand that. We didn't either until we knew what had happened.

I didn't want any big rumors running around as far as Harrah was concerned, so as soon as it was determined a kidnapping had taken place, I called Bill. He was in his home in Reno, and I woke him up. Bill didn't take phone calls personally at that time, but I got one of the help that he had there. He was somewhat perturbed—it was now about three in the morning. I said, "I got to talk to Bill. This is Gene Evans, and you know who I am. It's life and death. Get him and wake him up. Tell him I'm on the phone."

So in a couple of minutes Bill came on. Bill never, in his most violent mood, ever talked very loudly. He said, "What is this?"

I said, "Bill, Frank Sinatra Jr. has been kidnapped."

Now he came wide awake. He says, "What?"

I said, "The FBI is up here. We've got everybody in the country here. Frank Sinatra has been notified, and he's apparently on his way."

And he says, "Well, OK, I'll wait until I hear from you. You handle it. Let me talk to Holmes Hendricksen," who was club manager at that time. He talked to Holmes, and then between Holmes, myself, and a couple of others, we coordinated our involvement.

I told these guys, "Look, we're involved in this, and at this point in time, every newspaper in the country is going to say this is a publicity stunt." Some did. Here's a prime example: I called the Associated Press in San Francisco at about three o'clock or four o'clock in the morning–the desk guy there said, "What! Come on, what are you trying to pull here? What are you looking for, publicity?"

I heard this voice in the background say, "Who is that?"

And he said, "Oh, some nut up in Tahoe named Gene Evans saying that Frank Sinatra Jr. has been kidnapped."

The guy, who was the San Francisco bureau night manager said–I could hear him– "Give me that goddamned phone!" He comes on and he says, "Evans, this is so-and-so. What you got?" I told him. I found out later that this desk guy who answered the phone thought that we were just playing a game, and the night manager told him–I heard him say it– "Anytime you get a call from Evans, you take it," which I thought was great. [laughter]

Anyhow, that's how the whole story got broken.

Sinatra Sr. got involved in it. When I talked to him, he said, "Well, we don't need you anymore. You're out of here."

And I said, "No, I'm not out of here until such time as Harrah's is out of this. Then I'll be out, but not until then."

He says, "Well, I got my people. We'll take care of this."

I said, "Your people can take care of anything you have in mind for yourself, but you don't speak for Harrah's." [laughter] I was kind of cocky. I was very adamant about it.

Sinatra had brought up several PR people from Los Angeles with him, and they were from a top-flight L.A. firm. He says, "My guys will take care of this."

And I said, "They won't do anything as far as Harrah's is concerned." I said, "You don't speak for Harrah's. You can talk all you want to about your son and what you plan to do, and I can't tell you what to do, but you don't speak for Harrah's." And I said, "Until Mr. Harrah tells me I'm off of this, I'm here, and there isn't anything that you can do about it, Mr. Sinatra." I didn't call him "Frankie boy" or anything. I called him Mr. Sinatra.

As I recall, it all worked out–they paid the money and he was released; and they did catch the perpetrators, I believe.

Yes, they found them all down in the southern California area somewhere.

You must have handled dozens of news-breaking stories. Is there any way that you can possibly pick out the one or two top stories that you were involved in?

Well, of course, the Sinatra kidnapping was international news. Another thing that we were involved in was operating the press headquarters for the Winter Olympics at Squaw Valley in 1960. We had all the press in the world that were covering the Olympics stopping in there. We sponsored the headquarters for the press, and just about every story that went out mentioned Harrah's, which was quite a coup. But Bill Harrah was a generous man, and as far as press relations were concerned, I think Harrah's was considered probably the best place to go for covering the story, because we treated the press so well. I remember being elated that I was a part of all this.

Because I had been a newspaper man before joining Harrah's, I figured I would want to treat the press as I would want to be treated. We treated the press awfully, awfully good. It was Mark Curtis, my predecessor who later came back to work for Harrah's, who set up news contacts, press contacts with press agents (that's what they were called in those days) in San Francisco, Los Angeles, Chicago, and New York. The one I worked most heavily with then was a young man in San Francisco named Dick Skuse. Dick Skuse had been very much involved with the committee that had fought for the Olympics to come up to Squaw Valley where Alex Cushing was the primary winter resort operator—he was Cushing's PR guy then. He was hired by Harrah's to set up a PR office in San Francisco. Skuse had very good contacts in the Bay area.

The Los Angeles people, I knew very, very well, because they had a fellow by the name of Sam Wall who was there. And we had a young man in New York by the name of Jackie Cannon. Cannon was the brother of a very well-known New York news columnist who had all the contacts in the world on the East Coast. So Harrah's had a real network of top PR and news media. (Television wasn't that big then, but it was coming on, and I had made some very good contacts through the promotion we put on with the Harrah's unlimited hydroplanes.)

I believe of all the companies or businesses in the world, Harrah's, at that point in time, had the best media contacts of anybody, anywhere, anytime. Our involve-

ment in the 1960 Olympics was the reason for it, because we had every known major writer in the country—and in the world probably—come to the Olympics. Just about every one of them, at some time during the event, went through the Harrah's press relations headquarters. And, of course, Harrah was a great host.

Was the press relationship headquarters at Squaw Valley or at Harrah's?

It was at Squaw Valley. After the day's activities had concluded, we'd bring them down to the South Shore Room and have them as guests in the room, introduce them from the audience and, in general, give them a real V.I.P. treatment. It was kind of lobbying in another way! [laughter] But we had great coverage. That Olympics was one of the biggest coups, from Harrah's standpoint, for becoming known world-wide for anything in which it had ever been involved.

Of course, the Sinatra Jr. kidnapping was probably, in another way, a big thing too. I did everything in the world that I could to keep Harrah's clear of any involvement. I contacted all the press people I knew to put a positive approach on Harrah's involvement, because the first people that called were saying, "Hey, he was kidnapped from this sleaze gambling outfit, and it looks like it was probably set up by them," and that, "This is a publicity stunt, right?" This went on for three days, night and day. Finally we got the right spin on it, and it worked out to where we, Harrah's, weren't the bad guys.

The timing of the Olympics was so perfect because Harrah's had just expanded to the Stateline Club across the street, and they had just opened their South Shore Room.

Yes, the timing was perfect for the South Shore Room. It was really a kickoff for their expansion, and from then on, anything we did that had any significance at all, just the slightest thing, if we sent it out, the name Harrah's would get picked up. And, of course, that's what PR—press relations—are all about.

One important thing that I learned in my Harrah's association was picking out the "phony." And there were a lot of them running around there. But once you picked them out, you could learn to deal with them. You could turn them around to suit your best interest too. And then there were the good guys like Walter Winchell. I got to know Walter Winchell on a first-name basis, and a guy by the name of Frank Delaplane. I got to know all the top writers. Earl Wilson was a great guy. We had him out on several occasions, and I'd call him personally and got to know him on a first-name basis too. When I put a call in, they'd listen, and that was great.

I had a good name with the media that we dealt with. Being an ex-newspaper man, I knew how I would want to be treated, and I tried to treat the people that I dealt with that way. I never lied to them. I didn't want anybody to lie to me. We dealt in facts. And in the newspaper business, when you write a story, you're dealing with facts, not fiction. So anything that I would send out for Harrah's was based on fact, not something fictional or something that wasn't real.

The most important thing of this whole set-up was that Bill Harrah, for some reason, trusted me. I guess he figured that I could be a good spokesman for him with the media. I'd call Bill and say, "Bill, I need a comment from you. I have so-and-so who wants to talk to you."

And he'd ask me, "What about?" and I'd tell him, and he'd say, "Well, you tell him." I used to write a lot of things for Bill, only because Bill would say, "You write it. You know what I'm thinking." So I'd write it and run it past him, whatever it was, and he would OK it. Just about every time I'd get a call from the media, I'd get the same kind of reaction: "Well, you tell him. You know what I'll say."

"Well, goddamn it, Bill," I'd explain, "they want to talk to you, not me."

"Well, no, you tell them. You know exactly what I'd be saying anyhow. You always write it . . ." words to that effect.

So there's a lot of Bill Harrah quotes out there floating around in the world that were actually Gene Evans's quotes?

Well, it's possible. Yes, there are a couple of them, [laughter] but Bill was that way. Bill was very quiet, and he didn't like publicity for himself. He wasn't a blow-hard, wasn't a show-off. He walked into the room, and you wouldn't even know he was there most of the time. Look around, and there he was.

Bill was one real fine gentleman. I liked him very, very much. I think that was reflected in the book *Gambler's Money*, written by Wallace Turner. Turner contacted me for information about Nevada's gambling control bill because he was planning to include it in his book. After I told him about it, he wanted to know why I went to work for Bill Harrah. I gave him the background that Bill Harrah was the only person in gambling that I would work for. I don't know if that was good or bad as far as the media was concerned, but that's just the way that I happened to feel. Bill, I trusted as an honest man. Most certainly, Bill had some problems. Everybody has his problems. He had his idiosyncracies, but in dealing with the public, Bill was honest. And that was a key to this thing called gambling.

You eventually left Harrah's Club after working there for how many years?

Eleven years. I went to work in 1959 and left in the first part of 1970.

Earlier you said you didn't care to work for any gambling organization other than Bill Harrah, but you did go to work for Charles Mapes.

Yes, and I've thought about that many times. I made the comment earlier that there was no other gambler in the state of Nevada that I'd work for other than Bill Harrah. When I left Harrah's, I left for personal reasons, and I spent three months just doing nothing. I had been divorced. Day in and day out, I sat on this porch. Did nothing but eat, sleep, and play with my dog. And I looked at the river. It took me three months to unwind from having been on that thirty-eight-hour-day, seventeen-months-a-year tour of duty with Harrah's. God, you met yourself coming and going all the time when you worked at Harrah's. I was always between Reno, Lake Tahoe, and Carson City. Had to fly to Chicago, had to go to wherever on some deal. I was constantly on the go. So when I finally left Harrah's, I spent three months right here doing nothing . . . just unwinding. And that was the first time I ever went on unemployment compensation. [laughter] I did get a severance check from Harrah's, so I had maybe a couple of thousand dollars, and I did not need to work for the minute, so I unwound.

⟨⟩

In the course of the time I was at Harrah's, we used to put on golf tournaments, and we'd always invite Charles Mapes to the tournaments to play. I'd always play because I was basically the promoter for Harrah's, and I'd always be in a foursome. As it happens, I was in a foursome a couple of years with Charles Mapes. I had heard all sorts of stories about Charles Mapes and some of his irrational and idiotic behavior at times, but in playing with Charles in golf, I got a different feeling about him. And for whatever reason, I don't know whether he respected me or not, but I began to see him in a different light. I guess because I had been a legislator, he treated me fairly well. I didn't see or experience many of the things that I had heard about him from some of the other people. Truthfully, I found him to be basically a considerate, compassionate person. Later I saw him on a couple of occasions when he had been drinking. Oh, he drank . . . as did most of us in the business, and sometimes his demeanor would change

dramatically. I think that's how many of the stories concerning Mapes came about.

I can, in all honesty, say that Charles Mapes was the first man in all the time that I worked in the gaming industry, even at Harrah's, that said, "Thank you, Gene. Job well done," or something like that. Bill Harrah never did. Bob Ring, never. Once, I remember saying to Bob, "You know, there are two words in the vocabulary that I don't think you know."

And he says, "What's that?"

I said, "There are two words called 'thank you.'"

And he says, "What's the big deal with that?"

I said, "Well, every once in a while it helps to tell somebody that."

And he says, "Well, why should I have to tell you 'thank you' when that's what we're paying you for?"

I said, "No, you're not paying me for that—I do my job, and you don't have to. But when I go beyond my job and do things, which I'm doing now in certain areas, and they are outside of the scope of what my job description calls for—not just for me but anybody in this organization—a simple little 'thank you' will go a long way." Bob and I had that kind of an understanding, really, from then on. That was my attitude; that was my stance, right or wrong. I'm sure, however, that it cost me. I resigned from Harrah's not too long after that conversation.

11

JOSEPH FANELLI

*J OSEPH FANELLI was born in New
Rochelle, New York, in August of 1918. He
is a graduate of Cornell University.
Following service in the military during World War
II, he went to work for Kahler Corporation, a
subsidiary of the Mayo Clinic in Rochester,
Minnesota. There he met Bill Harrah and other
Harrah's executives who went to the clinic for their
annual check-ups. In 1971 he was invited to become
vice-president of food and beverages for Harrah's
Clubs. Fanelli was one of the first executives to be
hired by Harrah's from outside the organization.*

*For this oral history Mr. Fanelli was
interviewed in his home in Reno, Nevada. He was
very eager to participate in the project. The
interview was conducted in June of 1997 and was
done in one session.*

*Mr. Fanelli recalls his personal contact with
Bill Harrah and his job assignments. Of special
interest is his account of the time and effort that
were put into the planning of the Summit, Harrah's
five-star restaurant at Lake Tahoe, and the
attention that was given to its menu and services.
Mr. Fanelli, who stayed on at Harrah's for almost
six years after it was sold to Holiday Inns, also
discusses some of the differences between working for
the new owners and the old. This oral history*

*supports the widely-held belief that Bill Harrah
demanded perfection in all aspects of his operations
and suggests that the restaurants were an important
factor in Harrah's overall success.*

JOSEPH FANELLI: I was born August 8, 1918, in New Rochelle, New York. My father was a superintendent of the police building and the courthouse in New Rochelle. My mother was a housewife who occasionally worked. She was very active in the church; very active. I have a sister five years younger than I am.

I grew up in New Rochelle and left to go to college in Ashland, Virginia, at Randolph Macon. While attending college, I was drafted.

DWAYNE KLING: When you were in the military, I heard that you served in General Patton's division.

For a while, yes. That was very interesting. It was sure different from all the other units. There was more spit and polish and well-dressed soldiers. Everything was on a pretty high plane. I was in the quartermaster corps. My primary function was doing road reconnaissance for convoys. That entailed going ahead of the convoys and laying out routes for the convoys. Very interesting duty. After my discharge (I was a captain when I was discharged), I enrolled at Cornell University.

What was your major at Cornell?

Hotel administration. When I finished there, I went to work in Rochester, Minnesota, for the Kahler Corporation. The Kahler Corporation actually served the Mayo Clinic—we had a very fine hotel across the street from the Mayo Clinic.

Although Kahler Corporation was part of the Mayo Clinic, Kahler had—when I left—thirteen properties. (When I started, they only had two.) I was food and beverage director for the entire Kahler Corporation, and I traveled around from property to property, but I was headquartered in Rochester, Minnesota.

Was that where you met Bill Harrah?

Bill Harrah used to go to the Mayo Clinic, and he used to stay at the Kahler Hotel. He must have seen something he liked; I never did find out. I knew him, greeted him, and things like that. Later, one of his executives came to the clinic, and they made me an offer to go to work for Harrah's. At that time I turned it down. They made another offer later on and flew me out to Reno. I looked over the property and met all the people, Lloyd and Shep in particular. A short time later, my wife flew out to take a look at the school situation and the general area. She was very impressed. That made my decision easy. From the time I was first approached until I was hired was about one year.

Joseph and Kathryn Fanelli on their way to Middle Fork Lodge in Idaho.

After I came to work for Harrah, most of the Harrah's Club executives went to the Mayo Clinic on a yearly basis. Prior to that, Bill Harrah and Bob Ring were the only Harrah's people who went to Mayo on a regular basis. Also, Bill Harrah, when he was going to get married, would send his future wives to the Mayo Clinic for physical exams.

I had worked for Kahler for twenty-one years, so it was quite a major move for me to come to Reno. I gave it a lot of thought. I had four young children at the time, and it wasn't an easy decision, because the two businesses were entirely different from each other. Kahler was a medical setup, and here it was gaming—two totally unrelated businesses; but I never regretted it.

Did Lloyd Dyer and Shep actively recruit you?

Yes, but Rome Andreotti also spent a lot of time with me. George Drews, the chief financial officer, and I both came to work for Harrah's Club the same day in 1971.

Were you and George the first two people in top management that were ever brought into Harrah's Club from the outside?

Yes.

Were you aware of that when you went to work for Harrah's?

No, not really. I just felt I had a job to do, and I enjoyed the change. In the long run, it turned out to be very good.

How did you feel about the efficiency of the operation and the way the operation was run as compared to Kahler?

Well, Kahler was very similar. Very similar. I have to say Harrah's was more refined. They had a better organization from the standpoint of rating employees. Each employee was rated especially for the attention they gave to making the customer happy without hurting the business. We had a similar goal at Kahler's, but it wasn't carried out as well as it was here.

When you took over the food and beverage operation, did they have existing problems?

Well, I think Bill was unhappy with the food and beverage departments, and I think he came to the conclusion that they needed

one head of the organization, one that would encompass both properties: Tahoe and Reno. So I was it. I was in charge of both properties and of all the food and beverage operations. I must have done a decent job, because I never heard from Bill after that . . . I mean, in a critical way. That pleased me. (I reported directly to Rome Andreotti.)

Did anyone give you guidelines as to what Harrah's was striving for in their restaurants?

They wanted to upgrade everything, and they wanted consistency. I set food cost goals, but they had to meet the approval of Rome. I don't know who else beyond him—possibly a management committee or possibly Shep when he was president, or later on Lloyd when he was president.

Did Mr. Harrah have any special likes or dislikes in food that he would ask you to put on or leave off the menu?

No. He just wanted good food.

Was he a gourmet, or was he a meat-and-potato person?

Well, he knew what he liked, and whether he took the gourmet bend, I don't know. I know he liked hamburgers and hot dogs. [laughter] We were pretty well attuned to just doing the very best we could. We didn't say, "OK, Bill likes this," or "Bill wants it done this way." We just did the best we could, and usually it pleased him. When it didn't, you heard about it. He didn't come down hard on you; you just heard about it, that's all.

We used to send cooks out to his house, to the ranch, and to a lot of his functions, such as management meetings. I don't know officially what his policy was, but every entertainer who appeared here had one dinner at the ranch. We sent a cook out to prepare that, and we would do the menu and so forth.

So it was entirely your selection as to what they had for dinner?

Yes, unless he had a specific request at the time.

Did Bill Harrah or whoever was president, Shep or Lloyd, leave you pretty much alone to run your department?

Yes. Yes, they did. I had certain goals, and they left me alone, except Rome Andreotti. He was always on my tail.

Rome was on everybody's tail, wasn't he? [laughter]

You said it. I didn't.

Did you report to Rome all the time you were employed at Harrah's?

Yes. From the day I started until the day he died.

He was a hard-driving person. People either loved Rome or they hated him.

Well, I didn't hate him. I would have to say that working for him was tough, but at least you knew where you stood with him and what was expected of you.

Was he very demanding?

Oh, yes. He didn't think so, but he was.

I think his main goal in life was to please Bill Harrah and make Bill Harrah a success.

Yes, I think so. And I think that's true of all the executives at Harrah's, particularly before us "outsiders" came along. [laughter] Bill commanded a great deal of respect.

You just used the term "outsider." Did you really feel that way?

No. Somehow or other we just fit right in, both Drews and myself. I think I can speak for George–we were both completely absorbed into the organization. Some things you couldn't understand, but you went ahead and did what you were supposed to do.

Was Bill Harrah concerned with making a profit in the food and bar department, or was he more concerned with the quality of the food and beverage and the quality of the service?

Well, he was in the business to make money, I don't doubt. But I think it was his contention that if you supplied the proper surroundings, like a clean place full of courteous employees offering a quality product, the volume would take care of itself. And we were very much aware of the customer. Very much aware.

You were over both clubs, the entire operation, but did you have a food and beverage manager at each location?

Oh, yes, each place. Nothing changed there; each place had a manager. The only change came when the managers were suddenly responsible to me.

The South Shore Room at Lake Tahoe must have been a tough place to operate when you had upwards of 1,000 customers in to see the show.

That operation was very well organized. We had two kitchens. One served half the room, the other served the other half. You could hear a pin drop in the kitchens. They were immaculate, and they offered very, very good food in my opinion.

Bill Harrah did not allow serving during the show. Once the curtain went up, that was it. The room had to be clear of employees, except for those in charge of a certain area. The tables had to be cleared as much as possible, but you didn't stay over during the show to clear a table.

Seating was at 6:00 or 6:30, and the show was at 8:00, so you had to have everybody seated, served, and the tables cleared in less than two hours. I didn't think much of it at the time, because we did it, but in retrospect you say, "How the hell did we do it? How did we feed that many people?"

Were you involved with the opening of the Summit restaurant at Harrah's Lake Tahoe?

Yes, I was involved with the entire operation–the planning as well as its operation. It was a very fine restaurant, but I don't know about now. It was a five-star restaurant, and I would have to be modest and say that it was *among* the top restaurants in the state of Nevada.

Everything from the table settings to the menu to the service, all were different from anything else in this area. For example, our service plate was hand carved out of wood from the Philippines. It was carved in the Philippines and shipped here. We had a combination of settings, whereas, for example, Harrah's Steak House in Reno is all silver service. When we were doing the Summit, some preferred silver service, but I felt that we were a part of the environment up there. The environment consisted of trees–the outdoors, wood; the indoors, silver. So we stuck with that combination, and we had a unique table setting. And our menu was particularly designed. Aside from steak, there was nothing that was very common. Everything was a little extraordinary–different types of preparation and presentation.

Did you specialize in lobster or seafood?

Well, lobster we considered a common dish. [laughter] We did clay pot cooking, but we finally had to abandon that because it became so popular that we couldn't maintain a time schedule.

Was the menu changed frequently?

Pretty frequently. I would say it was done frequently for all the work involved in presenting the menu. A great deal of attention was paid to the service and the atmosphere; and the view, of course, from the Summit, was fantastic and exciting.

Were your offices in Reno?

Yes, but I spent a lot of time at Tahoe, especially during the planning of the Summit restaurant . . . although we did a lot of that in Reno.

You said earlier that the Steak House was open when you came to work there, but you must have refined that area.

Yes, we did to an extent. It was a good operation when we got here, and it was very popular among the locals. We used to, of course, send the high rollers down there. We only had about seventy seats at the time, and it was a highly-sought-after dining area.

I have heard that Bill Harrah had a private dining area there.

Yes, he did. It was beautifully decorated, and he could enter it through the kitchen, so he didn't have to go through the Steak House to get to it. It could seat about ten at one table, and we'd hold it for Bill to the extent that if he came in and wanted it, he had it, regardless of who we had to throw out. [laughter] A lot of people ate in there: the high rollers ate in there; management ate in there. If we had a particularly long list of people wanting to eat, we would use the room. It wasn't one of those things that "This is mine, nobody can use it."

What, if any, personal relationship did you have with Mr. Harrah?

Well, we had a very informal relationship. His first chastisement was, "I want to tell you my name is Bill." [laughter] (I used to call him "Mr. Harrah." Where I came from, everybody was Mr.; even if you worked for your best friend, he was Mr.) We really had a cordial relationship, a very relaxed relationship. Most of the business he wanted to talk about was conducted through Rome or some subordinate, but every once in a while I would be called up to his office, and we would talk personally about business.

How many restaurants or eating facilities did Harrah's have when you were there?

We had eight just in Reno and the same in Tahoe.

Do you recall how many employees were working under you at that time?

Oh, fifteen hundred in Reno and about the same at Tahoe. I worked real long hours. I didn't have to, but I *felt* I had to. I had people ordering food and ordering liquor for me, but I still had to tell them what to do. I had people hiring for me, but I had to oversee that hiring. A twelve-hour day or a ten-hour day was almost like a vacation. However, I enjoyed it, I really did. Looking back on it, it was fun.

Were you employed there when Bill Harrah died?

Yes. It had been a pleasure working for him, and I sure hated to see him go.

What was the feeling at that time? Was it, "Gee, what are we going to do now?"

Yes, I think so. That was our first concern. Our next concern was that whoever bought this company or whoever took over would be quality people.

Did you have the feeling that it would have to be sold in order to continue to operate?

No. Actually, speaking for myself, I didn't know. I just assumed at some point it would be sold. I didn't think it would come as soon as it did, but business is business.

I wonder if anyone realized at that time what an integral part of the organization Bill Harrah was?

Oh, sure. Sure.

He did seem to let loose of the reins to a degree in the last few years of his life.

Not really. He may have in the eyes of some people, but he didn't. He was still on top of everything, in my opinion. You would almost catch yourself saying, "Now, would Bill like this?" We knew by pleasing Bill, we would be successful, whether it was individually or as a company. He was an amazing man.

When Harrah's sale to Holiday Inns was finalized February 28, 1980, were there any changes as far as you were concerned, either personally or in your department?

Yes. There was a reassessment of what was quality and what wasn't. That was unfavorable. A lot of us felt that the sale of the auto collection was a big mistake. That was Bill's pet, and he did a magnificent job with it.

So, what was commonplace before became "quality" with Holiday Inns?

Oh, yes. The food didn't have to be as good, or the service didn't have to be as good. We didn't have to have crystal in the showrooms. A lot of things were hard for us to take, and that didn't help the operation.

How long did you stay with Harrah's?

Until 1985–fourteen years.

Were you asked to resign by Holiday, or did you just feel the time was right to leave?

Well, it was time to leave. I was a Harrah's man. I mean, there's no question about that. I think they quietly resented that. Also, they had a rule that you retired at sixty-five, and I had stayed on beyond that age, primarily because of the Atlantic City opening. The man who was supposed to run the food and beverage department at Atlantic City didn't qualify for licensing in the state of New Jersey, so there was only one recourse–I went to Atlantic City and got in the middle of that mess. Somehow or other, we got out of it, and we had a pretty good opening. It had been open about a year when I retired.

It was an extreme pleasure knowing Mr. Harrah and a very fine experience to have worked for him. He was just a fantastic man, and there were a lot of good people there, good people to work with. Bob Ring was a fine man–hell of a sense of humor. Top management–Lloyd, Shep, Rome, Holmes, Mark Curtis–were all fine people and contributed a great deal to the success of the company.

12

JOHN GIANOTTI

J OHN GIANOTTI was born in Helper, Utah, on October 12, 1928, and moved to Scotia, California, at an early age. He attended the University of Nevada, graduating with a degree in education. While teaching high school in the 1950s, he would work as a dealer for Harrah's during summer breaks. He eventually joined Harrah's full-time staff and stayed with the company, rising to become vice-president for community affairs.

For this oral history, Mr. Gianotti was interviewed in a hotel room in Harrah's Tahoe Hotel at Stateline, Nevada. He was an eager participant and was excited about the project. His allegiance to Bill Harrah, even so many years after Harrah's death, was obvious.

The interview was conducted in July of 1997 and was completed in one session. In it Mr. Gianotti reminisced about his role in publicizing the Winter Olympics of 1960 that were held at Squaw Valley, about the times he spent on the road as the motel representative of Harrah's, and about his work in promoting hydroplane races, golf tournaments, and the movie, Forty Pounds of Trouble. *Mr. Gianotti also discussed in depth his experiences in the community affairs department of Harrah's. Many people have blamed Bill Harrah for the pollution of Lake Tahoe, but Gianotti gives the*

reader an uncommon interpretation of Mr. Harrah as a protector of the natural environment. Indeed, Gianotti credits Harrah to a degree with saving Lake Tahoe. He asserts that Bill Harrah was one of the forces behind the creation of the Tahoe Regional Planning Agency, the Douglas County Sewer Improvement District, and the Gaming Alliance.

JOHN GIANOTTI: I was born in Helper, Utah, on October 12, 1928. My father was a doctor there at the time. My mother was from Missouri. We later moved to a small community called Scotia in northern California, where Dad was the company doctor for the Pacific Lumber Company. I spent most of my early years there. I have a brother, Ernest Gianotti, who's an attorney in Kona, Hawaii, and a sister who lives in Berkeley.

I grew up basically in Scotia, and I graduated from Fortuna High School. After graduation, I went to Menlo Junior College for two years and then transferred to the University of Nevada. I was there for three years and got a Bachelor of Arts degree in education. Then I taught and coached at Fortuna for approximately seven years, and

during the summertime I would work in casinos. I started working for Harrah's at Lake Tahoe in the early fifties. My first job was a cashier; second job was dealing; and then I went into various departments.

DWAYNE KLING: Please tell us of your involvement in the 1960 Winter Olympics at Squaw Valley.

Well, those were interesting times. I worked for Harrah's for about six months at Squaw Valley, and I did the public relations and liaison between the Olympic committees and various V.I.P.'s and people who we wanted to entertain during the two weeks of the Olympics. We purchased $85,000 worth of tickets which were later distributed to our

John Gianotti (far left) with members of the Russian ski-jumping team at the 1960 Winter Olympics. *"I worked for Harrah's for about six months at Squaw Valley, and I did the public relations and liaison between the Olympic committees and various V.I.P.'s and people who we wanted to entertain during the two weeks of the Olympics."*

V.I.P.'s, our guests, or other people who might want to see the Olympics. We also had a residence for Mr. Harrah, who attended the Olympics quite regularly (he and his wife), and we had a hospitality house which we used to take care of our V.I.P.'s and other people whom we invited to the Olympics.

It was a dream assignment. Just being a part of Harrah's and the fact that they had enough confidence in me to give me that kind of an assignment in Squaw Valley as a representative of Harrah's–actually the chief representative for Harrah's–in promoting the Olympics in any way we could was a big thrill. We promoted it very well, but we did spend a lot of money. In fact, we were the third largest contributor to the Olympic program. Nevada built a visitor's center, and California built a visitor's center–they were the two largest contributors, but we were the third largest contributor of actual dollars. The reason we were the third largest was because of the $85,000 worth of tickets we bought. I remember going to San Francisco to pick up the tickets, and all I had was a briefcase to put the tickets in and a check to the committee for $85,000.

It was a wonderful time, and it was a very good promotion for Harrah's, as we did bring a number of people into Lake Tahoe. And since it was 1960, we were just beginning to make an impact in the gaming industry. That was a big program, and I think it helped to publicize Harrah's and Lake Tahoe and the nice things we have here. And it certainly gave us an image–that was part of Mr. Harrah's plan.

What did you do after the Olympics ended?

They elevated me to public relations, and I became the liaison between the community and the casino.

Did you work for Lee DeLauer then?

Yes. I don't know how it came about, but one Saturday night someone said, "Would you mind developing a motel program?" And that motel program basically was to deliver to the motels ashtrays and matches and certain gimmicks that they could use. [Each item was decorated with the Harrah's Club logo, the idea being to attract patrons to the club from among the motels' guests.]

Bill Harrah never believed in doing things that would obligate people. He wouldn't try to buy somebody or entice them to do things–it was done as a goodwill kind of thing, and everybody loved the ashtrays and things like that. It was a big expense for a lot of those motel owners. We also used to give them ice buckets and lots of matches. It was successful, so it was extended.

We started in the local area, and then I expanded it to the north shore. I had my own delivery truck, which was another nice thing. They asked me to pick out the truck that I wanted, and that was my little car. I could drive it, and I could take it home. I could do whatever I wanted with it, which I thought was pretty neat for someone just starting off in the business.

Then we expanded it down to Mammoth. We did all the motels down there, and I would go there maybe once a month. It was a goodwill turn on the part of Harrah's, and they got a lot of exposure out of it. People would pick up the ashtrays, pick up the matches, and take them home, and we were constantly getting calls from motels for more items. It was a nice program, and it tied in nicely with the bus programs. Lee DeLauer was really the champion of the bus programs.

Did you ever get into the motels in Sacramento or Stockton?

No. We never went down that far. We really stayed in the Tahoe basin except for Mammoth, and we did do some in Gardnerville.

So it was more for the people who were in the Tahoe area already?

Correct. The ashtrays were something they could take out and put in their house. They would steal the ashtray, and then they'd take it home and it would be sitting on a desk and someone would say, "Gee, where did you get the ashtray?"

"Well, it's Harrah's." And that, basically, was the program. It was a good program, well worth the money spent on it.

We were the liaison between the motels and the casino. When Harrah's hotel was built, we didn't want to be in competition with the motels, so we priced everything out of their reach, and they were very, very happy with that. We were really the first ones not to undercut the motels in any way. They could establish any price they wanted to, but it was always way under ours. That was directly from Bill. He was thinking ahead; he didn't want to affect the community, and people really appreciated that. The groundswell was really good over that.

Later, when you got into the public relations end of the business, were you involved in Harrah's golf tournaments?

Yes. I was the coordinator for the women's side. [laughter] The men had their own schedules for their golf, and because the women didn't play golf, we needed to entertain the women. So I was assigned to handle the women's side of the golf tournament, and I participated in every golf tournament. I planned things for the women, you know: a day here, a day there, a tour of Virginia City, maybe a day of golf somewhere else where the men weren't playing. Fashion shows . . . we always had fashion shows. Things like that were my responsibility.

But you still got a chance to play golf yourself?

I still played. Yes, I worked that in. I played probably every one of the golf tournaments. Alex Stewart was the kingpin, and the second kingpin, equally in charge, [laughter] was Bill's sidekick, Bob Ring. And then we also had a golf committee.

Another thing that I was on the committee for was the baseball celebrity promotion. For about four or five years, we invited, in the off-season, major league baseball players to the lake. We'd probably bring in sixty to seventy major league ballplayers. Many of them are in the Hall of Fame now—people like Brooks Robinson, people like that. We did that through a guy by the name of Norm Gerdeman. Norm worked in a clubhouse for one of the major league teams, and it was because of his suggestion that we started promoting the ballplayers. Then the public relations department picked it up, because we wanted to get some exposure through people such as that.

There were so many things you couldn't do in the gaming business. You couldn't advertise gambling, but you could advertise things that you did. So baseball was one of our major promotions, and we did it for about three or four years. One year, we brought in the three greatest living left-handed pitchers: Lefty Grove, Warren Spahn, and Carl Hubbell.

Another project I remember was when we made a movie here called *Forty Pounds of Trouble*. Tony Curtis, Suzanne Pleshette, Stubby Kaye, and Larry Storch were all in the movie. They filmed a good portion of it here, and then, of course, they had a simulated set in Hollywood, which I went down to see, where they had the casino, and they filmed a lot of it there. I was assigned to the movie company and spent about a month with them, making sure that they were well taken care of, making sure they were comfortably situated here at Lake Tahoe, and seeing that they had everything they needed.

Harrah's Club—the marquee and the facade of the building—was all seen in the movie. It was really a very good movie, and it's a fun movie, even today, to see. Once in awhile, it'll come on the late shows, and it's worth watching.

For something like that, did the company contact Harrah's, or did Harrah's search them out?

Mark Curtis was the father of that project. I remember going to preview it in Reno. We went down for the opening deal, and the fact that they hadn't given Bill Harrah any credits was the first thing he noticed. [laughter] And that changed real fast, because Bill had been very giving when they were here.

✧

Harrah's was very active in community affairs. It was one of the biggest things that we did. Shep was very involved, and I was too. My title was director of community affairs, and later I became vice-president of community affairs. The job basically was to act as a liaison between Harrah's and the community and to join a number of Chambers of Commerce and to attend meetings. Then we formed a group of local people who were interested in doing something to save Lake Tahoe and also to protect the gaming interests there. We knew that if we didn't develop some environmental concerns here at Lake Tahoe, one day there would be no casinos here. The environmental movement was so strong that they would somehow find a way to punish us and maybe take us out. I can't remember the name of the group, but we had people from Glenbrook and from the north shore. And we got together and we sat down and we discussed various things that we should be concerned with in development and so forth. We knew it was important that the state of Nevada be involved in this, because we were trying to preserve the natural beauty of Lake Tahoe. Bill Harrah was, in my mind, the first to really invoke any environmental concerns or look at any environmental concerns at Lake Tahoe.

He wanted to do something to protect this lake.

One of the things I thought was very, very paramount to Lake Tahoe was the formation of a committee, headed by Maurice Sheppard, that later became the Tahoe Regional Planning Agency. Our committee went to the governors of California and Nevada, and we met a number of times with Governor Laxalt and Governor Reagan. So from that little community committee that we had came the idea for the Tahoe Regional Planning Agency and the need for the federal government to come in and stop development of things that we felt were major concerns. There were other people involved, but we just jumped right in there. Bill Harrah wanted us to be in on that.

It was my job to go to those T.R.P.A. meetings, but Bill had the final say on all decisions. A bi-state compact was eventually agreed on, and after we had got the ratification from both states, the actual signing of the compact by governors Reagan and Laxalt was done on the *Thunderbird,* which was Bill Harrah's boat. We took Governor Reagan and Governor Laxalt out on the middle of the lake, and they signed the compact out there, right on the state line. I'm not quite sure who put that together, but it was probably Mark Curtis. Mark probably told us, "Do it out in the middle of the lake." It was something that people would remember, and Harrah's was always thinking about the promotional value of an event.

If there is one thing I would like Bill Harrah to be remembered for, it would be the things that he did environmentally for this area. Besides helping to get the T.R.P.A. started, another thing that he did was get rid of the septic tanks here at Lake Tahoe. There was lots of talking about it in the committees, and finally one day he said, "Look, we need a sewer plant." Well, it was through Bill Harrah and Maurice Sheppard that we got the other two casinos involved in building Douglas

County Sewer Improvement District Number One.

We got together with Harvey's and Brooks Park, who at that time had Caesar's Tahoe, and Oliver Kahle.[1] What we did was we proposed and built the Douglas County Sewer Improvement District Number One, and I served on the board for fifteen years. Maurice Sheppard was the first board member from Harrah's, and then when he went on to become president of Harrah's, they asked me to serve on that board. We basically built the sewer plant. We also maintained it for many years, and it's still operating and will probably operate forever. It did a whole lot to save this area, and it saved the casinos, because it got everybody off septic tanks on this end of the lake. Bill Harrah paid most of the fees. The fees are based on usage, and most of the usage was from Harrah's.

Another environmental thing is that if you look at Harrah's hotel, it's still in earthen tones. I attended many meetings about the design and the plans for this hotel, and Bill didn't want to interfere with the environment here. He wanted the hotel to appear to be like a clump of earth, and if you notice, it still has the earthen tones. The exteriors were done like rivulets of clay–that was his idea. And he did all the floors here like the four seasons.

Another thing: when Bill first moved across the street, all this area out here was a paved parking lot. But we owned a little piece in the back–maybe five or six acres–and so we wanted to do something with the five acres. I can remember sitting in a meeting with Bill Harrah, and I suggested that the one thing we could do for our public image to show the community that we were environmentalists was to develop it into a parking lot and leave a lot of trees on it. And if you look at it now, there's still trees there. We lost a lot of parking spaces, and most people would probably, at that time, have chopped every tree down. But Bill left a lot of them standing.

Bill Harrah knew that if he couldn't get people here, we had no business. So he was

constantly involved–and I was involved–with U.S. Highway 50 to make it a better thoroughfare: to get slow traffic lanes, to get places where drivers could put their chains on, to get signing. The first sign on Highway 50 coming out of Sacramento had not given the mileage to Lake Tahoe. I made it possible to get us the first sign that said Lake Tahoe–I worked through the highway commission in California–and it's still there. It says, "South Lake Tahoe" instead of just "Placerville."

I guess this is not going to go anywhere where I can get anybody into trouble anymore. [laughter] We forced Harvey's to build the underpass under Highway 50 that connects Harvey's and Harrah's. We developed the underpass connecting Harvey's and Harrah's because Bill knew that this road could not maintain the traffic that it had there. We were getting 10,000 cars a day, and it couldn't take that traffic. Still can't, but he said, "One of the major problems we have is people crossing the road. Well, what about an underpass? Get on it." So we got on it, and we flat forced Harvey's to do it. [laughter]

I went to the governor and said, "Look, we're trying to do something for traffic up there. We're trying to get people through there and cut down the pollution." So the governor went to Harvey's and suggested that they go along with the underpass. The sad part of the whole program was that we could never get anybody to do something between Caesar's and the Horizon.

Bill Harrah felt that we should be doing something to get people through the belt. We worked hard to get a bypass road; I worked on it for years. We had it designed and ready to roll, and I still think it was a big mistake by the environmentalists not to go along with the environmental road. You'd never have seen it. It would have been up against the mountains amongst the trees. It was a meandering, beautiful two-lane highway which would have gone all the way from the base of Echo summit to Spooner Summit. It would have taken care of those people who didn't want to stop. It could have given them a way to avoid the high impact areas. I think it was a big mistake, but the environmentalists got in it, and they killed us.

They thought you would have to cut down too many trees?

That, and that it would invite more people to come to Tahoe. They didn't think that it would really get the people in and out of here. How wonderful it would be now to be able to go out of this parking lot and get on a road and go all the way out of this basin without traffic problems. Car pollution was a big thing then, but you never could convince them that driving at forty five miles an hour is not the pollution problem. Driving at five miles an hour is what causes pollution.

One of my jobs was to create better highways. I would work very closely with the highway departments of both California and Nevada to upgrade the condition of the highways and to make them safer. Obviously, Bill knew that better roads meant business for him, and he was always very safety conscious. All of his cars and all the company cars were up to the highest standards of safety and pollution. He initiated turn-on lights, lights that automatically come on when you start your car. He felt it was safer to drive in the daytime with your lights on. When you went down the road, everybody knew you worked for Harrah's because your lights were on. We used to laugh at it because we kept thinking, "Well, gosh, we're the only ones that do it." But it was known that it would save lives. Of course, in the next year or two, every car made will have their lights come on when they are started.

Bill Harrah was also a big supporter of the Highway 50 Federation. I was the president for about three years. Highway 50 starts in San Francisco and goes all the way to Ocean City, Maryland. Highway 50 has some major things on it that people should see. (At one time, it was called the Lincoln Highway, but that was changed to U.S. Highway 50.)

♦

People don't realize how isolated Lake Tahoe was in the fifties and even into the sixties. Roads got snowed in, and you were really isolated. It was pretty unheard of for a community this small to undertake a major project like founding the Barton Memorial Hospital. We opened with a thirty-five bed facility that later expanded to eighty-five beds and a brand new hospital. There was no doubt in my mind that our charge at Harrah's was to support this community and do the things that were good for this community, and the hospital was one of them. There were fund raisers in the South Shore Room for the hospital and lots of other programs, such as fashion shows and luncheons. I can't recall all of them, but we were very involved in it.

Lee DeLauer was probably as responsible for the Barton Memorial Hospital as anybody. He was on the original committee. I did a few things for them, and I'm still one of the original donors, as are a number of people from Harrah's. We're on the original group that elects the people to the board, and the original committees helped raise $600,000 in this little community to get that hospital started. Bill had some payroll deductible programs to encourage his employees to be a part of the fund-raising, and we raised a lot of money through those programs.

We did a lot of things without direction; we simply saw a need for it and jumped on it. My job was to stay in contact with and listen to what the community was doing, and if I thought we should do something, I would just go do it. Bill liked that. He liked you to get out and be a part of this community, and you didn't have to go ask anybody. Whatever you did, you would write it in a daily report, and if he had an objection to it, then he would tell you; but he very seldom did. In all my years at Harrah's, I can't remember ever doing something that he didn't agree with. He didn't have to give us a lot of directions; we knew what he wanted. He was a firm believer in delegation of authority, and he would allow you to grab the ball and run with it. You just knew what to do, and if you didn't, you wouldn't be working there. [laughter]

Did you have much personal involvement with Bill Harrah?

Yes, I did, but probably no more or no less than anybody else. (I think of all the people that I've ever been around, Bob Martin, Holmes Hendricksen, Lloyd Dyer, and Mr. Sheppard spent more time with Bill than anyone.) I would go to Bill's office a lot during the legislative sessions. I was the liaison between the casino and the legislature, and I remember we were the first casino—and that was because of Mr. Sheppard—to go to Carson City and lobby for the casinos. Shep later helped form a casino group that was an association of people who were in the gaming business. Shep would represent all the casinos, but we were actually the only casino that went to the legislature on a daily basis to make sure that we were involved in what was happening and what they were doing. Sheppard was our first lobbyist, and then when Shep became president, I took his job, and I was there every day.

Every once in awhile, when we had a major involvement with the state in regards to casinos, we'd call the association (or in the early days, we had to do it individually because there was no association), and we'd say, "Look, we've got a little problem here. I think you should come down here and meet so we can decide where we ought to go with this." We would say, "Look, we'll be happy to help you; we'll provide the expertise and so forth and so on." So Bill was very conscious of what was going on in the state, and there was nobody else in the casino industry following that.

Later I formed a group, because I felt there was a need for the casinos to get more involved in political situations, not only at Lake Tahoe, but in Douglas County and in Washoe County. I would go to probably 90 percent of the commissioner's meetings, but there were no other casinos there. The only time the other casinos would come is when I'd say, "Look, they're going to throw a tax on us, and I think we better sit down and decide what we want to do. Here are the ramifications. If you just want to let it slip by, then that's OK, but I think we need to be there to let them know that we don't agree with this and we want to study it." We did a lot studies for them, and we had the expertise to do it. That was not an unusual thing.

Going back to what I was saying about forming a casino group, I explained to them that it's bigger than just one person: "Bill Harrah can't do it, and I can't do it. We need the strength of this group to be able to determine what our future is in regards to the Tahoe Regional Planning Agency." (I sat on the advisory commission to the Tahoe Regional Planning Agency for maybe a year or so.) Our group was called the Gaming Association. Now it's the Gaming Alliance. We would meet maybe once every three months. If something special came up, then we would call a meeting and discuss things. As I understand it, they now have a major player that they pay a big salary to, and the casinos and the community are involved. And it all started because of Bill Harrah.

There are probably some people that think, "Oh, Bill Harrah ruined the lake," because he built a casino here and brought all the people into the area, but you are saying that he helped to save the lake and save the environment.

He would never "go around" the environmental thing, but he wouldn't fall prey to it either. He said, "Look, we have to be somewhere in the middle. We get something, they get something. We have to be willing to make substantial changes in our philosophy to make sure that we're not offending anybody." That's why we always had somebody on all those boards and groups, so that we knew exactly what was going on, and we would help if we could. He was always there to help.

Bill Harrah said, "Let's maintain what we have, because we're going to be under close scrutiny from the whole world as to what we're doing to and for this lake." It was a tough job for our public relations department to maintain the images that we thought were important. People are still working to save Lake Tahoe.

Originally, this hotel–Harrah's Lake Tahoe Hotel–was to be thirty-five stories. Our plans went in for thirty-five stories, and we would have got permission, but we decided that it was too offensive, so we dropped down to eighteen stories. Years later, I wished we had thirty-five stories, because we could have filled them up.

Now the other thing that we did–and Bill and Maurice Sheppard were probably the innovators of this–was we got this area red-lined. At the time when there were concerns about the growth of casinos, we went to the county commissioners, we went to the organization we had formed, and we went to the legislature and said, "Look, we want to control gaming, just like everybody else." It would benefit us because we didn't want any more casinos, and it also kept the casinos in the core area, and there couldn't be any more casinos developed. So in effect, we red-lined this area and that red line is in the compact of the Tahoe Regional Planning Agency. And they followed suit on the north shore.

We decided to red-line this area before the Regional Agency was formed. We did that by county edict and then T.R.P.A. picked it up and put it into their plan. I'm sure that's the way it took place. But the red-lining came out of Harrah's. We said, "Look, we have to control gaming."

Bill was really instrumental in kicking off this rapid growth, but he saw that there were going to be some major concerns. And I think in a lot of respects, he hit them head on.

Knowing that, "Yes, we're going to start attracting more people, but we want to be a part of making it comfortable for those people to come and enjoy and yet not ruin the lake. Because if we ruin the lake and its environment, we don't have anything." The national cry would have been just horrendous. So the public relations department at Harrah's had to do a pretty good selling job.

Harrah's image is still great–they are so lucky now to have that Harrah image. You know that little statue, that little bust of Mr. Harrah that they have in the Harrah's Hotel lobby downstairs? They ought to make it about one hundred feet high.

John, what do you remember most about Bill Harrah, or how should he be remembered in the gaming industry?

I appreciate that question, because I think probably no one [else being interviewed for this project] will allude to what I think his major contribution was and what I'll remember him for: his environmental concern, his concern over what direction the lake was going in regards to its deterioration, his involvement with the number of people coming in, his concerns about how his facility would look, his concerns about the property itself, the saving of the trees around where he had to develop parking lots, and the growth of the Douglas County Sewer Improvement District, which basically came from him. What I would like him to be remembered for is his environmental stance and his involvement in the environment. To me, that's one of the greatest contributions he made here at Lake Tahoe. I think the environmental movement was really passed on by Mr. Harrah and developed out of a lot of the concerns he had, and if it hadn't of been for him and his support, I think we would have been twenty years behind times. Bill was really the impetus behind a lot of the environmental concerns.

The community was another concern of Bill's. He was involved with the hospital and other things, too, that were community oriented. He wanted to be a part of the community. He didn't want to take anything out of the community; he wanted to be a part of it and meet the needs of the community. He was very, very strong in that area.

Well, this is getting off the subject and going back in time, but earlier you mentioned Captain Whittell's [2] boat, the Thunderbird. *Could you elaborate on that?*

Well, Bill was always interested in what properties were available, and I would take Bill Harrah around to look at properties like the Steve Bourne property, because he was interested in purchasing something on the lake. The Whittell story is that George Whittell owned 145 acres that fronted on Lake Tahoe. There was a big old castle on the property, and that's where the *Thunderbird* was housed. The *Thunderbird* was a major boat

on Lake Tahoe. It was forty-five feet long, and it had two huge Allison engines in it. I remember going down there to see about insuring it, and we were going to see if it would start. The boat had been in dry dock for twenty years, hadn't even been run. They put diesel in those two big old Allison engines, got the batteries to turn it over, and it started right up just like it had been running yesterday. [laughter] Bill restored it to what it is today. It's still on the lake, but Harrah's sold it later. It's just a beautiful, old, old boat.

Another thing we did that got a lot of national publicity for Harrah's was the hydroplane races. I was assigned to the hydroplane crew, and we'd travel to the Gold Cup races in Idaho, Seattle, and Detroit, and that got a lot of national publicity. Mr. Harrah's boat was called the *Tahoe Miss.* For years, Bill put on a major event here at Lake Tahoe which drew lots of people and got a lot of national and international coverage for Lake Tahoe.

Bill Harrah at the wheel of the *Tahoe Miss.*

Bill liked speed.

He always did. He liked his cars to be fast. [laughter] From Reno to Lake Tahoe, we never wanted any stop lights, nor did we want any speed limits. Bill didn't want *any* speed limits. He thought that was the one last freedom that we had in Nevada–no speed limits. We tried very hard–and that was one of my jobs as lobbyist–to not have a speed limit, and we did very well until they decided that we had a fuel shortage.

The federal government decided they were going to cut off all Nevada's funds if we didn't follow the federal speed limit. We knew of some ways to make them go *jump*, but we decided that the money to the state was more important, so the speed limit was imposed.

Do you recall why Bill got out of hydroplane racing?

Well, I think it was too costly. The motors were very expensive. They would blow up a motor, and it was sixty, seventy thousand dollars. And to do the traveling and all the things that needed to be done, I think it got to the point where he would rather put his money into his antique cars. He'd really served his purpose. He was like the Michael Jordan of hydroplane racing. The National Basketball Association would not be what it is if it wasn't for Michael Jordan, and hydroplane racing would not have been what it is today without Bill Harrah. He brought it to prominence.

Was the Villa Harrah part of the sale when Harrah's was sold to the Holiday?

No, Chase International, my company, just sold that property. It was located in the Skyline area of Lake Tahoe. It was a beautiful place, a wonderful place to entertain. He had hotel facilities for cooking and things like that. There were management meetings there, and it could seat 120 people.

The Middle Fork Lodge in Idaho will certainly verify Bill Harrah's personality in regards to environmental things. He would even have the garbage flown out of there. He would fly it back to Reno or Boise. They never disturbed anything on the site itself. They brought everything in by plane. They recreated that whole area back to its original look, and they never put anything into the river. He wanted that area to be environmentally sound.

That was a wonderful place to go, and everybody would rave about it when they went there–it was so natural, but it was very convenient. The hot springs were maintained, and it was really special. It was unbelievable how well he did that without taking anything out of the environment.

As a public relations person, did you bring customers up there?

Yes, we brought V.I.P.'s up there, and we brought political figures. Some people went there just for rest and relaxation. Some went there to hunt and fish. Probably two of the best fishing holes on the entire Salmon River were at Middle Fork. The Salmon River was within walking distance, and there was no motorized equipment except what was needed to come from the airport. He had three vintage cars that he would use to go pick the people up at the airport. He maintained the airport, and people would come in from the Forest Service, and they couldn't believe how well maintained it was, and how there was nothing damaged. It was just like it was one hundred years ago. There was a little bit of history up there. But that was his character and his thought process.

Did he use the lodge a lot as an individual?

Yes. I think his heart was in Idaho. He loved Idaho and the old property line, and he loved Sun Valley and, of course, he loved Stanley, Idaho.

He loved to fish. He'd go fishing every year with Bob Cole, who was a fishing guide. Later he hired Bob Cole to run the fishing operation and the hunting operation at the Middle Fork Lodge. Bob was very close to Bill Harrah.

Bill Harrah liked to look at new opportunities, and one opportunity that I was assigned to help him with was in Australia. I went to Australia four times for Harrah's to search out opportunities before they ever had any gaming. I spent 130 days in Australia, and I hired a consulting company to keep us up-to-date on what was going on. I went around to all of the major areas first and looked at the opportunities for gaming.

We were first interested in Melbourne. Once, a guy in Melbourne wanted us to look at his property over there, and it was in the spring, and I had plans to go to the Canadian Rockies and helicopter ski. I was just getting ready to go when I got a call from Sheppard, and he said, "We need you to go to Australia. Can you go?"

And I says, "Yes."

Instead of canceling the skiing trip, I gave it to Jimmy Palmer.[3] I said, "Here, you take it and use it. I won't be going." So that was the start of that. I just went over by the seat of my pants and met with this guy and then decided what we ought to be doing to find out whether we should be there or not. We were very close at that time to making a decision. It was just before Bill died, and when he died, that was the end of it.

Bill knew the need for going someplace else, but he didn't want to go to New Jersey because he thought that he would be tainted because of the mafia image. He was timid about going to Las Vegas, too. He didn't want to be around anything that might tarnish his image. In his own mind, he felt that that was not the place to be.

He was also going to build Harrah's Auto World on I-80 West. That was the next big thing. I remember the thing that astounded me was that he was looking at buying the *Spruce Goose*[4] and putting it in the lobby. It was astounding that the man could think that way. I thought, "Gee, have a nice lobby with some flowers in it," but he was going to buy the *Spruce Goose*! He wanted something spectacular. It's incredible, the way he thought sometimes. He was a real visionary; he was way ahead of people. And probably the biggest vision he had was when he came to Tahoe.

Bill Harrah died on June 30, 1978, and less than two years later, Holiday Inns took over the Harrah's Club operation. Was your job affected in any way, or were you personally affected in any way when Bill Harrah died or when the company was sold?

In the beginning, I could see the end for me was near. They had removed most all of the jobs that other people had. I think I was maybe one of the last ones to leave, next to Holmes Hendricksen, who stayed forever. I was with them for two years when they did away with my job, which they really didn't do away with, but that was the reason they gave for terminating me, which was fine.

I was vice-president of community affairs at that time, and they said they were no longer going to have that. But basically, they just did it in a different way. I could see some problems with my staying with Holiday Inns, because they had a whole new mode of operation, and I would have had to change my ways considerably. At that time, things were changing in the gaming industry anyway, and I said, "Thank you very much; you get on with what you have to do." I don't think their plan of operation was like what were we used to (service-oriented things and the like), and I'm sure many people have told you that.

So you retired about two years after the sale?

Yes. I left, and there were good feelings on both sides.

Did you work in the casino business after that?

Not at all. I did open up a couple of fitness centers. I always wanted to be in the fitness business. I was the president of a corporation called ProFitness in San Diego for about eight years. I now assist in the operation of a real estate company called Chase International, so I do a little bit of real estate. But I'm basically retired.

Notes

1. Oliver Kahle owned Oliver's Club.
2. Captain George Whittell was a large land owner in the Lake Tahoe area. Whittell High School is named after him.
3. Jimmy Palmer: a longtime gaming employee, he was employed as a pit supervisor at Harrah's in the fifties and sixties.
4. The *Spruce Goose* was the largest wooden airplane ever to fly. Built by Howard Hughes during World War II, it is now on display as a museum exhibit in Long Beach, California.

13

SCHERRY HARRAH

S CHERRY HARRAH, who was married to William F. Harrah for almost twenty years, was born "in the hills of Tennessee" in 1926. She married for the first time when she was fifteen years old. Later she moved to Toledo, Ohio, and won a beauty contest that resulted in her going to New York City and working for the John Robert Powers modeling agency. Eventually she left New York for Hollywood, California, to work for the Earl Carroll Vanities show. A short, unsatisfying movie career influenced her decision to answer an ad for "young beautiful girls" to work for Harolds Club in Reno, Nevada. Arriving in Reno, she began working as a twenty-one dealer.

Scherry Harrah was an enthusiastic participant in this oral history project. The interview was conducted in March of 1997 at her son's house on Del Monte Lane in Reno, and it was completed in one day. Mrs. Harrah was very gracious and showed the interviewer many photographs of her life with Bill Harrah. In her interview Mrs. Harrah reveals why she left Harolds Club to go to work for Harrah's and how she was introduced to Bill Harrah in 1947. Less than a year later they were married. She describes how their sometimes stormy marriage led to a divorce, reconciliation, re-marriage a short time later, and a final divorce after eighteen years of marriage.

Mrs. Harrah reminisces about the Horseless Carriage Club and the authentic costumes that she loved to put on for the many functions and treks that the club sponsored. Also remembered are the early days of Harrah's expansion at Lake Tahoe and her participation in the design and decoration of the Harrah's Lake Tahoe Hotel.

SCHERRY HARRAH: I was born in the hills of Tennessee on a twenty-acre ranch in 1926. The only way you could get to town was by horse and buggy or a boat. My father was a riverboat captain on the Tennessee River. When he died in 1928 we moved closer to town, to another place down by the Tennessee River.

I had four half-brothers and one sister, and they were all older than me–by the time I was born, my brothers had children that I played with. At the age of twelve my mother allowed me to move to Alcoa, Tennessee, to live with an aunt. I lived there until I became a teenage bride. I was married in January and turned sixteen in May.

When I got married, we lived with his parents until he got drafted into the army in 1941. After he was in the service, I lived with his sister in Toledo, Ohio, until she decided to move back to Alcoa. I wanted a particular job at the Unicast Corporation in Toledo, so I stayed there when his sister went back to Tennessee. You had to be eighteen to work there, and since I didn't have a birth certificate, I had one made so I could get the job.

DWAYNE KLING: What was your maiden name?

I hate to tell you this. [laughter] My father liked the midwife, and he gave me one of her names. He named me Mayme Kandis Lucille Teague.

What was your first husband's name?

Elmo Fagg. He was in show business, and he also worked in a warehouse for a grocery store. He was really a good entertainer. After he went to the service, he still had his trio. He would sing every Sunday morning in churches. When he came back from the service in 1945, I had grown up a little, and I didn't care to be married anymore.

While living in Toledo, I had won a beauty photo contest, and first prize was a job with the John Robert Powers modeling agency, one of the top agencies in New York City. I didn't like the job or New York City. For someone my age, being alone in New York was like an ant looking up at an elephant. It was overpowering. I was also a hostess at Longchamp's for a while, and then I decided I just didn't like New York, so I thought, well . . . the old saying is, "go west young man, go west," and I thought it should work for a girl, too. So I went to Hollywood.

In Hollywood, I met a photographer, and he told me that Earl Carroll was casting for "The Earl Carroll Vanities" to go on the road as a road show.

I said, "Gee, I can't dance or anything."

He said, "You don't have to. They'll teach you." So I went over and auditioned. They chose twenty-one girls out of three hundred to go on this road trip, and I was one of the twenty-one. After the road show we came back to Hollywood, and I went back to the same photographer, and he said, "Why don't you go see the King brothers?"

I said, "OK." So I met the King brothers, who were movie producers, and they were just super nice to me. They treated me like a little sister. I worked for them, but I also worked for different studios as an extra.

How many movies did you appear in?

I'm not sure how many. I worked just as an extra for the King brothers and for Columbia studios. One movie I was in was a musical called "That's My Gal," but so help me, I've forgotten who made it. [laughter]

One of the King brothers wanted me to go to acting school and to make a star out of me. One morning I went to his office, and he was sitting there laughing, and I asked him what was so funny. He said, "Well, there's an employment office up the street here. They are looking for pretty girls to go to Reno, Nevada, to be twenty-one dealers."

So I said, "Where is it?" and he told me.

The next day I went in and said to him, "Guess what? You were telling me about the place up the street, hiring people to go to Reno." [laughter] I said, "I'm leaving."

He said, "You got to be out of your mind."

I said, "Maybe I am, but I'm going to Reno."

That was 1946, and it was Harolds Club that had the office there in the Hollywood area. They were looking for beautiful girls.

Did you ever have any regrets that you didn't go on to become a movie star?

Oh, no. I didn't like the movie business that much. I just didn't like it.

After you were hired by Harolds Club in Hollywood, how did you get to Reno?

They actually paid your way here, and if you didn't like it they would pay your way back. I was here about two weeks before finally Mr. Smith said, "Are you going to go to work or not go to work?"

I said, "I guess I will."

I had never been around gaming, and I thought maybe I'd have to have a room upstairs to get a job downstairs. I wanted to make sure that I didn't have to do anything like that. [laughter] Then I went to dealing classes for three weeks, and I learned how to deal twenty-one, craps, and roulette.

When I came to Reno, Jessie Beck[1] met me at the bus station. She had a reservation for me at the El Cortez, so she went in, and she was gone a long time. When she came back out she said, "I don't know what happened. I had a reservation for you, but they say that they don't have a room."

Since I had been line captain and dance instructor for twenty-one girls on the Earl Carroll show, I said, "You wait here just a minute." So I went in, and I told that desk clerk, "This nice lady sitting out here in the car had reservations for me." I said, "Now I want you to find a room." And I went back out.

Jessie always wondered how I got the room when she couldn't.

I stayed there until I got an apartment. Then when the Mapes Hotel opened, I went there and asked them how much it would cost me to live there, and believe it or not, it was only twenty-four dollars a week. So naturally, I moved right in.

How long did you stay at Harolds Club?

Well, I went there in January 1946, and I went to Harrah's Club the last of 1947, so I stayed there almost two years.

Did you meet Bill Harrah while you were working at Harolds Club?

No. He had seen me going across the alley when I was going back and forth to have lunch, but I had never met him. When I started working for him, I think it was Warren Nelson that said Bill wanted me to meet him at the Wine House. I said, "OK." So I went over to the Wine House, and he was there. We were the only ones in the place.

He said, "What would you like to drink?"

I said, "Oh, I don't care. Whatever you're drinking." So he ordered a gin martini. [laughter] I didn't drink, so you can imagine what a gin martini did to me. [laughter] I tried to sip it a little bit, but there was no way I could drink it.

Finally Bill said, "Would you like something else to drink?"

I said, "Yes, a rum and coke."

Later he wanted to go out to the Deerhead Lodge on South Virginia, and about the time we got there, his girlfriend came screaming up in a taxi cab. [laughter] She caused quite a scene. He had been living with this lady for three years, but after that, he told me that she would be gone in three days. Sure enough, three days later she was gone, and then I was with him. But I couldn't go out with him all night and then work all day. The club thought it was time for me to do one or the other, [laughter] so I quit work, and we were married in 1948. We were married a little less than a year after we met.

Why had you left Harolds Club to go to Harrah's?

Well, it was the only place that had carpet on the floor, and it looked nice there. It looked cleaner and nice. The pay was about the same in all the places in those days. Everyone was paid from about eleven to thirteen dollars a shift.

Doesn't seem like much, does it?

Well, in those days we also made a lot of tips. We kept our own tips, and I would make anywhere from fifty to a hundred dollars a day in tips.

When you married Bill Harrah, was he drinking heavily?

When I met him he was an alcoholic–there was no two ways about it. It took me about three years to get him off liquor. We had squabbles about it all the time, and finally I told him, "You just have to quit. Your business is going broke," and I told him quite a few other things too . . . .

So he said, "Well, what do you want me to do?"

I said, "I want you to sober up, quit drinking, and go to work like other people do. Go to work nine to five and come home to dinner."

Well, he called his doctor, Vernon Cantlon, the next day, and he said, "I'm losing my business, I'm losing my wife, and I have to quit drinking."

The doctor said, "Well, you'll have to do what I ask you to do."

He said, "Why in the hell do you think I'm calling you?"

So, anyway, he went in a hospital for a week, and when he came out he was really not drinking anymore; and to my amazement, he moved to the Mapes Hotel. So I moved to the Mapes Hotel too.

A few days later he said, "I want to wipe my slate clean and start over again."

I said, "OK, what do you want to do?"

He said, "Well, let's get divorced, and then we'll get married again."

So, I said, "OK." I got an attorney and a witness and went out and got the divorce and went back home to the Mapes. After about a year-and-a-half we got married again, but we were never apart during the time we weren't married. We were always together during that time.

Did he ever start drinking again?

Nineteen sixty-nine he tried. When he quit he said, "Now, I might drink sometime in the future. If I can't handle it, I'll quit." So he had a few drinks after 1969, and he decided that he could handle it. So then he would have a couple of drinks at the dinner table and maybe a couple of glasses of wine, but that was it.

Do you remember Virgil Smith?

Well, yes. But his time with Virgil was before me. Bill never had what you might call close, close friends. He had acquaintances in the club, and Bob Ring of course was a friend, but he didn't have *close* friends. His friend was always the girl that he was with at the time. And he seldom talked. If he was at the bar and he wanted a drink, he would just motion.

He never smiled when he talked. It took me two years to get him to smile. He said that if he smiled at the camera, people would think that he was phony. So I said, "Well, would you rather be phony for about half a second or look like an old grouch the rest of your life?" So I got him to smile and got him to start talking.

Even when he was drinking he didn't smile?

No. Sober or drinking, he didn't smile.

Do you think Bob Ring was his best friend when you were first married?

I would say so. Bob Ring was seeing a lot of him at the club, and we had dinner at his home several times. Bob was very dear to him. Bob Ring and Bill Harrah came up from Venice together, and they worked together for many years . . . until Bill passed away.

Soon after your second marriage to Bill Harrah, he purchased the club at Lake Tahoe and began operating there in 1955. Tell us how it got started.

Well, what happened is that he bought the Pony Express Museum in Arcadia, California, in 1955 from Parker Lyon. He left me there to supervise the packing of the museum while he came to Reno and bought the place at the lake. The club was located in a Quonset hut at the state line, and he built around the Quonset hut and then tore the Quonset hut down. If it hadn't have been for Eddie Questa, the president of the First National Bank of Nevada, loaning him money, and Mrs. Vogel loaning him money, I don't think there would have been any lake club.

Who was Mrs. Vogel?

She was the mother of two of his best friends from Hollywood. One of the sons was named Fred Vogel. He came up to Lake Tahoe to operate the sports book.

So you were in Arcadia supervising the packing of the Pony Express Museum, and when you got back to Reno you found out that he had bought the Tahoe Club?

Yes. [laughter]

That must have been a little shock to you.

Oh, not really. Nothing Bill did surprised me, but he was the only one that believed that it would work, because at that time there were no hotels at the lake, and Harvey's was just sort of a hamburger place with almost no gaming at that time.

But Bill never closed in wintertime. He was the first person at Tahoe, either north shore or south shore, to remain open all year.

Yes. He started bringing up buses from Sacramento and other cities in California because he thought that the older people wouldn't want to drive in the ice and the snow. He made a package deal with Greyhound, and they would come up for a few hours and go back the same day or the same night. The club would have failed without the bus program.

There's an old saying, "Behind every great man there stands a woman." Tell us about your role in the early days of Harrah's.

My gambling knowledge came from a friend of mine named Dick Caskey. From him I found out all there was to know about cards and dice. In other words, I would know it if you were doing something wrong on the table. I could catch it. I also had an assistant, Mrs. Adeline Murphy. She would be at one place for breakfast, another place at lunch, and someplace else for dinner. She knew everything that was going on in town.

A lot of times people would call me when something wasn't right at the club. The first time I mentioned something to Bill, we had quite an argument. So I told him, "I'm never going to quarrel over this with you again. If I think you should check something, I'll put a note on your desk. If you want to check it, do it. If you don't, don't do it." And we never had a quarrel afterwards. I still kept leaving the notes even after the divorce in 1969.

We had a party when the hotel opened down here, and a reporter heard Mead

Dixon, Bill's attorney, say, "He doesn't know what's going on anymore."

The reporter said to me, "Do you want me to do anything about that statement?"

I said, "No, it's true. He doesn't have anyone telling him anything anymore."

In late 1948 the *Saturday Evening Post* did a story on the club, and in one of the pictures I was dealing, and it showed paper, trash, and cigarette packages all over the floor. It was really messy, and Bill just couldn't believe it. So I told him, "Why don't you clean this place up and keep it clean?" And he sure did! [laughter] But he hadn't noticed it until then.

When he quit drinking, Bill would look at things and say, "Look at this! Why couldn't I see that before?"

I'd say, "Because you were at the bar drinking and not looking for it."

♦

The Horseless Carriage Club was a club consisting of people who collected antique cars and would dress in authentic period costumes when they were driving or riding in their cars or when they were together. We joined when Bill bought his first antique car, a 1907 Maxwell, in 1948. (We bought it in 1947 but it wasn't ready until 1948.) Actually, he *thought* it was a 1907, but when we were in Los Angeles a nice gentleman by the name of Bud Catlett, who was a policeman in Sacramento, came up and very nicely told him, "Mr. Harrah, that's not a 1907; it's a 1911." And I think that's the last mistake Bill ever made about cars.

Some of the trips or tours that the Horseless Carriage group would take would last three to five days, and I guess I had the most extensive wardrobe in the world. In the daytime I would wear daytime costumes, and at night I would change. I loved to wear the period costumes.

The costumes and the wardrobe that you wore, were they actually the original old costumes or ones that had been patterned after the originals?

No, no. They were authentic. Authentic costumes.

And everybody in the Horseless Carriage Club wore them?

Well, if they could find them, they wore them, or they had them made. My first one was made because I didn't know where to get them.

You said those Horseless Carriage Club trips lasted four or five days. Did the people actually drive the old antique cars?

Scherry Harrah in an authentic period costume she wore at Horseless Carriage functions. *"Some of the trips or tours that the Horseless Carriage group would take would last three to five days, and I guess I had the most extensive wardrobe in the world."*

Oh yes. They drove their cars.

Did they ever make it up the hill from Reno to Tahoe?

Oh, sure. [laughter] No problem.

[It was thought that] he had 1,600 cars in the museum when he died, but I don't know what happened . . . after he died there turned out to be only 1,400. They had sort of disappeared.

Do you know how many there are now in the collection downtown?

Well, if they keep going like they're going, there won't be *any* left. The way they're running it, there's no way they can make it. They have too many chiefs and no Indians. The only thing that's keeping them afloat is the fact they keep selling off the cars, asking for donations, and selling certificates to the cars. Pioneer [Citizens] Bank has six certificates, and there's no way they can pay them back. Also, my son John gave them a million and a half dollars. There's no way they can pay him back either, but he's got a certificate for a Rolls-Royce.

Bill also owned an unlimited racing hydroplane, the *Tahoe Miss*. He drove it a lot, but he didn't drive it in races. We had different race drivers; Mira Slovak was the best. He was a commercial pilot for Continental Airlines. They finally told him that he had to stop driving hydroplanes, so he did, but he was our best driver. And the club finally told Bill that hydroplanes were a rich man's hobby, so he just finally got out.

I really wanted to drive a hydroplane, and one time Bernie Little, who owned *Miss Budweiser*, took me out for a ride. Those pylons came up so fast . . . that was the end of my asking to drive one. [laughter] Bill never heard "I want to drive" again.

Would you touch briefly on the expansion at Lake Tahoe?

Well, the place at the lake was supposed to cost three million, and it cost over five million. That was just the showroom. Bill had to keep going back to Eddie Questa for another fifty thousand and another fifty thousand until he got up to five million.

When we had the reception, Eddie Questa was standing right next to me, and everyone that came through the line was laughing at him. It really bothered Bill quite a bit.

They were laughing at him because he kept lending the money?

Yes. So when we got inside, Eddie was sitting across from us, and he told Bill, "If this thing doesn't go, I'm going wherever you go, wherever that is."

But if it hadn't been for people like Eddie Questa, the place would not be there. And everybody was paid back right on time. The payment for the place at Lake Tahoe was fifty thousand dollars a month. The bank wrote me a letter one time thanking me for the payments being on time. They wouldn't let him buy it unless my name was on the loan.

How big a part did entertainment—the dinner shows and the cocktail shows at Lake Tahoe and in Reno—play in the success of Harrah's Club?

They played a big part. Reno was more or less built on the dinner show, and so was Lake Tahoe. People would come to them all the time. But we didn't keep them over ten days or two weeks, because you needed new shows to get new business. Now they are trying to make it with buses and no big entertainment, and they keep those naked shows on too long. People are not going to take the time to see those shows, and they know that even if there was a good show, they'd have to eat someplace else, then buy a ticket and stand in line with a hundred other people. People are just not willing to do it, and most of the locals don't go anymore. I don't go anymore.

I wrote a letter recently to the local paper concerning this. If they don't get back to good entertainment, Reno's business is just going to keep going down.

So what you are saying is entertainment played a part in the success of Harrah's Club?

It was *the* part—the entertainers and the dinner shows. It was an added inducement for people to come from California, the northwest, and it was a place where the locals could go.

After the dinner show people would go gambling. The dinner shows would start at eight o'clock, and around 9:30 Bill wanted them out of the show so they could gamble. But the way it is now . . . several months ago Hilton mentioned that they had dinner shows, and I had guests here, so we went down to see the dinner show. Even though I didn't like it— it was the imitations of Sammy Davis and other stars—we went in, and they wanted you to be in at 6:00 or 6:30. So we went in at 6:00 or 6:30, and the show didn't start until 9:00. [laughter] So once you get out, you're not going to gamble.

Did you and Mr. Harrah go to every show?

Yes. When we were here we went to the shows. I told Bill Cosby, "I've seen your show of Fat Albert so many times I could do it."

We had a guesthouse called Villa Harrah that was located at Lake Tahoe in Skyland, and we frequently had the entertainers there for cocktails and dinner. I designed the plans for the Villa so a hundred people could be upstairs for cocktails and go downstairs for a sit-down dinner.

The house was that big?

Fifteen thousand square feet. It was real nice. The cook we had at the time said she could cook for fifty people, but above that she couldn't handle it. So for big dinner parties we would have the food prepared at the club, then bring it out to the Villa and send it downstairs on dumbwaiters, and it would be served just as if it came right out of the kitchen.

Did every entertainer that appeared at Harrah's come to the Villa Harrah for dinner?

Oh, sure, at least once during their engagement.

How many houses did you have in Reno for the entertainers?

The Interlachen was the only house that we had here in Reno, but we had two penthouses at the Arlington Towers.

Where did you host the entertainers in Reno? Where did you take them?

Either to the club or to our house on Del Monte Lane. My son John lives there now. He owns about 170 acres on and around Del Monte Lane. He owns the house where I live now. I used to live on Windy Hill, but I sold it. John has five houses down here, so there's no sense in my buying a house. [laughter]

Does your son Tony live in this area also?

Yes, he lives on Thomas Creek, a short distance from us. Tony's wife is into jumping horses, and John now is into the cutting horses. They're both involved with horses, and they plan to have shows there. They have built large barns and an arena for horse shows.

How old are your sons?

John is thirty-two this year, and Tony is thirty.

Was John Harrah named after Bill's father, John?

Yes, and Tony was named after Tony Hulman from Indianapolis. Mr. Hulman was

Sammy Davis Jr. holds John Harrah while Scherry Harrah looks on. *"Sammy was definitely a favorite. Sammy just loved everybody. And he was just like he was, not phony at all."*

such a nice man that Bill wanted to name our youngest son Tony after him. He was the owner and director of the Indianapolis Speedway for many years.

Did you ever go to any of the races at Indianapolis?

Practically every year. I liked it until I saw one of the drivers, a rookie, cause an accident, and a pro driver crashed in front of the stands and in front of the pit crew and burned to death right in front of us.

Who were some of your favorite entertainers?

Practically all of them. I guess Sonny and Cher were about the worst we ever had. They were not good houseguests. Sonny and Cher played Harrah's only once. They had a four-

letter word mouth, and they were not nice to the people who waited on them.

Practically all the rest of them, Belafonte, Bill Cosby, Sammy Davis, Jim Nabors, they were all really nice. Kay Starr, Patti Page, Carol Burnett, Lawrence Welk, Wayne Newton—I could go on and on. They were almost friends you might say. Sammy Davis especially. Bill was very friendly of course with Cosby, but Sammy was definitely a favorite. Sammy just loved everybody. [laughter] And he was just like he was, not phony at all. One time I went down to the dressing room—and they called white people honkies at that time—and I said, "Say, Sammy, there's sure a lot of honkies up there watching you tonight." Something like that would crack him up. It's like he didn't know that I knew that they called them honkies. [laughter]

Sammy Davis was such an outgoing person, and Bill Harrah was just the opposite.

Yes. But Bill liked him. They talked a lot. And Jim Nabors. And Cosby too. As a matter of fact, Cosby liked him so well that he named one of his daughters Harrah . . . one of her second names is Harrah.

The state of Idaho seems to have been very popular with you and Bill. Where did you spend most of your time?

We stayed in Stanley, which was the only place that we had at that time, and it was a remodeled log cabin. It was right in town, and Bill owned half of the town.

How big is Stanley?

It's small. I don't know what the population would be right now. But there was a grocery store there, and it had a garage, a motel, and a restaurant–everything that you could want. Bill also had a lodge on the middle fork of the Salmon River called the Middle Fork Lodge. We bought it and re-modeled it as a place where executives and entertainers could go to unwind. When we bought it, there were two houses. One was called the River House. Bill thought we should tear it down. I said, "Oh, no." I had the builders put a foundation under it and fix it up. Later, Bill had them build two other large buildings with five bedrooms and five baths in each house, so it's pretty big.

It's kind of just out in the middle of nowhere, and if you wanted to ride horseback it would take three days to get there. Another way would be to fly way up above there and raft down the river. The other way is to take a small plane from Boise–it's thirty minutes by small plane from Boise to the lodge.

We used to fly in to Boise and then take the Twin Otter from Boise to the Middle Fork. The Twin Otter was a really neat plane. It had huge wings, and it was sort of a bush-pilot

plane in a way. It'd stall and more or less come down like a helicopter, or it could just turn like a bird. You really felt safe in it, and you could land in a small area.

Did the Otter stay at the Boise airport most of the time?

No, it stayed mostly at Middle Fork.

Did you have pilots on call or on standby all the time?

We had four pilots on standby. We might use them every day, and then they might not work again for several days.

You mentioned earlier that you would go to Europe a lot. Did you use your planes to fly there?

No, we flew commercially.

It's been said that Bill Harrah's greatest love was his automobile collection.

It was [a great love], but his greatest love was the boys. He loved those boys like crazy. You can't believe it. When we were divorced, he said, "Well, when can I see the boys?"

I said, "Three hundred and sixty-five days a year, every day, four o'clock in the morning if you want to."

Sometimes he would call and say, "Could I take the boys away for a week or so?"

I'd say, "Two weeks if you want to."

After we were divorced we were exactly the same as we were when we were married, except we just lived in different places. He came for Christmas and all the holidays and birthdays and Thanksgiving. Sometimes he'd just call to say he was coming over. I never knew if he was going to be there ten minutes or two hours, but it didn't make any difference. It made it so nice for the children. They loved it.

His automobile collection started in 1948. Did he go look at all these cars himself, or did he have certain people who acted as buyers?

He had a couple of buyers to start with, and he had some buyers that went around looking for cars all the time. Also, they have a lot of antique shows, and we went to lots of those. There was one car meet in particular when the guy wouldn't sell him the car he wanted, so he bought the whole collection.

The 1907 Thomas Flyer that won the race around the world we bought from a man in Long Beach, but we weren't sure it was the actual car. A man named Mr. Schuster was the mechanic and driver on the race around the world, and Bill wanted to get Mr. Schuster to come out here and say that the car was the authentic car. Well, Mr. Schuster said that he's not spending that man's money to come out here to tell him that's not the right car. But Bill finally said to him, "If you come out here and get under the car, and if you can recognize the repairs, then will you authenticate the car?" So, Mr. Schuster came out here, and he got under the car and sure enough, it was the right car. And for three days he was in that car, out of the car, under the car, all day long, from the time they opened until the time they closed. It's still in town here at the automobile museum.

You were married to Mr. Harrah when he purchased the Golden Hotel and re-furnished it and re-decorated it. Did you play an active role in the planning and designing of the Golden Hotel?

No, not there, but I was involved with the hotel at Lake Tahoe. I designed the floor plans for that. Then after I designed the floor plan, Henry Conversano took over and did everything else.

What started it all was . . . when we traveled so much, Bill said, "If I ever build a hotel, every room is going to have two bathrooms," because I stayed in the bathroom so long. So when he decided to build the hotel

at Tahoe, he says, "OK, two bathrooms. You figure it out." Oh, my god! It took me forever to get two bathrooms into one room.

And I told him, "I think you need a service center on each floor."

He said, "I agree with you, because it will get the food to the rooms faster than if everything is in the kitchen. If they're all set up in one place, then the only thing that will have to come upstairs is the food."

When we traveled, we looked at everything in every hotel, everywhere we went. We heard that Hilton had a hotel in Switzerland with two bathrooms in each room. We could never find out for sure if it did or didn't, so we went over there to find out. They had two bathrooms, but they were suites, so they *didn't* have two bathrooms. One thing that always amazed me is that Harrah's never advertised two bathrooms to each room.

Do you think Harrah's was the first hotel to ever have two bathrooms in every room?

I know it was! I know it was. [laughter]

I also designed Villa Harrah, because I knew what we wanted. Then I told the architect, "Now I want you to build it exactly like Frank Lloyd Wright would do."

He said, "I wish you hadn't said that."

What were some of the other amenities of the Harrah's Tahoe hotel?

They had a little television in each of the bathrooms, and they had a fully-stocked bar in every room. Of course, you did have to pay for whatever you drank from the bar.

Do you feel a sense of pride in having taken part in designing such a great hotel, a five-star hotel?

Oh, I don't have too many feelings about anything along those lines. [laughter] In other words, to me that's something that's done and over. I don't live for the past. I just live for the future. The pleasure of my life actually was raising the boys.

After you were divorced, did you and the boys live in Reno or Tahoe?

We have a house in Skyland, South Tahoe, but we lived in Reno. We did everything that we wanted to do the same way. If we wanted to use the boat–the *Thunderbird*–all we had to do was call Bill and tell him when we wanted to go out and go for a spin, regardless of who else wanted it. It was there for me and the boys.

Did the boys go to school here in town, or did they go away to school?

They went to school here. John went to Switzerland one year. I think that's the biggest mistake I ever made, because he would call me every morning at three or four o'clock in the morning (because of the time difference), and he would say, "I just got to get out of this place. I want to come home." Bill wanted him there for the discipline, but I should have let him come home. He was twelve years old, and it was tough to be without your parents.

John absolutely insisted on me coming over there when it was time for him to get out. I said, "John that's kind of crazy. You're coming right home, and that's a long trip for me to make over there when you are coming home."

He said, "No, you have to come over here."

I went over there and looked at the place and everything, and he said, "Now, would you like to live here?" He just wanted me to see why he wanted to come home and see what he had been through over there.

Do you have any ideas on why Bill Harrah was such a perfectionist? Was he always that way?

Yes, he was always that way. I'm about the same way myself. [laughter] I might have

gotten it from my mother, because she was just immaculate all the time, but I hate to see things all messed up. I can't stand it. Bill and I thought alike. Practically everything that he didn't like, I didn't like; if I liked it, he liked it. For instance, I wouldn't want his family to come and stay for a week or two, and he sure wouldn't want mine to come and stay for a week or two, so we just didn't do it. We put them in the hotel.

Did you discuss much business at home or when you were traveling?

Well, after our first argument, I left things pretty much alone.

When Bill Harrah traveled, did you usually go with him?

Yes. He said that he liked his women to be right where he was all of the time.

So he wasn't the kind of guy that hung out with guys. Did he play golf or other sports?

He said he always wanted to play golf and learn how to dance, but he couldn't do either one. [laughter]

I hadn't thought of it until now–he sponsored many golf tournaments, but he never did play, did he?

No. Bob and Lucille Ring always took care of that. Bob Ring loved to play golf, and he played in all the tournaments.

Did Bill Harrah talk much at home or when you were by yourself?

Very little. Like I said, it took me a long time to get him to smile. If he was talking to Sammy Davis or somebody about the cars, then he would talk. He talked more about the cars than anything else.

After your second divorce in 1969, Mr. Harrah's public image seemed to change. Most noticeably, his hairstyle and his clothes. Do you have any comments on that?

Well, first he married Bobbie Gentry.[2] I moved [to a place on Juniper Hill] from Rancharrah, now owned by my son John, so Bill and Bobbie Gentry could move in. I didn't have to move—I moved because I had built the house around him, and I told him he could have the house. He appreciated that. And of course, I refused child support. I just didn't want it. They insisted that I take it, and I said, "I don't want it." And they said, "Well we have to give you something." So they wound up giving me eight hundred dollars a month. [laughter]

[Bill's marriage to Bobbie Gentry] lasted about two-and-a-half months or something like that. She was supposed to be appearing at the Queen's Theater in London, and Tom Jones was on the same bill. She got up about five or six o'clock in the morning for rehearsal, and she thought Bill would stay in bed, but he went down and sat in the back of the theater and found out that what they were doing on the stage was not in the script.

When they went to Stuttgart, Germany, Bill called me, and I said, "What's wrong with you?"

He said, "Nothing."

I said, "Well, something's wrong with you, because you don't sound right."

He said, "No, everything's fine."

I said, "Well you don't sound fine." (I could always tell by his voice if something was wrong.)

He said, "No, everything's fine." The next afternoon he was standing in my living room. It was all over.

Then Bill married Mary Berger, who was the one that got him looking like a hippie. I told his hair stylist, "Jerry, if you don't cut his hair, I'm going to." [laughter] Got him over that. Then Bill straightened up again, and he married a model. She used to model once in a while in the club. Her name was Roxanne. That lasted . . . oh, nine or ten months, I guess. (And I think he was married to Mary for about nine or ten months.)

After that Bill married Verna Frank, and they were married four years. She was married to him when he died. She had a son, and she wanted Bill to adopt her son, but he didn't want to do it. It was rather odd in a way, because the three children didn't get along at all. They would go to Idaho together, but they didn't get along. John and Tony haven't had any contact with Verna's son since Bill died.

It sounds like you two had a good relationship after the divorce.

Oh, we did. Just like I said, the only difference was we lived in different houses.

Didn't you buy a small casino after your divorce?

Yes. It was called the SH Corral, and it was really very nice. I just had three twenty-one tables and a lot of slots and a bar and restaurant and coffee shop. The food was just great. Bill came out one time, and he said, "I think you have a real nice place out here."

Did you work out there a lot yourself?

I would say most of the time.

You didn't deal twenty-one though, did you?

Yes, whenever I wanted to. [laughter] Finally it got to where sometimes I had to be there at two o'clock in the morning, and I didn't like it, so I just sold it in about 1975. I had it for about five years.

Did Bill Harrah ever worry about not having enough money to expand or not having enough money to make the loan payments on any of his different clubs or hotels?

He sure did. He'd wake up and—especially [when we were building] the place at Lake Tahoe—be covered with sweat.

Who was his most trusted financial person in the club?

Well, that would be Mead Dixon and Eddie Questa; and later, George Drews.

What do you miss most of the life you had when you were married to Bill Harrah?

Nothing. [laughter]

Don't you miss the entertainment or the hydroplane races? Not even the Horseless Carriage Club?

No. I'd had it! I had it all and I just wanted to get out. But every time he got married and divorced . . . well, then he would want to get married again. As a matter of fact, before his death—it was in November or October—he

wanted me to go to Switzerland and tour the Ferrari factory with him. I didn't go. I should have gone, because he really wanted to leave the club and everything to the boys and me. I knew that. But I thought, "Well, I could never be phony," and I couldn't start then. And I never needed very much. I didn't need fifty billion dollars.

Notes

1. Jessie Beck: Mrs. Beck, née Howard, worked for Harolds Club as a dealer and pit supervisor prior to marrying Fred Beck. After Mr. Beck's death, she operated the keno game at Harolds Club. She owned and operated the Riverside Hotel from 1971 to 1978.

2. Bobbie Gentry was born in Mississippi in 1944. She became a nationally known pop and country music star with the release of her first single, "Ode to Billy Joe," in 1967. Gentry often performed at Harrah's.

14

VERNA HARRAH

V ERNA HARRISON HARRAH, who was married to Bill Harrah at the time of his death in 1978, was born in Nampa, Idaho, on July 25, 1944. She grew up there and later attended Seattle University before applying for a job at Harrah's through an employment office in Twin Falls, Idaho. She was hired as a secretary, but when she got to Reno she discovered that she could make more money as a cocktail waitress, and so she transferred to the bar department. She worked at Harrah's for three years and never met Bill Harrah; only after she left and became a real estate agent did they meet.

Verna Harrah was a willing chronicler, recalling many memories of Bill Harrah and sharing with the interviewer pictures from their marriage . The interview was conducted in her movie production office on Rodeo Drive in Beverly Hills, California, and two sessions were required to complete it.

In this oral history, Mrs. Harrah tells of her whirlwind courtship and marriage to Bill Harrah at the Middle Fork Lodge in Idaho, and she remembers some of the many entertainers who appeared at Harrah's Clubs. Mrs. Harrah recalls many trips with Bill to Europe, Australia, New York, Indianapolis, and Russia and tells several interesting, and sometimes humorous, anecdotes about those trips. She also

relates the surprising thoughts that Bill Harrah had when the MGM Hotel opened in Reno in 1978, and she offers important information about his decision not to leave his automobile collection to the city of Reno or the state of Nevada. Finally, she gives an account of the last few days of Bill Harrah's life and the behavior of Harrah's attorney Mead Dixon on the trip back to Reno from the Mayo Clinic after Bill Harrah's death.

VERNA HARRAH: I was born Verna Harrison in Nampa, Idaho, July 25, 1944. My parents were both born and raised in Idaho. My father was the son of a lawyer and a state senator, and my mother was the daughter of farmers.

My parents grew up in Idaho, met in high school, and married quite young. I think my mother was nineteen, and my father was five years older. I have an older sister who was born about five years after they were married, and I have a brother who is ten years younger than I am. I grew up in Twin Falls and went through high school in Twin Falls.

I am not currently married, but I have a son, Richard, from a marriage prior to my marriage to Bill, and I have an adopted daughter from a marriage after Bill. Richard lives here in the Beverly Hills area. He wants to go back to school, and he wants to be a writer. He's actually very good. He's very talented, and he's very, very artistic. He's done wonderful things with his life. He's worked for Steven Spielberg, he's worked for me, and he's worked at Warner Brothers Music. He loves writing, and he loves his music. He's a wonderful guitarist, but when he goes back to school, I think it's going to be to study writing.

My daughter is fourteen, and she's at Crossroads, which is a private school in Santa Monica. We live in Beverly Hills. I also have a home at Malibu beach, which I am, at the moment, trying to sell. It's just too far out. It's absolutely the most beautiful home I've ever seen—it's just an incredible house on eight acres right on the beach—but we seldom go there because I work all the time. I work every day, and Sam (my daughter) is here in school, and her friends are here, and so she doesn't like to go out there. And if she doesn't go out, then I'm not going to go out.

DWAYNE KLING: What did you do after you finished high school?

I went to Seattle University. When I was there for about two years, I had a fall which

resulted in a life-long problem for me—I have kidney disease resulting from the fall. At least, that is what we think caused it. I was born with only one normal kidney; the other one was really small. My mother was also born that way and has had no problems in her life. My son was born with only one normal kidney, and he has a bad problem, unfortunately, but his function is fine.

My problems started after my fall when I damaged my kidney. Twenty years later I lost the function completely, and then I went on dialysis for ten years. It will be two years this December since I had a successful kidney transplant.

After my fall in Seattle, I had to go home, because I was really quite ill. I was having a lot of problems with my kidney. I did try to go back to school in Idaho—I tried going back to Idaho State in Pocatello, but it just never happened. I never finished school. I ended up in Reno and got a job at Harrah's.

How did it happen that you went to Reno and got a job?

Bill really loved Idaho people. He was a big fan of the state and of the people, and he really liked the idea that the employees that worked at Harrah's were different than they were anywhere else—they were all fresh, young, college-looking or college-educated kids. He thought that by going to states like Utah and Idaho—especially Idaho—that he would get the kind of employee that he wanted. He didn't care that they had absolutely no training; as a matter of fact, he preferred that.

I had had an unsuccessful marriage that lasted a very short time; I had a son, and I wanted to get out of Idaho. Harrah's had an employment office in Twin Falls, and that was a way of doing it. So in 1968 I packed my son up, and off we went to Reno. It was really easy.

I had applied for a job as a secretary and was accepted, but when I got to Reno and saw how expensive everything was, I didn't really think I could make it on the salary. So I went into cocktails and made much better money there. I did other jobs. I was Harrah's first [corporate airplane] stewardess, and I posed for a lot of photographs for their brochures, advertisements, billboards, and that sort of thing.

I got my real estate license and left Harrah's in 1971. I had never met Bill Harrah the entire time I was there. I never even met him when I flew in the company airplane as a stewardess, because Bill never liked having a stewardess. He just flew by himself.

Were you studying real estate while you were working at Harrah's?

Right. When I got my license, I quit and went to work selling real estate, and that's how I met Bill Harrah. [laughter] A woman that he was dating was buying a house through me, and he wanted to see the paperwork, so she introduced me to him. I showed him the contract, and he looked it over, and we started talking: "You're from Idaho. Oh, and you're left-handed, and . . . ." All those good qualities. "Oh, you're a Republican. Oh, my god," you know, "this is too good to be true!" [laughter] We just got along so well that I wasn't really that surprised when he called me a couple of days later and invited me out to dinner. At first it was just kind of, "Oh my god, Bill Harrah's taking me out to dinner," and I really didn't think too much about it other than, "Wow, this is really amazing." [laughter] But he just became my best friend. He was truly my best friend, and it was amazing how much we were alike and how much we had in common.

The "best friend" part is interesting, because I've asked people like Lloyd Dyer, "Well, who was Bill Harrah's best friend?" So many people have claimed to be his best friend. Mead Dixon claimed to be his best friend.

I know. I know. [laughter]

And people have said, "Oh, Bob Ring was his best friend." But Lloyd said that he felt Bill Harrah was happiest in his life when he was with you, and he felt that you were his best friend.

Yes, that's true. I was surprised at how many people were his "best friend," but people like to think that–people that knew him and loved him felt that way about him. Bill was a very private, shy man, and I was too. I guess that's why we clung to each other in so many ways. I mean, at big parties and so forth that we had to go to–Don Rickles used to make jokes about it–we'd prop each other up because we were both so shy. [laughter]

How long did you know Mr. Harrah before you got married?

A year, almost to the day.

Do you think he had a friend other than you?

No, not really. He had a lot of acquaintances and a lot of people he cared about very much. Probably the person he cared about the most was Bob Ring, but we didn't socialize with him that much. Bill was funny about people. I mean, he had a lot of acquaintances, but even when he went on business meetings with other executives, and they did not take their wives, I always went. I was always with him. I think in the entire time that we were together before he died, there was only one night when we were apart. And we were constantly on the phone. [laughter] So we were together almost every single day.

Do you remember who the witnesses were at your wedding?

Yes. For me it was my sister, and for Bill it was Bob Hudgens, Bill's assistant. I wanted to get married at the Middle Fork Lodge, because that was a place that was so special to us, and it was in Idaho. We were married in the original cabin there on the property. We didn't really take that many people with us, because it's small, and we didn't want a big wedding. Just my family and Bob Hudgens, his assistant, that was all that were there.

You must have felt almost like a fairytale princess.

No kidding! I came from a family of very moderate means. We weren't poor, but we certainly were just average folks.

Did you travel a great deal with Mr. Harrah?

Yes. We were in the air much of the time, but it was amazing–when I went back and looked at my photographs–how family-concerned and oriented he was, because so many of our trips included the children. In looking through my photographs, there were times when we would go without them, but they were with us a great deal of the time. He was really amazing with those boys. I have pictures of him back-packing. I'll show you. You'll see how he was.

He would bring John, Tony, and Richard[1] on trips?

Yes–many, many times; many, many trips.

That's interesting, because you don't hear about that side of Mr. Harrah.

I know. I have pictures that are so endearing, that will show you a completely different man.

Did you go on the back-packing trips too?

I certainly went on all the river trips. We went on a river trip every year, but he did take one back-packing trip with them where they back-packed from Stanley to Pettit Lake Canyon. That hike is over the mountains, and it's a long hike. I didn't go on that one, because I really wasn't strong enough to do that.

And he was sixty years old at least.

I know, but when they got there, they drove back. They were going to spend the night at Pettit Lake, and I waited for them in Stanley–I thought I was going to see them the next day. [laughter] But when they got there, they drove back! They came in looking so pitiful and so bedraggled . . . . They were just dragging in, and they were so filthy that when I opened the door, I just had to start laughing. They were so cute.

Did you travel to Europe frequently?

We went to Europe every year, sometimes more than once, and most always on an antique automobile trek. We were in Australia once on an antique car rally. We did the London-Brighton Run every year, and once we were in South Africa. The London-to-Brighton Run was always such fun. I hope I get this right . . . before 1914, you couldn't drive an automobile in London unless you had a man on horse out in front of the car waving a flag saying, "Here comes an automobile. Watch out. Here comes a car." They changed the law in 1914, so every year from 1914 on, they celebrated by driving cars–and they had to be 1914 or older–from London to Brighton.

Every year we'd take this run. Of course, the cars never had tops in them or heaters, and it was always the middle of the winter, and you would freeze to death. When we got to Brighton, we would stay in this really wonderful old hotel that's only opened in the winter for this run. Brighton is on the sea, and it is really a summer resort town. They have a black tie, big gala event at the end of this run, and then you spend the night there. You get a room, and you go up and change your clothes, and you're cold and wet. I got to tell you something–this trip is a hardship. I mean, this is not for sissies. [laughter]

Now, Bill had a tremendous sense of humor. He was a bit corny, but I loved that about him. He got these huge glasses, and he put windshield wipers on them so he could see. The glasses were a joke, but you almost needed them. [laughter] He was very cute. Very cute.

We always had a car following us, a car with extra parts and mechanics that could help us if we broke down. That part was legal, but sometimes these old cars just couldn't make it, and they would quit. The whole idea was just finishing the run. You didn't care who got there first. There was only one year when we didn't make it. Bill almost didn't go to the gala that night; he was so upset. They just could not fix the car. I said, "You know, we have to go. This is traditional, and it's like being a bad sport."

He said, "You're right. You're right."

Did you go to England just for that run and then come home, or did it tie in with a trip to Europe?

Generally, it did tie in. We would always go to places where Bill knew friends that had cars. We would stay with Baron Raben, for instance, in Denmark, and what a trip that was. He had this huge castle and his little car collection, and what a treat he was. We stayed right in his castle, and it was an exciting experience.

I have to tell you, I was so terribly unsophisticated about the world. Baron Raben had this big, huge, crystal bowl completely full of caviar on ice. In those days, I never had tried caviar, and I was sitting there when the Baron puts this big dollop of caviar on this little biscuit and hands it to me, and I've got this thing, and I think, "What am I going to do with this?" And I had to eat it, and I just thought I was going to die. I couldn't imagine how I was going to eat this. And then at night, it was the same thing. They would have sturgeon that I don't think was even smoked. It was just raw sturgeon. He was a wonderful man, really interesting man, and there were a lot of people like him, that I would meet.

Cars were usually the reason for our trips, almost everywhere we went. Bill was the west coast dealer for Ferrari, and we went to the Ferrari factory in Italy, and that was fasci-

nating. He had other dealerships as well. I'm not sure exactly which ones now, but I think he had the BMW and Mercedes local dealerships. The Ferrari was for the entire western part of the United States.

We also had a lot of car tours in upstate New York, and we would tie the tours in with trips to New York City. We would go to the Broadway shows, and we always went to Frankie and Johnny's, sometimes every night. Frankie and Johnny's used to be a speak-easy during prohibition. I still go there when I go to New York. You go up this little tiny stairway, and then you have to push a buzzer to get in. It's just like it used to be in that respect, and it has the best steak in the country.

Bill tried desperately . . . . He knew Johnny, and he would say, "Johnny, I want these steaks. I want them just like this. I want them for the showrooms and for the Steak House. These are the best steaks in the world."

And Johnny'd say, "Oh, sure." But, what Johnny didn't tell him was how he seasoned them, or how he cut them. Bill never could get the exact recipe for the seasoning. That was Johnny's little secret. He wasn't going to give it up. But we would go there almost every night. It was definitely Bill's favorite place to eat in New York City.

When you went on these trips, did you fly commercial, or did Bill Harrah take his own plane?

We generally took his plane. We usually took the GII when we went to Europe. We did fly commercial a few times, but we usually did take the GII. When we went to Australia, we took the GII. I don't recall why, but we did. We stopped in Tahiti on the way over and Fiji on the way back. Sometimes we would take the Concorde to Europe. (He really wanted to see if there wasn't some way that Harrah's could buy a smaller version of the Concorde. He says, "Well, just think of it. We could go to Australia in no time." [laughter]) On these trips it was usually just Bill and myself. In the United States he always had a security [person] with him, but not when we went to Europe. Then it was just the two of us.

Was he afraid for his well-being, or did he want somebody there to help him and do things for him?

I think that Bill was concerned. Because of the business that he was in, he was concerned about being kidnapped. I'm too naive about that sort of thing to know whether it was warranted or not, but he certainly felt that it was, and I know that when people are drinking, and they're gambling and losing money, that can make for a dangerous set-up. There were times when we were threatened, and so he always had security for the children. My son had security, and his boys had, and Bill did too. I really didn't, but I didn't need security: I almost never went anywhere. [laughter] I spent an awful lot of time at home during the day, but we went out almost every night.

We went to every opening of every show, and then on the nights when there wasn't an opening, we'd maybe have dinner with one of the show's stars. If I went out during the day, it was usually just to have lunch with a girlfriend, so I rarely ever felt the need for security, and I don't think Bill was too concerned about it either.

We traveled back and forth between Reno and Lake Tahoe a great deal, and he drove himself all of the time. He loved to drive, so we'd have security follow us; and, yes, he always had security, but, yes, he loved to drive. Loved cars. [laughter]

Did you have any love for cars, or did you fall in love with cars after you fell in love with Bill?

Well, I certainly appreciated them more, because he taught me so much about them . . . although, I must say, I forgot it very quickly. But you know what I loved? I loved the fact that he loved it so much, because it was just so endearing to see someone be so in love with something. I wish that I felt that way towards some hobby.

Bill was enamored with cars his entire life. When he was a child, riding on a bicycle, a car knocked him over, and he was sprawled out on the street. His mother came running out, and he says, "Mother, Mother. What's an IF?" as they are carrying him to the hospital. It was an Isotta-Fraschini. He didn't even notice that he'd been thrown off the bike. [laughter]

Bill went out to his auto collection almost every day. When he was with me he had the same itinerary every day. He'd get up about the same time, have his breakfast, go to work, go to the office; then he would leave and go to the car collection around 4:00 and stay for an hour. Then at 5:00 he would go see his boys for an hour, and then he would come home and we'd have dinner. It was always the same.

So, he saw his boys almost every day?

Every day. Every single day . . . and the automobile collection every day, yes.

I've heard it said that he loved his family first and the car collection second.

Right. As a matter of fact, when we were at Mayo Clinic, and he was getting ready to go in for surgery, the nurse said, "Mr. Harrah, I understand that your first love in life is antique automobiles." And he says, "Nope, that's my second love. This is my first . . . ."

Pointing at you.

Yes. [laughter] That was very sweet. But every night when he'd go to bed, he would go through stacks of magazines. He subscribed to every antique automobile magazine, and that was his reading material.

He evidently knew every car in the collection. Clyde Wade told me that if something was just the slightest bit wrong, he could spot it almost immediately.

He'd know, and he would know if it was authentic or not. He knew every detail. As a matter of fact, he had more knowledge of antique automobiles than anybody in the world.

Right before he went into surgery, Bill knew that he was going to die. I don't know how he knew it, but he knew it. When I look back now, there's no question in my mind. There were so many things that he did, so many things he said. He said, "Do you believe in an afterlife?"

I said, "I don't know. I'd like to believe in an afterlife."

And he said, "Well, you know, I think that there must be something, because I know so much about antique automobiles. Where does that knowledge go? It must go somewhere." He figured that that knowledge couldn't just dissipate. It had to go somewhere.

But he never expressed a great deal of concern or worry to you when he went there. He didn't say, "Gee, I don't know if I'm going to get out of this alive or not?"

He did say that to me. He did say that to me. He talked about it a few times. Once in Idaho, he said, "I don't think anything's going to go wrong, but if anything should go wrong, is there anything that is special to you? Is there anything that you would like?"

And I just couldn't talk. I said, "Well, how can you even talk to me about this? You know, if you feel that there is going to be a problem, just don't do it. Let's just not do it. You don't have to do it."

He says, "Well, I think I have to do it."

Perhaps he'd been advised that he had to have an operation?

I guess so. I don't know. But I was completely left out of that part of it. I guess I was too young. Today, I would never be left out of a decision like that. Not that it would make any difference. You always have to do what they want you to do, but at least I would have liked to have had some knowledge of it and discussed it with someone.

In the hospital, he said, "There are two things that I want to tell you and to talk to you about." One was that he had been giving it a lot of thought, and that if anything went wrong, he said that he wanted to be buried in Idaho. He said, "Now, I've looked around, and I don't like the graveyard in Sun Valley or in Ketchum–it's right next to the highway, so I don't like it there. I can't be buried in Stanley, because there's no police there, and there will be grave robbers," he says. "So I'm going to leave it up to you. Take your time." he says. "I've investigated. You can take your time. There's no deadline as to when I have to be buried, so you take your time."

The second thing he wanted me to know was that the years with me were the happiest years of his life. Those were the two things that he wanted me to know.

After he died I had such a difficult time making anyone believe that he wanted to be buried in Idaho, because, obviously, they wanted him in Reno. I just wish that he had shared it with someone besides me. [laughter]

Where is he buried?

Hailey, Idaho. We had homes in Sun Valley and Stanley, so that area, to me, seemed like where he should be. I didn't want to go to Boise or Twin Falls–they were too urban, and Hailey really has a charming cemetery. It's a marked grave, and it's cared for, so it's not like someone's going to desecrate it. To me, Hailey was the right choice, but when I moved from Sun Valley, they asked me if they could move him to Reno. Mead Dixon and Scherry Harrah were the two who were giving me the most trouble about it. They thought that it was something that I wanted because I was there. I said, "You don't understand. This was his last request. There's no way I can let you move him back to Reno."

Bill loved Idaho. We would go to Middle Fork Lodge even in the winter. We had a Christmas there one time, but we would spend a lot of time there in the summer. And a lot of times we'd spend a whole month in Stanley.

Did he keep in touch with the business while you were there?

Oh, every day. As a matter of fact, he had one of the first ever fax machines. I had never seen anything like it–this paper rolling through with all the numbers. Every day, yes. He absolutely would never lose contact with the business. Then if he had questions, he would call Shep or Lloyd Dyer or whoever was in charge. He was on the phone every day.

❖

We also went to Tucson every year. Bill had a friend there that owned a lot of old Franklin cars. His name is Tom. Tom was a bachelor. His family had left him some money, so he didn't have to work, and all he cared about was his cars. He had, literally, built his house around this Franklin, because he only liked Franklins. He had put a Franklin in his living room and built his house around it.

Once he bought a new Franklin, and the big deal was we all had to decide what color it was going to be, what color we should paint it. Most Franklins are black, but I guess he could paint it dark green or something, I don't know. But we all had to write a secret little ballot. I mean, he really was the biggest nerd on the planet! [laughter] We enjoyed him, and Bill really got such a kick out of him–he really enjoyed being with him.

We went to Tucson every year, and we stayed in this wonderful hotel that I can't remember the name of anymore, it's been so many years. We would spend a week there, and at night Bill and I would catch up on all the movies. We would always go right before the Academy Awards show, and we would catch up on all the movies that we hadn't seen that had been nominated for an award, and

then we would go–I mean this is so, so terrible–eat Mexican food!

We were both such fanatics–we watched our weight all year long. I mean, he would weigh me every single morning and then weigh himself and then write it down. It was always written down. We would get on this big huge scale with the big arrow, like one of those where you put a penny in. We were always very weight conscious, the two of us, and he made me even more than I was. (I'm neurotic enough without that.) But when we were in Tucson, we just let everything go. At every movie we would eat popcorn, and if we went to a movie and they didn't have popcorn, we wouldn't stay unless he could go get it at another theater or get the security to go into the other theater and bring it to him. It was really cute. [laughter] And we would have Mexican food every night, and then we would go to Baskin-Robbins, and we'd each get a pint of ice cream!

❖

We went to the Indianapolis 500 race with Jim Nabors every year. It was something that the two of them really enjoyed doing together. Bill was almost as big a star in Indianapolis as the races. They all knew him. He would go down to Gasoline Alley along the track, and he would spend time with the racers. We stayed in the same hotel the drivers stayed in. It was very small, kind of like a Motel 6, not big and classy but very close to the racetrack. So it was all the drivers and Bill and Jim. It was great fun for Bill.

Art Smith[2] mentioned in his book that when we would come into town we would be met by the police, and they would bring us into town with their sirens going; when we would go home, they would take us back to the airport the same way. That's absolutely true. I don't know how Bill swung it. [laughter] Every year that's what happened, and I really have to tell you it was a luxury. We were the only ones that got [that treatment], so it was a luxury from that aspect, but it was almost impossible to get into the racetrack on that day because the city was so jammed. I just don't know how you would have done it any other way. We never would have got there on time, that's for sure! [laughter]

An event called the Concours d' Elegance takes place in Pebble Beach, California, every year. They judge the most elegant antique automobile. I don't know what all the requirements are, except that the cars must be absolutely authentic–there cannot be any parts that are not genuine. The cars have to have all original parts, and [the "best of show" winner] has to be the most elegant of cars. Bill was invited every year, and every year he won.[3] Bill always brought a different car, but every year he would win, because every year he always had the best car. (If you would go to an antique automobile auction, and a car went on the block to be auctioned, and they said, "This is a Harrah restoration," it went for far more money because, obviously, it was the best.)

One year Bill didn't win. He should have because he had the better car, but I think somebody felt like, "Well, this is getting to be ridiculous. We're going to give it to somebody else."

Bill got very upset. His feeling was, "It doesn't matter if you win every year. If you have the best car, the best car should win." He wouldn't go back–for two years in a row, he wouldn't go back. He wouldn't enter a car.

They became very upset: "Mr. Harrah, please come back. We really want you to enter. It isn't a competition without you. It doesn't have the prestige without you."

He said, "Well, I'm sorry. I'm just not going to do it, because if the best car doesn't win, then you're not legitimate."

They said, "We promise you that if you'll come back, the very best car will win."

He said, "OK." So he came back, and, of course, he won. [laughter]

Earlier you mentioned that Bill Harrah asked you, "If you could go anywhere in the world, where would you want to go?" What was your answer?

I said to him that I would like to go to the Soviet Union. I had always been fascinated by communism, and I wanted to see what living in a communist state was like. There was a lot of fear in those days. It was before the Reagan years, and there was a lot of fear about Russia taking over the world. You would read some things that sounded like life wasn't great there; but other times, you'd read they're so advanced, and they've got this, and they've got that, and they've got a man in space. There was so much of that kind of fear that I wanted to see what it was really like.

We went, and it was enormously disappointing. What a pitiful place it was. In those days–and I know that things are quite different now–you really couldn't go anywhere without a K.G.B.. Even on your floor at the hotel, they had K.G.B., and your room was apparently wired. As a matter of fact, some people would come into the room and say they had to change the light bulb, and they *kept* having to change the light bulb. We figured it was because the sound wasn't coming through properly. [laughter]

We went over there just as ordinary tourists, but we should have gone in an official capacity. I know Bill could have arranged it. We just didn't know any better. We had too much luggage, and we were too rich, and we were just not popular at all. We were not liked, so we made a lot of mistakes–we just didn't know how to go to the Soviet Union. We got tickets for the Moscow circus, and we got tickets for the ballet and a couple of other things. We were supposed to be there for five days, but we left early. There was only really one place to eat, and that was the hotel. In those days they didn't have restaurants that you went out to; or if they did, we certainly didn't hear of it. The first night we were there, we were supposed to go to the circus at 8:00, and so we wanted to have dinner at 7:00. We went into the dining room, and as we were walking in, they said, "You can't come in to eat."

"Why?"

"Well, Henry Kissinger's here, and nobody's allowed in the dining room."

And we said, "Well, OK. We'll come back at 8:00."

Of course, everybody knows everything. They know who's there, they know what you're doing, and they say, "You can't eat at 8:00. You're going to the circus."

Bill says, "Well, I'm not going to go without dinner. I'll just give my tickets to the driver." So he went down and gave his tickets to the driver, and, of course, the driver was almost afraid to take the tickets. You know, "My god, you're giving me the tickets!"

So we were punished. We were then not allowed to do anything else. Our ballet tickets were taken away from us, and all of our other plans that we had arranged were taken away, and the only thing we were allowed to do was to go on a bus tour. We had a private guide who took us on this tour. She was Jewish, and she said there was a lot of anti-Semitism in Russia. Not from a government point of view—they were allowed every job like anyone else—but from the people themselves, there was a lot of anti-Semitism, and she really wanted to get out of the country. I felt bad for her, and I felt she was kind of sick. Her lips were sort of purple like she needed medical care.

You just felt really sad that you couldn't do something to help. She was talking about the fact that they really didn't have any fresh vegetables, and we were driving by a store, and in the window there were all these vegetables. So I said, "What about those vegetables?"

And she says, "If there ever is anything like that, people line up around the block for four blocks and wait in line for hours to get what they have, like oranges or vegetables."

I said, "But look at all those beautiful fruits in that store, and there is no lines."

And she says, "Those aren't real. They're just for the tourists to see." So she was really very honest with us.

We were actually in Russia only three days. We left two days early simply because they really didn't allow us to do anything, and we were so unpopular. We realized we did everything wrong. When we first got into the country, we wanted to change money, and as soon as we got off the airplane we asked the woman where to change money. She said, "Well, there's this place over there. You go over there, and you change money."

So we went over there, and we had all this luggage, and the person looked at us, and he says, "No."

Bill says, "Well, what do you mean no?"

And he says, "No, I'm not going to do it."

So we went back to the woman that we talked to who sent us over there, and we said, "He won't give us any money."

And she says, "What do you mean he won't give you any money? Of course, he'll give you some money." So she walks over and talks to him, and he's talking to her, and they're talking back and forth, and she turns around and says, "You're right. He won't give you any money." She walked away. [laughter]

I said to Bill, "I'm so sorry. I'm so sorry I drug you here." But I've been back many times since, and it's a little different now.

❖

You met every entertainer that came into Reno or Lake Tahoe and spent a great deal of time with them. Was that enjoyable time for you in most cases?

Oh, yes. Absolutely. I can't ever remember an occasion when it wasn't. All the entertainers had enormous respect for Bill, and Bill really liked them. He really enjoyed that part of the business. I think like most people, he was probably a little star struck. Frank Sinatra was, by far, Bill's idea of the biggest star, and he was so thrilled when Frank decided to come to Tahoe and do that back-to-back performance with John Denver. But every time we were with Frank, it was always, "Mr. Harrah. Mr. Harrah."

And Bill says, "Why don't you call me Bill?"

And Frank said, "Because, sir, I just have too much respect for you." It was really wonderful to see that. Bill called him Frank and, eventually, it became Frank and Bill because we were with him a lot. We became very close friends, and the Sinatras are still very close friends of mine. We never had any bad experiences. Now, there were, I'm sure, times when we weren't with Frank when he could have caused problems for some people, but, never, never for us. We just always had wonderful experiences.

Bill had a reputation of treating the stars that was unequaled in any other casino. He hired stars that would work nowhere else. He didn't pay the most, but he treated them like royalty. He treated them, he said, like he would like to be treated himself. He knew the birth dates of the stars and their families. He knew what they liked to drink. He knew what they liked to eat. He gave several of them a Rolls-Royce or a Ferrari. He gave them what they wanted, whether it was a house on the lake or a stay in the star suite. He treated them like royalty, and they loved him for it. It's one thing to have to just go to work and have a job and put your time in; it's another thing to really feel like you're on vacation. Bill made them feel like they were on vacation.

It's been said that Sammy Davis Jr. was closer to Bill than a lot of the other entertainers.

Jim Nabors was very close; and on a personal level, we were friends with Bill Cosby. Bill Cosby, in the early days, went to Bill for a loan. He had been turned down everywhere else because he was, at that time, having trouble gambling. (This is not a secret—he tells this story, so I don't think it's a problem for me to repeat it.) Everyone turned him down except Bill, and Bill said, "Absolutely." And Cosby never forgot it. He never forgot it and would do anything for Bill, so that friendship was very close.

When entertainers were appearing at Harrah's in Reno, we would have them in our home. If they were at Lake Tahoe, we would have them to the Summit for dinner. (We also traveled with some of them. We went to New York a lot with Frank and Barbara Sinatra.)

Once, Steve Martin was in our home at Villa Harrah, and I thought he was in a bad mood, because he never said anything. He really was very, very quiet; and Bill being quiet, and myself being shy, it was a very quiet evening. [laughter] It was painful, really, but now I know Steve, and I know that he is shy. It wasn't that he was in a bad mood at all. He really is a very, very shy man. It's just incredible how a person can be one way on stage, just this enormously funny man, and then, in person, be so completely opposite. Don Rickles is Don Rickles—on stage or off stage, he's the same. He's a sweetheart of a man, and he doesn't have a mean bone in his body. He is hysterically funny on stage or off, but not Steve. [laughter]

Willie Nelson I adored, but I don't think Bill ever quite "got" Willie. [laughter] You know, Bill was such a perfectionist. I mean, the show had to start at exactly 8:15. It couldn't be 8:16, and it couldn't be 8:14. With Willie Nelson, when the curtain would rise, there wouldn't be anybody on stage, or maybe his mother would be sitting on the stage drinking a beer, and Bill just didn't get it. I kept saying, "I'm telling you, Bill, this guy is really, really talented."

Willie's band would start to wander in whenever, and Bill would just say, "I don't get this. This can't happen." So they talked to Willie, and they talked to Willie, and he'd go, "OK. All right. All right," and then just never do it. [laughter] But I loved him. I thought he was wonderful.

Wasn't Bill Harrah an intelligent enough businessman to realize that even if he was late, he was still bringing in crowds of people?

You don't understand. Even knowing that, there's nobody could do it. Bill just would not allow it. He would absolutely not allow it! It just couldn't happen. They had to be there on time. Yes, he was a good businessman, but he felt there was always somebody else that was just as good as Willie Nelson. It took awhile, but Willie finally got there on time. But it did take awhile. [laughter]

Debbie Reynolds tried her best. In those days, she'd say, "Bill, I'm . . . superstitious. I just don't want to be there at 8:15 because I'm superstitious."

He says, "Debbie, 8:15."

She said, "OK." [laughter]

I can't imagine that any of Bill's managers were ever late coming to a meeting with him, because everybody was very aware of how important punctuality was to him. To him, it was a matter of respect. He wouldn't be disrespectful to someone else, because he really felt that time was all you had. He felt it is your most valued asset. If you wasted somebody's time, that was a crime in his mind, so he would never do it to anyone, and he would never expect anybody to do it to him. If you respect a person, you are not late.

Was Bill a perfectionist in his home life also?

Yes, and he was married to someone that was the exact opposite. [laughter] He was just such a Virgo. Everything on his desk, every little pen, everything was lined up. Everything was neat as a pin. He was absolutely amazing that way—so organized. Every year, when we would go to Europe, he'd get his clothes made for him at Brioni's in Rome. He would be there for seven days, and he would get, maybe, fifteen suits made, and he would have two long-sleeve shirts and two short-sleeve shirts made to match each suit, and he'd have a tie to match the outfit.

But Bill couldn't really put anything together (he was sort of color blind), so everything was hung together and numbered. There would be Brioni one, and then there would be Brioni two, Brioni three, Brioni four; and then every shirt would be Brioni one, two, three or four, so you'd know that it went with that suit. And on top of that, every jacket had a card attached that was made up at Harrah's,

and it would have date, time, and a person's name on it. It would say, "On December 12, dinner with Sammy Davis," so then he would never wear that suit with Sammy Davis again. Now, this is a very anal person! [laughter]

By having these outfits all matched up and ready to put on, he saved a lot of time. Could time management have been part of the reason for organizing his clothes?

I suppose you could say that was true. It certainly helped him in that respect. I think it was a great idea, a fabulous idea, but I could never do it. I tried. I even had photographs taken of my clothes, but I just couldn't get it together. I still would love to do that, but even now, I have trouble; what blouse goes with this suit, et cetera.

Sometimes when I would get ready to go out, I would put on something, and I wouldn't like the way it looked, so I'd throw it on the floor. Then I'd grab something else, and he'd come into my room to see if I was ready—and I was never ever late—and he'd say, "I don't see anything. I have blinders on. [laughter] I don't see anything." It was very sweet. I must say he really never, ever got mad at me, but I certainly lived differently than he did.

I've heard a lot of stories about Bill Harrah's notebook.

It used to frighten me, because sometimes when we'd be talking, he'd take the notebook out and start to make notes. He always wore a shirt with pockets, and he kept this little notebook in his shirt with a pen, and I would think, "Oh my god, I've done something wrong. [laughter] What is he writing?" And then I would always tease him about it. I'd say, "'This wife is going to go?' Is that what you're writing? Is that the note? [laughter] Or is it, 'She talks too much.' What is it? Is it, 'Remind myself to get of rid of Verna when I get home'?"

So he'd be talking to you, and he might be making notes on a car driving by or something else?

Right. If a clock was five minutes fast, he made a note on that. We would be walking the property, and he would be making notes. It's really the only way to do it. When you're managing so many things . . . I mean, when you think about the car collection, the casino, the house, the airplanes–how else do you do it? It's just mind boggling, so he had to do it that way.

We were at a dinner party one night at the house. One of the executive's wives (I loved this woman; she was one of my closest friends) was there, and the two of us probably had too much to drink, and we were gab, gab, gab, gab. Never stopped talking, the two of us. After the party, Bill made a note, and I said, "What? What?"

I'm not going to mention anybody's name, but Bill said, "I'm going to tell so-and-so he can't bring his wife to another dinner party."

And I said, "You're what? How can you say that? Why, she didn't talk any more than I did. I talked more than she did."

He said, "She talked too much and didn't allow the star to be the star."

I said, "Bill, nobody talked more than I did. If anybody's to blame, it was me."

He says, "Yes, but what you said was interesting." [laughter]

We were best friends, and so being quiet together was OK. I love to read; I've always been a reader. (I think that's why I'm pretty good at my business, because all my life I've read; and I read a lot of commercial novels, so I know commercial taste.) One time, when I was reading a book, Bill came in. It was in the evening, and he walked in the room, and I was reading. He stood and looked down at me and said, "From now on, I forbid you to ever read a book when I'm in the house." And I looked at him, and–I couldn't help it–I started to laugh because it was just so funny. It was just so outrageous. I mean, it was so outrageous! I said, "I don't think you can prevent

me from reading. I think that's against the law." [laughter]

He just got very huffy, and he walked off. He walked into his office, and I went back to reading. I just couldn't take it seriously. Pretty soon, he walked back into the room, and he said, "You're right. You can read anytime you want."

I said, "Well, you know something, Bill–if you want to talk, I don't mind putting my book aside when you're home. If you want to sit down and be together and talk, that's great. I can always read when you're gone." I guess what he was trying to tell me was that he was feeling lonely, and he wanted to talk. That was his way of telling me. [laughter]

Bill made me laugh all the time. People who are very bright generally see the world humorously. They can laugh at themselves, and there were many times when he would see humor in situations and laugh at himself or at the situation. He never laughed at people (he was just too kind a man to ever do that), but he did find things very funny. When you're so in tune to someone the way we were with each other . . . we could sit in a room, and somebody could say something, and we would both react the same way. We'd look at each other, and we just knew what we were both thinking. He was very funny. He had a great wit. He had kind of a Bob Newhart sense of humor.

⟡

One thing that was really interesting about most of the executives that worked for Bill was the way they felt about him–they just bent over backwards to do whatever it was that he wanted. They loved what he represented and loved the fact that he had such integrity and that he wanted the best. Not only did he expect the best from them, but he gave the best of himself, and so they respected him for that. Somebody mentioned to me, "You know, I have so much respect for Mr. Harrah that I would do more for him than I would do for myself or even my own family."

Bill's word was absolutely as good as gold. It was his bond. He was incredibly honest. If he said he was going to do something, he would take out his little notebook so that he wouldn't forget; and I can guarantee you, it was done. It was absolutely done to the smallest little thing, such as some woman saying, "Oh, Mr. Harrah, I love those cocktail napkins with 'Harrah's' on them. I would sure like some for my bridge party." He'd make a little note, and she would get those in the mail.

He made people proud, and he always would say to someone, whether it was the lowest janitor or the highest executive, "You're doing a great job." He really appreciated everything, and they loved that. He appreciated every single person. As far as he was concerned, Harrah's was a family, and that's how he made people feel.

[Among the top people at Harrah's], Bob Ring was Bill's closest friend, going back almost to his childhood. Bob came to Reno with Bill in the early days, and so they always had a special relationship. Maurice Sheppard was leaving as president when I came in, but Bill had enormous respect for him. Shep was stepping down, and that's when Lloyd Dyer came in as president. Lloyd was always a good friend, and I know that Bill relied on him a lot. Holmes Hendricksen is one of my closest and dearest friends of the group, and I know Bill just thought the world of him. He was head of entertainment, and Bill had enormous respect for him.

Bill felt Rome Andreotti was the smartest casino operator in the world, bar none. Rome knew more about casino operations and gaming than any other human being on the planet. Rome married one of my closest friends, and the four of us went to Europe together. I never really got to know Mark Curtis that well. He wasn't around much. Maybe he was close to Bill at the office, but I really didn't know him that well.

Bob Hudgens was Bill's assistant, and I certainly got to know him. I mean, he even went out and bought my tennis shoes—this was

the kind of thing he did. He would give orders to Lloyd Dyer, and then he would go out on his lunch break and buy my tennis shoes. [laughter] Bob did everything. He was just sort of a high energy, kind of nervous person, so it was hard to get close to him on a more personal basis, but he did everything. He and Cindy Wade did all of Bill Harrah's errands.

Mead Dixon . . . Mead was tough. I mean, we all talk about Mead. I had a difficult relationship with Mead on a personal level when Bill died. When Mead got sick and knew he was going to die, he started writing me long letters, and I didn't know what to do, because we were pretty much estranged. He was very strange to me when Bill died. For some reason, he really resented the fact that Bill left me so much money. I don't know why, because Mead and I didn't know each other that well when Bill was alive, so there wasn't anything personal; couldn't have been anything personal. He just decided that somehow it wasn't right. [laughter]

Before Mead died, he wanted to make up and say he was sorry. He started writing these long letters, and I would write him back, but it was difficult because I didn't quite know what to say. I mean, I was nice and I was pleasant, but you know . . . he caused a lot of people a lot of pain. Yet, Mead was brilliant, he really was. One thing that Bill always said about him is, "Mead Dixon's an asshole, but he's *my* asshole." [laughter]

Mead went with us on a trip to Australia, and he was extremely difficult on the trip. (Bill wanted to go into the casino business in Australia. He certainly never wanted to go to Las Vegas, and I know he would never have wanted to go into New Jersey, because he never wanted to be in an environment that had unions. Australia had no unions, so it was very attractive to him. He wanted to go into business with a gentleman named Sir Reginald Ansett, who owned an airline there. Casinos then had to be 50 percent or 51 percent owned by an Australian resident or citizen.) When we got home, Bill was ranting about Mead day after day. He said, "Why did he do that? Why did he act like that? I can't understand it! What is it with this guy?" Then Mead gave him the official report of the meetings that they had had, and Bill thought it was brilliant. That's when he said, "Look at this. The guy is brilliant. He might be an asshole, but he's *my* asshole." [laughter] Mead was obnoxious. That's a good word for him.

Did you and Bill Harrah ever discuss casino business?

Yes. I was really interested in every aspect of his life, so we did discuss business. We were the best of friends, and best friends talk about everyone and everything. [laughter]

Bill was very proud of the fact that the hotel in Tahoe was the most beautiful hotel, at that time, in the world, and it was the most expensive hotel to be built per square foot. It was, without a doubt, the creme de la creme of all hotels. Every room had two bathrooms. People would ask him why, and he would give different answers. The one answer he would give if a person was talking business was, "If the woman isn't ready to go downstairs and gamble, she has her own bathroom. The guy can get ready really fast and get downstairs, and it makes us more money." That was his answer, which really wasn't the truth. The truth of the matter was he just liked the idea of giving people what he would have liked to have had himself if he were in a hotel.

Bill was very proud of that hotel, and he was proud of the fact that Tahoe was the largest casino in the world under one roof until MGM came to Reno. When MGM was building that huge casino, Bill got very quiet. It troubled him that MGM was coming in, and he wondered how it would affect the town and how it would affect Harrah's. One day he walked up to me, and he said, "You know something, I really don't mind being second. It's OK." I had never realized that it was on his mind so much that MGM was going to be bigger than Tahoe. It never even occurred to

me that that would bother him, but all of a sudden, he says, "You know something, it's OK. I've come to terms with it. I don't mind being second."

Bill had a lot of expansion ideas. There were things he wanted to do for the car collection. He had this beautiful museum in mind—he was such a visionary. Bill wanted to have a casino tied in with the car collection, and he wanted to have amusements for kids (which is exactly what's happened in Las Vegas), and he would have been out in front, the very first. Reno would have been bigger than Las Vegas. He was, absolutely, a man ahead of his time from the very beginning of his life to the end. The Auto World was his dream, and they let it go.

Verna and Bill Harrah at the opening of the MGM Hotel-Casino, May 3, 1978. *"When MGM was building that huge casino, Bill got very quiet. It troubled him that MGM was coming in, and he wondered how it would affect the town and how it would affect Harrah's."*

Did you notice any difference between Bill's interest in the club from the time when you first got married and the last year or so of his life?

Yes. He always got his report, he always kept up on that, but he was spending more time away from the club and more time with his family. He knew that he had an aneurism, and he knew that he could go just like that! He had aneurism surgery before he met me, and he knew he had a problem. I had my problem too, so we both went to Mayo Clinic every year.

Just to give you an example of where his mind was at at that time—I was very concerned about the car collection, because I was afraid that when he died it would be sold. I said to him, "Why don't you buy the car collection from Harrah's and turn it into a private foundation?"

And he says, "Because, Verna, it's my hobby. It's not yours. It's not the boys', and I wouldn't do it to either one of you. When I'm dead, I don't care what happens to the collection. It's my hobby." When people would cry and feel so bad about the collection after it was gone, I would try to make them feel better by telling them that story. That's how Bill was.

Did he ever think of donating it to the state or to the city, or did that subject ever come up?

I don't think so, because Bill really didn't leave any money to charity. It just isn't the way he thought. He just felt like the auto collection was his, and when he was gone, "It'll go to somebody. The cars will dissipate, probably, but they'll go to people who love them."

When you and Bill went back to the Mayo Clinic in June of 1978, did either of you have any feelings of how dangerous the operation would be?

Hindsight is always so much clearer. I really didn't think when Bill went in for surgery that there was that much danger, but looking back before that and thinking about how he was reacting to things–taking his little dog and walking the property and looking at everything, and the way he talked and so forth–I can see that he seemed to have a feeling of . . . I don't know whether doom is the right word. He seemed to have some sort of an innate feeling about it, but at the time, I didn't feel that way. As a matter of fact, we talked about going on the river in July. That's something that we did every year–river rafting with the boys. I really didn't sense anything. Now, when I think back, and I think about how Bill was acting, I can see that he, certainly, had a forewarning.

Bill told me that he had made sweeping changes in his will–that he had left the Stanley property to me and a couple of other things. He put the Sun Valley house in both of our names. (He changed that because it was only in his name, and he signed a quit claim and put it in my name as well.) Bill said just in case anything went wrong with the surgery, he wanted to make sure that all the ends were tied up; but I really didn't think that was terribly unusual, because I do that too—every time I go in for surgery, I make sure that my will is exactly the way I want it, so I really didn't think anything of it at the time. I just thought it was something that people do. He told me he was doing that, and he didn't want just Mead Dixon's input. He wanted other people that he had a lot of respect for, so he brought in outside attorneys to look at his will and to go over it when we were in Stanley, right before we went back to Mayo for the surgery.

When you went back to Mayo Clinic, did anyone go with you?

It was just Bill and myself. The next morning, before he went into the surgery, I was there with him when they took him in. When I knew that it wasn't looking good, I called Cindy Wade to fly out to be with me, and she came right out. Cindy and I had a really wonderful relationship during the time that Bill and

I were married. We talked on the phone all the time. She told me everything that was going on in the corporate world. She'd give me all the gossip, because Bill was not a gossip at all. Bill never said anything. I got everything from Cindy–who was getting along with who; who was sleeping with who . . . you know, all of the executive floor gossip. [laughter]

I was really worried, and I just had to have somebody to be with me, so I called Cindy. I knew Bill was going to die, because the doctor was telling me that sewing his blood vessels was like sewing wet tissue. They just kept falling apart, and they gave him blood transfusion after blood transfusion after blood transfusion. Then when we lost Bill, I went into . . . I guess everybody handles things differently. Some people are very stoic, and I'm usually a very stoic person. Under most circumstances, I'm very sort of English–the stiff upper lip and all of that. I was brought up that way, but, for some reason . . . I don't know, I just collapsed.

When Bill died . . . I mean, I just couldn't believe it. Dr. Smith took me to his house and gave me some kind of sedative to calm me down. I was sedated, and I was lying on his sofa talking to them, and I just kept saying over and over again how important it is to always tell the person you love every day that you love them, because you never know. Then the phone rang, and it was Larry Thompson, Jim Nabors's manager. (Bill had told Jim that he was going to Mayo Clinic for surgery, so Larry called to find out how he was doing.) When they said, "You're wanted on the telephone," I went to the phone and just started crying.

Larry was the only person I ever talked to. Later, Mead Dixon spread the rumor that I just started calling everybody and telling them that Bill was dead, which was absolutely not the case. The only other phone call I made was to Cindy Wade, and that was before Bill died.

Cindy was there when Bill died; and then, of course, Mead flew out before Bill died, and Mead was calling his brother, who was a doc-

tor. Mead didn't believe anything Dr. Smith was telling him. Mead was trying to take over everything. He would look at the chart, and he would copy down things from the chart. Then he'd run out and make a phone call to his brother. Then he brought his girlfriend in with him. He had her come, and I was just completely pushed out of the picture.

When Bill died and we flew back–this is a terrible thing to say, but I'm just going to say it because this is how I felt–it was almost like a celebration. Mead sat in the airplane with his girlfriend, and I was sitting there, curled up in the side of the chair. He never talked to me. I was just a mess. I was completely distraught, and they just sat there and drank and laughed and ate, and it was just like a celebration. Champágne. I mean, it was unbelievable. It was unbelievable and so unbelievably rude to me. He never said a kind word. He never showed any remorse.

Were you aware of the fact that he was going to be, according to the will, "Bill Harrah" now that Bill Harrah was dead? [4]

No. I knew nothing; I'd never seen the will. I mean, I knew nothing. I just couldn't believe it. This man I hardly knew. I'd only been on one trip with him–that was when we went to Australia, and he was drunk most of that trip. He came on to all the women, and he was really outrageous on that trip. And now, even on the day of Bill's death, not to be just a little bit kind . . . . It was remarkable.

Well, of course, he did become Bill Harrah as far as controlling the company, so he was the kingpin of the entire operation from that day forward.

Yes, that's right, but at the time I just didn't understand it. I mean, they were literally, the two of them, laughing and eating and drinking. To me, it was just like a celebration. Neither one of them even acknowledged that I was on the plane. It was unbelievable. In my life, I've never, ever been treated like that before or since.

Who called him to come out there? Did Cindy call him?

I certainly didn't call him. And I can't believe Cindy called him. He must have called the hospital and asked for a status report.

And then he spread this rumor all over town, "Verna called everybody–let everybody know that Bill was dying." I never called. I called Cindy Wade. That was it. I didn't even call my family, I was in such a mess.

When you arrived back in Reno, did you have anyone you could lean on and draw strength from?

Just my family, my mom and dad. They came out and stayed with me. And, of course, I had my son. Richard was twelve, and he was so cute. I was such a mess that my girlfriend came over to get Richard to take him to a movie so I could sleep. The doctor had given me some Valium, and I spent a lot of time sleeping, so she took Richard to the movies, and Richard said, "I can't go to the movies."

She said, "Why not?"

He says, "I don't want to ask my mother for any money, because we are now going to be poor." [laughter] It was so sweet.

Were you involved in any of the funeral arrangements?

Well, Scherry Harrah had gone to the funeral home and picked out the casket. She had gone in and said, "I'm Mrs. Harrah, and I'm making all the arrangements for the funeral." They said OK. Then I was called and told what was going on and that I was to come down to the funeral home immediately. I knew that Bill wanted to be buried in Idaho, so I wanted more of a western-looking casket than the one she had chosen. I picked out a different one, and I said I wanted the casket closed, and they wanted it open. I mean, there were a lot of things like that.

Everything I wanted was honored, but then a lot of the family started calling me, telling me that a lot of things that were in the house really belonged to them. Scherry called and said everything really belonged to her: the dishes were hers; the silver was hers. Then Bill Harrah's stepmother would call. She'd say Billy really loved her; was really in love with her.

I'd say, "I know he loved you."

And she says, "Well, you know, I really wasn't left that much money, and he was really in love with me–not just 'loved' me." You know, that sort of thing. [laughter] Oh boy, there was a lot of that stuff going on!

Do you remember the funeral, or were you in a state of shock?

I remember that John Denver sang a beautiful song, and I still have the tape. The song is called "Singing Skies and Dancing Waters," and it was just wonderful. I really don't remember too much about it other than that; and that there were just an awful lot of people that were there, and that they came out to Rancharrah after the funeral.

How was the estate divided?

It was pretty much split between the boys and myself. I think they might have gotten a little more than half, like 55 percent, but it was pretty much right down the middle.

After Bill Harrah died, Mead Dixon became chairman of the board, and evidently the first thing he looked into was the sale of Harrah's. Were you, as a 50 percent owner of Harrah's, consulted?

No, not at all. No. I had the right to the money, but I certainly had no control of the company. That was all given to Mead in the will. He did talk to me about the interest that Holiday Inns had expressed–he hoped that the sale would go through, because he didn't have a lot of confidence that without Bill, Harrah's could be run the way that it was before, and he felt that the estate needed the money to pay taxes, to pay debts, and so forth.

He didn't feel that the management team in place at Harrah's was good enough to run it?

He wasn't that confident, no. That was his opinion, right.

Was there any one quality or trait or combinations of traits that you could say made Bill Harrah such a successful business man?

I think that one thing that most people who are very successful in life have in common is that it is never about money–if it's about money, they can never reach that degree of success. It's really about the game and the love of the game, and Bill had that in spades. He never was concerned about whether he was going to succeed or not . . . fear of money or losing everything. It was just the game and his vision and his integrity. You really have to have that, because people have to trust you.

He wanted people to be treated the way he wanted to be treated himself. He said that over and over and over again, and he wanted people to want to come back because, "Wow. At Harrah's, it's so fantastic. I'd rather stay here than across the street."

I miss him. I miss him more than anything.

After he died, did you stay in Reno?

No, I didn't. That was a very difficult time for me. There was a lot of in-fighting going on at the hotel, and every day I'd get a phone call from Cindy or Bob Hudgens. I don't think anybody really realized what I was going through. Everybody was just concerned about what *they* were going through. [laughter] That's natural and normal, but I was having such a difficult time handling Bill's death. It was just too much, and so I thought the best thing I

could do was to move to Sun Valley. I needed that time to heal, so I took my son and moved to Sun Valley. Bill had bought me a home there the year before. It was a beautiful, beautiful home, and I just considered that place to be a healing place, and I wanted to get away from everything in Reno, so I packed everything up, and we drove to Sun Valley.

Why did you pick Sun Valley instead of Stanley?

I didn't want Richard to go to school in Stanley. I wanted him to have a really good education. Sun Valley had a private school, Sun Valley Community School, and it was an excellent school.

I never went back to Reno to live. I would go back for a day or two for business; a couple of times I would go to a dinner show or something, but very rarely, and I still don't go to Reno often.

How long have you lived in southern California?

About ten years. I'm a movie producer. I started about five years ago, never knowing exactly where it would take me or whether I'd be successful. I decided that I would put a certain amount of money that Bill would feel, "OK, this is risk money, and if I lose it all, that's fine. This is the amount, and I'll take it to the table, and if I lose, I go home, right?" I went in to it with that in mind. I don't finance any production; I just finance development, and we're just doing so well, I just can't believe it.

Well, I know recently you produced Anaconda, *which was a top money maker.*

Yes. It was my first movie, and we just did great business. We are well past the hundred million dollar mark. They took out a big ad for us in *Variety* a few weeks ago, so it's very exciting. [laughter] Our second movie's going to be with Universal. It has Penny Marshall directing. We have a big name, hopefully, that will star in that, and then the one after that will be with Warner Brothers. It's a big action adventure, and then there's one at Paramount. It's a political thriller that is just beginning. Then Columbia wants to do *Anaconda II.*

The only way to really make money as a producer in this business is to own the negative, so I have plans to make three movies where I will sell off the domestic rights to one of the studios and then sell off the foreign rights and do gap financing. That way I can retain the negative. I still won't be putting up any of my own money, but it's just another way of holding on to more of the distribution rights. It's a little more difficult to get it set up, but it's well worth it.

Who, ordinarily, gets negatives?

The studios, and they will retain the domestic rights. They will have the negative for the first showing, but then I will be able to retain the negative, and years down the line, the rights to television and so forth will be important.

The name of our company has been changed to Middle Fork Productions, in honor of Bill. Obviously, I could never have done any of this without him, and Middle Fork is where we were married. When I mentioned to my staff that I wanted to name the company Middle Fork Productions in honor of Bill, they were all absolutely thrilled with the idea. I had been kind of nervous about bringing it up, because I thought they'd say, "Oh, that's a terrible name," but, they loved it. This summer I took them all to Idaho, and we took a river rafting trip. We went in at a little place about an hour from Stanley, and then we ended up in Middle Fork Lodge and spent the night there. The next morning we flew to Sun Valley and then back to Los Angeles. It was an amazing trip. The fellow that took us on the trip was a little bit nervous about all these Hollywood types. He was afraid that they wouldn't be able to handle the river, but we all became close friends. It was a little differ-

ent than the way Bill and I used to do it, where we would go on those big, huge, massive boats. We were on little floaters, and we actually did a lot of the rowing ourselves, and it was a bit different. We put up our own tents, and everybody loved it.

The thing that always amazed me the most about Bill was that nothing was impossible. Often airplanes couldn't land in Tahoe because of weather, so Bill always wanted the stars to be transported up there from Reno in a limousine. Sometimes the roads were very bad, especially in the winter, and the limousine would slide all over. It would be better to have a Jeep four-wheel drive, so he built a Jeep limousine—he built a Jeep, and he stretched it out. It was the funniest looking thing you ever saw, but it was a four-wheel drive Jeep limousine, and it even looked like a Jeep.

Nothing was ever impossible for Bill. I think that's the thing that I admired about him so much. We'd talk about things like, "Oh god, wouldn't it be wonderful if" this or that, and it was never impossible. There was always a way. We just talked about *how* we were going to do it. Not *whether* or not we could do it. He was an amazing man and so much fun.

Notes

1. John and Tony are Mr. Harrah's two adopted sons. Richard is Verna Harrah's son from a prior marriage.

2. Art Smith was president and CEO of the First National Bank of Nevada (now Wells Fargo Bank) for many years. His oral history was published by the UNOHP in 1996 with the title *Let's Get Going.*

3. Mrs. Harrah's enthusiasm for her husband's efforts is commendable. Bill Harrah did, indeed, have remarkable success at the nation's most prestigious competition for classic cars. The National Automobile Museum's records indicate that he entered twelve cars between 1962 and 1978, taking "best of show" four times.

4. Bill Harrah had named Mead Dixon the executor of his estate, which was made up almost entirely of stock in Harrah's. As executor, Dixon controlled the stock, and shortly after Harrah's death he met with the board of directors to ask that they elect him chairman of the board. They did, thus making him the most powerful person in the company.

15

HOLMES HENDRICKSEN

*H*OLMES HENDRICKSEN was born on April 23, 1933, in Holyoke, Colorado. His family moved to Gooding, Idaho, when he was less than a year old, and he grew up there. Hendricksen first worked at Harrah's Lake Tahoe in the summer of 1956 when he was attending college, and he returned the next summer, never to leave the Harrah's organization. He started as a busboy and then transferred to the cashier's cage, was promoted to supervisor, rose to club manager, and eventually was named a vice-president. He worked for Harrah's for thirty years and spent a great deal of time with Bill Harrah over those years.

For this oral history, Mr. Hendricksen was interviewed in the offices of the William F. Harrah Trust in March of 1997. He was an especially enlightening and informative chronicler, and his interview required two sessions. It gives us an in-depth look at Bill Harrah and Harrah's entertainment department and entertainment policies, including information about many of the headline entertainers who appeared at Harrah's and details about how they were selected and the salaries they were paid. Hendricksen tells us why casinos will never again have the type of entertainment policy that was in effect at Harrah's from the 1960s through the early 1980s.

The daily report that was such an integral part of the Harrah's operation is also described and analyzed, and personal anecdotes about Harrah are told, many of them revolving around his need for perfection in every facet of the operation.

HOLMES HENDRICKSEN: I was born in Holyoke, Colorado, April 22, 1933. I lived there for just a year, and then we moved to Burley, Idaho, lived there for a year, and then moved to Gooding, Idaho, which was really where I was raised and where my parents made their home until they passed away.

My dad ran a small men's clothing store in Gooding for many years. He later sold that and ran a couple of car washes in Twin Falls, Idaho. My mother worked in the businesses as a bookkeeper-accountant. They were very small, family-owned businesses with only three or four employees.

I had one brother and one sister. My sister died seventeen years ago from asthma, and I have a brother that's two years younger than me that lives in Texas. I'm married, and we have one son who is seventeen and is a junior at Galena High School.

DWAYNE KLING: What year did you start work for Harrah's, and how did you happen to apply there?

I was in graduate school at the University of Utah, working on a master's degree in physical education. I had a fraternity brother whose mother and father worked at Harrah's at Lake Tahoe. (Their names were Hal and Beaulah White.) I was looking for a summer job, and [my buddy called his parents] about a job for me. They said, "If he will come to Tahoe, we'll get him a job in the cashier's office."

At the end of winter quarter at Utah, which was in late March, I quit school and came to Lake Tahoe, thinking I had a job in the cashier's office. When I arrived there was no job, mainly because there was no business. However, Mrs. White ran the coffee shop, and she was able to give me a job as a busboy. I worked as a busboy for about six weeks, and then Pat Francellini gave me a job in the cashier's office. This was April of 1956.

I worked through the spring and summer in the cashier's office, and then right after Labor Day returned to Salt Lake to continue my schooling. I went two more quarters at Utah, working on a master's, and then quit again at the end of the winter quarter to return to Tahoe in April of 1957. I went to work back in the cashier's office and stayed at Harrah's for thirty-eight years.

How many years were you a cashier?

After six years I became a shift supervisor, and then I became the credit manager. I was the credit manager for about three or four years, and then I went into the pit for a short time–about a year and a half. When I was in the pit, I was a shift manager for a while. Then in 1964, I became assistant manager of Harrah's Tahoe when Curly Musso was the manager. I was assistant manager for about two and a half years, and when Curly retired I took Curly's job as the general manager; had that for four years. Then in 1971 I moved to Reno and was put in charge of entertainment.

To go back to Harrah's in the 1950s and 1960s, do you recall the type of person that worked in the casino business in that era?

Well, the one thing that everybody did was work their tails off. Everybody knew that from the middle of May until Labor Day, you were going to work seven days a week. There weren't any days off, and an eight-hour shift was a luxury; plus you worked ten or twelve hours most of the time, and sometimes you pulled double shifts. If you only worked eight hours, that was great. [laughter] There was no overtime, as far as pay goes. It was all straight time. Time-and-a-half was unknown. Everybody got paid for when they worked, but that was all.

It wasn't unusual during those summer months to work three or four months without a day off. That was the norm rather than the exception, for every department. We would try and schedule the women for a day off, but the guys would all work seven days. The reason was the influx of business was so great in the summer compared to what it was in the winter that you really didn't have the luxury of putting on all these extra people for a short period of time. By the time you got them trained, the summer was over.

In 1957, Harrah's at the lake expanded from its original location, the old George's Gateway Club (which was known as the Lake Club), across the highway to the old Sahati's Stateline Country Club. Harrah's purchased that, then purchased the Nevada Club and the Tahoe Plaza. In 1959, when the east side of Highway 50 became our main location, the Lake Club became a problem. The east side was our main operation twenty-four hours a day, twelve months out of the year, and the Lake Club became a part-time operation (weekends, summers), and then eventually it was sold to Harvey's.

Were the weekdays in the winters of the late 1950s and early 1960s very busy?

Very, very quiet. [laughter] Anybody that headed up a department became a master scheduler. By that I mean we did everything we could to not lay off people. Everybody got their working hours cut back, but everybody worked weekends; and through the fall and winter and the early spring months you hoped that you didn't get snowed out on the weekends, so you could work everybody for three shifts on Friday, Saturday, and Sunday, and then they could get by during the week. We had lots of married couples working for us, and we would go to the couples and say to the wife, "If you would only work Saturday night for us, then we'll guarantee your husband five days a week." We made every effort not to lay off people, but we really cut people back on their hours and their shifts.

We had a policy of sending people home, which was very difficult, but every department did it. Sometimes you would send people home after two hours, and sometimes you

would send them home after four hours or six hours, and you'd even send them home after seven hours so you didn't have to pay them for the eighth hour. We would send people home during the week, sometimes every day, which would be very discouraging. Then we'd turn right around on Fridays and Saturdays and ask them to work overtime, because that's the only time we did any business. The attitude of the employees was outstanding. People didn't like it; people had financial struggles because of it, but that was just the nature of the business.

Even though we didn't have much business, we had more business than anybody else at Lake Tahoe. Then in December of 1959 we opened the new South Shore Room and started a policy of continuous shows. That helped our business considerably. Also by then we had our bus programs going, and between the bus programs and the show promotions . . . we did a lot of promotions that would encourage people to go to the second shows for half-price or two-for-one packages or "Invite a Friend" or whatever. We had all kinds of names for them, but they were all giveaways on the second shows, Sunday through Thursday. After a couple of years, those programs really got going, and it wasn't unusual for us to have eight or nine hundred or even a thousand people for a second show on a Monday, Tuesday, Wednesday, or Thursday night—maybe 70 percent of them were freebies, but we got bodies in the shows. We would have maybe 450 in the dinner show and 900 in the second show.

Do you recall any of the people that worked in the pit during the 1950s and 1960s?

Yes, we had some great old-timers: Ovlan Fritz, Sharkey Begovich, Lou Latasa, Al Childers, Chet Edwards. [Most came to us from other casinos]—very few had transferred up from Harrah's in Reno. Buddy Howland had worked for Harrah's in Reno; also Ken

South Shore Room

An image of the South Shore Room at Lake Tahoe, from a Harrah's photograph folder.

Watkins, Andy Marcinko, and Lee DeLauer. Lee was in public relations and advertising. A couple more were Joe Kowalchuk and Bill Leary. Bill's wife, Lorraine, worked in the cashier's office.

Harrah's Club had a lot of men and wives working together, and this was unique in the gaming industry at that time. Many casinos were afraid that there was going to be collusion between the husband and the wife. Harrah's had no problem with that?

No. However, an effort was made not to have them work the same shifts. Couples like Buddy and Bev Howland and Kenny and Ivine Watkins did not work the same hours.

Part of it, too, was that to ask somebody to move to Lake Tahoe at that time was difficult.

Housing was extremely difficult in those days. We created a huge problem–"we" being Harrah's–in that we insisted that everybody live on the Nevada side to give us a voting base in Douglas County. But there was practically no housing on the Nevada side–everybody was living in California, because that's the only place there was housing. Eventually we almost forced people and just put pressure on them to move, especially if they were supervisors or in management. It wasn't a situation of, "You move or you lose your job," but it was real close. There were plenty of threats! [laughter]

⋄

In the 1950s and 1960s, you really didn't think about hours; you just worked. And if you became a supervisor at even the first level, then that automatically took you out of hours. In other words, that never was a consideration; you just worked.

Every department manager and assistant department manager, or whatever their title was, checked in with the switchboard operator when you hit the hotel or the casino to let her know you were there. When you left to go home, you told her you were on your way home. The operators had everybody's home phone number, and there were never any qualms about calling somebody at home at any time of the day or night. It didn't matter whether it was ten o'clock at night or one o'clock in the morning or seven o'clock in the morning, you called people. You called them to come in to work or for whatever situation needed their evaluation. It was mandatory that you have a home phone, which was difficult to get at Tahoe then.

⋄

During the years that I was general manager at Lake Tahoe (1967-1971), we had an entertainment committee. The entertainment committee was made up of the general manager from Reno and myself, Mr. Harrah, Bob Ring, Rome Andreotti, Mark Curtis, and Shep. Also, the vice-president of entertainment, Pat France, and the entertainment director, Dick Lane. That was our entertainment committee.

Basically, the entertainment committee worked this way: The director of entertainment and the vice-president of entertainment would do all the homework. They would find out who was available; they would find out what the prices were. It was their job to go out and see who's hot and who's cold and who's on the rise and who might do business; who had just played Vegas, who had done well or done badly and whatever—then bring that information back to the committee and make

a recommendation to the committee as to who they would buy.

Bill Harrah felt very strongly that it was his obligation to see all the openings for all the shows. If he was in town, he would catch every opening. In those days we opened a show every two or three weeks, and many times I would get a phone call from Reno asking if I would have dinner with Mr. Harrah that night, since he was coming up to see the show and didn't have anybody to have dinner with. (I was the only unmarried member of management at that time, and Mr. Harrah was going through a series of divorces.)

Over a period of two or three years, I sat through numerous dinners with Bill, and sometimes I would go to Reno to attend a Reno opening with him. If I got a phone call, and they said, "Would you come down to Reno and see the opening down here?" the answer was obviously yes. It wasn't, "I really don't want to go to Reno, and I don't care about that show." It was, "Yes. Oh, certainly! I'd be happy to!" [laughter] I think that probably played a part in my selection as the vice-president of entertainment in 1971.

They had decided to make a change. Pat France had been the vice-president of entertainment, and just out of the blue they asked me to take over entertainment, which I agreed to do, although I didn't want to at all. We had just received our approval to build a hotel at Tahoe. We had done extremely well up there for the last few years with no rooms at all, and I was really looking forward to having a hotel to work with. My personal preference was to live and work at Tahoe, and I really didn't want to move to Reno. I also didn't want to get in the entertainment business, because what little exposure I'd had to it was mostly bad. I knew that you were dealing with a bunch of people that were difficult to deal with. I knew that there wasn't much loyalty in the entertainment department or entertainment industry.

I didn't know anything about entertainment, and I really didn't want to move to Reno, but I agreed. I said, "OK, I will do it," but I made myself a promise that I would do it for just one year, and, assuming I still didn't like it and didn't want to do it, that I would ask management if I could go back to Tahoe. I knew that I wouldn't be able to go back in my same job, as they obviously would have another general manager up there, so I just decided, "I'll take any job they give me up there." But I never had enough nerve to make that demand, and as time went on, I gradually began to like the entertainment business. I learned it, and I learned it probably from three people: I learned it from Dick Lane, who was the entertainment director. And then Dick left, and Doug Bushousen became the entertainment director, and I learned it from Doug. And I learned it from my secretary, Judy Starley. She had been secretary to Pat France for several years and was quite knowledgeable. So with the help of Dick and Doug and Judy, I learned the business after a few years.

Somewhere along the line—I really don't know whether this was Bill or Bob Ring or Rome or whomever, or collectively—but somebody making the decisions decided that if you were a manager, if you could handle people, you could *learn* whatever you had to learn in order to handle another department. When I came down to take over entertainment, not only did I not know anything about entertainment, but I also took over public relations and advertising. That was all being headed up by Mark Curtis. Mark was a brilliant manager and a brilliant idea man in advertising, public relations, and things in that field. I knew absolutely nothing and learned a tremendous amount from Mark over the years. Even though he reported to me, he was the one that was doing all the teaching. I'm not sure how it developed, but Harrah's wasn't hesitant about putting people in areas where they had no expertise. They had confidence in the people themselves, and it proved out in a large majority of cases.

✧

We used to keep track of all of our competition—we used to do hourly head-counts in the casinos of our competitors. Also, we saw almost every show that came to the entire state . . . well, almost the entire state. We didn't run off to Elko, and we didn't run off to Battle Mountain if they had a new lounge act that we had never heard of. [laughter] But any of the major stuff, either in the lounges or in the big rooms in Vegas, we made a point to go see it. If we were to talk about anything appearing in Vegas, we knew what we were talking about—we had seen the show. We didn't always get right down there when a new show opened, but we would see it before it closed.

We had our own policy: you didn't buy anything that you hadn't seen. Even today, most people don't do that—which, to me, is quite dumb. We didn't buy anything we didn't see. I used to tell our people the best dollars that we can spend are the ones we spend when we go out and look at acts, because 80 percent of the stuff you see is bad, or it doesn't fit us, or we wouldn't be interested. It's just as big a plus to see it and know that you don't want it as it would be to see something that's really great.

Doug or myself or Dick Lane, depending on who was there at that time, would go see the acts. Then we would have an entertainment meeting, and the meetings were probably once a month or maybe once every six weeks or maybe every two weeks if there were a lot of decisions to be made. We might even have two meetings in three weeks, and then not have a meeting for a month. There was no set schedule.

Did Bill Harrah go to most of the meetings or all of them?

Yes. Absolutely. Bill thought entertainment was very important to our success and very important to our image. It would be my judgment (or Doug or Dick's—whoever the entertainment director was) when we had enough things to talk about, to have a meeting. First thing we would do was check to see if Bill was in town, and then we'd pick, for example, Thursday. Then we would see if everybody was available. If they were, we would call a meeting. (Sometimes we'd have them at Tahoe; sometimes we would have them in Reno.) Then we would prepare the agenda. The agenda was sent out far enough ahead of time so that everybody would have a chance to read it and think about it, and then we would have our meeting.

(Meetings would last generally less than an hour. Bill had a thing about meetings going over an hour–he didn't like meetings to last more than one hour. Once in a great while we'd have a long agenda that might take more than an hour, and then we would run that by Bill to let him know that this may take more than an hour, to warn him. Otherwise, he would get up at the end of sixty minutes and leave.) [laughter]

In the meeting, we would lay out all of what I call our homework. We saw so-and-so, and we saw so-and-so, and we saw so-and-so. So-and-so did this, and so-and-so did that. Business was good. This is the kind of customer that I saw in the showroom. So on and so forth. The material is dirty; we don't want them. Or maybe we can get them to drop this material, or so on, and we'd go through all that. Then we would answer the questions from the committee. We'd tell them what the price was; had to be within our budget. And then we would make a recommendation to the committee: "This is who we think we should buy." And the committee would either approve it or not. Probably 90 percent of the time they just went ahead with our recommendation.

Did Bill Harrah have input as far as asking questions about the show?

Yes, but not a lot. Bill listened a lot and said very little, but he would raise questions.

Over a period of years there were many repeaters. Lawrence Welk, of course, came every summer for several years, and a lot people, like Jack Benny, used to come annually. Why did they come back so often?

Everybody made a mystery out of that, and there was no mystery. If somebody did good business, we brought them back. (Sammy Davis Jr. worked for us for twenty-eight years. He appeared hundreds of times. Sammy did more shows for us than any other single artist, I'm sure.) And if they didn't do good business, we didn't bring them back. If it was a borderline situation, then we would try and take into account the time of year that they played.

An act had a much bigger problem with drawing a crowd in February than it did in the middle of August. In the middle of August, everybody's successful. We would say, "We played this guy three times now, but we've never given him a summer date. Maybe we ought to give him a summer date so he really has a chance." Also, we would monitor what was happening in their careers: Did they have a new show on television? Do they have a new album out or television show appearance, or are they going to do a movie? Was their career going up or down? That was our job to find out.

Did you monitor only the body count in the show, or did you monitor in some way the receipts or the gross gaming revenue?

Oh, we monitored that, but mostly it was very unsophisticated. In other words, we'd ask the general manager, "How was the business when Sammy Davis was here? Was the pit business good or bad?" Welk was a great example. Welk drew a lot of people, but they weren't big gamblers. There was probably some slot play from these people, but it was a show that fit our image. We were the only casino he played, and we got a lot of plugs from him on his television show. We did finally have to drop Lawrence when the business finally fell off to where his customers were so old the second shows weren't filling up. [laughter]

He's the one person I remember who had the longest lines into the showroom.

Yes, because the people would all come early for a "good seat."

We were going to drop Lawrence the same year Mr. Harrah died. We decided to keep him one more year, just because Bill had passed away and we didn't want to dump him. So we brought him back. We literally brought him back one year more than we had planned to do because of the timing of Mr. Harrah's death.

Bill respected every one of the entertainers. He respected them because of their talent and their drawing power and the fact that they could put people in seats, and because of whatever they did on stage. Bill used to just be in awe of what they could do. Bill wasn't comfortable up in front of people, wasn't really a good speaker; he was well aware of that, and he knew he couldn't get up and do that. He was just amazed that people could get up and entertain people. He had a tremendous amount of respect for Bill Cosby, Sammy Davis, Jim Nabors, Don Rickles, Liza Minelli . . . and I'm leaving out people, but those were favorites of his. Also, Mr. Welk was a big favorite. Danny Thomas and Bill were good friends. Bill wasn't really close to any of them, but those were some of his favorites.

Bill attended every opening that he could when he was in Reno and Tahoe. He really felt it was his job, and he *always* went back to talk to the entertainers and thank them for being there. It didn't matter who it was, the routine was the same. With entertainers that he knew, it was a much more comfortable situation. For him to go down and visit with Sammy was not a big deal–Sammy looked forward to it, and Bill looked forward to it, and they got along fine.

For Bill to go and visit with an entertainer that he really didn't know, that was something that I orchestrated. That was my job. I always attended, and I always filled Bill in on whatever information I had to make him more comfortable. He wanted to know as much as he could about the artist, so he'd be comfortable talking to him. He didn't want to be embarrassed about anything, and he didn't want to be asked a question that he wasn't prepared for. These visits were very short (ten, twelve, fifteen minutes), and if things weren't going very well, which many times they weren't, then I would look at my watch and say, "Bill, you know, we've got to get going. We've got something else we have to do."

After a show many entertainers are drenched in sweat, and they have to get out of their clothes and take a shower. Some of them are just out of breath or kind of excited or coming down a little bit; but we always alerted the artist that Mr. Harrah was coming down, and if the artist needed to shower and change and needed fifteen minutes or twenty minutes, then Bill understood that. Each one of them was different. Part of my job was to know if we were going to walk right in after the show and the artist was going to be waiting for Bill, or if he was going to be in the other half of the dressing room trying to cool off.

Do you have some entertainers that were your favorites?

I always felt that I didn't have the prerogative to have a favorite. That wasn't my job. If I had a favorite, then I really wasn't doing my job. Obviously, you have people that you get along with better than other people, and you have people that you're comfortable with and people you're uncomfortable with. But that's in any line of work. So . . . I will leave that at that. [laughter]

Were there ever any entertainers that you tried to get and you couldn't?

Oh, yes. There were many acts that *didn't* fit our budget, or we were outbid by other casinos. We had a very generous budget for both our properties, Reno and Tahoe–certainly very competitive with what everybody else in the area was paying; however, many times not as much as they were paying in Las Vegas. So if there was an act down there that we couldn't get because of money, then we just couldn't get them; that's all. But our assignment–"our" being me and the entertainment director–our assignment was to get the best, biggest name that was available at all times. Every time we went to fill a spot, we were to fill it with the biggest name we could get, but that had to be within budget. The budget changed as time went on, just as all things change, but we were always competitive; and because of relationships that we developed with many of the artists, and because of the way Mr. Harrah treated them, we were able to buy acts for less than what they were getting in Vegas.

Some acts would work for us for less money than they might get at Caesar's or the Sahara or someplace else in Vegas, mainly because we had several perks. We had two jet aircraft, and it was our policy to fly the entertainer to and from the engagement if they wanted it. We also had great company cars they could use. We had two Rolls-Royces in each location and a backup third car, a Cadillac, available for them. We had a house at each location plus a suite in the hotel for them. We also had a domestic staff to cook for them and take care of them. It was part of my job, and the people that worked for me, to do our homework on these artists. We had to know what they smoked and what they drank and what they ate and what they didn't eat. We knew all about their families; we knew when their birthdays were, and we knew what their wedding anniversaries were, and we remembered those things.

If an artist was going to work for us in June, and we found out that they're here and they're going to have a birthday, then we did something about it–made sure we had a birthday gift for them or something. If the guy's wife had a birthday during that time, and she was going to be here, we made sure we remembered that. If they had a special event in their family–if there was a bar mitzvah or a wedding or a funeral or whatever–then I was there, assuming that I was invited. Most of the time I was, so I went to a lot of functions in Los Angeles or wherever. We showed up out of respect. If it was a funeral, we showed up out of respect; if it was a bar mitzvah, we showed up because we had a nice gift for the young boy. If it was a wedding, then we showed up with a very nice gift for the wedding. And if it was a divorce, why, whatever, you know! [laughter]

The person that usually showed up was you?

Almost always. Yes, a big part of my job was to attend functions. Most of them were in Los Angeles because most of them lived there. You attended a lot of charity dinners, you bought a lot of tables for charities, and you took ads in programs congratulating people on this and that. If we had an artist that won a Grammy, we would take an ad in the *Daily Variety* and *Hollywood Reporter*, congratulating Glen Campbell on winning a Grammy (or something like that) from all your friends at Harrah's. And those were the kinds of things that developed the relationships. The artists were extremely loyal to Bill, and it was our job to make Bill look really good.

Were all those things you've mentioned unique to Harrah's?

They were unique in that we did more of it than anybody else. Other casinos did the same thing. Probably the second casino that did a lot of that was Caesar's, but I would say we were probably a little more thorough, a little more detailed, and we did more of it . . . which meant we spent more money on it.

Did you give every entertainer a gift at the end of their engagement?

No, and a lot of people thought we did. There was no policy. We gave gifts from time to time, but there was always a special reason—maybe a birthday, maybe an anniversary, maybe ten years working for Harrah's, or maybe they had done a benefit or an appearance for us.

Yes, we gave a lot of gifts, but that was probably exaggerated. I mean, the public thought that Bill was just lavishing gifts on these people all the time, which wasn't true at all. We did give cars to Wayne Newton, Bill Cosby, Sammy, and Rickles and some other people, but there was always a reason for it–a specific event or a milestone. There were other gifts, but it wasn't like every time somebody closed, they got a gift from us. That wasn't the case.

The thing that made my job easy was that I had the authority to do all of this. Bill didn't have to approve it. The way you worked with Bill is you told him what you were going to do, then he'd tell you whether he liked it or not. You didn't ask Bill for an OK. You just went ahead and did it and let him know about it.

One of the first things that happened when I got the job as vice-president of entertainment was I went in and I made a huge mistake. I had a question–and I don't recall the question–but I asked Bill what he wanted to do. Bill very seldom ever got upset, never used profanity; but he got a little bit upset, and he said, "You are running entertainment. You tell me what you're going to do." That was my job: to read *Bill* well enough to *know* what he wanted to do! [laughter]

I remember once when we played Roger Whittaker here in Reno . . . Roger did great business for us. I had taken Roger out to play golf, and there's a particular set of golf clubs that he'd been trying to get–hadn't been able to find one. So we were able to get it for him and gave it to him as a gift. It wasn't a big item;

it wasn't a big deal, but he was just absolutely thrilled with the set of golf clubs that we gave him. When I told Bill about it, and this is after the fact and everything, Bill just lit up and thought that was just wonderful that we would do something like that. Bill never asked, "What does it cost?" or anything like that. He really equated the value to the company, because it created a relationship.

Were there any stars that he could not get along with that he kept bringing back?

Oh, yes. We never once did *not* play somebody because Bill liked him or didn't like him. We bought many acts that Bill didn't really like. I used to kid Bill. I'd say, "Well, Bill, you don't have to go see him."

And he'd kind of laugh, and he'd say, "Yes, but you know I will."

It was always a business decision: Are they good for the casino? Will they do business? Will our customers like them? And believe me, Bill really wasn't a big fan of country music. He was from the old school: stars should wear a tuxedo. The acts that he really related to were Sinatra and Tony Bennett and Dean Martin and everybody that wore a tuxedo. He thought that was the way you performed in a nightclub. When we started playing country acts, and the country acts dressed the way they did and do now, that was tough for Bill to accept. But there wasn't any problem. He said, "If they do business and our customers want to see them, that's what we should do."

I remember Willie Nelson's first show. We had been pursuing Willie for probably a year. I had seen him in Nashville a couple years prior to that and kind of kept track of him, and I had seen him in concert, and he was just getting hotter and hotter. Finally, Joe Francis, the general manager at Lake Tahoe, and I went to Indianapolis to see Willie in concert at the Market Square Arena—maybe twelve, thirteen thousand people just all going crazy. I wanted Joe to see what he was going to be getting at Lake Tahoe.

Then I went to Bill. Bill knew who Willie was, but I took in about three albums to show Bill how Willie dressed and how his band dressed. Bill was really from the old school, where he thought everybody ought to wear a tuxedo and certainly a coat and tie. I explained to Bill that Willie didn't dress that way, that the way he dressed was the way he was pictured, that his band looked that way or worse, [laughter] that we couldn't change it, that we couldn't ask him to dress up, and that was it. Bill agreed; he understood, so we finally made a deal.

On Willie's opening night Bill was there . . . . First of all, the show didn't start on time, which was really a problem with us, because we started everything right on the second. When the show finally started about ten, twelve minutes late, the place just exploded. People were dancing and trying to stand on the chairs, everybody was on their feet, and about 20 percent of the audience were wearing cowboy hats. (That was another thing that bothered Mr. Harrah. He thought anytime you were inside you should take your hat off. In fact, we had a policy of that for many years in our restaurants–hostesses had to ask the guys to take their hats off.) Then about halfway through the show, Willie's mother, who had come up for the opening, just kind of drug a chair out from backstage, sat off in the corner watching the show–on stage. Quite visible to the audience. I just about died. I thought, "Oh, my God, Bill's going to just hate this."

When the show was all over, people were screaming and hollering, and I was waiting for Bill's comments. As was our procedure, I went up and sat with him for a minute or two after the show was over until the room started to empty out, and then I would take him downstairs to the dressing room area and introduce him to the star. I'm sitting there with Bill, and I asked him what he thought of the show. He said, "The guy can really sing, can't he? And the people love him."

I said, "Yes," and that's all he said. [laughter] We went downstairs, I introduced him to Willie, and nothing was ever said. Later on, I worked out the problems with Willie on where his mother could sit and his being on time. [laughter] Everything worked out great. Willie was a joy to have around, and the business was phenomenal. We were the first casino he'd ever played. We had a long-time relationship until Holiday Inns just decided that they did not want to spend that kind of money, and Caesar's offered Willie more money than what we were paying, and he went over to Caesar's.

❖

I don't recall the year, but we had an opportunity to bring out the Rockettes from Radio City Music Hall to do a production show, and the show would play for six weeks. It was in the wintertime; I think the show opened late January and probably finished February or early March.

We began to negotiate the deal, but one of our problems was that there were thirty-six Rockettes on stage at Radio City Music Hall, and our stage wasn't big enough to accommodate them. We had to cut them down from thirty-six to twenty-four. This really bothered Bill; he said, "Everybody knows that there are thirty-six Rockettes." Well, everybody *doesn't* know, but Bill certainly knew. We finally convinced him that twenty-four girls on our stage, because of the size of the stage, would look like lots and lots of people–it would certainly fill up the stage, and our customers wouldn't be disappointed.

It was very costly to bring out this many people, because you not only brought the twenty-four girls, but you brought a whole production team, also. There were boy dancers, there were lighting people, choreographers, a big group of costume people, and everything needed to do the whole show. The Radio City people asked us if we wanted to bring any backup dancers in case a girl got sick or got hurt or something like that. They assured us that they had lots of girls sitting back in New York that they had costumes for that knew all the routines, and that a phone call to a girl in New York would get her out there the next day. All she had to do was get on a plane and fly to Lake Tahoe, and she was ready to go right in the show. They really didn't feel that it was necessary to have any backup girls. Doug Bushousen and I made the decision, "OK, we don't do it then. We'll see if we can save some dollars."

Anytime we opened a production show, if we felt the show wasn't really as sharp as it was going to be after a couple of performances, I would go to Bill and say to him, "Bill, I really don't want you to see this show opening night. Why don't you wait a couple of days, give the kids a chance to get settled in and to get comfortable?" And he would always agree. So I asked him to wait a few days to see the Rockettes.

He says, "OK, but tell me when I can see the show."

Then a couple of the girls got sick with the flu, and all of a sudden we were on the phone trying to get the replacements out of New York. The timing was . . . they had one of those huge east coast blizzards that closed all the airports in New York–Kennedy was closed, La Guardia was closed, and Newark was closed for about two days. The girls couldn't get out of the east coast to get back here, and we had about three girls missing.

Bill decided after about three days he wanted to see the show, so he came in. The very first thing he did was count one, two, three, four, five. [laughter] There wasn't twenty-four, and after the show we heard about it. Traditionally, the day after Bill had seen a show, I would go in and see him in his office to get his comments. His comment on the Rockettes was, "Why don't we have twenty-four?" [laughter] And I explained. Bill very seldom lost his temper, but he was *very* upset.

The worst thing you could tell Bill was, "Well, we tried to save a couple of bucks," so I got myself in a lot of trouble with him. We finally got girls out there. We not only brought out the replacements, I think we brought five additional girls that we paid the entire time, standby, just in case anybody got hurt or got sick. Bill's comment to me, and I'd heard this before, was, "I don't lie to my customers. If we tell them we're going to have twenty-four Rockettes, then I expect to have twenty-four Rockettes. Twenty-two or twenty-three isn't twenty-four." And he was very upset about it. He didn't talk to me for two or three weeks–I would have daily things for Bill, and I would take them in to Bob Hudgens, his assistant, and Bob would get Bill's comments for me, but Bill wouldn't see me.

Everybody thought I was going to get fired. I mean I was . . . like the guy with leprosy around there. [laughter] Everybody said, "Boy, Holmes is really in a lot of trouble with the boss!"

About two or three weeks after the incident, I went in with my list of things for Bob Hudgens. Bob just looked at me like I was nuts and said, "Well, why don't you go ask Bill? What are you talking to me for?" [laughter]

So I said, "Fine."

I went in to see Bill, and everything was just normal. "Hi, how are you?"

"I'm fine." Like boom, boom, boom–never mentioned it again.

Were there ever any acts that Harrah's was forced to terminate, either because of conflicts or because the entertainers weren't drawing anybody? Did they ever just close anybody off?

Yes, we had a couple over the years that, because of their behavior or their material, we had to terminate. We just paid them off. Our policy was if we had to fire them, we would, but we paid them in full . . . . Very few over the years, considering the number of acts that we worked and the number of shows. I'm not saying who they were! [laughter]

Harrah's was well known for its star quality, and for the fact that Bill was so tough on nudity, bad language, and "blue" material. Was there ever anybody that refused to tone down their act? Or were there people that you didn't even present, because you knew that their material was objectional?

There were people that we would ask to take out certain portions of the show or lines in their performance, and if we had problems with them, we just didn't bring them back. There were also people that we never bought because of the kind of material that they did. We had a policy called "No Blue Material." There used to be a sign in the dressing-room areas in both facilities that said entertainers couldn't do any material that couldn't be done on television–no blue material. That eventually changed, and Bill was the one that changed it.

For many years we had small production shows in our lounges, and then we went to nude shows on the second show in the lounges, and Bill was the one that suggested a policy change. He said, "Times change." He said, "What's wrong with doing it as long as you tell people what you're going to do? It's an adult situation–you obviously don't let anybody in that aren't adults. They've been doing it in Vegas for years, and there's nothing wrong with it as long as it's in good taste."

I remember the meeting that Bill suggested we think about that. There were about seven of us sitting around the table with startled looks on our face, because none of us would have had nerve enough to suggest it. But Bill was the one that suggested it. "What's wrong with it?"

Well, the customers were aware of the show's content. They had a choice.

Yes, that was Bill's thinking. The room is going to be totally closed off. You're not going to offend anybody. You're going to tell people what kind of a show it is, so they make the decision whether they want to see it or not. He says, "What's wrong with it?" And he said, "We can have standards. We can still monitor what they do. We don't want any simulated sex acts or anything like that."

Over the years we softened our approach on the material, too, because times change. I mean, television changed–look what they're doing on television now as to what they did twenty-five years ago. Bill's response was, "What's wrong with changing?" He always said he'd like to be the first guy on the block to change, not the last guy. And in most cases he was–not just in entertainment, but in everything.

Who was the highest paid entertainer that ever appeared at Harrah's?

We didn't have a highest-paid entertainer, because we had a top-of-the-room that we paid many, many people. We had a flat number; that was our top, and we never paid anybody one dollar more. I can vouch for that. I made a personal promise to Sammy Davis that we would never pay anybody more than we paid him. Sammy always got the top.

Did other people get the same as Sammy Davis?

Oh, yes–Sinatra, Liza, Willie Nelson and many others, but no one got more than Sammy Davis.

We had a top-of-the-room both in Reno and at Tahoe. It was different in the two locations because of the size of the room. Reno had four hundred seats, and we had a thousand at Tahoe. One of the advantages that we had in buying was that we could promise people, "Nobody'll be paid more than you."

Vegas was a totally different deal. Everybody was trying to be the top-paid act, and the thing about the entertainment business, there are no secrets. *Absolutely* no secrets. There isn't anything you can't find out. One of the easiest things to find out is how much people are paid. When we said, "Nobody will get more than you. We're offering you the top-of-the-room. That's the *most* we can offer you; can't offer you any more . . ." we lost some people because of that, but very few. Most of them would work for our number, and it might be less than what they were getting someplace else, but they knew that nobody else was making more.

What was that top figure?

It peaked out at Tahoe at two hundred thousand a week, and it peaked out in Reno at seventy-five thousand a week.

You mentioned earlier how much Bill Harrah liked Sammy Davis and, of course, Bill Cosby. Were there any racial problems in the early days before you took over entertainment? Did you have any racial problems?

No. We bought, probably over the years, every black act that was out there, and there certainly was never any problem. Everything we bought was based totally on who was hot and who was doing business.

One thing I remember so much about Harrah's is that there were entertainers you'd never heard of, and all of a sudden they came out with a big hit, or a new TV show, and Harrah's had them the next week or next month.

I think that just speaks well of the people that ran our entertainment. That really speaks well of Bob Vincent and the guy before Bob Vincent, Candy Hall, and Pat France and Doug Bushousen and Dick Lane. These were guys that were all really doing the same thing, which was doing their homework. If you *did* your homework, you *knew* what was

happening, because, again, there are no secrets.

I remember when I was assistant manager at Tahoe, and Roger Miller got hot. He was the hottest thing in the country, and we had him booked at Tahoe. None of us in the non-entertainment departments knew who in hell Roger Miller was, and I'm going to guess that it was probably Pat France or Dick Lane that hired Roger. It might have been Bob Vincent; I'm not sure. But somebody had to know that this guy was really happening.

As I remember, I was in San Francisco on vacation. I had a lot of friends down on the North Beach that used to come up to Tahoe all the time to play, and they all wanted reservations to see Roger Miller. I said, "Well, that's not a problem. I'll set it up for you."

So I called the club and they said, "We don't have any reservations. We're sold out!" [laughter] I think that just speaks well for the system, not being afraid to go out and spend money looking at acts.

Probably the biggest shortfall nowadays is most of the entertainment directors sit in their office, they look at a bunch of videos, and they don't get out of their office and go do things. Our policy of not buying anybody before you saw them answered a lot of questions. If you were interested in somebody, you got on a plane, and you went to see them. Period. That's probably what I did 60 percent of the time. A lot of my time was just spent looking at acts. It didn't matter where they were, and it didn't matter what the situation was. You just went to look at them. You didn't want to go to an entertainment meeting trying to explain an act that you hadn't seen! [laughter]

One of the biggest acts ever to appear at Harrah's was the back-to-back billing of John Denver and Frank Sinatra in the 1970s. How did that come about?

That was probably–at that time–the biggest nightclub act that had ever been put together. Denver was *huge*–playing twenty-thousand seaters and selling them out consistently. He had number one records, and he was just red hot. Sinatra had come out of retirement about two years before that, so he still had a little bit of heat on him. The two people that put it together were Mickey Rudin, who was Sinatra's attorney, and Jerry Weintraub, who was Denver's manager. They were close friends. They got the idea to put them together, and they called us. The reason they called us was our relationship with Sinatra and Mickey Rudin. I had a very good relationship with Rudin and still do. And they said, "Would you guys be interested in this?"

Obviously we said, "Yes, and we'll provide the facility." Mark Curtis and I went to Los Angeles and met with Jerry and Mickey, and we put the whole thing together in one meeting. We committed a large amount of money to publicize it and advertise it. I explained to both people that I didn't have any extra money other than the top of our room.

So they both got the top-of-the-room?

No, no. They split it. Mark put together a fantastic advertising campaign, and we went literally all over the world with it. We went to Montreal, because Montreal was the site of the Olympics that year. We took outdoor boards at the airport and on the road from the airport to Montreal. We took outdoor boards in London, just so Sinatra could see it. We painted buses in Los Angeles, and it really put us on the map entertainment-wise.

The first engagement John did the first show, and Frank did the second show. Then the next year we did it—that was the appearance called back-to-back—John would open the show, and Frank would come on and finish the show. Then John would come out, and they'd do a closer together. But when John would do the first show, and Frank would do the second show, it wasn't unusual for Frank to do a walk-on on John's show or John to do a walk-on on Frank's shows.

Frank would stop in the middle of the show to do his little talk piece and get a cocktail, and then John would walk out with a glass of milk because of his image at the time. The two artists got along fine. There were no ego problems; there were no billing problems, which is just absolutely phenomenal, because you don't have to tear your hair out over who gets first billing. Frank just said, "Give it to John—whatever he wants." And John was the same way—"Whatever Mr. Sinatra wants, that's what he gets." [laughter]

It was "Mr. Sinatra" and "John?"

[laughter] Yes! Anyhow, we just happened to be in the right place at the right time. We did have a relationship with Mickey and Jerry, and that's what I think created it. But it was their idea; it wasn't anything we dreamed up.

Did some of the entertainers have multi-year contracts?

No. That was a misconception. We didn't have anybody under contract other than their next engagement. Now, we did have an agreement with Sammy Davis that as long as he worked northern Nevada, he would work for Harrah's, but other that that we didn't have any long-term agreement.

On the agreement with Sammy, there was no money involved or anything like that. It was just a mutual agreement that if he worked northern Nevada, he'd work for Harrah's. Sammy wanted it, because it bothered him a little bit that we signed Sinatra. I think Sammy was just a little afraid that Sinatra was going to take some of his thunder away. That never materialized, but we did have that agreement, just to give Sammy a little publicity after all the publicity that happened when we signed Sinatra.

The media always gave the impression they had a great friendship. Were they truly great friends?

Oh, they were great friends. There wasn't any doubt about that. You bet. There was a love affair between the two of them; but you have to understand, they're both entertainers, and they both have egos that were bigger than this room. Sammy didn't begrudge Frank anything. He was happy for Harrah's that we had signed him, but he didn't want it to take away from his situation.

Lounge acts can sometimes be as important as a headliner. Possibly the greatest lounge act to appear in any casino in Reno, Tahoe, or Las Vegas was Louie Prima and Keely Smith.

Louie and Keely first worked for us in the summer of 1958 in the old South Shore Room at the lake—what we called the Lake Club in those days. Candy Hall was the entertainment director at that time. I was working in the cashier's office, and I recall that they were

just a phenomenal hit. They filled the place up at two o'clock in the morning. It was just amazing.

Later on, when I became assistant manager and then general manager, they worked for us. I knew all of them really well. I knew Louie and Sam Butera, and the guys in his band were really good friends of mine. I played a lot of golf with them; we had a lot of dinners together. I also knew Keely and have seen her within the last two years at Las Vegas. She and Sam Butera work together down there.

Louie and Keely were an exciting act. As their career got a little hotter and hotter, they became a big room act, and I would say in about 1961 or 1962 they appeared in the South Shore Room a couple of times as a headline act. They did phenomenal business, and then Louie and Keely separated. They got a divorce, and the act kind of cooled off. Louie

l. to r.: Phillip "Curly" Musso, Mary Kaye's husband, Isadore, the Mary Kaye Trio (Mary Kaye, Frank Ross, Norman Kaye), Holmes Hendricksen, and Lloyd Dyer.

had two or three other girls that were leading the band; Gia Maione was one of them. I don't recall some of the other names. But they worked for us again in the lounge. Then Louie's health went downhill, and he eventually died in New Orleans.

Our budgeting process was such that we had a top figure for every room, and it was really pretty simple. We had a top figure for the big room at Tahoe, which was considerably more than the top figure for Reno, mainly because of the size of the room. Both lounges were pretty much the same size-wise, so they had a comparable top figure. As time went on, that figure grew a little bit all the time. Then when we started doing revues, that escalated the price paid in the lounges. Yes, we had a top figure. In the days when Louie and Keely were playing the lounges—and other groups, like the Mary Kaye Trio, Earl Grant, Duke Ellington, and the Harry James band—the top price was fifteen thousand a week. Then we went to seventeen-five.

The lounges were a very important part of the history of gaming in Nevada. They attracted a lot of people. They afforded people a format to see famous people, great musical acts, and great comedy acts at a really reasonable price. The charge in many of the lounges was just the cost of a drink or a two-drink minimum. The lounges over the years changed from wide-open lounges—which I personally think is the best format, because it creates a great atmosphere and a great sound out in the casino—to closed-in venues. As they got bigger, they closed them in, and they really became small showrooms. Later, as the years went by, they took out the lounges. The feeling was that that space was probably more valuable as casino space. So, there was a time when there were very few lounges in any of the casinos, either here or Las Vegas. Now they've come back again, and the open format seems to work the best. I think they're an important part of the casino business. I think they attract people, but more important, they create a great atmosphere for having a good

time. Music's very important, and it creates an atmosphere that I think is conducive to really showing your customers a lot of fun.

The lounge acts were also definitely a hook to keep customers in the casino longer, especially in the late hours. Your headliner, your top act in the lounge, generally would go on from ten o'clock to eleven o'clock at night, and they would do a second show—in the early days they used to do three shows a night—around midnight or one o'clock, and the third show might be two o'clock in the morning. We would schedule them so that when the people came out of the South Shore Room at Tahoe at 1:30, our top act would be on stage performing at that time. It would hold the customers; it really would.

Were there ever any acts that you wanted to hire for the lounge and they wanted to be in the big room?

Oh, yes. That happened occasionally. Some of the lounges in Vegas were much bigger, and the acts were working for a little more money than what we were paying in our lounge. It wasn't unusual for a lounge act in Vegas to get twenty to twenty-five thousand a week. We might have a fifteen-thousand top or a seventeen-five top. But again, our argument was, "We're not paying anybody any more than what we're paying you. You're getting the top of the room. This is our policy determined by the size of our room and the kind of business that we attract. We're not high rollers. We're not Caesar's Palace. We're Harrah's." If they wouldn't take it, it didn't bother us. We were prepared to say, "We're sorry, but good luck to you. Goodbye." It didn't bother us at all, because we enjoyed a great reputation in the entertainment business.

My line has always been: "I was very fortunate and very lucky to enjoy quite a well-thought-of reputation in the entertainment business. It cost Bill Harrah a lot of money—he paid for everything that made me look good." [laughter]

You were a hero on his money?

Yes, a hero on Bill's money. That's exact truth. We did a lot of things for the artists, did a lot of small favors, did a lot of big favors, and we did a lot of considerate things. They all cost money, and Bill approved them all, but I was the guy that enjoyed the relationship, because that was my job. I was the go-between, and I was the contact, but Bill paid for all of it. There wasn't much that was free.

After Harrah's Club was sold to Holiday Inns, were there any immediate entertainment policy changes made?

No, there were no immediate changes. When the Holiday management came, in they directed us to continue doing just exactly what we were doing. There were some raised eyebrows about some of the things we did, and they felt that probably we were a little too generous with some of the perks. But, no, there were no immediate changes.

When Bill Harrah was alive, you just did something and then went to Bill and told him about it. Did that change when he died? Did you have to get permission to do things?

No, we continued right on. The gentleman that took over when Holiday Inns came into the picture was Dick Goeglein. I would run things by Dick as to what we were doing and so on and so forth and make him aware. We still had budget parameters, and we didn't do anything other than what we'd been doing, and we didn't spend any more money than what we'd been spending.

Things stayed the same probably for a couple of years after Holiday Inns got into the picture. Then things started changing a little bit, slowly. Budgets started coming down a little bit and so on and so forth.

Not too many years ago, casinos began to operate under a theory that each department should be self-

sufficient. In early years, casinos operated under the theory that departments, such as food/beverage, rooms, entertainment, et cetera, were loss leaders, and that their main job was to get people into the club, and that the gaming revenue would naturally follow. Currently, each department is supposed to show a profit. What are your thoughts on that approach?

I think what you've stated is true. In the "old days," I don't think anybody *wanted* to run some of these departments at a loss, but you did.

It also depended on how your accounting worked. In other words, the income from the dinner shows and second shows was tremendous, as far as income goes, and that all went to our food and beverage department; it didn't go to the entertainment department. So the entertainment department had a huge loss, but beverage and food could look pretty good because of the prices that they were able to get on dinner shows and second shows. I don't disagree with the *thinking* that every department should be a profit leader. I think if people want to run their businesses that way nowadays, it's their prerogative. However, I do disagree with it personally. I think, as an old-timer speaking, too many of the people in the casinos run the properties as hotels with casinos, which to me is backwards. They're supposed to be casinos that have a hotel.

Nowadays, a lot of the entertainers price themselves out of business. You still can run entertainment . . . you're not going to make any money with it, but you could run entertainment and break even. There certainly isn't going to be a profit, but we always used it as the vehicle to get our name out there. In other words, Harrah's was associated with great entertainment.

Our entertainment was the vehicle that got us millions and millions of words of publicity. We got free advertising; we got on television and on radio and in newspapers because of the events that we did and the people who we had playing. There are only so many things you can advertise, and some places choose not to go with entertainment. They advertise great food at low prices or great rooms at low prices or free this or free that. That's fine; that's their business. We just decided to go with entertainment. Why, I don't know, but I don't think it was because Bill liked entertainment. I think at that time it was a good decision to make. It might not be a good decision to make nowadays. It might not be very realistic nowadays. I don't really know, but it gave us a vehicle to hang our hat on, and it gave us an image.

The things that were true twenty-five years ago might not be true today. Times have changed so much. Money is totally different. Television has changed our lives so much. Twenty-five years ago, television wasn't that big a thing in everybody's life. I think now, today—and this is really a personal thought—it's without a doubt the most demanding, creative, dictating factor in our lives. It keeps us up to date with what's happening in the world immediately, twenty-four hours a day. It tells us what we like and don't like, what we're going to eat, what we're going to wear. It tells us what the fads are, what's hot, what's cold. Television dictates our lives to us. And in that same respect, it dictates our entertainment choices and values. That's why our business changed so much.

In the old days, an act was created and then slowly, slowly got better and bigger and then finally happened. Now, it is not that way. An act now is a rock band that gets a hit record, and in thirty days they're a huge smash, and they're selling twenty thousand seats. Then three years from now, they're out of the business. Things have really changed.

As far as Harrah's and entertainment, it was a chosen path, and Bill gave us the tools to make it work. If we didn't have the leeway, if we didn't have the houses and the airplanes and the relationships with these people, none of it would have happened. Bill was smart enough to be comfortable with his image, and he was smart enough to say, "Go do it." It

happened to work, but it may not be the way to go now.

You have to remember that twenty-five and thirty years ago a federal law prevented you from advertising gambling or gaming. (We called it "gaming;" they called it gambling.) You couldn't advertise that you had twenty-one, craps, roulette, slot machines, and keno. It was against the federal law. So when you advertised, you used words like "Nevada-style entertainment" and "Nevada excitement" and so on. Everybody knew it was gambling. Bill's approach was, "Everybody knows we're in the gambling business. We have casinos, and we just happen to hit on entertainment." Now, other places use food and cheap rooms, and there are different ways to go. We just decided entertainment was the way to go. I think that still works today.

I don't think anybody gets in their car in Sacramento or Portland or San Francisco or San Jose and drives up here for a great buffet, and I don't think they'll come up here for a nineteen-dollar room. They'll come up here for something to do that's fun and exciting, something that isn't available in their area. Shows can be part of that. I don't think that's the total answer, but you have to give people something that they don't have. The one thing that entertainment's always done is that it gives people an excuse—Joe Blow will tell everybody that he's going up to Tahoe or Reno or Vegas to see a show, when in his mind he is saying, "I'm going to go up there and kick the crap out of that crap game." But he doesn't tell everybody that. He says, "We've got to go see Barry Manilow," or, "We've got to go see John Denver."

One strange thing about gambling is that we get a tremendous amount of word of mouth advertising, and pretty much of it is positive. When people win, they talk about it; they tell everybody about it. If they *don't* win, what do they say? "Well, I broke even," or, "I had a great time." They don't go around telling everybody, "I got my brain beat out." A lot of people tell their friends, "We're going to go see some shows, and we're going to have some great dinners, and we're going to do this and that." They don't tell the banker, "I'm going to go up to Reno and lose all my money." [laughter] They say, "We're going up to Reno to have some wonderful food in the restaurants up there."

Now you're allowed to advertise gambling, so a lot of places do. But I still think you have to hang a hook out there and offer them something that's strong enough to get them to come over the mountain. I really do. I don't think a buffet will do it, and I don't think the cheapest room in town will do it. You have to offer people the total package; I think the casinos that are most successful offer the total package–great service, the places are clean, good food, fair prices, maybe shows, and security. Very important nowadays.

And dinner shows . . . I would love to see them come back, but I think it's unlikely that they ever will. It's an era that probably just passed us. Somebody might do it, might be the only one in town and might have a little bit of an edge, but there're so many limitations–the space is a big thing; providing kitchens is another. To have the right kind of kitchen is mandatory. It is almost impossible to remodel an old place to put in kitchens without destroying your whole facility, so you'd almost have to build it from scratch, and I think it's very questionable whether it would be successful or not. It was at one time, but I think it's something that may have gone by the way.

Are there performers out there that can do those shows? Yes, and there're performers whose price the casinos could handle. You're not going to bring Bruce Springsteen in, and you're not going to bring Michael Jackson in, and Neil Diamond isn't going to play a casino nor is Barbra Streisand, but there are acts out there that will work that are affordable. However, one of the biggest things in the entertainment industry that's changed is that the acts just won't do two shows a night anymore.

One of our stipulations when we bought was you work two shows a night, and you work seven days a week. That's fourteen shows a week or twenty-eight shows for two weeks. The acts just aren't conditioned to doing that anymore. Also, a lot of your acts that are out there that are still working, that will still do some business, physically aren't able to do it. They're older, and they just can't do it. They really can't. That's why in today's casino situation, any room under a thousand just isn't big enough.

If you were to build a new casino and to build a showroom, probably the ideal situation would be to have fifteen hundred seats, and to feed fifteen hundred or a thousand people dinner is almost an impossibility. To have good food and good service, it's just really difficult to do. We were able to do it because our showrooms were small, but nowadays I think to have anything less than a thousand seats just isn't practical.

With twelve hundred or thirteen hundred or fifteen hundred seats, you can charge enough so you can pretty much pay for the entertainment. The act gets all the money, but that's no different than it was thirty years ago. The act always got all the money. It's not a profitable business. There are some casinos that make a little money on their entertainment, and there are some that break even, but there are a lot of them that lose money because of bad buying practices and because they don't know how to run entertainment.

There are some casinos that play a lot of entertainment and make money on it all the time. They create a huge marketing tool, and that is really what entertainment is supposed to be–it's a way to wave your flag to get people's attention. The one thing that's never changed about the entertainment business is people are still interested in seeing celebrities. Whether it's a famous singer or a famous comedian or a famous movie star or a famous football player, they love celebrities. Celebrities bring people to casinos.

Do some casinos lease out a show, make a deal with a booking company?

Yes. The Reno Hilton has a deal with the Bill Graham Company in San Francisco, and they provide all the shows in the Hilton outdoor arena and some of the shows inside. I don't know the terms of the deal, but the deal is: They book the shows, they put up so much money for the expenses, and the Hilton probably has a small share in the sale of the tickets, so there's probably a real small profit margin there for the Hilton or maybe a break-even situation.

It must take a lot of headaches away from the property.

Yes, it does, but it also does something to me that is just absolutely wrong, and that is, you give up control. You don't have any say-so in who appears; you don't have any control over the act once they get there. You're at the mercy of the act and the Bill Graham people. That's something that we didn't ever like to do. Mr. Harrah had a policy of no partners. We did everything ourselves, which I think is the best way to go.

Ascuaga's Nugget has a package where you eat in a restaurant, and then you go to the show. What are your thoughts on that?

I think those programs are quite successful, but it's necessary to have plenty of restaurants. You can't have just one restaurant. If you have a property as big as the Nugget, with as many restaurants as they have, then I think it's a very good package, very attractive to the public, and I think it works.

They do a very good job of buying over there. They have a good selection of people. It's kind of ironic–all the people that used to work for us at Harrah's, now work over there. Harrah's, now, just really doesn't want to be in the entertainment business and certainly doesn't want to be in the "name" business.

So the conclusion is that dinner shows, as they were, will never return again?

Well, my guess is that they won't.

❖

With Bill there was never any gray area to speak of. Everything was black and white. Everything was exact. You either did it, or you didn't do it. You had a meeting at ten o'clock; you didn't have a meeting at 10:02. If he wanted everybody there at 10:02, he would have called it at 10:02. You had it at ten o'clock, and to him 10:02 wasn't the same. He was exacting, and he was a killer on time. I used to have to explain to him why a show went thirty-five, forty seconds late.

And he was a perfectionist! I will tell a story that I've told many, many people. When I was in charge of entertainment and of advertising/public relations, Bill used to come in about nine o'clock, and he would go out to the automobile collection about 11:30 or 12:00, have lunch out there, and spend the afternoon at the automobile collection. One day he brought in an ad that we had run in the newspaper that said, "A thousand cars on display at the automobile collection." He told me that he'd just come from the collection, and that a couple of the cars were being worked on. He says, "You know, we're painting a 1917 Chevrolet." And he named another car, and he says, "You know, we're doing new upholstery on that, and we pulled them out."

I said, "Fine."

He said, "Well, that means we've got only 998 cars out there. We don't have a thousand." He says, "I don't lie to my customers. If I tell them a thousand, I want there to be a thousand cars out there."

And I had worked with Bill enough to know that I only had one answer, and that was, "Bill, I'll get back to you." [laughter]

So the next day I go to Bill, and I said, "Bill, we can't change our advertising every day, as you pull cars in and out of display."

And he said, "I understand that."

I said, "What if we come up with a word that says 'approximately' or 'about' or something like that, so we're not held right to a thousand?"

Bill said, "That's fine. Just make the change." That's an example of the way he thought.

I'll give you another example of Bill's exactness: if you were one of the so-called company execs, and you were traveling, and the company airplanes were going in the direction that you were going at the same time, you could always get a ride if there was space available. Bill flew a lot in the company planes, and if there was room, and the schedule worked, you could always get a ride if you checked with Bob Hudgens or one of the secretaries to make sure that it was OK with Bill. The thing that you understood was, if there was a ten o'clock flight, that meant that you were at the hangar at 9:30, and you loaded your luggage at twenty minutes to, and at about fifteen minutes to, the pilots cranked up the plane and pulled out and sat at the end of the runway. A ten o'clock flight to Bill was wheels in the well just lifting off the runway *at* ten o'clock. Not five minutes after, not five minutes before, but at ten o'clock. And that's what an on-time person he was.

The only other person that I met like that is Frank Sinatra. Frank is very prompt and very much aware of time. Frank was one of the few entertainers you didn't have to worry about being up on stage and ready to go, because he was ready to go long before the show was ready to go. [laughter]

Detail was very important to Bill. Little things were just as important as big things, and it was a great education for all of management. You learned discipline, and you learned to pass that on to the people that worked for you. To me it's a very, very positive thing as far as business is concerned. People used to ridicule or make fun of the fact that he wanted all the lights to be on—every light had to be on, but it was just another part of the whole picture. If one light is out, there's something wrong—it's not perfect.

And Bill managed his time like nobody I've ever run across. He had a schedule that ran thirty days ahead continuously. It started about eight o'clock in the morning, and it finished about eight o'clock at night. It was broken up in half-hour units, and everything was scheduled. His haircut was scheduled three weeks ahead of time; his shoeshine was scheduled . . . . If he was going to get a manicure, if he had a meeting at the automobile collection, if he had a meeting with Bob Ring or any of his managers or management, everything was scheduled. It wasn't very often that you could catch him without getting on his schedule, but if he was open, he was certainly available.

Lots of times when I'd schedule entertainment, I would go in to see Bob Hudgens or Cindy Wade and say, "When is the boss available?" I mean, this might be a Monday morning, and they would say, "Well, when do you want to have the meeting?"

I'd say, "As soon as possible."

They'd say, "Well, it looks like Wednesday afternoon at three o'clock is available, or Thursday morning at 9:30 is available." Something like that.

In his last years, Bill traveled a great deal. He went to Idaho a lot—he loved his place up in Sun Valley, and he loved the Middle Fork Lodge. He spent a lot of time up there, so that made the demands on his time, when he was in town, even a little more difficult.

When I first went to work at Harrah's, there was a sign in the personnel hallway. It said, "Do the impossible: please everyone."

He had a great feel for his customers. If I heard him once, I heard him I don't know how many times: his question would always be, "What do our customers want? What can we do to give them what they want?" And we gave them things, and we did things that Bill didn't like, that personally he didn't care for. But if our customers wanted to do it or were asking for it, that's what we would do.

⟡

Holmes, let's talk a little bit about some of the people at Harrah's Club, especially at Lake Tahoe, that had an impact on your growth and your personal success.

I think the two guys that influenced me the most and were very helpful were Curly Musso and Frank Perez. Curly was one of the original owners of George's Gateway Club, which Harrah's purchased in 1955. His partner was George Cannon. Curly started out as a floorman for Harrah's. He later became a shift manager and eventually general manager. Curly was extremely good to me, and I worked for him in a lot of different capacities. I eventually became his assistant manager from about 1965 through 1967. When Curly retired, I became the general manager.

Frank Perez had been one of the part-owners and operators of the old Nevada Club, which was next door to the Stateline Country Club. Frank went to work for us as . . . in today's terms, you'd probably call him a casino host–he had total authority over extending credit and comps to good customers. A very knowledgeable guy in the gaming business, and a guy who brought *years* of experience from gambling boats off the coast of southern California and from casinos in Palm Springs in the late 1930s.

Frank also brought with him very close connections with several casinos in Las Vegas. This opened the door for us to get accurate credit information about customers that would walk in the door who would not be established with us, but be known to us as a player. Frank would be able to call his friends in Las Vegas, and we would get credit clearances or information on these customers. He was an old-time gambler and a very

ethical man, and I learned a great deal from him.

Both those guys were really from the old school, Curly having been in the gaming business in Vallejo many years before he came to Tahoe. I probably learned more about the gambling business from them than from anyone else, but there were many people that really played an important part in Harrah's growth in those early years at Tahoe. Besides Curly and Frank, Rome Andreotti played a very important part. He headed up all the gaming. Bob Ring certainly played a major role in management. Bill Harrah, although he was involved in everything, wasn't very visible, but we did see Bob and Rome all the time. They were really the two guys that carried the message. Maurice Sheppard also played a real important part. A lot of changes as far as company policies and a lot of employee benefit programs came into existence while Shep was president.

As the company grew, more people came on board, we got more sophisticated, and a lot of things developed. Personnel departments developed, and industrial relations departments developed. As the departments grew bigger, it was necessary to change, and Bill wasn't afraid to change . . . Or to copy things being done by other successful businesses.

We weren't the best-paying place by any stretch of the imagination, but there were perks that [Harrah's management] had that other places didn't have: we had company cars, we had profit-sharing programs, and we probably had better medical programs than many of the casinos. Some didn't have any medical programs at all. We were one of the first ones to do that, and our total benefits package was certainly a lot more attractive than most of the casinos.

Bill pioneered a lot of things that were unheard of in those days in gaming. Paid vacations for all the employees was unheard of in the gambling business until he started it. The benefits that are standard nowadays in any kind of business, in many cases Bill was the one to pioneer them in the gaming business. [In other casinos] there was no overtime; there were no bonuses—bonuses were for the top guy, and that was it, until Bill came along.

[Most of us were very loyal to Bill Harrah.] Bill didn't understand why you couldn't run a casino just like the Bank of America ran their business, or Sears, or any other big, successful corporation. Why couldn't you use the same management policies? Why couldn't you train people? Why couldn't you have the same structure and everything? I think that one of the key elements behind his success is that Bill wasn't afraid to copy. He was an innovator in many, many ways, but if somebody across the street had something that was really good, Bill used to say, "There's no reason why we can't do it, too." Bill was very innovative on a lot of things—on employee cafeterias and uniform programs and parking for the employees. All these things became standard at Harrah's long before they were accepted by other companies.

Well, it was such a pleasant place to work in so many ways. I think that was the main reason he never had any union problems . . . although, wasn't there a union in the stagehands or the lighting department?

We had an election, and we lost it; but then within two years we had another election, and the union was voted out. That was in the middle or late sixties. Bill didn't like unions at all; made no bones about it. He felt that we didn't need them. He felt that if we took good care of our employees, and if we were fair to our employees, that the employees wouldn't feel that they needed a union. And that was very important with Bill. He felt very strongly about it, and I'm sure that was one of the reasons for all the benefits and all the programs that we had.

Bill felt very strongly that he didn't need anybody else to tell him how to run his business—that he would run it the way he wanted to run it. He felt that it was important to be fair to the employees, and he was very intent on creating great working conditions.

One of the most important policies he ever instigated was promoting from within. I'm the best example in the world of that, and many, many other people are too. Harrah's gave us a chance to get into other areas and to be promoted.

Harolds Club got credit for a lot of things . . . which I'm sure were true, and the credit is all deserved. However, Bill Harrah didn't get as much credit as he deserved for the many innovative things he did as far as the employees were concerned; also for the way he treated his customers and the facilities he offered the public. He certainly was one of the leaders when gaming started to move out of the dark, sinister business that everybody thought we were in, into "It's legal. It's wide open. We're not ashamed of what we do; let's let the public know, and there's nothing wrong with these places."

How did Mr. Harrah keep up with daily events?

We always used to complain that we spent more time reporting what was going on than we did managing. In some cases it was probably true.

All the areas were organized into departments. Every department had a department head, and every department had somebody in charge on that particular shift. When the shift was finished, somebody wrote a report as to what happened. At the end of twenty-four hours, or at the end of three shifts, that information was all compiled in what we called a day book, and by ten o'clock in the morning it had to be on Mr. Harrah's desk in Reno, Bob Ring's desk in Reno, Rome Andreotti's desk in Reno, and the two general managers' desks.

When I was a general manager at Lake Tahoe, I knew by ten o'clock in the morning what had happened in Reno the day before, and people in Reno know what had happened the last twenty-four hours at Tahoe. This was in great detail. If there was a coffee maker that blew up in the kitchen, we knew about it. If there was a guy that beat us badly in the casino on graveyard, we knew about it. If somebody hit the thousand-dollar jackpot in the slots, we knew about it. And if somebody hit a twelve thousand-dollar keno ticket, we knew about it. If a parking lot attendant dented a fender in the parking lot, we knew about it. If the men's restroom on the casino floor got plugged up, and we had to shut it down for three hours, we knew about that.

If something happened in the casino that was unusual, the shift manager automatically picked up the phone and called his boss, who was either the assistant manager or the general manager. Depending on the severity of the event, the general manager then called Rome or Bob Ring at home. Even if it was two o'clock in the morning and some guy beat us for thirty-five thousand dollars, you called Rome at two o'clock in the morning, woke him up, and told him, or you called Bob Ring. Now, whether they called Bill Harrah or not, I don't know. On certain occasions they would, but most of the time, no. But if somebody was injured (a customer or an employee), you called the people in Reno and let them know. If we had equipment failure, if the power all went out at Tahoe, or a gas line was broken and we couldn't cook anymore in the kitchen, you called everybody and let them know.

We had another method of reporting things in the casino where we used a code, and the code was related to winning or losing. We would pick words that had ten letters that would correspond with one, two, three, four, five, six, seven, eight, nine, zero. Then if somebody had won five thousand dollars on the twenty-one game, the shift manager would put that in code in his report. This was

one of the ways of making management aware of the exact amounts that were involved all the time . . . but the maintenance manager would have that same report on his desk, and he *wouldn't* be aware of how much money that was. It was a confidential code that was used only by the casino people in top management. This code would be teletyped or just typed up on reports. Also, we used to have daily couriers that went back and forth between Tahoe and Reno a couple of times a day, and they would carry information back and forth. It was a great way to keep upper management aware of winners and losers.

Many high management people in Harrah's and other casinos were promoted out of the cashier's office. That includes people like yourself, Lloyd Dyer, Doyle Mathia (who was the vice-president in charge of the automobile collection for a long time), Dennis Small, and your brother Lowell. Do you have any idea why so many former cashiers became prominent in upper management?

I think it was the nature of our organization at that time. First of all, we were small enough so that everything kind of started and ended in the cashier's office. That was the central bank for the casino. None of the gaming areas got their money to operate with until it was issued by the cashier's office. When their shifts were over, the money came back into the cashier's office to be counted and logged and reported on, and those numbers went up to the business office. I think mainly because of the interaction between the cashiers and all the other departments that handled money–food and beverage, keno, slots, pit–we had great exposure to the entire casino.

As cashiers, we used to relieve people in the restaurants and cashiers in the premium booth. We would issue new bar banks for the bar department and keno banks, and we would issue the bankrolls for the pit, the twenty-ones, the craps, and the roulette. Any promotion that was being run generally involved money, and, therefore, we were involved in setting it up or tearing it down or putting it out or bringing it back in. So I think exposure to all those other departments broadened our education, and we got to know about the whole operation, not just the cashier's office. I think that's probably the number-one reason.

And also in the games, you would make the bankrolls; you would make the fills and sometimes even deal.

Yes. In the early days, when we first bought the Stateline Country Club, we would operate it on weekends, and sometimes we would open that place with three or four hours notice. If the weather was good and all of a sudden it looked like there were a lot of people coming up Highway 50, we'd open it. We would run across the street, *literally*, to the cashier's office and get the cashier's office open. Then we would go out on the floor and . . . I mean, I opened many a twenty-one game. I also opened crap games, and I wasn't a twenty-one dealer or a crap dealer, but I stood there behind the table. [laughter] The pit people were on the phone calling dealers in, and as soon as a dealer would come in and take me out, then I'd go open up another twenty-one game.

I remember the first time I saw you standing behind a crap table, I said, "Hey, he doesn't know how to deal craps." [laughter]

But I lost plenty of money shooting craps! [laughter]

After working so many years in the gaming industry, what do you miss about not being involved in it on a day-to-day basis?

I miss the association. It's a great business with great people in it. You develop friendships and relationships over the years, and I miss that. I really do. It's an exciting business. There never is a dull day in the gaming business. Every day is different, and it's fun. I miss that, but when your time is up, your time is up. That's all. Time to do other things.

If you owned a hotel-casino today, what part would entertainment play in your method of operation?

It would play a big part. I think it's absolutely necessary. I don't think you can give the place away, but with the expansion of gaming, the entertainment element becomes even more important. Right now, with all the Indian casinos . . . .

One thing about our business is that twenty-one pays the same here as it does in an Indian casino in Washington. And the hard eight on the crap game probably pays the same. All the games are the same; the slot percentages are basically all the same. So I think you have to offer them something in addition to that, and that is where Nevada has the big edge, because they've got the facilities, they've got the room. So, if I were to own or to operate a casino, I would have to give people something more than that little Indian casino up in Washington gives them. And I think entertainment's the key. I don't think it's the whole thing, but I think it's a very important piece of the pie.

16

RUSSELL MCLENNAN

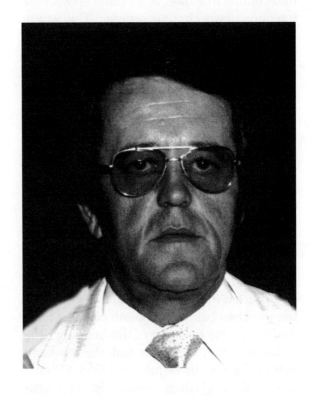

*R*USS McLENNAN *is currently (1999) vice-president of special casino promotions for Harrah's Tahoe. He was interviewed in his office in July of 1997. He was a cooperative and expansive chronicler, and the interview required two sessions.*

McLennan was born January 8, 1936, in Concord, California. He was first employed by Harrah's in April of 1959 as a change person and was sent to dealer school a few months later. His oral history interview contains a description of the dealer schools and explains why Bill Harrah decided to have schools. He also discusses his early days in the pit, work schedules, the salary program in effect at that time, some of the pit bosses, and, in some detail, Harrah's policies and procedures and the necessity for them.

Other subjects include the successful junket programs from Mexico and the Far East that Harrah's employed for many years, and the problems that they eventually created. McLennan suggests that many "new" methods of marketing and promoting of casinos are really only a variation of the old. He also describes special casino programs available to the good customers of Harrah's, not only in the Reno-Lake Tahoe area, but in the many Harrah's locations throughout the United States.

This oral history interview gives the reader a look at how Harrah's has changed over time, for both employees and customers, as seen through the eyes of one of the very few casino employees who have been with Harrah's for forty years or more.

RUSSELL McLENNAN: I was born in Concord, California, on January 8, 1936. My dad worked for Shell Oil company, and my mother was a housewife and worked part-time. Dad had close to thirty years with Shell. He died in 1962, and my mother died in September of last year. I had three sisters and one brother, and I lost a brother and one sister—my youngest sister. I grew up in Concord and graduated from Mount Diablo High School there. After graduation, I went straight in the army, and I was in the army from 1954 to 1956.

After I got out of the military, I went to work for Lincoln-Mercury in Concord. Then a friend of mine, Russ Armstrong, talked me into coming to Tahoe, and I came up with the intention of working one summer. That was in April of 1959, and I've been here ever since. My first job was carrying change on swing shift, but I didn't plan on staying in slots. I was just waiting for a dealer's position to come open.

In June, two months after I started work, I got a chance to go to dealing school. (I didn't have to pass any tests; I just had a brief interview.) Harrah's had in-house dealer schools, and I went to the six-week school for four hours a day while still working in slots. Jim Erwin was teaching the craps school, and his wife, Ruby Erwin, was teaching the twenty-one school. The classes had about twenty to twenty-five people in them.

I started in the pit in the summer of 1959, the weekend before the Fourth of July. (They opened up the new part of this building[1]—the California end; the south end—the weekend before the Fourth of July of 1959.) When I started dealing, there were a lot of Vegas dealers here, and I think that Bill Harrah had started the dealer schools because he wanted to get away from hiring Vegas dealers. He would rather train his own.

DWAYNE KLING: Did Harrah's have trouble with some of the Vegas dealers?

Absolutely.

What kind of trouble did they have?

Deciding who the bankroll belonged to, Bill Harrah or them.

They'd borrow some money once in a while and not repay it?

A little lunch money and a little cocktail money. But Harrah wanted procedures and policies followed, and he wanted all his dealers trained the same, so that everybody dealt the same way. It was easier for the catwalk to follow and easier for the floormen to follow—if a dealer deviated from procedure, it stood right out. The dealers coming from Vegas, and even some of the experienced dealers from Reno, either didn't follow the procedure or *couldn't* follow the procedure, so consequently, Harrah moved into more in-house training.

❖

In the beginning, from 1959 to about 1963, we worked straight through from Memorial Day to Labor Day with no overtime for those days. We had no days off, and we worked twelve, fourteen, sixteen hours on occasion, but we never balked at working.

Harrah's used to have three different pay rates, depending on the time of the year. The first year I came in the pit was the last year of the three rates. I started in slots at $14 a day, and when I came in the pit, I started the first month at $17.50, and then I went to $20. In the summer—I believe it was around the Fourth of July—you'd jump $2.50 on your high rate. It went $20, $22.50, and $25, and then they quit doing that the following year and went to a year-round rate with the tops at $27.50.

After they went to the year-round rate, if you were a top dealer, you got the $27.50 year-round and the box man got $32.50 and was in on the tips. I think the floormen started at $35. I went on the box in 1962, and I worked one year on the box and then went on the floor.

So it wasn't a very good job to go from a box man to a pit boss. You got a $2.50-a-day raise and no tips.

No, it wasn't; but shortly after that, they went to $40.

The interesting part is that Harrah's paid so much more money in summertime.

That's right. They had to, or the dealers would go across the street, which was what happened when the Sahara Tahoe opened. For years, Harvey's paid a couple bucks more than we did, so we'd always lose a few to Harvey's. Then when the Sahara Tahoe came in, they started offering more money, and we lost a good-size group of people to Sahara.

Did Harvey's Wagon Wheel have a dealer school?

They didn't have to, because they hired ours. [laughter] As did Harolds Club in Reno. After the Harrah's schools became popular around the gaming industry, Harolds wouldn't hire a dealer unless they had worked at Harrah's, because they knew they were well trained. They followed the procedures. They knew the game well, and they were first in line to get a job at Harolds when Harolds was the premiere place to work . . . Harolds had the best tips.

So, many of Harrah's dealers worked for other casinos?

Thousands. Thousands, and after they started getting rolling here, expanding so fast, we would do several schools a year. In the spring, we'd have a school for in-house help– slot employees, bartenders, waitresses, whatever, they could go to our dealer schools. Then in the summer, we'd hire college kids and run the crash course. We'd do two weeks, eight hours a day, for college kids and turn them out as dealers.

So Harrah's had kind of a reservoir of in-house employees that they were ready to insert behind the games immediately when business picked up?

Yes. On Memorial Day, we turned out the first group. Then we started getting the college kids in May, early June . . . have them all ready for the summer. We didn't have a hotel in those days, so the business was much more volatile. You'd hire a ton of them for the summer, and they'd go back to school in the winter; and, consequently, we got to hire a lot of those back for the following summers. Gary Arbentrout is an example. He ended up being one of our corporate attorneys and later the general manager in Las Vegas. He was a dealer here for five years in a row in the summer while he was going to college.

Harrah's, for the first few years, operated just the Lake Club. Then they operated the Stateline Country Club and the Lake Club, and there came a time when just the Stateline Club was open year-round. Do you recall when that happened?

In July of 1959–Harrah's was getting ready for the Olympics in 1960, and they closed the Lake Club in the winter and kept the Country Club open. In December, when the showroom opened, we left the Lake Club closed except on weekends or holidays, but we'd open the Lake Club in the summer all the time. The Lake Club was sold to Harvey's around 1966. It had been called the Thrifty Gambler for about two years, and it was the Lake Club for quite some time before that. (It was called the Thrifty Gambler because we lowered the limits on all the games. We had fifty-cent tables, and we had twenty-five-cent crap games and ten-cent crap games, and I believe we did that for about two summers before it was sold to Harvey's.)

As the amount of table games were reduced in the wintertime, a lot of people who were box men or even pit supervisors during the summertime went back to being dealers.

Some of them did go back to dealing. When I was on the box, that happened to me a few times, but once I went on the floor, I never went back to dealing.

Around 1963 was when we went on the salary program. A certain percentage of the floormen were salaried, and that was a six-day salary. You worked six days every week, minimum, and it wasn't unusual to accumulate days. You didn't get paid for the extra day if you worked seven days; you accumulated that comp time. It wasn't unusual for guys to have thirty or forty days of comp time coming at the end of the summer.

Did they always get the time off?

Not always. Some guys took advantage of it, but lots of us didn't. I never did catch up.

So come November and December, they'd say, "You have twenty days comp time." And you could say, "OK, I'll take ten days off."

That's right. Or I'd work four-day weeks or five-day weeks.

I remember in 1962, 1963 that ten-hour shifts were commonplace.

Commonplace, and we also had many twelve-hour shifts. We got a gal that's having a retirement party tomorrow night, and she's been here forty years—Flora Boyaji. Her and Marie Scott and Madeline Mueller, those gals would work double shifts like you would a straight eight-hour shift. They would work a double and not blink an eye, and they weren't getting that time-and-a-half either. They were getting time-and-a-half pay after eight hours, but not for the sixth and seventh day.

These things were happening only a little over thirty years ago. A lot of times, people don't realize what advancements have been made. Tell someone now that they would have to work sixteen hours a day for straight time, and nobody would do it.

You'd be in court. [laughter]

Who were some of your mentors as you were learning the gaming business? Were there any old-time pit bosses or supervisors you patterned yourself after or that you admired, or were you your own man?

There were some that you didn't really care for. You didn't pattern yourself after some of them. [laughter] You'd want to choke them. Sam Revty . . . I mean, they didn't come any worse than him. Homer Wall and Elio Martini were good dealers, but they weren't the friendliest bunch in town, and they kind of tortured you when you were a young dealer. They wouldn't give you a whole lot of help. They would rather kick your ass then help you. But there were a lot of good people around, too.

Were there a lot of older, experienced bosses that had worked in Reno?

We had a group that came out of Elko (Rube Whittaker and Hal White and Harold Akey and that bunch), and then you had a bunch from Fallon. I guess Hal White was a Reno guy, too—I think he worked in Reno for a long time. It seemed like every once in a while, we'd get another group of guys from one particular town, and they'd bring a couple of their buddies with them. You had a Fallon group, you had an Elko group, you had a Reno group, and each guy that came brought his own guys with him.

Did they all get along?

No, not hardly. [laughter] Not hardly.

Was there was some friction between some of the cliques?

Lots of it. Absolutely.

Did it have any bearing on the promotions?

[laughter] Big time. Big time. It had everything to do with promotions. They'd take care of their own group. The Elko group would want to take care of their group, and here comes Fallon, "Well, what about this guy from Fallon?" And then you had Aaron Dimmit. Aaron Dimmit was a Fallon guy. Al Childers, Chet Edwards, and Ovlan Fritz were all from Fallon. Then there was the Vallejo group, Curly and Willie Musso, and thank God there was only a couple of the Vallejo guys.

Some of those people that you mentioned, of course, were skilled in dealing what would be considered illegal.

Extremely. [laughter]

But they didn't do anything illegal for Harrah's Club?

They didn't have to. This was like a retirement job for them. They didn't have to worry about getting beat up every day working here or getting closed. And they were an asset, because they were very experienced guys.

Did some of them teach the younger pit supervisors what to look for when somebody's turning the deck or dealing seconds?

They were good about it that way, but you had to be on the right side of the fence with them.

◇

A lot of the people like myself that hired in here in 1959 kept their jobs because of the anticipation of a lot of business from the winter Olympics; and, as you know, it didn't materialize on this end of the lake. We carried a lot of help through that winter that probably wasn't necessary, and we wouldn't have carried so much if it hadn't been for the winter Olympics.

Business was *so* volatile from winter to summer until we went to the hotels. When Harrah's Reno opened that hotel down there, they realized we should have one up here too. Harvey's already had a hotel, so their business didn't fluctuate like ours did, but once the lake got a couple of hotels, then the business kind of leveled out. We didn't have the big highs and lows, especially where the help was concerned. Not as many lay-offs. You could make more straight schedules.

Could you give me a little run-down on how you advanced through the Harrah's management chain?

I think it was around 1965 or 1966 that I became a "number one" in the Thrifty Gambler. A "number one" is in charge of the pit for an eight-hour shift. And from there, I think it was about 1972, I became a shift manager. A shift manager is in charge of the entire casino for an eight-hour shift—the entire building, all departments. From there I went to casino manager, and now I'm vice-president of customer development. I've been a vice-president for ten years.

Did Harrah's have management seminars or training programs for their managers?

Still do. They're ongoing all the time. Some are in-house, some are out-of-state. Some managers have been sent to college courses for six, eight, ten, twelve weeks. Hector Mon, president of Harrah's Nevada, was sent to Pepperdine College for a year.

How often do you attend seminars?

Quite frequently. They may last three days, or they may last five days, but they're ongoing. Some are on the property; sometimes we go outside the property. One year we had the senior management meeting in Fort Lauderdale. Two or three times we've had it in Memphis or Orlando. We've had them scattered across the country.

Were these started when Bill Harrah was running the operation?

That's when they started. After we went public and the Holiday group came in, they've been more consistent and more intense.

—◇—

Harrah's training and Harrah's policies and procedures for dealers were a major part of their success. Other casinos now have tried to copy us. In the last few years, we have had to go outside to hire upper-echelon people because we have been raped so many times by new properties opening. We are constantly training new people. Since this last gaming proliferation has taken place all over the country, different companies continually draw from ours, and we've lost so many people over the years that we're continually training new ones.

Rome Andreotti wrote most of the procedures for the pit. Different department managers, when they had a problem, would come up with their own procedures, but all procedures and policies had to be OK'd by Rome.

What are some of the pit procedures on a twenty-one game?

They covered, among other things, how the dealer held her deck, where she held her deck, how many times she'd shuffle a deck, how many times she'd strip a deck, turn the deck . . . all facets of the game. There were procedures pertaining to everything on crap games. All the procedures were set, and that's what many of the early dealers didn't like about them. They wanted to total bets, pay on and off bets, and that was strictly against policy and procedure.

Did every dealer on every shift in both Reno and Tahoe deal exactly the same?

They were exactly the same, and any new floorman knew the policies and procedures as well as the dealers did because he had been trained the same way; and that's why they promoted from within for so many years. We still have the same procedure books, and our crap schools right now are almost identical to what they were thirty-five years ago.

We do pay on and off on a crap game now, and we can total some bets on a crap game now, but if a guy broke in here thirty-five or forty years ago, everything is basically the same. Our dealer schools are pretty much handled the same all the way, although we don't have as many. There was an article in one of the gaming magazines a while back stating that Harrah's is "The Harvard of dealer schools."

Did the other departments also have procedures that they followed?

They all had a set of procedures that they followed just like they did in the pit. The only difference today might be that we have different cash handling techniques. In the cashier's office, when they go to the vault for money, there have been certain areas of change in that respect; but it's still policy and procedure in every department. You can go to maintenance, and maintenance has a book that says what day they check what generators, at what time they check certain compressors, and at what time the refrigeration units get checked. Every department has their own set of procedures.

When you were a supervisor, did you do a building inspection?

Shift managers and number ones would walk the building inside and out every shift looking for discrepancies. When Doyle Mathia was the shift manager and I was the number one–the shift supervisor–Rome would come up every Tuesday morning, and we wanted the building to look great. So Doyle Mathia walks the building inside and out. He says, "You check the inside. I'm going outside to check for burned-out lights." We never wanted lights burned out. If a light was burned out, you didn't wait till the next shift came on to change it. You'd change it when you spotted it. So we get done checking, we come back in, and everything's fine.

Rome walks through the front door and walks over to the cashier's office, where Doyle and I are waiting for him. He walks in, points up and says, "You got a light burned out."

Doyle Mathia says, "Grab it, Rome. I'll guarantee you it's still warm." [laughter]

Rome lived for Harrah's; he devoted his life to the place. Every waking hour, he was thinking Harrah's, and nobody gave more of himself, as far as I'm concerned, than Rome did. If you owned a casino yourself, you would hope to have someone devote as much time to his job as Rome did. He was as important to Harrah's as Bob Ring was. Bob was loyal, and he was more outgoing and better with the customers than Rome. Rome was all business; there were no games to be played with Rome.

If a dealer broke policy or didn't follow procedure, how was that handled?

You'd tell them then, and if they continued to do it, they'd be written up in the pit book. I can't recall anybody being fired over it, but you followed the procedures. It said, "Shuffle the deck three times." When it first started, it was three to five times; now it's three times. It was three to five times, and if they did it seven times, they heard about it.

Did the pit work in conjunction with the catwalk or the surveillance department?

When I first came here, the catwalk was kind of an independent group. If you wanted someone observed, you could call the catwalk at any time. I think they reported to security originally and then started reporting to the general managers.

Did they ever call down to a pit boss and say, "That girl's shuffling the deck seven times"?

Many times; and sometimes personalities got involved in that. When a guy in the catwalk would be pissed at the floorman, he'd ride the floorman pretty hard or write him up, and then the floorman would be complaining about the guy in the catwalk. (That's why the reporting structure changed from security to the general manager. That way there was only one stop to make.) Yes, they got some petty little games going up there, and they'd nitpick sometimes. Some guys in the catwalk would nitpick over minor details–dealers talking too much to a customer and stuff like that–but basically you could work pretty close with the catwalk, especially if you knew of an incident coming up or you heard of an incident that might be happening. You could work with them closely that way.

Were the catwalk people well-trained in the gaming business?

Not really. They knew the policies, they could read the book, they could follow the procedures, but that was about all. They'd call you up and say, "Oh, Flora's not shuffling the deck right," inferring that you were working in the pit and did not see it. Then you'd go stand there and waste fifteen minutes watching and find that the dealer was doing nothing wrong. You had to kind of pick through it, but we got through it all right.

What were some of the things that made Harrah's different from the other casinos?

I think Bill Harrah was more emphatic about how everybody treated the customers. You could get fired out of here quicker for insulting a customer or being rude to a customer than you could for any other thing, other than stealing money. Customers were that important to Bill. He was probably the first guy where the customer was always right the first time, not only in gambling, but also in restaurants and, later on, hotel rooms. He took that to a new level, and it's still practiced the same way now.

As you went higher up in Harrah's organization, did you have much personal contact with Bill Harrah?

None. When a show opened and he was in town, he would drive up here to catch the opening show, but he would walk through and never say a word to anybody. He'd nod to you if he caught your eye, but I never had a conversation with the man. He gave me a little arm wave one day as he was walking by, and it took him fifty feet to get his arm back down. [laughter] He never said a word to you when he walked in. He might nod to you, but if there was something wrong, you heard about it the next day–not from him, but from Rome. Rome would call the general managers and tell them what Bill had seen and go from there.

I was a shift manager for five or six years before Bill Harrah died. In fact, I was probably a casino manager when he died, and I never had any conversations with him. We'd go to the Villa Harrah once a year, and he'd have a party for the upper management and give a very brief speech, welcome you there, and that was the extent of it. Shake your hand coming through the door, but not much for conversation. Bill was always a gentleman– never had a bad word to say to anybody, and he didn't hassle you. He didn't come in here

trying to pick the place apart. He walked by, and if he saw something out of the ordinary, he would get back to Bob Ring or to Rome, and you'd hear about it the following day. As far as hassling you, he never did. Never did.

That's different than a lot of other casino owners.

Yes. Harvey Gross ranting and raving and drinking at the bar. Here, it was out of the question. Never happened here.

Did you ever run into him at any of his Idaho properties?

He owned the Middle Fork Lodge on the Salmon River in Idaho, and I was up there a lot on hunting trips. In fact, I was in the first group that went in there to use it. There were only four or five hundred acres there, but it bordered the primitive area, and if he didn't hunt on that land, they would give it to an outfitter guide. So he had to have somebody there to hunt it, and he brought in a guy named Bob Cole from Idaho to take care of the lodge. When he realized hunting season was approaching a week later, and that the Idaho Fish and Game was going to give the primitive area to an outfitter to hunt if it wasn't hunted, he sent four of us up there. Aaron Dimmit, myself, Fred Naugle, and Joe Curry went up and hunted it.

For years after that, I would take customers up from here or Reno. I ran into Bill one time up there with Bobbie Gentry. I was trying to get out of Middle Fork Lodge to come back to Reno, and the plane was late getting in, and finally when it did show up, Bill and Bobbie were on the plane. Before they could take us out, the plane had to go back out to Boise to fly a piano in for Bobbie Gentry, so she could play the piano while she was there. So we were late getting out of there. I saw him there on a couple of other occasions, but again, just passing: "Hello. Goodbye. Did you have a good time?" Very little conversation.

There was also great fishing on the Middle Fork—salmon, trout, and steelhead fishing. That's why Bill bought that lodge. Originally, it was him and Scherry who used to go up there and fish out of Stanley, Idaho, and he liked it so much up there that when the lodge became available, he bought it. I fished there on a couple of hunting trips. When we got done hunting elk, deer or bear, we'd go up the river and fish a little bit; but I never went up there just to fish.

Do you still take customers on hunting trips?

I take customers on dove hunts to Mexico, fishing trips to Alaska, golf trips to Monterey. We still do a lot of that, but we don't do the lodge anymore. They gave it to the Nature Conservancy.

—◇—

What is the difference between the employee of today and the employee of earlier days at Harrah's?

Oh, I don't think they take as much pride in their work today. When we were dealing, you didn't dare ask anybody how much a bet paid on a crap game. You figured it out yourself, and it was a big deal to you because of peer pressure. If somebody you were working with had to tell you how much a horn bet paid, it went all through the club, and everybody knew about it. You had a little more pride than that. You wouldn't dare let somebody else make your pay-offs for you. Now these kids here deal for five years and still can't remember what a horn bet pays, what the limits are on the table, or the limits on the numbers. They don't seem to care about it. It's more of a carefree attitude now.

We would never dream of not showing up for work. We would not dream of coming in late. We'd better have a damn good reason for being here late, and the no-show without even a phone call in was unheard of. You could also get your ass fired for it. If you work somebody a twelve-hour shift now, they cry for a week. You try to change their days off, they're upset

over it. It's really a lot different than it was, but I think that's a way of life in any business, not just here.

And the supervisors don't the take the job as serious as we did; they're not concerned—they don't believe that there's anybody out there trying to cheat anymore. They think that's all stories from the past. It still happens, but there's a different breed of people that you're working with now. The customer has changed too.

Do people strive for a promotion like we did when we were young?

Yes, but not as much. As an example, we've got a craps crew on graveyard that are lifetime dealers. There's one in there that's a thirty-five-year dealer; there's a thirty-year or twenty-five-year dealer, and these are guys with families. You would think they would want a promotion, but they don't. They don't want the pressure of the job. They don't want the responsibility that goes with it. They would just as soon have a nice, carefree, dealing job.

When we were breaking in, the big thing was to put a coat on, be a pit boss.

That's right, and you got a drink stamp when you put on a coat. That was important. [laughter]

Today there is a department called marketing, but years ago, they used to call it advertising. What's the difference?

It's the same old whore in a new dress. I'm not a marketer by a long shot, and I don't know how to tell you, but they are kind of a different breed. I think sometimes they're looking at the wrong people, the wrong group of people, the wrong mass. I think if you already have a good product to offer the customer, it's too bad that you have to spend that much money on it to get them here. Our marketing budget is huge. And I think sometimes we overemphasize the same program. Instead of changing with the times, I think we stay in the same mode too long. I know I'm not putting that very clearly to you.

What I'm picking up is that you're marketing to a certain group, whereas in advertising, we used to just throw it up on billboards, radio, and TV and try to reach everyone.

Well, in marketing you're trying to find the higher-end customer, too, which is right, but I'm just not sure that we have come up with anything new in several years. It seems like it's the same old story in a different language. It just doesn't seem to have changed as fast as the business has changed.

In your program, though, you're in marketing to a degree when you take somebody golfing in Monterey.

In the casino marketing part of it, yes. But as an example: Steve Wynn. I don't think he has as big a marketing budget as we do. He built a volcano out there, and he did his marketing through a volcano. In Vegas, what could you do to put 5,000 people in your front door four, five, six times a day any better than that volcano has done?

Good point. Yes, very good point.

We haven't done anything here—and when I say "here," I mean the whole marketplace, the four major casinos we have here—that really stampedes the door, OK? Steve Wynn puts a volcano out there [in front of his Mirage Hotel-Casino in Las Vegas], and in the course of four hours or four different eruptions, you've got 25,000 people standing at your front door watching. That's his marketing program. He'll take them out of your place to watch his place. I don't say all 25,000 people walk through the Mirage, but it's a good opportunity for them if they want to. They're at your front door.

When you take somebody to play golf in Monterey or to Alaska to go fishing, are those proven, established, longtime customers?

Yes, they're high roller customers, but I'm taking eight, ten, twelve of them at a time. I'm talking about marketing to a mass to really affect the market count, the head count up here. I don't believe any of these casinos have done anything revolutionary to draw people to this market. We're handicapped with no airport. (We have an airport, but we can't bring in any big flights—there are noise restrictions, environmental concerns.) It's a tough market to bring people into, and that's why Vegas is so popular—traffic from every airstrip in the country can get to Las Vegas. You want to come to Tahoe, you have to go to Sacramento, San Francisco, Oakland, or Reno; and either way, it's an all-day trip for a person from the East Coast.

Let's talk about employee benefits. Have they changed a lot in the last forty years?

I don't believe there's a casino in the country that offers the benefits that Harrah's does or ever did, for that matter. I mean, from day one you are insured. We have dental insurance and eye care. We have high-end medical coverage, paid holidays (your birthday is still paid), retirement fund, the 401K that matches you dollar for dollar. I think Harvey's does fifty cents on the dollar or twenty-five cents on the dollar. Harrah's matches it dollar for dollar. So between your retirement fund, your 401K, and stock option plans, the benefit plan here is outstanding, and that also came from Bill Harrah.

Another benefit, one of the best raises we ever got, was when we went from a six-days-a-week salary to five days a week at the same salary. They didn't give you the pay cut. They left you at the same pay rate, and you only had to work five days. I had thirteen years of six-day salary, and now if somebody works six days in one week, they think it's a big penalty.

Years ago, we used to have just a few high-limit players. What's going on now in Harrah's?

It's a night-and-day difference. In the days you and I are talking about (in the 1950s and 1960s), the high rollers were Art Berberian, Jack Androvich, Alex Spanos, Ferdie Sievers, and not very many others; but now I have lots of them. As an example, our biggest table limit in the 1960s was $500, and we had one of them. This weekend, we had at least a dozen $100 minimums and, I think, three $500-minimum twenty-one tables. Five-hundred-dollar minimum to $5,000 maximum.

With so many of your tables having $500 or $100 minimums, do you even have a two-dollar table on the weekend, or is five dollars as low as you go?

Mostly five dollars. We'll have some three-dollar tables. We're talking three or four, but other than that, it's all five dollars and up. They're full, but we used to have fifteen crap games too. The craps is kind of a dying game now. You know, people laugh at me, but I think the army had a lot to do with that. The draft was a breeding ground for crap players, and everyone learned to play craps in the service. We used to have big keno play, but slots ruined the keno. Years ago, the biggest slot jackpot was $5,000, and $25,000 was the keno maximum. Now keno has a $100,000 maximum, and in some places, one million dollars, but the difference is, you've got three hundred slot machines out there where you can win a million dollars. We've got 1,600 or 1,700 machines out there, and there are probably three hundred of them or more that you can win one million dollars on with a pull of a handle, so why chase a keno ticket when you can play a slot machine and win that much?

Another thing that's changed all over northern Nevada, and Las Vegas quite a bit, too, is the entertainment.

We used to have shows seven nights a week, two shows a night, and we had all main headliners; but now, as we said, the employees don't want to work that much, and neither do the entertainers. Take Neil Diamond as an example. Why should he come up here to work for $300,000 a week? Two shows a night, seven days a week–why should he do that when he can do a one-night concert in Sacramento in the Arco Arena and make half a million dollars? One-night stands, two-night stands, and they make themselves one million dollars and get the hell out of town.

You can't pay an entertainer $300,000 and $400,000 a week and pay that bill off of a dinner show. The cost has become prohibitive. So now we do shows for three nights only. We just had the Gatlin Brothers for three nights. We'll have Don Rickles back, and we have Neil Sedaka coming back for two or three nights. It's tough to get name entertainment that people will travel a distance to see, so we do more revues–revues that last four, five, six, eight, ten, twelve weeks–for a lot less money. Vegas has done away with most of their headliner rooms. There's a few of them; I think the Sahara still has one. The Mirage, of course, has Siegfried and Roy. That's a forever-popular show, but most casinos in Vegas have done away with them too.

How many years ago did you break away from the pit and get into special casino promotions?

About seven years ago. I've always been tied in with the customers and got to know a lot of them over the years, so it was no big deal. I was a casino manager at Harrah's Tahoe for fifteen years, and I'm probably the only one left here now that has a large customer following. We've expanded our V.I.P. department in the last few years to handle the bigger volume of high rollers. Basically, all high rollers have to come through my department. We treat them right and we try to upgrade the players. I report directly to the general manager of Harrah's Tahoe, Pat Denehy, and I have about thirty people in the department.

Dan Orlich was in basically the same type job at Harrah's in Reno, but he was running more junkets. He was in charge of the junket operation when we had our own planes. He was bringing in high roller junkets, and we do all that ourselves now. We don't have as many junkets as we used to. We're more of a one-on-one, and we'll work with our other properties. The V.I.P. department in Joliet, as an example, brought in forty, fifty, sixty customers last week for the Fourth of July celebration, and they'll bring in a group for the golf tournaments. For New Year's Eve, all the different properties will bring a group of seventy to eighty people.

Then you'll do the same thing. You'll send some of your customers to Joliet?

Well, it's hard to send anybody to Joliet, and it's hard to send them to Tunica. There's not much there anymore. But last year, we took groups to New Orleans. We'd go down to New Orleans, spend a couple nights there, and then take them to Dallas for a football game when they were playing the 49ers.

We don't have junkets per se, other than our special casino groups that come from our other properties, but we still have a few reps in the network, and we might be getting back into that in the future. We have very few outside reps that bring in junkets as we used to know them, because the reps all have to be licensed now, too. Also, with the junket reps, we like them to be loyal to our properties. An outside junket rep, as we know them, has a group of customers that he'll take wherever the best deal is for him. He might take them to the Bahamas, or if he got a better deal out of Resorts in Atlantic City, he would go to Resorts International. So it's whatever the best

L to R: Sammy Davis Jr., Debbie Reynolds, Bob Hope, and Russell McLennan. *"We used to have shows seven nights a week, two shows a night, and we had all main headliners."*

return is for the rep. That's why we kind of like to do it with our own properties–if I have a customer here that wants to go to Atlantic City, I can call our hotel out there. They take care of him for me just like he would be taken care of here, so it's important to the customer too.

Harrah's, before they sold to the Holiday Inn and maybe afterwards, had a private air fleet.

We got rid of all of that. We had two jets and a King Air and the Grumman Otter, but we got rid of all the airplanes. The cost was prohibitive. If you've got a $100,000 player in Los Angeles, that plane costs you $2,000 or $2,500 an hour to fly him to Tahoe or Reno. So how many $100,000 players do you have in Los Angeles?

So Bill Harrah did it more for entertainers and for prestige purposes?

Entertainers, convenience, and prestige.

Harrah's Club developed a customer base in Mexico and in the Far East. Were you involved in that at all?

Yes, we had customer bases there, and we lost them with the devaluation of the peso. It really killed the Mexican program. Caesar's has stuck with it pretty good, but it was very, very expensive. And the same with the Asians. By the time you fly them over here–they all want to fly first-class–the expense of coming here is tremendous. (We paid for their plane tickets from the Orient.) With the Mexicans–some of them–we'd go down to pick them up with the jet. There again, the expense was prohibitive. You could only carry twelve passengers.

The devaluation of the peso killed our Mexican groups. We still get splinter groups of them. I just took six of them to Alaska last month fishing, so we still get splinter groups of them, but as far as junkets out of there, no.

Vegas gets that business now because of the convenience, if nothing else, plus the mega-casinos, of course, and the big fight promotions. You come to Tahoe from Mexico, it's an all-day trip by the time you fight the Reno Airport. Vegas to Mexico is just a matter of hours.

Ninety percent of the Asian market goes to Las Vegas too, but we never were heavy-duty in the Asian market. We had a group that used to come, but not a big-number group. They had big limits; they were big players; but we didn't have the number of people to justify that one. Plus, the Asians would go to Vegas first. They'd make that stop in Vegas first, pick up airfare down there, then fly up here and want another airfare here. So I mean, the expense was too much.

When Holiday Inns took over the operation of Harrah's, was there any effect on your job responsibilities?

Not really. I was a casino manager then, and I was in the customer end of the business then, too. The customer-oriented programs were not really touched at all. We were always top-heavy in upper management, and they were the ones that got cut in that shuffle. As far as the customer contact people, they weren't touched. We weren't bothered at all by the takeover. Holiday felt that if you don't have a customer, you don't have a business, so the customer departments weren't affected.

A few days ago, you started your thirty-ninth year with Harrah's. Is there any Harrah's employee who can challenge your length of service?

One–Bob Sterling. He's in the food and beverage department. He's got me by about ten months, I think.

Ten months. Are you going to outlast him? [laughter]

I hope so, but he's looking pretty healthy. I don't know.

People ask me, "How many club managers have you worked for?" And I basically tell them, "All of them." The only one that wasn't here was Eldon Campbell, who went to Harvey's about the same time I got here; but from then on . . . Curly Musso and Pat France . . . I mean, I've been through all of them. I figure that it averages about one club manager every three and a-half years.

You have seventeen years with Holiday and twenty-one with Harrah's.

That's it. In Reno, Carmel Caruso and probably four or five others down there have similar numbers. I think Dick Henry is still down there, and there might be four or five of them down there with forty years plus.

A lot of people that started here in entry-level positions wound up running casino businesses. A lot of them started here as change aprons, crap dealers, or twenty-one dealers; and it's not just at Harrah's that they've become managers, but other companies too. It's all from Bill Harrah—where else are you going to track it from? Where else would you get that kind of opportunity?

I think another thing about Harrah's is that people such as yourself were given the right to make a decision. You didn't have to wait for somebody to tell you to do something, you were given a chance to expand your capabilities and your potential.

It's even more so now than it was when it was Harrah's, in that respect. You have a little more leeway now to make those decisions. Years ago, everybody said, "Well, Rome had to approve everything." I think Rome would have probably rather had you do it if he could have counted on you to do it instead of waiting for him to make the decision for you. I think you could have done it yourself then, even in those days, but nobody wanted to take the

chance to do it, to make that decision. They'd rather have somebody else do it for them.

Note

1.   This "building" is the present location of Harrah's Tahoe Hotel-Casino.

17

DAN ORLICH

D AN ORLICH was born December 21, 1924, in Chisholm, Minnesota. He grew up there, and after completing high school attended Northwestern University as a member of the Navy V-12 program. Orlich came to Reno in June of 1947 to play football for the University of Nevada. That led to a part-time job at Harolds Club in 1948. Following a professional football career with the Green Bay Packers, he returned to Reno and Harolds Club.

Orlich was hired by Harrah's Club in 1972 as director of special promotions, and that eventually led to his being named vice-president of that department. He retired from Harrah's in 1986. In this oral history he gives a detailed description of various junkets brought into Harrah's, especially those from Asia and Mexico, including the various types of junket "reps" and how they were paid. Another subject covered by Mr. Orlich is what is known as the "calculated win." This method of evaluating a player, which was developed by Orlich

and George Akmon, is a system that does not rate the customer by what he wins or loses, but by how much money the customer "puts into action in a given time."

DAN ORLICH: I was born December 21, 1924, in Chisholm, Minnesota. I'm divorced and have three children—two girls and a boy. Dori will be thirty-two March 18, Dana will be thirty-one November 15, and my son, Simo, will be thirty November 13. Dori lives in Reno, and Dana lives in Seattle; she's married to Dan McGwire. My son lives in San Diego.

My parents are both immigrants. My dad came to the United States in 1915, when he was twenty-four years old, to avoid being inducted into the Austrian army. My mother was two years old when she came to the United States in 1904. They were married in 1922.

I have two sisters who are twins, a year and a half older than I am, and I have a younger brother, Mike, a year and a half younger. Then there's the baby, Sam—he's six years younger than I am.

My mother went right to Minnesota because her father and mother were there. My dad went to Gary, Indiana, worked in grocery stores and hardware stores. He soon learned there was a huge Serbian settlement in northern Minnesota in an iron ore mining area, and he decided he would go there. Those old Serbians could hardly read and write the English language, so they emigrated to where the Serbian communities were, and there was a big one in northern Minnesota. Being uneducated and hardly able to speak the language, they went where the hard labor was.

DWAYNE KLING: Well, you got out of there pretty quick.

I got out right after high school, 1942. But there was a war—we all had to leave. [laughter] On December 7, 1941, I was a senior in high school when the Japanese attacked Pearl Harbor. I was only sixteen years old then, but I turned seventeen on December 21. When I graduated in June of 1942 I was awarded a scholarship to Northwestern University, so I went there as a civilian and later enrolled in

the navy V-12 program. They had a marine detachment, and I joined that portion of the program. I had spent my freshman year as a civilian, and on June 1, 1943, we all became activated, and I was in the marine corps officer training program. We were on active duty, we were in uniform, and we lived in barracks.

I spent two semesters at Northwestern, and then our entire detachment was transferred to Penn State. I spent two semesters there taking both academic courses and military courses, and I was permitted to play football. I had only played four games for Penn State when our detachment was called to boot camp at Parris Island. From there we went to Camp Lejeune, and then I went to Quantico for officer training. I got my commission on August 14, 1945, one day before Japan surrendered. Suddenly there were *thousands* of second lieutenants without jobs.

I was assigned to a casual company at Camp Lejeune with nothing to do—just sit there and wait for a new assignment. I asked if I could get out of the marine corps and go back to school, and they agreed, but all of a sudden I got orders to go to Washington, D.C., to the Marine Corps Institute. The CO was Colonel Donald Kendall. He was the brother-in-law of the commandant of the marine corps, and he was a basketball nut. He *loved* basketball! He lived and breathed it. He had been going through the records and discovered that I had played basketball and was six-five and weighed 220 pounds, so he had me transferred to Washington, D.C. to play basketball. [laughter] What a military career! Anyway, when the basketball season was over, he asked if I wanted to become a regular marine, and I said, "No. I want to get out. I want to finish up school." So they discharged me in April of 1946.

I went back to Northwestern and stayed there the school year of 1946-1947. In June of 1947 I said, "I think I'll go out west and see what's going on out there."

Two former Northwestern football players had come to Nevada earlier that year, and they said, "Why don't you stop in Reno? They have a *gorgeous* little school–only about twelve hundred people." So on my way to Sacramento I stopped, and I talked to Jake Lawlor, and I talked to Joe Sheeketski, and they said, "We'll give you a full scholarship if you want to come here."

Joe Sheeketski, the football coach, had coached at Iowa, and he probably had seen me play. They just took one look, and they said, "Come on." Jake Lawlor was the basketball coach, and he said, "You're also going to play basketball." I said, "Fine."

After the school year of 1947-48, I started working for Harolds Club on June 11, 1948. I was on the GI Bill, and that paid seventy-five dollars a month. The athletic scholarship took

Dan Orlich in action with the University of Nevada Wolf Pack football team in 1948. *"I had played football in 1947, and we only lost two games that year, but in 1948 we had a* superb *team."*

care of my room, board, and tuition, but I wanted extra spending money, so I went to work.

Duke Lindeman, my roommate, was a football player at the University of Nevada, and he worked at Harolds Club as a bouncer. He went to Chuck Webster, who was a shift manager, or Jim Hunter, the assistant club manager–I'm not sure who–and said, "Dan wants a job." They said, "Bring him down." So that summer of 1948 I worked at Harolds Club as a bouncer. I quit when school started, but Duke didn't. Duke decided he wanted to work one more week, and Sheeketski said, "You either come to school now, or you're off the team." And Duke said, "The hell with you," and dropped out of school.

I had played football in 1947, and we only lost two games that year, but in 1948 we had a *superb* team. At one time, just before the Santa Clara game, we were ranked seventh in the nation in the UPI poll. Stan Heath was the quarterback; Tommy Kalmanir was a halfback; Dick Trachok was a halfback. Oh, we had a tremendous team! If we'd have beaten Santa Clara we were the odds-on favorite to go to the Sugar Bowl to play Georgia. When we lost to Santa Clara, we got the Harbor Bowl bid there. We played Villanova, and we lost 27 to 7. The year prior to that, on January, 1, 1948, we played in the Salad Bowl and beat North Texas State.

Didn't Joe Sheeketski work for Harolds and Harrah's?

He worked at Harrah's Lake Tahoe, and he was also a crap dealer at Harolds. Pappy[1] hired him to be a crap dealer during the summer of 1948–just a publicity stunt of Pappy's.

I graduated in February of 1949, and I worked at Harolds Club from February of 1949 to June of 1949. Then my sister got married, so I went back to Minnesota to attend her wedding, and from there I went to Green

Bay, Wisconsin, to play for the Green Bay Packers.

Curly Lambeau, coach of the Green Bay Packers, had come to the Harbor Bowl game to see Stan Heath play, because Stan was nationally famous. (He had set some passing records that were unheard of in those days.) During the game, Lambeau looked over some of the other guys on the team, and when the game was over–before I even had my clothes on–he came in and asked if I wanted to play. I said, "Yes, I'd love to play," and he handed me a contract. I said, "I can't sign that contract until the basketball season is over because I'm going to be on the basketball team." It was my understanding that if I signed that contract, automatically I'm a pro. So he said, "Keep it. When the basketball season is over, sign it." When it was over, I signed it, sent it to him, and I became a Green Bay Packer.

Now, there was another guy by the name of Joe Bach, who was born and raised in the same town as myself. He was about my mother's age. He was a coach with one of the New York football teams–I think the New York Yankees, who the year before that were the Boston Yankees; neither team survived. He asked me if I would play for them, and I turned him down. I wanted to play for the Packers. They had had fantastic seasons in the 1930s, and during the war, in the 1940s, they had won a couple of championships. Fact is, they were the only team that won three championships in a row in the 1930s. Also, I was very close to home–Green Bay is ninety miles north of Milwaukee, so I'm going to say I wasn't more than three hundred miles from my home.

So you went to Green Bay, and your first season at Green Bay was 1949?

Right. The season ended in December, but I did not come back to Nevada then. My dad had a grocery store in Chisholm, Minnesota, so during the off-season I worked

there. I worked there from January until the season began again in August.

So you played for the Packers in 1949, 1950, and 1951?

Yes. And in February of 1952 I came back to Nevada. One of the reasons I came back was that I was in the marine reserve, and Korea was going full blast. I was a lieutenant in the marine reserve, so I figured, "I'm going to go back to Nevada and have some fun until they call me." Well, I kept throwing away my requests for reserve training, and shortly thereafter I received my discharge. So I stayed in Reno the rest of my life.

While I was waiting to be called up by the marines, I went to work again at Harolds. The opinion in those days was, a casino job is not a permanent job, it was something to *work at.* And suddenly I start getting promotions and start getting more money, and that's when I said, "Holy mackerel, I hope the marines don't call me." [laughter] So they didn't, and that's the reason I'm still in Reno.

[From 1952 to 1971 I was at Harolds Club, first as a craps dealer, and then, after 1953, also as a public relations representative and competition trapshooter representing Harolds. Harolds Gun Club was established in 1953. It soon became the home of the most prestigious trapshooting meet in the West, the Golden West Grand, held in May of every year. I became Harolds' house shooter, successfully representing the club all over the country at trapshooting meets. At the same time I rose through the ranks, eventually becoming a casino manager. Pappy died in 1967, and in 1970 Howard Hughes's corporation bought Harolds. Things changed. In 1971, I left Harolds Club.]

I was off for a year after leaving Harolds, and Bob Klaich and I tried to put a couple of deals together–couple of hotel casinos . . . one at the lake, one here in Reno. They fell through. Off for a full year, I decided I had better go back to work, so I called Lloyd Dyer at Harrah's. He said, "I'll get back to you."

As I recall how it happened, Lloyd was the senior vice-president or executive vice-president of administration. Rome Andreotti was executive vice-president of operations, and Maurice Sheppard was the president. Lloyd went to Rome, and Rome said, "We don't hire from the outside." Then Shep got wind of it and said, "Call him in and let's talk to him." So they called me in, talked to me, and said "Come to work."

They hired me as a promotion person, but I wanted to work in the pit for a while to become familiar with their policies and procedures for dealers, because they were very different from what they were in Harolds. At Harolds, you flew by the seat of your pants. Harrah's was much more business-like, and I wanted to learn policies and procedures and get to know just how they operated.

They put me in the pit for a short time, but what they really wanted me to do was re-start the junket program that Lee DeLauer had previously run, and which didn't pan out.

I was named director of special programs. (A director was a level below vice-president and one level above a department manager. You might say directors were junior officers. They were the persons in charge of departments.)

The hotel was already open—it had opened in 1969, and they had tried a junket program at that time. When they handed me the papers, the reports on it, I looked it all over, and I could see things that could and should have been done to the program. They gave me about six months to report back to them with what I thought should be done to create a successful program.

Harrah's had already discussed a regular fly-in program comparable to Las Vegas junkets. We continued to build on that program, and we set up some strict guidelines—much stricter than they had in Las Vegas. By that I mean the limits were higher,

the gaming requirements were higher, the complimentary privileges were less, and they had to qualify as good gamblers. It was a good program. At first, nobody thought it would work because it was too restrictive, but when you have a hotel like Harrah's at Lake Tahoe, which is very sought after, you have no problem getting people to go there.

What size were the junkets you brought in?

We flew some in on Harrah's planes. The Falcon held nine customers, and the GII held fourteen preferred customers. When you only have nine or fourteen customers, and when you're flying an airplane that costs three thousand dollars per hour to operate, they have to be pretty good players. We would bring regular customers in on commercial airlines, and of course, if they qualified, we would refund the price of their commercial ticket.

We also had a charter program with United Airlines. That was one of the most interesting things I ever did with Harrah's. We were going to use airplanes that they had in their fleet but not presently in use. They asked us, "Where do you have junket reps?" And we said, "Well, we have one in Vancouver, we have one in Portland, and we have one in Seattle. We have one here, and we have one there." Then United took airplanes out of their fleet and gave us an absolute beautiful schedule. For instance, start with a group in Vancouver. Bring them to Reno. Take them home, then stop in Portland. Bring the Portland people to Reno, then go to Seattle. Our down time was practically nil. It was just a fantastic program. But it deteriorated for the reason a lot of other junkets deteriorated. You have representatives who become lax, and they start putting friends and girlfriends and non-gamblers on the flights, resulting in an unprofitable trip.

Were those players tracked?

Absolutely. They were tracked. They had identifying pins or symbols, such as little dice pins or little card pins, and the pit supervisors, slot supervisors, and dealers recorded their play. We had their names before they arrived, with their credit limits. It was a fairly sophisticated system.

George Akmon, who was my assistant, and I devised a rating program which was entirely different than win-loss. You may have heard of it; it's called "calculated win." You would determine, for instance, how many hands a twenty-one dealer can deal in an hour, how many rolls of the dice on a normal dice game in an hour, and how many spins on a roulette wheel. Then you would determine the player's average bet, and then you would calculate the percentage that a particular game would hold. The rating system had nothing to do with whether a player won or lost. If a man would bet $150 for one hour on a crap table, you were going to hold, theoretically, a known percentage of that money. It didn't have anything to do with his win or loss.

Our philosophy was, "You're bringing these people here to play; and if they play, you know that come December 31, you're going have won money for the year." If a player provides you with good action, that's all you have a right to expect. In a lot of casinos, a man had to lose before he would get any complimentary privileges. We never operated that way. All he had to do was give us good action—we knew what it had to be—and if he did that, there was no question we would come out ahead. We started that system, and then a guy wrote a book in Las Vegas and gave us credit for developing the system. There were many variations of it. Eventually the system went to New Jersey and, to my knowledge, this is the system they still use.

Tracking programs started in Vegas, God knows how long ago. Then all you had to do was write twenty-five hundred dollars in markers. It didn't work out, because it doesn't

take a genius to know that *anybody* can write markers, buy them back; write them again, buy them back. You could write fifty thousand dollars worth of markers, but that doesn't show that you played.

The initial problem we ran into with *our* system was the accuracy of the dealers. When you have one big crap game going with fifteen people on it and money all over the place, the dealer's got other things to do besides determine what this man's average bet is. So on a game like that, if there were, say, eight or ten players with pins, we knew that those people had to be tracked, and floormen would come up and help out.

How long did the junket program with United Airlines last, Dan?

It probably lasted six to eight months. It gradually deteriorated because of the time constraints placed on the representatives. You can't tell a junket rep, "You have five weeks to produce this group," because sometimes maybe he can't do it. So in order to meet the quota, he would start putting in non-players just to fill it. Eventually George Drews, vice-president of finance, who was a watchdog on everything that I did, came flat out and said, "The program is not carrying its own weight." So we had to cancel it. But about that time we got into a junket program in Mexico and one in Hong Kong.

How did you bring the players in from Mexico and Hong Kong? Were those commercial flights?

Most of them were commercial. One year we had a gigantic Christmas program up at Lake Tahoe. I occupied 95 percent of the hotel for a period of about three weeks over Christmas and New Years with junkets of just Mexican players. They were the cream of the Mexican gambling crop. There were players with two, three, four, five-hundred-thousand-dollar and one-million-dollar lines of credit, and *they played.* They'd sit in that baccarat room for hours and hours and hours.

Also, we would have seven, maybe eight, GII flights per year at fourteen passengers per flight. Our GII flights were strictly stag. By stag I mean just the gambler, no guests. Occasionally, we had a woman with a ten thousand or fifteen thousand line of credit, and she could get on that airplane.

We would also have a couple of Falcon flights a year. On the spur of the moment, my rep, Marcos Berkman or Mauricio Cats, would call and say, "Dan, is the Falcon available? I have six people who want to come up." And we'd send it out. Of course, I had to share those airplanes with Holmes Hendricksen, vice-president of entertainment, who used the Falcon for the entertainers. But Holmes was always so easy to get along with. He was a hell of a guy to work with, simply because he was so accommodating. Everybody knew he had first choice of the planes because Bill Harrah worshiped entertainers.

Whenever Frank Sinatra wanted the GII to go wherever, it was available to him. But if I had a flight scheduled, Holmes never just took the plane. Sometimes he'd say, "Dan, is it absolutely necessary that you have that GII?"

And I'd say, "Not absolutely."

He'd say, "Can you charter? I'll OK it with Bill."

And I would say, "Yes, I can charter."

He'd say, "OK, go out and get your charter." And then I would go out and find a comparable airplane that could accommodate nine, ten, twelve, fourteen people.

Sometimes it would go the other way. He would have a flight scheduled, and I would say, "Holmes, I just got a call from Mexico. I got fourteen of the top players ready to go."

He'd say, "You've got the plane. I'll find other transportation." And that's the way we did it.

But there were people who were jealous. "Who the heck's this guy Orlich, for Christ's sake? He's just a director and he has primary responsibility for those airplanes?" And, in

two seconds flat, Bill Harrah sent a memo– "Following are the priorities for the GII and the Falcon: Bill Harrah, Dan Orlich, Holmes Hendricksen, Lloyd Dyer." He went right down the list. Nobody ever said a word again.

So, you were ahead of Lloyd Dyer, president of the company?

On priority for the airplane, yes, because they knew the type of customer I was putting in there. Tom Yturbide, general manager of Lake Tahoe, was my number-one advocate. At Lake Tahoe we would put $1.7 million to $1.8 million on the bottom line every Christmas. From, say, December 16 to January 5, we did that much business.

Did the Mexican people bring cash or checks?

They all had checks because they all had bank accounts in Texas, but mainly we used markers. They were more in the form of IOUs, which are legal documents in Mexico. They were made out in dollars. At first, we did it in pesos, and then we did it in dollars so that we could collect dollars. The peso had a way of going amiss, and then, of course, just like everybody else in the business, we took a "dumping" because of the devaluation of the peso.

❖

Harrah's put on two or three golf tournaments a year at Tahoe and a couple here in Reno. They were Bob Ring's special pride and joy. He put on, in my humble opinion, one of the *finest* golf tournaments that I have ever seen in the history of the gambling industry. They were absolutely superb.

People used to pick up the phone, call Bob, and say, "Please! I've got to be invited to your tournament." The galas they held in our convention center every night were out of this world. I was very, very impressed until I saw the figures. Then you could see that it was just a big show, and it was costing Harrah's too much money.

Typically, if you don't put the reins on such events, they come to a point where they can't make any money, I don't care how many players you have. The number of celebrities gradually kept increasing, until at one time there were 35 celebrities in a tournament, of say, 140 people. And celebrities cost a lot of money. Joe Namath was here, and Joe DiMaggio, and names like that . . . they were all here.

And the door prizes kept getting better and better until the tournaments were costing you more than you could ever have a right to expect in return. They would give ladies jewelry. They would give every entrant a brand new set of golf clubs and a golf bag–seven, eight, nine hundred dollars apiece. And they gave watches–thousand-dollar watches–as prizes for winning the tournament. They would give big TV sets. Everyone in a foursome would win a prize, so you go down five places, and that's twenty prizes. They were absolutely first-class. I went to a few tournaments as an invitee in Las Vegas, and they couldn't compare–*could not compare!*

Didn't Bill Harrah give away a Rolls-Royce every year?

He gave away several, and he gave away several hole-in-one prizes. Finally, one year when they got the bill, they just said, "These golf tournaments are getting out of line. We have to stop them." Then they were turned over to us. We did it in conjunction with our reps and with our casino managers.

John Cerutti was our Texas rep, and one of our better reps, and he was also a bonafide junket man. He knew what he was doing. He was an operator, and he did a lot of thinking for himself. He devised promotions–he would say, "I have thirty-five customers who would love to play golf, and here is what I can guarantee you." Then we would put together what we'd call the Longhorn Open or the Texas Longhorn Open or whatever.

And then another junket rep would hear this and would say, "Well, I've got the following . . . ."

And I would say, "OK, you show me what you have, and then we'll give you a golf tournament." And the big tournaments, the big galas that Bob Ring had put on, simply disappeared.

A lot of people don't realize a junket develops good players, and then you more or less take them out of a junket group. A superb player just picks up the phone, calls you, and says, "I'm coming in with my wife. Are we all set?"

And you say, "Come on in."

If a customer did that, I had a special arrangement with my junket reps that I would give them their fee anyway. You want a junket rep to last, you can't beat him out of his fee. You just can't do it. He has developed that player, and he deserves to be paid.

Is that how they got paid? Did they have a flat salary plus a commission based on the player's action?

Right. We had a fee structure where the rep would get paid the following amount for this kind of a player and this for that kind of a player and so on. If he really got a superb player, then he'd get a little bonus.

Did the rep usually come with his players?

Oh, yes. We insisted that he come with every group of ten or more. And of course, we had rules and regulations, which no other casino had. Typically, on Las Vegas junkets, the representative took care of his group–he'd comp for them; he could sign for them; he could increase their credit limit. He could do a lot of things. We absolutely said no to all of that.

We told the reps, "Our casino will take care of all the casino players."

One of them said, "What am I? Just a host?"

And I said, "Right, that's all you are." The reps would try to go in the pit like they do in Vegas, and we would absolutely not permit that. But when they got used to our way, they saw that it was easy. "Hey, this is duck soup. We don't have to do anything."

If a player got out of line or something like that, the rep didn't have to take care of it. We took care of it. But we would go up to him and say, "Now, this guy was a problem. You instruct him before he gets on your next flight that if he does it again, he's out of here."

Did you frequently put on special shows for the junket people in the convention center?

We sure did! I'll tell you the one the Texas group absolutely adored—Willie Nelson. Whenever we would have Willie Nelson, we would give the Texas rep priority on rooms and groups to bring to the lake. For instance, we'd call the Tulsa rep and say, "Willie Nelson's in town, and we are going to bring your group in six weeks later. A group from Texas is going to take your place." The Texans always got to see Willie Nelson.

Did you have special dinners for the junket players?

No, not really. But on the top floor of Harrah's at Tahoe we had the finest restaurant I have ever been to. It was called the Summit.

We had a lot of problems with our so-called maitre d's up there. They knew exactly when our groups were coming in, and they knew they were full comp, especially the Mexicans. They wouldn't bother to give them menus. They would simply walk up and say, "My name is so-and-so, and I will order your dinner for you." They knew full well they were going to get big, big tips. We ran into problems, and we fired several just because of that. A party of four might have a bill of over twelve hundred dollars. But no question about it, it had great, good food, and it was one of the number-one drawing cards at Tahoe.

How many airplanes did Harrah's have in their fleet?

Harrah's had, when I first got there, the Jet Commander, which could carry six passengers. They had the De Havilland Otter, which was used to fly back to Harrah's Middle Fork Lodge in Idaho, and they had a couple of Cessnas.

The Otter could not be used for junkets. It was a big old workhorse used to fly supplies, employees, et cetera, to the lodge. The Jet Commander was kind of Bill's private airplane, and he traveled in it a lot, but we did use it for junkets sometimes, even though it only seated five customers. Shortly after I got there, Harrah's purchased the Falcon, which held nine passengers, and the GII (the Gulfstream II) which was originally designed for twenty, but Bill Harrah wanted it plush, so he re-designed it with extra amenities and plush areas so that it held fourteen passengers comfortably.

The aviation department reported to me only because you can't have everybody reporting to the president. If there was a problem in that area, they would come to me, and then I would ferret it out, straighten it out, and report back with an answer. I didn't know an airplane from an automobile, but eventually the department did report directly to me, mainly because I used the airplanes more than 90 percent of the time.

Where were the airplanes based?

Harrah's had the GII and the Falcon in Reno, and the Otter was pretty much stationed in Boise. The Cessna was stationed in Boise and at the Middle Fork Lodge.

Were there any planes based at Lake Tahoe?

No, but we used the Lake Tahoe airport quite often, and that's very interesting. The GII, of course, is one of the noisiest airplanes in the world, and if you're not familiar with the airport at Lake Tahoe, it's kind of cut into a gorge. When that GII took off, it rattled windows for miles. [laughter] The pilot, Bill Blackmore, a tremendous guy, was a hotshot pilot. He would drop a group off at Lake Tahoe, and then he'd fly the plane back to Reno. He would take off and point that GII straight up, and it could climb two thousand feet a minute on one engine. So he would have both engines wide open, and he would take that thing up, and within minutes the phones at Harrah's would be ringing off the hook. The poor FAA had to call the complainers and say, "I'm sorry. We cannot insist on Harrah's noise abatement because that airplane isn't big enough." [laughter] (You had to have x number of seats before you had to take off slowly across the lake.)

Bill used to "cowboy" that thing. I still razz him. Spoke with him yesterday, and he said, "Dan, you've never flown an airplane, so you wouldn't understand, but when you can point a private jet straight up like that, you can't resist."

✧

Had you ever met Bill Harrah before you went to work for him?

I had met him only once before I went to work for him, but I used to see Bill at the Prospector's Club with his management group. Every year since 1953, I would go to Arizona for trapshooting, and I had a doctor friend in Phoenix who I went to high school with. He was an internal medicine man who had a very close friend at the Mayo clinic who was Bill's doctor, and together they had developed a new system for EKGs.

My friend asked if I knew Bill Harrah, and I said, "I know who Bill is." (This was when I was at Harolds.) "I see him on occasion."

He said, "Well, the next time you see him, just tell him Dr. Smith says to say hello."

And so, I'll never forget it, we're at the Prospector's, and I'm in my big black suit, and there Bill is sitting over in the corner. I get up, and I start walking to that table. All the eyes are looking at me like, "What the hell is this?" and I stop right next to Bill. I said, "Mr. Harrah, I have a message for you from Dr. Smith. I met him in Arizona, and he wanted me to give you his best regards." [laughter] I don't know, maybe they thought I was a hit man.

That was the only time I'd ever talked to Bill before I went to work at Harrah's, and after I went to work for him, I seldom had any dealings with him. I don't think anybody but Lloyd, or maybe Rome and Bob Ring, saw much of Bill. He was not a hands-on guy, but you knew exactly what to expect from him. Bill was a martinet, a perfectionist, and he knew what was going on at all times.

Here is an example [of Bill's attention to details]: Everybody from the director level on up had a company car. If you're the president, you're allowed this kind of car, if you're a vice-president, you're allowed this kind, and if you're a director, you're allowed this kind. *Except* the director of entertainment. Because he dealt with the entertainers, he's entitled to a Cadillac. Well, I had an occasion once, when one of the limousines broke down, to take five Mexicans from Lake Tahoe to the airport, and I took them down in a company Wagoneer. Bill heard about it, and he said, "You're taking our top Mexican customers in a Wagoneer? How often do you have occasion to transport passengers?"

And I said, "Very often. I go to Lake Tahoe twice a week and I almost always have a customer in the car."

"Why didn't you tell us?" he said. "Our good customers all ride in Buick Skylarks. You go get yourself a Skylark." Well, that created a little bit of a stir with some people simply because I was only a director, but eventually they understood.

Were the company cars yours to do with as you wished?

Oh, yes. They were yours twenty-four hours a day. You were told what you could get. The garage manager would say, "Go down and look at the following . . . ."

You would go down and look at them and tell him, "That's what I want." Then the next day, you would come to work, and there it was. You drove it, and it was yours. You brought it home. It was your car, but you didn't have to pay any insurance, and you didn't have to service it, buy gas for it, or maintain it. It was a definite benefit. Hell of a benefit!

A lot of people have said that Bill Harrah strongly believed in delegation of authority.

No question about it. You can't compare him to Pappy Smith. Bill had his top guys, and he was there as the chairman. He would have his meetings, and they would report to him, but as far as giving assignments or things like that, Bill never had to do that. Bill definitely delegated authority.

Did you have a great deal of freedom of decision when you attained the position of director?

Yes, I did, because my position was very unique. I was kind of over there all by myself, and I did so many things off of the premises. At one time, we had forty junket reps scattered all over the United States, Mexico, and Canada, and I had to do business with all those people. Now, had all of my business been done on the property, I probably would not have had as much freedom as I did. They gave me a lot of freedom simply because I would talk to this guy, and if I couldn't make a decision or had to get permission to do something, it was too late. That did happen on several charters.

It took about six weeks to get a charter. You had to reserve the airplane, get the price, decide who was going to be on it, establish their lines of credit, and research their history of play. Then you would put a report together, and you'd give it to Rome. OK, he would look at it. By the time he would say, "OK, do it," it

was too late. So, we lost a couple of charters because of it. Then after a while, when they were comfortable with me, I would go in and say, "Everything looks good," and Rome would say, "Then go ahead and do it."

Did you go to the areas where the junket people were located?

I went initially, just to meet them. I went to Pennsylvania, and I went to Mexico to hire a rep and to open up an office there. I also went to Hong Kong and met with Rome and Lloyd; but as a rule, I didn't go to the junket locations.

You had the good fortune of working in high-level management in two of the greatest casinos in northern Nevada. Can you compare Harolds and Harrah's as casinos, or in any way compare their owners, the Smiths and Mr. Harrah?

The biggest comparison would be the ease with which the Smith family ran Harolds Club. Nothing really complicated; comparable to flying by the seat of your pants. Whereas at Harrah's, everything was defined. It was operated more like a business, and I'm not being derogatory. Now, I don't think that had anything to do with their personalities. As you know, Pappy was outgoing, blustering, always selling Harolds Club. Bill Harrah was very, very remote, very straight. He just did not want the limelight.

Customer relations–they both had the same philosophy in customer relations. Treat them properly; treat them right. Customer comes first. Maybe Harrah's was not as blatant as Harolds Club, where the customer was never wrong. That was Pappy. But let's say the comparison, as far as customer relations, was very close when compared to the rest of the casinos in the state of Nevada. I went to plenty of them that were downright rude towards customers–that was just the way they were. But Harrah's and Harolds were parallel as far as customer relations. They treated them with dignity and respect, and they were genuine. They were honest about it. And of course, Bill, being the martinet and perfectionist that he was, did everything he could to ensure that the customer would be treated like a king when they came into his place.

Of course, there were differences in how the two clubs operated. Harolds, when they had a meeting, it was spur of the moment: "Let's meet." At Harrah's we had scheduled meetings from the director level on up once a month. Bill Harrah tried to attend all of them because this is where he was in contact with his managers. There were about eight or nine vice-presidents, there were thirteen directors, and of course, Rome and Holmes as executive vice-presidents. Lloyd Dyer was also an executive vice-president, and Shep was the president. Later on, when Shep left, then Lloyd became the president.

Who chaired the meeting—the president of Harrah's or Bill Harrah?

Usually the president. Bill would never chair. He sat there and listened and very rarely offered opinions. The meetings were mainly to let everybody know—even though there were reports on top of reports—what was going on with them, their scope of management, and also what was lacking at Harrah's. "Here's where we're going. Here's what we want to do, and here's what we expect to do," and things like that. They were very informative.

With what I did, you very rarely were in touch with the administrative directors at Harrah's, whereas Harolds was a "Ma and Pa" store—you were in contact with everybody. There weren't that many top managers. There was only the Smith family, Guy Lent, the business manager, and Jim Hunter. Then there was the purchasing agent, and then you went down to the shift manager, the bar manager, and that was it. But Harrah's had the hotel, they had the bars, they had the casino, they had the restaurants, they had the

aviation, they had all of those departments, plus all the operation departments. I definitely was in contact with the operation departments on a daily basis, but the others I didn't see too often. And these monthly meetings put you all together.

Was there any one thing that Bill Harrah and Harold Smith or Pappy Smith expected, or even demanded, from their upper management employees as far as loyalty?

Well, Dwayne, I think loyalty's implied. When you get a position of authority, it's implied that you're going to be loyal to them, but we all know cases in the industry where that wasn't true. When I had my meeting with the Hughes people after they took over, I said, "The Smith family earned my loyalty. Right now, you people are paying for it." I said, "In time you will have earned it, or I will not be here." I think that's top management. You earn that respect, and through that, loyalty's implied. It's automatic. You just give it to them.

Were there any management theories or policies that were similar between the two northern Nevada gaming giants, such as customer relations or entertainment or promotions?

Well, we have hit on customer relations. They were both friendly. "We love our customers, and we're going to do the best we can for them." Entertainment, they both went for entertainment. But unfortunately, Harolds facility wasn't anywhere near what Harrah's was. As we discussed earlier, I don't think Harolds showroom could hold sixty people, but it was good entertainment. Harrah's, of course, had their great, big, huge showroom.

Harolds had bar entertainment, and they had the gun club . . . and Pappy's doubling of the bets[2] was, in my opinion, one of the best promotions there ever was. Everybody copied it or tried to copy it. No other casino would've ever dreamed up such a thing, but this was Pappy's philosophy. And all of a sudden, Harrah's saw that it was one hell of a thing, so they started doing it. Pappy was a very innovative guy. As far as dreaming up ideas, he was far and beyond anyone else and, in my opinion, better than all the promoters in the state. Pappy's the one who took it out of the green eye-shade era and brought it out into the open.

What do you feel were some of the reasons that Harolds Club became static in the late sixties while Harrah's Club just continued to grow and expand?

It's very difficult to pinpoint the exact reason, but Pappy's death was a big factor simply because Pappy was the driving force—not 100 percent, but he was the driving force. And I just don't think Harold Sr., Harold Jr., or Raymond had any intention of taking over and making Harolds Club grow. I think they had had it. They were willing to get their money out of it and let somebody else take over.

And about the same time Harrah's had taken over the Golden Hotel, they were expanding their entertainment, and they were getting ready to build their new hotel.

Yes. Harrah's, before that, was just another little old dinky casino like some of those across the street and smaller than Harolds. Just a regular casino ... but they decided that the future of this business is in hotels, promotions, and big-name entertainment. Harolds did not. Harolds just remained static.

Harrah's had to go public in order to build all these things. They had to sell stock; they could not have borrowed that kind of money. And of course, that's what all the other hotel/casinos in the business did. If Harolds Club had decided to go ahead with their hotel plan and their big-name entertainment, they would've had to go public. They would've had to sell stock. It could not have been a family operation, because, to my knowledge, they didn't have that kind of money.

Both casinos were innovative for a long period of time, weren't they, Dan?

There was no more of an innovator than Pappy. And we don't want to compare Pappy with Bill Harrah, because Bill is modern and Pappy is from the old school. Pappy was such an innovator that when he was going to go to Las Vegas, they sent him a message, "Stay in Reno. We can't compete with you." Which is probably the best compliment ever paid the man.

Dan, you're the only person who was in top management in both Harolds and Harrah's when they were purchased or taken over by another major company. Were there any similarities or differences in the two takeovers?

They were *not* similar. The first takeover of Harolds by the Hughes people in Las Vegas was a casino being taken over by casino people. Carl Cohen and Jack Pieper and those people were casino people all their lives. They had preconceived notions of how a casino should be run, whether it be in Vegas, whether it be in Reno, or whether it be in Podunk. And that's what they brought to Harolds. That is what they tried to force down our throats.

When Harrah's was taken over, they were taken over by a motel chain, Holiday Inns. They knew little or nothing about a casino. They were smart enough to buy the number-one casino in the industry at that time. And they flat-out said, "Why should we change what's working?" They came in, and they spent hours and hours and hours with all of us, asking for suggestions. It was just beautiful. There was almost no pressure. Oh, there was some occasionally when top management came in, and Lloyd Dyer had to leave because they had their own guy. That part was very similar. When Hughes took over Harolds

Club, the top guys had to go, and they put in their own people. And in both cases there was anxiety. Having been through the Harolds Club thing, I figured, "Well, here we go again." Two times in my life is more than a guy had the right to expect. But it wasn't very difficult at all. The transition of going to work for Harrah's from Harolds was much greater than the transition of working with the people who bought Harrah's. That was very smooth—very easy. In my humble opinion, they brought in a lot of good ideas even though Harrah's was a very well-organized, very well-run casino business. They brought in a lot of ideas from the outside world that we had never thought of before.

Let's face it, Holiday Inns was the largest motel chain in the business at that time. They had a lot of smart people. They brought in a lot of smart planning people and promotion people, and they got it out of the pure casino business. They got it more international, and you can see what's happened. Look at it. They are all over the world.

Prior to Bill Harrah dying, Harrah's was moving toward Atlantic City, but very slowly—very deliberate—typical of the way they did business. Holiday Inns comes in, and it's, "Here's an opportunity. Let's go." And away they go. Then they hire people, put them in place, and then they go on to the next one. Now, I don't know if that's the proper way to do it, but that's just a difference—a difference in how Harolds, Harrah's, and Holiday Inns did business.

Another difference between Harolds and Harrah's might have been their theories on bringing in outside help.

That's right. When Pappy died, Harolds Club just went flat. Instead of hiring someone and saying, "Come on in, outsiders, come on in. You're a hell of a promoter. We'll take care of the casino. You make sure that this place expands." That didn't happen. It just didn't happen. And when they put Harold Smith Jr.

in there, Harold Smith Jr.–God bless him, he's not here to defend himself–he was not a manager, he was a playboy. And it's not his fault. That's the way he was brought up. He didn't have any fantastic ideas on how to build the business up, how to promote, how to keep the thing running. That just didn't dawn on him.

But Bill Harrah surrounded himself with top management people from the inside and outside. Bill struggled for a long time in the regular casino part of it until such time as he got some outside brains. "What can I do?" and this is what they told him. He was not afraid to get outside help, well-educated help, people who'd been in promotion and in the hotel business and in all industries. He went out and got them, and he built himself a tremendous organization, and he sat up there and watched over everything.

It's interesting that Pappy was offered the help of a restaurant executive, Paul Debus, and he didn't want outside help. He was going to do it himself. On the other hand, Bill Harrah went out and actively sought outside help.

Absolutely. Bill had a vision: "This is what I want to do." Whether he was advised, I don't know, but he said, "I can't remain this way forever. I'm going to build a hotel. I'm going to have top-name entertainment. I'm going to build the largest hotel/casino in the business." And he set out to do it. He went public. He went out and hired expert help. Where do you get a hotel manager if you don't have a hotel? Outside. You got to go outside. That was one of the major differences between the two clubs–Harrah's went "outside" for help and advice, Harolds did not.

At one time, weren't Harolds and Harrah's about the same size or even smaller than most clubs in town?

Yes, and they literally took over the town. I remember distinctly when the Hughes people took over Harolds Club, and we had just been introduced to Jack Pieper. We were in a meeting, and he said, "Well, no wonder you had all the business in the world. You had the location."

I stood up and I said, "Jack, in the 1930s when your father ran a casino, you know where downtown Reno was? It was Center Street. It was the Bank Club and the Palace Club." I said, "Harolds Club and Harrah's changed it to Virginia Street."

What effect did the merger of Harrah's and Holiday Inns have on your specific duties at Harrah's Club?

It didn't have any effect. I still did the same thing, except Holiday Inns had a slightly less restrictive policy toward bringing in the high-limit players. They wanted me to bring in more: "If your program is so successful, why aren't you in more cities?" And of course, you had to explain to them that you can't be in every big city in the world. But it did give me a little more leeway as to what I did. Not that Harrah's restricted me—it's just that when I first came to work at Harrah's, they didn't know who I was except from being across the way, and they kind of watched what I did for awhile. Then when they were at ease with what I did, I could operate pretty good. But they had a restrictive policy: "We don't want this program to get too big." And Holiday Inns had a different viewpoint. They were at ease with me because I had been with Harrah's for a long period of time.

Was your budget changed?

Yes, it was increased. I was given, for instance, the go-ahead to go into different cities. Then our people would get together, and we would present our budget, and we would say, "OK. Do you want us to go to the following places? This is what it's going to cost. This is what we're going to bring in." Then the decision would be made, and we pretty much stayed with it.

In 1983, which was a little over three years after Holiday Inns took over Harrah's, you were promoted to vice-president of special casino programs. What responsibilities did that position entail?

Nothing really different from what I was doing as a director, except I was given managers to do what I previously did, and now we had a program going in Las Vegas, and we had a program going in New Jersey along with our Reno and Tahoe programs. I was overseer of all four of those programs, but duty-wise, I did pretty much the same.

In May of 1986, Harrah's decentralized their properties. A lot of the job positions were eliminated. Some people were terminated and some people transferred. Were you involved in that situation?

Yes. What happened was the putting into action of the philosophy that Harrah's had discussed many times. Decentralization means each property now runs itself. They're not run by a central location. Reno had been the headquarters, and all the vice-presidents and the directors of all the various functions were in Reno. Now, each property had its own managerial people running their departments. The person in Reno who was in charge before the merger either took a job at one of the properties or he was eliminated. That's pretty much what happened. I don't know how many, but there were several jobs lost.

I had the opportunity to go to Lake Tahoe, which I turned down because I was going to be sixty-two in December, and I just went to Phil Satre, the president, and said, "Phil, rather than go anywhere, I'll retire in December." He was very receptive and thanked me for it. I had a company car which they gave to me, and I purchased all my stock options and all the restricted stock was given to me—just outright given to me, which I thought was very nice. This took place in May of 1986, and they kept me on in an advisory capacity until January 1, 1987.

It seems you were treated very fair.

Simply because I didn't fight it. I just didn't fight it. Many Harrah's people were very bitter. They thought Harrah's was not treating them properly. I'd been through this before, so I just said, "Hey, whatever you want to do, that's fine with me." [laughter] That was the end of my *active* gaming career. When I had my retirement party, Harrah's gave me their famous gold card as a gift. The gold card is something Bill Harrah began presenting many years ago to a lot of Harrah's favorite customers and favorite people—not necessarily customers. What it amounted to was complimentary privileges in the bars, the restaurants, the hotel, and the showrooms. It still carries on. Mine was given to me by Phil Satre when he was the chairman of Harrah's. I have the next to the last gold card with Bill Harrah's signature. Mark Curtis, former vice-president of advertising/public relations, got the last one with Bill Harrah's signature. When I left in January of 1987, there were twenty-seven gold card holders still living. I have no idea what that figure is now.

Do they give them out anymore?

No. To my knowledge, Mark Curtis got the last one.

Now that your active gaming career has ended, do you still go to Harrah's on occasion?

Oh, yes. I stay in touch with them. I'm not even close to being in an advisory capacity, but I still feel like I'm one of the family.

Notes

1.   Raymond I. "Pappy" Smith founded Harolds Club in Reno. He named the casino after his son, Harold Smith Sr., who became general manager upon Pappy's death in 1967.

2.   On a regular (but unscheduled) basis, Pappy Smith would randomly visit different table games throughout Harolds Club and double the wagers of anyone playing at a particular table. This practice became well-known and was an effective promotional tool for the casino.

18

MAURICE SHEPPARD

MAURICE SHEPPARD was born in Longmont, Colorado, on May 24, 1917. His family moved to Reno when he was young, and he grew up there and graduated from the University of Nevada. After service in the air force in World War II, he returned to Reno and started work at Harrah's as a bookkeeper in the spring of 1946 at a salary of fifty dollars a week. He worked for Harrah's for almost forty years and was president of the company from 1969 to 1975. Succeeded by Lloyd Dyer as president, Mr. Sheppard was Harrah's vice-president for community affairs from 1975 until his retirement in 1982.

For this oral history, Mr. Sheppard was interviewed in the offices of the William F. Harrah Trust in March of 1997. The interview was completed in one session. In it, "Shep," as he was known to his friends and associates, describes Harrah's early methods of operating, the development of the daily report, the monetary problems of an expanding Harrah's, and early methods of financing. He also discusses how he became president of Harrah's and how John Harrah, Bill's father, took a very active part in the first years of Harrah's operation in Reno.

Mr. Sheppard also recalls the close association he had with Lloyd Dyer, the man who eventually replaced him as president of Harrah's. They worked

hand-in-hand in many real estate transactions and in searching for financing.

Maurice Sheppard was in poor health at the time of this interview, and he passed away a few months later. Regrettably, his condition at the time made it impossible to conduct a lengthy interview in depth with the man who would otherwise have been perhaps the best single source of information about the operations of Harrah's Clubs from 1946 to 1980.

MAURICE SHEPPARD: I was born in Longmont, Colorado on May 24, 1917. My father was the manager of a Woolworth store there before being transferred to Reno. My mother and father were later divorced in Reno.

I was an only child. I grew up here and went all through school here, graduating from Reno High School in 1936 and the University of Nevada in 1940. After graduation, I went to work for an airplane factory in San Diego before the war, and when they started drafting, they wouldn't take me because of my job. I had to quit my job to get into the army air force. I was sent to finance school at Lake Forest, Florida, and I was in the accounting department the entire time I was in the service.

I met my wife, Audrey, when we were both in the air force, and we were married right after the war was over. When I was discharged from the air force, I came back to Reno, and in March of 1946 I went to work for Harrah's. That was the first job I had after the war.

DWAYNE KLING: How did you happen to apply at Harrah's?

I can't say there's any reason why I did it. I had to start looking for a job someplace, and I went to Harrah's. There were some people working there that I knew, and that may have been the reason I went there, and when I married my wife, I had to have a job. [laughter]

L to R: Maurice and Audrey Sheppard and Joseph Fanelli at Harrah's South Shore Room in October 1976. *"I met my wife, Audrey, when we were both in the air force, and we were married right after the war was over."*

What was your first job at Harrah's?

A bookkeeper for fifty dollars a week. I had many jobs after that, but mostly in the accounting department down in the basement. There were two or three of us in there, usually. One fellow was Red Farnsworth, and he did the payroll. He would come in at the end of each shift and get the time cards, and then he would go someplace in the club and make the basic payroll. Then he would go home, and at the end of the following shift, he'd be in again; and then the following shift, he'd be in again. How he ever worked it, I don't have any idea.

Everybody got paid at the end of each shift?

Well, not everybody. Some of the people were on regular salaries, like myself and Bob Ring. But all the people that were working on the floor–the dealers, pit bosses, et cetera–were paid cash at the end of each shift, right out of the cashier's cage. They would just line up and get their pay at the end of every shift.

Did they deduct withholding tax?

Oh, sure. Mr. Farnsworth just figured it out. If you were making $20.00 a day, he'd withhold it and pay you $18.50 or whatever.

Do you remember when they stopped paying them every day?

No, I can't remember exactly, but I remember . . . they had to talk them into it because they were so used to getting paid every day. They weren't very happy about getting paid once a week; and actually, daily pay was one thing that worked well for the house. There was a saying in every joint in town that as soon as they get their money, they go over and have a drink or two, and then they walk over and start playing the table games or the slot machines. So a lot of the money we were paying the employees came back to us right away.

Were you involved with the counting of the drop boxes every eight hours?

No, there was a crew that did that. They had a different group that would take the boxes into the office on the ground floor. I needed to have the figures right away, because I did the daily financial statement, and I had to have it completed and up to John Harrah (Bill's father) by ten o'clock in the morning or else I got my ass chewed. [laughter]

Bill would look at the report, but, John was the one who was keeping an eye on it. However, John was really never communicative. John didn't have anybody report to him, and he had nothing to say to me about the operation at all. Whatever he had to say, he would say it to Bill, but Bill just delegated everything. I had a lot of outside help, though, from Semenza, Kottinger and McMullen, an accounting firm that was with us all the time. If I had any problems, I could always go to them.

From that daily report that I started, I had all the information I wanted. I knew what the salaries were for salaried people, and I knew the daily receipts from the food and bar department and when they would empty the slot machines, and I could figure out what they made on the slots. The games were the easiest, because I had all the figures.

My whole idea of the daily report was so we would know exactly what was going on. It worked out pretty good. At the end of the month, I'd always check it, and we were not too far off on profit and loss. And it wasn't that difficult to do, so if they finished the count around 8:30 or something like that, then I could get it all put together and get it up to John by ten o'clock. (Bill wasn't as eager to look at it as John was, and Bob Ring didn't care to be involved in it in any way at all.)

What did Bob Ring do in those days?

Well, Bill Harrah and Bob Ring had worked together for a long time in southern California. They had card games and a circle game, and when Bill came up here, he brought Bob along. Bob hung around the place all the time and did everything.

Did he deal, or was he a pit boss?

No. There was a fellow that worked for Harrah's named Rome Andreotti, and he was a heck of a great guy. He knew more about gaming than anybody in Reno. He had spent his whole life doing it, and so Bill left the gaming up to him, so far as rules and procedures.

Did Harrah's have a club manager in those days other than John Harrah and Bill Harrah?

They didn't have, really, but Bob Ring could have been considered the manager. And Bill was there quite a bit of the time. Probably, just by walking through the place, he could tell how the club was doing.

It's been said that Bill Harrah drank a lot and gambled a lot in the forties . . . .

Well, he didn't do a lot of drinking in the club. I think he did a lot of drinking in other places, and he did a lot of gambling, too, but I don't remember ever seeing Bill drunk.

Did you know a gentleman named Virgil Smith?

Yes, he was a friend of Bill's. He was in the club quite often. He didn't have anything to do with running the place, but he gave Bill advice on this, that, or the other. He was an old-timer; he and Bill were old-timers together.

⋄

I eventually became the office manager, and when the Lake Tahoe club opened in 1955 I kept the records for both clubs.

So, by that time you were the controller of the entire operation?

Well, you might say that, yes. I kept the same records of the club at the lake as I had been keeping for the club in Reno, and in the same manner. I got all the figures—all the slot machine figures, all the gaming figures, keno, bingo, and everything that we had—and along with the daily report I also issued a P & L (profit and loss) statement every month. I had several employees working for me at the time, and I was in touch with them quite often. We had weekly . . . maybe not weekly meetings, but pretty close to it at Lake Tahoe and Reno. Time was divided for everybody between the two places, but the club at Lake Tahoe took more time at the outset, because it was larger than the Reno facility.

When Bill Harrah went to purchase something (for example, when he purchased the Lake Club), did he consult with you to see if Harrah's had enough money to purchase it, or was that pretty much an independent decision?

Oh, he was very independent, because he had so many friends that he could borrow money from. He didn't have a problem to buy the place. People thought a lot of him. They knew that they could depend upon him to pay them and so forth, so he didn't have a lot of problems in raising the money for the lake club.

Bill had a good reputation, and he didn't lack the ability to get money for expansion from the First National Bank of Nevada or wherever the best interest rates were, but it worried me when he did things like that. You know, I had to pay the bills, and sometimes it was tough. [laughter] I hated to see the winter months come, particularly at the lake.

Did you have monetary problems in the wintertimes, especially at Lake Tahoe, when the weather was bad?

Oh, yes. One time we just didn't have any business at all at the lake. One year, I forget exactly what year . . . my God, it was just a disaster! I thought, "How are we going to get by? How are we going to make it this year? I hope we don't have to go through this again." There was just absolutely no cash flow.

When Bill opened the place at the lake, the bankers and all the other people said, "You're making a mistake. You'll never make it up there. You'll never make it." Well, hell, you can see what he did. [laughter] He opened up the doors for everybody else up there too.

You must have had a hard time getting from Reno to Lake Tahoe in the heavy snow storms.

I sure did, but Bill furnished us all with cars that could get through the snow and everything else. [laughter]

◆

Bill Harrah used efficiency experts, on occasion, to give him ideas on how the company should be run.

He might have talked to some of them. After all, when he started out, he didn't have experience in gaming. He didn't know anything about anything other than what he and Bob did down in southern California, and that couldn't compare, in any way, with what was going on up here, so he would get the information he needed the best way he could.

When did you become president of Harrah's Club?

Well, that was a rather sorry sort of a thing. Bill called me in one day in 1969 and told me that he wanted me to take Bob Ring's place as president. Bill didn't ever like anything that was distasteful or hard to do, so it was my job to go up and say, "Bob, effective tomorrow, I'm the president, and you're out." How would you feel? That was tough. It was really tough, but that's the way he wanted it, and that's the way it was. Bob and I still got along fine after that, because he knew as well as I did where it was coming from. It was coming from

Bill himself, not from me. I wasn't doing it, and it really was a shock to me too.

◆

I hired Lloyd Dyer a long, long time ago. There were two fellows applying for the position of vice-president of finance and real estate, and I had asked for somebody that was good at accounting. The fellow that hired all the people recommended somebody else, and I said, "No. I want Lloyd." So I got Lloyd. [laughter]

Were both Lloyd and this other person already working at Harrah's?

Yes, so it was a big promotion for Lloyd. Lloyd got into the job right away. He got into doing the daily reports, and he did everything that I did, and it went real well. Initially he was spending some time at Lake Tahoe, but he wasn't up there on a full-time basis. I thought that I would put him up there and let him

Maurice Sheppard at the Middle Fork Lodge.

handle the Lake Tahoe finances, and I'd take care of Reno, but it didn't work that way at all, because I needed his help down here. I used Lloyd a lot in real estate transactions because he was good at that . . . better than I was. And then Bill got to like him a whole lot, too, which was helpful to me. [laughter]

Do you recall any master plan that Bill Harrah and yourself ever discussed, i.e., "I want to expand here. I want to go on this side of Center Street, and then I want to go down and buy the Overland or buy the Palace"? Were long-range plans ever discussed, or did things just happen?

Bill didn't say, "This is what I want to do," but he knew what he wanted, and he had it in his own mind. He had his plans all made up, and there wasn't any way you could change what he wanted to do. He was going to do it his way, period! I had an awful time trying to get in to him to say, "Bill, I don't think we should do that." It's like when he went to go to Lake Tahoe, the bankers were all saying, "Bill, you're making a mistake. You shouldn't go up there." But, of course, he did go. I mean, he took a stand, and that's the way he did it. He had his mind made up to do it, and so he's going to do it.

When Bill opened the first club at Lake Tahoe, there were those places across the street, so he just bought out the competition. He just kept buying them out. He did the same thing in Reno, even going back to his bingo parlors. He would buy a property or lease a property to eliminate his competition.

We had weekly management meetings, and Bill conducted them. When Bill was there, that was it. He was the boss, period. But he let you bring up whatever you had to bring up. Sometimes we had an agenda–can't say that we had one all the time, but I used to try to get agendas: "Let's get it all down so we know what we're going to talk about. Let's write it all down." But he was going to do it his way. It really didn't make any difference whether anybody agreed with it or not.

[laughter] Bill and I also met on an almost daily basis and discussed things, but other than in meetings, I spent very little time with Mr. Harrah.

Bill Harrah would ask you to do something or tell you he was going to do something, and it would be up to you to implement it.

Yes. But on the big moves . . . boy, he would be having secret sessions with whoever he was dealing with, and then all of a sudden it would come out to you. For the most part, that was what he liked to do; but on the other hand, if he needed help, he would have meetings with top management and get as much input and information as he could.

19

JOSEPH SNYDER

*J*OE SNYDER *was a dealer and pit supervisor in Nevada gaming for over forty years. He worked on the south shore of Lake Tahoe for several years, not only at Harrah's but also at the Tahoe Village and Harvey's Wagon Wheel. For this oral history project he was an enthusiastic chronicler and very willing to talk about subjects that many chroniclers didn't care to discuss, such as cheating in casinos. The interview was held in Mr. Snyder's home in Carson City and was completed in one session.*

Joe Snyder was born in Richmond, Virginia, in 1927. He and his family moved to the Los Angeles area when he was a young child because his father, who was running illegal gambling in Baltimore, was getting too much "heat" from local law enforcement officers. The father later relocated to Reno and worked for Bill Graham and James McKay at the Bank Club. In the summer of 1947, Snyder went to work at the Tahoe Village for the infamous Woods brothers. The operation was a "flat store," and it was there that he got his first training in the field of casino cheating.

Snyder recalls his days as a dealer at the Palace Club working for the legendary "Baldy" West. Later, while in the military, he used his training in cheating to make extra spending money. When he got out of the service in 1955, Snyder went to Lake Tahoe to work at the Wagon Wheel. He tells of being terminated from the Wagon Wheel and going to work for Harrah's in 1962. He then describes in

detail the type of action that Harrah's was getting and the pros and cons of working for Harrah's. He also makes the observation that in a gambling house no one is irreplaceable except the customer.

This oral history interview contains valuable information about how, prior to the state gaming commission coming into being, some casinos took advantage of players.

JOSEPH SNYDER: I was born in Richmond, Virginia, in 1927. When I was a young child, we came west to Los Angeles because of problems that my dad was having in the east. He was in gaming in the Washington, D.C. area and in Baltimore, Chicago, Philadelphia, all over. The games were illegal, of course. It was during the Depression, and today they'd probably call him a "street hustler." I probably learned how to spin a roulette wheel before I knew what one and one was. [laughter]

Dad was very knowledgeable in table games, and when he came west to Los Angeles, he became involved with a consortium that had the largest racehorse book in the city, located in the basement of the Pantages Theater on Hollywood Boulevard. He eventually got out of race booking in Hollywood because of problems with the law enforcement and because some of his partners went to Vegas. He did stay in Los Angeles and started speculating in real estate, but on the side he always had some kind of a little game or race book going. So I lived primarily in the Los Angeles area until 1941.

DWAYNE KLING: Was that when your dad went to Vegas?

Well, yes. It was a funny or an unusual incident. We had gone back to Chicago for a racehorse meet at Washington Park, and when the season was over with, we started west. We were going to go into Yellowstone National Park, and we missed the turnoff. I got sick in Salt Lake City, and we spent a couple days there, and then we came into Vegas late in 1941. I was still sick, and we spent an excessive time in Las Vegas, and that was when, you might say, that we established our residence in Nevada.

So, you traveled with your dad when he went to Chicago? Did your mom travel with you too?

We always traveled as a family, yes. Dad was boss of the family. He might come home at five o'clock at night and say, "We're leaving for Chicago in the morning. Pack." And we'd go. And the marriage lasted about thirty-five years. My mother was in her early fifties when she passed away from cancer.

In Vegas, Dad had games in what was then called the Slot Machine Arcade—it is now part of the Golden Nugget or Steve Wynn's Nugget. I guess he lost the lease, and we moved to Reno in June of 1942. In Reno, he went to work for Jack Sullivan at the Bank Club, and he was there for probably, six or seven years. Bill Graham and Jim McKay owned the Bank Club at that time, but they were serving time in prison for mail fraud. Harry Bond was the casino manager, and the casino was a three-way partnership with Jack Sullivan.

Did your dad know Jack Sullivan when he came to Reno?

I don't know what the connection was. Somebody, possibly, had recommended him, or they might have heard of one another from connections around various states that had illegal gambling. Anyhow, he was offered a job, so he took it.

He was a boss and a shift manager for several years. When he left the Bank Club, he went over to the Palace Club for a short period of time. The Palace was owned by Baldy West. In 1947, when I got out of the merchant marine, Dad went to Lake Tahoe and ran a place on the south shore of Lake Tahoe called the Tahoe Village. It's now the administrative buildings for Douglas County. It was first the Tahoe Village, then it became the Casino D'Paree, and in later years it became Oliver's Club. Oliver Kahle was the last casino owner of the property.

The Woods brothers owned the Tahoe Village. There were three brothers. Denny is the only one that I can remember. One was a banker out of New York. He financed it. The other two brothers were out of Oregon.

So, your dad went to Tahoe Village to work there, and you went along with him?

Yes. That was my first job in the gaming business. My dad and a gentleman by the name of Jack Hogue had taught me how to deal twenty-one; craps I just learned on my own. I started out as a stick man. Everyone started as a stick man. I was a clean-up individual because the dice game was flat, and they had to have some place to clean the dice up in the event there was any heat. So I wore a jacket with large pockets, and if there was trouble, they would dump the dice in my pocket, and I would walk off.

Would you elaborate on the duties of a "clean-up" man?

Originally the box man was the bust-out man. He had the bowl of dice in front of him, and he would switch the dice in and out of the game on the first roll. Sometimes it was done by the stick man; and, if the stick man was doing the clean-up or the busting out, he had to clean the dice up in the event there was a problem–take the phony dice out of the game and put the squares back in.

Did they change the dice all the time or just according to what kind of play they had?

It was strictly according to what type of play they had, because you couldn't change the dice all the time. If the heavy action was on the "do" side, then they'd put in the "don't" dice, and they'd usually wait two or three rolls to see which way it was going to go, because you usually had "do" action and "don't" action and "field" action and "come" action. You wanted to see if the square dice were running in any type of pattern. Were there more bets on the odd numbers, or were there

more bets on the even numbers? Then you would determine what to do, what dice to use.

You were saying that ordinarily the box man would take care of getting the dice in and out, yet you went to work as an outside stick man.

Well, the only reason that I wound up with the job is because my dad was running the casino. I just started picking up various things, and I'd be told to do various things. You'd never question it–that would be the end of the story. Sometimes, if they had a good player on the twenty-one game, you would sit down on third base, and you'd draw the card off so the player couldn't make their hand or the dealer wouldn't go broke.

So, he was not dealing off the top of the deck? He was dealing the second card and was taking a peek so that he knew what that top card was?

Yes, right.

Did you, as the person taking the hit, make the decision, or did the dealer make the decision?

The dealer made the decision. They'd signal me to hit or not hit.

Did your job have any title?

No. There was no moniker as far as I was concerned. I was just there as a convenience to them. [laughter] I was only twenty years old, but I didn't have to worry about the gaming enforcement checking my age. The south shore of Lake Tahoe came under the jurisdiction of Washoe County. Washoe County police used to come up once in a while and you were supposed to have a Washoe County card, which I didn't have, but I acquired one when I came down to Reno to go to work. You didn't have to show any proof of your age. You just go in and fill a form out, and it said how old you were, and you put down twenty-one, and you were issued a police card.

So even though it was in Douglas County, it was still under Washoe County jurisdiction?

Yes. All they had at Lake Tahoe at the time was a constable, and the gambling was only open three months of the year. Gaming opened Memorial Day and closed Labor Day. After Labor Day, you could shoot a cannon off and not hit anyone.

You make it sound like a player very seldom left with any sizeable amount of money.

Very seldom. If they did, they had to be playing on the opposite side, and if anybody was in the gaming business, they knew better than to play on the opposite side.

Did the customers ever wise up? Did they ever figure out they were getting taken?

There was an incident at Tahoe Village when a gentleman out of Oregon or Washington had lost a sizeable amount of money on a crap game. He picked the dice up, and he said—of course, he had the bad dice—"Hey! You guys are cheating me." Well, they wound up chasing him around the casino to get the dice away from him, and he finally dropped the dice on the floor. When the dice got picked up, we made the switch and laid them on the table and convinced him that the dice were square. There were several incidents like that.

There was another incident at the Village where they beat a fellow for $10,000. It was about six o'clock in the morning, and he went back to his room, but prior to going to his room, he wrote a check on a Los Angeles bank. Well, as soon as he wrote the check, Dad gave an employee named Eddie enough money to go to Reno in an automobile, get on an airplane, and go to Los Angeles with the

check and cash it before the customer got out of bed.

When the customer did get out of bed, he came back to the casino, and he said, "I think that I was taken advantage of. I'm going to stop payment on the check."

My dad says, "Be my guest. We've already cashed your check."

And he said, "How could you cash my check?"

Dad says, "Well, we flew an employee down to Los Angeles and cashed the check." And the customer was a little surprised at that.

I remember another incident that my dad told me about where they had beat a fellow for a sizeable amount of money. They went to the bank . . . we'll hypothetically say that the check was for $10,000. Well, the guy only had $9,500 in his account, and they were informed that the check wouldn't clear, so my dad made a $500 deposit in the man's account so the check would clear. There were always ways to get around situations, but I don't know if you could do it today or not because of secrecy and the way that credit is classified.

On the twenty-one games, I don't imagine people ever knew they were being cheated. They might have thought they were being cheated, but a good card manipulator is hard to catch.

Oh, no. You could suspect it, but you couldn't prove it. If they were using the peek, it would be one thing. If they were using sand, it would be another. Of course, there are several ways to mark a deck, and oftentimes a man on the outside will try to sand the deck so that he'll know what's coming off the deck.

This is 1947. Was cheating more prevalent in Lake Tahoe than Reno?

It was more prevalent at Tahoe because it was seasonal. It existed in Reno in the smaller casinos. In the major casinos, it didn't exist. I think the inception of the gaming commission and the gaming control board really cleaned up the gaming business. And I would say that the illegal activities ceased around 1955, 1956 on the south shore because of Harrah's Club. Harrah's Club was one of the first really legitimate, clean operations on the south shore, and some of the old-time gamers or gamblers could see that volume took precedence, and the way that you treated customers so that you could have repeat business was very important. Volume overcomes everything.

Of course, when that heavy cheating was going on in the thirties and forties, as we said earlier, it was only a three-month time span, and the casinos felt that they had to get that money any way they could.

That's right, yes. Yes, you only had approximately one hundred days, and you had to make your payroll. They had big shows at the Tahoe Village in 1947. We had Ted Lewis, Sophie Tucker, Leo Carillo, the Marx Brothers, and the Ritz Brothers. They were all top names, and even though they weren't making what they are now, they were still making fabulous wages.

When the owners or bosses would make those big scores and beat somebody out of $5,000, or $10,000, did they come by and give a little something to the dealer?

They always took care of the help. I remember working in a few places where they'd make $1,500, $2,000, $3,000, which would be a pretty fair night, and the boss would go to the cashier's cage and get a handful of twenty-dollar bills and walk around and put a twenty-dollar bill in everybody's hip pocket . . . maybe forty dollars, which was two days' wages. You could do a lot with a twenty-dollar bill.

Back then, your rent was only eighty dollars a month, so forty dollars or fifty dollars went a long way. When I first went to work at the Wagon Wheel back in 1955, they used to come around all the time and, on major

holidays, put an extra twenty-dollar bill in your pocket. And if you were on the floor, a supervisor, they came around at the end of the year and gave you a bonus. You always "hit a keno ticket" around Christmas time–anywhere from two to five hundred dollars, which was a lot of money.

Tahoe Village was no different than anywhere else at Lake Tahoe as far as going for the money?

No, of course not. Sometimes there was casino jealousy because of the quality of play that one casino would get over another. Rather than getting what would be classified today as grind action–dollar, two-dollar action–the Cal-Neva on the north shore would be getting five, twenty-five, and one-hundred-dollar action, maybe one-thousand-dollar action depending on the situation and the quality of clientele. The clubs would try and bring in different entertainers to get a better quality of clientele.

Well, were there a lot of dealers who were just average dealers that weren't mechanics or weren't capable of manipulating the customer?

There were a lot of dealers that never knew that they were working in a flat store. The dealers that knew were an asset, and they helped the mechanic. And when I say they "helped" the mechanic, I mean there is a difference between keeping the dice in the center of the game so that you're anticipating what the box man is going to do versus somebody that's inexperienced that'll take the dice and put them in the center of the table and whip them back to the customer.

After you were in the business for six months to a year, you could anticipate what was going to happen, so you just laid everything in front of the box man; and if they didn't have a box man, the stick man was the "heavy." But it wasn't something that went on every roll of the dice. My dad had a philosophy that you knock out the big bet and give everybody a square roll on the small action. So a man bets you five dollars, you don't want to get the five dollars. You want to let the dice take the natural course. Now, you get a man that comes in and bets you five hundred dollars from the shoulder, you try to get that five hundred dollars. You let him roll a couple times on the square, or maybe you have a progression player so you're not trying to knock out those bettors five or six hands in a row.

When they came around and gave you some extra money, did the dealers that were dealing on the square and that weren't involved in manipulating get cash money too?

Oh, yes, sure. It wasn't determined on what you did. It was determined on how good a shift or night or day that they had.

So, you didn't get any more money if you'd help beat somebody out of $5,000? You didn't get any more than the average dealer?

No. Well, *I* might have. [laughter]

After the first summer at Lake Tahoe, where did you go when they closed up for the winter?

I went back to Reno and went to work at the Palace Club, where they didn't cheat the customer. When I went to work at the Palace Club for Baldy West he told me—I'll never forget his words—he says, "Well, kid, now you're going to have to learn how to deal craps, because there is more to the game than just taking the money. Some people win once in a while."

Another one of the things that Baldy impressed upon me was, "You don't insult a dime player. You insult the big player, and you treat the dime player"—they don't have any more dime crap games—"with more respect than you do a hundred-dollar player." The reason for that is the dime player is not going to make any big score. The hundred-

dollar player, he might beat you out of something, and we don't want him to beat us out of anything, so if he would win three or four hundred dollars, we'd try to insult him and get him off the game unless he was a professional player. A professional player, you can insult them, and they're not going to leave anyway if they're on a run. [laughter] Of course some gamblers, if they're far enough ahead, they're looking for an excuse to get the hell out of there anyhow with their winnings.

That was in the days before there were chips on the games—we dealt silver dollars. If somebody bet a hundred dollars, we had silver dollars that were banded in twenty-dollar stacks, and you would give them five banded stacks of silver dollars. We had two-hundred-dollar limits, so you'd push out two hundred dollars in banded silver dollars.

Harolds Club, I think, was one of the first clubs that came out with chips. The mistake with Harolds Club was in the denominations—he had five-dollar chips, ten-dollar chips, and twenty-dollar chips. Later he went into five-dollar chips and twenty-fives and hundreds, which made it easier to deal. Harolds Club was possibly the only place that ever had twenty-dollar chips.

When you worked at the Palace for Baldy West, did your dad work there, too?

No. I worked at the Palace until possibly the fall of 1948, and then my dad bought the Rollo Casino in Douglas Alley. He had that a couple years, and then he sold it.

I went to work at the Cal-Neva in Reno when it first opened. Worked there a couple years and was laid off during the winter. I had a friend that was in Sacramento—Lock Richards. He was working in Sacramento on a river boat, and he got me a job down there, and I stayed there for a year. I got a divorce, and then I was drafted in the army during the Korean War. When I got out of the army, I knocked around San Francisco with my dad for about six months, and then I got married and moved back to Reno in 1953.

Did you do any gambling or operate any gambling games in the military?

I gambled every day, usually craps or twenty-one. All you had to do was lay a blanket out and come out with a couple of pairs of dice, and you were in action.

I never did anything on crap games other than blanket roll and then try to lay a bet down after a point had been established. I would try and bet the "don't" for even money. Sometimes you got called on it; and if you got called on it, then if it was four and ten, instead of laying two-to-one, you lay them three-to-two. Even money on the six and eight, because the average player didn't know any better.

We used to shoot on the bunks. What you do is, you lock your six and aces together so that you can't crap on the first roll, and that gives you an edge. You can catch your seven-eleven on the first roll, but you can't crap on the first roll; and then, once you establish your point, you lock your six-aces together so that the same combination is coming up.

On a blanket roll the dice don't hit a solid surface. You roll them up the hill on a blanket, they roll back down, and it's just like a wheel. You always keep the blanket tight, and if you roll the dice up one way, they're going to roll back the same way. They aren't going to wobble the way they do on a hard surface.

I played some twenty-one, and I always tried to be the dealer. If I wasn't the dealer, I had the game papered—I would have the deck marked so that I knew what was coming off the deck. I used sand. If I got a leave, I'd go home and fix up five or six decks and put them out around the barracks—just leave them laying around. Anytime there was a game that you wanted to play in, you played, but I never put a deck in the game. Never broke a new deck. It was always there. You knew your deck. If you didn't see the sand, then you didn't play.

Were these several different military locations, where you played?

Primarily, Fort Ord was where I played. I did very little card playing on the ships. The dice were a different story, because you didn't have to do anything—just play the percentage. Going overseas, I won a hundred a day for seven days, and coming home, I did the same thing. I'd try to win a hundred, two hundred a day. I'd win twenty or thirty dollars in one game and go to another game. On troop ships, you always had more than one crap game going, and that was the story. You just moved from game to game, and you'd be surprised how gullible people are. You walk up to them and say, "Hey. Five dollars they don't six," and six is a point.

The guy says, "You're on!"

And then sometimes, I'd walk up to the game when four or ten was the point, and I'd say, "Five dollars they don't."

And the guy would say, "Hey! That's a two-to-one bet."

"OK. Ten to fifteen."

"OK, you're on."

If they didn't take the bet, you didn't lose anything. You couldn't get faded [covered], and that's the end of the story. I made a couple dollars along the way. I was never short of money.

I was drafted in December of 1950. My military career was from December 1950 until November of 1952, and I came back to Reno Easter of 1953 and went to work at the Bank Club. Brad Hewins was running the Bank Club at the time, and he gave me a job, and I stayed there for a good period of time. Then John Hickock was the owner of the Picadilly at the time, and I worked for John for about a year running the Picadilly, and from the Picadilly, I went back to the Bank Club. From the Bank Club, I went to the Colony Club. I was at the Colony Club for about seven months, then went to south shore Tahoe in 1955.

When you were working around Reno during that time, do you recall going into Harrah's Club?

Yes. It was a clean operation. It was probably one of the cleanest operations in town as far as environment, the appearance of the help, and the rules and regulations. I think that Harrah established some excellent rules, because when you're working with a lot of employees and you instill in them that they have to follow the rules, it's easier to protect the games. When Harrah went to Tahoe, he was very emphatic that the rules be followed. One of the main duties of a supervisor was to correct procedure rather than correcting a mistake—to be sure that procedure was followed at all times.

Did the old established people in gambling, such as Brad Hewins or Baldy West, make fun of Harrah's, or did they even comment?

I think the major comments about Harrah's were made when he opened at the lake in 1955. He had the largest casino with the most games, and they felt that he would not be able to fill all those games with customers. He proved them wrong. I'm sure he had his problems in the winter, but he had a bus program that helped increase business; and, of course, the south shore eventually grew to the extent that they put in a four-lane highway to the south shore which helped increase business even more.

I went to work at Harvey's Wagon Wheel in 1955, just prior to the opening of Harrah's Club. I worked for Harvey's from 1955 through 1962, and during that time Harvey had verbally committed himself to sell to Harrah. He had scheduled a meeting to sell the Wagon Wheel, but when he got to the sidewalk, he turned around and came back. He decided not to sell, and, of course, as Harrah got bigger and better, Harvey went

right along and got bigger and better too. Harvey benefited from the Harrah's overflow.

Harrah's bought up Sahati's Country Club, and they bought Itaha's, which is Sahati's spelled backwards, and then they bought the Nevada Club. After acquiring the Nevada Club, they acquired the Blue Mirror Motel on the California side, and they turned that area into a parking lot.

In 1962, I got laid off at the Wagon Wheel, so I went over to Harrah's, and I worked the summer, winter, and fall, and the early part of the spring of 1963 as a dealer. Then I was promoted to box man and then promoted to a floorman. I stayed at Harrah's and worked myself up to a pit shift supervisor and went through a few of the expansion stages with Harrah's Club.

In 1969, there was a large exodus of employees from Lake Tahoe to Las Vegas. I think the majority of the employees that left in 1969 went to Vegas because of job opportunities and an increase in pay. None of the casinos in northern Nevada were excessive payers. A box man in Harrah's was making thirty-five dollars a day; a box man in Las Vegas was making forty or fifty. I started out as a floorman at Harrah's at thirty-five dollars a day and finally went to fifty-five dollars after approximately nine years, but I went to Vegas and was immediately hired for sixty.

There was a big difference, and it's still like that today. You're lucky if you can make $100 to $110 a day in Reno in 1997, but you can go to Vegas and make $150 to $175, and your living expenses are no higher down there than they are up here. In fact, they're probably cheaper because of the year-round warm weather. You don't need two or three wardrobes. You don't have to winterize your automobile. You don't have a large utility bill, although in the summertime you do have an air-conditioning bill in Vegas that you don't have up here.

When you went to work for Harrah's, what were the noticeable differences between Harrah's and other casinos?

Quality of play. I would venture to say that I probably dealt to more money in one day dealing at Harrah's Club than Harvey would get in a week–no question or no doubt in my mind. I can't recall all the players' names, and I think that would be insignificant anyway, because a lot of them would not be alive today, but they were quality players. They were individuals that could lose ten, fifteen, twenty thousand dollars and go have a steak dinner, and it wouldn't bother them one bit.

What do you think that Harrah's did to get that quality of player that Harvey didn't do? Neither one of them had hotel rooms at that time.

Joe Snyder with his wife, Nina, at an employee's party in 1966.

I think that it was the personal attention that was given quality players. The environment was cleaner, and there was no question or doubt that they were getting a fair shake for their money. And I think entertainers such as Red Skelton and Liberace had a significant impact when Harrah's first opened. They were all high-quality Hollywood entertainers, and when a good player would come to see the show, Harrah's always paid his bill. But so did the customer–indirectly.

Did you notice any difference in the knowledge or the skill of the gaming people working for Harrah's as opposed to some of the other clubs you worked for earlier in Reno?

Well, in the first place, Harrah's had college students for dealers and teachers on the security force, so it projected a clean, courteous operation. That was a big difference. As far as gaming knowledge, there was no doubt that some of the old-timers had far more gaming knowledge than Harrah's Club employees, but the thing is, Harrah didn't want them because he wanted to project the clean, pretty image. And volume overcomes a lot of mistakes. I remember years ago at Harolds Club–and when I say years ago, I'm talking about during the forties and fifties and sometime in the sixties–Harold Smith said, "We sometimes have to win the money two or three times, but we eventually win it." So volume and consistency overcome mistakes on the dealer's part that are legitimate mistakes.

So Bill Harrah went about it completely differently from some of the old-time gamblers?

Oh, he sure did. It hasn't been too long ago that I read in a magazine article that Harrah's Club has probably turned out more dealers and supervisors that have gone on to become a success than any other casino. That shows that what might have been thought as being wrong thirty years ago has turned out to be right today with today's operations.

In 1969 there was a mass exodus from Harrah's Tahoe to Las Vegas, and there were always people going to the Wagon Wheel. With all these people leaving, did it have any effect on the success of Harrah's Club?

No, because there was always someone to step in and take their place that had been trained in Harrah's Club policy. I think that a lot of people made a mistake by leaving Harrah's. There was a period of time that I thought that I had made a mistake by leaving. There's an old saying that people that live in the forest can't see the forest for the trees, and promotional opportunity existed at Harrah's Club that I couldn't see.

In gambling, no one is irreplaceable except the customer. I think Harrah's had a philosophy that there were two groups of people that were very important for a successful operation, and it depends on which position that you want to put them in: the employees and the customer or the customer and the employees. Without the customer, the best employees in the world can't perform their duties, and this is what I think Harrah's instilled in the employees. The customer comes first.

Bill Harrah definitely believed that the customer comes first, but don't you think he took pretty good care of the employees too?

You've put me on the spot there, because I've always had the theory that one of the reasons for Bill Harrah's success was his lack of keeping up the wages for his employees. He always had a low pay scale. Also, Harrah's, for years, was the only casino that I know of that allowed its employees to gamble within the area where they worked and make a draw of 50 percent of the wages that they had coming so that they could gamble. Therefore, you have the employee locked in. He owes his soul to the company store, and Harrah can always pay them what he wants to, because he knows they're going to gamble and be broke the majority of the time. During the nine years I worked there, I knew a lot of employees who never made a move because they were broke.

Well, let me interject one thing: Harolds Club was the same way.

That I wasn't aware of.

Yes. Harolds Club actually encouraged you to play when you got off work. But what you're saying is true—I remember people getting off work and playing all the time.

I would also like to add that if Harrah could keep you broke, it was fine, and he benefited from it. If you look at it realistically, when he allowed you to gamble within the casino or area that you worked, he was getting free help.

Also, Harrah had the summer and winter pay scale. You got $25.00 a day in the summer time and $22.50 in the winter. I also remember when I first went to work, they started me out at $22.50, and they said, "In thirty days, you'll get a raise to $25.00." Well, I think it took from the beginning of summer until the beginning of the next season to get $25.00, and then I never got the $25.00. I got promoted. [laughter] They'd start you out at $32.50 on the box, and then they'd give you a share of the tokens; or you could go on the floor for $35.00 a day and not get any tokens. Well, the guy that made the $32.50 and a cut of tokes was better off than the floorman. And they not only had the summer/winter rate, but in the wintertime when business was slow, you'd come to work and work two hours and they'd send you home.

If you got to work two hours. Sometimes, you didn't even get to work two hours.

Yes. The first year that I worked there, I burnt a clutch out going to work because of the snow. I worked two hours and got sent home. I could have stayed home and not worked those two hours and saved my clutch until the next day. [laughter]

I don't think I have any regrets about leaving Harrah's. I could have probably stayed with them thirty years, but I don't think I'd have been any further ahead than I am now . . . . Might be a little further ahead with their retirement program if it made any money.

You worked for Harrah's for about nine years. During that time there was a lot of expansion in the club. Do you feel that any one individual was instrumental in that success?

No, I don't. I think it was the times. The whole gaming industry was growing, but if I were to credit anybody with a portion of Bill Harrah's success, it would probably be Rome Andreotti and Bob Ring.

I think the big explosion of gaming for Bill Harrah was when he opened his hotel rooms. From what I understand, their drop doubled when they opened the hotel rooms, and that was in Reno, not at Lake Tahoe. That was in Reno, because he expanded in Reno room-wise before he did it at the lake. In fact, Harvey Gross had a hotel at the lake before he did. I think timing had a lot to do with Harrah's success, plus good management.

During your nine years at Harrah's did you ever actually talk to Bill Harrah?

No. Even when I was a pit shift supervisor, I never talked to him. Probably saw him eight or ten times during my course of employment. Used to see his dad, John, more. I used to see John at Lake Tahoe–John's wife would hang around and play twenty-one, but Bill was in Reno, primarily. I did see him one night at a show; in fact, we sat at the same table. I was there for enjoyment, and he was there to rate the show. I don't think his pencil or pen stopped during the entire show. He took notes all night.

20

CINDY WADE

*C*INDY WADE worked at Harrah's for almost twenty years, the last few as Bill Harrah's executive secretary. For this project she was a very cooperative chronicler and went to great lengths to provide details and information that she thought would be of interest. The interview was conducted in the offices of the William F. Harrah Trust in August of 1997, and it took two sessions.

Mrs. Wade was born in Cedar Rapids, Iowa, on May 4, 1939. Along with her family she moved to Portland and then Seattle before coming to Reno in 1961. The first job she had in Reno was that of a secretary at Harrah's garage when it was located on Lake Street. In this oral history interview she leads us through her various positions at Harrah's, culminating with her job as Bill Harrah's private secretary.

Mrs. Wade goes into detail describing her duties and responsibilities as Mr. Harrah's secretary. She recalls a few of his idiosyncrasies and relates several anecdotes about him, even naming his favorite TV program. She also remembers the many trips that she and her husband, Clyde, took with Mr. Harrah and his various female companions.

An especially interesting and enlightening section of the interview tells of the last few days of Mr. Harrah's life. Mrs. Wade was called back to the Mayo Clinic and was there when Harrah died. She

was also on the plane that brought Verna Harrah and Mead Dixon back to Reno after Mr. Harrah's death, and she has an interesting account of what happened in the plane.

This interview contributes to our understanding of the behind-the-scenes Bill Harrah. Mrs. Wade possibly knew Bill Harrah even better than some of his wives, and she openly shared personal information about him with the interviewer.

CINDY WADE: I was born in Cedar Rapids, Iowa, on May 4, 1939. My father was in the newspaper business, and prior to that he had been in the bakery business. My mother had been a school teacher before they married, and when they started a family, she retired and was a housewife most of her life. I have a sister, Mary Sue, who is three years older than I am and a little brother, Terry, who is thirteen years younger than I am.

We moved to the country west of Portland, Oregon, when I was six. I went to a two-room grade school there. When I was just starting junior high school, we moved to Washington—I generally feel like I am from Seattle because that's where I spent my junior-high and high-school years. After high school I worked for a couple of years, went to college about a year, and then I worked and took night courses before moving to Reno in 1961.

I rented an apartment from a fellow by the name of Jay Barker. He owned a forms company, Barker Casino Systems. His property for me was next to Rancharrah on Talbot Lane. He didn't have a job available, and he recommended that I go to Harrah's because he said it was the best casino operation in town. He also told me Bill Harrah was a reformed alcoholic who had got so seriously into running his business properly that he had sent his wife, a former twenty-one dealer, to finishing school for some culture.

When I interviewed for the job, there were two or three openings—one in public relations, one in purchasing, and one in the garage. I like clerical work, and I thought that purchasing would be interesting, but the interviewer—and I wish I knew who that was so I could go back and thank him [laughter]—said, "You really ought to go check out Harrah's garage." I thought it would be processing parking tickets or something, but he said, "I'll take you down there, and then you make up your mind if you want the purchasing or the garage job."

He walked me down to the Lake Street garage. It was in the middle of the block across the street from the Santa Fe Hotel, between a couple of rundown buildings. When you walked in, there were modern limousines like Rolls-Royces and Mercedes parked on either side. Down the ramp was where they were serviced. We went up the ramp toward the back. There were antique cars parked all over, and it was stunning! I'd never seen anything like that before.

To the right was the office where I was interviewed by Sidney Strong, the research director. There was a chassis of a small car right outside the office. It was all copper and brass, and it gleamed. It had one cylinder which was water-jacketed, and it looked like a work of art. I interviewed with Sidney and his assistant, Nadine Ross, and we hit it off great, so I went to work for them.

We were at that location about six months. There was a wonderful library there where Sidney and Nadine researched the cars before they were restored. As time went by, I got a chance to do a little researching myself, which I just loved. The end of that year they moved the collection out to the former icehouse in Sparks.

About the time they were moving the collection, they hired a young man by the

A work area at the Harrah's Automobile Collection. *There were antique cars parked all over, and it was stunning! I'd never seen anything like that before.*

Clyde Wade at work on a classic automobile. *"[Clyde] was a mechanic, and I thought he was cute because he looked like Elvis Presley. . . . I was hooked."*

name of Clyde Wade, who I eventually married. He had just gone to work for the collection. He was a mechanic, and I thought he was cute because he looked like Elvis Presley. I found out from another employee that he liked me. I walked into the employee cafeteria one day, and he was drinking coffee, and when he saw me he choked on it. I just thought that was so endearing, and I was hooked. [laughter] We started going out. Clyde was out of town a lot driving the big car hauler for the collection, but one day about a year after we met he came back from a real long trip, and we just went to Carson City the next day and got married.

DWAYNE KLING: Did Bill Harrah used to come into the garage on Lake Street quite a bit?

Yes, he did, but more so when the collection was in the icehouse. In those days everybody was just so in awe of him that when he would walk in, everybody would just kind of stiffen up, and it created a different kind of atmosphere. When I say everybody, I mean all the employees and all the managers. He used to come in the office and talk to Sidney, but I never had much in the way of conversations with him for some time. For the first couple of years, I was just busy with the job, and I would be up in the library. I'd bump into him once in a while, and he'd always say, "Hi," but that was it.

My first memorable conversation with Bill Harrah was when I had just had our first baby, and I was on six weeks leave of absence. I was in the cafeteria to have lunch with Clyde and to show off our new daughter. The baby was still asleep, and I had set the baby seat on one of the tables in the cafeteria. Mr. Harrah came in and was going over to sit down at a table, when suddenly I realized that he had turned in my direction, and I just wanted to melt into the wall. Everybody had always said, "Don't ever strike up conversations with Bill. If you ever do get into a conversation with him, don't ever talk to him about children or show him pictures. He hates kids." (At that time, he and Scherry were married, and they had no children.)

You always had all these instructions from people about how to act around him, and so here he was, coming over, and I thought, "Oh, is he going to throw me out of here because I have this baby with me?" [laughter] My heart was pounding. He walked over, and I was hunkered down, trying to hide. He stood right above me, and I had to look up and acknowledge that he was there. He was looking at the baby, and he asked, "Is that yours and Clyde's baby?"

I said, "Yes."

And he said, "Well, is she a good baby?"

I said, "Oh yes. She's just perfect."

"Well, does she sleep like that all the time?"

He asked me about half a dozen questions about the baby, and I thought, "What is this? This isn't the Bill Harrah I'd been hearing about for two or three years." And then he just kind of walked off. You know, he had this little, quiet way of just kind of walking off. [laughter]

❖

I loved the library. It grew a lot while I worked there. When I didn't have clerical work to do for them, Sidney and Nadine allowed me to go in the library and try to learn

to do a little research. I had no background or anything that qualified me to do that, but with their help, I kind of got into it a little bit and learned a lot about cars. One of the fun things I got to do was to maintain a list of the cars. It had year, make, body style, body builder, serial number, motor number, and the name and address of the person from whom the car had been purchased.

The library was wonderful because Bill Harrah had collected so many old magazines. Probably more importantly, from the research aspect, were the catalogs and especially the owner's manuals that accompanied the car when it was purchased. They gave all the specifications of the cars. Those were just so important to researching the car.

When Bill bought a car and it would come in, usually the first thing that would happen was Sidney and Nadine would go out and take down all the vital statistics of the car—measure the wheelbase, wheel size, body style, motor, and serial number, et cetera, and then they'd research it in the library. Many times they would discover, after doing the research, that it wasn't the year that the owner had said it was, or it was a different body builder or a different size of motor.

Sidney and Nadine would build up a manual with photocopies of the information from the car catalogs and owners' manuals for the mechanics so that when they started tearing the car down, they could check in the manual and know how to put it back together again. Over the years, that manual became very enhanced—when it started out, it was just a few pages, but by the time my husband was in charge of the auto collection, that was a very big, thick book, sometimes more than one volume.

They were always out buying material for the library. The staff got better informed and did better research. I didn't always work out at the collection, but when I would return and see what was in the manuals ten or fifteen years after I worked for Sidney and Nadine, I was amazed. I believe that those manuals are in great demand. They went with the cars when they were sold, and they are invaluable to the new owners. If people who own an old car can get their hands on a Harrah's research manual for the same make, year, and model, it's like gold.

When Harrah's developed an NCR system in the accounting offices, I got to drive the Model A truck downtown to update the list, and I became acquainted with the internal auditor at the time, who was new at Harrah's. His name was Vern Petty. The accounting manager was Dub Cunningham, and I got along well with both of them. After I had worked out at the collection about five years, while I was on leave of absence for our second baby, I got a call from Vern Petty. They had an opening, and he wanted me to come to work for him. He was the controller, and this job was the secretary to the controller. I jumped at the chance because I like doing accounting work. I loved statistical typing, which is pretty rare.

I was the secretary to the controller for about four years. I went to work for him in the Byington Building. Later they renovated a building on Center Street across from the Cal-Neva, and then the whole business office moved from the Byington Building over to this building on Center Street. We had the controller's office, auditing, accounts payable, accounts receivable, and the programmers. The personnel office was in the adjacent building.

Soon they were in the throes of installing a new computer system—one of these big mainframes that stood on the floor; the cabling was in the floor. That was an interesting era, getting the computer going. We had about five programmers and the old-fashioned, card-punch system. We thought it was pretty sophisticated at the time. [laughter] It's a dinosaur now.

I had our third and last child after I had worked for Vern for a couple of years. I came back from that leave to work for Vern, but he

quite abruptly left Harrah's. He was forced out because he had formed a partnership in a slot machine company, and Harrah's management said he had a conflict of interest. I was pretty upset because I liked working for him. Dub Cunningham was still there, and I think he took over as controller. I respected him, but it just didn't seem the same.

I talked to Ken Gooding at the auto collection (he was the research supervisor there), and they had an opening for a librarian. I thought it would be fun going back out to the collection, but I wasn't sure if I could be a librarian or not. I certainly had no qualifications whatsoever, but then nobody who had worked in the library was a credentialed librarian. It wasn't that type of job; it was more just indexing. I had five or six employees who did the indexing. When I had a little extra time, if the research department needed a little help doing research, why then I got back into doing some research.

I did that for about a year, and then I got an opportunity to work for Maurice Sheppard. He had just become president and when he needed a secretary, somebody recommended me. I worked for him for about a year and a half, maybe two years. At that time they were just opening the Reno hotel, and they were making plans to build the hotel at Tahoe. Also, the company was going public—they had to go public to raise the money. There was a gentleman by the name of David Shuldiner from New York who was very involved with the public offering, and he met with management frequently.

So, you were right in the middle of all that, as far as writing correspondence and memos?

Well, Shep was not the kind of person who put much in writing. He was a one-on-one type person. He liked to sit down and have personal meetings. I didn't do a lot of secretarial work for Shep. It just was not his style.

Shep was a nice person. He was difficult to work for, but he treated me right and I liked him. However, I just didn't have a lot to do, and I found I was quite bored. Fortunately, or unfortunately, while I worked for Shep, Mr. Harrah went through a succession of secretaries and a divorce or two. [laughter] He liked to have attractive, single young ladies in his office, and they weren't always well endowed with secretarial skills, so Bob Hudgens, who was Mr. Harrah's assistant, started bringing work to me with Shep's OK. I appreciated the work, and I built up a nice relationship with Bob Hudgens. I like to be busy, and he appreciated my being available and willing to do the work.

There was a little incident with their executive secretary, and she was terminated on the spot. I had just completed some work for Bob, and when I brought it in and gave it to him, he got up, closed the door, and said, "When do you want to go to work for Bill and me?"

I was quite surprised, because he'd not made any kind of an indication that he wanted me to work for them, and I certainly wasn't cute and available. [laughter] I was married with children. I guess they were both pretty fed up and just wanted someone who could do the work, but I had this problem—I worked for Shep. I said, "Is there any chance that I could work for you guys and Shep also? There's not, as you know, much work to do for Shep, and I am a little concerned about his reaction." (I didn't think it would be a big difference for Shep. There just was no work in his office.)

Bob said, "No, that couldn't be," because if I happened to be busy doing something for Shep and wasn't available for Bill, it would cause problems. It had to be for them or for Shep, one or the other.

I told Bob that I was going to have to think about this overnight. There was no way I was going to be able to tell him immediately, although I knew what I wanted to do. I told him I would let him know in the next day or so, and I asked him to think about how we

were going to deal with Shep if I went to work for Bob and Mr. Harrah. (Shep could be a very difficult person.)

I was not so much concerned for myself as I was for my husband's position at the auto collection. He was, by that time, the assistant manager, and I didn't want to put his situation in any jeopardy. There always was quite a bit of resentment of the automobile collection by the management downtown because the collection spent so much money; so naturally, the people who ran the collection were not in the best of favor. I went home and talked it over with Clyde. Of course, I knew that I would be absolutely stupid to pass up an opportunity to work for Bill Harrah. I knew I could do the work, and I was sure I would like working for Mr. Harrah.

Mr. Harrah took a month-long trip to Europe each year, and the climax of the trip was the London-to-Brighton Run. While I was working for Shep, Clyde and I went on the London-to-Brighton Run one year—Clyde was the mechanic and Mr. Harrah drove the car. Mr. Harrah was married to Mary Berger, and the four of us went on the Brighton Run together. That was when we got to know Bill Harrah personally, although Clyde had already gotten to know him fairly well out at the collection.

The London-to-Brighton Run was a trip that not an awful lot of people who worked at Harrah's got to experience. It was just pure enjoyment traveling with Bill Harrah, and he had so much fun when he was driving the car. He was fun. We'd go out to dinner, and he'd tease. That was my first trip to Europe, and it was kind of a landmark experience because we both came away with the feeling that we had developed kind of a special relationship with Mr. Harrah.

When I discussed Bob's offer with Clyde, he said not to worry about the thing with Shep. He didn't feel that it would be a problem as far as his job; and as it turned out, it wasn't. So the next day I told Bob that I would like to work for him and Mr. Harrah, and I said, "Now, what do we do about Shep?"

Bob said, "I'll go in and talk to him."

Well, Shep was a very emotional person, but he was super-controlled, and he had a hard time expressing himself and his emotions. When Bob told him that he and Bill wanted me to go to work for them, Shep said, "Well, I'll think about it, and I'll let you know." So in other words, it wasn't my decision or their decision, it was *his* decision. [laughter]

I think that was on a Thursday or Friday, and Shep didn't render his decision until the next Monday. I was a wreck, but I went to work on Monday morning wondering if I should show my face. Shep came in my office, and he said, "You start working for Bill and Bob today." And that was it, period. I think I moved into their offices immediately, and Shep didn't speak to me again for a year.

What were some of your specific duties with Bill Harrah?

Everything. He never answered his phone directly—I screened all of his calls. When the mail came in, I had to anticipate what he intended to do with the correspondence. Harrah's was very departmentalized. If it was correspondence that had to do with the public offering, I would put a route slip on it: "To Shep from Bill Harrah. Please handle and advise." Something like that. If the correspondence had to do with, for instance, somebody complaining about a big loss down at the tables, then it was routed to Rome: "To Rome. Please handle and advise," or maybe, "Please discuss." Occasionally, he'd disagree with the way I thought it should be handled, and he'd have me change it, but it was usually pretty routine. He strongly believed in delegating, but if it was a letter to him that shouldn't be delegated, I would draft a proposed answer, and he would approve or edit it, and I would type it for his signature. *Everything* was typed,

including telephone messages and slips that everybody else would handwrite.

I handled Mr. Harrah's scheduling. Bob devised a form on a legal-sized sheet of paper, one for each month with spaces for each day. I typed in all of his appointments, everything he was going to do for six or eight months ahead of time, and we revised constantly. He referred to it daily.

Was Bob Hudgens involved in the scheduling of appointments also?

Yes. A lot of my work was at Bob's direction. After Harrah's went public, Mr. Harrah had more cash available, and he needed to invest some of that money. He acquired a large apartment complex down in Florida, and he bought property in Stanley, Idaho. Bob became involved in dealing with the management of these properties, which required quite a lot of traveling, so I took over more of Bob's duties as time went by. I purchased anything he needed. If he wanted a little flashlight on the bedstand for getting up in the middle of the night, we'd buy a dozen of them and send one to the house in Stanley, one to the Villa at Tahoe, one to Rancharrah, et cetera.

He visited someone's home once where they had these individual guest soaps. He thought they were so nice because people could just wash their hands and throw the soap away. Bob didn't know where to go get them, so I went shopping and bought dozens of them and then sent them to all of his homes. He was always so interested in innovations.

Well, he bought a lot of gifts for entertainers. Were you involved in that?

Not really. Holmes and Adeline Murphy, known to us as "Murph," were the ones who catered to the entertainers' needs and whims. They had some kind of a sheet that was distributed whenever the entertainer was coming so that everyone was aware of their likes and dislikes—what to have on hand in the entertainers' houses where they stayed and in the dressing rooms. I was more involved in buying gifts for his family, for his current wife, his ex-wives, and his children. I would also buy gifts for the office and household staffs for Christmas and birthdays.

I would buy, probably, a couple hundred birthday cards at a time so that he didn't have to go shopping for them. I maintained a list of birthdays—everybody in the executive offices, his friends, and all his relatives. Every time there was a birth date, I'd send in about half a dozen cards that I thought would be appropriate, and then he'd pick out the one he liked. I would fly in the company plane to San Francisco or L.A. to buy cards. [laughter] I'd go down to L.A. at Christmastime to shop for his family.

I went on shopping trips with Mr. Harrah and his wife. Clyde and I went to the Indianapolis 500 and the Middle Fork Lodge in Idaho. We went to Europe with him three different times, one time for five weeks. The trips were pure pleasure for me. [laughter] I did very little secretarial work when we traveled. He usually checked in every couple of days with Bob to see what was going on, to find out what the numbers were in the casinos and that kind of thing. Once in a while he'd have me call Bob, but I hardly ever did any secretarial work at all. When he was on those trips, he thoroughly relaxed and got away from it, and so did we.

And he went on that London-to-Brighton Run almost every year for several years?

He did. I'm not sure when he started, but he'd been going on it for several years before Clyde and I went with him. I went two years in a row with them. Then I didn't go for quite a few years, but Clyde went, always as the mechanic. Mr. Harrah took guests if the car could hold extra people. The last time I went was the first time Mr. Harrah did not go. It was in 1977, the year before he died. He told Clyde, "I've been going every year. Why don't you and Cindy go, and you drive the car?"

That must have been exciting for Clyde.

Oh, it was, and it was so much fun. I enjoyed going with Mr. Harrah, but that was such a special thing that he did for us. I will never forget it. We had a wonderful time. The Brighton Run is not a race, it's a reliability run. We made it with no problems every time I was on the Run, but several times they had car trouble, and Clyde would be in his suit, and he'd have to work on the car. I remember one time the clutch went out. It was slipping real bad, and he said, "I couldn't fix it so I took dirt

Clyde and Cindy Wade and friends on the London-to-Brighton Run in 1977. *"Clyde drove a Panhard-Levassor in 1977. It's a French car, with the surrey top and fringe and picnic baskets on the side. Some friends who had helped store the car over in England rode with us."*

and threw it in on the clutch just to give it something to grab onto." And they made it to Brighton. [laughter]

Did Mr. Harrah always take the same car?

Oh, no. It was always a different car. That 1903 Packard chassis that was in the garage on Lake Street the first day I interviewed for the job with Sidney and Nadine was the first car that I rode in on the London-to-Brighton Run. I remember arriving at Brighton in the Packard. They announce on a loudspeaker when each car arrives because people bring their cars from all over the world. They said, "And here comes Mr. 'Hurrah' from 'Hurrah's' Club in Reno, Nevada, in his 1903 Packard." [laughter]

Clyde drove a Panhard-Levassor in 1977. It's a French car, with the surrey top and fringe and picnic baskets on the side. Some friends who had helped store the car over in England rode with us. We did the formal banquet after the Run, and then we went back to London that night. Sometimes we had stayed at the Metropole Hotel in Brighton, but that year the car was trucked back, and we rode back to London in a limo. (When you worked for Mr. Harrah, you always did everything first-class.) When we walked into the hotel lobby, we were on a high and decided to send Mr. Harrah a telegram. It said, "We made it. Three hours and so many minutes. Great run. Clyde, Cindy, and Panhard." [laughter] We had a lot of fun doing things like that, and I know he liked it because Bob told me later that Mr. Harrah had shown it off to Lloyd Dyer.

How was Bill Harrah in the office?

I was a little uneasy when I first started working for him. The first morning that I was in my new office, I could hear him come shuffling down the hall. He had this little shuffle type of walk, and I thought, "Well, is he going to acknowledge me or what?"

I looked up, and he was standing in the doorway, and he kind of rapped on the door a couple of times real lightly and said, "Gee, I'm glad you're here."

And I said, "Well, thank you. I'm really glad to be here."

Bob had prompted me that I was to give him a couple of minutes to settle in. Then I'd bring his coffee and ask him if there was anything he wanted me to do. He would usually ask me to sit down, and then he'd whip this little three-inch by five-inch card out of his pocket. He didn't like to waste paper, and it just fit into his pocket. Sometimes it was pieces of paper that had these little printed notations on them. I'd sit down with my pad, and I'd start writing, and just those notations from that little piece of paper would keep me busy all day. It was just amazing, and I looked forward to it because I like to be busy, and there was always something new and different.

Mr. Harrah would be very business-like most of the time. When he would arrive in the morning, I'd know he was there because I'd hear this little, quiet rap on the door. He wouldn't say anything, and he'd go on into his office. It was usually strictly business.

I was always Mr. Harrah's secretary—I never called him Bill. Everybody called him Bill but me. People who had never met him called him Bill, but I never could. He was Mr. Harrah, and I was his secretary, but once in a while, we'd get into a conversation about something other than business. His time, often, was tight, and the executives would be waiting to meet with him, but if things were a little slow, and if I could get him talking, he'd start telling me stories. He'd wave his arms, and he'd just go on and on. It was surprising how much he would talk when it was a one-on-one situation, but he never was good in crowds or at parties.

One time Clyde and I were at a party, and Mr. Harrah and Verna showed up. We got so tickled because he started following us around. I think maybe one reason that we got along so well is because I am the same way.

I'm not an outgoing person, and I tend to cling to Clyde. I can't go up to a stranger and start talking. I think, "What do you talk about? I don't even know this person, so what is there to talk about?" and I believe Mr. Harrah felt the same way. But if it was just the two of us, I could get him going sometimes.

Usually Bob Hudgens and Mr. Harrah went to lunch together. There was a private dining room in the Steak House where they ate lunch. Once in a while, he'd like to go to one of the other restaurants, but normally his routine was to go down to the private dining room. When Bob was not there, he would take me to lunch with him. Once in a while, there would be executives coming down the hall, and I always wondered if they showed up right at noon, purposely, on the chance that Mr. Harrah would invite them for lunch. More than once, Mr. Harrah came out of his office, and there would be an executive standing there, and he would poke his head in my office and say, "Well, are you ready?" and I'd grab my purse, and we'd go off to lunch and leave whoever it was standing there. [laughter] There was a little remote on the table for him to signal that he was there, and a waitress would come through a door and take our order and leave. Then he'd turn on the TV for the news, or sometimes we would chat; but at 12:30, the *Andy Griffith Show* came on, and that was the end of the conversation. We watched *Andy Griffith* re-runs while we ate. He loved that program. He would say, "Oh, good. It's a black-and-white one. That means Don Knotts will be in it." He didn't like the later ones as much. He said more than once, "You know why this show is so good? It's because the casting is perfect."

So we'd eat and watch TV, and if we'd get done eating and the program wasn't over, we would watch it to the end. Sometimes I'd look over, and he'd be kind of nodding off. He was a person who could relax instantly. A few times, I walked into his office when he was pushed back in his chair sleeping, but when he woke up, he would be perfectly alert.

❖

Most people were really afraid to make Bill Harrah angry, and some of them made the mistake of avoiding telling him things that they thought would make him angry, which made him angrier when he found out. Some would lie to him, and of course, that was the worst thing in the world you could do. My way—and it seemed to work with him—was that if I did something stupid or made a mistake, I would, at the first opportunity, go in and tell him about it, and he was always so accepting of it. He'd just say, "Oh well, you know, that was dumb, but I do dumb things too."

One time we disagreed about something, and I knew I was right, and he knew he was right. A couple days had gone by, and he acted pretty miffed about it. I suddenly figured it out—it was just like a light bulb went on, and I went right into his office, and I told him, "Remember when we were talking about such and such? I was wrong! You were right."

And he just smiled, and he said, "Boy, that's a relief. I was really mad at you." Then he said, "I really thought I was getting to be just a crabby old man." [laughter]

We had a lot of fun in the office. Mr. Harrah had a wonderful sense of humor. You just had to know how to get through to it. When he was serious and he didn't want to be bothered, you were serious too, but if you could sense that he was in a lighthearted mood, you could just really have a lot of fun with him. When we traveled with him, he liked to put us on every once in a while. One time we went up to his suite to have dinner with him, and he opened the door, and he had this brilliant scarf tied around his neck. He had it tied in a big bow around his neck, and he was standing there, and I thought, "Oh, am I supposed to say something about that or not?" He was just standing there grinning, and I said, "Well, hi, Mr. Harrah. Are you ready to go to dinner?" Finally he burst out laughing. He says, "You're not going to say anything about my bow are you?" [laughter]

I think everybody knew he had this thing about fat people. He didn't like to see overweight people. There were overweight people that he liked, but he just did not think that people should be overweight, and he didn't want overweight employees hired. Of course, his friend Bob Ring was pretty roly-poly. Well, one day I got a call from somebody who told me that Mr. Ring had broken his arm. I told Mr. Harrah as soon as he came in that day. I said, "He's fine, but he's going have his arm in a cast and in a sling for a while."

And he said, "Well, how did it happen?" Well, how it happened was he was riding in a golf cart, and it turned a corner real fast, and he just kind of fell out. When I was telling Mr. Harrah about it, I was picturing Mr. Ring just kind of rolling out of that golf cart, and I started laughing, and pretty soon, Mr. Harrah started laughing, and we both had tears running down our faces, we were laughing so hard. It just struck us both as so funny. He told Clyde about it that afternoon, and he said that I had tears running down my face. Well, he did too! [laughter]

Is it true that he had a scale on the fourth floor where people had to weigh in?

Yes, he did. It was in the conference room for several years. They always went through these fads. For several years, there was this weight thing, and everybody was supposed to put their weight down; but there were also all those other little, funny idiosyncracies. If there were people with moles or anything on their face down in gaming, or if they had disfigurements on their hands, Mr. Harrah didn't think that they should work there because it would be offensive to the public.

Then there were the little things like the scotch tape. There was a policy that you could not have scotch tape showing on anything. It had to be double-stick scotch tape, and I even had to wrap gift packages with double-stick scotch tape underneath so that you couldn't see the scotch tape. There were written company policies—all pictures had to be hung with two hangers so that they wouldn't get crooked. When the turtleneck shirts or sweaters were popular, there was a company policy about how high they could be, like one-and-a-half inches and no more.

I'm sure he felt that way about it personally, but I always wondered if he even realized that these things went down the line to every single employee. It probably got passed on down because Mr. Harrah had walked into somebody's office one day and said, "Gee, that looks tacky with that Scotch tape sticking up there. Why don't you use double-stick Scotch tape?" Well, then, the next thing you know, there's a company policy written up about it.

I've heard that he didn't like mustaches either.

I think that's right, yes; and there were very few bald-headed people working for him.

I doubt that something like that was written down in any procedure. It would have been too discriminatory.

Well, probably so . . . even more so now. Back then I'm not so sure, but I know it definitely was understood in the personnel department. In some instances, an exception was made for people who didn't have contact with the public or who didn't represent Harrah's away from Harrah's.

Do you have any insight as to why Mr. Harrah was such a stickler for details and a perfectionist?

I believe it was part of his character. I think his whole life is kind of indicative of that, even in his marriages. He used to ask me about Clyde's and my family life. He was curious about how we lived, how we raised our kids, did I have help at home? I told him, "Yes, I have help. I've got three kids and a husband." [laughter] We would all do housework on Saturdays. That was beyond him. I think he had always been raised with some household help in the house.

I got the impression, over the years, that marriage to him was just like business. The way he applied himself to a marriage was you have these certain jobs to perform in a marriage and in raising your children. It's hard to explain, but he seemed to me to apply his business principles to his marriages, and I think that's why there were sometimes problems, because if the marriage didn't meet his expectations, then it was over. It wasn't successful, and so you didn't expend any more effort on it, you just did something different.

He would tell you the bottom line of what he wanted accomplished, and you were expected to figure out how to do it. He was a master at manipulating people without them even knowing it. You didn't sit there and discuss, "Well, I could do this, I could do that." Just do it. Just get it done. He didn't want to be bothered with the details. If it was building a hotel, I doubt if he really concerned himself with much of the details of the actual building. He just wanted the hotel built, and it had to meet his expectations of a fine hotel.

He was not a complex person. I look at these Harrah's Trust offices here today, and they look lush compared to his office, which was rather utilitarian. And I had the worst office in the executive offices on the fourth floor of the old F.I.B. [First Interstate Bank] building. I had this little, cramped office lined with file cabinets and a Steelcase desk. This is not a complaint, but people would walk in, and they'd look around kind of surprised and say, "Well, is this your office?" [laughter] Mr. Harrah's office was redecorated once by Henry Conversano, the decorator of the hotels. First he had to sit down with Mr. Harrah and kind of go over his routine, what he liked. He really didn't make all that many changes, and certainly, it was not ornate. Eventually, Bob Hudgens moved into a

bigger office, and I moved into Bob's old office, which was larger, but my furniture looked like it was from the Salvation Army. Clyde had an extra wooden desk at the collection that was bigger, and he traded with me for my old Steelcase because they needed it for the library. I had to horse-trade because there was no budget for new furniture.

Was there any single thing, one person, that contributed to the success of Harrah's?

I think it was Bill Harrah and his consummate business sense which he applied to every aspect of his life. He did it with the casinos, the cars, and his personal life. He just applied business sense to everything. If he tried some kind of a business venture and it didn't work out or it wasn't going well, he'd just say, "Well, OK, this isn't working. We'll try something else, or we'll try it a different way, or we'll just stop and do something different." He went on to the next person, the next business venture, the next car, the next marriage. [laughter] No regrets, no remorse.

He was very curious about everything. I remember when the plastic Ziploc bags came out, there had been a commercial on TV, and he came in the office with that written on his little piece of paper and asked me to get him some. He wanted to see what they were like. Well, they weren't even on the west coast yet. They were on the commercials on TV, but we couldn't find them in Reno, and it took us a week or so to finally get those darn Ziploc bags. We had to have a contact on the east coast buy them and mail them to us so he could see what they were like. [laughter]

Was he visionary? Do you think he had long-range plans on a lot of these things?

No, I don't think he considered himself a visionary, and I didn't think of him as a visionary. I think he went very much day-to-day, but the way he applied his business sense to everything made things evolve. If it didn't work, then scrap it, forget it, and do something else.

Was Bob Ring very active in the business when you were there?

When I went to work there, I believe he was the general manager of Harrah's, and I think he was pretty active at that time, but by the time I went to work for Mr. Harrah in the executive offices, Bob Ring was, I think you'd say, semi-retired.

The best thing about Bob Ring was that he was a great PR man for Harrah's. He knew all of the employees on a first-name basis. I think of him as Mr. Harrah's alter ego. Mr. Harrah didn't go out and say, "Hi, how are you?" slap you on the back, and all that kind of thing. Bob Ring did that for him. It was understood that they were very close friends. Although they did almost nothing, socially, together, they did have a caring friendship.

Were there any specific individuals that you were associated with or that were prominent in Harrah's Club that you'd care to talk about?

Well, I never really knew the executives at Harrah's very well. I hope to think that I did my job well enough so that we all got along. I was so involved with Mr. Harrah's little center of activity that I didn't mingle with the other people on the fourth floor very much. I was too busy, and I wasn't that kind of person. When I got off work at 5:00, all I had on my mind was to go home to be with my family. Many of the secretaries in the executive's offices liked to socialize in the casino or the Prospector's Club. It just never interested me, so I never developed any kind of a social life with them.

I feel I had a good working relationship with Lloyd, with Holmes, Rome, and George Drews. Rome was an interesting person. When I was working in the accounting offices, everybody was afraid of Rome. He was the enforcer, kind of the "mean guy." He fired a lot of people, and he did all these draconian things. I wasn't afraid of Bill Harrah, but I was kind of afraid of Rome, and Rome turned out, to me, to be just a big pussycat. [laughter]

I never had much contact with any of those guys, other than when they needed to meet with Mr. Harrah. They would check in with me before Mr. Harrah would get there in the morning. When Mr. Harrah would arrive, I'd tell him, "Rome wants to see you," or "Holmes wants to see you."

And he'd say, "OK. Let me see Holmes first. I want to talk to him about such and such, and then after Holmes, I'll see Rome." One time I forgot to tell him that Holmes wanted to see him, and he left. Holmes came down and wanted to know if Bill was mad at him. I said, "No!"

He asked, "Well, then are you mad at me?"

I said, "No, why?"

He said, "Well, I was supposed to see Bill."

And I'm going, "Oh, no!" I felt so terrible; but you know, he understood and was very nice about it. Rome didn't see Mr. Harrah very often. After Lloyd became president, he and Holmes were the ones who had the most contact with Mr. Harrah.

I want to say something about Rome and then go on to somebody else. I didn't know Rome very much at all, but I will never, ever forget what he did after Mr. Harrah died. It was such a devastating thing to everyone. I didn't even know if I should come to work or stay home or what was going to happen. I came to the office and just sat at my desk with the door almost closed. I didn't know what to do or what to say; and, of course, everybody else felt the same way. The door opened a little bit, and Rome was standing there, and he came over. He gave me a big hug, and he said, "What can I do for you? Can I babysit your kids? Can I go shop for your groceries?" I mean, this was the guy that was feared or hated by many employees. I will never forget that gesture from Rome.

Another person, of course, who was influential in Mr. Harrah's life was Mead Dixon. Mead had a sort of dual personality. Away from Mr. Harrah, he came across as very egotistical and mean-spirited. He criticized everything and everyone. But around Mr. Harrah, he was just the perfect attorney to the point of being "oily."

One thing that really bothers me is that I feel that Mr. Harrah was fooled by Mead, that he was kind of taken in over the years. Whenever Mr. Harrah would marry or divorce, there would have to be a new will, lots of paperwork, and I was the notary. In these wills, I noticed that first, Mead was the attorney. In the next one, he became, I believe, one of the trustees of the estate. Eventually, he was the executor of the estate. It never really agreed with me, but it was none of my business.

In the last will, Mr. Harrah had a codicil added naming Clyde and me guardians of his sons, John Adam and Anthony, if anything should happen to him and to their mother, Scherry. Mr. Harrah didn't say much about it to us. Mead Dixon called me and told me Mr. Harrah wanted that changed, but didn't tell us how it came about. At that time, Scherry liked Clyde and myself very much, and I think Scherry influenced that, but I'm not sure.

Wasn't Mr. Harrah married to Verna at the time?

Yes, he was. Verna was very upset after Mr. Harrah died and she found out about the codicil. One thing that concerned me was, before Clyde and me, Bob Hudgens was the guardian of the boys. I love Bob Hudgens, and I didn't want him to feel that Clyde and I had usurped any territory of his or anything like that. It bothered me, but I don't think it bothered Bob at all. [laughter] Bob is not a person to raise kids. Thank heavens it never happened, because I think Clyde and I would have had a difficult time raising two more kids.

I went to Mr. Harrah and talked to him about the codicil. I said, "If there's any money involved as far as support for the children or anything like that, I don't want to have anything to do with it, and Clyde doesn't either. Please have Bob handle that end of it." So that's the way the codicil reads. Bob was in charge financially, and Clyde and I would have raised the boys.

You were saying that Mead Dixon kept coming further up the ladder in regards to the estate.

Yes, he just kind of eased his way in. I was disappointed in Mr. Harrah that it was OK with him. On the other hand, who should it have been? I have no idea. I know one person that he liked very much was Judge Bruce Thompson, one of the estate trustees. To me, he would have been a good person to have been his executor.

Or maybe he could have had a three-man executor?

Right. That would have been good. Any of the executives on the fourth floor would have done just about anything for Mr. Harrah, and they would have been just fine collectively. Also, and maybe I'm totally off base on this, but one thing that's always bothered me is that Verna got a half, and John got a fourth, and Tony got a fourth. I thought it should have been a third and a third and a third, but that would have given Scherry control then, because the boys would have had two-thirds. Mead never would have allowed that. With Verna with 50 percent and the boys, together, with 50 percent, nobody had a majority, and Mead had all the control.

I felt like Mr. Harrah had adopted those boys and raised them, but he was not the "father-of-the-year." Here again, back to the business thing. He was well-intended and loved and cared for them, but he just didn't have a real good parenting instinct. I didn't observe it anyway.

When John was in school in Switzerland, Mr. Harrah would come in in the morning, and he'd say, "Well, John called me at 3:00 in the morning because it was daytime for him. Would you call him back and find out what the problem is?" Clyde and I ended up going to Switzerland to visit John because he was not coping well. He was just a normal kid, and he was homesick. He finished the school year there and then came back here and went to Reno High. He just wasn't happy there.

But you and Clyde went, as opposed to Bill Harrah himself?

Yes, as his secretary. See, there's the business thing. That was part of my job. I hired tutors for the boys if they weren't doing well in school; we went to Switzerland to see John when he was having problems; I talked to their teachers. That was my job.

Mead Dixon did Mr. Harrah's legal work, and while I was at Harrah's, he handled the second divorce from Scherry . . . also Bobbie Gentry, Mary, and Roxanne. I have a problem with some people who allude to the fact that they knew Mr. Harrah well when I knew, in fact, that they didn't. I also have a problem with those who alluded to being part of the reason for his success. There were a couple of wives who felt that way, and Mead Dixon had that attitude. It came through, to me, in his book[1] that Mead credited himself for very much of Mr. Harrah's success, and I just do not believe that. I do not believe that Mead had anything to do with the success that Mr. Harrah had in developing Harrah's. I'm not sure at what point in time Mead came strongly on to the scene, but I never felt that he was that involved in the operations of Harrah's to be able to credit himself with any of the success of Harrah's.

Was Mead ever actually employed by Harrah's, or was he just Bill Harrah's personal attorney?

Well, he definitely spent a lot of time as Mr. Harrah's personal attorney, and I guess he did act as Harrah's attorney. The law firm of Vargas Bartlett & Dixon was involved in Harrah's operations, but that's really beyond my scope because I wasn't involved in that.

Talk a little bit more about John Adam Harrah and Tony Lee Harrah, the children that Bill and Scherry adopted. Were you working for Mr. Harrah or Harrah's when the children were adopted?

I was working for Harrah's. I believe I was in the accounting department at the time. Of course, anything in Mr. Harrah's life was always of great interest to the employees, and people were saying that Mr. Harrah had adopted a little boy. Clyde was around the boys, John Adam and then Tony, before I ever was because Mr. Harrah would bring the boys to the collection. He and Scherry also took the boys on car tours. Probably the first time I was ever around John and Tony was on a car tour. It was the first one on which I accompanied Clyde, and we also took our two small children. It was a tour around Lake Tahoe, and Scherry, Mr. Harrah, and their boys were along. They were toddlers, and the four children played together when we stopped along the way.

How long was it between the time that John was adopted until Tony was adopted?

About a year, I think, and they were both newborns when they were adopted. Harrah's had a house organ called the "Harrah-scope," and they had a picture of the family–Mr. Harrah, Scherry, and the baby, John Adam– which I thought was very nice. Mr. Harrah was such a mystery to most of the employees.

Did he spend more time at home with his family after the boys were adopted?

I don't know, because I wasn't working for him before he had them. When I became his

The Harrah men and their Bugattis. *L to R:* Bill Harrah in a 1927 Type 35B Grand Prix, John Adam in a Type 52 Electric Kids Bugatti, and Tony Lee in a Type 52 replica. *"Clyde was around the boys, John Adam and then Tony, before I ever was because Mr. Harrah would bring the boys to the collection. He and Scherry also took the boys on car tours."*

secretary, the boys were probably around five and six. He seemed to me to be a homebody. He had his routine, which he followed fairly closely every day. He would come into the office by about 10:00 and would usually stay, have lunch, and then go out to the auto collection and spend the afternoon, then go home. He almost always had the current entertainers for dinner at Rancharrah once during their appearance at Harrah's, but otherwise he didn't seem to have a busy social life. His routine didn't change much day-to-day, and I do believe he probably spent time with the boys in the evenings, but I don't know what happened at home.

Had he divorced Scherry just before you became his secretary?

No, he married Bobbie Gentry after Scherry. Then he married Mary Berger. He was married to Mary for a year or two. Their divorce was the first one that I went through with him. [laughter]

Did his divorce or his divorces affect his time with the children?

On most weekends he'd go to Scherry's to visit the boys. They would spend some time at Rancharrah, but I really can't remember an awful lot about that. I know that they'd be at Rancharrah once in a while. They were pretty established with Scherry, and he'd go visit them there. Scherry's friend, Bob Jackson, was wonderful with the boys. Mr. Harrah took them to dinner shows once in a while, and to Stanley and to Middle Fork Lodge.

Did you personally know all of his wives?

Not all of them. I really didn't know any of them very well except Verna. We went on that London-to-Brighton Run with Mary, and I talked to her on the phone quite a bit, but I didn't know her very well.

I met Bobbie Gentry after they were divorced. She was entertaining at Harrah's, and she came up to the office. Mr. Harrah brought her in my office and introduced us, and we chatted for a few minutes. That's the only time I ever met her. I did talk to her on the phone occasionally. She was always extremely nice.

I didn't know Roxanne Carlson very well, although I think I had something to do with Mr. Harrah getting together with her. Mr. Harrah would be at loose ends without a companion. He didn't like to be alone, and he needed a crutch, so to speak. When the entertainers came to dinner, he wasn't going to sit there and have dinner with them by himself—he needed a lady to be there with him. That was very important to him. And when we went on the long trip to Europe, a young lady went with us. He wasn't married at the time, and she was just kind of along for the occasion. [laughter]

One day Bob and I were in the office, and there was an occasion coming up when Mr. Harrah didn't have a date. Bob and I were discussing it, and I said, "You know, I have a very good friend who handles the fashion shows in the restaurants. She said that a model, Roxanne Carlson, told her that she'd like to meet Bill Harrah, and she's tall and good looking."

Bob said, "I'll find out who she is!" I regret it now, but I didn't know it was going to end up in another bad marriage. Roxanne was just in it for what she could get out of it. [laughter]

Could you tell me why you think Bill Harrah married so many times in his later years?

Well, I think there were a couple of reasons. The basic reason, in my mind, is this business attitude he had about everything. If a marriage wasn't working out for one reason or another, then he got divorced and went on to the next. He didn't seem to dwell on it or have any regrets.

Several of the marriages got in trouble when the wives appeared to become bored and became involved in activities that were not compatible with Mr. Harrah's plans. One or two wanted to start up business enterprises of their own. He expected them to adjust their lifestyles to fit his, not the other way around.

Also, after Scherry, he became attracted to my friend, Betty, who was his secretary when he and Scherry got divorced. He pursued her to the point that she was overwhelmed. Betty is a very nice person, highly principled, and she was married. He lavished her with gifts and put on the pressure until she did divorce her husband. She had four children, and she was very torn up over the situation. Mr. Harrah was big on giving huge, diamond, marquise-shaped engagement rings, and one day she came in to show me her ring and told me she had agreed to marry him. But she was in tears about it. Several months later, she gave back the ring, re-married her husband, and left town. We have always remained friends.

While I was his secretary, Mr. Harrah asked me to meet with Betty in an attempt to get her to reconsider. She wouldn't consider starting up the relationship again under any circumstances because she just simply didn't love him. It was very difficult for her, because she had not had an easy life, and this man threw Ferraris and money and a $100,000 engagement ring at her. When she considered all the material things he had to offer and what it could have done for her children, the whole affair had a profound effect on her life. It even affected my life. It was one thing about Mr.

Harrah that I did not like, because it was not fair.

Do you feel that he really, truly loved her a great deal?

Well, I don't know if he really loved anyone. I don't know if he really had that emotion within him. I do think that she could have been good for him. They liked the same things—she liked cars; she loved fashion and dressed well; she wanted to travel.

Do you feel it had an influence on the rest of his life as far as his later romantic relationships or his marriages?

Possibly. Over the years, he would ask about Betty, even when he was married to other ladies. I know he never forgot her.

Or to put it another way, did Mr. Harrah's personal life spill into his business life?

No, not at all. For instance, when he divorced Mary, I went out to Rancharrah and notarized her signature on the divorce papers. When I brought them back, he was sitting in his office just antsy, ready to get that one over with and go on to the next. [laughter] That was his attitude, and I don't recall his demeanor or his emotions or anything changing. He'd meet a new lady and start taking her out and want to get married again. However, that was another thing that bothered me—he always did the same things with the same women, over and over. It was like déjà vu.

First of all, he wasn't particularly choosy, just whoever was available. The first date was invariably a dinner show. Then he'd take her to Los Angeles or New York on a shopping trip. They would spend maybe $3,000 or $4,000, $5,000 on clothes and jewelry. Then he'd have her to dinner at Rancharrah to help entertain an entertainer, and then it was a trip to Europe, and then they'd get married. Every time he would take a date to a dinner show, he

would have the photographer take pictures to memorialize the "special occasion." The smiles in the photos always looked the same, just different faces. He had a way of reaching over and touching their knee, and each one thought it was special between them. It seemed very sad to me.

He appears to have set routines for all aspects of his life. He didn't have to plan his social life—he knew he was going to do those things.

That's the way it seemed to me. He hired an efficiency expert after he was married to Verna. Verna is a very vivacious and sweet person. She had a son and wanted to try to have more of a family life, and she wanted Mr. Harrah to have more time to spend at home, so we hired an efficiency expert. He spent several days going around with Mr. Harrah on his daily routine, and then he interviewed Bob Hudgens and me individually. After reviewing the schedule and how we dealt with his activities, he concluded that there was very little that he could suggest to find more time in Mr. Harrah's life, because it was already about 100 percent allocated. There was no wasted time. He was impressed with how efficient Mr. Harrah was with his time and how efficiently the office ran. By that time, we had a couple more girls working in the office, and we had the staff busy all the time.

I've heard that the last four or five years of Mr. Harrah's life, when he was married to Verna, were the happiest times of his life.

I remember a discussion Bob Hudgens and I had about that. This may sound terrible, but we agreed that Verna did the best job.

Why do you say it sounds terrible?

The business thing. Verna had a job just like the rest of us, and she did it very well. Don't forget that he and Scherry were married for a lot of years, but he and Verna did get along much better than he'd gotten along with most of the previous wives after Scherry. However, Verna was thirty-something, and this was already her third marriage, and I did sense that Verna was getting restless the last year. She was spending a lot of time with a group of friends, and his wife was supposed to be at home and be ready to go to Europe, look nice, make the right conversation, and "play the role."

Verna got him very interested in Idaho. Of course, she was from Idaho, and she loved it up there. They bought the home in Sun Valley and a cabin on a lake outside of Stanley.

Verna and I were on friendly terms, but it was an edgy situation for me. Verna was very friendly to me, and I was very comfortable being around her because she was so nice, but there were problems. She had to send her son, Richard, to a private school in California, and there was a lot of friction because he lived at Rancharrah, but Mr. Harrah's sons couldn't.

Now, Mr. Harrah didn't like his wives having their own business. This had happened with Scherry. She wanted to do this cosmetics thing and several other enterprises when they were still married. I wasn't working for Mr. Harrah when he was married to Scherry, but I heard rumors that this had caused problems, that he didn't like his wives getting out and getting involved in businesses. But they did get bored. Roxanne got involved in something, maybe a nursery school, and Mary got involved in physical fitness programs.

Mr. Harrah was more comfortable with Verna, but then the winter before he died she called me to tell me about a bookstore in Ketchum that she wanted to buy. I said, "Well, who's going to manage it?"

She said, "Well, you are." She even bought me a book, which I still have, *How to Buy and Manage a Bookstore*, and it started making me real nervous. I loved working for Bill Harrah. I'm not a workaholic, but I'm always doing something, and he kept me busy all the time. I would get energized when he'd walk in the door. My life was my family and working for Mr. Harrah.

I said to myself, "Well, wait a minute. I have a husband and a family here in Reno. My home is in Reno. I'm Mr. Harrah's secretary. How am I going to run a bookstore up in Ketchum, Idaho?"

I told Bob, and I asked him, "What am I going to do?"

He said, "I know about it. She called me at home on a Sunday and said, 'Cindy and I are going to Ketchum tomorrow to inventory this bookstore that I'm going to buy.'" I cried that night. I was very upset. It was about a month to six weeks before Christmas, and I not only had all of my shopping and everything to prepare for Christmas for my family, I had to do all of Mr. Harrah's shopping. It was a very busy time of the year, and here we are going to Ketchum the next day to inventory a bookstore.

So we went, and I ran the calculator, and we inventoried this little bookstore. Halfway through it, I started thinking, "Why does she want to buy this place?" It was run by hippies. Half the books were worn and dogeared because they had loaned them out to their friends. A lot of ski-bum types lived in that area, and it was just a little hole in the wall. I couldn't figure it out.

At the restaurant for dinner that night, Verna suddenly said, "Cindy, I don't want to buy that bookstore. That's not the kind of bookstore I want."

And I thought, "Oh, thank God! I'm getting out of this gracefully." The next morning, I called Bob Hudgens, and I said, "Hey, we're coming back. We're not buying the bookstore."

Bob was relieved. However, that wasn't the end of it. She said she still intended to buy a bookstore, but she was going to shop around for the right one, so I tried to square away with her gently. I said, "I don't know how I can do my job here and take care of my family and manage a bookstore in Idaho."

She said, "Well, I'll get Marilyn to do the day-to-day operation, and she can report to you."

Marilyn was a housekeeper at Rancharrah, and I'm going, "Ungh! This is getting worse all the time." [laughter] But that was kind of the beginning of the end. Just a few weeks later was when Mr. Harrah went back for his physical at Mayo Clinic, and then he had to go back for the surgery and all that, so I think it was a kismet kind of thing. I don't know if they would have been married to each other for a long time if he hadn't died when he did. I am probably cynical because of the experiences of having dealt with so many of his marriages and divorces.

Did Bill Harrah look at a wife as a friend because he didn't have many friends?

Well, that's true, and they all influenced him in some way. With Mary, he got into the physical fitness thing and the health food supplements. After she was gone, the physical fitness thing ended to a certain extent. Verna got him to buy the places in Idaho.

I was surprised that Verna did not know a lot about his prior life. He was such an interesting person. He didn't always want to talk about everything, but if I could get him going, I could get him to talk about a lot of things that happened in the old days. He even told me about the child that he and Thelma[2] had that died. I'd heard that he'd been in a car accident and had broken his neck, but I didn't know that Thelma had been in the car and had a miscarriage because of this accident. The baby was stillborn. I think he said that the cord was wrapped around the baby's neck.

After Mr. Harrah died, Verna read about Thelma in the paper. She didn't even know he had been married to Thelma, and she was shocked. She asked me if I knew about Thelma, and I told her Thelma lost his only natural child, and she seemed to be upset on learning this.

Do you think that there was anyone that he talked to? Were there any automobile people that he was close with?

I think he considered Bud Catlett a good friend of his. When I went to work at the collection, Bud bought the cars, and I think he eventually became the manager. He was the head buyer for a long time, and he bought many of the cars when the collection got started. He had a good friendship with Mr. Harrah, but here again, I don't think they had a social life going on the outside. They did the tours together and just had a great time. I know Mr. Harrah thought fondly of Bud and considered him a good friend, but I don't think they ever had any kind of a–to my knowledge–social life outside of the cars or the collection or tours.

Possibly, he really didn't have a personal life or someone that he "hung out with."

I would say that's correct. I can't think of any single person that he really went out and drank beer with or went fishing with or shot ducks with or anything like that. He was more of a private person.

You had kind of a different role than most employees there because you were an executive secretary, and yet you were also the spouse of the general manager of the Harrah's Automobile Collection. Did the two positions ever generate any friction between you and other employees or the other top management wives?

Yes. At times, it was kind of like walking a tightrope. I know Clyde was conscious of the fact that guys might be saying, "Well, he's married to Bill Harrah's secretary, you know. You can see how he got his job." I felt animosity from some of the secretaries, a little discomfort from the wives. The secretaries, I think, felt like I had it made because my husband was a director, so I had this "in" with Bill Harrah.

I didn't have too much contact with the executives' wives. However, Verna was real good at getting Mr. Harrah to invite people over to the house other than the entertainers. She was trying to have a more normal life and to develop a social life, and for two or three years they had a patio party out by the pool at Rancharrah, and anybody from a director on up was included. As Mr. Harrah's secretary, I wouldn't have been invited, but as the wife of Clyde, I *was* invited. Some of the other secretaries didn't like that, but there wasn't anything I could do about it. [laughter]

I have to tell you one funny little story about Clyde working at the collection and me working downtown for Mr. Harrah. When Clyde was going to leave Harrah's Automobile Collection (HAC), his secretary would call me and say, "Clyde's leaving. He'll be back at 2:00," and I would type up a little message and give it to Mr. Harrah. He would usually stay downtown until he knew Clyde would be back in his office, and then he'd go out to HAC. If I wasn't in my office, the executive office receptionist would answer my phone and take the message.

Once we had a new receptionist who didn't know the reason for these messages. She knew that Clyde and I were married, and she was taking these messages from Clyde's secretary to let me know whenever Clyde had left HAC. [laughter] One day I walked into the ladies' lounge, and everybody was laughing. She had told them that I had a real good way of checking up on Clyde. I knew where he was every minute because I had his secretary informing me. [laughter]

In June of 1978, Mr. Harrah went back to the Mayo Clinic in Rochester, Minnesota. Did he go there on a regular basis?

Yes. He went there annually, unless there was a problem . . . which most of the time there was not a problem.

Did he also have a doctor in town that he went to for minor things?

No, not really. In years past, he had gone first to Dr. Vernon Cantlon and then to Dr. Ed Cantlon, but once he started going to the Mayo Clinic, I don't believe he had a doctor in town.

When he went to the Mayo Clinic in June of 1978, was that a regular check-up or did he have an inkling that he had a problem?

Well, if my memory serves me correctly, his regular appointment was in January of 1978. During that appointment they found a very serious problem. He had had surgery for an aortal aneurism about five years previous, and when he went back in January of 1978, they found that the artery in that same area was failing. He had to go back and have a second surgery for an aneurism which was forming below where the first one had been. When we talked about it, he told me that his arterial disease had been caused mainly by his smoking and drinking in his younger years, and there was no going back.

I don't recall why there was such a lapse there before he had the surgery. He made a trip to Europe, and I remember I was very concerned about his making the trip. I asked the security who went with him to, "Please don't let him carry anything heavy." I was very concerned about him lifting anything. Verna did not go on that trip. I believe he went to the Ferrari factory in Italy but mainly to pick up John Adam from the school in Switzerland. The trip was in May, and it seems to me that it was a short trip and that he took the security.

So when Mr. Harrah went to Mayo Clinic, he knew he was going to be operated on for the repair of the aneurism?

Yes, he did. He knew that he was going to have this surgery. Just he and Verna went back there, and not very many people knew about it. He didn't want anybody to know about it. I believe he told Lloyd Dyer because it was necessary for the business for Lloyd to be aware, but there were very few people who knew why he was going back. I, of course, was aware of the seriousness.

He had to have considerable testing done before he was to have the surgery. They probably left Reno on a Friday, and I believe it was on Sunday that Verna called me. She sounded real upset because he was so nervous. This was not an overly emotional man, usually, and it upset her . . . which, of course, upset me. I decided that I wanted to be there. I was thinking about the situation for the sake of people like Bob Hudgens, and I thought maybe I could create a little communication there.

I called Bob Hudgens that night, and he called the guy in charge of the aircraft. Harrah's plane was already in Rochester, but at that time Modern Classic Motors had their own plane. It was a King Air, and Bob got the pilots up in the middle of the night while I packed, and then Clyde took me out to the hangar. It was midnight or 1:00 a.m. It was a strange experience. I was so uptight. I couldn't sleep all night, and I flew back all by myself in that plane to Rochester, Minnesota.

The pilots drove me to St. Mary's Hospital, and I found Verna, who was with Dr. and Mrs. Ralph Smith. Dr. Smith was not the surgeon, but he was Mr. Harrah's regular doctor there. We all went in the room to see Mr. Harrah, and he was pacing the floor. He did not have the surgery that day.

Verna and I had dinner that night, and he was scheduled to have the surgery the next morning, Tuesday. We arrived about 8:00 a.m., and I think he was scheduled to have the surgery about 9:00 a.m. They had got him up real early and prepped him, and he was catheterized, and I remember going in the room, and he had tubes and things attached to him. He had on a hospital gown, he was pacing the room, and everybody was just really nervous, but the operation got delayed. The surgeries that were scheduled before his went longer than they had anticipated.

I called Bob Hudgens because I knew he'd be on pins and needles. I had promised Bob I would call him immediately if there was anything to tell him or when Mr. Harrah got out of surgery. Dr. Smith followed me out of the room. I had had quite a bit of contact over the years with Dr. Smith because Mr. Harrah had entertained him and Mrs. Smith quite a bit. He'd taken them to Middle Fork Lodge and various places, sent the plane back for them, and I did all their travel arrangements, although I had never actually met either one of them. He followed me to the phone, and when I got off the phone, he was very serious. He said, "You know, Cindy, I really don't want Bill to have to go through this. I wish we didn't have to do this, but we have no choice." And my heart just sank. I got a very bad feeling just from the look on his face and the tone of his voice. So anyway, we went back in.

Mr. Harrah was pacing up and down all the time and just an absolute wreck. The wife of Verna's doctor, who was a non-stop talker, started to get on everybody's nerves. I remember seeing Mr. Harrah waving his hand toward the door, and Verna and Mrs. Smith and this other lady started leaving, and I said, "Do you want me to go, or do you want me to stay?"

And he said, "No, you can stay."

You were the only one left?

Yes, and we just talked a little bit. He wanted to know if I had talked to Clyde and how the swap meet was doing. He asked who was watching my kids. He also asked me if I had seen Betty lately and how she was doing. Then they came back, and we had to leave because it was time for the surgery.

Verna and I said, "Well, we think we'll go have a Bloody Mary." We'd had Bloody Marys the night before.

And Mr. Harrah said, "Well, you have a Bloody Mary for me too." So we had two Bloody Marys. [laughter] Then it was a long, long, long wait. It seemed endless. I think it was evening before they came in and said that he was out of the operating room and that they had put him in intensive care. We went in to see him, and he was hooked up to all those machines and lights, and he looked pretty bad.

Was he conscious of the fact that you were there?

No, he was not. We went back to the Kahler Hotel, and the next morning we went to the hospital early. He wasn't doing well. His vital signs were slipping a little bit, and it just wasn't looking very good. I immediately got on the phone and called Bob Hudgens, and I told him that I thought he ought to come to Minnesota.

Bob showed up that afternoon with Mead Dixon and Joe Fanelli. I believe by the time Bob got there, they had told us that Mr. Harrah was going to have to go back in for more surgery. He was bleeding internally. The way Dr. Smith described it to me is that his arteries were in such deteriorated condition that the stitches were pulling loose. I believe he had surgery Thursday morning, and he had not, to my knowledge, gained consciousness during that whole time.

After that surgery was when they said that it appeared that he was picking up a little bit; but his kidneys were failing, so they brought in some specialists to see what they could do to save his kidneys or what they could do to handle the situation if he survived. During that time when he seemed to be improving, he did appear to gain consciousness a little bit. Verna was talking to him, and it seemed to me that he appeared to acknowledge that she was there. He was pretty held down with all those tubes and everything, but it seemed to me that he was aware that she was there. He just made a few little sounds like he was trying to say a few words, and that was about it.

Were Mr. Hudgens and Mr. Dixon and Mr. Fanelli also in the room?

They would come in and go out, and we would come in and go out. Verna spent most of the time there, but as you can imagine, it was an extremely wearing thing on all of us. By that evening, things were starting to get worse again according to the doctors, and Verna just kind of went to pieces. She was just about in a state of collapse. There was a hotel right across the street from the hospital, and a couple of the men said, "Well, let's take Verna over and give her a couple of sleeping pills." Dr. Smith said that nothing was going to happen that night, but Verna wouldn't go until she made me promise that I would stay there, and I told her I would.

They took Verna across the street, and everybody left, and they found me a little room where I could lay down. I couldn't sleep, but I rested–and I'd go in and check on him. I remember his feet kept getting uncovered, and I'd cover them up because they just felt like ice cubes. He appeared to be unconscious, and so I just checked on him all night long.

Sometime in the early hours of the morning, I sat down in a chair in his room. I had a blanket wrapped around my shoulder and I guess I fell asleep, because the next thing I remember was that Mead or Bob or someone was touching me on my shoulder. I had fallen asleep in that chair, and when I woke up everybody was in the room. So then it was just a long, long day of waiting for him to die.

There didn't appear to be any hope. It was just a matter of time when he would pass away. He was on life-support systems, and the day before Verna had said, "Well, we ought to just disconnect everything."

And I said, "No, you shouldn't do that yet because there still is a little ray of hope here." I just didn't feel like it was time yet, and I don't think Dr. Smith did either. Then the next day, sometime later in the afternoon, I believe, was when they said it would be OK. Verna gave her permission, I think, although I don't remember that, and they unhooked him, and he was gone. Actually, I think we went outside the room, and they went in to unhook him. I think we were just right outside the door. It was real tough. It was not easy for anyone.

Did someone then contact Reno, contact the management team or Lloyd Dyer?

Yes. I'm sure Bob Hudgens and/or Mead had been in touch with them all along. When he was gone, we all went back to the Kahler Hotel to Mr. Harrah's suite, and we all just kind of sat around there like zombies. It was real strange. It had started storming terribly, and it got real dark, and there was lightning while we were still at the hospital. It was eerie.

My next memory is being in Mr. Harrah's and Verna's suite, and everybody was sitting around. Several other people had arrived that afternoon. June Hudgens had come to give Bob support. A lady by the name of Gwen had been on the plane with June. I did not know who this woman was, and I got June off in a corner, and I said, "Who is that lady?" She said, "Well, that's Mead Dixon's girlfriend."

I called Clyde as soon as I was able to be alone, and he was not in his office. They were putting on a car show and swap meet, so I had him paged out in the field at the swap meet. And someone called Scherry. It might have been me, but I don't think so.

When we were sitting in the suite talking, trying to think who should be notified, somebody said, "Mr. Harrah's sister needs to know." So I got volunteered to call Margaret Schroeter, Mr. Harrah's sister, which was not an easy thing to do. I had, I think, met her once in my life, but I had talked to her on the phone quite a bit, and so I told her, and she was very gracious. That was the end of that day.

Did you all fly back to Reno the next day?

Yes, we did. We all went back on the Harrah's plane–Verna, Bob and June, Mead and Gwen were on the plane. Joe Fanelli probably stayed to help with arrangements. I don't recall him being on the plane.

There were two things I remember about that plane ride home. One was Mead Dixon's attitude, which was very difficult for me to deal with because he was not in the same mood as the rest of us. He was upbeat. He was smiling and cheerful and "huggy" with his girlfriend, and the rest of us were about as low as we'd ever been in our lives. There was such a contrast. I still have the impression that everybody was just so unhappy and remorseful and concerned. I'm sure everybody was thinking about their future, too, and Mead just had a totally different attitude. It was disturbing to me because I just didn't see how anybody connected or involved with Mr. Harrah could be that cheerful, but then I didn't know what was coming down the track, and he did. He was very positive and upbeat.

The other thing I remember was I thought about the shopping I had done for Verna's birthday, which was the end of July. Mr. Harrah died on June 30, the end of Harrah's fiscal year. We had some wonderful gifts that we had purchased for Verna's birthday, and I thought, "My gosh. What's going to happen? All this stuff is going to go into an estate, and what happens then?" I asked Bob if there was any way to get these things to Verna right away, before all this estate business started, because they were from Mr. Harrah.

I had acquired several gifts, including a gorgeous ruby ring that we had had made, but it was not paid for. I asked Bob if there was some way we could handle that so that Verna could end up with it, and he said, "Yes, we'll figure out a way." And then later on in the week when we had a little bit of our senses about us, we sent a check for the ring.

It just happened that Frank Sinatra was appearing at Harrah's on Verna's birthday. Verna, Clyde, and I went to the Frank Sinatra show. We went to the house first, and we gave her the gifts that were from Mr. Harrah, posthumously, which was kind of an emotional thing, but I think she liked it. There were also some pewter pieces for their home in Idaho. She had been wanting pewter to display in an antique piece of furniture that she had bought for the house. And the ring had turned out beautiful. We went to dinner in the Steak House, saw the show and had cocktails with Frank Sinatra after, but still it was a sad birthday.

Let's return to your flight back to Reno from the Mayo Clinic. What happened when you landed in Reno?

When we pulled into the hangar, I remember seeing Lloyd and Holmes and a few other of the executives waiting for the plane. Clyde was kind of off to one side. I got off the plane, and Clyde hugged me, and we left. Everybody was, of course, commiserating with Verna, but we just got out of there and went home. That was Saturday, and I changed my clothes, and I spent the weekend pulling weeds. That was my therapy. I just was out there pulling weeds all weekend. It was all I could do, and I was wondering if I was even supposed to go to work on Monday. What was everybody supposed to do?

Bob called me Sunday night. I picked up the phone, and he said, "Bill's back."

It didn't sink in, and I said, "What are you talking about?"

He said, "Well, they brought him back. They brought him back on the Harrah's plane."

And I said, "Well, OK. What are we supposed to do?"

He said, "Well, everybody needs to be at work tomorrow morning, and we'll start getting things sorted out." So I went to work on Monday morning, and it was so strange because everybody kind of had their doors half closed. The executive floor was like a tomb. It never was a real bustling place, [laughter] but that day it was deadly quiet up

there. People who came up on the floor with reports and things like the day book didn't even want to look you in the eye. I didn't want to look at anybody or talk to anybody. Then Rome came down and hugged me and offered to babysit my kids and buy my groceries or whatever, which was very touching to me.

Finally, I heard talk about the funeral arrangements. Maybe the next day, I was invited into the conference room to kind of help out with what I could on whatever I thought would be good as far as the arrangements, but I was so out of it, they must have thought I was crazy. I had nothing to offer. I believe Holmes said something like, "John might read a poem." And I wasn't sure who he was talking about. I thought he was talking about John Adam, but he was talking about John Denver. Well, I never called these people by their first names, and I didn't have a clue who he was talking about.

Lloyd and Holmes mainly were the ones who made the funeral arrangements, and I believe Joan Dyer helped also. (I really didn't do anything until after the funeral. Then Bob Hudgens and I had to get to work cleaning out all of Mr. Harrah's offices.)

The services were held at Saint John's Church just down the street from our home. We took our children. Verna had said that Clyde and I should sit with the family. Well, I didn't think it was proper for us to sit with the immediate family, but we chose a pew about three or four rows back, and Scherry was there next to us. Clyde was an honorary pall-bearer. I don't remember an awful lot about it. I remember Carolyn O'Callaghan, the governor's wife, was looking for a place to sit, and I guess the ushers didn't know who she was, and they seated her in a chair out on the side aisle. It was real embarrassing. [laughter] A few little snafus like that, but it was a nice service. John Denver sang and George Vargas delivered the eulogy.

*After the funeral was over, did you and Bob
Hudgens get busy cleaning out the desks and
cleaning up a lot of paperwork?*

Yes, and Mr. Harrah had offices all over.
I cleaned out the offices. He had an office at
HAC, one at Villa Harrah and Rancharrah. I
just pretty much packed things up and sent it
all to the warehouse. It's probably still there
somewhere. Then the appraisal had to be
done, so they had me accompany the
appraisers to Rancharrah and to Idaho to
Stanley, Middle Fork Lodge, Sun Valley, and
to the Villa at Lake Tahoe.

*How long did you stay at Harrah's after Bill
Harrah died?*

I believe I was there for another year and
a half. I believe I left in January of 1980. I was
in my old office for a short time, and then
Lloyd needed a secretary, so I moved to his
office. I worked for him for about a year and a
half, during which time Mead moved into Mr.
Harrah's office and took control.

Then we started hearing that Harrah's was
going to be sold to Holiday Inns. Of course,
this would have all kinds of ramifications for
Clyde and me. There he was at the collection,
and we knew that a new owner would not
maintain the collection the way Mr. Harrah
had done it, or even keep it, and so we knew
that the end was coming one way or the other.
It was a year and a half, then, when Holiday
Inns finally took over.

I left when Mr. Goeglein came in. He was
around for a few days, and the next thing I
knew, Joe Specht, who was in charge of
Harrah's industrial relations department, took
me to lunch and told me what was going on.
He told me that Holiday Inns was going to be
buying Harrah's and that I had to be thinking
about what I was going to do. I was the only
salaried secretary at Harrah's. All the rest
were on a daily wage, and I made quite a bit
more money than the other secretaries.
Obviously, there was no way I was going

maintain my status quo. That wasn't much of a
concern, but I had to make the decision
whether I wanted to stay at Harrah's, and I just
couldn't imagine staying there.

I had two considerations. I couldn't face
the letdown of working for anybody else at
Harrah's after having worked for Mr. Harrah.
The other consideration, of course, was
Clyde's situation. I remember one time Mr.
Harrah and I talked about nepotism, and I
said, "Well, have you ever considered it a
problem, Clyde and me both working for
you?"

And he said, "Oh, no! I think it's great. I
think it's to my advantage, because I feel like
that gives me more leverage over you guys."
[laughter] It did, but I just had a feeling that
there was not going to be that same attitude
with new people coming in. A new broom
usually sweeps clean, and I just felt that the
best thing for me to do was just to leave.

Mr. Goeglein had been on the floor there
and had been in and out of Lloyd Dyer's office
for a few days prior. I knew this was it—that
Lloyd was not going to stay in that office. I
think he left, and the next day I met with Joe
Specht and told him, "I'm leaving. I'm going
to have to quit."

I went back over to my office, and I
cleaned out my desk. I had a few little things
that I put on the desk of one of the other
secretaries—a little statue or something that
she had admired—when she was out of her
office. I was back clearing out my desk, and
she appeared in my door looking at me, and
she knew I was leaving.

I didn't really say many goodbyes, except
I did go say goodbye to Rome. He'd been so
kind to me when Mr. Harrah had died. I
called Bob Hudgens and told him I was
leaving. He had been made a vice-president
of something like real estate. That was kind of
a token thing, I think, that Lloyd and the
management had done for Bob. It didn't last,
but I believe that's what he was doing when I
left. Bob tried talking me out of leaving, and I
said, "This is it. I'm out of here."

Notes

1.   *Playing the Cards That Are Dealt: Mead Dixon, the Law, and Casino Gaming.* Reno: University of Nevada Oral History Program, 1992.

2.   Thelma Batchelor was Bill Harrah's first wife.

21

CLYDE WADE

C LYDE WADE worked at Harrah's Automobile Collection (HAC) for over twenty years and was general manager when Harrah's was sold to Holiday Inns. He may know more about the automobile collection of Bill Harrah than anyone alive. Mr. Wade was a little hesitant to be interviewed for this project when first asked, but he eventually proved to be a very informative and helpful chronicler. The interview was conducted in the offices of the William F. Harrah Trust in September of 1997 and was concluded in two sessions.

Mr. Wade went to work for Harrah's in December of 1961 and remained with the company until 1986. In this oral history interview he describes his rise through the organization and recalls many of the employees of Harrah's Automobile Collection, or "the HAC" as it was commonly called. He also remembers many trips that he and Bill Harrah took to attend auto swap meets, runs, and auctions, including trips to Africa and the London-to-Brighton Run on which he served as Mr. Harrah's mechanic.

Of special interest is Mr. Wade's description of the steps of restoring automobiles for the HAC, including factors determining the order in which the cars were restored. Details of the sales, the auctions,

and the disposal of Mr. Harrah's automobile collection are also revealed. Finally, Mr. Wade furnishes the reader with important eyewitness information about the final days of the collection.

CLYDE WADE: I was born March 13, 1940, in Fallon, Nevada. We lived there until 1942 and then moved to Reno, and I've been in Reno since. My father worked for Dodge Construction Company, and my mother was a homemaker. I have one sister seven years older than me and one sister seven years younger. My youngest sister died nine days before her first birthday from meningitis. In Reno, we lived on Linden Street, which is a block south of Franktown Corners. My grandparents, in fact, homesteaded the Franktown Corners property.

When I was in high school, when the Harrah's Automobile Collection was on Lake Street, I used to go see Kay Downs, who was the collection's librarian at the time, and charm her into letting me see some of the factory literature and the photographs and those sorts of things. I enjoyed looking at those old cars. I recall seeing a 1910 Mercer, a beautiful old car, and I'm thinking, "My God! Where in the world did they ever find fenders?" I didn't have a clue that they made them. I didn't have a clue. This thing was just absolutely beautiful, and it was bright yellow, canary yellow–it's called Mercer Yellow, a real vibrant color, a real loud color. I'd stop by every night and look at it. It was there probably a month. It was roped off and everything; you couldn't touch it, of course, but it was just a beautiful thing. But anyway, I used to visit there when I was young. I guess I've always been a car nut.

After I graduated from Reno High, I went into the RFA, a military reserve program. We were called six-month wonders because we were on active duty for six months. When you came out, you went to weekly meetings. You were on two-and-a-half-years active standby, and then you went to inactive standby. Military life was not my idea of having a good time–I disliked having to be at a certain place at a certain time and doing things that you didn't want to do. Of course, that's the way they teach you discipline in the military. As much as I disliked it, I have to admit it was probably one of the best things I ever did.

DWAYNE KLING: What did you do in the military?

I always was a fan of cars, and I went in as a mechanic and worked in a motor pool. I've seen some pretty poor mechanics, but I saw the worst in the army. [laughter] I can't believe some of the things they did. Maybe they couldn't get a job on the outside, so they stayed in the army.

I was at Fort Ord through boot camp, and then I went to school there; and I have to admit, the military schools that you go to for training are excellent. From there I went to Camp Roberts, and I was there for the duration.

I got out of active service in August of 1958, and I worked for A. Carlisle and Company as a delivery boy. I bagged groceries at the Safeway Store at Virginia and Mount Rose, and then I started to work for Reno Ready Mix and then ABC Block. I operated a fork-lift; I used to fire the kilns; I used to do maintenance and change dies for different blocks. I could change a set of dies in less than an hour–no one else had ever done it that fast, but I just had a knack for doing it. I did that, and I loaded trucks and took care of customers on weekends. They put me in the office on Saturdays, and I would handle the office and write orders and fill orders and so on.

In October of 1958, Jim Gullihur's[1] son and I were going deer hunting up north of Gerlach, and so I got to talking with Jim, and he started telling me about his restoration job on Dr. O'Brien's L29 Cord. I couldn't believe that you could take an old rusty car and make it like a new car. I was impressed. The next thing you know, I wasn't working much when I got a telephone call from a friend, and he asked if I would like to go to work for Harrah's Automobile Collection working on Model Ts.

I went, "Well, sure." So I finally went to work on December 19, 1961.

For three days I didn't do anything (they had nothing for me to do), but there were some beautiful cars that they'd acquired from J. B. Nethercutt, who owns Merle Norman Cosmetics. The one that stood out in my mind the most was the 1938 Rolls-Royce Sedanca DeVille Phantom III, which is a V-12. The colors were like butterscotch and cream. It was just beautiful. It had whitewall tires, and it was just a beautiful thing. I remember walking around the shop, and the floor was pink, and it was shinier than the top of this table.

Where was the shop then?

It was in Sparks in the old icehouse. Mr. Harrah had a few cars there at that time. The restored cars were inside the main room. There were some cars out on West Second Street, and some were at a warehouse on Timber Way. When I went to work, he had about 350 cars counting all locations.

The HAC opened to the public January 25, 1962, shortly after I went there. We had about 150 cars on display. We had to wax and

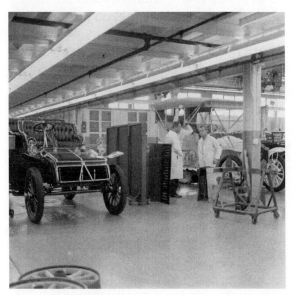

"I remember walking around the shop, and the floor was pink, and it was shinier than the top of this table."

polish all the cars, and we had to literally shovel cork out because Showroom One was where they had stored the ice. We swept the floors and then painted the floors pink—they didn't want to spend the money to put a concrete surface in there. Then we put runners down for people to walk, and we only had guided tours.

Jim had me work right next to George Herman. I started as what they called a "unit mechanic." George was the master mechanic, and he was excellent. George had a wooden leg. He had lost his leg on one of the street cars in Reno when he was a young boy about twelve years old. He said he was just out riding and horsing around, and he stuck his leg out, and it hit a light pole and broke it, so they had to amputate it. He was a very knowledgeable guy, and he taught me so much!

I was very thankful for just having the opportunity to work for such a great man (as Bill Harrah.) I'd never worked for anyone who had such a fetish for cleanliness, honesty, and quality standards. I'd never seen anything like that before in my life. Even with the old guys like George Herman, it was the trickle-down effect. I mean, everyone had the same standards. If you didn't maintain the same standards, then you didn't last; they got rid of you.

There were probably ten to twelve mechanics working there, but shortly after I went to work all hell broke loose, and I don't know why. I don't recall anything other than they were having some cash flow problems downtown, and so they made them get rid of some mechanics. Well, it was a good excuse to get rid of who they wanted to get rid of, but they left George alone. They left me alone. They fired the guy that was next to me, and then they fired a guy two stations down from him and across the shop. Then they cut three or four more loose, so they really did a housecleaning, and I thought, "Well, I guess tomorrow's my day," but it didn't happen.

How soon after you went to work there did you run into Mr. Harrah?

Well, I was really confused at the time. There was a guy named Ora Fezler, and he used to say, "There goes the boss."

"Well, who was that? You mean Jim, the porter?"

"No, no, no. This is the big boss."

I said, "Well, who's that?" Well, that was Lee Jellison—he was the general manager. There was also Bud Catlett. I was really confused.

Then when Bill Harrah came in, Fezler said, "Now there's the *big* boss. The big, big boss."

And I'm going, "Well, who's that?"

"Well, that's Bill Harrah."

"Oh, really?" There were all these bosses. I didn't know what it was all about, but George did; and as I got older, I learned from him what the chain of command was. I knew I was way down on the ladder, but I didn't care. I was just happy to have a job.

The first three days I was at work, they didn't assign me to anything, and I thought, "Man, I'm not used to this." You know, you have to keep yourself humping and busy or you don't have a job, so if you saw something that could be done, you just did it. So I walked around for three days wiping up oil spots and dusting off cars and that sort of thing and apparently impressed someone. No one told me to do anything, but I did anything to keep busy.

I went over and started helping Barney Martini. He was a mechanic there at the time, and I started helping him on this real pretty blue-and-black Model A Coupe. Then for the next two or three days he assigned me to a guy named Fred Covol. We started inventorying motorcycle parts and that sort of thing, and then next thing you know, we were moving cars from warehouses. They were getting them out of the Second Street warehouse and moving them to A Street in back of John Ascuaga's Nugget.

The HAC did most of their buying from about 1965 to 1969–that's when they really started buying cars. We had thirteen warehouses [full of cars] in addition to the cars that were on display. We started with a small showroom up front in the icehouse, and then they built a tin building, which was Showroom Three. Later we opened that up, and we put the Fords there. Then they built Showroom Two, and we filled that with cars and started getting rid of some warehouses; and when they built Showroom One, we put another 300 to 350 cars there, plus we had the boat and aircraft building out there and a plating shop.

Counting the craftsmen, about how many people were working in restoration?

About seventy. That would fluctuate up and down, and by the time you added staff and the cleaning department, security and so on, we had about a hundred and fifty employees.

I went from being a unit mechanic to being a master mechanic. Then I was thinking it would be nice to know more about the cars, so in about 1968 I transferred to the library and became the assistant library supervisor.

Doing research in the library was fun, but I lost a five dollar bet to Bill Harrah on an Elto race car known as "Miss Pepsi." It had an outboard motor for power like a motorboat motor (they used to convert those), and Bill said they could get, like, fifty horsepower out of it.

I didn't believe that. I said, "No way! Thirty is more like it." I even did some research, so I was pretty sure of myself.

He said, "Well, OK. Would you like to bet?"

And I go, "Sure. How much do you want to bet?" So we agreed on five bucks. Mr. Harrah came down with his assistant one night and researched it himself, and he made a copy and sent it to me. It wasn't fifty horsepower, but it was forty-nine and a half, so I clipped my five bucks to the copy and said, "It's close enough for me," and paid my bet. [laughter]

It taught me a lesson. I never lost another bet with him, because I made damn sure I knew what I was talking about or I wouldn't bet. Then it got to a point where he wouldn't bet with me anymore either. But it was fun, and there weren't too many people that could do that.

Mr. Harrah got to know me, and I became the only guy that was always put on a hot job. If we were doing a Franklin to go to the Franklin track, or if we were doing a CBS TV special, I was the first one they would come to, because I never said no. They could always rely on me. Once when the fire system went down at the A Street warehouse, I took my dog up there and did fire watch all night and then came to work the next day. I just never said no.

Once they sold Harry Belafonte a Rolls-Royce, and they called him and asked him if he still wanted the car, and he said, "Well, tell you what. I'll be in New York City on Friday," and this was, like, Wednesday. He says, "If you can have it there by Friday, I'll take it," which he thought was safe. He didn't think we could make it. Well, Del Schultz, who was a truck driver, and I went non-stop from here to New York City in two and a half days. I remember getting pulled over in Ohio and getting a speeding ticket, and they made Del drive. They told me I wasn't very alert. We were tired, because I wasn't used to sleeping sitting up in a truck and staying awake all night, and he wasn't either. So anyway, we managed to get it there. We had three days to do it, and we got it there in two and a half. After we got there, I couldn't go to sleep. I was wired. All I could see was white lines coming at me.

Did Belafonte take it then?

Yes, he took it; and ironically, they had to repossess it, and I thought, "Man!" You know,

having to go through a grueling situation like that, and then the guy turns around and flakes out on them. I thought that was pretty bad.

I left the HAC for about a year and went into my own business. We thought we had an opportunity to make a lot of money, so I left, and Ken Gooding and I became partners. We restored a 1911 Pope Hartford for Harrah's, and at the same time did one–built the body and everything–for Ken Gooding; and we restored a 1913 Mercer Raceabout for Roger Ellis. Then I remember driving over to HAC to pick up some parts, and Bill Harrah was walking across the yard. I was talking to the restoration supervisor at the time, and Bill just sort of passed by. Well, the next time I came over, they had the manager out there, Ray Jesch, and he says, "They're jumping all over me. They said that Bill Harrah said that it would be nice to see Clyde back here working again."

At that time I had had about enough of business with a partner, and we weren't going anywhere big, so I went back to work for the collection. I was there maybe six months as a mechanic again, and then I became the assistant restoration supervisor. Soon we were working on a Ford that was hopped up like one Bill Harrah had had when he was in high school. It had Chrysler wheels on it and dual carburetors and a cam . . . an overhead-valve head, and that sort of thing. Bill's high school car would do eighty-two miles an hour, and he wouldn't allow the restoration Ford to be considered finished until he drove it at its advertised speed. So I went to work on it. One of the things that was happening was it was bending push rods, so I had them make some push rods out of chromium alloy. We went to three eighths instead of quarter inch, and that took care of the problem.

I took the Ford out and drove it. Bill saw me driving it back in, and he says, "How fast will it go?"

I said, "Eighty-four."

He says, "What did you do?" and I told him all the things that I had done. He just grinned, and he says, "That's funny, I had to do the same thing to mine." [laughter] That was how I started to get to know him.

I used to pull those late shifts, and being single at the time, I used to go and eat in the cafeteria. It was, like, a dollar and a half for a steak dinner or lobster tail. I mean, they really put it out for you. I'd go in and say, "Wow!" I used to go down to the HAC just for the food. I was always there.

I was working on a Franklin one night and having a bad time. We'd paid money to have new bearings put in it, and I pulled the pan down, and none of that work was done. The Franklin had an oil pump with all these lines going to different mains and parts of the motor for pressure oiling, and in addition to discovering that new bearings hadn't been installed, I was having a hell of a time trying to get this fitting to go on the other fitting. It just wasn't working. I come firing out from under the car cussing and getting mad, and I look up, and there is Bill Harrah standing there in a grey suit. He says, "Are you having a bad time?" I said yes. I told him about it, what I'd found and so on, and we got to know one another more.

Then when I was a truck driver I got to know Mr. Harrah even better. We were back at one of the Franklin meets, and I was sitting there having lunch with Scherry, Paul Larios, (the assistant manager), Paul Larios's wife, and Bill Harrah. We were having ham sandwiches and Cokes when this guy drives up in a fire engine–this thing was about forty feet long, and I said to Scherry, "Geesh. I sure hope Mr. Harrah doesn't see this, because I don't know how in the world I'm going to get that thing in the van."[laughter] She thought it was funny, and she told him. I thought I was going to really get in dutch, but he just kind of laughed at it.

Bill Harrah was a totally different man when he was away from his casinos. One thing that impressed me–me being just a truck driver/mechanic kind of guy at the time–was at a Holiday Inn in Rocky Mount, North Carolina. These guys were going to have lunch, and they wanted to know how many, and he included me, the truck driver, in this lunch with all the big shots. I'm going, "Wow!" Of course, I kept my mouth shut and just listened, but it was like he didn't forget me. I didn't forget him either.

I always had his luggage, and on this tour the truck was much faster than the cars were, so the mechanic that was with me at the time was supposed to ride with Bill Harrah and take care of the car if anything went wrong. We came to a low bridge. We were thirteen feet, six inches high, and back East, many bridges and tunnels were twelve feet, six, so you had to really pay attention or you could be in real trouble. Mr. Harrah was aware of what the height restrictions were, and so he asked the mechanic what he thought I would do, and he says, "Well, if I know Clyde, he's going to divert. He's not going to take a chance."

I took another route, and when I got to where they were staying, I didn't know where to park this big thing. It was fifty-five feet long, and I'm going, "Wow! Where am I going to park this thing?" So I found this little street, and I tried to pull off the highway, and I got stuck in the sand. Well, the tires turned about half a turn, and it went "vroom," like that, right down in it, and that was it. I was all upset because I had gotten stuck, and I had to go over and tell him that I'm sorry. I said, "Your luggage is going to be late." I started going into detail about what I had done, and he says, "OK. When you get it handled, just bring our luggage up."

On the same trip I even got the general manager, Lee Jellison, in trouble–not intentionally, but I managed to do that quite a bit. One day Bill Harrah crawled up in the cab. I had the air conditioner going, but it wasn't cooling the air, so he says, "How long has it been like that?"

I said, "I don't know. It's been that way since I left Reno."

He says, "Well, from now on, if something like that happens, you get it fixed right away."

And he must have jumped on Lee about it–Lee was in charge of the modern transportation as well as the antique cars and dealerships.

Lee came to me and told me, "The next time Bill asks you a question like that, tell him it just happened."

I says, "I'm not going to lie. There's no way I'm going to lie."

You get caught lying to him, and that would be the end of that.

So he says, "Yes, you're right."

That's sort of how I operated. Everyone could always depend on me, and I was always there. My job came first, and my wife, thank god, was understanding and went along with it. She always considered me the breadwinner. I did a lot of overtime, and at that time, you didn't get paid time-and-a-half. When we bought our first house, which cost $16,300, I think my take-home pay for half a month was $524. There was just the two of us at the time. My check went into the bank, and we lived on Cindy's, and we were pretty frugal. We had a baby on the way, and so we wanted to have our own home, and that's how we got to doing it.

Cindy was a secretary when I met her. When I went to work at the collection, she was already there, working in the research department. She was Sidney Strong's secretary, and Sidney had an assistant who was Nadine Hobblett–that wasn't her name then, but that's her name now. That's where I met Cindy. I found out later that she had said to Nadine, "Boy, you should see what they hired now!" She didn't like me. [laughter] I had the greasy hair, and I always wore white Levis, and I don't know . . . she just took a dislike to me.

There was a gal working in the parts room named Mary, and Cindy and Mary were always having coffee together, so I started working on Mary to get to know Cindy, and I managed to get Cindy to go out with me. On our first date we went bowling, and that's how we broke the ice, and then I took her out. And god, I couldn't afford it, I'll tell you. I was making, like, twenty-one dollars a day, and I took her to Eugene's for dinner. From there, we went to the Mapes Hotel and saw one of their floor shows and one of the small shows down on the first level there, and that's how it started.

So you were moving along in the organization . . . ?

Well, no. To be frank, things were going bad–things were not happening with Lee as the general manager. When B.H. was unhappy with something, he would take a bold step, so he hired a management consulting firm to come in and study the HAC and make recommendations.

At the time, I was up at Middle Fork Lodge . . . another tough duty that I always had, taking care of maintenance on the old cars that were up there. We'd go up there whenever they needed something . . . twice a year or something like that. I was fortunate enough to be the leader of the pack, and I remember flying in with Rex Lanham, a welder, and one other mechanic. Bill Harrah and Scherry were there waiting to pick me up and take me back to the lodge. We made a pass, but Rex had to pull out because the wind was blowing us.

(It was really touchy at that altitude to get in and out of there, and you couldn't take too many chances. You couldn't land in the middle of the day because it was so high, the air was too thin. In fact, one pilot crash-landed taking off in the upper hayfield, and we ended up burying the airplane up there because Bill Harrah didn't like it in his hayfield. The guy had a broken back, and he crawled on his hands and knees all the way down to the lodge, which was a good quarter to a half mile.)

But getting back to the story, on the second pass we pulled out, and Bill Harrah said to the other mechanic, "Well, looks like Clyde will be spending the night down at Big Bend," which was a ranch that Rex Lanham owned. Rex Lanham used to own the Middle Fork, and he sold it to Bill Harrah. Rex used to fly in all the supplies and materials that we used.

When we finished up what we were doing, I took some time off at home, and then I headed back in to the HAC. My supervisor says, "They got a guy here. They're doing a management study. They want to talk to you. Watch what you say, because he's carrying a hidden microphone." The guy's name was Bob Mariscale, and he interviewed me. I told him what I'd been told, because I knew that B.H. had requested this study. I told Mariscale what I had been informed of and told him that I'm not going to say anything any different, so we go off to have lunch at Miguel's. We talk about the business and what I knew about it and what was going on, and I told him Bill Harrah would only come out to the collection in the evenings. He wouldn't come out during the daytime because he was so unhappy with the way things were going.

Mariscale supposedly reported—he didn't put it in writing, but he told them—that I was the only one out there that was promotable. I immediately went from assistant shop supervisor to technical assistant to the general manager, and Doyle Mathia was named the general manager. Lee had been demoted, and Paul Larios got demoted to a lead man from assistant manager.

Doyle Mathia was not an automobile person, was he?

Not at all, but he was a good administrator. He was an excellent administrator. He had done some sort of a study or something at Lake Tahoe, and it had worked out great. It had something to do with unions, and he nailed it. He's a very bright guy, and

even Bill Harrah liked him. He and Bill got along fine.

So he was put in there as an administrator, and you were actually running the restoration part of the collection?

Yes, and Harry Volpi was there. He was the boat and aircraft manager.

So then you were reporting to Doyle Mathia?

Yes and no. He was my direct report, but I also had a dotted-line relationship direct to B.H. when it came to talking about restorations.

What happened when I got promoted was I'm walking across the yard wearing my shop coat, and everyone is gone. I mean, Lee isn't there. Ray Jesch got canned. Paul Larios was demoted. I was the leader of the pack, and Jim Edwards was there and some of the other guys, so I just took care of the shop, and that was that. Well, I remember walking across the yard there at about 8:30, and in drives Shep in his Wagoneer and then this guy driving a Volkswagen station wagon. He was a grey-haired guy, but he looked fairly young, and that was Doyle Mathia. Shep stopped me right out there in the middle of the yard—there was no office or nothing—and he said, "I guess you know that we've made some changes out here. This is your new boss, Doyle Mathia. You're promoted to technical assistant and report directly to Doyle, and these are your job duties: you're going to be in charge of . . . ."

I'm *absolutely* dumbfounded. I go up into the shop after this meeting is over, and it still hadn't sunk in. Doyle told me to take my shop coat off because that wasn't my function. [laughter] But I'm still running the shop, and so I go up into the shop . . . . If we borrowed a part off of a car in the warehouse for duplication, we had to put a tag on it, the date that the transaction took place, who did it, and what car it was borrowed for; and there was a memo with the same information that had to go to Bill Harrah. He got the original, and anybody else involved got carbon copies of it, and one was put in each car's file so it could be tracked. (If ever something happened and you wondered where the part went and the tag was missing, there was still a memo in the file that you could follow up on. It was just a paper machine out there at the HAC.) So I was up there, and the shop secretary wrote up one of these memos, and she says, "Well, who do I direct it to?"

I said, "Send it to me with a carbon copy to Bill Harrah," and so she typed it up. I signed it, and she distributed it.

Jean Brundidge, at the time, was B.H.'s secretary, and she told me, "Mr. Harrah came out smiling, and he says, 'Hey, look at this. This guy's really going places. He's already writing memos to himself.'" [laughter]

The next day I had lunch with Doyle, and he said, "You know what? This is the last time I'm going to tell you to take your shop coat off." And he's telling the other supervisors this, "This is three times I've told him to take his shop coat off," and so the third time, I took the shop coat off. [laughter] I remember going up in the front office, and I really hadn't any idea what the hell my role was. It hadn't sunk in at the time. I was sort of in shock because I can't imagine management coming out here and doing this sort of thing with all these guys that were the big shots when I went to work there, and were still the big shots in my view. I had more authority than a lot of them did now. This was quite a change, and it was difficult—at the time there was a lot of jealousy because I was so young.

Did Doyle stay there very long?

Yes. I think he stayed there for a little over a year, and then he got promoted to Harrah's management. You know, he's a bright guy, and of course, I made him look good too. [laughter]

I can tell you, there's a couple of times that I got my fanny chewed personally by Bill Harrah, and this is one of them. We had one Model T that we couldn't get to quit boiling, so we were never going to be able to finish this thing. In my new position, I told them, "Put another head gasket in. I want two of them in there instead of one to lower the compression, and it won't boil." So they did it, and damned if it didn't work; but it didn't have the power that it used to, and when I went out driving the car with Bill Harrah, I heard about it. (He wouldn't drive a car until I approved it, and the same thing was true when I was just assistant shop supervisor. He used to run out of gas, but he never ran out of gas when I was in charge—when I said the cars were ready to go. He liked it that way.)

◇

Shep told Doyle he wanted to know how much it would cost to restore all the cars that needed restoring. So we made these charts. [Wade lays a chart on the table.] See here, this is the equipment number, the year and the make of car, and what the condition is. The condition of this car is a five. A condition five was acceptable for display only, so it wasn't a *really* good car. A one was a perfectly restored car. And the location shows it is in the shop. The chart was continually changed, and we had to put out a new one once a month. [This is said while Wade rolls out another chart.]

So basically, you had all the cars listed here on this computer printout?

Yes.

You had the car location code, and you had the condition of the car, and the conditions were one through five?

No, one through nine. Nine meant it was undergoing restoration, so the thing was probably disassembled, and then when it was approved, it either got a one, two, or a three.

So, one was completely finished?

Yes, and authentic. Two meant it was an authentic, complete restoration, but it had something wrong with it, like the wrong lights or something like that. Four was a little less than that, and a basket case was like an eight, and a nine was undergoing restoration. If you bought a new Ford, for example, you'd give it a one. How could it not be a one if it was a brand-new car? So it was either original, new condition or authentic restoration.

Then it would tell what the model was. It was a new Super Six we're looking at in this case. This says what the purchase price was. They paid $895 for it. The body style was a Sport Roadster, and the fair market value was $9,000. The body maker was Murray. Then over here, it gave the serial number, the motor number, and the license plate number. And then over here, it shows how many cylinders, the brake horsepower, advertised horsepower; and then over here was the date that we bought the car—in this case, it was June 1960—and who we bought it from.

So this was all kept current every month?

Every month, yes. It was ongoing, and the responsibility lay on the research supervisor.

Basically, it's an inventory of the cars.

Yes. And then once a month, I'd have to take the restoration costs by equipment number, and I provided the business office with this every month—how many man-hours. They tracked material costs and that sort of thing, but I had to give them the man-hours, and any time that they would have a change, they had to put out a report. They wanted to know how much the collection was worth, so we had to do that too. [Wade is paging through charts.]

Well, was there an actual budget for restoration? Did someone say, "You can spend so much this month," or, "You can spend so much on this particular automobile"?

Yes, we had a formal budget, but it could be bent a little. One time I got Shep in trouble when he wanted a study done but had not discussed it with the old man, with B.H. I felt uneasy about this.

If I knew something, I wouldn't volunteer the information to Mr. Harrah, but if he ever asked me, I would tell him, and he knew I would tell him the truth. Not everyone was like that, not even Doyle. Bill Harrah and I had some discussions that got some of the big shots in trouble. In fact, it damn near got Shep fired when he wanted this study done.

I'd take each car by condition. A number-one restoration would average 3,450 man-hours. That's an average car; that's not an easy car. A simple car, like a Model A, you could probably do in about eighteen, nineteen hundred hours. Then you'd get into, like, a Bugatti Royale or something, and it might take you 8,000 man-hours. We had one car that had over 12,000 man-hours, but we literally built the car, and it took ten years.

I took all these cars by condition and projected out what these different types of restorations were, because I was familiar with them, and forecast the cost of doing this. I had literally every secretary at HAC working on this, and I had the papers up and down the hallway because we didn't have a Xerox machine that would sort them and collate them. So we put them together in a book report form and sent them to Shep. (Doyle helped me on this.)

Then I gave a blind copy to the old man, and he put a note on it that said, "See me." I went back in, and he says, "What is this?" I told him that I had been asked by Shep to put this report together, and I thought that he should know about it.

He says, "Don't you ever do anything like that again unless you discuss it with me first!" Period.

Cindy and Clyde Wade in front of a restored Bugatti Royale. *"[A] Bugatti Royale . . . might take you 8,000 man-hours [to restore]."*

I said, "Yes, sir!" [laughter] I told Doyle what had happened, and of course they were pissed at me because I gave the old man a copy. They had to answer to him, I'm sure. When you sneak around doing things like that . . . it makes you wonder about your executives. I wasn't trying to protect my fanny, but I just felt he, as the owner, should have an idea what the hell was going on.

Well, there had to be friction between the hotel-casino part of Harrah's and the collection because Bill Harrah liked the collection so much more. He knew the casino generated the money, but he got so much more enjoyment out of the collection.

There was no love between us and the guys downtown. The guys downtown figure they're generating the money and we're spending it, and they didn't like us at all. We were putting on those boat races up at Tahoe, and we sponsored Ferrari races at Stead, and, shoot, it was just all spending money and not generating any revenue.

We used to report to Rome Andreotti, and he was a son-of-a-bitch to report to. Oh, tough! Rome didn't like me, and I didn't like Rome. Everything that we wanted to accomplish or get done, you had to write a report. All we did was do studies and reports and then send it to him, and he'd change this and change that and send it back. Why, hell, from the time you started to the time you finished reporting, the project could have been done.

Bill Harrah called me in the office one day, and he says, "What's the problem around here?" (That's while Doyle was still there.) "How come things don't get done?"

And I said, "You really want to know?"

He says, "Yes."

I said, "It's Rome."

He says, "Well, what do you mean?" and I told him about all of the roadblocks the guy would throw up at us. He says, "Well, what do you recommend?"

I said, "I recommend that we report to the president. Then if there's a problem, it's just between you and the president, and it's not going to be you and Rome and then the president or whoever. If there's a problem, then you two can sit down and decide, and you don't have to bother anyone else, and you can just get a one-on-one."

He said, "Well, that's a good idea," so it got changed immediately.

Another thing happened once when we were coming back from a Brighton Run shortly after I was promoted, and Doyle was still there. We had bought a collection of early race cars from George Waterman, and we paid a lot money for them. George Waterman wanted us to make the payments over ten years because it worked well for him tax-wise. We didn't have the budget to do it, but we did it anyway, and then we were able to work it out. We paid so much money for these cars. We paid $85,000 for the 1911 Fiat, which was a lot of money. We only paid $40,000 for the Duesenberg, the last Duesenberg we bought.

And then, of course, you had the restoration charges.

The restoration quality was not what B.H. would have liked. Shep was legitimately concerned about it, so he told Doyle that if B.H. wanted to restore one of these cars, to let him know about it, and Doyle passed that information down to me.

Anyway, B.H. and I were coming back from the Brighton Run, and on the way home we were selecting the next car for Brighton.

He says, "We got the 1903 Napier. We paid $63,000 for that. The 1903 Napier is the oldest surviving English race car known to exist. We'll leave it over in Beually," which was the museum in England that Lord Montagu [Lord Edward John Montagu] owned. "We'll leave it over there for a year." We had to get it out before a year was up, because if it stayed there for more than a year, then we had to pay huge taxes on the value of the car.

So I get back, go back to work in Doyle's office, and he says, "How was the trip?" So we went over all of the what-fors that went on and the fun things that were positive, and I gave him a rundown on it, and that was that. The next day B.H. called me in the office and laid it on me what car we were going to restore—the 1903 Napier. I said, "That's one of the Waterman cars, so we're going to have to run this by Shep before we start restoring it."

He turned about as red as a beet, and he was pissed! He says, "What do you mean?" And so I explained to him what I had been told. We were supposed to go drive cars immediately after this, but he got torqued. He was *pissed!* He turned around, and his phone was on his credenza behind him, and he reached down and got it and dialed 3-0-4.

Well, 3-0-4 was Shep's number. The old man said to Shep, "I'm on my way down there. You be in your office when I get there." I thought, "Oh, shit!" So I went for a drive by myself, because I knew I was going to get my throat cut. [laughter] I knew I was going to get shot right between the eyes and be out of there. I go back to the HAC, and I drive into the shop and get out of the car, and there's Doyle pacing back and forth. [laughter] He goes, "Well, do you think Bill will approve it?"

"Yes, I think he'll approve it."

He's skirting around it a little bit, and then he finally says, "By the way, what did you tell Bill?" I told him what I told Bill. He says, "Well, I didn't tell you that."

I said, "Bullshit! You think I'm making it up? You're damn right you told me."

He says, "Well, Shep doesn't know if he's going to have a job tomorrow or not."

And I said, "Neither do I." And I never heard another word about it. Apparently they got it straightened out, and we both had a job the next day, but it was scary as hell to me.

I've heard the words the "Gold Star List" and the "Red Star List." Does that tie in with rating the condition of the car?

It started out that way, and it was Bill Harrah's idea. When he was walking through the showroom, he didn't always know if the car was a one or a two, so we'd fix a gold star on it if it was a gold star restoration or a red star if it was a red star restoration. A gold star was the absolute tops in restoration or a factory original.

Of all those hundreds of cars, who decided what car was going to be a number one or a number two?

The research department would usually designate what a car was going to be, but it always was subject to change predicated on what I thought or what Doyle thought and what B.H. had decided.

In the early days did Bill Harrah actually drive around looking for old cars to buy?

Yes. In fact Bill Craig, who was our Duesenberg expert when I first went to work there, had just a horrendous supply of Duesenberg parts in Oakland under his house. If we ever needed Duesenberg parts, then we would contact Bill Craig, and he'd make a trip to Oakland and bring the parts back. But the point is that he showed me a picture of a car and an actual receipt where Bill Harrah paid him $400 for a Duesenberg. Now, we don't have the car any longer, so I don't have a record of it, but I did, in fact, see the signature, and I'm sure that Bill Craig probably still has it today. He used to carry it

around in his wallet. So, yes, Bill Harrah used to go buy the cars.

Rip, who was a truck driver, used to go pick up the cars. He told me that B.H. bought this Model A Phaeton, and it was supposed to be a complete car, but the guy took the headlights off and wanted $125 for the pair of headlights. Rip reported this to Mr. Harrah, and Mr. Harrah told Rip not to come back with the car. He says, "If you come back with the car, then I'm going to can you." I mean, he felt that strongly. So the guy blew the deal.

Bill Harrah sometimes purchased cars himself in the early days, but later on he brought in a gentlemen named Bud Catlett as his buyer.

Yes. He and Bud met on a tour back when we had the Maxwell. Bud was very knowledgeable with old cars, and he and B.H. started talking, and they became pretty good friends over the years.

And another interesting thing that not too many people know is how the library got started. It got started because Bill Harrah bought a 1907 Maxwell, and then after he got into buying and liking old cars, he decided, "Maybe we should start buying factory literature when we can so we'll learn more about what we're buying." Well, it turned out that this 1907 Maxwell had mostly 1911 parts on it, and they were able to identify this through research. That was actually how the library got started.

A short time later, Bud Catlett came to work as a buyer. Bud had been the first to point out to B.H. that the 1907 Maxwell had a lot of wrong parts. Then they had to hire people to go through and read the literature; and I mean, we're even talking periodicals. If they ran across an article on a 1911 Empire that had photographs, they would save it. In its day, everything was in drawers and file cabinets or wood cabinets with glass doors.

For the life of me, I can't figure out why in the world they just didn't take the whole damn thing and make a little bit more room for the library in the National Car Museum. We had duplicate stuff, which I agree, yes, you could sell duplicate stuff or triplicate stuff and still maintain integrity; but to take that wonderful museum library and literally put it into cardboard boxes made absolutely no sense to me. It was a real screw-up on somebody's part.

Did Bud Catlett also have people working for him that would go out to different parts of the country?

We would have different individuals that we knew were car buffs, like Eli Williams in Salt Lake City or god knows who all in California. And if we ever had a car offered to us, we would always send one of those guys to look at it. We would pay them their expenses and a little bit of money for their time, or in most cases the people would donate their time. We'd have them on a retainer, so much a year, and they'd go look at the cars and make a report and send photographs and so on, and then we'd make a determination whether or not to buy it. And I will tell you this too, that if you think for a second that Harrah's Automobile Collection did not influence the market, you're dead wrong, because the last Duesenberg we bought, we paid $40,000 for it, and it sold at auction for $280,000. That was the last one we bought, and I remember Doyle having to stand his ground to get that.

The last Duesenberg we bought had belonged to George Whittell at one time. It was a 1929 Duesenberg. We didn't buy it from Whittell, but it was one of his cars. [Clyde is looking at charts.] OK, we bought a 1929 Duesenberg in 1972 from George Newhall in San Francisco, who owned, I believe, a publishing firm in San Francisco, and we paid $40,000 for it. We had it valued for the auction at $140,000, and it went for $280,000.

Was that an auction held after Bill Harrah had died?

Yes. And I know of Duesenbergs selling for $3 million but now the price of Duesenbergs is probably down to $650,000 to $700,000. They've really gone downhill.

Did Bill Harrah ever want something so bad that he just said, "Get it."?

Yes. When Jack Nethercutt offered his collection of cars, and I think it was around forty cars, he felt there was only one guy that he knew that could come up with the money right away, and that would be Bill Harrah. So he called B.H. and asked Bill if he'd like to buy his cars. Bill said yes, he'd be interested. "How much?" and it was, like, $150,000 for all of these wonderful cars, and Bill Harrah says, "Well, OK. I'll call you back." So he calls a meeting and tells the money guy–Bill Harrah referred to Andy Iratcabal as "the money guy"–he wants to buy these cars, and he needs $150,000. The problem was that Nethercutt needed it the next day, and Bill Harrah didn't have airplanes and that sort of thing then.

So they had this meeting, and Andy tells B.H., he goes, "Wow!" He says, "I don't know how we're going to do it. Where are we going to get the money?"

Well, it ticked B.H. off, and he said, "Andy, it's not your job to tell me whether I can or can't do something. It's your job to see the money's there if I want to do it." That's the way it went, and B.H. got the money and put it in his car in a briefcase and drove all night and gave Nethercutt the money the next day.

When the famous Schlumpf Collection was put up for sale, they wanted $28 million for 660 cars. Did Bill Harrah buy any of that collection?

No. I used to get assignments from Bill Harrah directly. He called me in and said, "We're negotiating on the Schlumpf Museum. We're going to go over and see it." It was one of those cloak-and-dagger things where it wasn't open to the public. We were going to make a deal out the back door if we could, but it didn't work out.

It was the same way when we were negotiating to buy the *Spruce Goose*.[2] Bill Harrah would call me and he'd say, "Blah, blah, blah. This is what we're doing. How are you going to move it, or how are you going to handle it?" That's basically the way it went.

The same thing happened when we bought the Rockefeller Collection. Doyle and I went up to see a guy that was one of the directors for the college and negotiated the deal. We got the entire Rockefeller Collection for $4.3 million. The collection was in Petit Jean Mountain Museum in Morrilton, Arkansas. It was right there on the grounds where they used to keep the Santa Gertrudis bulls. (They were huge things. They weighed, like, 1,600 pounds, and they were just beautiful.)

I was called in after we bought the collection to go handle the transfer. They asked me how many guys I needed to go with me to inventory this so we weren't ripped off, and I said, "One. What you got to worry about are the little things, so I want to take a photographer. All it's going to do is psych them out. Forget about the cars—we already know what cars we're going to get; they're not going to take a car. What we got to be concerned about is anything that's small that they can pilfer and go out the back door with before we can do anything about it. So the first thing I'll do is go down with the photographer, and we'll just start snapping photos, and that will end that. You know, psychologically, everybody will think that everything's been photographed, and they won't take anything." And near as we can tell, nothing got taken.

When we got there, we wanted to see what it was like, so we drove to the museum in Morrilton, but it was closed. We looked through the glass and turned around and were walking away when the night watchman comes out, and he says, "Oh yes, you want to come in and see it?"

We said, "Yes, would you mind? We came all the way from out-of-state, and we thought it'd be nice to see it while we're here, and we won't be here long. So if you wouldn't mind, we'd sure appreciate it."

He said, "Sure, no problem. That will be three dollars each." Well, I picked up on what that was all about, and so I paid the guy the six dollars, and he let us in. We took some photographs just like we were tourists and asked questions, and he freely answered them, and we left.

The following morning, I go in to meet Buddy Holzman, the museum director, gave him my card—back then big shots had their photographs on the cards—and told him I was from Harrah's. Of course I got the welcome mat. I asked him if we could go in his office and have some privacy for a couple of minutes. I says, "You know, we own the collection now. I want it closed immediately, and I want all of your help sent home. The only thing we want here is security. And speaking of security, who was the guy that was on duty last night after you guys closed? Did he turn in any money?"

He says, "No."

I said, "He didn't turn in six dollars?"

He says, "No, I don't think so," and he goes and checks, and he says, "No, he didn't turn in any money."

I said, "OK, especially him. I don't want him here, period." So we just went down there and started photographing, and about two days later we were flying home, and it was a done deal.

Were you working for Mr. Harrah when he bought the 1907 Thomas Flyer?

Oh, sure. We got that from Austin Clark in Long Island. Clark used to have sugar plantations in Cuba, and when this guy with a beard came out of the jungles and took over Cuba, he lost the plantations, so he had to sell some cars.

George Schuster and Scherry Harrah with the 1907 Thomas Flyer. Schuster had driven the car around the world in 1908. *"At first he doubted that it was the real car. But when we lifted the body off, he walked over, and he looked where he personally had made a repair on the frame . . . and the tears started down his cheeks because he realized it was the real car."*

I went back to bring back a load of cars; and after I loaded the cars to come home, I had to ship some fire trucks, so we had to deal with the railroad. That's like dealing with an ex-wife. I mean, it just doesn't happen fast, and none of it is easy going. We were there for so long we got to know the family.

Later on Bill Harrah flew George Schuster Jr. to Reno to inspect the Thomas Flyer and verify its authenticity. Schuster had driven the car in the race around the world in 1908.

Yes. At first he doubted that it was the real car. But when we lifted the body off, he walked over, and he looked where he personally had made a repair on the frame where it had been cracked—he'd put a plate in there and made this repair, and the tears

started down his cheeks because he realized it was the real car. I believe he had a heart attack while he was there, and he was in the hospital for a while, and B.H. took care of that.

Bill Harrah wanted to restore the car to the condition it was when it finished the race. When we were painting it, you couldn't have shiny paint because it's going to be oxidized and beat up from being in that race. So it was pretty tough, and it went against everything that we had done before. We usually tried to make everything perfectly bright and shiny.

You always had a beef going between the painters and the mechanics, because the mechanics would chip the paint, and the painters would have to go back and repair the damage. My goal was always to do a car without the painters having to come back, and the closest I ever came was on a 1931 Ford

Deluxe Delivery. (It turned out so nice, by the way, that they retired it.) I only put three chips on the entire car when I was restoring it, and that was when I was putting the doors on. The painters liked me because I didn't really beat them up too bad. [laughter]

Bill Harrah was well know for his attention to details and cleanliness. Was his automobile collection handled the same way?

Oh, man, let me give you an example. We were restoring this car right here, this 1904 Franklin. [Mr. Wade points to photo.] You see the grille in that? That's the original grille. They had taken it out of the car because it had some pieces missing, and rather than repair it, they just made a new grille. This was when Paul Larios was the guy that was in charge of the restoration, and he reported to the manager, Ray Jesch. Anyway, Bill Harrah goes out into the body shop, and he sees them making this grille, and he asks them, "What's that for?"

"That's for the 1904 Franklin."

"Well, why are you making a new one?"

"The other one had some pieces missing."

"Where's the other one?"

"Well, it's down in the welding shop."

"Oh, OK." So he walks down to the welding shop. There was another body man down there, Johnny Turche, who had come over from Lake Street. He used to paint all of B.H.'s Ferraris, so they were on a one-on-one basis. B.H. asked Johnny, "Where's the grille out of the 1904 Franklin?"

And Johnny said, "Oh, that's down there," and he took him over to show it to him.

He says, "Well, can't that be fixed?"

And Johnny said, "Yes."

He says, "Call Larios and have him come out here." So he called Larios, and Larios came out there, and the old man made him take out that brand new grille, repair the original one, and put it back in. That's the way he was.

We've been looking at the computer printout on all the automobiles. Yet Mead Dixon said when he looked at the automobile collection, there was no inventory list. Is that true?

Yes. There was no inventory. In fact, that was a big problem with the accounting office, because there was such value at the HAC, and there was no way that you could inventory it.

I had an internal audit out there, and we're going through all these parts, and they're going, "How are we going to inventory this?"

I said, "Well, why don't you guys tell me how? I don't know how." Why shoot, we had engines and all kinds of things.

For years and years, we had the warehouse on Timber Way, and that was the same thing–we had no inventory. If we had 350 chamber pots in the Pony Express Collection, we had no inventory of the 350 chamber pots. At Timber Way, it was fenced off, and vehicles like high-wheel bikes or motorcycles or that kind of stuff, they were inventoried. But a parts inventory? No way. It was impossible. How in the world are we going to inventory 749 window handles? I mean, who in the hell is going to come out and count? Who's going to do this? I'm not going to do it. If you want the inventory, you come do it.

The parts were sorted, and the parts were on racks. They were easy to find. If you needed a hubcap for this particular car, you just had to go back and look, but to inventory it all would have been a monumental task. We'd have spent hundreds of thousands of dollars fooling with that, and I didn't think it was worth the effort, personally. There were smarter guys than me working for Harrah's, and they couldn't tell anyone how to do it.

The collection contained items other than automobiles that a lot of people aren't aware of. There were things like motorcycles, airplanes, and of course, the Pony Express Museum. How did Bill Harrah get into those areas?

You know, we would buy complete collections. In the Petit Jean Mountain Museum, we had goat carts and pony carts. We had things that came along with the automobiles. It wasn't that we were intentionally looking for anything particular, but it was a large museum. It all went together, and B.H. was one that didn't like selling stuff too much.

Did he like motorcycles too?

Yes. I'll never forget this: We had an auto-ped. It a little one-cylinder motor that drove the front wheel. When you put the handle down, it would stop; and when you raised the handle, that was the way the drive would work. Well, Bill Harrah rode that damn thing all over the yard there.

We had just finished this Henderson motorcycle–and it has an in-line, four-cylinder motor. The spark plugs are on the side, but they didn't have rubber cups like they do today; they were just metal. Well man, let me tell you, get your leg too close to it and that thing will start biting you. So I told B.H., "When you ride this, you better ride bow-legged because . . . ." He did, and he was a good sport. He was a good sport. Fun guy.

We'd go into a meeting, and Bill Harrah had a thing about associating a person with their car. That's how he would remember them, and we would go into a meeting, and he would describe someone, "Who's that guy that had that 1931 Dodge, and it was yellow and kind of was . . . ?"

"Oh, you mean Mr. Feltonburger?"

"No, it wasn't a common name like that." [laughter] That was his sense of humor.

We bought this 1908 Franklin, and it had a little, round hood and a great big, high body on it. We bought it out of the *L.A. Times* and brought it up, and it had termites in it of all things. Christ, we were afraid they were going to infiltrate the whole thing. We restore this car, and as we're on the finishing touches, they

were trying to get this thing to run right. The problem they were having was it was smoking–man, you wouldn't believe the blaze of blue smoke this thing was leaving! The reason it was doing it was because of the way that Franklin had designed the motor: it had an extra set of valves in the exhaust manifold that you really didn't need, and it was trapping oil there, and it was just causing this God-awful smoke. You couldn't see the highway.

They were trying to put miles on it going down I-80, and you couldn't see the damn highway. Coincidentally, that was the year that the government had just started having emission controls, and they had white cars . . . . I forget the name of the department, but whoever they were, these officials saw this damn thing going down the highway, and just out of curiosity they followed it into HAC. I'm coming across the yard, and here comes this thing just blazing smoke, and behind it is this official car with a seal on the door.

They follow this thing in, but it was just curiosity on their part. "What in the world is this thing making all this damn smoke?" [laughter]

While they were there, Bill Harrah drove up in his Ferrari. When I get back to my office, there's a call: "Bill wants to see you."

He says, "What was that all about?"

I said, "Oh, that. That was the Department of Agriculture in the city of Sparks, and they wanted to know if they could either rent or lease the 1908 Franklin for mosquito abatement this summer." [laughter] I thought I was the funniest thing around, and he just sat there and stared at me. [laughter]

Along with the automobiles, the motorcycles, and other things, Bill Harrah had quite an airplane collection. The Ford Tri-Motor especially garnered a lot of attention. Would you comment on that?

I have to say that was an incredible restoration. The driving force behind it was Bill Harrah, but I think Harry Volpi deserves a lot of the credit. Harry had been with B.H. for a long time before I was ever there, and he was in charge of the restoration. They had quite a talented crew back then. It was probably one of the most expensive restoration jobs that went through the place. It took four and a half years and a half million dollars *at cost.* They bought the Tri-Motor in Caldwell, Idaho. It had been ground-looped in New Mexico at one time. One of the features of the Tri-Motor was it had a corrugated skin, which was part of the strength of the aircraft. But when it was ground-looped, it was so damaged that the original corrugated skin was removed, replaced with a smooth skin . . . and then they drilled additional holes for rivets so that the new skin could be installed. We were going to replace the smooth skin with the original-type corrugated skin, but because we wanted it to be certified to fly, the FAA told us, "No, you have to make a new framework. It needs new structural pieces as well." So the only thing on the airplane that wasn't replaced was the fuselage. Everything else was new. When the people from the Air and Space Museum in Washington, D.C., came out and examined the restoration, they said it was absolutely a fabulous job. They said, "It's the finest Tri-Motor in the world."

To fly the Tri-Motor, we had to hire a pilot from Johnson Flying Service who had a lot of hours under his belt. On its maiden flight it flew over Reno, and then we took it out a couple more times after that. Also, TWA rented it and flew it back East, then to California, and then back to Reno. We later flew it in and out of Middle Fork Lodge, and that was a dangerous landing field. Bill Harrah wanted to fly into Middle Fork in it, and we highly recommended that he not go. He was there to watch it land and take off, and everything was fine, but it was an iffy situation. I've flown into Middle Fork when you couldn't see the wing tips on the DeHavilland Twin Otter. They would reverse the pitch on the props, and it would go down just ever so slow until they'd find a hole in the clouds to go through and look around below. If that wasn't the right canyon, they'd turn around and find the hole and fly back out again. It was spooky, but we had some incredible pilots.

How many old airplanes did Bill Harrah have?

He had about thirteen. Some of them we got rid of because the restorations were going to be far too expensive. After we went public, we had $200,000 a year to spend for car purchases. Anything we sold went into the kitty also, and we could use that to buy additional vehicles.

So by getting rid of the airplanes, he picked up some cash to buy some more automobiles?

Right. We always tried to upgrade the collection, buy a better car. Whatever we sold went into the kitty. The constant upgrading kept the activity going, which also influenced the market.

Did Bill Harrah hold auctions here?

Yes. First we tried a livestock auction company from Fallon—I think it was in 1962—but it just didn't work too well. So then we tried advertising cars for sale via sealed bids, and we would do an auction over the phone between the two highest bidders. Someone would arbitrate between the two to arrive at which one would pay the highest price. That was OK but sort of clumsy, so then we got into auctions.

Bill Harrah would go to the auctions, and of course everybody wanted to rub elbows with him. By then he was world-renowned, and the result was that there were a lot of people going around saying they knew Bill Harrah when indeed they didn't. Let me give you an example. Cindy has a relative who came to a swap meet. He told Cindy, "I had lunch with Bill today."

And she said, "What did you have?"

"Oh, we had watermelon."

"Well, what did he have to say?" Well, he didn't have anything to say. What happened was they sat at the same table. Bill Harrah came in, and he had his piece of watermelon with whoever he was with, and that was it. We used to hear a lot of that kind of story.

What did you sell off in the auctions?

Usually we sold off our duplicates. Once in a while we would come across a car that had some real problems–for example, a 1947 Volkswagen. We had one undergoing restoration that had been crashed. It was in bad shape, and there was a tremendous amount of work to do on it. We found one advertised for sale, which we bought for $1,000. We were looking at up to 3,450 man-hours to restore the bad one, and why spend that much to restore the wrecked one? Here is a good one for $1,000. So just shut down the restoration and sell it for what you can.

We had a "want" list of cars. I'd say that probably more than half of them don't even exist now or never did exist, but we had them on the list anyway. We wanted a Russian car like a Zif or a Zin, but they were not obtainable. Bill would read about a car or have a discussion with somebody or somebody'd ask him, "Do you have this?" or, "Do you have that?" And no, he didn't have it. He wanted to have the world's largest automobile collection and a car representing every country that built one. He was also looking for something different. There were over 4,000 different makes, and if you throw in trucks, there were over 6,500 different makes.

We had a lot of one-of-a-kind cars like the Adams-Farwell, the only one known to exist. We had a Henry Grey, the only one ever built. It wasn't much of a car, but we had it. We also had a Julian. The Adams-Farwell involved kind of a funny story. The chassis was restored but didn't have the body on yet. What was so unique about it was that the crankshaft was rigid, and the five cylinders would revolve around the crankshaft. To start it, you would get the cylinders to start spinning and "cachoo, cachoo, cachoo." I was at my work bench two stalls away from the car, and Bill Harrah was there with his coat off–and he was in a white shirt, a tie, and grey pants. The mechanic started this damn thing up, and it started throwing oil on him and everyone and everything else around it. Everyone scattered, but they finally got it going.

In the Adams-Farwell the driver could sit in the back seat and put the kids or the mother-in-law or whoever up front; or he could move the steering wheel and the controls up front and put everybody in back and drive it from the front. That's why it is called a "convertible sedan." A typical convertible sedan is a sedan that has a convertible top that folds down, but it has side windows. If it has no windows, then it's a Phaeton; but in this case, "convertible" would sure throw you off. [laughter]

I went to some auctions around the country. I bought some cars, but we had car buyers, and that was their job. We had every major newspaper clipped every day and sent to Bill Harrah. He would check off those he wanted looked into, and we bought a lot of cars that way. If all the car buyers were on a trip to buy a car or on vacation, I would go.

I remember when Bill wanted me to go to an auction and buy a Porsche that was made the first year of production and also a Model T that was a year that we didn't have and another car that was too rough. When you went to look at a car, you had to call him, describe the car to him, and discuss it with him. He'd say, "Well, OK, go ahead and buy it if you can get it for this." You didn't do it entirely on your own. We bought the cars, and after they arrived, we would research them, and occasionally it would turn out that they weren't what they were represented to be. So then I had to call the seller and say, "Hey, you sold us a bogus car." They usually took them back, no problem.

I went to England with Bill and Verna and Rome Andreotti and his wife to buy a very rare Weymann-body Stutz. What made it attractive was that it was the only supercharged Stutz known to exist, and Weymann used to import them into England and race them. In 1929, Bentley came out with a Speed Six, which is an extremely fast car, and the only way Stutz could compete with it was to put a supercharger on it, so they mounted one in front of the radiator. They had three cars they were racing, and two of them developed problems, but they were able to take parts off the other two and keep the third one going. It was way out in front during the race, but it lost high gear and had to finish the race in second, and so it lost. But still, it was a very good, rare car.

I think we started negotiating to buy the Stutz about 10:00 a.m. Bill had said he wanted to spend 19,000 pounds. In rough dollars, that was about $43,000, something like that at that time. Well, I was negotiating this thing, and Bill Harrah was just down the hall, three or four rooms around the corner. I went to his room and asked him questions and then went back for some more negotiating. Well, we got down to within 350 pounds of having a deal, and I'm going, "Nope." I was authorized to go to 19,000 pounds and they wanted 19,350 pounds. I said, "All right, I'll tell you what. You restore race cars, so why don't we do this? We'll pay you the 19,000, and then I'll send you the chassis of an early Hispano-Suiza to restore. It's a fifty horse." (For 1904, that's a lot of horsepower.) I was able to convince them, and we made the deal.

All the while during the negotiating, Bill Harrah's calling me. [laughter] I'm on the phone saying, "I can't talk to you right now. I'll probably be finished up here in another ten minutes, and I'll call you." He sent Rome and his wife and Verna to go have lunch. He was so antsy. He wanted this car so bad, he was in there pacing the goddamned floor waiting for me to finish the deal.

When we finished, I still had to go to Mr. Harrah's room and get the money. We had arranged for the cash the day before, so I went in and told him the deal and why it took so long, and he was just shaking his head, and he said, "I love it!"

I said, "You told me 19,000, and this is what I did."

And he said, "OK, that's good."

What was the purpose of the swap meets?

Well, primarily at swap meets at that time, we were able to acquire needed parts. We had a "parts wanted" list for cars that were going to be restored. After research completed their verification of the car, they'd make up a list of parts that were missing or incorrect. Then we would photograph those parts from the literature or another car and put together a parts-buying book to take to the swap meets. We acquired a lot of parts here at the Reno swap meets and didn't have to spend as much money to travel all over the country for them.

There must have been a lot of people who didn't read *Hemmings Motor News* or had no idea what we wanted, because if people knew what we wanted, their prices would go up. To give you an example, I went back one year to Hershey, Pennsylvania, where they had a big gathering. They had about seventy-five acres of parts, and it was a swap meet and a car exhibit. Well, Mr. Harrah had seen a sign there that he wanted. It was a brown, white, and powder-blue porcelain sign mounted on four-inch-thick concrete. We were buying any porcelain signs there, which drove the prices up. Well, this guy was holding out because he knew who our buyers were. One of our guys went over to try and buy it, and he wanted $900 for it; and then another of our guys went over to try to buy it, and now he wanted $1,000. So I said, "Let's wait until Sunday. He doesn't know me from a sack of wheat, and I'll go buy it."

I went over there on Sunday and bought it for $750. And then I sent one of the guys over for a receipt, which we had to have for accounting. The seller said, "Goddamn it, I knew I should have held out." [laughter]

The next year, everybody brought their signs, and their prices were very high, but we already had what we wanted, and we weren't buying. Those kind of things went on. We even got to the point where we used walkie-talkies to verify things. We saved steps and got more work done and were a lot more efficient. We got some negative publicity off of that. A newspaper called *Old Cars* referred to us as "transistorized locusts," so we dropped that. [laughter] We had to come up with another idea, and we decided that four guys would each respond to a different color light on a light bar mounted on the back of the tractor-trailer. If Bill Harrah or somebody wanted to talk to a certain person, we would flip on his light, and he'd come back to the van. They'd converse, and then he'd go back and do whatever had to be done.

Did you ever go on any trips with Bill Harrah just for fun?

Yes. Bill was not married when Harrah's went public, and Cindy and I spent a month with him and his friend in Europe. If I can remember this sequentially, we went to Portugal, Spain, Majorca, Italy, Switzerland, France, England, and then we came back home. We stayed at the Ritz in Paris, the Gritti Palace in Venice, and the Savoy in London. Bill was totally different in a situation like that. He was fun! We had to take a couple of vehicles—one for the luggage and one for the four of us. Or we'd take two taxis if we didn't have a limo there, so we would split up the luggage—and half of it would go with us, and the other half would go with him.

We were checking into the hotel in Geneva, Switzerland, and our room got finished first. Of course, we asked them, "Well, would you like to go on up and use our room until yours is ready?"

He said, "No, no, just go ahead. Our room will be finished in a few minutes. Don't worry about it." He said, "I'm not going to walk around with you today. I had a problem last night."

I said, "Oh, what's that?"

He said, "Well, I ordered a Coke from room service, and when the waiter brought it in, the Coke fell off of the tray right on my big toe and broke it." [laughter]

We had a black chauffeur who owned a Cad 75 limousine. He was very well educated and well spoken—nice guy, very polite and knowledgeable. He drove us all over in the limo, and B.H. sat and just chatted with him for two or three hours and let us go do our thing.

I went to South Africa with Bill in 1975. He had found out I really wanted to make the trip, and he called me in, and we talked about shipping the car, and he said, "You're going, aren't you?" So of course, I did. It was a tour. We had finished the restoration of a 1918 Dual Valve Pierce Arrow. (It had experimental hydraulic brakes. The first production hydraulic brakes were in a 1921 Duesenberg.) We shipped the Pierce Arrow to South Africa on a ship. It was supposed to arrive in Durbin on such and such a date, but it got into a big hurricane and had to turn around and return to port. Then they had to take it off of that ship and put it on another one. I went over there early, of course. When I arrived, I went to the people that were supposed to accept the car, and I asked, "Where's the car? I need to get it ready for B.H."

"It hasn't arrived."

"Where is it?"

"Well, we don't know. We haven't heard from anybody."

Bill Harrah was on his way to someplace else with Verna, and I'm going, "Holy shit! What am I going to do now?"

Finally, I got hold of the shipping company, and they told me the story about it. They said, "It isn't going to be here for another week."

William F. Harrah (inset), who built the Reno and Tahoe Harrah's casinos, also enjoyed the hobby of collecting old cars. He gathered together the world's greatest collection of antique cars for display in Reno. His facility also housed an extensive restoration garage and the largest library of research material in the world.
(Dondero Photos)

A first-day issue commemorating Bill Harrah's automobile collection. The cover was designed by Don Dondero.

The tour would be over by then, so what am I going to do? I couldn't get a hold of B.H. because he was traveling, so I found a guy who owned a collection of about maybe fifty cars, Waldy Gravenstein. We flew to Bloemfontein to look at his collection, and I selected a 1928 Packard Roadster. I figured, "Well, it's American. Mr. Harrah would be familiar with it, it's a half-way decent car, it runs, and it's trustworthy, so let's just do it."

I was supposed to pick up Bill at the airport, and when I wasn't there, he knew that something was going on. He left a message for me to call the minute I got in. When I checked in I said, "The car isn't here, and they're not sure that it's even going to be here in time for the tour, but I'll keep checking. In the meantime, I borrowed a 1928 Packard Roadster for you to use," and that's what he did.

There were all these rumors going around that we really didn't ship a car, that we just said we were shipping a car and we rented one just to go on the tour. I told B.H. this rumor that I had picked up that was going around, and he said, "Where is the car?"

I said, "Johannesburg. It'll be in Johannesburg tomorrow."

He said, "Get it off the boat." That was two days before the end of the tour. So I hired a chauffeur and a Jaguar XJ6 sedan and got the car. The guy in customs wasn't going to release it, and it had to be released before Friday because they're closed on the weekend. I had to go clear to the director of shipping in South Africa to tell him that the guy in customs didn't want to release the car. So he called up this customs agent that's blocking us from getting the car and chewed him out and made him do it. Well, that guy didn't like me even a little bit when I showed up to pick up the car. They had to break the seal and go through all the paperwork, and he ground me up big time.

Then I had to get some gas—it has a huge gas tank on it—and then I drove it out of town.

This car could run seventy-five miles an hour with no problem at all, so I drove to the Guidini Spa where Bill had a bungalow, and I opened the cut-out, which bypasses the muffler, and it just roared. So I roared up and the car is magnificent, you know. It's nice and clean and shiny and new. It's just far superior to any other car on the tour. I drove up and asked, "Where's Mr. Harrah's room?"

He says, "The bungalow over there," and I saw the Packard sitting out front. So I roar over there, and Bill came out with a grin on his face, and everybody was saying, "What a beautiful car! Blah, blah, blah," and we just kind of let them go at it.

That evening, we were to drive it to dinner. It has an electric starter on it, and the starter would barely turn it over. Mr. Harrah said, "Well, I haven't been checked out in it yet, so why don't you drive?"

And I said, "OK." So I got in it, and it went [making sounds of an engine trying to turn over], and it fired up, and we drove to dinner. We left it parked outside, and people just gathered around it oohing and ahhing while we were in having dinner. We had one bottle of wine, and then we had another bottle of wine, and pretty soon Bill and I were feeling pretty good. He was so happy how this had culminated. [laughter]

When the banquet was over, we got into the car. He sat beside me, and Verna was in the back seat. I turned it over and the battery was getting kind of low, and then it finally roared to life. I'll never forget it, he reached over and patted my knee, and he said, "Good show, Clyde. Good show." [laughter] He really enjoyed the thrill of driving it the last day of the tour.

On my trip over, I had written a speech for him to give at the end of the tour. They even treated him badly there, because we had sent our clothes out to be pressed, and they were late coming back. If his clothes didn't come back in time from the cleaners, he wouldn't be there to make the speech. So again, they thought we were just mousing on

them. Well, it turned out that the clothes did show up at the last minute, so Bill showed up, made the speech, and everything went over just great.

After we would finish a trip or a tour like that, as soon as we got back to work, it was all business again. Cindy and I could deal with that.

I've heard that people in the automobile collection called him "B.H.", and with people in the casino or the hotel, it was always "Mr. Harrah" or "Bill Harrah."

Only when we were talking to each other did we refer to him as B.H.–when he wasn't in our presence, we would refer to him as B.H. If you mentioned his name in public, people's ears got big, so we just used B.H.

Of course, you knew him well enough to call him "Bill."

Yes. But at first, when I wrote him memos, it was "Mr. Harrah," or when I was called into his office, I always referred to him as "Mr. Harrah," even after my promotion. Then one day he held a memo up, and he said, "From now on don't call me Mr. Harrah. Call me Bill."

"OK." And then from that day on it was "Bill."

Did he have any special friends that were collectors?

There were a few. There was a guy who had owned a cigar factory in Tampa that had burned down. He was an expert on early Rolls-Royces. It wasn't like they were pals or anything like that, but there were some people that he enjoyed talking to. One of these gentlemen collected Cadillacs, and he had a seat on the New York Stock Exchange, and he would visit B.H. His name was Al Rodway. He was a real character.

When celebrities such as Bill Cosby came to Reno, did he go through the collection with them personally?

Sometimes he did; but most of the time, I did. Sammy Davis Jr. wanted to go around with B.H. We had a White Steamer painted white, and we had a Black–that's the name, a Black. It's like a little buggy with a little one-cylinder motor on it. We purposely put them side by side. We had the white White and then the black Black. Sammy Davis Jr. was touring through, and he picked up on this, and he said to Bill, "Bill, how come you've got the White before the Black? The Black should be before the White." So one of my assignments was that each time Sammy came out, we put them side by side. We'd switch them, and then when he'd leave, we'd switch them back. I couldn't forget to do that either, or I would get into trouble.

Well, he probably didn't like to go around the collection when it was open to the public, because people would stop him.

In his later years, he did. In fact, I would go around with him. He'd have a five-by-seven piece of paper, and he would quarter it and take notes on it. I had to keep track of everything that we ever talked about on an eight and a half by eleven legal pad, and it usually would be three or four pages of assignments.

So when you walked around with him, you were making notes all the time?

Oh yes, and adding it to my list. When I would finish one–it had the date that I was given the assignment and what the progress was and the date I finished it–I would send him a memo that it was finished and delete it off of the list, and he had to have a copy of my list. The guys downtown couldn't believe it, because I even had things like widening Glendale Avenue. I was even put on a committee to study the forms in Harrah's so that we could go with fewer printed forms. When they found out downtown what my assignments were, they were amazed. Rome just about flipped out when he found out some of the things that I was involved with that B.H. had asked me to do. I was on a hop and a skip all the time.

Could you explain what the London-to-Brighton Run was and some of your experiences there?

Yes. Prior to 1904 in England, there was a law that said if you're going to drive a motor car, you had to have someone walk in front of the car with a lantern and warn the people that one of these automobiles was coming. In 1904 they abolished that law, and you were able to drive without having this person walk in front of you. So to celebrate this each year, the Royal Automobile Club has this run from Hyde Park in London to Brighton.

What is the difference between a race and a run?

A race is when you're competing for the fastest time. This was a run because they made you do it in a designated amount of time. If you get there too early, they'll disqualify you, and they've got spots along the way where they will check you and make sure that you're not getting there too soon.

I'll tell you a bit of humor that most people don't know. At one time in the early 1970s . . . they had these great big, huge glasses that were sold in costume stores. B.H. said he wanted those, and so I got a pair of them, and I had these huge prescription lenses made by his optometrist, and we put little windshield wipers on them. So at the Run we are sitting out in the damn rain in a 1901 Packard when he turns on his glasses, and these wipers start going. [laughter] Everyone got a kick out of it. He had a great sense of humor.

Were there certain types of cars that had to be in this run?

No car was allowed newer than 1904. After they verified the year, the Veteran's Car Club of America, V.C.C.A., gave you a plaque saying that your car had been verified. They don't have to re-verify it if you decide to send it over another time. But we never sent the same car twice. We took a different car every year, and I was there eight times.

In 1977 Bill invited Cindy and I to go by ourselves. He said he wasn't going, and he invited us to make the Run in his place.

One year was kind of hectic. We had rented garage space from a guy, and when we got over there, the doggone Panhard had popped the valves. The heads on a valve had broke off, so I'm trying to find a valve to put in it. It was on a weekend, and this guy with the garage doesn't even have a valve machine! He didn't have reamers; he didn't have anything! So I started welding the heads on it with a torch, and then I ground it down by hand and put it in. I drove the car around and it had the power, and I lapped the valves with dirt off the floor. I had used Carborundum that was a little too coarse, and I had to mix it with dirt, but I got the job done.

I called B.H., and I said, "OK, you want to come test drive this?" He showed up, and we made one lap around Hyde Park. We're going to go around another lap, and I'll be damned if another valve didn't break. So, all right, back to the garage. They wanted me to go have lunch with them and also dinner, but I had to work on that damn car, and I said, "I can't do it." So I welded the other one on, and I drove it. It was going around fine.

Then the day of the run, the four of them (Bill's guests were Lloyd and Joan Dyer) are in the car and starting on the run. They just make it across the river there by Big Ben, and it shot craps, and it was the same thing. It broke another valve, and I said, "We're out of it. I can't do anything about it anymore." So they jumped in the limousine and went on to Brighton.

In Brighton they always had a gala, and we always rented a room and spent the night there. Bill Harrah forgot his bow tie for his tuxedo, but I didn't forget mine, so I said, "Well, here. Just take mine, and I'll get another one." All the shops were closed.

I was a little bit late getting there, but when I showed up for the banquet, he said, "Oh, you got a tie. How'd you do it?"

I said, "Well, all the shops were closed, and I couldn't find anything open, but I was riding in the elevator back up to my room, and I noticed that this room service guy had a bow tie. So I bought it off of him." [laughter] Bill thought that was great, and he used to go around telling the story.

The first World Car Classic was held in 1971 in Japan, and Bill Harrah sent, I believe, thirty cars to that festival. Did you go over to Japan with him, or did you prepare the cars to go to Japan?

Well, I wanted to go, but I didn't get to. Everybody went but me—Doyle Mathia, Jim Edwards, and Mark Curtis went. Everybody in the world went but me. I had to stay and take care of the business, but that was OK. I didn't have any ill feelings toward it. I would have liked to have gone and wasn't able to do it, but I had my rewards, and I had no problem with that.

We had a mess with those cars. We polished all the brass and put on stuff to protect it, but the cars got shipped in the open salt air. Oh my god, they were a mess when they got there. Not only that, we sent the guys over with quite a lot of money, but in Japan, expenses are so high that they ran out of money early, and I had to wire more money to them. [laughter] So I'm getting in trouble because I'm the guy asking for it, but what do you do? In fact, the guy that put on the show over there—I can't remember his name now—I think he committed hari-kari because the show went bust. We still got our money plus expenses from the company, but nobody's ever heard from or seen him since.

Prior to Mr. Harrah's death, he'd planned on opening an attraction on West I-80 to be called "Harrah's Auto World." The project, of course, was canceled after Mr. Harrah's death. Were you involved in the planning of the project at all?

Oh, are you kidding? We talked about that for years, and we spent hours and hours on that. In fact, I took anyone supervisory (who had anything to do with it) that I could take away from HAC to Middle Fork Lodge, because a lot of them had not been there. We got up there, did some brainstorming, and came up with some great ideas, which we presented to B.H. He went for it. We set up a big room where the old car parts were, a kind of war room. We made blocks of wood with car names on them and scaled them so that we could figure things out.

We always talked about having an introductory film or something to introduce the people to the collection before letting them go on through. I said, "Why don't we just have one of these mannequins like Abraham Lincoln in Disneyland, only it would be Bill Harrah?" No one thought he would go for it, including the guys downtown. I said, "Well, I'm going to ask him anyway." So I went in and explained it, and he said yes. I went beyond that. I even contacted the guy that built Lincoln for Disney. I flew him up to Reno, and we discussed it. It would cost $1,000,000, and it never materialized, but Bill would have done it. Now it is possible that a conversation with me could be fed into the computer, and they could make my voice sound like Bill Harrah, and you'd think you were talking to him. I mean, that's how far we could have gone with it, but then it didn't happen.

You feel the project was realistic, but I've had many downtown people tell me that it wouldn't have made any money. It couldn't have stood alone.

Right. That was always a bone of contention, but who's to say it wouldn't work?

Yes, it was going to cost a lot of money to do it, but money was being appropriated to build it. They were going to have to do it in three phases because they couldn't come up with the money to do it all at once. Bill Harrah called me in his office, and he wanted to know my opinion, and I said, "Once you build a hotel along with your casino, then you can take care of your customer base, and your profits will go sky high. You've proven it here, and you've proven it at Tahoe. So I'm thinking that maybe if we increase the size of the gaming, then maybe we don't have to do this in three phases. We might be able to do it in two or possibly even one."

He said, "We want to build rooms, and we want every room to have a view. We'll have different prices of rooms. We'll have rooms like Holiday Inn, and then we'll have our kind of rooms, and then we'll have suites. And every seat in every restaurant will have a view." I mean, it would have been quite a place. They had a model of it over on Lake Street. I don't know what happened to it.

When Bill Harrah died, the Harrah's Auto World project died because Mead Dixon didn't want to build it. Did anyone really want to do it after Bill Harrah died—other than yourself, of course?

No. From the very beginning we never believed that we would get any backing from downtown. It seemed as though when it came to spending large sums of money on automobiles, they didn't want to do it.

Did Mr. Harrah ever discuss with you what he thought would happen, or what he would like to have happen to the collection after his death?

I don't think he discussed that with anyone. He never discussed it with me. I don't think he wanted to see those numbers. It is my belief, however, that when O'Callaghan was governor, there was a time that if anything happened to Bill, he wanted to leave the collection to the state. They weren't interested, so nothing was done about it. I don't think he ever gave any consideration beyond that for the city of Reno or anyone else.

We would have open houses at the collection, but it was tough convincing him to let the public in for free. With that many people, we thought we were going to have a tremendous security problem. Over 14,000 people in three days visited the collection, but it turned out to be less of a burden security-wise to us than it was on a daily basis. There were days when we would have very few people go through there, but when we held the open house, there were so many people that there was a steady stream, and people wouldn't stop and spend much time in one place. They just sort of wandered through. One had to walk between three and four miles to look at every car; going through each showroom and down every row.

So people were just taking cursory glances at the collection?

Yes, and the people behind them kind of nudged them along.

It sounds like when the full collection was here, Reno wasn't that interested in either viewing it or operating it.

Well, I don't know that it was ever presented to any of the powers that be. We used to have these swap meets, and I think Sam Dibitonto was the mayor who forced us out of Reno. We ended up going to Sparks. The reason was that we called it a swap meet, which was intended to involve parts and cars and that sort of thing, but he had seen people selling t-shirts, so he didn't believe it was a "true" car swap meet. I don't understand his logic on why he let this function go away, or rather chased it away, when it would bring in so much money to the area. We brought in 45,000+ people in a week, which at that time was a lot of people. We moved from over here

by the airport, Wooster High School, over to the Sparks High School, which didn't work out as well, but it worked. There are a lot of car collectors around the world who still reminisce about the swap meets.

Do you recall how many vehicles were in the collection at the time of Bill Harrah's death?

I couldn't tell you exactly. There were bicycles, motorcycles, airplanes, boats, cars, trucks, fire engines, and trains–all modes of transportation–so we always referred to them as vehicles, and that way we made the claim of the higher number of vehicles. In fact today, there's a collection in Washington state that is larger than Harrah's was, and it's all cars. I've not seen it, but I understand that nothing is for sale, and it is open to the public one day a year. [laughter]

Could you estimate the value of the collection at the time of Bill Harrah's death? Did anyone ever make an offer to buy the entire collection?

Yes. I recall that right after Mr. Harrah died, a gentleman who was in harness racing and also owned the largest coal mine in the United States was interested. He was located in Pennsylvania, and his name was Lloyd Arnold. He offered $30 million, which was not accepted–for what reason, I don't know.

Who actually refused to take it?

That was Mead Dixon. In looking back, you wonder why. [laughter] I mean, that's roughly 10 percent of what he sold the entire company for, and I learned after Harrah's had been sold to Holiday Inns that they had no idea that the collection was included. They didn't know until three days later that they were buying the collection.

When Mr. Harrah died, did you have any idea that the club, and therefore the collection, would be sold?

As far as the collection went, I always suspected it. There were never any steps or precautions made to save it. I know that the executives downtown didn't favor it. The ones who really enjoyed it, of course, were the people at the HAC and Mr. Harrah and a few people on the outside. But from the Harrah's hierarchy, no, they could better use the money for gaming and building hotels. And they were trying to get into gaming in New Jersey and looking at Australia, so they could have used the money there.

Did Mead Dixon ever express any interest in the collection?

No. I guess the best way to put it would be that he tolerated it because he had no choice but to deal with it. Then when he had this thing going with Holiday Inns, it wouldn't be his problem. There would be a hue and cry the minute that it was decided to sell, which there was. There were a lot of people that raised some real Cain over it. I know people today who won't stay at a Holiday Inn because of it. They're still boycotting it.

Did Mead Dixon ever consult with you or ask you your opinion about anything relating to the collection?

Oh, yes, but there was never much of any significance. Having operated it for so many years, not really having made any money at it, I think it was just something to gather a little information that might make Holiday Inns a little more interested in it.

I was really baffled when I learned that Holiday Inns didn't know that the cars were included. I learned that from a Holiday Inns executive who I worked with for about nine months after the sale. We tried to figure out what could be done with it and how we could make it profitable. We looked at all sorts of properties around Reno, but the construction cost was so high that it would have been very difficult. We were looking at Holiday Inns maybe taking over a building. There was consideration for several different properties around town, one of which was the casino that was going to be built over I-80, and the steel and so forth was already in place. That was a possibility, but it would have been so expensive that there was no way it could be justified.

Did you ever buy any more cars after Mr. Harrah died?

I can't recall buying any, but we sold a lot. We put out catalogs in 1983 or 1984. I think over a two-year period we had three auctions. I had made up a list of 500 cars to donate to a foundation, which included many of the premiere cars like Bugatti Royales, Duesenbergs, and one-of-a-kind cars, of which they donated about 100 right off the bat just to get it started.

After we finished the third auction, I made a comment to my boss, who was a Holiday Inns senior vice-president, "With the money that we made on this auction, just think what we can do with the fourth one." All I got was a grin, so that told me the story that there was probably going to be another auction. But they didn't do it publicly. As it turned out, they started cutting back the personnel at HAC and so on, so it'd be really difficult to put on an auction. The cost of an auction plus the auctioneer is really high. One buyer came in represented by Ken Gooding, who used to be an employee, and the few remaining choice cars were sold for $26.75 million. They were bought by General William Lyon, who was from southern California around the L.A. area.

Jerry Moore, from Houston, was contacting me at that time. He was interested in making an offer also. We put the numbers to it, and we didn't feel that it would be workable for more than $25 million, because some of the best cars had already been sold. There were two cars where we were far apart on value. They were the 1933 Weymann Duesenberg that we had bought from George Whittell, which had 2,000 original miles, and the blue and silver Bugatti Royale. That's what made the difference, and that's why Jerry Moore wouldn't go for more.

General Lyon, as I understand it, was to buy the collection, keep the key cars that he wanted, and sell the rest. That way he would get all his money back and end up with those cars he chose for little or no investment. They bought a 1929 Miller front-wheel-drive race car for maybe $350,000 or so and sold it before the cars ever left Reno for $1 million. So, you know, there was a lot of money to be made. The ironic part of it was, when they were selling the company, we were never consulted. We were always kept out of it. I mean, they never really wanted to know what we had to say.

How many automobiles were in the collection, roughly, when Harrah's was sold?

I believe 1,363 automobiles; and then if you threw in everything else, it was just short of 1,500 vehicles.

And how many cars are in the foundation's collection now?

About 250, but not all of them came from Harrah's. I think there's approximately 175 that were donated from Harrah's. From the list that I had prepared for donation, Holiday Inns rated them from the most expensive to the least expensive and donated from the bottom up.

So out of the roughly 1,363 cars when Bill Harrah died, there are now approximately 175 still in Reno?

Right. Yes, and I think that after all the dust had settled, the HAC was probably sold for somewhere around $65 million. It was sold in three public auctions plus private sales here and there, and at the end, all the parts,

everything that was left including the shop equipment, was sold. I wasn't involved with that, but they sold that in lots out in the yard. I think Bill Anderson of the Ponderosa Ranch bought a lot of the equipment, the cabinets from the library, and the file cabinets, including the wooden cabinets with the glass doors.

So Holiday Inns has nothing left of the automobile collection now?

I think they've got a couple of cars. They've got a Wills Sainte Claire. I don't know if they still have the Cretor's popcorn wagon that we used at the collection. I believe they have the second bronze, pony-express-rider statue, and it's in the Memphis headquarter's building. We had two made. One of them is at Lake Tahoe at the Tahoe hotel, and Holiday Inns took the other one to Memphis.

So they actually got rid of the collection except for one or two cars and a statue?

Yes, they may have a few knick-knacks or something, but I don't know for sure.

Did you stay working for Holiday until they sold off the collection?

Yes. During the auctions we had headphones, and I would communicate with the auctioneer. At one auction, a *Road and Track* photographer took a photograph of me and referred to me as the "great disposer."

We had a portrait of Mr. Harrah at the entrance to the collection, hanging where people could see it going in and going out. Apparently something happened during the auction, and one of the little hooks came out of the framework, and it was hanging down. One of the workers took the portrait down and leaned it against the wall in the main shop area in back of the little trash container. Well, this photographer found it and took a photograph of it. It was published nationally with the caption, "Out With the Old and In With the New." It was awful. That was the end of the photographer's career with the HAC as far as I was concerned, and we still don't get along today as a result of it. It had nothing to do with referring to me as a "great disposer." I was there and helped put this thing together, and I saw it materialize, and then I had to turn around and get rid of it (because that was my job), or I could leave. I hung around to try to save as much of it as I could, and that's why it took six or so years before I left.

It must have been a very emotional thing for you to sell it, having to break it up and dispose of it.

Yes. I went to work on December 19, 1961, and on January 25, 1962, we opened the doors to the public. I was there almost from the beginning, sweeping floors, cleaning out the old ice building, and I polished cars, moved cars. My god, I moved cars for years. I did a lot of that.

A lot of people wonder, "How long does it take to restore a car?" I used to have to report all those hours to the accounting department, so I can quote them pretty good. An average restoration, the way the HAC did it then, was to make them no better than they were when they were new and no less than what they were when they were new. They were not intended to be perfect. Automobiles are not perfect, so we strived to make them like they were when they were on the showroom floor.

An average restoration would take 3,450 man-hours. The fortunate thing for us in the early days is that we were paying from a low of two dollars and forty-two and a half cents an hour plus benefits and taxes to a high of about $3.50 an hour for a master craftsman mechanic. We also paid for their coveralls, uniforms, et cetera. This was opposed to farming out restorations and paying $10 or $15 an hour. Today, there are people who charge $50, $60 dollars an hour, but not many people are restoring cars now.

So a master craftsman in that time frame got paid $3.50 an hour?

Yes, that was good money. That's when a dollar was a dollar.

When I got promoted, I had to come up with some ideas on what was wrong and what we could do to improve production. Mr. Harrah wanted to know what I felt was wrong, and I said, "Well, if you look at all the jobs that we're working on and you divide it by the manpower we have, we've got three or four cars assigned to each guy, but he can only work on one at a time." I recommended that we just work on ten or twelve cars at a time, concentrate on them and get them done, then bring in another ten or twelve. After I had been able to spend some time on it, I told him, "Here's another problem. This car may need a lot of wood work. This car may need a lot of body work, and this car may need a lot of mechanical work; but what's happening is just because you want to do this car, this car, this car, and this car, we're loading down the wood shop, and we've only got four guys working in the wood shop. We're not doing it right. You need to allow me to put cars in a priority that you want done so we can maximize our performance and keep everyone going."

It seemed to make sense to him, so I asked him to give me a list of his priority one hundred cars. By doing that, we would finish anywhere from one to as many as possibly three cars a month. On an average, I'd say one a month, but usually we'd hit about fourteen cars a year, and that was pretty good with the manpower we had.

The longest restoration that we were involved with was a 1937 Bugatti. It took us ten years to complete it. It was a beautiful coupe. We painted it a mustard and cream, and it went to Pebble Beach and won "best of show." The car had stayed in storage a long time because a body-maker who we used quite a bit had done a lot of incorrect work. The headlights, the hood, the front fenders, and the back of the body, everything from the windshield back, had to be modified. A doctor brought a two-tone green Bugatti exactly like ours to one of the swap meets, and we made patterns and took photographs of it. It worked just great for us, and we finally finished the car, but that's why it took so long.

On the other hand, the fastest restoration was related to my being a session leader at an American Management Association training seminar. The A.M.A. theory was that a session leader didn't make a statement or answer questions but asked questions and led the group to solve its own problems. The session leader did things like planning, communications, controls, and organizing. I was the first session leader, and as it happened, everyone from the director level up through and including the president of the company was to attend. One of the things that they taught you was to not assign an unattainable goal, because that would adversely affect morale.

Is this before or after Harrah's had been sold?

Before. This was Bill Harrah's project. When I addressed the maxim about not assigning an unattainable goal, my boss, Doyle Mathia, who was the general manager of the HAC, got into it with Joe Specht, who was from industrial relations. Joe claimed that I had assigned an unattainable goal of restoring a 1926 Pontiac.

How that came about was one Monday morning in 1975, Mr. Harrah had called me into his office and told me, "We're doing a commercial on Pontiac Grand Prix cars." He said, "We have a 1926 Pontiac, which is the first year of production for Pontiac, and it would be nice to have it in the commercial. How much time do you need to restore it?"

I replied, "Well, that's an unfair question. I haven't even seen the car." I said, "When you come back this afternoon, I'll give you a number."

He said, "OK."

I took all the department heads, the two supervisors from the shop and one from research, the chassis and final assembly leadman, paint leadman, body leadman, fabrication leadman, wood leadman, everyone who would be working on the project, with me to the warehouse where the car was stored. We had to literally dig it out. I told them, "I want the worst scenario. I want to know how many hours and what problems each of you see. How many hours is it going to take?" After we compiled it all, I spent pretty much the remainder of the day determining if we could even take this thing on.

Sure enough, about 3:30 or so, Mr. Harrah showed up and called me into his office. He was really good at manipulating people, giving you the monkey. So he asked me, "What did you decide?" [laughter]

I said, "I need five days."

And he sat back in his chair and grinned, and he said, "OK."

I said, "But there's a condition."

And he asked, "What's that?"

I said, "That you don't get involved."

And he grinned again and said, "You got it." Sometimes we'd be involved in a project, and Mr. Harrah would see something that he would want to change, which would just totally foul up the project; and after all, we only had five days. I told him that I'd already had the car pulled out and taken to the steam-clean rack. We'd already started on it because I could see the handwriting on the wall, and we were going to go for it.

Getting back to the management training seminar, Joe Specht and Doyle disagreed over this unattainable goal. Doyle was trying to defend it, but he really didn't know much about car restoration so he said, "You're going to have to talk to Clyde about it."

Here I was up in front of all these vice-presidents and the president, and I'm nervous anyway, so the way I put it to Joe Specht was, "Alright Joe, why don't you come out on Friday at five o'clock, and I'll give you a ride in it." Well, that put everything down, and that was it.

On Friday at five o'clock, Joe Specht showed up. I didn't think he would, but damned if he didn't show up, and we were late. We drove him out of there at five minutes past five o'clock on Friday. [laughter] Of course, we used our best people and our most versatile people for the job. We had employees who could do more than one thing, and we had enough personnel at the time to where we could run two shifts and, at times, a third if we needed it. This actually turned out to be for the people in the shop–the craftsmen–a hell of a morale booster.

(Joe Specht was in Industrial Relations. I never did like that department. What they would do is go around and talk to all the sourpusses and the bad mechanics or bad employees that were there and get them to say something derogatory about someone in management, and then you had to write a damn memo defending yourself and how you were going to change it and on and on and on; and of course, all that went to Rome. So I really didn't care for that department.)

⋄

I stayed at the HAC until 1986. I had a friend who knew the president of Holiday Inns at the time who told me that my longevity would be about two years. It lasted about six, much longer than I expected.

There were many people and groups that would approach me who were really unhappy and wanted to save the collection. The owner of Tandem Computer, Tom Perkins–who's just a great guy, a very intelligent guy, and forward looking–wanted to buy the collection. In fact, he put a group of people together to buy the collection. (I found out that Holiday Inns had talked to them about me going with it, which made me feel like I was just another piece of furniture that went with the collection.) They intended to keep it in Reno, but it was a complicated deal. I think they were going to eventually sell cars. There were also people from the Banford Tractor Company of England that were interested.

I feel that selling the collection was a big tragedy, a tremendous loss. There was a time when they considered it could be a Smithsonian West or something like that, but there were a lot of false promises: "We're going to do this, that, and the other thing." Different individuals represented people who were interested in buying it, and there had to have been half a dozen people that were really serious about it, but nothing materialized. I suspect Holiday Inns figured they could realize more by selling it piecemeal and donating part of it rather than selling it intact.

Wendy's was interested in it. In fact, their representative was a good friend of the collection. We had a meeting at my house over that–three guys and I went over the numbers. I don't have any idea of Holiday Inns' attitude. The chairman of Wendy's "felt sure as heck that they were going to get it," but it fell through, and I don't know what was involved.

My business now is restoring automobiles. I have my oldest son working with me, and at one time I had nineteen people working for me. But the restoration business has deteriorated over the past few years, and I don't see that to be a long-range thing to continue doing.

Notes

1. Jim Gullihur was hired by Mr. Harrah in 1948 to restore automobiles. He was the first employee of Harrah's Automobile Collection.
2. The *Spruce Goose* was the largest wooden airplane ever built. Constructed by Howard Hughes during World War II, it flew only once before being permanently hangared. It survives as a museum exhibit in Long Beach, California.

22

EDWIN J. WESSEL

*E*D WESSEL *was employed by Harrah's for almost forty years, the majority of them as a pit supervisor. Born in Salt Lake City in 1934, he moved to Ely, Nevada, at an early age. He attended the University of Houston and the University of Nevada and served in the military prior to going to work for Harrah's as a change person in the summer of 1958. In this oral history interview, Wessel traces his rise in the Harrah's organization. After going to dealer's school and becoming a dealer, he soon became a pit supervisor and eventually the pit manager of Harrah's Reno club.*

Mr. Wessel was a willing and enthusiastic chronicler. The interview was conducted at his home in Reno and was completed in two sessions. It gives the reader a unique look at the world of gaming. Wessel describes in detail some of Harrah's regular customers and some of the company's eccentric employees. Of special interest are stories relating to

cheating in casinos and how the methods of catching and convicting cheaters have changed over the years.

EDWIN J. WESSEL: I was born in Salt Lake City, Utah, on January 8, 1934. My dad was a mining engineer and had some mines just south of Wendover in the Gold Hill mining area. He took my mother to Salt Lake, and I was born there. A week later, I went back to Gold Hill with my dad, mother, and my four-year-old brother, Gordon.

I have four brothers and a sister, Patty, who's two years younger than I. My oldest brother is Gordon. My brother Norman retired from Bell Telephone about five years ago, and my brother Dale is retired from the power company. My youngest brother, Ted, lives in Battle Mountain and owns a Chevron station there. The rest of them live in Reno, with the exception of my sister, who lives in Las Vegas.

I grew up in Ely, attended grade school, and graduated from White Pine High School. I was first introduced to gambling at the old Bank Club in Ely. Bud Simpson owned it, and that became a hang-out. I believe I was under-age at the time I started going in there, like most people. But nobody seemed to care in those days, and I think I probably played my first hand of twenty-one when I was about seventeen years old. [laughter] A lot of kids did. If you lived in Ely there wasn't much else to do, and I think they just closed their eyes if you looked old enough.

Ely during those years was dominated by Kennecott Copper—the Ruth copper pit, and the smelter and a mill in McGill. The people that lived there had company-owned houses. They paid maybe fifteen dollars a month for a three-bedroom house and bought their groceries at a commissary, and they had plenty of money to spend. All of them had new cars and a house full of nice furniture. So gambling in Ely prospered, and the Bank Club was the main one, of course. I mean, they did really well there. There was one other casino in Ely—the Capital Club—and it was owned by the same people. Shortly after World War II, it burned to the ground, so that

just left the Bank Club, which really flourished.

Kennecott eventually went out of business because the toxic smoke and the tailings from the mill were destroying that whole Steptoe Valley, and the environmental control people closed them down. Then, of course, the Bank Club started going downhill and so did the Hotel Nevada. Simpson moved the operation over there and closed the Bank Club. They had maybe three twenty-one games, a crap table, one roulette, and a few slots. It was a very small operation, but on Friday and Saturday nights it sometimes was as busy as you might see some of the casinos in Reno in the early days. I mean, everybody from Ruth and McGill went to Ely and the Bank Club and blew all their money and had fun, and Monday they were back at work. [laughter]

DWAYNE KLING: When you finished White Pine High School, what did you do?

I went to the University of Houston in Houston, Texas, where I studied mechanical engineering. I had a scholastic Jesse Jones scholarship that helped me. I think it was only $300 a semester, but in those days, $300 went a lot further than it does now.

I stayed there for two years, and then I was having too much fun. Although my grades were good, my money started running out, and since I was putting myself through college, as were two other guys from Ely—a guy named Tom Jayo, who is a Basque guy and a close friend, and Carl Jansen—we just said, "Well why don't we just transfer to the University of Nevada in Reno?" And we did. Actually, Carl transferred to BYU.

So did you spend the summers in Reno?

I'd go back to Ely and work at different jobs. Gosh, I had all kinds of jobs in Ely. [laughter] I did everything. I worked in a service station, gandy danced on the railroad, worked in the mine, worked in the mill.

I think what made me appreciate a job in gaming was that when I was working on the bull gang at the mill, they sent me up to what they called the "grizzlies." They handed me some wire goggles and a sixteen-pound sledge hammer, and we went up to the top of the very first crusher, which is a big jaw crusher; and they had railroad rails spaced about seven or eight inches apart. It had a big machine that turned an ore car upside down, and it spilled onto these grizzlies, and most of the rocks went down. But the ones that didn't, I was directed to go out there and swing that sixteen-pound sledge hammer and make little rocks out of big rocks. [laughter] I tell you, I got in really good shape from that.

But I did all sorts of things during the summer. I worked in the oil fields for a Houston geophysical company. I was running gravity meters and seismograph work, and . . . oh gosh, I did everything. Anything for a dollar, make enough money during the summer to go back to school the next year and pay my tuition and board and room.

I never did graduate from the university. I had enough credits, but not in the right subjects. It was always my intention to graduate, but before I could do that I spent two years in the United States Army. I was stationed at Fort Douglas, Utah, and then I was transferred to Fort Ord, California, and spent four weeks there. Then I was transferred for basic training to Fort Lewis, Washington, and then I was transferred to a Nike-Hercules Missile Battalion in Los Angeles.

I worked out of Fort McArthur, near San Pedro, and had an office in Van Nuys, California. We did the radar placement in the mountains surrounding Los Angeles for Nike-Hercules. I had a nice job. I was exempt from the usual army duties like K.P., guard duty, et cetera, mainly because of my engineering background. I had worked for several engineering firms—F. W. Millard and Son, civil and mining engineers, and I worked for Malone Engineers in Reno. In fact, I worked for the university, doing surveying on their experimental farm south of town. So I had a variety of experience before I got into the gaming business.

When you got discharged from the army, did you come back to Reno?

Yes. I came back to Reno, and it was my intention to go back to the University of Nevada that fall. I got out of the army on June 13, 1958. Jobs were really scarce during that time. Most of the engineering jobs were not available because of the loss of government contracts by North American Aviation, Northrop, and Marquardt. These companies were really hurting, and there wasn't much chance to get a job in my own field, so a friend of mine, Rusty Crook—he is now on the school board in Washoe County, but he was a craps dealer in Harrah's at that time—said, "Well, gee, why don't you come down to Harrah's, and we'll fix you up with a job?"

Jim Jeffers worked in personnel, and I had gone to school with him at the University of Nevada. I thought I'd work a couple of weeks and just have some fun and earn some money.

Ed Wessel with his wife, Mickey, in 1962.

So Jeffers hired me, and little did I know that job would last for forty years.

I started on June 28, 1958, and my first job was a change man on graveyard shift. There were all those bells ringing and lights going on for the jackpots, and I felt like a mouse in a psychology experiment . . . you know, in a maze where they turn the lights on and feed you for a while, and then they'll turn the lights on and not feed you. It was a very frustrating experience. [laughter]

I worked one or two nights as a change man, delivering change to the slot machine customers. Then the third night, my boss—I think it was Dan Hoffman, who still works there repairing slot machines and is eighty years old—said, "You're a mechanical engineer?"

I said, "Well, of sorts. I guess so."

He said, "You think you could fix these slot machines?"

And I said, "Ah, sure, piece of cake." So they made me a key man, and I worked as a key man and got a three-dollar raise. I think when I was a change man I was making $11 a day, so $14 a day was pretty good. It went quite a ways in those days.

Did you work six days a week?

Oh, yes. Gosh, I worked at Harrah's six days a week for twenty-five years. I don't think I ever called in sick once during that entire time. Once, when my dad passed away in 1979, I had to take three days off. But other than that, I don't think I ever missed a day's work in all that time.

How long did you work as a key man?

I was on keys for maybe two and a half months, and then a craps school was posted. It was too late to enter the university and I thought, "What the heck; I'll put in for craps school." They made me a craps trainee, and I attended a six-weeks craps school which Carmel Caruso taught. He was also a dealer.

(Caruso was a former University of Nevada football player–played center on teams under coach Joe Sheeketski when Stan Heath was the quarterback and setting national records. To this day he keeps reminding me that I'd have never made it if it hadn't been for him, and I'm eternally grateful! He's still there. I think he's been there forty-five years.)

I attended school for six weeks, and in October or the first part of November, I became a craps dealer. Starting pay for craps dealers in those days was $16 a day, and the top pay was $22.50. To get $22.50, you not only had to deal craps, but you had to deal twenty-one and roulette. If you didn't deal two other games, then the most you could make, I believe, was $20 a day plus tokes. Seems to me that tokes in those days used to run $12-$15 a day. So it wasn't too bad.

Did the dealers split their tokes?

When I first started dealing, they were on a twenty-four-hour split, which was pretty nice. But I think within six to eight months, they started splitting tokes by shift. Graveyard always has been the best shift for tokes. There's fewer people working the shift, and most of them in those days were leftover from days and swing shift. The customers—most of them were drunk and rowdy. [laughter]

Yes, they were either drunk or had money or both.

Yes, yes, that's exactly right. And being drunk . . . most drunks are generous, and so the graveyard dealers did really well. It was the best money shift.

Harrah's had taken over the Frontier Club from Pick Hobson in 1956 and expanded in 1957. It was a period of very rapid growth in their customer base, and they were starting to become recognized as a major competitor. Of course, Harolds Club in those days had all the business. Harold Smith and Pappy regarded Harrah's as an upstart that was never going to amount to much of anything. [laughter] Harold always referred to Bill Harrah as "Mister Harrah," with the implication being Bill thought he was better than the other casino owners.

Do you remember any of your bosses on graveyard?

Yes. I dealt graveyard for maybe a year, and the shift manager on graveyard was Bull DeMarco, who was a very colorful person and eventually became a very close friend of mine. In fact, I have devoted several pages in the humorous book that I've written, *The Jokers Were Wild,* to Bull DeMarco and how we felt about him. He was an ex-bouncer and one of several people who came into the gaming business in Reno from Steubenville, Ohio.

Bull had worked in the steel mills in Steubenville, and he came out here looking for something a little better. The dealers and everybody just loved him. He was about five foot, ten inches, looked like a professional wrestler, balding and very stocky. He was nobody to fool around with. In fact most times, anybody got out of line on the shift, he didn't bother to call in one of the bouncers or security officers. He just grabbed the guy and ran his head through the back door, just like a regular bouncer. But he had a heart of gold, and the girls, the ladies who were twenty-one dealers on the shift, just loved him.

Their first encounter with him, most people were afraid of Bull. He had a gruff manner, but a heart of gold and a real fatherly attraction after you got to know him.

Ruf Olszowy, who was assistant general manager in 1959, was also from Steubenville, Ohio. Andy Marcinko was from Steubenville also. Andy was at Tahoe, and he came to Reno as a shift manager around 1959 or 1960. Andy was a former baseball player. There were a couple of other guys from Steubenville. I don't recall at this moment who they were.

The other place a lot of the people from early-day gaming came from was Montana—Great Falls and Butte, Montana. There was

Maggie McGuire, Pete Savage, Howard Farris, and Clyde Bittner. Also, there's an old guy that I used to go hunting and fishing with that was a hell of a nice guy, Maury Humber. In fact, his dad used to own a casino in Butte. He was just like the rest of them. He had a bunch of wonderful stories—a colorful guy. He worked as a roulette dealer and had been a pit boss in Butte.

Another Montana guy was Maury Pew. Maury was a good friend of Bill Harrah's. In fact, they tell me before Harrah's bought the Frontier Club that Maury ran the race book at Harrah's—the sports book. (Harrah's was half the size of the Virginia Street Club at that time.) One year Maury went on a Horseless Carriage tour to Europe with Bill Harrah, and the other guy that went with him was the bingo manager, Cecil Parke.

Maggie McGuire was a very colorful person and another person that I've written extensively about. He was a very funny guy, and he was loved by everybody at Harrah's. He was from Butte.

When they closed the gambling up in Butte, a guy named Bob White and his friend hitchhiked to Elko and went to work for Newt Crumley Sr. He told me they started out as twenty-one dealers at $8 a day. They spent a year or two in Elko, and then they came to Reno and worked in the old Palace Club about the time Warren Nelson was there.

Bill Panelli was also from Butte. He was a friend of Bill Harrah's. Bill Harrah said he always looked like he was Chinese. He had a white crew-cut, and he wore a visor, the type old-time gamblers wore. He had also been a faro bank dealer at the old Bank Club and a boss at the Palace Club. Bill was a former fly-weight boxer, grew up in Sparks, Nevada, and went to work at Harrah's in 1946. He became a personal friend of Bill Harrah's. When he passed away, Bill Harrah gave him a "Rolls-Royce" funeral. The only other person to get that treatment was Wayne Martin, former club manager during the early years. In fact,

Wayne Martin and Bill Panelli lie side-by-side in the mausoleum . . . two very fine people.

I owe some of my education as a pit boss to Bill Panelli, who taught me a lot of the cheating moves in his garage over in southwest Reno in the middle of the night during the late 1950s. The shades were drawn, and it was like he was divulging the king's secrets.

—◇—

In 1958 I worked the left side of the dime game at Harrah's next to the air curtain on Virginia Street for six months. Anybody that could raise a dime was up there playing. We'd call them spooks. Spooks were people who were very low-class, like street people, who literally made a nuisance of themselves by their presence every day. If the dice got hot or we had a new dealer on the table, those spooks would come out of the woodwork. [laughter] All of a sudden, they would appear.

I can remember every one of these spooks that played on that game for the six months that I was on there. The first player was a guy we called Scaley. Scaley had a skin condition, like dandruff, but it was all over him. His skin literally fell off on the layout. It was disgusting. We'd take the brush and just brush it off. Next to Scaley was this old man named Charley. Charley always had this brown overcoat on, and hollering at us all the time, insisting he'd gotten a wrong payoff. Next to him was a room waiter at the Mapes called Vince, who always had a tuxedo on underneath an overcoat, and he wore a gray hat with a dark band on it. He looked like a bookkeeper more than a waiter, and he was another one that just made your life miserable. Then we had Curly, who was kind of a white curly-headed guy with a flushed face and a short temper, and he was a room waiter also.

These were all nicknames, of course. We rarely knew anybody's real name. We had dubbed them with a name so we'd know who we were talking about. These guys were all playing their dimes, and god! I used to have nightmares about them.

Oh, and then there was Moe, who was a window washer at Edise's Jewelry across the street on the corner of First and Virginia. He was in there every day. A little short guy. *Mean* disposition, always causing trouble. It was just a miserable existence. Then there was Henry next to him. Henry was a shill in the poker game in a little joint that was at the end of Lincoln Alley. He had kind of a nice disposition, but he was another one who was always trying to take advantage of your mistakes. When these guys tried to steal a bet, we would take the stick and smack their hands. If they caused any trouble over it, the bouncer threw them out.

Then there was Blossom, who was an old lady about eight-five years old, who wore what appeared to be homemade dresses. She had a real white complexion with rouge on each side of her cheek for a little color, but a nice old lady. Next to her was a little red-headed gal who always stood in the middle, so she could hang over the proposition bets. If eleven rolled, you'd see this dime chip drop out of her hand right onto eleven, which paid fifteen-to-one. We called her "Big Red" even though she was a short woman.

These people were all addicted to gaming, and if they could scrape up a dime they would be there. In a lot of cases, they were either homeless or winos, and they were all looking for an edge. If the dice got hot, there would be so many people crowded on that table that you worked your *butt* off! Occasionally, a good player would buy a spot at the table, during a hot hand, for five or ten dollars from one of the dime players.

Next to Blossom was this peroxided blonde woman we called May, who happened to be Henry's wife. She was all right. She worked in the card room, too–the poker room in the alley there. Then we had a guy we called Winnemucca, because he was from Winnemucca–a toothless old guy, and always talking. Next to him was Angelo. Angelo's family owned a ranch around Reno somewhere, and he would sleep between the times that he shot the dice. You would have to wake him up when it was his turn to shoot. You'd send him the dice, and he'd hold them in his hand, shake them a little bit, then he would toss one up in the air about a foot and a half, catch it, shake a little more, and then finally shoot. [laughter]

Next to him, and the last one that I can remember on the game, was a guy named Scotty. An old man who was probably eighty-six years old and smoked a pipe that he never lit and kept it in his mouth. And consequently, we had tobacco all over the table. So we had tobacco all over one end of the table, and at the other end, there's Scaley with his skin all over the layout. Oh! It was a miserable existence. I *hated* it!

Those people were there every day?

Yes! I'll swear that they lived in the casinos. I mean, we're talking 1958, forty years ago, and I distinctly remember every one of them. I remember their personalities and . . . . Oh, gosh, it was quite an experience!

Ed, would you give us a quick rundown of your job history at Harrah's Club, from the time you started dealing until the present day?

I dealt for about two years. During that time I learned twenty-one and roulette, and it's kind of amusing how I learned twenty-one. I was dealing craps one day. Maury Pew, who was an old-timer and former race book manager at Harrah's first club, was one pit boss in my pit, and the other pit boss was Maggie McGuire. Maury told me to go relieve a twenty-one game, and I said, "I don't deal twenty-one."

He said, "What do you mean, you don't deal twenty-one? You're a crap dealer, aren't you?"

And I said, "Well, I think I am."

He says, "Well, you deal twenty-one. Can you count to twenty-one?"

I go, "Yes, sure—frontwards and backwards."

And he says, "All right, go over there and relieve that twenty-one game."

From being around casinos and twenty-one games, I knew pretty much how to deal the game and, of course, knew how to play it. He says, "Come here, I'll show you how to shuffle." So he showed me how to shuffle, and I relieved the game, and Maggie come over and put his two cents worth in and told me something he wanted done that I wasn't doing. So I learned twenty-one in about two minutes. [laughter]

If you dealt craps, you could deal anything. That was the attitude in those days. So I became a twenty-one dealer, and like most crap dealers, I have hated twenty-one since that day . . . probably know as much about it as anybody, as far as protecting the game, but I still hate it to this day.

I learned roulette on my breaks. Instead of taking my twenty-minute break that we got every hour, I would spend two or three of my breaks pushing chips. The wheel dealer knew why I was there, so she would show me how to deal the game and the payoffs and things like that. That's how I learned twenty-one and roulette.

Two years later, Harrah's tried an experiment where they wanted to take somebody who had a college education and make a supervisor out of him, so I was promoted to pit boss. I first worked as a box man, but only for a week. Then they called me up and asked me if I wanted to be a pit boss, and I said sure. But I didn't think the rest of those guys down there were going to be too fond of the idea. Most of the other pit bosses had been dealing for years. A pit boss, in those days, was a job that was well respected. It was a job that everybody wanted.

Who told you of your promotion?

It wasn't Rome Andreotti, but I think it might have come from him. He pretty much made all the decisions. Al Fontana was the general manager at that time, but Rome pretty much ran things at both Reno and Tahoe.

Those first few nights as a pit boss I had a couple of things happen to me. About an hour into my shift, one of the twenty-one dealers had a problem, and I went over to straighten it out. A drunk had missed a double-down card, and I told the dealer what to do. This drunk said, "Who the hell asked you?"

The dealer said, "Well he's the pit boss."

He says, "Pit boss? He looks like a little f———ing kid to me." [laughter]

So Duke Downs, who was a guy from Fallon, Nevada, and my partner that night, made a little hand motion with his fingers toward the bouncer, and the bouncer ran over and grabbed the guy off the stool and took him by the nape of the neck and seat of the pants and ran him through the casino, hit his head on the back door, and pitched him out in the alley. The bouncer came back, brushing off his hands, and Duke says to me, "Well, it looks like he found out you were the boss." [laughter]

I said, "My god, I've got this kind of power?"

And Duke says, "That's the best way to handle those guys. Anybody that gives you any shit, just call the bouncer. Get rid of him. You don't have to put up with that." If you caused trouble in the casino in those days you took your life in your hands.

About three hours later, a guy named Chuck Kossol, who was a fairly new pit boss himself, was working with me. This guy down at the end of the pit, a twenty-one player, kept watching me and watching me, and he was fooling around with the cards. So I went to Chuck, and I said, "That guy's up to something."

He said, "Ah, don't worry about it. He looks all right to me."

As it turned out, the next night Johnny Howells, who was the head pit boss, came in and threw me the deck and said, "Find out what's wrong with this deck." There was an

extra ace in the deck, and it was evident that the guy had mucked the cards.

As it turned out, this guy was my brother's neighbor. About six months later, I'm helping my brother build a fence, and this guy says, "You work at Harrah's, don't you, as a pit boss?"

I said, "Yes."

And he says, "I got to you one night, you remember?" And he laughed. I got a real good initiation on my first night as a pit boss.

I worked several different shifts. I never knew from one day to the next what shift I was going to be on. I can remember one time I was on swing shift, working from nine at night to five in the morning. One Saturday night I kissed my wife goodbye and left for work. When I got to work the schedule comes out, and I'm due in at four o'clock in the morning on graveyard. Hell, I don't get off until *five* o'clock. [laughter] So I went to Bill Goupil, who was the shift manager, and I said, "I got a problem here."

He says, "What the hell is your problem?"

I said, "I'm due in at four o'clock, and I don't get off until five."

So he arranged to give me an hour off between five and six o'clock, and then I worked until noon. I got home at one o'clock in the afternoon. Mind you, I'd gone to work at nine o'clock the previous night. My wife wanted to know, "Where in the world have you been?" I had been gone for sixteen hours.

In those days if you complained, they'd just tell you, "Hey, you don't want to work? Stay home!" That's the way it was: "Take it or leave it." I had a couple of kids, and I had to keep working.

I worked as a floorman on all shifts for about three years, and on swing shift I was relieving the shift supervisor, a guy named Joe Francis, who had come from the Primadonna casino. Joe was from Jackson Hole, Wyoming, and he was a pretty colorful character who later became the general manager of Harrah's Tahoe. Joe helped me an awful lot, taught me a lot of things. When they needed a shift supervisor on day shift, Joe came to me one night and said, "Well, you ready to take over day shift?"

I said, "What do you mean?"

He said, "We want to promote you."

And I said, "Well, if you think I can handle the job, sure." So I was promoted to shift supervisor and moved to day shift. I had gotten used to swing and really liked it, but of course you've got to work where they schedule you if you want to be promoted. So I went to day shift and worked as a shift supervisor there for about two years. The first week, I fired five twenty-one dealers for giving help to players. I saw them from the lookout tipping their hole cards.

A short time later Harrah's expanded and took over the old Golden Hotel. The day that they took over, the pit manager, Sam Silverberg, was promoted to shift manager, and they made me the pit manager.

What did the pit manager's job entail?

The pit manager was the pit department manager. He had full control over and responsibility for the pit. Mert Smith was assistant general manager at the time, and I recall a conversation with him right after I took the job. He said, "I want you to know one thing. You are in charge. You make the decisions. Somebody needs to be fired, you fire him. If you want to hire somebody, you hire him. Disciplinary action—you make those decisions or do it in conjunction with the shift supervisor that's involved." He also said, "But I want to know everything that's going on." In fact, he warned me, "I want you to know right now, if I find out from somebody else what I should have found out from you, you got a big problem. But as long as you make the decisions and you take the responsibility, we'll get along fine." I had a real good working relationship with him, and I admire Mert to this day. He was a very competent person, and he afforded Harrah's a lot of leadership in Reno.

Did he believe in delegation of authority?

Oh, yes. In fact, he'd catch me every once in a while putting in too many hours, and he would say, "How many hours did you work yesterday?"

I'd say, "Well, I had to do this or that, and I worked twelve hours."

He'd say, "Did you take your day off?"

And I'd say, "Yes, but I had to come in for . . . ."

He would interrupt and say, "Listen, if you get rundown because you're working too many hours, you're not going to be any good to yourself or us. You take your day off, and you try to get done everything that needs to be done within eight hours." That was very welcome news. [laughter]

The pit manager also made the budget for the department. Harrah's was set up like a regular business—you had a budget that you were expected to keep, and you would forecast what the hold was going to be on twenty-one, craps, and roulette and also forecast the volume. Volume was expected to increase about 10 percent a year. If it didn't increase, you would be called into the assistant general manager's office, and Mert Smith would say, "Hey, why is this?" They'd make an allowance variance if there had been a big snowstorm or something that kept the business out, but if you didn't have an excuse, then they would look at it as though you hadn't done your job.

I was thinking the other day about something that's really lacking at Harrah's these days. When Bill Harrah was alive, if there was a problem, you would have to write a memo as the department manager or shift supervisor explaining what happened. Who was responsible? What did you do about it? How are you going to prevent it from happening in the future? These memos were circulated to everybody on the management committee at that time. The first person to see it was the assistant general manager, then the general manager, and then it went to Rome

Andreotti and Bob Ring and everybody–even Bill Harrah. And if they had any questions about it, you'd write another memo, and you'd fill them in on whatever details were lacking.

Didn't you also have to keep some kind of a ratio between your wages and the drop?

Oh, yes. They called it the wage ratio. It was the ratio of the labor cost of the people you had working for three shifts to the volume for the three shifts. (At that time there were about 300 people in the department.) The volume was the amount of total drop (money) divided into what the wages had cost for that particular day. As I recall, an ideal ratio was about 3.4 or 3.5. There were variances to it– like if somebody came in and lost a huge amount of money, of course, they would take that into consideration. But basically it worked, and it worked real well.

Every operating department manager was responsible for his department's wage ratio. It was looked at daily, monthly, and yearly, and if there were any problems with it, you, as the department manager, would have to give an explanation for it and make proper adjustments. If it got too high, then that meant that you're paying more wages than what was needed for that volume, and you had to cut back. You had to cut your work force– reduced hours, whatever. It was a very effective control. I think it was something that contributed greatly to Harrah's success.

What was your next job after pit manager?

When Mert Smith, who I had a great rapport with, was promoted to general manager, Bob Contois, who was slot manager while I was pit manager, was promoted to Mert's job and there seemed to be some bad blood between the two of us. There didn't seem to be anything that he and I could resolve, and after I had a couple of run-ins, I finally went to Mert and said, "I can't take this

guy anymore. Just put me back on the floor. I'll work wherever you guys want me to work." But Mert talked me out of it and told me what a great job I had done.

(That was a period, the early 1960s, when card-counting was really causing a heck of a lot of problems. It was a new thing, and the card counters were beating us up with end play on twenty-one decks. [laughter] I had put Mert in touch with a guy named Bill Godecki, who was a math professor. He could count cards as good as anyone–he used the Thorpe count, and he counted aces, others, tens, and the five count, which is the ultimate Thorpe count. One day he put on a show in Rome Andreotti's office, and everybody was there except Bill Harrah. It was a revelation to them. Of course, they were very grateful to me, and after that we put in a lot of safeguards, some of them at my suggestion, to beat the counters. The best one, of course, was not dealing the last third of the deck, when they could determine, through card counting, exactly what remained in the deck.

(A good card counter couldn't lose; they could only win. So Mert was really grateful to me, and eventually I helped teach everybody how to count cards–the floor people in Reno and some of them at Tahoe.)

So Mert talked me out of stepping down. He said, "No, no, no. I'll take care of this guy. You just do your job. You do a hell of a job." Et cetera, et cetera, et cetera. So I went back, did my job, and the situation improved for a little while.

Six months later, I went on vacation. When I came back, why, I was a regular pit boss, and Joe Francis was pit manager! [laughter] That was all right with me–the difference in pay wasn't that much in those days.

After I worked on the floor for a while, I worked in personnel as a senior personnel representative. A gal named Helen Mooney and myself staffed almost the entire new Harrah's hotel in Reno: pool boys, health club manager, bellhops, maids, maintenance, everybody. I worked in personnel about three months, getting ready for the hotel opening.

We staffed the hotel, and it turned out to be a heck of a success. I, of course, knew a lot about the gaming business, and I tried to place only people that I thought would make good Harrah's casino employees. Unions were something that Bill Harrah was not fond of at all. You couldn't ask direct questions about them, but through your interviews you could find out if people were sympathetic toward unions or thought that unions were the right way for a business to handle their employees.

I enjoyed working in personnel, but I also enjoyed going back to the gaming, getting back into the pit. Gambling gets in your blood. Who wants to sit behind a desk when you can be out there on the floor—where the excitement is—having fun? After a few years in the gambling business, particularly if you work swing, your worst fear is having a nine-to-five job behind a desk back in Missouri or Kansas somewhere where they roll the streets up at nine o'clock. [laughter] That's one of the reasons I didn't go back into mechanical engineering. I know what it's like to work in a little cubicle, and the only person you see is your boss a couple of times a day. Sit there behind a drafting board. Sometimes I'd wake up in a cold sweat dreaming that I had that kind of a job. After working in gambling, and particularly being a boss, I could never work anywhere else.

It was an exciting life. Every day is the same, but every day is different, and something exciting or interesting is always happening. Sooner or later it seemed like everybody you read about in the newspapers would show up.

I was there when they filmed *The Misfits*.[1] John Huston, Eli Wallach, Montgomery Cliff, and Clark Gable were all there. And those people accept you like you're part of show business. They don't treat you like they treat other people—particularly the stars at Harrah's. Bill Cosby'd come in and deal twenty-one and sit around the baccarat room, and he would

tell stories, and it was exciting—you feel like you're in the mainstream of life. It's just been a wonderful life and almost forty years for me now.

◆

When I first got promoted, I knew the way to be successful in the business was to learn as much as I could about it, and particularly to learn about cheating. Crossroaders were running rampant throughout the industry at that time. I mean, they were stealing a good portion of the bankroll. But people like Bill Panelli (who taught me all these things in his garage at night), Maury Pew (who taught me quite a few things, and a guy named Hal White, who was from Elko . . . . They all taught me something, and because of them I started catching a lot of thieves.

After I caught two or three thieves, all these old-timers accepted me into their fold. Then I made some other contacts, like Don Ramos of the Reno Police Department. Don was a detective, and he was in charge of taking care of the downtown area—cheaters and scams in the casinos. If he knew some guy was in town, he would call me (I worked swing shift), and he'd say, "Hey, so-and-so is in town. Keep an eye out for him." I'd run to this Rolodex where we had all the known cheaters' pictures, and I'd look at that guy, and I'd memorize his face, and when he walked in the door I had him.

I believe I became one of the foremost authorities on cheating in northern Nevada. When they were going to open up gambling in Puerto Rico in 1968, I remember sitting down one night in a conference room with Dallas Seevers, who was in charge of identification at the Reno Police Department, Captain Hart, assistant chief, and a guy named Art Miller, who was at Tahoe in law enforcement for a long time. We set up a "Black Book" for Puerto Rico. It listed all the cheaters. We listed everybody who was deceased, who was still active, this kind of a cheater and that kind—we set up the whole book. And god, that was an experience! I wish

I had taped that meeting. Those guys would start telling stories from their early years in Reno, with different types of thieves and all the cheaters, crooks, and murderers. I got more of an education there, as far as cheating goes, than I ever got anywhere else.

I'll tell you an interesting story about a cheater. I guess it must have been about 1962 or 1963–I was working swing shift in the area right below where the old Terrace Room Restaurant was located. It was about 9:30 at night, and I was one of the pit bosses in that pit. I was watching this twenty-one game, and when I stepped outside the pit to get a better look, I saw this great big old guy sitting on third base. He couldn't see me, because I'm only five feet, eight inches tall, and I was hiding behind some players on a table exactly opposite him. As I looked over, he made a cheating move, bringing his cards into his other hand. He had a sixty-dollar bet out there and turned up a blackjack.

I felt sure he had mucked the cards, so I called security and said, "Get behind that guy." This guy must have weighed 280 or 290 pounds, about six foot five, six six–he was sitting down, but he looked huge. And when he covered his cards I couldn't see anything.

Most of the time a cheater isn't that good at it. You can see part of the card, a little bit of the color of the back of the cards, but I couldn't see anything because his hands were so big! He was one of the biggest guys I'd ever seen in my life. But he had mucked the cards, so I got two of the bouncers, and I said, "Go over there. This guy just ran his own cards into the game and got paid for a blackjack. Just keep him from going anywhere while I get some more help." I also called over to the other club on Virginia Street, and I said, "Send security over here. I got a guy who mucked cards over here." They ran over and grabbed the guy.

When the cheater went to stand up, and he saw those guys standing alongside of him with their blue uniforms and stars, he knew he had been had. He tried to pass the mucked cards back, but there was a bouncer in back of him and not his partner–who was supposed to be there for just such an occasion. So the bouncer grabbed the cards, and in doing so, he just bent the hell out of the guy's forefinger, and we found out later he had broken it.

Nobody had ever, as far as I know, been arrested on a cheating charge. But when I got a hold of Mert Smith, he says, "Well, why don't we try arresting this guy?"

I reluctantly went, "Well, OK."

So we held him. Major Inch, who is a friend and quite a colorful character, was the shift supervisor on swing shift that night. He is a real nervous type, but a hell of a nice guy. He came running over there, and this guy was standing up. Major looked up at him, and he says, "Oh, my god, Ed, can't you catch somebody a little bit smaller?" [laughter]

We called the police, and Don Ramos showed up to make the arrest. I had to go along with them to the police station, and this guy's in the back seat, handcuffed and glaring at me. When we get down to the police station, the booking sergeant takes one look at him, and he goes, "What did you bring him down here for?"

And Don Ramos said, "Well, he mucked cards at Harrah's."

The sergeant said, "Well, listen, the best thing to do with these kind of people is push them down the stairs a couple of times. Just don't bring them down here."

I told him, "If you want to push that big son of a bitch down the stairs, why don't you go right ahead. I'm not going to." [laughter]

Don Ramos told me, "The guy kept complaining about his finger, so they took him to Washoe Medical and had it x-rayed, and he had a broken finger. The bouncer shouldn't have done that; this guy is just a big, dumb guy."

And as it turned out, this guy was two weeks out of San Quentin. When Don learned who he was, he told me, "He's not dangerous, but he's got some friends that are really bad asses. They're going to get him. You wait and see."

A week later, two guys staged a fight over in the same area at about 11:00 p.m., when Jerry was on duty. (The bouncer's name was Jerry Elsey.) When he went over to break it up, they both turned on him and beat him up. Broke both his collarbones and left him in a heap on the floor. He was off work for three months. You can believe I was looking behind me for a long time after that.

When we went to court, his lawyer, the judge, and everybody in the courtroom, they're looking at us like, "What the hell's the difference? You're wasting our time." Like, "You casino guys stole the money to begin with. You're gamblers and all he did was steal the stolen money." It was just that kind of an attitude. The trial was postponed, and before it could come up again, they caught this guy crawling through a window at the Circle RB Restaurant on West Fourth Street as he was robbing the place in the middle of the night. He went to Nevada State Prison for life as a habitual criminal.

In the gambling industry, there are the terms "inside cheater" and "outside cheater." In your many years of gaming, have you found that most of the cheaters are outside people—in other words, people not associated with the casino—or inside people?

Most of the outside cheaters in the early days were people who we knew or had some history of cheating. They were what we refer to as crossroaders, and that's how they made a living—cheating the games. A lot of them were people who were busted out of casinos—ex-dealers, ex-pit bosses—who were dishonest, and they couldn't work because their police cards had been lifted. So they've got their skills, and they'd go around Nevada to every town, even the small towns (which were really susceptible in a lot of cases), and cheat the games for a living. But after a few years, we'd get to know most all of them. Occasionally, there would be some unknown person, but in most cases, they were people that we knew, like Andrino, Baliotis, "Blondie" Johnson, Tony Rozzetti, the Galloper (Cliff Judd), and Mike Sarkis.

As to cheating from the inside, we used to catch a lot of them. In a lot of cases some guy would get next to one of our twenty-one dealers, usually a single gal with two or three kids, kind of a plain-looking gal, and wine and dine them. The next thing they knew, they thought they were in love with the guy. Then he'd propose that they do something wrong and dump the game to either him or one of his friends. Then the dealer would say, "Well I can't do that. I've got to have my job. I mean, if I get caught, I'm going to get fired."

Those guys' standard line was, "Well, what the hell is more important, me or the job? You either do it or you never see me again." Of course, once they did something, which usually was just tipping a hole card (telling them what was in the hole), then they've got them. Once they do something small, then pretty soon it leads to some really bad stuff like flashing the next card, which will empty the tray out in a hurry. If you know what the next hit card is, it doesn't matter what the dealer's up card is.

Most of the cheating involved collusion?

From the inside, yes. Then there are the chip stealers. I think I've caught every type of chip stealer there was. One guy was sticking the chip back of the tack on his tie, a twenty-five-dollar chip every break. Another guy took chips off between the fingers in the palm of his hand. Another guy stuck chips in his mouth and went on his break with them in there. Another guy put chips in his mouth, gets out his handkerchief, clears his hands, and spits it out in his handkerchief and puts the handkerchief back in his rear pocket. He was a crap dealer. I figured out what was going on by watching from the lookout. I went downstairs, and his handkerchief was just sticking out just a little bit, and I reached out and grabbed it, and a twenty-five dollar chip came flying out.

Also, there were guys who would recruit dealers and run a little cheating school. They'd teach them to flash the next hit card. Or they would mark cards and have somebody come in, sit down, and play it off. They would also teach them how to peek at the next hit card, and signal the card to the "agent." And, oh, gosh, dozens of other cheating methods too numerous to go into at this time.

Was this happening all over Reno or all over Nevada?

Oh, it was all over Nevada. You never knew who would get recruited by these guys. Glen Grayson was another one who had a school. These guys would run schools because they were too well known to do the cheating themselves. They would recruit people and then give them back part of whatever they stole as payment. Then after a while we would get to know them. Once in a while they'd try disguises, but that didn't work too well. Most of the bosses in those days, in the sixties, were pretty sharp guys that had been around the block a few times. [laughter] Nobody's fool.

A cheater would take his life in his hands when he came in to some of those places. These bouncers would take you in the back room and really work you over. (Harrah's was probably the least offensive that way.) I'm talking about the Palace and the Bank Club. You go in the Bank Club when Bill Graham, McKay, Sullivan, and those guys ran that place and cheat one of their games, you may not go home. You could end up *dead* or with broken arms or broken fingers. I used to see those bouncers in the Bank Club and the Golden. They'd get a hold of somebody, especially a cheater, and they'd just beat the living hell out of them. I mean, you didn't want to get caught.

It's amazing those cheaters had enough guts to go back in again.

Yes, and some of the dealers too. Harrah's never beat up on anyone, but if you were a dealer in the Bank Club or the Palace and they caught you stealing, they'd work you over. You'd not only lose your job and could never work in gambling again because they would pull your police card, but you'd get yourself hurt *real bad.*

Other cheaters I could mention were the D'Annas—Rusty D'Anna and his dad, Julius, and a brother, Ortega. There were three or four of them. Harrah's even hired Rusty one time, accidentally. [laughter] They hired him in the slot department as a key man. I didn't see him, but one of the other guys did and tipped them off. Of course, they fired him right away.

Once Rusty got caught cheating in the Palace Club, and he ran out the door. The bouncer chased him all the way down Commercial Row, across the railroad tracks, over to Fifth or Sixth Street. He must have chased him for three or four blocks.

It seems to me in the sixties there was at least one or two cheating instances every night on swing shift in Harrah's. In fact, there are several very prominent people in Washoe County now, who were busted for cheating in the casinos during the 1950s and 1960s.

You don't hear about it that much now.

No. You see, to cheat a casino now is a felony. You could go to prison for it. Also, the sophisticated means of confirming that you were cheating, like the closed-circuit TVs, have made it easier to prosecute. Now everything is on tape. I've been to court with several cheaters that I've caught, and it's plain as day. You don't have a guy sitting up in the lookout looking down at a game and then going to court as a witness to tell them what he saw. Now they take the tape to court, and they go through it step by step. On a twenty-one game, they watch the hit-stand patterns, you know—for example, hitting into stiffs when the dealer's got a six or less up and getting a card that improves his hand. Well, how does he know that that card is not a breaking card?

You can explain all that to the average jury. You can go over it step by step and show them, "Here's what they did to the deck." For instance, if the cheater has crimped aces through fives, then every time you see that crimp and you're sitting there with a stiff, sixteen or less, you know the card with the crimp on is going to help your hand. So you take the card. If you don't see the crimp, you know it's a breaking card, so you don't take it.

The gaming commission agents are pretty sharp. They are used to presenting evidence, and most of them are ex-law enforcement agents. They know exactly how to present a case in court under questioning by the prosecuting or defense attorney, and they just lay it out. Harrah's ended up with several convictions since 1982. There are several enforcement agents that I have taught cheating methods on twenty-one, baccarat, craps, and roulette.

Prior to 1982, there were no surveillance cameras to speak of, and it was pretty much our word against his word. What we would do is get two or three of us to witness the same thing. We'd go up in the lookout, and we would all witness the incident, and then we'd present our case. But it was tough to get a conviction prior to about 1982.

And the judges were usually against the casinos.

Yes. A lot of people thought casinos were just a legal way of robbing people. Also, a lot of people thought that everybody that worked in a casino was a loser in life or a shady character. They thought all the old men were alcoholics and all the women were divorcees and probably hookers on the side.

One thing about Harrah's was that Bill Harrah and the people who ran Harrah's, the top executives of Harrah's, demanded that the conduct of every employee be above average. One of the things on the list of reasons for termination is "conduct unbecoming a Harrah's employee." They had strict standards.

Also, if you worked for Harrah's for more than five years, and you go to the bank for a loan, you got special consideration as opposed to other casino employees. In fact, they wouldn't hardly loan money to people working in certain casinos. [laughter] Generally, the public had a very poor perception of people who worked in the casino industry.

I have a lot of college friends who would come in and see me, and even though I was a pit boss or a shift supervisor or a department manager, they would just look at me just like "Gosh, what happened to you?"

I remember one night a guy came in, and he was from the bank next door, First National Bank. He was just above a teller, where they give you a title instead of a raise. He was from Ely, and he'd gone to the University of Nevada when I was there. I was working with a pit boss, Bill Campbell, who was a real nice guy. We were talking, and this guy came up, and he says to me, "Gosh, Ed, when are you going to get yourself a real job, a bank job, like I did?"

Bill Campbell looked at him and said, "Listen! He (meaning me), makes more on the side in one night than you make in a month at that goddamned bank!" Well, it wasn't true, but it sounded good.

Did the pit department in those days work closely with the surveillance?

Most of the times surveillance just had a bunch of old guys who couldn't stand on their feet anymore. They'd maybe been pit bosses, but they weren't real sharp. The pit bosses, in most casinos, were the real experts. Most of the times when we'd call the lookout, we were just getting them to verify what we already suspected or knew. If we had a really strong suspicion, we would either go to the lookout ourselves, get somebody to replace us on the floor, or get one of our buddies and another pit boss to go up there and check it out and tell the guy in surveillance, the lookout, what to look for. Then after he saw what we told him to look for, he could be a witness if we wanted to go to court. During the seventies we did try to prosecute if we caught somebody and thought we could make it stick.

Harolds had a lot of good people, and Harolds pit bosses used to work up in surveillance.

Yes. In fact, the guy who was head of the lookouts at Harolds Club was a friend of mine, LaVerl Kimpton, and he was a smart guy. He had a very high I.Q., and he knew everything that was going on. He and I got together one time and traded stories.

In Harolds Club, the lookouts ran that pit. If they called down and said such-and-such was happening, the floor manager or assistant floor manager was more or less obligated to do what they told him to do. The opposite was true with Harrah's. The shift manager and the pit bosses, the knowledgeable ones, they ran this thing, and they controlled the cheating suspects and how situations were handled.

How did Harrah's strict pit procedures come about?

Ruf Olszowy wrote the original procedures, and they were pretty simple. Just little things. Historically speaking, the George S. May Company from Chicago (business engineers) set up the original procedures for every position at Harrah's in August of 1952, but they were very brief until Ruf wrote those procedures for dealing. First he just made a list of things he wanted people to do, and as the years went by, they became formal. Every game had procedures, and most of the time these procedures were written to protect the game and the dealer from cheaters and to protect the house from cheating from the inside.

We expect dealers to do certain things: We expect them to hold the deck a certain way; if they aren't holding it that way, it opens up an opportunity to flash a card. To prevent that we have a procedure that states the deck is to be held at a forty-five degree angle. It's like a mirror. They look right at the back of the card, and they hold it up high enough so that if the cards are daubed, the cheater who is sitting down at the twenty-one game cannot see it. Of course, they got around that. They'd get a buddy to stand behind them and read the daub, and then if they saw a daub, they'd nudge the chair, and the guy would take it as a hit card if he had a stiff.

Another procedure has the dealer covering up the end of the deck with the forefinger on the deck hand. By covering the end of the deck, if a player has crimped the cards—aces through five, for instance—he cannot see the crimp prior to hitting. If I'm a cheater and I'm a crimper, and I'm crimping the end of the cards, I'm going to find myself a dealer who doesn't cover the end of the deck. So we write a procedure so that everybody holds the deck a certain way as I outlined, and that eliminates a problem. It also supposedly eliminates her (the dealer) from exposing it on purpose.

We also have procedures on how to shuffle. I've seen dealers hop the cut, which means they false shuffle so the cards that they've dealt are in the same order. Or they set something up during the pickup, and then the false shuffle keeps it that way. Then they stick the cards out to be cut by their agent, who might be the only person on the game, and he refuses to cut. Hopping the cut really isn't a cut. They put the cards right back where they were.

I've also seen dealers roll the deck. That is when they know what the cards are that have been dealt, so they just reach out, pick the cards up, turn the deck over, and bring it up and deal the same cards out again.

All the procedures were written to protect the house and the game. I don't know of any except appearance standards that *weren't* written to protect the house. The pit boss looks at a dealer and sees if they are following procedures. If the dealer isn't following a certain procedure, then we start looking to see if something bad is happening.

Sometimes dealers got on each other's nerves by breaking procedures. Dee Roulias was a little Greek guy—looked like a jockey. He must have been in his early sixties. He'd been a pit boss, but he'd gotten in a beef with somebody and had been put back dealing. A lot of times he wouldn't keep his mind on what he was *doing*. He'd run over the other dealer. By that, I mean he would return the dice to the shooter before the other dealer had completed their work.

Well, in the late fifties and early sixties, Harrah's had very few lady crap dealers, so they thought if they put a lady on each table, that would be an inducement for women to come over and play. So Dee is dealing with a lady named Sue Sly. Sue must have been six feet tall, and Dee is about five-foot-four and a little skinny guy. Dee had the stick and was calling the dice. Sue's just working like hell over there and got all kinds of action, and Dee sends the dice out to the shooter. Sue gave him a look that'd kill. Then she held her hand out to the shooter and said, "Give them to me." She took the dice, walked over to Dee on the other side of the table, dropped them in his shirt pocket, and she said, "Run over me again, and they'll be up your ass." Dee didn't *dare* say a word; Dee never ran over her again.

Were policies and procedures strictly enforced, and who enforced them?

Everybody was responsible to see that the dealers followed procedures, particularly on twenty-one. On craps, it was a lot more lax. In the early days, there were roulette procedures, but they didn't enforce them like they did on twenty-one. Of course, most of the cheaters were twenty-one cheaters. Everybody felt it was really important that the game be dealt in a manner that protected the house and the game from cheating.

Each pit boss had an assigned pit, but we did what we called a crossover. If your buddy walked down to the other end of the pit, then it was understood that you would go to the other, and we'd just "cross over." It gave you a little diversion. We only got one break in those days, a one-hour break, and it's hard to stand there in an area like that for so long. Now they get two forty-minute breaks, which is pretty nice. To stand in one area for four hours was just excruciating! [laughter] Pain!

The pit bosses in the pit were responsible to see that people were following procedures. The lookouts were looking for mistakes, too, and they'd have a little quota system up there in the lookout. They'd call the pit and say, "Hey, so-and-so did this or that." And the big deal was you never passed the buck to the lookout and told the dealer, "The lookout said you did such and such a thing wrong." We couldn't say that. We had to say, "Hey, you paid this or that." Well, the dealer knew full well that you weren't standing there watching her, so it had to come from up there.

Lookouts helped a lot; and of course, when we're watching a game, and we see somebody's not doing something the way they were supposed to, we'd go over there and correct it. It was just understood that, at Harrah's, that's the way the games were dealt, and if you didn't want to deal that way, you wouldn't be there too long. You almost had to go someplace else one way or the other. Either you straightened out or they got rid of you.

Every once in a while I would take a trip around town and watch other club's dealers. And a couple of times I would go in the Bank Club in Ely, and later the Hotel Nevada, and watch those dealers; and a couple of times during the early 1960s, I had to just turn my back. I tell you! [laughter] They were not only not following proper dealing technique, but I saw a couple of other things that I better not go into.

What were some of the things that made Harrah's different from the other clubs?

The big thing that made Harrah's different than everybody else was that Bill Harrah and Scherry Harrah wanted to make it a family type of business where the people who worked there were proud that they worked there. They had a process for selecting personnel that was as high as any regular business anywhere. Also, the employees' behavior was important. If your wages were garnisheed twice, you lost your job. If you went out and started a fight at another casino, or if you played twenty-one someplace else and you did something wrong, and those casino people there knew Harrah's policy, they'd call in. And hey—that was conduct unbecoming a Harrah's employee, and we fired them. We strictly enforced all of those standards. Over a period of years, the people at Harrah's were head and shoulders above all the employees at every casino except maybe Harolds Club.

Harolds Club had lots of good employees.

Yes. They had really good employees and long-term employees also. Those jobs at Harolds Club were so good. Their dealers went for their own tokes. I knew about ten of them that were high-limit dealers at Harolds Club, and Harolds Club had all the big business in Reno, all the high rollers. I would say in the sixties and seventies, those jobs were probably $70,000, $80,000-a-year jobs, if not more. Frankie Eamigh's husband, Dean, worked at Harrah's, and I'll tell you what— they had new cars every year, and he never had less than a thousand dollars in his pocket at all times. And he didn't make that kind of money at Harrah's. And Bessie Hoyt's husband, Jack—a Harrah's pit boss—became an owner of the Horseshoe Club.

Dealers' jobs were hard to get at Harolds Club. If you were a high-limit dealer at Harolds Club, that was your table. The only way they could take it away from you is if you did something dishonest or you died; then, of course, somebody else got it. Even the reliefs on the table were the same. They didn't need a schedule.

Those dealers had great loyalty to Harolds Club, and Harrah's developed that same loyalty. People there were proud of the fact they worked at Harrah's. I can recall somebody would say, "Where do you work?", and I said, "Harrah's!" It was something to be proud of because of the standards for personnel and the impeccable integrity of Harrah's itself. Everybody knew that it was run like a regular business, and there were not shady things going on at Harrah's.

I was just telling somebody the other day some of the people that I know that worked at Harrah's. They are chairmen of the boards of big gaming casinos, like Tom Yturbide (the chairman of the board and president at Harvey's) and Larry Wolfe (who's president, chief executive officer of the MGM in Vegas) and Steve Greathouse (who's chairman of the board of the Alliance Gaming Corporation).

I remember Rome told me one time when Atlantic City first opened up that they had a meeting of the casino executives from all the casinos in Atlantic City, and he knew them all. They were all ex-Harrah's employees. In Las Vegas, Mike Ensign, who's the vice-chairman of the board of Circus Circus, is a close friend of mine. He used to work for me on my days off when I was a shift supervisor at Harrah's during the 1960s. And Tony Alamo, who is the president of the Luxor and the senior vice-president of Circus Circus Enterprises, is an ex-Harrah's Reno pit boss, supervisor, and pit administrator. And by the way, Mike Ensign's son, John, is the United States representative from Nevada.

These are just a few throughout the industry, which says a lot for Harrah's and the caliber of people that they trained at Harrah's during the sixties and seventies and probably the first part of the eighties. Mike Ensign and Tony Alamo are millionaires. As I recall,

Mike started in Ely, I think, as a check racker. Made eight dollars a day or something like that. Tony came here from Cuba with a shirt, the clothes on his back, and that's it. He had two jobs. He dealt at Harrah's, and he was an orderly at Washoe Med. Now he owns shopping centers. [laughter] (I covered for him. You weren't supposed to have two jobs in those days.)

If you had to make a list of any specific individuals that were responsible for the success of Harrah's, could you do that, or would the list be too long?

It would be long. First, I would name Rome Andreotti. He was a sharp guy. I remember being in a meeting one time, and he was expressing himself, and I looked at him and thought, "You know, here's a guy, if he had the motivation to do it, could have been a United States Senator." He was a person who had charisma in everything; he got things done, and his integrity was beyond reproach. I thought he was great.

I fired Rome's sister, and she deserved to be fired. You know what he said? "She caused all kinds of problems." You know what Rome told Mert Smith? He said, "You tell Ed to do what he has to do, and you guys leave him alone." After that, he never mentioned it, but he never passed the pit that he didn't come over and speak to me and shake my hand. And in later years, when they had the Holiday Inn people coming in, he brought every one of them over and introduced them to me. That's the kind of guy he was.

The day I fired Rome's sister, Tony Alamo came into the office. I was pit manager, and we had a memo book for things that were happening. The word spread fast. You know, "Ed Wessel fired Rome Andreotti's sister." So Tony's looking at the memo book, and I see him over there looking at me out of the corner of his eyes. I'm sitting at my desk, and I go, "What's the matter, Tony?"

He says, "You got guts!" [laughter]

And Bob Ring. God, what a loveable guy he was! I mean, from the first day that I worked at Harrah's, he never forgot my name, and he always stopped and talked to me. Everybody in the industry had the greatest amount of respect for him. He was like a goodwill ambassador for Harrah's. And of course, he was Bill Harrah's best friend. He did a lot to shape Harrah's in the early days.

Another important man was Mert Smith, who was the general manager of Reno. I had such a good working relationship with him when I was department manager of the games department. I recall a conversation I had when I was first promoted to that position. I was sitting in his office, and he told me, "I want to make it very clear to you . . . ," he said, "You run this department. You make the decisions." And he said, "I'm here to counsel you. If you need to talk to somebody, you come down and talk. Don't write me any memos. You just come in here. We'll talk it over."

I had a lot of respect for Mert. He was very competent. He wasn't a real outgoing person, but he was very intelligent, and I think he helped shape Harrah's during the early years.

Did you ever have any personal contact with Bill Harrah?

Not really. He would walk by, and as you well know, he would acknowledge your presence. I believe he would kind of mouth my name as he went by and just lift his finger up a little bit and wave at me. And he'd just go like, "Hi," although you couldn't hear it. It was inaudible.

But I got a kick out of his dad, John. In recent years, I've mentioned John Harrah in different conversations I've had with people, and they'll say, "John Harrah! Did Bill Harrah have a father?"

And I'd say, "Yes, and he was a very congenial guy, and he would sit around the bars—not regularly but on occasion—and talk."

Well, I've heard he took an active part in the club in the 1940s, when it first opened.

Yes, he did. I was looking at an old "You and Your Job," and I saw John Harrah's picture in there, and he was listed as advisor. When I first came to Harrah's in 1958, John Harrah counted the drop. In those days the shift manager had first count on his shift, but John Harrah would be in there to assist them. That was a very trusted position in any casino, so John would count the drop with the shift managers just to keep them honest. Other than doing that, I don't know of any other active role that he had.

John was always visible, and he was around the club a lot. He was a nice old gent. I enjoyed him. I can recall when it was his birthday, and he was eighty-six years old. The joke around Harrah's Reno was that he was now "eighty-sixed." He was very good natured, and everyone liked him a lot.

Was Bill Harrah visible a great deal?

He was very visible. If you worked day shift, you'd see him go to his office upstairs above the Virginia Street club. Later he would walk down to Lake Street. They had a garage there where he kept his car. You'd see him in the morning and night and once in a while during the lunch hour, but for the most part, I always thought that Bob Ring actually ran the place.

I want to tell you a few things that they attributed to Bob Ring. First was the cleanliness of the place. I mean, we were all in a panic that everything was clean and that all the lights were on. They were fanatics about the lights. If you had a burned-out light in your area, and Bob happened to see it, you would hear about it. He would walk through the club, and he would spot ten things wrong. Then he would call Al Fontana, who was the general manager before Mert Smith, and then he would pass the word down, and then you kind of got a little chewing out: "How come

you didn't call somebody about that light?" Or dust. No dust on anything. And of course, Harrah's didn't settle for second best. I mean, if you couldn't do it first-class, you didn't do it, and that was clearly understood by all the supervisors and managers of Harrah's.

Do you feel that that came from Bob Ring?

I think it was Bill Harrah, who I've heard was a perfectionist. And I think Scherry Harrah had a lot to do with it. Of course, Bob Ring . . . he was such a classy guy, too, that I think it was just their nature not to settle for second best.

The Nevada Club, which was right next door, was so rundown. We used to laugh at the layouts. I mean you couldn't even see the lines on the crap tables. They'd use them until they were *ragged*. Of course, most gamblers didn't care. They were only interested in trying to win a bet. Harrah's was just the opposite. It was the shift manager's responsibility to go through the facility every day and check for everything. If there were pictures or something promoting a certain event, you didn't put thumb tacks in the corners. You didn't use Scotch tape on anything–you used double-stick masking tape on the back of it, and it was stuck on the wall just like it was a framed picture. And in Reno we have terrific winds, and the wind was forever blowing the letters off the marquee, so our people would go up there in windstorms putting those damn letters back up there.

There was one little thing that used to just drive me nuts during the 1950s and 1960s. We had stage entertainment on Virginia Street, and when they would periodically take a break, a curtain would come down. During the break we would play canned music over the PA system. The music was activated by a switch on the pit podium. It was the pit boss's responsibility to turn the music off when the entertainment began, and I don't know how many times I got caught leaving the music on. Then I would hear, "How come you left the music on? I don't care what you were doing, when that curtain's up, that music better be off." Al Fontana, Bob Ring, and even Bill Harrah would notice it. They checked it every time they came through the casino.

One night Dee Roulias was working with me, and this was about the second week I was on the floor. It was Saturday night, and we were talking about something that was going on in the pit. All of a sudden, he jumped three feet off the floor and ran over there, and I said, "What did you do?"

He said, "Just the most important thing you're going to do. When that curtain comes up, you turn that damn music off, or so-and-so's going to come over here and chew you out."

Dee was a ham radio operator, and he had offered to make a switch that turned the music off when the curtain came up; and when it come down, it turned it on. But Bob Ring told him, "You've got nothing else to do, you just take care of it. It keeps you alert." [laughter]

And all the carpet! Of course, Harrah's was the first Reno club other than the Riverside and the Mapes to have a carpet. Nobody else had carpet. That was really a big thing. I think they put that in around 1956, but it could have been sooner—it could have been 1955. The carpet always had to be in perfect condition, no rips or worn places. There was certainly no duct tape like I see at Harrah's these days. And of course, *clean.* They took those carpet scrubbers and heavy-duty maintenance men on graveyard, and they'd scrub those things until they practically wore them out cleaning them.

I think the lake club was even more particular about those things. I remember going up there for employee parties. They would give us tours of the kitchen areas, the back of the stage, the dressing rooms, and everywhere. Everything was just as sparkling and clean and first-class as it was outside for the customers, and the employees' lounges were the same way. It was a philosophy that there wasn't anywhere that any guest, patron

of the casino, couldn't go in and have the same impression of Harrah's behind the scenes that they had when they were out in the gambling areas.

Another thing—there was no red ink! You don't use red ink for anything. That's a deficit. That's losing. You'd think in terms of winning, positive thinking. And "closed" signs. I mean, Bill Harrah, I know personally, had a phobia about "closed" signs, having failed in business once in Reno when they had a wrong location. He didn't put "closed" on anything. If it had to be closed, just close it, but don't put a "closed" sign on it.

One of the other things that made Harrah's were the dinner shows. There was no blue material by entertainers. By blue material, I mean off-color jokes, bad language, or sexual innuendos. That wasn't acceptable to people with class. They didn't use that type of language. People could bring their children to a dinner show and not be offended by the language.

And of course, if there were things wrong, there was the day book that every shift kept. Any problems that you had during the shift or any things that had to be changed, or if something was broken and you had it fixed, that was reported. You mentioned what was wrong, who was responsible, what did you do about it, how you are going to prevent it from happening again. It was all right to have a problem, but don't have it more than once, or *you're* going to have a problem.

Another thing I remember is that they occasionally hired people from the outside, but for the most part it was promotion from within and very strictly so. On occasion, somebody would be hired from the outside, and they wouldn't quite do things our way, and the excuse was, "Well, they're not 'Harrahized' yet." That was the term that I used to hear, and everybody knew what that meant. If you were "Harrahized," you were used to doing things right. And that's exactly the way it was. It just became second nature to have things right and have things clean and aboveboard. That was Harrah's.

What are some of the biggest changes you've seen in the gaming industry?

When I first came to Harrah's in 1958 there were really lots of good people there. They wanted to please the boss. In later years we went through the anti-establishment, anti-family phases and the Vietnam War, and the people we were training were different.

When I first came to Harrah's there were certain visual impressions that you left the gaming patron with. Number one, everybody had to have fresh, clean, well-groomed clothing–a clean white shirt every day. It wasn't until about 1960, or maybe late 1959, that pit bosses started wearing suits. Before that the only person who wore a suit was the shift manager. Dealers and bosses all wore these white shirts that you got from wardrobe at a cut-rate price–you'd have "Harrah's Club" embroidered in red on one side and your first name on the other. You had to have your hair cut; there were no mustaches; they didn't hire bald people; they didn't hire people with facial scars.

I'm sure most of this came from Bill and Scherry Harrah. They were trying to overcome the negative stigma that was attached to gaming and people who worked in gaming. It was really a good thing, and I think Harrah's was instrumental in doing it. Of course, Harolds Club, with their western outfits and everything, they used to look *sharp*. Harolds and Harrah's were trying to live down the stigma and stereotype of people who worked in casinos, with the old visor and the little rubber bands around your arm, like you've got tricks up your sleeve and you're going to mess with the cards, and things like that.

Also, there was no gum chewing. One thing that I got a kick out of when I first came there, they allowed dealers to smoke on dead games. If you had a dead game, you could smoke. But I remember Al Fontana, the general manager, sending down a memo that said, "The next time a twenty-one dealer on a dead game is smoking a cigarette that blows smoke in the customer's face, there will be no more smoking." A few weeks later the *Saturday Evening Post* magazine did a story on Harrah's and their success and some of the new things that they had implemented, and how the gaming business was being run like a regular business. Two of the things they mentioned were no gum chewing and no smoking cigarettes while you're on duty. Well, the day the magazine came out, that was the end of the smoking.

What are the differences in supervision currently as compared to forty years ago?

The quality of the supervisors is different. In those days, you were the boss, and to be a pit boss you had to know what you were doing, and you were respected. It was a revered position. When somebody got promoted they'd say, "Did you hear so-and-so's going to be wearing a suit?" People were impressed, and we made good money by comparison to the rest of the trades. Most of us were on six-day salary, and that additional day's pay helped out.

You had to deal with the employees and the customers. You had to handle drunks, you had to handle cheaters. You had to know when the games were being cheated. You had to know what to do about it once you determined the game was being cheated. You had to deal with dishonest employees, who were maybe "dumping a game" to a customer. (That's the casino phrase for dealers illegally helping a customer, like flashing the next card coming off so they know whether to hit a stiff with it or not.) There was so, so much to do. And, oh, the fights in the casinos! You had to know how to handle these drunks. I found out very early in my career not to challenge drunks, because if you did, you had a fight on your hands or you had to call the bouncer, who really roughed him up.

Over the years, when cheating in a casino became a felony and with the new surveillance systems, things became easier. Also, it's not fashionable to get drunk anymore. I very rarely see any drunks. The quality of supervision and being able to handle all types of situations isn't as important as it used to be.

Casinos these days are more interested in cutting costs than they are in having a real competent person as a boss. They just want somebody that can get by, but they do keep a few people who really know what's going on to take care of major problems and to intercede on behalf of the weaker supervisors.

So, the supervisors today aren't as knowledgeable as they were?

No, they aren't; and they don't have the respect that they used to have either. I'd like to think that I have the respect of most of the people that know me, but some of the pit supervisors today are just laughed at. The customers, the dealers, and the other pit bosses don't have any respect for them.

I think a guy named Danny Troye said it all: When Harrah's was experimenting around 1963 or 1964, they wanted to cut the starting wage for a pit boss, and they put a few guys in there who just didn't have it. So Danny stood up in a meeting and he said, "Let me tell you something. Bargain basement supervisors are no bargain." And he was absolutely right. If you are any kind of a thief or crossroader when you walk into a casino, you know in two minutes whether that pit boss standing back of those tables knows what the hell he's doing or not. Those inexperienced guys cost Harrah's a hell of a lot more than the few dollars they were trying to save in wages.

Pit supervisors now try to be gaming people, but nobody really understands the gaming patron unless at one time he has been a gaming patron, and he's gone out and lost more than he can afford. I came close a couple of times myself. I went out and got caught up in something. Maybe you've been drinking, and you lose more money than you can afford. You're sitting there trying to be a gentleman, and you've lost most or all of your paycheck—you can't pay your rent, and you don't know what you're going to tell your wife when you go home; but you sit there and smile and try to be a gentleman. Then some jackass pit boss, who doesn't know what he's doing, comes up and gives you the glad hand and tries to make jokes with you. This is a common occurrence now.

Most of the supervisors now have never gambled. In the early days, everybody gambled. You just got caught up in it. We couldn't play on our own games, but we'd go to Harolds Club, or wherever, and play. So I knew what it felt like to sit there and lose and still try to maintain your demeanor and act like a gentleman. People these days, they don't know this.

Have employee benefits improved since you started in gaming?

Oh, yes. In the early days you didn't get a vacation. Now people over twenty years at Harrah's have five weeks vacation; and after fifteen years, four weeks; ten years, three weeks. The first year is a week, and then the second year, I believe, it is two weeks. When I started, there were no paid vacations at all.

Dealers got paid overtime if they worked more than eight hours, but you didn't get overtime pay when you worked six days in a week. As I recall, we've always had good group health insurance. The first one we had was Mutual of Omaha. Jesse Area and Bert Area had Mutual of Omaha in Reno, and they had the Harrah's account. I remember when I became eligible, Jesse came around and said, "OK, you're eligible for insurance. Here, sign this card." I was very grateful for insurance, especially because I was married and had children.

Another benefit at Harrah's are the eight paid holidays. When I started, you worked Christmas, Thanksgiving, or any holiday for straight time. Now if you work a holiday, you get paid time-and-a-half, or if you are on salary you get a complimentary day off.

In the gaming business, did Harrah's lead the way in employee benefits?

Yes, they did. I'll tell you how that came about. About 1964, the culinary union was trying to organize casinos, and Harrah's became a target for them. A guy named Chuck Handley started the union in Las Vegas, and they began trying to sign up dealers or any type of casino personnel: bartenders, maintenance people, et cetera. So what we tried to do—it wasn't my idea, but I had a big part in carrying it out—was to give Harrah's employees everything that they would get under a union plus just a little bit more.

Bill Harrah, when he first came to Reno, could care less about unions. He didn't care whether employees were union members or not. In fact, quite a few of his bartenders were union members. However, on the Fourth of July in around 1954 or 1953, as a show of force, the union called out all the bartenders. You can imagine a casino with no bartenders and the volume of business that casinos had in Reno on the Fourth of July in those days. The casinos had owners, pit bosses, and everyone tending bar just to get by until the strike was over.

It pissed Bill Harrah off so bad that he made up his mind that he would never have a union in the place and that his employees would not have a need for one. Handley's group tried very hard to organize Harrah's, and that's when we started the paid vacations, the paid holidays, and anything from a benefits package that a union might propose.

We started training our supervisors, and I had a big part in the training of how to deal with employees, so they wouldn't have what

was a dirty word around Harrah's—a grievance. They liked calling it a complaint. To handle these complaints, they set up what they called the board of review, which I think was one of the greatest things that Harrah's had and a big deterrent to unions.

Before the board of review, I was a dealer on the graveyard shift, and Bull DeMarco was the shift manager. I was going on a break, and Bull was in an argument with a twenty-one dealer. He wanted the game she was dealing dealt a certain way, and she was giving him some static about it. When he tried to tell her something, she started walking away, and he said, "Just keep right on going."

She says, "What did you say?"

Bull said, "I said you just keep right on going. You don't have time to listen to me. You just go on. Don't come back." And that was it. She was fired.

I'm sure that's the way most casinos in those days, and maybe some to this very day, are run. I mean, if you don't like somebody, or they don't do what they're told to do, they're gone; but after Harrah's established its board of review, if you had an argument with your supervisor or you were terminated for reasons you didn't think were just, you took it to the board, and you had your own employee representative. If you were a dealer, there was an elected dealer representative. In fact, I was the second one they ever had, when I was a dealer. I was a dealer representative for about six months, then Bessie Peterson took my place after I was promoted to pit boss.

On the board there was an employee representative, a person from human resources (an employee counselor), and a member of management. All three had an equal vote. I have sat on probably 200 board of reviews in various management positions, and I can only think of one that I didn't think ended up with a fair and just decision. It has a great reputation among the employees. It is a very fair thing. In fact, the story goes, and I believe it's in Bill Harrah's oral history, that Bill fired his gardener or somebody he didn't like, and the guy took it to a board of review and beat him. Bill accepted the decision and put him back to work. The board of review worked really well. It gave employees everything that a union could possibly have given them, and they didn't have to pay any dues.

The threat of that particular union went on for maybe three years. Finally, Handley got picked up on a felony charge. I can't recall what it was, whether it was breaking and entering, embezzlement, manslaughter, or something like that. And of course, that broke their back, and the threat was really over for a long time.

❖

In the early days it was all cash play. The marker play came later. In fact, I was instrumental in changing the way markers were handled. When Dr. Wayne Pearson got into the Nevada State Gaming Control audit, he liked the way Harrah's handled markers. In the forties and fifties, if you had a marker, it was kind of a gentlemen's agreement between the pit boss, the shift manager, and the player. And of course, things got lost in between, and I think a few palms were being greased.

For example, at the shift change, the dealers would change, the pit boss is gone, and the amount on the card that was kept on the pit stand would suddenly show repayment. There was no way to track or verify the repayment. To eliminate this, I proposed that there be a double-check method, where every transaction had to be called into the cashier's. Everybody resisted it at the time, which was about 1965. In fact, the cashiers didn't want to do it at all. They had a budget to keep, and they had to put on an extra cashier.

My method went like this: If you had a transaction with a customer, credit or marker play, you not only had to keep a card and lammers on the game, but you had to call it in to the office. Then the cashier wrote it on a duplicate card, and you took his initials, and he took yours. When it was paid back, the same thing occurred.

When my method hit the pits, there were a few people who were really in shock. Half of their livelihood was cut off. A couple of shift managers and a few pit bosses were pretty upset. Of course today it's all on computers—it's pretty hard to take advantage of the house with marker play, and every casino in the state uses the same method.

The players were different in the late 1950s and early 1960s. I remember people like Nick Sahati, who would play all seven hands on the table, and when he'd lose a bet, he'd slam his hand down onto the table. He would play $500 on a hand. I remember one time this gal, Rosemary Primm, was dealing to him, and he'd lost every bet. Well, he took both arms and hands and slammed the table so hard that her glasses fell off the end of her nose and hit the table.

We also had players like Harold Smith and Eddie Sahati. And, oh gosh! I remember there was a Frenchman we called François who played nothing but $500 a hand, and he would get those $100 chips stacked up like he's building the Empire State Building. And oh, they used to sweat him out. He was an old stoop-shouldered man. He'd walk along, and his gray hair would stream out behind him in the wind. A very colorful person. And we had Scotty Yamamoto, who was a big farmer from the Sacramento valley. He played $500 on a hand all day and all night.

Another one of our high-limit players was Bill Fong, who owned the New China Club. When he would come in, he'd have a whole entourage of people following him. He'd have wads of hundred-dollar bills in both hands, and usually he would have too much to drink. When he'd win, he'd throw money to his people or hand it off to them.

When Harold Smith would come in, he'd have wads of hundreds. I remember one incident with Harold Smith. It was about two or three o'clock in the morning when he started playing, and he was about half tanked-up. He started hollering at me, "Call Dan

Orlich. Call Chuck Webster, and tell them I'm here."

And I said, "Harold, I'm not your secretary. I'm a pit boss."

He says, "You want my business or not?" He'd give me a hard time. Most of the time he'd play cash, but sometimes he would want a marker, and he'd say, "Oh, I've got the money in my hand." So we'd mark it up, and when he lost we kept marking it up. I remember one time he owed about $30,000. He throws me a bundle of money, and he says, "Here, count it! You got nothing else to do." So, I stand there and count the money out while he's sitting there muttering to himself. He was kind of a pain the neck.

But the biggest games that I remember were on craps. We had a guy named Jacobson who owned Schenley Whiskey, and he played heavy. Paul Butler—who owned Bella Vista Ranch and was a major stockholder in Standard Oil and IXL Foods and Wilson Packing—was a regular player at Harrah's. He always played on markers. He would usually settle up at the end of the day, either write a check or pay cash. And if he reached our limit, he'd run over to Harolds Club and get some more money and come back.

We had four or five crap tables on Virginia Street, which was our only club at the time. Then we opened up where Andreotti's Cafe is now, down below there. We called it the old pit four. I think it was 1961. We had two crap tables over there. But for the most part, all the high-limit play was in the Virginia Street club. We started out with two- and four-hundred-dollar-maximum flat bets. We had double odds on craps. At the time, the Mapes and the Riverside were both in full swing, and a player could only get single odds there. Harolds Club also had double odds. If someone like Paul Butler wanted to play on a different game, we would change the limit just for them.

In the sixties, the high-limit tables were a dollar to five hundred dollars flat with double odds, and most of the high-limit play would go to those tables. I remember one Washington's Birthday in 1961, we had Joe Conforte, who owned Mustang Ranch (a house of prostitution) playing; we had an old guy that owned a meat-packing house; we had Mr. Jacobson, who owned Schenley Whiskey; we had a Harrah's bus boy, who had hit a $25,000 ticket; and we had Harold Smith—all playing craps at the same table. Halfway through the shift there were so many hundred-dollar bills in the drop box on that table that the paddle was standing up, and they had to take the box off and bring out a new box.

There were no five-hundred-dollar chips in those days, and if a game would get hot and the players would start winning, it was really a sight to see the racks in front of the players get filled with hundred-dollar chips all the way around. I know there's some hellacious big games these days, but because of markers, the public doesn't realize the amount of money that's changing hands. But in those days, you did.

When I first started dealing in the fifties, it was a novelty to see a hundred-dollar bill. Tourists would walk through the club, and they'd see somebody buying in for a couple of hundred dollars, and they would look at those hundred-dollar bills and go, "Wow! I've never seen one." Now, people walk in, buy in a thousand dollars, and it's no big deal.

Were the high-limit players rewarded with complimentary entertainment shows or meals?

Before we had a showroom, we didn't even have restaurants. In fact, a lady came in the other day, and it jolted my memory on what Harrah's used to do. If a boss wanted to buy your meal, they sent you to the Grand Cafe. John Petrinovich, a good friend and later an employee of Bill Harrah's, owned the Grand Cafe. This lady still had a little slip to go to the Grand Cafe for dinner. The high rollers that Harrah's had before we got a hotel were put up in Newt Crumley's Holiday Hotel.

So you fed the good players in Petrinovich's Grand Cafe, and you slept them in Crumley's Holiday Hotel?

Yes. If there wasn't a vacancy there, we put them in the Mapes or the Riverside, who were only too glad to have our high rollers.

And when entertainment came along, then you could put them into shows?

Yes. Of course, we always had stage entertainment, cabaret-type entertainment, lounge acts.

Thinking back to those days, it was just like an adult Disneyland. There was a stage in the back corner of Harrah's on Virginia Street with twenty-four-hour entertainment, and people like Sam Butera and Louie Prima—they made that place jump. It was just like a *party*. It was a party atmosphere. Harolds Club had their Silver Dollar Bar, and Ernie Primm, he had a little combo off in the corner over there. But Harrah's had class entertainment.

I remember Wayne Newton—he must have been about sixteen or seventeen years old—playing on Harrah's stage bar. I remember coming to work one night, and Duke Downs says to me, "Take a look at the marquee."

I looked over there at the entertainment list, and I said, "Oh, Wayne Newton."

And he said, "Yeah, that *fat* little kid with the high voice . . . for two weeks." And he was disgusted. Two years, three years later, you couldn't even get a reservation to see him at the Headliner Room because he was so popular.

Then there was Denis and Rogers, this couple from England. They called him the Roy Rogers of England. They were delightful people. People used to get out of church on Sunday mornings, and they'd gather around

Harrah's bar just to see them. Netta Rogers always had on a formal dress, and Johnny Denis always dressed in fancy, western clothes. They were just delightful! Very entertaining.

At two or three o'clock in the morning, when Sam Butera, Keely Smith, and Louie Prima would come on, dealers from all the rest of the casinos congregated in Harrah's and just stood around the bar and drank and played twenty-one and raised hell and had a good time. It was *party* time. It was exciting.

Another group that appeared was Gaylord and Holiday. I was a very young pit boss, and they would sing this song that they had made up, called "Pit Boss." It was about a pit boss sweating out a twenty-one game, and he grabs the deck from the dealer and jumps in there. When they would sing that song, everybody would turn around and look at me. Supposedly, the song was written about me, but I have my doubts about that. If it was, I didn't get any money out of it.

Some of the other acts there during this time were Judy Lynn and Her Cowgirls, a Hawaiian revue, and Harry James. Harry James liked to drink, and one morning Bill Mann and I were sitting with him at the bar when he decided he had to call his wife, Betty Grable, who was appearing at the London Palladium. He had promised her that he would call on that night. He had the bartender bring the house phone over, and he called Betty from Harrah's house phone on Bill Harrah's phone bill.

So he's talking to her, and he said, "Just a minute." And he hands the phone to Bill Mann, another pit boss. And Bill said something, and then they hand it to me, and I said, "Hello."

And she asked, "Is Harry behaving himself?"

And I said, "Well, sort of. [laughter] Nice talking to you," and handed it right back to him. But it was just a whole different world.

Harry James had a full band there, on that little stage. I mean it was deafening!

Everybody wouldn't fit on the stage, so they would have the rest of the band down below. I mean it was *deafening.* I think my hearing is affected to this day. And there was Ray Anthony, and of course, we had Nick Lucas. He was the old stand-by, filled in during the slow hours. "Tiptoeing through the Tulips." And Red Coty, he played the organ and the piano.

Then later on, after we bought the Golden in 1966, we opened the Headliner Room. Eddie Fisher opened the room. In fact, Eddie Fisher was in about a year and a half ago, and I didn't recognize him. He is married to a Chinese lady who was with him, a very nice lady, and they live in San Francisco. He was playing on the twenty-one table adjoining the baccarat table, and someone said, "That's Eddie Fisher over there."

I said, "No, it's not."

I went over there and started talking to him, and it was *him*! I couldn't believe it. He said, "Don't you remember me, Ed? I opened the room."

And I said, "Oh, yeah!" When he started talking, I recognized his voice. And so I said, "You know I never told you this, but I named my daughter, Cindy, because of your song, 'Cindy, Oh Cindy.'" And he was just *thrilled.*

So he started telling other people in his party, "You know Ed. He's worked here for years. He named his daughter after my song." And he acted like he was flattered. Of course, I was flattered that he made such a big deal about it.

All the big entertainers came to Harrah's: Kay Starr, Liberace, Danny Kaye, Robert Goulet, Jack Benny, Debbie Reynolds, Sammy Davis Jr., and of course, Bill Cosby. They were personal friends of Bill Harrah. They were around all the time. Bill Cosby'd come out and deal twenty-one, and people would come to Harrah's just to have something to tell their friends back home.

They'd say, "Oh, yeah. I was up at Harrah's Tahoe or Harrah's Reno last week,

and Danny Kaye was playing there (or Bill Cosby or Liberace)."

And their friends would say, "Oh, wow! Did you go? Did you go see him?"

"Yes, I saw him. Bill Cosby even dealt to me." It was just a party atmosphere that I think is seriously lacking any more.

Now Harrah's doesn't have entertainment as we knew it in those days. Do you think the lack of entertainment has anything to do with the drop in business in Reno and Lake Tahoe?

Yes. Absolutely! We used to schedule around these entertainers. We knew which entertainers were going to draw–like Mitzi Gaynor: I don't know why, but she and Debbie Reynolds attracted an affluent crowd. So at show break-time and the nights that they were appearing, we'd beef the schedules up, and I can never remember a time that it didn't work out. The entire schedule was based around what time the show started, what time it ended, how long they were going to be on. And the shows had to end on time. Bill Harrah wanted them to end at a certain time, because so many things were contingent upon tables being opened and the lounge shows starting when those people would come out of the show. And those pits and the games right next to where the show exited would fill up in a hurry. The customers were all feeling good. They'd probably had some champagne or wine, and they'd been put in a happy mood. They were ready to play and to have some fun.

Harrah's was better than Hollywood or New York or any place! They had it *all.* Holmes Hendricksen, who was the executive vice-president of entertainment, was a personal friend of all the entertainers, and they would work for Harrah for less money than they received from someone else. I remember Sammy Davis Jr. had tables outside his dressing room for himself and all the people in his show, and they would be served lobster, big prawns, anything you can think of, *just* for them.

Bill Harrah had class in everything that he did, and those stars loved it. They'd go someplace else, and they were not treated as well. It was hard to beat Bill Harrah's style, and they couldn't wait to get back. They would laud Harrah's in interviews that appeared in magazines, newspapers. Every time they were on stage, they would say good things about Harrah's and how well they were treated, how much class Bill Harrah had. All Holiday Inns had to do was continue that program. They had one of the greatest drawing cards of anything that could be dreamt up. It was built right in, but they destroyed it.

You were employed by Harrah's for many years both before and after the sale to Holiday Inns. In fact, Holiday Inns bought Harrah's Club or took over Harrah's Club in 1980, so you've been with them now going on seventeen years. There are probably a lot of differences between Harrah's operation and the Holiday Inns' operation. What are a few of the most obvious ones that you'd care to mention?

Well, in all truthfulness, when most of us who were "Harrahized" found out that Holiday Inns had bought Harrah's, we all shuddered. I don't know about you, but I'd stayed in a couple of Holiday Inns. We compared Harrah's rooms with those rooms that we stayed in at Holiday Inns, and there was nothing to compare. We all shuddered and just thought, god help us! We knew that they settled for second best, and we weren't second best. We were first-class.

I remember Doug Oien, the comptroller or vice-president of finance of Harrah's, was a *sharp, sharp* guy. He did all the budgets. When I was department manager, he helped me with my budget. He had been promoted to comptroller, but when he found out Holiday Inns was taking over, he quit. I don't recall who went to him and talked to him. It might have been Lloyd Dyer or Maurice Sheppard,

and they said, "Doug, we need you. Don't quit."

He said, "I don't work for any second-rate outfit like Holiday Inns."

When I asked him about it, he said, "I mean it! I work for Harrah's. They're a first-class outfit, and I'm not going to work for anybody less." Doug ended up president of a casino in Laughlin.

After Holiday took over, there didn't seem to be a lot of changes at first. But then things changed, and they started doing things their way. And if you started talking too much about Harrah's, it wasn't good. In a couple of meetings, I said, "That's not the Harrah's way of doing things. We don't do things that aren't first-class." (This was perhaps two years after they took over.) And I was told in no uncertain terms by an assistant general manager, "Holiday Inns *owns* Harrah's. Harrah's isn't owned by Bill Harrah."

The sale also started affecting the class of our clientele. The good ones slowly started disappearing. A lot of those people with money that Harrah's had cultivated were no longer coming in. The golf tournaments at Harrah's—they were *the* golf tournaments in the state of Nevada to go to, and this covered Vegas. You weren't *anybody* unless you got invited to Harrah's golf tournaments, up at Edgewood or here in Reno, or the New Year's parties. And the people with money, Harrah's catered to their every little whim.

About a year and a half after Holiday Inns took over, they got rid of their airplanes. They kept the Otter that flew into Middle Fork, Idaho, but they got rid of both the big jet and the smaller jet. Nothing happened all at once. It was just kind of taking this away and taking that away. I had the feeling that they thought nobody would notice. Well, people without class didn't notice, but those with class did, and Harrah's suffered financially as a result.

Then they did away with most of the automobile collection. They never realized that they had the biggest draw in the world. The whole country is car crazy. My wife is from Virginia, and we used to go back there when I was pit department manager—and really thought I was hot stuff—and I always thought, "Well, these people, they are really going to be pumping me for information about casinos—what goes on, and what it's like to be a pit boss and be the head of all the gaming." Well, they didn't care nothing about me. They wanted to know about the Harrah's Automobile Collection. Everybody had heard of it, and that's all they wanted to know about. They didn't give a damn about me or the gambling. Those cars properly displayed and intact would have drawn people from all over the world.

They could have rotated the collection through their other properties, especially on the East Coast. Would have been a terrific draw. I remember when they sent a bunch of them over to Japan. Those cars were better received over there than they had ever been in this country. And at times, Bill Harrah had cars displayed off-property. He went to Europe on Horseless Carriage tours, and people came from everywhere to see them—especially the Duesenberg and the car that had a wooden body and was hidden in the sewers in France during World War II. Bill Harrah acquired it and brought it here. The car was worth three or four million dollars.

Well, you stayed with Harrah's after Holiday Inns took over, and you're still working there as a pit supervisor.

Yes. Most of the time I'm in charge of baccarat, which is the kind of a game I love. It's the "in" game among most casinos today. The Vegas casinos figure if their baccarat doesn't do well, their casino is not going to do well. They get a lot of groups in from the Orient that are really high rollers. Of course, Harrah's doesn't enjoy that type of play. Over the past few years, I've just been a baccarat supervisor and actually, a glorified pit boss. Nobody is trained in supervisory methods.

I feel guilty about saying things about Holiday Inns. They had goals and objectives that Bill Harrah didn't have, and that was to become the largest gaming company in the world. First they opened in Atlantic City, and then they took over the Riverboat in Las Vegas. Of course, Holiday Inns was spun off a few years back, and Harrah's is now owned by HET, as it's called on the stock exchange—Harrah's Entertainment Company. And Bass Corporation of England owns Holiday Inns now.

When it's all said and done, had Holiday Inns not taken over Harrah's, they wouldn't have enjoyed the widespread success they have now. I believe there are eighteen or nineteen casinos owned by HET, and they tell me the net worth is something like $2.5 billion. Up until this past year or past couple of years, with the advent of the mega-resorts in Las Vegas, Harrah's was considered the premiere gaming company in the world. And had Bill Harrah lived, I have serious doubts it would have gone any further than Las Vegas, perhaps Atlantic City, and the net worth of the company would have been a hell of a lot less.

And, of course, the success of the stock—I have a 401K program that Holiday Inns put in, and they were very generous to match dollar for dollar up to 6 percent of your salary. I have a substantial amount saved through that, and the stock has split a couple of times. Actually, perhaps I am better off because of the sale, even though I didn't like it, and I don't think Harrah's is doing as well as they could. I think they've now lost their competitive edge and their personal touch.

I was reading today's paper, and I saw that the Eldorado opened a new showroom that seats 550 people. Don Carano made a statement that I think says it all. I'll read it to you: "Carano predicts the show will bring a party atmosphere, stirring the senses, bringing back memories, and putting fans in a jubilant mood." And that's what casino gaming under Bill Harrah was all about—excitement.

Harrah's, at this time, does not have a party-like atmosphere, and I don't perceive it happening anytime in the future. The Eldorado, with their new showroom, and the Silver Legacy—that is where Harrah's should be competitive, but they're not. They're not willing to invest in this market which they consider flat.

But I wouldn't have traded my life at Harrah's for anything else. There are thousands of people that I know and thousands that I consider personal friends through my association with Harrah's. It's been very rewarding.

Note

1. *The Misfits* was a 1961 movie starring Marilyn Monroe and Clark Gable. It was partially filmed in Reno and the Reno area.

APPENDIX

Reference list of frequently-mentioned Harrah's employees and executives:

Rome Andreotti served as an executive vice-president from 1966 to 1971 and was Harrah's executive vice-president of operations from 1971 to 1984.

Eldon Campbell was the first general manager at Harrah's Tahoe from 1955 to 1958.

Bob Contois worked at Harrah's Tahoe and Reno in the slot department starting in 1955, and he became the club manager of Harrah's Reno in 1979.

Mark Curtis was appointed the vice-president of public relations in 1977.

Lee DeLauer held several jobs at Harrah's, including director of public relations and director of community affairs.

Gene Diullo was Harrah's first keno manager in 1957.

George Drews started with Harrah's in 1971 as a controller and later became vice-president of finance.

Lloyd Dyer was first hired by Harrah's in 1957 and served as president of the company from 1975 to 1980.

Joseph Fanelli was working for the Kahler Corporation at the Mayo Clinic when he was hired by Harrah's in 1971 as the vice-president of food and beverage.

Red Farnsworth was a longtime employee of Harrah's who started as a cashier in 1946 and was instrumental in developing the personnel office. In 1961, he was named vice-president of public relations and special projects.

Bud Garaventa was hired by Harrah's in 1956 and worked in the slot repair department for many years. From 1971 until the early 1980s, he was director of gaming for Harrah's.

Bill Goupil was the assistant general manager at Harrah's Tahoe from its opening in 1955 until 1957.

Holmes Hendricksen started at Harrah's in 1956 and rose to become vice-president of entertainment, a position he held from 1971 to 1995.

Bob Martin was hired by Harrah's in 1952 and was later named a vice-president and general manager.

Bob Ring was the general manager and president of Harrah's for many years and worked there the longest of any employee–from 1938 until 1992.

Maurice Sheppard, a longtime Harrah's employee, was president of Harrah's from 1969 to 1975.

Cindy Wade served as Bill Harrah's private secretary from the early 1970s until Mr. Harrah's death in 1978.

Clyde Wade was the general manager of the Harrah's Automobile Collection from 1973 until 1986.

GLOSSARY

The gaming terms in this glossary were defined for us by Dwayne Kling. Some non-gaming terms are included in the list as well. When using the glossary the reader should keep in mind that these terms have evolved informally from within the gambling subculture. Their meanings are often imprecise; they may have meanings not listed here; and their use may be idiosyncratic or specific to certain times and places in the history of gaming in America. In other words, this glossary is the best that we can do, but we offer no guarantees that it has application beyond the context of this book.

agent, *n.* A cheater working with a dealer to cheat a casino.

bill acceptors, *n.* Devices built into slot and video poker machines that accept paper currency (e.g. $1, $5, $20, and $50 bills).

blanket roll, *n.* A controlled roll of the dice made on a blanket or a bed.

box man, *n.* A person who supervises the craps game and is responsible to the pit boss.

breaking card, *n.* (Twenty-one) A card that will give a player or a dealer a total over twenty-one, thereby causing the player or dealer to lose.

brush games, *n.* (Keno) A game in which the keno writer marks the ticket with a brush in the traditional Chinese style (as opposed to the method currently used by most casinos in which the writer marks the ticket using a black crayon).

bust-out man, *n.* A cheater who specializes in switching crooked dice in and out of a game.

catwalk, *n.* In early casinos, an area in the ceiling above the casino floor, usually concealed by one-way mirrors through which one could observe the games. In most casinos this type of observation has been replaced by video surveillance. (Also called a "lookout.")

clean up, *v.* To take illegal dice out of a game.

coin bank, *n.* A cabinet with drawers in which a change person stores the portion of his/her bankroll that is not currently in use.

come bet, *n.* (Craps) A bet on the next roll of the dice after a point has been established.

conditioning, *n.* (Keno) The procedure of inscribing, on the right-hand side of the ticket, the total price of the ticket, the number of ways, and the price of the ways (i.e., it describes the player's wager).

crimp, *v.* To mark cards by bending them slightly to allow identification of a card.

crossroader, *n.* A person who cheats casino games.

daub, *v.* To mark cards with coloring to allow identification of a card.

daybook, *n.* A daily report in which supervisors enter anything of importance that happens in a twenty-four-hour period.

dead game, *n.* A game that is open but has no players.

deuce dealing, *n.* A form of cheating in which the top card of the deck is not dealt, but rather the second card, or deuce, is dealt.

do side (to bet on the), *v.* (Craps) To bet the dice will pass (or win).

doing something, *v.* Cheating a game.

don't side (to bet on the), *v.* (Craps) To bet the dice will not pass (or win).

double odds, *n.* An "odds bet" taken by a player at twice the original bet.

draw, *n.* 1) A keno ticket with the winning numbers punched out for a given game, used as an overlay by keno checkers to determine winners and payoffs; 2) A specific keno race, game, or drawing.

drink stamp, *n.* An instrument used by a pit boss to authorize free drinks at the bar.

drop, *n.* 1) The total amount of cash handled plus the markers drawn at a game during a given time frame; 2) The amount of money emptied from a slot machine.

drop box, *n.* A receptacle under a gaming table in which currency used to buy chips or tokens is deposited (or "dropped") by the dealer.

eighty-six, *v.* To ban from a casino.

end play, *n.* A wager made with very few cards left in the deck, when a card counter could have an advantage.

eye in the sky, *n.* An observation post (or person in that post) used for purposes of monitoring casino activity.

field bet, *n.* (Craps) A bet that covers the numbers 2, 3, 4, 9, 10, 11, and 12 and pays double on 2 and triple on 12.

flat, *adj.* Illegal or crooked (relative to casinos or particular games).

flat bets, *n.* A bet that pays even money.

flat dice, *n.* Dice which are not true cubes (i.e., crooked dice).

floor man, *n.* A person who supervises a specific area of gaming (e.g., slots, pit games).

from the shoulder (to bet), *adv.* To make a high first bet.

full comp, *n.* A situation in which every item is complimentary (i.e., there is no charge to the customer).

GII, *n.* The Gulfstream II airplane, which was introduced in 1966 and was the first corporate jet capable of transporting up to sixteen passengers (plus crew) at jet airliner speeds.

going for the money, *v.* To cheat someone out of his/her money.

heat, *n.* Pressure from authorities or customers.

HAC, *n.* Harrah's Automobile Collection.

heavy, *n.* A person who engages in an illegal action during a game.

high roller, *n.* A bettor of high and consistent action.

hit a keno ticket, *v.* To win on a keno ticket.

hitting into stiffs, *v.* (Twenty-one) Taking a card when one's current total is 12 or over.

hold, *n.* The amount of money won by a slot machine or a table game.

horn bet, *n.* A one-roll bet on the craps table covering the numbers 2, 3, 11, and 12.

Horseless Carriage Club, *n.* A group of antique automobile owners and enthusiasts who would meet for gatherings dressed in period clothing.

key man, *n.* A person working on the casino floor who performs minor repairs on slot machines and in some cases pays jackpots.

lammer, *n.* 1) A small disc used to indicate the amount of credit extended to a player; 2) A disc used to designate the value of a chip or a check, usually on a roulette wheel.

layout, *n.* The cloth covering on a gambling table.

lookout, *n.* (See "catwalk.")

marker, *n.* An instrument used to extend a certain amount of credit to a player.

mechanic, *n.* A dealer who manipulates the tools of the trade (e.g., dice, cards) in an illegal manner for the express purpose of altering the outcome of a game.

Megabucks, *n.* A dollar-operated, progressive slot-machine game, linked via network to casinos throughout Nevada.

microfilm, *v.* (Keno) To make a film record of tickets as they are written to discourage cheating.

Middle Fork Lodge, *n.* The lodge, bought by William F. Harrah in 1965, which was rebuilt and remodeled to be used as a quiet retreat for Mr. Harrah, his guests, and his employees. It was located on the middle fork of the Salmon River in Idaho.

muck, *v.* To illegally enter extra cards into a deck.

number one, *n.* (Keno and pit games) Person who is in charge of a department for an eight-hour period (comparable to a shift supervisor).

on and off bets (to pay), *v.* (Craps) To use a dealer's shortcut method of paying a player's come bet that is coming off a number at the same time that the same player's new wager is going on that number.

peek, *v.* To sneak a look at the top card of the deck.

point, *n.* (Craps) A number established by the shooter on the first roll of the dice.

premium points, *n.* Points formerly awarded by Harrah's as a bonus when a player hit a jackpot. (See "premium tickets.")

premium tickets, *n.* Tickets that were printed in different numerical amounts corresponding to premium points and could be redeemed for merchandise at a premium booth.

progressives, *n.* A group of two or more slot machines electronically linked to share a single, common jackpot payoff amount. The payoff "progresses" as coins are inserted into any of the linked machines.

proposition bets, *n.* (Craps) One-roll bets or bets on the "hard ways" (i.e., on numbers 4, 6, 8, and 10).

Quartermania, *n.* A quarter-operated, progressive slot machine, linked via network to casinos throughout Nevada.

Rancharrah, *n.* The Harrah residence in Reno.

read the table, *v.* To count the bankroll, or the total amount of chips, on a table.

reel strips, *n.* Strips, usually made of plastic, which are attached to the reels on slot machines. The arrangement of various symbols on the reel strips (e.g., cherries, bells, and bars) determines the payoffs on the machine and therefore affects the percentage of the slot machine.

repayment, *n.* The paying back of a credit marker.

sand, *v.* To mark the edges of playing cards with sandpaper. The location of the sanded area allows the cheater to know the denomination of a card.

score, *v.* To win a lot of money.

shift manager, *n.* The individual in charge of an entire casino for an eight-hour shift.

shift supervisor, *n.* The individual in charge of a particular department for an eight-hour shift.

spotting, *v.* Marking the numbers on a keno ticket.

squares, *n.* Legal dice.

station-operated game, *n.* A keno game for which bets can be taken at an annex or "outstation".

stick man, *n.* The dealer who calls a craps game and moves the dice to the shooter.

stiff, *n.* (Twenty-one) A hand that could go over twenty-one if a player or dealer takes a hit.

store, *n.* A club or casino.

take and pay, *v.* (Twenty-one, craps, and roulette) A procedure in which a dealer collects the losing bets before paying the winning bets.

third base, *n.* The last position on a twenty-one game.

tokes, *n.* Tokens, monies, or chips given to dealers by players as gratuities or tips.

totaling of payoffs, *n.* (Twenty-one, craps, and roulette) The procedure in which a dealer, when paying a player who has won more than one wager on a single decision, pays one total amount rather than paying each wager individually.

track, *v.* To keep records on the amount of gambling action received from particular customers.

unit, *n.* (As in "unit bet" or "unit deal") A fixed amount through which bets are made (e.g., "He bets in five-dollar units.").

Villa Harrah, *n.* The Harrah guesthouse at Lake Tahoe.

way tickets, *n.* Keno tickets with the spots grouped so that two or more arrangements are bet on by the player.

whip the dice, *v.* (Craps) To send the dice back quickly.

INDEX

PHOTOGRAPH CREDITS

HARRAH'S BINGO PARLOR, Harrah's Reno, and Harrah's Tahoe: *Courtesy of University of Nevada Special Collections*; Harrah's billboard: *Courtesy of University of Nevada Special Collections* ; Lee DeLauer: *Courtesy of Mark Curtis* ; Horseless Carriage Club parade: *Courtesy of Don Dondero* ; Villa Harrah: *Courtesy of William F. Harrah Trusts* ; John Gianotti: *Courtesy of Joan and Lloyd Dyer*, Bill Harrah aboard the *Tahoe Miss*: *Courtesy of William F. Harrah Trusts*; Scherry Harrah (on chapter page): *Courtesy of William F. Harrah Trusts*; Holmes Hendricksen: *Courtesy of Joan and Lloyd Dyer*; South Shore Room: *Courtesy of Dolores Codega and William F. Harrah Trusts*; "Curly" Musso, the Mary Kaye Trio, Holmes Hendricksen, and Lloyd Dyer: *Courtesy of Joan and Lloyd Dyer* ; Dan Orlich: *Courtesy of the* Reno Gazette-Journal; Dan Orlich on the football field: *Courtesy of the* Reno Gazette-Journal; Harrah's Automobile Collection work area (one car): *Courtesy of Don Dondero* ; Bill Harrah and sons with Bugattis: *Courtesy of Scherry Harrah*; Harrah's Automobile Collection work area (multiple cars): *Courtesy of Don Dondero*; George Schuster and Scherry Harrah with Thomas Flyer: *Courtesy of Scherry Harrah* ; First-day issue stamp: *Courtesy of Don Dondero.*

Every Light Was On

Text formatting was done by Linda Sommer, while the design and file preparation were completed by Mary Larson. Electronic pre-press files for this book were composed at the University of Nevada Oral History Program using Adobe Pagemaker 6.5 and Adobe Photoshop LE. The primary font is Baskerville BE Regular.